Lecture Notes in Computer Science 7173

Commenced Publication in 1973
Founding and Former Series Editors:
Gerhard Goos, Juris Hartmanis, and Jan van Leeuwen

Roberto Bruni Vladimiro Sassone (Eds.)

Trustworthy Global Computing

6th International Symposium, TGC 2011
Aachen, Germany, June 9-10, 2011
Revised Selected Papers

Springer

Volume Editors

Roberto Bruni
University of Pisa
Computer Science Department
Largo Bruno Pontecorvo 3
56127 Pisa, Italy
E-mail: bruni@di.unipi.it

Vladimiro Sassone
ECS, University of Southampton
University Road
Southampton SO17 1BJ, UK
E-mail: vs@ecs.soton.ac.uk

ISSN 0302-9743 e-ISSN 1611-3349
ISBN 978-3-642-30064-6 e-ISBN 978-3-642-30065-3
DOI 10.1007/978-3-642-30065-3
Springer Heidelberg Dordrecht London New York

Library of Congress Control Number: 2012936825

CR Subject Classification (1998): K.6.5, D.4.6, C.2, F.4, E.3, D.2

LNCS Sublibrary: SL 1 – Theoretical Computer Science and General Issues

Typesetting: Camera-ready by author, data conversion by Scientific Publishing Services, Chennai, India

Printed on acid-free paper

Springer is part of Springer Science+Business Media (www.springer.com)

Preface

This volume contains the proceedings of TGC 2011, the 6th International Symposium on Trustworthy Global Computing, which was held during June 9–10, 2011 in Aachen, Germany, co-located with CONCUR & QEST. Informal pre-proceedings were available to the participants at the conference in electronic form and the papers in this volume have been further improved by the authors, by taking into account the feedback received at the conference.

TGC is an international annual venue dedicated to safe and reliable computation in the so-called global computers, i.e., those computational abstractions emerging in large-scale infrastructures such as service-oriented architecture, autonomic systems and cloud computing. The related models of computation incorporate code and data mobility over distributed networks that connect heterogeneous devices and have dynamically changing topologies. The TGC series focuses on providing frameworks, tools, algorithms and protocols for designing open-ended, large-scaled applications and for reasoning about their behaviour and properties in a rigourous way. The first TGC event took place in Edinburgh during April 7–9, 2005, with the co-sponsorship of IFIP TC-2, as part of ETAPS 2005. TGC 2005 was the evolution of the previous Global Computing I Workshops held in Rovereto in 2003 and 2004 (see LNCS vol. 2874) and the workshops on Foundations of Global Computing held as satellite events of ICALP and CONCUR (see ENTCS vol. 85). The last four editions of TGC were co-located with the reviews of the EU-funded projects AEOLUS, MOBIUS and SENSORIA within the FP6 initiative. They were held in Lucca, Italy (TGC 2006); in Sophia-Antipolis, France (TGC 2007); in Barcelona, Spain (TGC 2008); and in Munich, Germany (TGC 2010); see, respectively, LNCS vol. 4661, LNCS vol. 4912, LNCS vol. 5474, LNCS vol. 6084.

The main themes investigated by the TGC community are concerned with theories, languages, models and algorithms for global computing; abstraction mechanisms, models of interaction and dynamic components management; trust, access control and security enforcement mechanisms; privacy, reliability and business integrity; resource usage and information flow policies; contract-oriented software development; game-theoretic approaches to collaborative and competitive behaviour; self-configuration, adaptation, and dynamic components management; software principles and tools to support debugging and verification; model checkers, theorem provers, and static analyzers.

TGC 2011 received 25 submissions out of which the Programme Committee (PC) selected 11 regular papers to be included in this volume and be presented at the symposium. To guarantee the fairness and quality of the selection, each paper received at least three reviews. Additionally, the programme included five invited speakers:

- Michele Bugliesi (Venice, Italy)
- Mariangiola Dezani (Turin, Italy)
- Matthias Hoelzl (Munich, Germany)
- Kohei Honda (Queen Mary, University of London, UK)
- Bernd Werther (Volkswagen AG, Germany)

Mariangiola Dezani, Kohei Honda and Bernd Werther also contributed full papers to the proceedings based on the achievements presented in their lectures.

We thank the Steering Committee of TGC for inviting us to chair the conference and all PC members and external referees for their detailed reports and the stimulating discussions that emerged in the review phase. We thank all the authors of submitted papers and all the invited speakers for their interest in TGC. We want to thank the providers of the EasyChair system, which was used to manage the submissions, to carry out the review process including the electronic PC meeting, and also to assemble the proceedings. We thank Giorgio Spagnolo for administrating the website, Barbara Koenig, Joost-Pieter Katoen, Sander Bruggink, Mathias Huelsbusch and the local organization of CONCUR & QEST for their help and the project ASCENS for sponsoring the event.

February 2012

Roberto Bruni
Vladimiro Sassone

Organization

Programme Committee

Roberto Bruni	University of Pisa, Italy
Konstantinos Chatzikokolakis	Eindhoven University of Technology, The Netherlands
Rocco De Nicola	University of Florence, Italy
Sardouna Hamadou	University of Venice, Italy
Christos Kaklamanis	University of Patras and RA CTI, Greece
Zhiming Liu	United Nations University, Macao
Alberto Lluch Lafuente	IMT Institute for Advanced Studies Lucca, Italy
Matteo Maffei	Informatik, Saarland University, Germany
Dusko Pavlovic	Kestrel Insitute and Oxford University, UK
Sanjiva Prasad	Indian Insitute of Technology Delhi, India
Alejandro Russo	Chalmers University of Technology, Sweden
P.Y.A. Ryan	University of Luxembourg
Vladimiro Sassone	University of Southampton, UK
Maria Serna	Universitat Politecnica de Catalunya, Spain
Emilio Tuosto	University of Leicester, UK

Additional Reviewers

Acciai, Lucia
Bettini, Lorenzo
Bravetti, Mario
Calzavara, Stefano
Chen, Zhenbang
Del Tedesco, Filippo
Gabarro, Joaquim
Godskesen, Jens Chr.
Haj Hussein, Sari
Hedin, Daniel
Kramer, Simon
Loreti, Michele
Milazzo, Paolo
Morisset, Charles
Riely, James
Saraswat, Vijay
Tiezzi, Francesco
Valencia, Frank
Wang, Shuling
Zhao, Liang

Table of Contents

A Reputation System for Multirole Sessions*

Viviana Bono[1], Sara Capecchi[1], Ilaria Castellani[2], and Mariangiola Dezani-Ciancaglini[1]

[1] Dipartimento di Informatica, Università di Torino, Corso Svizzera 185, 10149 Torino, Italy
[2] INRIA, 2004 Route des Lucioles, 06902 Sophia Antipolis, France

Abstract. We extend role-based multiparty sessions with reputations and policies associated with principals. The reputation associated with a principal in a service is built by collecting her relevant behaviour as a participant in sessions of the service. The service checks the reputation of principals before allowing them to take part in a session, also according to the role they want to play. Furthermore, principals can declare policies that must be fulfilled by the other participants of the same service. These policies are used by principals to check the reputation of the current participants and to decide whether or not to join the service. We illustrate the use of our approach with an example describing a real-world protocol.

Keywords: concurrency, communication-centred computing, session calculi, session types, reputation systems.

1 Introduction

Building on [8] and [10], where flexible role-based multiparty sessions were introduced, we address the question of accomodating dynamic interaction policies in sessions with multiple roles and a varying number of participants for each role, taking into account the histories of principals. The *history* of a principal is a trace of its past interactions with other principals within service sessions. A *service* is an abstraction for a multiparty interaction point, where partners play predefined roles and behave according to a precise communication protocol. A *session* is an activation of a service. Histories are used to build principals' *reputations*. For each service, only the principal's history relative to that service is significant for her reputation in the service. This reputation is checked against the service access policy, before that principal is admitted in a new session of the service with a given role. It is also checked by other potential participants before they engage in a session involving that principal.

Our aim is to provide an enriched role-based session calculus able to deal with principals' reputations, together with a type system ensuring that classical session properties, such as communication safety and progress, continue to hold in the presence of these new features. While borrowing most constructs and typing rules from [8], and notably the *polling* operator that allows a principal to concurrently interact with all principals

* Work partially funded by the ANR-08-EMER-010 grant PARTOUT, and by the MIUR Projects DISCO and IPODS.

R. Bruni and V. Sassone (Eds.): TGC 2011, LNCS 7173, pp. 1–24, 2012.

playing a given role in an ongoing session, our calculus departs from [8] in that it distinguishes between the notion of *service* and that of *session*, allowing multiple sessions for a single service. We believe this may help modelling real-world scenarios. Think, for example, of an online shop, where there are principals who play the role of sellers and principals who play the role of buyers (notice that each principal may play both roles). The online shop is a service with two roles, "seller" and "buyer". These two roles are of different nature. Sellers should in principle always be available for a transaction with a buyer. Therefore they join the service in a stable way, in order to be present for several successive sessions. We call this a *stable join*. Buyers, instead, might want to join a service only for a single session, to purchase a specific item from some seller. We call this a *one-shot join*. To fix ideas, one may view the initialisation of the service as the start-up of the online shop, the stable join by a seller as the opening of her activity in the online shop, the one-shot join by a buyer as her connection to the online-shop site, the initialisation of a session as the start of an interaction among the sellers and buyers which are currently present in the online shop.

Other points of departure of our calculus with respect to [8] have to do with the introduction of histories. Thus, some constructs of [8] had to be refined in order to account for histories and reputations. For example, in our calculus there are two kinds of sending constructs. The first, denoted !, is the standard message send, while the second, denoted $!^\bullet$, represents a *relevant* message send, whose content must be stored in the history of the sender. Moreover, we offer a *choice* primitive for selecting one principal among the best ones for a given role (according to a given policy), if any.

Histories are exploited at various stages of the interaction:

- at service join, to allow the service to select the principals who will take part in future sessions and to allow a principal wishing to join the service to evaluate the reputation of the current participants and proceed or not with the join accordingly;
- at session initiation, to allow the service to select among the stable participants those who will take part in the session, by testing if they satisfy some condition;
- in a poll operation, to allow a participant to interact only with participants which satisfy some condition;
- in a choice operation, to allow a participant to select one of the best participants according to some criterion.

As regards the type system, the main novelties with respect to [8] are the addition of an existential quantification for the choice operator, and a variation of the universal quantification for the polling operator, as in our case polling does not collect all principals in a given role, but only those verifying some condition based on their reputations.

An interesting feature of our calculus is its ability to regulate a principals' participation in a service according to her reputation: if a principal behaves "badly" as a participant in some service, this may result in a restriction of the possible session roles offered by the service to that principal.

The paper is organized as follows. In Section 2 we introduce our approach by a motivating example. In Sections 3 and 4 we present the syntax and the semantics of our calculus. Section 5 defines the type system. Section 6 establishes the properties of our calculus. In Section 7 we draw some conclusions and discuss related work.

2 Example

Let us take a closer look at the online shop example introduced in Section 1. At any time, a buyer can choose among the current sellers according to some criterion, in order to purchase a specific item. For instance, the buyer may ask for sellers who are fast in delivering their products. This selection can be done by inspecting the past behaviour of sellers, that is, their history, assuming that the shop records all histories in a dedicated registry. The selected seller then sends to the buyer the price of the item. The buyer sends back either a positive or a negative answer, represented by the labels `OK` or `KO`, which become part of the buyer history. In case of a positive answer, the seller sends to the buyer the delivery time, which is recorded in the history of the seller and is liable to be tested in future interactions. In case of a negative answer, the transaction aborts.

In this scenario, there can be an arbitrary number of buyers and sellers, joining the online shop dynamically (this join is subject to an acceptance condition imposed by the service, and depending on the histories of the applicants). After a number of buyers and sellers have joined the service, a shopping session can start, in which all the present buyers and sellers may interact concurrently. Therefore, the online shop may be seen as the concurrent execution of several buyer-seller conversations, each of which is abstractly specified by the *global type* G of Figure 1. The global type G starts with a universal quantification over buyers, followed by an existential quantification over sellers satisfying the criterion `fast`. The former represents the spawning of a separate interaction for each buyer, while the latter represents the choice of one of the best sellers according to the criterion `fast`, i.e. one of the fastest sellers (for this choice to be possible, we assume that for each criterion, there exists an ordering on reputations parametrised on this criterion). Hence, interactions only occur between a buyer and the selected fastest seller, and each of these interactions proceeds in parallel with the others.

For simplicity, we only consider send actions to be relevant for the reputation here. One may argue that this restriction is reasonable since the value of a message is produced by the sender and the receiver does not have any control over it. Note however that, in some practical cases, a received value could be relevant for the reputation of the receiver (for instance, a notification from a bank could only be sent to trusted clients).

Buyers and sellers can participate in the online shop service in different ways. The participation can be one-shot: usually buyers join the shop when they want to buy some item and leave it when they have completed their purchase. By contrast, sellers are likely to have a more stable presence. As long as they want to sell their products, they are part of the service and they replicate their behaviour for each shopping session. However, nothing prevents the shop to include stable buyers and one-shot sellers. In other words, stability is a property of the join operation, not of the roles themselves.

$$\begin{aligned} G = \forall\, \iota : \mathit{buyer}.\exists \iota' : \mathtt{fast}(\mathit{seller}).\ & \iota \to \iota'\langle \mathtt{Item}\rangle; \\ & \iota' \to \iota\langle \mathtt{Price}\rangle; \\ & \iota \to^{\bullet} \iota'\{\mathtt{OK}.\iota' \to^{\bullet} \iota\,\langle \mathtt{Deliver}\rangle; \mathrm{end}, \\ & \qquad \mathtt{KO}.\mathrm{end}\} \end{aligned}$$

Fig. 1. Global type for buyer-seller interaction

$$\mathsf{B} = a[\texttt{b1} : \mathit{buyer}](y).\ \{\ y\exists(\iota : \texttt{fast}(\mathit{seller})).\ \{y!\langle\iota, \texttt{item}\rangle;y?\langle\iota, (x).\ \texttt{if}\ \texttt{OK}(x)\ \texttt{then}\ y!^\bullet\langle\iota, \texttt{OK}\rangle;y?\langle\iota, (x_1).\mathbf{0}\rangle\ \texttt{else}\ y!^\bullet\langle\iota, \texttt{KO}\rangle;\mathbf{0}\rangle\}\ \}$$

$$\mathsf{S} = \bar{a}[\texttt{s1} : \mathit{seller}](y).\ \{\ y\forall(\iota : \mathit{buyer}).\{y?\langle\iota, (x).y!\langle\iota, \texttt{price}\rangle;\ y?\langle\iota, \{\texttt{OK}.y!^\bullet\langle\iota, \texttt{deliver}\rangle;\mathbf{0},\ \texttt{KO}.\mathbf{0}\}\rangle\rangle\}\ \}$$

Fig. 2. Buyer and seller processes

Possible processes describing the buyer and the seller are given in Figure 2.

Process B describes a principal b1 who wants to join just one session of service *a*, playing the buyer role (b1 : *buyer*). Once the session starts, b1 asks (using channel *y*) for one of the fastest sellers. This is done via the choice construct $y\exists(\iota : \texttt{fast}(\mathit{seller}))$, which chooses among the participants in a given role one of the best according to a particular criterion. The selection over sellers is performed by inspecting their histories (that is, their delivery times), since *a* records them in a dedicated registry. After the selection, the buyer sends a request for a specific item and waits for the price of the item from the seller. Then, according to the price, she will answer either OK or KO: in the first case, she expects one further input (the delivery time), while in the latter the conversation ends immediately.

Process S describes a principal s1 who wants to join the service *a* in a stable way playing the role of a seller (s1 : *seller*) (the act of joining a service *a* in a stable way is expressed by $\bar{a}$, to distinguish it from the act of joining *a* only for one session). Once the seller has joined the service, she waits for the request of an item from all the present buyers. This is realised by the poll constructor $y\forall(\iota : \mathit{buyer})$, which spawns in parallel a copy of the seller for each buyer, where the variable ι is replaced by the buyer identity.

Note that the send construct $!^\bullet$ corresponds to the arrow $\rightarrow^\bullet$ in the global type and represents a relevant send whose content must be stored in the history of the sender.

This example can be extended by adding two roles: *goldBuyer* and *goldSeller*. Gold buyers can decide whether to buy an item or to ask for assistance. Gold sellers offer additional assistance and sell the same items with an extra cost to cover assistance. Gold sellers may want to interact only with gold buyers who tend to respond positively (i.e., who accepted the proposed price most of the time in their previous interactions), qualified as keen gold buyers. Gold buyers must select either the label BUY or the label AST to indicate the kind of interaction requested. If a gold buyer wants assistance, she

$$G' = \forall\,\iota : \texttt{keen}(\mathit{goldBuyer}, \iota).\exists\iota' : \texttt{fast}(\mathit{goldSeller}).\iota \rightarrow \iota'\{\ \texttt{BUY}.\ \iota \rightarrow \iota'\langle\texttt{Item}\rangle;\ \iota' \rightarrow \iota\langle\texttt{Price}\rangle;\ \iota \rightarrow^\bullet \iota'\{\texttt{OK}.\ \iota' \rightarrow^\bullet \iota\,\langle\texttt{Deliver}\rangle;\mathrm{end},\ \texttt{KO}.\mathrm{end}\}\ \ \texttt{AST}.\ \iota \rightarrow \iota'\langle\texttt{Problem}\rangle;\ \iota' \rightarrow \iota\langle\texttt{Solution}\rangle;\mathrm{end}\}$$

Fig. 3. Global type for gold buyer and gold seller interaction

$$\begin{array}{l}\mathsf{GB} = a[\mathtt{b1} : \mathit{goldBuyer}](y).\ \{\ y\exists(\iota : \mathtt{fast}(\mathit{goldSeller})).\\ \qquad \{\ \mathtt{if\ alright\ then}\ y!\langle\iota,\mathtt{BUY}\rangle;y!\langle\iota,\mathtt{item}\rangle;y?\langle\iota,(x).\\ \qquad\qquad \mathtt{if}\ \mathtt{OK}(x)\ \mathtt{then}\ y!^{\bullet}\langle\iota,\mathtt{OK}\rangle;y?\langle\iota,(x_1).\mathbf{0}\rangle\\ \qquad\qquad\qquad \mathtt{else}\ y!^{\bullet}\langle\iota,\mathtt{KO}\rangle;\mathbf{0}\rangle\\ \qquad\qquad \mathtt{else}\ y!\langle\iota,\mathtt{AST}\rangle;y!\langle\iota,\mathtt{problem}\rangle;y?\langle\iota,(x').\mathbf{0}\rangle\ \}\ \}\end{array}$$

$$\begin{array}{l}\mathsf{GS} = \bar{a}[\mathtt{s1} : \mathit{goldSeller}](y).\ \{\ y\forall(\iota : \mathtt{keen}(\mathit{goldBuyer},\iota)).\\ \qquad \{y?\langle\iota,\{\mathtt{BUY}.\ y?\langle\iota,(x).y!\langle\iota,\mathtt{price}\rangle;\\ \qquad\quad y?\langle\iota,\{\mathtt{OK}.y!^{\bullet}\langle\iota,\mathtt{deliver}\rangle;\mathbf{0},\\ \qquad\qquad \mathtt{KO}.\mathbf{0}\}\rangle\rangle\\ \qquad\quad \mathtt{AST}.y?\langle\iota,(x').y!\langle\iota,\mathtt{solution}\rangle;\mathbf{0}\rangle\}\rangle\}\ \}\end{array}$$

Fig. 4. Gold buyer and gold seller processes

selects one of the fastest available gold sellers and sends her an AST label to ask for help, then specifies her problem and waits for the response. Figure 3 gives the global type G' for gold buyers and gold sellers, starting with a universal quantification on buyers satisfying the condition keen, and Figure 4 shows the incarnations of principals $\mathtt{b}_1$ and $\mathtt{s}_1$ as gold buyer and gold seller, respectively.

Consider the following process, where the components B, S, GB, and GS are defined in Figures 2 and 4:

$$a\langle G \mid G', \mathtt{rel}\rangle \mid \mathsf{B} \mid \mathsf{S} \mid \mathsf{GB} \mid \mathsf{GS}$$

Here process $a\langle G \mid G', \mathtt{rel}\rangle$ represents a service with name a (the name of the online shop), global type $G \mid G'$ and join condition rel. The global types G and G' are given in Figures 1 and 3, respectively, and the condition rel (standing for "reliable") expresses different requirements for the join of a principal in the different roles:

- any principal can join a session of the service as an ordinary buyer or seller;
- only principals which have a long enough record of successful transactions can join sessions as gold buyers and gold sellers.

We notice that even if we collect in the histories only OK/KO answers for buyers and delivery times for sellers, this information is enough to check interesting properties. Indeed, histories are evaluated in different ways by the conditions keen and fast expressed by participants and by the condition rel associated with service a:

- rel checks the number of successful transactions of gold buyers, while keen checks the percentage of successful transactions over the total number [1];
- rel checks the total number of transactions completed by a gold seller (that is, the number of values in her history, no matter whether single values are good or bad), while fast checks the average time of delivery.

At runtime, the initialisation of a service will create a dedicated registry for recording the relevant behaviour of principals, thus building up their history in the service.

In the first session, principals $\mathtt{b}_1$ and $\mathtt{s}_1$ can only play the roles of buyer and seller, respectively, so principal $\mathtt{b}_1$ can only buy, without requesting assistance. After some successful sessions $\mathtt{b}_1$ and $\mathtt{s}_1$ will be able to play the roles of gold buyer and gold seller too. Then, principal $\mathtt{b}_1$ will have the possibility to ask for assistance.

[1] Note that it is possible to compute the percentage of failed transactions only for buyers, and not for sellers (because the label OK/KO is sent by the buyer, and only received by the seller).

After being promoted to gold buyer, a principal must keep up her reputation: only gold buyers who continue to satisfy the `keen` condition are allowed to interact with gold sellers. After a "bad" behaviour, in order to play again the role of a gold buyer, a principal must rebuild herself a "good" reputation as a buyer.

The above system only includes one buyer-seller pair, and one gold buyer-seller pair. In a more realistic scenario, there would be several participants for each role, differing from the processes B, S, GB and GS only for the id (`b1`, `s1`) and the exchanged values.

3 Syntax

We assume the following sets: *value variables*, ranged over by $x, y, z \ldots$, *service names*, ranged over by $a, b, \ldots$, *principals*, ranged over by `id`, `id'`, ..., *principal variables*, ranged over by ι, $\iota', \ldots$, *roles*, ranged over by $r, r', \ldots$, *sessions*, ranged over by $s, s', \ldots$, and *labels*, ranged over by $l, l', \ldots$.

The syntax of processes is given in Table 1. It uses the auxiliary definitions of Table 2 and the types of Table 3. The syntax occurring only at runtime appears shaded.

As hinted in the previous section, participants can either join a service in a *stable* modality and be present in all the sessions of the service (which start after they join and end before they leave), or join a service for exactly one session in a *one-shot* modality.

A new service is always opened by an initialiser of the form $a\langle G, \phi \rangle$, where G is a global type and ϕ is a mapping from histories and roles to truth values, representing the condition a principal must satisfy in order to be accepted as a participant with a given role in service a. The initialisation of service a creates a service registry $a[\mathscr{H}, \mathscr{O}_1, \mathscr{O}_2, \phi]$, where the *history set* $\mathscr{H}$ records the current mapping between principals and their histories, $\mathscr{O}_1$ and $\mathscr{O}_2$ are (initially empty) parallel compositions of *offers*, representing the participants who joined the service in a stable or one-shot modality, respectively.

Once the service a has been initialised, principal `id` can join the service in role r using $\overline{a}[\mathtt{id} : r, \mathscr{C}(\tilde{r})](x).\{P\}$ or $a[\mathtt{id} : r, \mathscr{C}(\tilde{r})](x).\{P\}$, becoming respectively a stable or a one-shot offer. The join is only allowed if the principal `id` does not already appear with the same role among the current offers, and if the histories associated with the other

Table 1. Processes

$P ::=$	Processes	$\mid P;P$	Sequential
$\mid a\langle G, \phi \rangle$	Service Init	$\mid \mathtt{if}\ e\ \mathtt{then}\ P\ \mathtt{else}\ P$	Conditional
$\mid \overline{u}[\mathtt{id} : r, \mathscr{C}(\tilde{r})](x).\{P\}$	Stable Join	$\mid \mathbf{0}$	Nil
$\mid u[\mathtt{id} : r, \mathscr{C}(\tilde{r})](x).\{P\}$	OneShot Join	$\mid X$	Recursion variable
$\mid \mathtt{quit}(u, p)$	Service Quit	$\mid \mu X.P$	Recursion
$\mid \mathtt{quit}\langle c \rangle$	Session Quit	$\mid (\nu a : G)\ P$	Service restriction
$\mid c!^*\langle p, l\langle \mathscr{I} \rangle \langle e \rangle \rangle$	Send	$\mid (\nu s)P$	Session restriction
$\mid c?\langle p, \{l_i\langle \mathscr{I}_i \rangle (x_i).P_i\}_{i \in I} \rangle$	Receive	$\mid s : \mathscr{B}$	Message buffer
$\mid c\forall(\iota \notin \mathscr{I} : \mathtt{C}(r, \iota)).\{P\}$	Poll	$\mid a[\mathscr{H}, \mathscr{O}, \mathscr{O}, \phi]$	Service registry
$\mid c\exists(\iota : \mathtt{B}(r)).\{P\}$	Choice	$\mid a\langle s, \mathscr{P} \rangle$	Session registry
$\mid P \mid P$	Parallel		

Table 2. Auxiliary definitions

u	$::= x \mid a \mid b \mid \ldots$	Service Id.
p	$::= \mathtt{id} : r \mid \iota : r$	Participant
$\mathscr{I}$	$::= \emptyset \mid \mathscr{I} \cup \mathtt{id} \mid \mathscr{I} \cup \iota$	Princ. Set
c	$::= x \mid s[p]$	Channel
v	$::= \mathtt{true} \mid \ldots \mid a \mid s[\mathtt{id} : r]$	Value
e	$::= x \mid v \mid e \wedge e \mid \ldots$	Expression
m	$::= (\mathtt{id} : r, \mathtt{id}' : r', l\langle\mathscr{I}\rangle\langle v\rangle)$	Message
$\mathscr{B}$	$::= [\,] \mid \mathscr{B} \cdot m$	Buffer
$\mathscr{O}$	$::=$	Offer Set
	$\mid \mathbf{0}$	Nil
	$\mid [\mathtt{id} : r](x).P$	Offer
	$\mid \mathscr{O} \mid \mathscr{O}$	Parallel

h	$::= () \mid h \cdot (l\langle\mathscr{I}\rangle\langle v\rangle, r)$	History
$\mathscr{H}$	$::= \emptyset \mid \mathscr{H} \cup (\mathtt{id}, h)$	History Set
$\mathscr{P}$	$::= \emptyset \mid \mathscr{P} \cup (\mathtt{id} : r)$	Part. Set

Conditions

$\mathtt{C}(\rho, r, \iota)$	$::= \phi(\rho \upharpoonright \iota, r)$	Single
$\mathtt{C}(r, \iota)$	$::= \lambda\rho.\ \mathtt{C}(\rho, r, \iota)$	Poll
$\mathscr{C}(\rho, \tilde{r})$	$::=$	Basic
	$\forall\iota.\ \mathtt{C}(\rho, r, \iota) \mid$	$r \in \tilde{r}$
	$\exists\iota.\ \mathtt{C}(\rho, r, \iota) \mid$	$r \in \tilde{r}$
	$\mathscr{C}_1(\rho, \tilde{r}) \wedge \mathscr{C}_2(\rho, \tilde{r}) \mid$	
	$\mathscr{C}_1(\rho, \tilde{r}) \vee \mathscr{C}_2(\rho, \tilde{r})$	
$\mathscr{C}(\tilde{r})$	$::= \lambda\rho.\ \mathscr{C}(\rho, \tilde{r})$	Join

principals present in the service satisfy the set of conditions $\mathscr{C}(\tilde{r})$ expected by id, what we call the *policy* of id. Moreover, the history of principal id in the service registry must satisfy the acceptance condition ϕ for the required role (in order to get started and allow fresh participants, some conditions must be satisfied by the empty history). Indeed, when a principal joins a service, her history is not necessarily empty, since she could have already joined and quit the service before. For stable join, the acceptance condition will be checked also at the start of each session. We call P the *body of the join.*

The join is implemented by registering the participant in the session registry as the offer $[\mathtt{id} : r](x).P$. The service a can be abandoned by the stable participant p by $\mathtt{quit}(a, p)$.

A service registry $a[\mathscr{H}, \mathscr{O}_1, \mathscr{O}_2, \phi]$ can initiate a session by creating a new session name s and a session registry $a\langle s, \mathscr{P}\rangle$, where $\mathscr{P}$ records the session participants. The offers in $\mathscr{O}_1$ whose histories satisfy the predicate ϕ for the required role (evaluating each offer's reputation) and all the offers in $\mathscr{O}_2$ will join that session. A session represents a particular instance or activation of a service. Session initiation replaces the variable x in the body of each offer $[\mathtt{id} : r](x).P$ with the corresponding session channel. Session channels are temporary channels created at the start of a session, and their lifetime is that of the session. Each participant has just one session channel and this is her only means for interacting with the other participants within a session.

The output process $c!^*\langle p, l\langle\mathscr{I}\rangle\langle e\rangle\rangle$ sends to p on channel c the value of expression e labelled by the constant l and the set of principals and principal variables $\mathscr{I}$. The symbol $!^*$ stands for two different kinds of send, ! and $!^\bullet$: ! is used for standard send, while $!^\bullet$ is used to send a message which will be registered in the history of the sender within the service register. The input process $c?\langle p, \{l_i\langle\mathscr{I}_i\rangle(x_i).P_i\}_{i\in I}\rangle$ expects from p on channel c a message with a label l in $\{l_i\}_{i\in I}$ and a set of principals and principal variables $\mathscr{I}$ in $\{\mathscr{I}_i\}_{i\in I}$. If $l = l_i$ and $\mathscr{I} = \mathscr{I}_i$, the value of the message will be replaced for the variable x_i, which is bound in P_i.

Table 3. Global and local types

G ::=	Global Types	T ::=	Local Types
$\mid\ p \to^* p\{l_i\langle U_i\rangle.G_i\}_{i\in I}$	Label. Mess.	$\mid\ !^*\langle p,\{l_i\langle \mathscr{I}_i\rangle\langle U_i\rangle.T_i\}_{i\in I}\rangle$	Selection
$\mid\ \forall\,\iota \notin \mathscr{I} : \mathtt{C}(r,\iota).G$	Univ. Quant.	$\mid\ ?\langle p,\{l_i\langle \mathscr{I}_i\rangle\langle U_i\rangle.T_i\}_{i\in I}\rangle$	Branching
$\mid\ \exists\,\iota : \mathtt{B}(r).G$	Exist. Quant.	$\mid\ \forall\,\iota \notin \mathscr{I} : \mathtt{C}(r,\iota).T$	Univ. Quant.
$\mid\ G \mid G \mid G\ ;\ G$	Paral., Seq.	$\mid\ \exists\,\iota : \mathtt{B}(r).T$	Exist. Quant.
$\mid\ \mu\mathbf{x}.G \mid \mathbf{x}$	Rec., Var.	$\mid\ T \mid T \mid T\ ; T$	Paral., Seq.
$\mid\ \varepsilon \mid \mathrm{end}$	Inact., End	$\mid\ \mu\mathbf{x}.T \mid \mathbf{x}$	Rec., Var.
		$\mid\ \varepsilon \mid \mathrm{end}$	Inact., End
U ::= $S \mid T$	Message Types	S ::= $\langle G\rangle \mid \mathrm{bool} \mid \mathrm{string} \mid \ldots$	Sorts

Polling $c\forall(\iota \notin \mathscr{I} : \mathtt{C}(r,\iota)).\{P\}$ allows interaction between c and all the principals ι not belonging to $\mathscr{I}$ that instantiate the role r and whose history satisfies the condition $\mathtt{C}(r,\iota)$. Process P (the *body of the poll*) is replicated for each such participant.

Choice $c\exists(\iota : \mathtt{B}(r)).\{P\}$ returns P where ι is replaced by one of the best principals with respect to criterion $\mathtt{B}$ among those playing role r in the session, that is, one of those enjoying the best reputation with respect to $\mathtt{B}$, if any. For instance, if r is *seller* and $\mathtt{B}(r)$ is $\mathtt{fast}(\mathit{seller})$, the choice $c\exists(\iota : \mathtt{B}(r)).\{P\}$ returns P where ι is replaced by one of the fastest sellers, unless there is no seller. This presupposes that for each role r of a service, and for each criterion $\mathtt{B}$ applicable to r, there exists a partial order $\sqsubseteq_{\mathtt{B}}$ on histories, parametrised on $\mathtt{B}$. For instance, $h \sqsubseteq_{\mathtt{fast}} h'$ means that the average delivery time recorded in h is less than or equal to the average delivery time recorded in h'.

Messages have the form $(\mathtt{id} : r, \mathtt{id}' : r', l\langle\mathscr{I}\rangle\langle v\rangle)$, including sender, receiver, label, set of transmitted participants and value as in [8]. Messages exchanged (asynchronously) in session s are stored in the message buffer $s{:}\mathscr{B}$.

Parallel and sequential composition, conditional and recursion are standard. The restriction $(\nu a : G)P$ creates a shared service name that can be used as a reference for a service specified by G, while $(\nu s)P$ represents a new session instance.

Histories h are built by recording some of the labels and values that are sent by the principals, together with the roles the principals belong to. A history set $\mathscr{H}$ is a set of pairs $(\mathtt{id}, h)$ associating a history with a principal $\mathtt{id}$. Histories are used to measure principals' reputation, that is, to check if principals satisfy the conditions and the criteria expressed in join, poll and choice operations. We project history sets on principals as follows:

$$\mathscr{H}\restriction \mathtt{id} = \begin{cases} h & \text{if } (\mathtt{id}, h) \in \mathscr{H}, \\ () & \text{otherwise} \end{cases}$$

Therefore, if ρ is a history set variable, $\phi(\rho\restriction\iota,\ r)$ expresses a condition (*single* condition) on the history of principal ι in the history set ρ relative to the role r. We denote by $\mathtt{C}(\rho, r,\ \iota)$ a single condition and by $\mathtt{C}(r,\iota)$ the abstraction with respect to ρ of a single condition. We use $\mathscr{C}(\rho,\tilde{r})$ for conditions (*basic* conditions) obtained from single conditions by universal or existential quantification on principal variables and by closure under conjunction and disjunction. Lastly, $\mathscr{C}(\tilde{r})$ is the abstraction of a basic condition with respect to ρ. For example, $\mathscr{C}(r_1,r_2)$ could be $\lambda\rho.\exists\iota_1.\phi_1(\rho\lceil\iota_1,r_1)\wedge\forall\iota_2.\phi_2(\rho\lceil\iota_2,r_2)$. For processes we adopt the following simplifications, already used in the example of Section 2: we omit empty sets of principals, we omit labels if there is a unique branch (i.e., we write $c!^*\langle p,v\rangle$, $c?\langle p,(x).P\rangle$), we omit empty values (i.e., we write $c!^*\langle p,l\rangle$, $c?\langle p,\{l_i.P_i\}_{i\in I}\rangle$), we use $\iota{:}r$ as short for $\iota{:}\mathsf{C}(r,\iota)$ when $\mathsf{C}(r,\iota)$ holds always true, and we omit roles for quantified principal variables (i.e., we write ι in the body of a quantification on $\iota{:}\mathsf{C}(r,\iota)$ or $\iota{:}\mathsf{B}(r)$). The writing of types is simplified in a similar way.

A process is *initial* if it does not contain free variables and runtime syntax.

To sum up, the syntax of our calculus differs from that of [8] for the following features:

1. we distinguish services and sessions, allowing multiple sessions for a single service;
2. we associate histories with principals participating in services;
3. we associate acceptance conditions with services, allowing them to filter out "bad" principals;
4. we associate policies with principals, allowing them to join a service only if the reputation of the other principals already present in the service satisfies the policies;
5. we add conditions to quantifications, allowing a participant to interact only with selected partners;
6. we offer a choice primitive, allowing a participant to choose one of the best principals (according to some specified criterion) among those playing a given role in a session.

4 Semantics

As usual, the operational semantics is defined modulo a structural equivalence $\equiv$. We assume the standard structural rules for processes [16]. Among the rules for buffers, we have one for swapping independent messages, i.e., messages with different sender or receiver. Moreover, the following rule

$$(\nu s)(a\langle s,\mathscr{P}\rangle \mid s:[\,]) \equiv \mathbf{0}$$

is useful to garbage collect ended sessions.

The reduction rules are given in Tables 4, 5, 6 and 7. We briefly comment on them.

Rule [ServiceInit] initialises a service by reducing $a\langle G,\phi\rangle$. It creates a *permanent* session registry $a[\emptyset,\mathbf{0},\mathbf{0},\phi]$ where the history set is empty, and two (initially null) groups of offers are created: the first is the parallel composition of all stable offers, that is, offers by participants who will be present in all sessions of the service, unless they behave "badly" or decide to leave the service. The second is the parallel composition of all one-shot offers, that is, offers by participants who will join one session only of the service and then leave it.

Rules [StableJoin] and [OneShotJoin] perform the registration of a participant as an offer associated with a service, in a stable or one-shot way, respectively. The applicant specifies: i) her identity `id`, ii) which role r she wants to play and iii) her policy, i.e. which conditions $\mathscr{C}(\tilde{r})$ must be satisfied by the histories of the principals that are already present. The join is successful if:

Table 4. Reduction rules I

[ServiceInit]
$a\langle G,\phi\rangle \longrightarrow a[\emptyset,\mathbf{0},\mathbf{0},\phi]$

[StableJoin]
$\bar{a}[\mathtt{id}:r,\mathscr{C}(\tilde{r})](y).\{P\} \mid a[\mathscr{H},\mathscr{O}_1,\mathscr{O}_2,\phi] \longrightarrow a[\mathscr{H}\flat\mathtt{id},\mathscr{O}_1 \mid [\mathtt{id}:r](y).P,\mathscr{O}_2,\phi]$
if $\mathscr{C}(\tilde{r})\mathscr{H}$ and $(\mathtt{id}:r)\notin\mathscr{O}_1\mid\mathscr{O}_2$ and $\phi(\mathscr{H}\upharpoonright\mathtt{id},r)$

[OneShotJoin]
$a[\mathtt{id}:r,\mathscr{C}(\tilde{r})](y).\{P\} \mid a[\mathscr{H},\mathscr{O}_1,\mathscr{O}_2,\phi] \longrightarrow a[\mathscr{H}\flat\mathtt{id},\mathscr{O}_1,\mathscr{O}_2 \mid [\mathtt{id}:r](y).P,\phi]$
if $\mathscr{C}(\tilde{r})\mathscr{H}$ and $(\mathtt{id}:r)\notin\mathscr{O}_1\mid\mathscr{O}_2$ and $\phi(\mathscr{H}\upharpoonright\mathtt{id},r)$

[SessionInit]
$a[\mathscr{H},\Pi_{i\in I}[\mathtt{id}_i:r_i](y_i).P_i \mid \Pi_{j\in J}[\mathtt{id}_j:r_j](y_j).P_j,\Pi_{k\in K}[\mathtt{id}_k:r_k](y_k).P_k,\phi] \longrightarrow$
$(\nu s)(a\langle s,\{\mathtt{id}_i:r_i|i\in I\cup K\}\rangle \mid \Pi_{i\in I\cup K}P_i\{s[\mathtt{id}_i:r_i]/y_i\} \mid s:[\,])\mid$
$a[\mathscr{H},\Pi_{i\in I}[\mathtt{id}_i:r_i](y_i).P_i \mid \Pi_{j\in J}[\mathtt{id}_j:r_j](y_j).P_j,\mathbf{0},\phi]$
if $\forall i\in I.\phi(\mathscr{H}\upharpoonright\mathtt{id}_i,r_i)$ and $\forall j\in J.\neg\phi(\mathscr{H}\upharpoonright\mathtt{id}_j,r_j)$

[ServiceQuit]
$\mathtt{quit}(a,\mathtt{id}:r) \mid a[\mathscr{H},\mathscr{O}_1,\mathscr{O}_2,\phi] \longrightarrow a[\mathscr{H},\mathscr{O}_1\backslash(\mathtt{id}:r),\mathscr{O}_2,\phi]$

[SessionQuit]
$\mathtt{quit}\langle s[\mathtt{id}:r]\rangle \mid a\langle s,\mathscr{P}\cup(\mathtt{id}:r)\rangle \longrightarrow a\langle s,\mathscr{P}\rangle$

1. the histories associated with the principals already present in the service satisfy these conditions, checked by $\mathscr{C}(\tilde{r})\mathscr{H}$;
2. the participant is not already present as an offer, i.e., $(\mathtt{id}:r)\notin\mathscr{O}_1\mid\mathscr{O}_2$, where we define:

$$(\mathtt{id}:r)\in\mathscr{O}\Leftrightarrow\mathscr{O}\equiv\mathscr{O}'\mid[\mathtt{id}:r](y).P \text{ for some } \mathscr{O}',P$$

3. the principal id has a history satisfying the predicate ϕ for role r, i.e., $\phi(\mathscr{H}\upharpoonright\mathtt{id},r)$ holds.

In the resulting service registry, id will have exactly one history since the update of a history set with a new principal is given by:

$$\mathscr{H}\flat\mathtt{id}=\begin{cases}\mathscr{H}\cup\{(\mathtt{id},(\,))\} & \text{if } \mathtt{id}\notin\mathscr{D}(\mathscr{H}),\\ \mathscr{H} & \text{otherwise}\end{cases}$$

where $\mathscr{D}(\mathscr{H})=\{\mathtt{id}\mid(\mathtt{id},h)\in\mathscr{H}\}$.

Notice that, for preserving the order of communications, no channel occurring in the bodies of the joins should occur in the processes which follow the joins. This is assured by the typing rules for the join constructors (rules ⌊StaJoin⌋ and ⌊OSJoin⌋ in Table 10). For example using [OneShotJoin] and [Par] (see Table 7) we could get:

$$a[\mathtt{id}_1:r_3](y).\{\,s[\mathtt{id}_1:r_1]!\langle\mathtt{id}_2:r_2,\mathtt{true}\rangle\,\};s[\mathtt{id}_1:r_1]!\langle\mathtt{id}_2:r_2,5\rangle\mid$$
$$a[\emptyset,\mathbf{0},\mathbf{0},\phi]\longrightarrow s[\mathtt{id}_1:r_1]!\langle\mathtt{id}_2:r_2,5\rangle\mid$$
$$a[\{(\mathtt{id}_1,(\,))\},\mathbf{0},[\mathtt{id}_1:r_3](y).s[\mathtt{id}_1:r_1]!\langle\mathtt{id}_2:r_2,\mathtt{true}\rangle,\phi]$$

In this way, the participant $\mathtt{id}_2:r_2$ could receive first 5 and then true from $\mathtt{id}_1:r_1$, instead of receiving first true and then 5, as expected.

Table 5. Reduction rules II

[Send]

$$s[\mathtt{id}:r]!\langle \mathtt{id}':r',l\langle\mathscr{I}\rangle\langle v\rangle\rangle \mid s:\mathscr{B} \longrightarrow s:\mathscr{B}\cdot(\mathtt{id}:r,\mathtt{id}':r',l\langle\mathscr{I}\rangle\langle v\rangle)$$

[SendR]

$$\begin{array}{l} s[\mathtt{id}:r]!^{\bullet}\langle \mathtt{id}':r',l\langle\mathscr{I}\rangle\langle v\rangle\rangle \mid \\ a[\mathscr{H}\cup(\mathtt{id},h),\mathscr{O}_1,\mathscr{O}_2,\phi] \mid s:\mathscr{B} \end{array} \longrightarrow \begin{array}{l} a[\mathscr{H}\cup(\mathtt{id},h\cdot(l\langle\mathscr{I}\rangle\langle v\rangle,r)),\mathscr{O}_1,\mathscr{O}_2,\phi] \mid \\ s:\mathscr{B}\cdot(\mathtt{id}:r,\mathtt{id}':r',l\langle\mathscr{I}\rangle\langle v\rangle) \end{array}$$

[Receive]

$$s[\mathtt{id}:r]?\langle \mathtt{id}':r',\{l_i\langle\mathscr{I}_i\rangle(x_i).P_i\}_{i\in I}\rangle \mid s:(\mathtt{id}':r',\mathtt{id}:r,l_k\langle\mathscr{I}_k\rangle\langle v\rangle)\cdot\mathscr{B} \longrightarrow P_k\{v/x_k\} \mid s:\mathscr{B}$$

where $k\in I$

Table 6. Reduction rules III

[Poll]

$$\begin{array}{l} s[\mathtt{id}:r]\forall(\iota\notin\mathscr{I}:\mathtt{C}(r',\iota)).\{P\} \mid \\ a\langle s,\mathscr{P}\rangle \mid a[\mathscr{H},\mathscr{O}_1,\mathscr{O}_2,\phi] \end{array} \longrightarrow \begin{array}{l} \Pi_{i\in I}s[\mathtt{id}:r]!\langle \mathtt{id}_i:r',\mathtt{YES}\rangle \mid \\ s[\mathtt{id}:r]?\langle \mathtt{id}_i:r',\{\mathtt{YES}.P\{\mathtt{id}_i/\iota\},\mathtt{NO}.\mathbf{0}\}\rangle \mid \\ \Pi_{j\in J}s[\mathtt{id}:r]!\langle \mathtt{id}_j:r',\mathtt{NO}\rangle \mid \\ s[\mathtt{id}:r]?\langle \mathtt{id}_j:r',\{\mathtt{YES}.\mathbf{0},\mathtt{NO}.\mathbf{0}\}\rangle \mid \\ a\langle s,\mathscr{P}\rangle \mid a[\mathscr{H},\mathscr{O}_1,\mathscr{O}_2,\phi] \end{array}$$

where $\{\mathtt{id}_i \mid i\in I\} = \{\mathtt{id}' \mid (\mathtt{id}':r')\in\mathscr{P} \wedge \mathtt{C}(r',\mathtt{id}')\mathscr{H} \wedge \mathtt{id}'\notin\mathscr{I}\}$
and $\{\mathtt{id}_j \mid j\in J\} = \{\mathtt{id}' \mid (\mathtt{id}':r')\in\mathscr{P} \wedge (\neg\mathtt{C}(r',\mathtt{id}')\mathscr{H} \vee \mathtt{id}'\in\mathscr{I})\}$
if $\iota:r'$ occurs as subject in P

[PassivePoll]

$$s[\mathtt{id}:r]\forall(\iota\notin\mathscr{I}:r').\{P\} \mid a\langle s,\mathscr{P}\rangle \longrightarrow \Pi_{\mathtt{id}':r'\in\mathscr{P}\ \mathtt{id}'\notin\mathscr{I}}P\{\mathtt{id}'/\iota\}$$

if $\iota:r'$ occurs only as object in P

[Choice]

$$\begin{array}{l} s[\mathtt{id}:r]\exists(\iota:\mathtt{B}(r')).\{P\} \mid \\ a\langle s,\mathscr{P}\rangle \mid a[\mathscr{H},\mathscr{O}_1,\mathscr{O}_2,\phi] \end{array} \longrightarrow \begin{array}{l} s[\mathtt{id}:r]!\langle \mathtt{id}':r',\mathtt{YES}\rangle \mid \\ s[\mathtt{id}:r]?\langle \mathtt{id}':r',\{\mathtt{YES}.P\{\mathtt{id}'/\iota\},\mathtt{NO}.\mathbf{0}\}\rangle \mid \\ \Pi_{j\in J}s[\mathtt{id}:r]!\langle \mathtt{id}_j:r',\mathtt{NO}\rangle \mid \\ s[\mathtt{id}:r]?\langle \mathtt{id}_j:r',\{\mathtt{YES}.\mathbf{0},\mathtt{NO}.\mathbf{0}\}\rangle \mid \\ a\langle s,\mathscr{P}\rangle \mid a[\mathscr{H},\mathscr{O}_1,\mathscr{O}_2,\phi] \end{array}$$

where $\{\mathtt{id}_j \mid j\in J\} = \{\mathtt{id}'' \mid (\mathtt{id}'':r')\in\mathscr{P} \wedge \mathtt{id}''\neq\mathtt{id}'\}$
if $\mathtt{B}(r')\mathscr{H}\mathscr{P} = \mathtt{id}'$

[NoChoice]

$$s[\mathtt{id}:r]\exists(\iota:\mathtt{B}(r')).\{P\} \mid a\langle s,\mathscr{P}\rangle \longrightarrow a\langle s,\mathscr{P}\rangle \qquad \text{if } \nexists(\mathtt{id}':r')\in\mathscr{P}$$

In case of stable joins, we cannot allow free channels at all, as explained below when rule [SessionInit] is discussed.

Notice that our double join mechanism, with possibly multiple sessions associated with a single service, prevents new participants from intervening in the middle of an ongoing session. In this way, we avoid the need for a locking policy, as required in [8] to assure safe synchronisation.

Rule [SessionInit] initiates a session by reducing $a[\mathscr{H},\mathscr{O}_1,\mathscr{O}_2,\phi]$. It creates a fresh session name s, a session registry $a\langle s,\mathscr{P}\rangle$ and an empty message buffer $\mathscr{B}$ named s, like the new session. The participant set $\mathscr{P}$ contains:

1. the identities and roles of all the offers in $\mathscr{O}_1$ whose histories satisfy ϕ;
2. the identities and roles of all the offers in $\mathscr{O}_2$. We do not check the reputations of participants in $\mathscr{O}_2$ since they were good at the moment of the service join and these participants may be active for one session only.

The new session activates the offers in $\mathscr{O}_1 \mid \mathscr{O}_2$ listed in $\mathscr{P}$ by replacing $s[\mathtt{id} : r]$ for the private channel of the offer with identity id and role r. The resulting session registry does not have one-shot offers and it has the same stable offers. Note that if $[\mathtt{id} : r](y).P$ is a stable offer with a good history, then we get $P\{s[\mathtt{id} : r]/y\}$ for all s created by reducing the service registry. Therefore, in order to preserve channel linearity, our type system requires that y is the only free channel in P (see rule $\lfloor$STAJOIN$\rfloor$ in Table 10).

Rules [ServiceQuit] and [SessionQuit] allow a participant to leave a service or a session, respectively. When quitting a service, the participant is cancelled from the stable offers (if among them), but she remains in the session registries when present. When quitting a session, the participant is cancelled from the session registry.

In both cases the participant's history remains in the service registry. The cancellation from the stable offers is defined by:

$$\mathscr{O}\backslash(\mathtt{id} : r) = \begin{cases} \mathscr{O}' & \text{if } \mathscr{O} \equiv \mathscr{O}' \mid [\mathtt{id} : r](y).P \text{ for some } \mathscr{O}', P \\ \mathscr{O} & \text{otherwise} \end{cases}$$

Rule [Send] describes the standard asynchronous send, implemented by putting the message in the message buffer s.

Rule [SendR] describes the asynchronous send of a relevant message, which must be registered in the history of the sender. Again, the message is put in the message buffer s. The intention of recording the message sent is expressed by the programmer by using the symbol $!^\bullet$. The history h of principal id is extended by the pair $(l\langle\mathscr{I}\rangle\langle v\rangle, r)$.

Rule [Receive] specifies the reception of a matching message from the buffer, and the selection of the corresponding continuation.

The most subtle rules are those for the poll and choice operators. Before examining these rules in detail, we start with some observations. Note first that, in a global type, each communication occurs between two participants of the form $\iota : r$ and $\iota' : r'$, whose principal variables ι and ι' are both quantified, either universally or existentially. A universal quantification on ι in role r may either be simple, as in [8], or *conditional*, i.e., controlled by a condition $\mathtt{C}(r, \iota)$ on the history of ι, which will hold only for some of the session participants (possibly none). Its effect is to spawn in parallel all participants satisfying that condition. An existential quantification on ι in role r is always conditional, i.e., guided by some criterion $\mathtt{B}(r)$ on the history of ι. Its effect is to spawn exactly one participant among those best satisfying that criterion, if any. Now, if both the principal variables ι and ι' are conditionally quantified, this means that each role imposes some condition on the other, and hence some potential interactions between the two - possibly all - should be filtered out. Only the "good pairs" of participants, where each partner satisfies the condition required by the other, should be allowed to interact. Now, the fact that a condition is satisfied by a participant can only be checked by the partner requiring that condition. Hence a cross-checking is necessary. For this reason, in the rules for poll and choice, each participant sends a message YES to all participants that are "good" in her view (because they comply with her policy) and a message NO to all participants that are "bad". Symmetrically, she waits for either YES or NO from both good and bad participants. For example, suppose that b1 and b2 are the only *goldBuyer*s in session s, and that b1 is a keen *goldBuyer* and b2 is not. In this case, a *goldSeller* s1 who wants to interact with all keen *goldBuyer*s will send YES to b1, NO to b2 and wait for either YES or NO from both b1 and b2. The interaction between s1 and b1 will start only if s1 receives YES from b1. For this reason, the body P of the poll with b1 replaced for ι must be guarded by the reception of YES from b1.

Using gB and gS as short for *goldBuyer* and *goldSeller* we get:

$$s[\mathtt{s1}:gS]\forall(\iota:\mathtt{keen}(gB,\iota).\{P\} \longrightarrow \begin{array}{l} s[\mathtt{s1}:gS]!\langle \mathtt{b1}:gB,\mathtt{YES}\rangle \mid \\ s[\mathtt{s1}:gS]?\langle \mathtt{b1}:gB,\{\mathtt{YES}.P\{\mathtt{b1}/\iota\},\mathtt{NO}.\mathbf{0}\}\rangle \mid \\ s[\mathtt{s1}:gS]!\langle \mathtt{b2}:gB,\mathtt{NO}\rangle \mid \\ s[\mathtt{s1}:gS]?\langle \mathtt{b2}:gB,\{\mathtt{YES}.\mathbf{0},\mathtt{NO}.\mathbf{0}\}\rangle \end{array}$$

For instance, if b1 only wants to interact with fast *goldSeller*s, and s1 is not fast, then b1 will reply NO and the interaction will not take place.

This discussion explains the "agreement protocol" in the reduction rule [Poll]. However, there is a further subtlety to take into account. Notice that a quantified principal variable ι may be sent in the content of a message, as part of the set $\mathscr{I}$. As explained in [8], this is essential to avoid ambiguity in the routing of messages. A paradigmatic example is a forwarder:

$$\forall\, \iota_1 : r_1.\forall\, \iota_2 : \mathtt{C}(r_2,\iota_2).\iota_1 \to \iota_2\ \mathtt{OK};\forall\, \iota_3 : \mathtt{C}'(r_3,\iota_3).\iota_2 \to \iota_3\ \mathtt{OK}\langle \iota_1\rangle$$

If the message sent by ι_2 would not contain ι_1 and there would be more than one principal in role r_1, then the participants in role r_3 could not predict the number of messages they should receive, which is $n_1 \times n_2$, where n_1 is the number of principals in role r_1 and n_2 is the number of principals in role r_2 satisfying condition $\mathtt{C}(r_2,\iota_2)$.

Now, we want to argue that if a principal identifier is transmitted in a message inside the body of a universal quantification, then this quantification cannot be conditional. Indeed, since such a quantification would occur both in the sending and in the receiving process, and the history of the transmitted principal could change between the time of sending and the time of receiving, a mismatch could arise if the quantification were allowed to be conditional, thus invalidating the property of communication safety. For example, if b1 : *buyer* sends to s1 : *seller* all the names of reliable couriers, and c1 : *courier* is reliable when b1 sends the message, but no more reliable when s1 receives it, then the message would remain forever in the buffer. For this reason the typing rules of Section 5 guarantee that all principal variables which occur in messages are universally quantified without conditions.

To formalise these concepts, it is useful to distinguish the two ways in which a principal variable ι may occur in a process P. We say that ι occurs in P:

- as *subject*, if for some role r, P contains a subprocess $-!^*\langle \iota : r, -\langle - \rangle\langle - \rangle\rangle-$ or a subprocess $-?\langle \iota : r, \{-\langle - \rangle(-).-\}\rangle$;
- as *object*, if P contains a subprocess $-!^*\langle -, -\langle \mathscr{I}\rangle\langle - \rangle\rangle$ such that $\iota \in \mathscr{I}$, or a subprocess $-?\langle -, \{-\langle \mathscr{I}_i\rangle(-).-\}_{i\in I}\rangle$ such that $\iota \in \mathscr{I}_i$ for some $i \in I$.

Table 7. Reduction rules IV

$[\mathsf{If}-\mathsf{T}]$
$\texttt{if true then } P \texttt{ else } Q \longrightarrow P$

$[\mathsf{If}-\mathsf{F}]$
$\texttt{if false then } P \texttt{ else } Q \longrightarrow Q$

$[\mathsf{Par}]$

$$\frac{P \mid Q \longrightarrow P' \mid Q'}{\mathscr{E}[P] \mid Q \longrightarrow \mathscr{E}[P'] \mid Q'}$$

$[\mathsf{Congr}]$

$$\frac{P \equiv P' \longrightarrow Q' \equiv Q}{P \longrightarrow Q}$$

Clearly, the cross-checking described above is sensible only if the quantified principal variable occurs as subject in the body of the quantification. This is always true for well-typed processes in the case of existential quantification. For this reason, in rule $[\mathsf{Choice}]$ participant $s[\mathtt{id}:r]$ sends $\mathtt{YES}$ to a principal of $\mathscr{P}$ playing role r' and having one of the best histories according to the criterion $\mathtt{B}(r')$, and $\mathtt{NO}$ to all the remaining principals of $\mathscr{P}$ playing role r', and then she waits for $\mathtt{YES}$ or $\mathtt{NO}$ from all of them. Rule $[\mathsf{NoChoice}]$ is used when there is no principal in role r'.

Similarly, if the quantified principal variable occurs as subject in rule $[\mathsf{Poll}]$, participant $s[\mathtt{id}:r]$ sends $\mathtt{YES}$ or $\mathtt{NO}$ to all principals of $\mathscr{P}$ playing role r', according to whether their histories satisfy the condition $\mathtt{C}(r',\iota)$ or not, and waits for $\mathtt{YES}$ or $\mathtt{NO}$ from all of them. Instead, if ι only occurs as an object in the body of a universal quantification, we apply rule $[\mathsf{PassivePoll}]$, which simply spawns in parallel copies of the body with identifiers replaced for the principal variable, as in [8].

A last observation is that a quantification of a participant which does not occur in the body is useless and for this reason our type system does not allow it.

In the contextual rule $[\mathsf{Par}]$ the *evaluation contexts* are defined by:

$$\begin{aligned}\mathscr{E} ::= & \ [-] \mid \mathscr{E} \mid P \mid \mathscr{E};P \mid (\nu a:G)\mathscr{E} \mid (\nu s)\mathscr{E} \mid s[\mathtt{id}:r]!^{*}\langle \mathtt{id}':r',l\langle\mathscr{I}\rangle\langle\mathscr{E}\rangle\rangle \\ & \mid \texttt{if } \mathscr{E} \texttt{ then } P \texttt{ else } P \mid \mathscr{E}\wedge e \mid v \wedge \mathscr{E} \mid \ldots\end{aligned}$$

We assume that bound names in $\mathscr{E}$ and free names in Q are disjoint in rule $[\mathsf{Par}]$. Notice that the standard contextual rule:

$$\frac{P \longrightarrow P'}{\mathscr{E}[P] \longrightarrow \mathscr{E}[P']}$$

is derived from rules $[\mathsf{Par}]$ and $[\mathsf{Congr}]$.

5 Typing

5.1 Types

The syntax of global and local types is given in Table 3. The main novelty with respect to [8] is the addition of the existential quantification. Moreover, our universal quantification is different, as our polling construct does not accept all principals in a certain role, but only the ones verifying a given condition based on their history. Therefore, we concentrate on these two kinds of global and local types and refer the reader to [8] for the other kinds.

The projection from global types to local types is defined as in [8] but for the case of quantifiers, which is given in Table 8.

Well-formed global types must satisfy all conditions given in [8], i.e., they must be syntactically correct, projectable and linear.

5.2 Typing Rules

As usual, to type sessions we use a session environment, ranged over by Δ, which associates local types with channels, as well as a standard environment, ranged over by Γ, which associates sorts with value variables, global sorts with service names, roles with principal variables, and session environments with process variables.

$$\Delta ::= \emptyset \mid c : T \qquad \Gamma ::= \emptyset \mid \Gamma, x : S \mid a : \langle G \rangle \mid \Gamma, \iota : r \mid \Gamma, X : \Delta$$

Table 9 gives the typing rules for expressions and participants, taken from [8].

Our typing for processes assures that the joins and quits of two different principals cannot be *sequentialised*. This condition means that if there is an order among the actions of different principals, this must be made explicit via some communications, and should not be hidden by a sequentialisation (for instance, in the example of Section 2, we want to allow the same principal to perform some actions first as a *seller* and then as a *goldSeller*, but we do not want the actions of principal `b1` to depend on the actions of principal `s1`, without informing them both).

There are two kinds of typing judgments for processes. The most liberal judgment is $\Gamma \vdash P \triangleright \Delta$: it says that under the assumptions in Γ the channels in the process P have the local types prescribed by Δ. The judgment $\Gamma \vdash_{\mathtt{id}} P \triangleright \Delta$ assures also that `id` is the only principal occurring in P. This is used to guarantee the condition discussed above.

Table 8. Projection of quantified global types

$$(\forall\, \iota \notin \mathscr{I} : \mathtt{C}(r,\iota).G) \upharpoonright (\mathtt{id} : r) = G\{\mathtt{id}/\iota\} \upharpoonright (\mathtt{id} : r) \mid (\forall\, \iota \notin \mathscr{I} \cup \{\mathtt{id}\} : \mathtt{C}(r,\iota).G) \upharpoonright (\mathtt{id} : r) \quad \text{if } \mathtt{id} \notin \mathscr{I}$$

$$(\forall\, \iota \notin \mathscr{I} : \mathtt{C}(r,\iota).G) \upharpoonright (\mathtt{id} : r') = \forall\, \iota \notin \mathscr{I} : \mathtt{C}(r,\iota).G \upharpoonright (\mathtt{id} : r') \text{ if } r' \neq r \text{ or } \mathtt{id} \in \mathscr{I}$$

$$(\exists\, \iota : \mathtt{B}(r).G) \upharpoonright (\mathtt{id} : r) = G\{\mathtt{id}/\iota\} \upharpoonright (\mathtt{id} : r)$$

$$(\exists\, \iota : \mathtt{B}(r).G) \upharpoonright (\mathtt{id} : r') = \exists\, \iota : \mathtt{B}(r).G \upharpoonright (\mathtt{id} : r') \qquad \text{if } r' \neq r$$

Table 9. Typing rules for expressions and participants

$$\frac{}{\Gamma \vdash \mathtt{true}, \mathtt{false} : bool}\ \lfloor\text{BOOL}\rfloor \qquad \frac{\Gamma \vdash e_i : bool \quad (i = 1,2)}{\Gamma \vdash e_1 \vee e_2 : bool}\ \lfloor\text{OR}\rfloor \quad \ldots$$

$$\frac{}{\Gamma \vdash \emptyset}\ \lfloor\text{PSE}\rfloor \qquad \frac{\Gamma \vdash \mathscr{I}}{\Gamma \vdash \mathscr{I} \cup \{\mathtt{id}\}}\ \lfloor\text{PSI}\rfloor \qquad \frac{\Gamma \vdash \mathscr{I} \quad \iota : r \in \Gamma}{\Gamma \vdash \mathscr{I} \cup \{\iota\}}\ \lfloor\text{PSV}\rfloor$$

$$\frac{}{\Gamma \vdash \mathtt{id} : r}\ \lfloor\text{PA}\rfloor \qquad \frac{\iota : r \in \Gamma}{\Gamma \vdash \iota : r}\ \lfloor\text{PAV}\rfloor$$

Table 10. Type system $\vdash_{\mathtt{id}}$

$$\frac{\Delta : \text{end}}{\Gamma \vdash_{\mathtt{id}} \mathbf{0} \rhd \Delta}\lfloor\text{NIL}\rfloor \quad \frac{}{\Gamma, X : \Delta \vdash_{\mathtt{id}} X \rhd \Delta}\lfloor\text{RVAR}\rfloor \quad \frac{\Gamma, X : \Delta \vdash_{\mathtt{id}} P \rhd \Delta}{\Gamma \vdash_{\mathtt{id}} \mu X.P \rhd \Delta}\lfloor\text{REC}\rfloor$$

$$\frac{\Gamma \vdash u : \langle G \rangle \quad \Gamma \vdash_{\mathtt{id}} P \rhd y : G \upharpoonright (\mathtt{id} : r)}{\Gamma \vdash_{\mathtt{id}} \overline{u}[\mathtt{id} : r, \mathscr{C}(\tilde{r})](y).\{P\} \rhd \emptyset}\lfloor\text{STAJOIN}\rfloor$$

$$\frac{\Gamma \vdash u : \langle G \rangle \quad \Gamma \vdash_{\mathtt{id}} P \rhd \Delta, y : G \upharpoonright (\mathtt{id} : r) \quad \mathtt{ns}(\Delta)}{\Gamma \vdash_{\mathtt{id}} u[\mathtt{id} : r, \mathscr{C}(\tilde{r})](y).\{P\} \rhd \Delta}\lfloor\text{OSJOIN}\rfloor$$

$$\frac{\Delta : \text{end}}{\Gamma, a : \langle G \rangle \vdash_{\mathtt{id}} \mathtt{quit}(a, \mathtt{id} : r) \rhd \Delta}\lfloor\text{SERQUIT}\rfloor \quad \frac{\Delta : \text{end}}{\Gamma \vdash_{\mathtt{id}} \mathtt{quit}\langle c \rangle \rhd \Delta, c : \text{end}}\lfloor\text{SESQUIT}\rfloor$$

$$\frac{\Gamma \vdash p \quad \Gamma \vdash \mathscr{I}_j \quad \Gamma \vdash e : S_j \quad \Gamma \vdash_{\mathtt{id}} P \rhd \Delta, c : T_j \quad j \in I}{\Gamma \vdash_{\mathtt{id}} c!^*\langle p, l_j\langle \mathscr{I}_j \rangle\langle e \rangle\rangle; P \rhd \Delta, c : !^*\langle p, \{l_i\langle \mathscr{I}_i \rangle\langle S_i \rangle.T_i\}_{i \in I}\rangle}\lfloor\text{VSEND}\rfloor$$

$$\frac{\Gamma \vdash p \quad \Gamma \vdash \mathscr{I}_i \qquad \Gamma, x_i : S_i \vdash_{\mathtt{id}} P_i \rhd \Delta, c : T_i \quad \forall i \in I}{\Gamma \vdash_{\mathtt{id}} c?\langle p, \{l_i\langle \mathscr{I}_i \rangle(x_i).P_i\}_{i \in I}\rangle \rhd \Delta, c : ?\langle p, \{l_i\langle \mathscr{I}_i \rangle\langle S_i \rangle.T_i\}_{i \in I}\rangle}\lfloor\text{VRCV}\rfloor$$

$$\frac{\Gamma \vdash p \quad \Gamma \vdash \mathscr{I}_j \quad \Gamma \vdash_{\mathtt{id}} P \rhd \Delta, c : T_j \quad j \in I}{\Gamma \vdash_{\mathtt{id}} c!\langle p, l_j\langle \mathscr{I}_j \rangle\langle c' \rangle\rangle; P \rhd \Delta, c : !^*\langle p, \{l_i\langle \mathscr{I}_i \rangle\langle T \rangle.T_i\}_{i \in I}\rangle, c' : T}\lfloor\text{CSEND}\rfloor$$

$$\frac{\Gamma \vdash p \quad \Gamma \vdash \mathscr{I}_i \qquad \Gamma \vdash_{\mathtt{id}} P_i \rhd \Delta, c : T_i, x_i : T \quad \forall i \in I}{\Gamma \vdash_{\mathtt{id}} c?\langle p, \{l_i\langle \mathscr{I}_i \rangle(x_i).P_i\}_{i \in I}\rangle \rhd \Delta, c : ?\langle p, \{l_i\langle \mathscr{I}_i \rangle\langle T \rangle.T_i\}_{i \in I}\rangle}\lfloor\text{CRCV}\rfloor$$

$$\frac{\Gamma, \iota : r \vdash_{\mathtt{id}} P \rhd c : T \quad \mathtt{ubi}(T, \iota) \wedge \mathtt{noo}(T, \iota)}{\Gamma \vdash_{\mathtt{id}} c\forall(\iota \notin \mathscr{I} : \mathtt{C}(r, \iota)).\{P\} \rhd c : \forall\, \iota \notin \mathscr{I} : \mathtt{C}(r, \iota).T}\lfloor\text{POLL}\rfloor$$

$$\frac{\Gamma, \iota : r \vdash_{\mathtt{id}} P \rhd c : T \quad \mathtt{ubi}(T, \iota)}{\Gamma \vdash_{\mathtt{id}} c\forall(\iota \notin \mathscr{I} : r).\{P\} \rhd c : \forall \iota \notin \mathscr{I} : r.T}\lfloor\text{POLLALL}\rfloor$$

$$\frac{\Gamma, \iota : r \vdash_{\mathtt{id}} P \rhd c : T \quad \mathtt{sub}(T, \iota) \wedge \mathtt{noo}(T, \iota)}{\Gamma \vdash_{\mathtt{id}} c\exists(\iota : \mathtt{B}(r)).\{P\} \rhd c : \exists\, \iota : \mathtt{B}(r).T}\lfloor\text{CHOICE}\rfloor$$

$$\frac{\Gamma \vdash_{\mathtt{id}} P_1 \rhd \Delta_1 \quad \Gamma \vdash_{\mathtt{id}} P_2 \rhd \Delta_2}{\Gamma \vdash_{\mathtt{id}} P_1; P_2 \rhd \Delta_1; \Delta_2}\lfloor\text{SEQ}\rfloor \quad \frac{\Gamma \vdash e : \mathit{bool} \quad \Gamma \vdash_{\mathtt{id}} P_1 \rhd \Delta \quad \Gamma \vdash_{\mathtt{id}} P_2 \rhd \Delta}{\Gamma \vdash_{\mathtt{id}} \mathtt{if}\ e\ \mathtt{then}\ P_1\ \mathtt{else}\ P_2 \rhd \Delta}\lfloor\text{IF}\rfloor$$

$$\frac{\Gamma \vdash_{\mathtt{id}} P_1 \rhd \Delta_1 \quad \Gamma \vdash_{\mathtt{id}} P_2 \rhd \Delta_2}{\Gamma \vdash_{\mathtt{id}} P_1 \mid P_2 \rhd \Delta_1 \mid \Delta_2}\lfloor\text{PAR}_{\mathtt{id}}\rfloor \quad \frac{\Gamma, a : \langle G \rangle \vdash_{\mathtt{id}} P \rhd \Delta}{\Gamma \vdash_{\mathtt{id}} (\nu a : G)P \rhd \Delta}\lfloor\text{RES}_{\mathtt{id}}\rfloor$$

Table 11. Type system $\vdash$

$$\frac{\Gamma \vdash_{\mathtt{id}} P \rhd \Delta}{\Gamma \vdash P \rhd \Delta}\lfloor\mathrm{NOid}\rfloor \qquad \frac{\Gamma \vdash a : \langle G\rangle}{\Gamma \vdash a\langle G, \phi\rangle \rhd \emptyset}\lfloor\mathrm{INIT}\rfloor$$

$$\frac{\Gamma \vdash P_1 \rhd \Delta_1 \quad \Gamma \vdash P_2 \rhd \Delta_2}{\Gamma \vdash P_1 \mid P_2 \rhd \Delta_1 \mid \Delta_2}\lfloor\mathrm{PAR}\rfloor \qquad \frac{\Gamma, a : \langle G\rangle \vdash P \rhd \Delta}{\Gamma \vdash (\nu a : G)P \rhd \Delta}\lfloor\mathrm{RES}\rfloor$$

Table 10 contains the rules for the system $\vdash_{\mathtt{id}}$, which we briefly comment.

The session environments for **0** (rule $\lfloor$NIL$\rfloor$) can only contain the types ε and end: this is enforced by the premise Δ : end, which means that all types occurring in Δ are either ε or end. Rules $\lfloor$RVAR$\rfloor$ and $\lfloor$REC$\rfloor$ for recursion are standard.

As usual, rules $\lfloor$STAJOIN$\rfloor$ and $\lfloor$OSJOIN$\rfloor$ check that the local type of the participant channel coincides with the projection of the global type for the required role. Moreover, to type a stable service join we require that the participant channel is the only channel in the body of the join. This is necessary in order to assure that the application of rule [SessionInit] preserves the linearity of channels, see page 12. Peculiar to our system is also the condition in rule $\lfloor$OSJOIN$\rfloor$, stating that all channels but y in P have types terminating by end or by a recursion variable. The reason for this restriction is to prevent channels in P from being used in processes following P (see the discussion at page 11). To this aim we define the predicate $\mathtt{ns}(T)$, letting $\dagger$ range over $\{?, !^*\}$:

$$\mathtt{ns}(\dagger\langle p, \{l_i\langle \mathscr{I}_i\rangle\langle U_i\rangle.T_i\}_{i\in I}\rangle) = \textstyle\bigwedge_{i\in I}\mathtt{ns}(T_i) \quad \mathtt{ns}(T \mid T') = \mathtt{ns}(T) \wedge \mathtt{ns}(T')$$
$$\mathtt{ns}(\forall\, \iota' \notin \mathscr{I} : \mathtt{C}(r, \iota').T) = \mathtt{ns}(\exists\, \iota' : \mathtt{B}(r).T) = \mathtt{ns}(\mu\mathbf{x}.T) = \mathtt{ns}(T' \;;\; T) = \mathtt{ns}(T)$$
$$\mathtt{ns}(\mathbf{x}) = \mathtt{ns}(\mathrm{end}) = \mathtt{true} \quad \mathtt{ns}(\varepsilon) = \mathtt{false}$$

We then extend this predicate to session environments by letting $\mathtt{ns}(\Delta) = \bigwedge_{c:T\in\Delta}\mathtt{ns}(T)$.

A participant may ask to quit a service (rule $\lfloor$SERQUIT$\rfloor$) at any point. She will cease to take part in the service starting from the first session initiated after her withdrawal. Instead, rule $\lfloor$SESQUIT$\rfloor$ prescribes that a session may be quit only after the participant has terminated her task.

The system types communications on channel c with participant p allowing different labels, sequences of participants, values and continuations (rules $\lfloor$VSEND$\rfloor$ and $\lfloor$VRCV$\rfloor$). Also the exchange of channels can be typed (rules $\lfloor$CSEND$\rfloor$ and $\lfloor$CRCV$\rfloor$). Notice that the type system does not allow sending a channel with $!^\bullet$ since there is no meaning in putting a channel name in the history of a principal. Moreover, the session names occurring in channels are restricted and therefore, in order to do that, we should enlarge the scope of these restrictions, making it impossible to use the current structural equivalence to cancel exhausted sessions.

The typing of a quantification requires a unique channel in the session environment (rules $\lfloor$POLL$\rfloor$, $\lfloor$POLLALL$\rfloor$ and $\lfloor$CHOICE$\rfloor$). As argued in the previous section, participants that occur in messages (i.e., that occur as objects in processes) should be universally quantified without conditions on their histories. There is another condition that must be satisfied in order to avoid message ambiguity: participants who are universally quantified should appear (either as a subject or as an object) in every communication occurring in the body of the quantification. In order to check the above conditions, it

Table 12. The predicates ubi, noo and sub

$$\mathtt{ubi}(\dagger\langle p,\{l_i\langle\mathscr{I}_i\rangle\langle U_i\rangle.T_i\}_{i\in I}\rangle,\iota)=\begin{cases}\mathtt{true} & \text{if } p=\iota:r \text{ for some } r \text{ or}\\ & \iota\in\mathscr{I}_i \text{ for all } i\in I\\ \mathtt{false} & \text{otherwise}\end{cases}$$

$$\mathtt{ubi}(\forall\,\iota'\notin\mathscr{I}:\mathtt{C}(r,\iota').T,\iota)=\mathtt{ubi}(\exists\,\iota':\mathtt{B}(r).T,\iota)=\mathtt{ubi}(\mu\mathbf{x}.T,\iota)=\mathtt{ubi}(T,\iota)$$
$$\mathtt{ubi}(T\mid T',\iota)=\mathtt{ubi}(T\,;\,T',\iota)=\mathtt{ubi}(T,\iota)\wedge\mathtt{ubi}(T',\iota)$$
$$\mathtt{ubi}(\mathbf{x},\iota)=\mathtt{ubi}(\varepsilon,\iota)=\mathtt{ubi}(\text{end},\iota)=\mathtt{true}$$

$$\mathtt{noo}(\dagger\langle p,\{l_i\langle\mathscr{I}_i\rangle\langle U_i\rangle.T_i\}_{i\in I}\rangle,\iota)=\begin{cases}\mathtt{true} & \text{if } \iota\notin\mathscr{I}_i \text{ for all } i\in I,\\ \mathtt{false} & \text{otherwise}\end{cases}$$

$$\mathtt{noo}(\forall\,\iota'\notin\mathscr{I}:\mathtt{C}(r,\iota').T,\iota)=\mathtt{noo}(\exists\,\iota':\mathtt{B}(r).T,\iota)=\mathtt{noo}(\mu\mathbf{x}.T,\iota)=\mathtt{noo}(T,\iota)$$
$$\mathtt{noo}(T\mid T',\iota)=\mathtt{noo}(T\,;\,T',\iota)=\mathtt{noo}(T,\iota)\wedge\mathtt{noo}(T',\iota)$$
$$\mathtt{noo}(\mathbf{x},\iota)=\mathtt{noo}(\varepsilon,\iota)=\mathtt{noo}(\text{end},\iota)=\mathtt{true}$$

$$\mathtt{sub}(\dagger\langle p,\{l_i\langle\mathscr{I}_i\rangle\langle U_i\rangle.T_i\}_{i\in I}\rangle,\iota)=\begin{cases}\mathtt{true} & \text{if } p=\iota:r \text{ for some } r,\\ \mathtt{false} & \text{otherwise}\end{cases}$$

$$\mathtt{sub}(\forall\,\iota'\notin\mathscr{I}:\mathtt{C}(r,\iota').T,\iota)=\mathtt{sub}(\exists\,\iota':\mathtt{B}(r).T,\iota)=\mathtt{sub}(\mu\mathbf{x}.T,\iota)=\mathtt{sub}(T,\iota)$$
$$\mathtt{sub}(T\mid T',\iota)=\mathtt{sub}(T\,;\,T',\iota)=\mathtt{sub}(T,\iota)\vee\mathtt{sub}(T',\iota)$$
$$\mathtt{sub}(\mathbf{x},\iota)=\mathtt{sub}(\varepsilon,\iota)=\mathtt{sub}(\text{end},\iota)=\mathtt{false}$$

is handy to define three predicates on local types and principal variables. The predicate $\mathtt{ubi}(T,\iota)$ is true if all selections/branchings in T contain ι. The predicate $\mathtt{noo}(T,\iota)$ is true if no selection/branching in T has ι as object. The predicate $\mathtt{sub}(T,\iota)$ is true if there is at least one selection/branching in T having ι as subject. More precisely, letting $\dagger$ range over $\{?,!^*\}$, these predicates are defined by the clauses in Table 12.

Table 13. Typing rules for runtime processes

$$\frac{\Gamma\vdash P\triangleright\Delta}{\Gamma\vdash(\nu s)P\triangleright\Delta}\lfloor\text{SesRes}\rfloor\qquad\frac{\Gamma\vdash\Delta\triangleright\text{end}}{\Gamma\vdash s:[\,]\triangleright\Delta}\lfloor\text{EBuff}\rfloor$$

$$\frac{\Gamma\vdash P\triangleright\Delta,y:T}{\Gamma\vdash[\mathtt{id}:r](y).P\triangleright\Delta}\lfloor\text{Off}\rfloor\qquad\frac{\Gamma\vdash\mathscr{O}_1\triangleright\Delta_1\quad\Gamma\vdash\mathscr{O}_2\triangleright\Delta_2}{\Gamma\vdash\mathscr{O}_1\mid\mathscr{O}_2\triangleright\Delta_1\mid\Delta_2}\lfloor\text{ParOff}\rfloor$$

$$\frac{\Gamma\vdash s:\mathscr{B}\triangleright\Delta\quad\Gamma\vdash v:U}{\Gamma\vdash s:(\mathtt{id}:r,\mathtt{id}':r',l\langle\mathscr{I}\rangle\langle v\rangle)\cdot\mathscr{B}\triangleright\{s[\mathtt{id}:r]:!\langle\mathtt{id}':r',l\langle\mathscr{I}\rangle\langle U\rangle\rangle\};\Delta}\lfloor\text{SMess}\rfloor$$

$$\frac{\Gamma\vdash\mathscr{O}_1\triangleright\Delta_1\quad\Gamma\vdash\mathscr{O}_2\triangleright\Delta_2}{\Gamma\vdash a[\mathscr{H},\mathscr{O}_1,\mathscr{O}_2,\phi]\triangleright\Delta_1\mid\Delta_2}\lfloor\text{SerReg}\rfloor\qquad\frac{}{\Gamma\vdash a\langle s,\mathscr{P}\rangle\triangleright\emptyset}\lfloor\text{SesReg}\rfloor$$

To type the poll (rules $\lfloor$POLL$\rfloor$ and $\lfloor$POLLALL$\rfloor$) in such a way that we avoid ambiguous messages, it is necessary that ι occurs in all selections/branchings of T, condition assured by $\mathtt{ubi}(T,\iota)$. Moreover, if the poll is conditional (rule $\lfloor$POLL$\rfloor$), then ι cannot occur as an object in T. For this reason we require $\mathtt{noo}(T,\iota)$ too.

In rule $\lfloor$CHOICE$\rfloor$ $\mathtt{sub}(T,\iota)$ assures that ι occurs at least once as a subject in T, and $\mathtt{noo}(T,\iota)$ assures that ι does not occur as an object in T.

For typing the sequential composition of processes, in rule $\lfloor$SEQ$\rfloor$ we use the sequential composition of session environments defined by:

$$\Delta;\Delta' = \Delta \setminus \mathscr{D}(\Delta') \cup \Delta' \setminus \mathscr{D}(\Delta) \cup \{c : \Delta(c);\Delta'(c) \mid c \in \mathscr{D}(\Delta) \cap \mathscr{D}(\Delta')\}$$

Rule $\lfloor \text{PAR}_{\mathtt{id}} \rfloor$ (as well as rule $\lfloor$PAR$\rfloor$ in Table 11) uses the following parallel composition of session environments:

$$\Delta \mid \Delta' = \Delta \setminus \mathscr{D}(\Delta') \cup \Delta' \setminus \mathscr{D}(\Delta) \cup \{c : (\Delta(c) \mid \Delta'(c)) \mid c \in \mathscr{D}(\Delta) \cap \mathscr{D}(\Delta')\}$$

Notice that a service initialisation cannot be sequentialised, since it cannot be typed in the system $\vdash_{\mathtt{id}}$, but only in the system $\vdash$ (rule $\lfloor$INIT$\rfloor$ in Table 11).

The rules of Tables 10 and 11 are enough for typing user processes. For typing runtime processes, we extend the syntax of local types with *message types* of the shape $!\langle \mathtt{id} : r, l\langle \mathscr{I} \rangle \langle U \rangle \rangle$ and use all the rules in the tables above plus the rules of Table 13. We notice that the rules for typing the registries are simpler than the corresponding rule in [8], thanks to our distinction between services and sessions.

6 Properties

Our calculus enjoys type safety, which is obtained from the properties of subject reduction (Subsection 6.1) and progress (Subsection 6.2). Moreover, there is an interesting relation between the local types and the possible future reputations (Subsection 6.3).

6.1 Subject Reduction

In order to state the subject reduction property, we need to define a reduction relation on session environments, which describes how these environments evolve during process execution. Table 14 gives this relation, which mimics the sending and receiving

Table 14. Reduction of session environments

$$\{s[\mathtt{id}:r] :!^*\langle \mathtt{id}' : r', \{l_i\langle \mathscr{I}_i\rangle\langle U_i\rangle.T_i\}_{i\in I}\rangle\} \Rightarrow \{s[\mathtt{id}:r] :!^*\langle \mathtt{id}' : r', l_k\langle \mathscr{I}_k\rangle\langle U_k\rangle\rangle;T_k\} \qquad k \in I$$

$$\{s[\mathtt{id}:r] :!^*\langle \mathtt{id}' : r', l_k\langle \mathscr{I}_k\rangle\langle U_k\rangle\rangle, s[\mathtt{id}' : r'] :?\langle \mathtt{id} : r, \{l_i\langle \mathscr{I}_i\rangle\langle U_i\rangle.T_i\}_{i\in I}\rangle\} \Rightarrow \{s[\mathtt{id}:r] : \varepsilon, s[\mathtt{id}' : r'] : T_k\} \qquad k \in I$$

$$\{s[\mathtt{id}:r] : \forall\, \iota \notin \mathscr{I} : \mathtt{C}(r',\iota).T\} \Rightarrow \{s[\mathtt{id}:r] : \Pi_{i\in I}!\langle \mathtt{id}_i : r', \mathtt{YES}\rangle;?\langle \mathtt{id}_i : r', \{\mathtt{YES}.T\{\mathtt{id}_i/\iota\}, \mathtt{NO}.\varepsilon\}\rangle \mid \Pi_{j\in J}!\langle \mathtt{id}_j : r', \mathtt{NO}\rangle;?\langle \mathtt{id}_j : r', \{\mathtt{YES}.\varepsilon, \mathtt{NO}.\varepsilon\}\}$$
where $\forall i \in I \cup J.\mathtt{id}_i \notin \mathscr{I}$

$$\{s[\mathtt{id}:r] : \forall\, \iota \notin \mathscr{I} : r'.T\} \Rightarrow \{s[\mathtt{id}:r] : \Pi_{i\in I} T\{\mathtt{id}_i/\iota\}\} \qquad \text{where } \forall i \in I.\mathtt{id}_i \notin \mathscr{I}$$

$$\{s[\mathtt{id}:r] : \exists\, \iota : \mathtt{B}(r').T\} \Rightarrow \{s[\mathtt{id}:r] :!\langle \mathtt{id}' : r', \mathtt{YES}\rangle;?\langle \mathtt{id}' : r', \{\mathtt{YES}.T\{\mathtt{id}'/\iota\}, \mathtt{NO}.\varepsilon\}\rangle \mid \Pi_{j\in J}!\langle \mathtt{id}_j : r', \mathtt{NO}\rangle;?\langle \mathtt{id}_j : r', \{\mathtt{YES}.\varepsilon, \mathtt{NO}.\varepsilon\}\}$$

$\{s[\mathtt{id}:r] : T\} \cup \Delta \Rightarrow \{s[\mathtt{id}:r] : T'\} \cup \Delta'$ implies
$$\{s[\mathtt{id}:r] : \mathscr{T}[T]\} \cup \Delta \Rightarrow \{s[\mathtt{id}:r] : \mathscr{T}[T']\} \cup \Delta'$$

$\Delta \Rightarrow \Delta'$ implies $\Delta \cup \Delta'' \Rightarrow \Delta' \cup \Delta''$

of values and channels. The sets of identifiers in the reduction rules for quantifiers are arbitrary. In this table, we consider types in Δ modulo an equivalence relation reflecting the equivalence relation on buffers, and we define type contexts $\mathscr{T}$ as:

$$\mathscr{T} ::= [-] \mid \mathscr{T} \mid T \mid T \mid \mathscr{T} \mid \mathscr{T};T$$

We need to start from a well-typed initial process in order to assure that participants respect the prescriptions of some global type. We say that a process P is *reachable* if there is a well-typed initial process P_0 such that $P_0 \longrightarrow^* \mathscr{E}[P]$.

As usual for session calculi, the reduction of processes gives rise to the reduction of session environments.

Theorem 1. *If P is a reachable process and $\Gamma \vdash P \rhd \Delta$ and $P \longrightarrow^* P'$, then $\Gamma \vdash P' \rhd \Delta'$ for some Δ' such that $\Delta \Rightarrow^* \Delta'$.*

6.2 Communication Safety and Progress

As usual, communication safety assures that every receiver will find an appropriate message in the buffer and, conversely, that every message in the buffer will be fetched by a matching receiver.

Definition 1. *A process P is* communication safe *if:*

- $P \equiv \mathscr{E}[s[\mathtt{id} : r]?\langle \mathtt{id}' : r', \{l_i\langle \mathscr{I}_i\rangle(x_i).P_i\}_{i\in I}\rangle]$ *implies that* $\mathscr{E}[\mathbf{0}] \longrightarrow^* \mathscr{E}'[s : (\mathtt{id}' : r', \mathtt{id} : r, l_k\langle \mathscr{I}_k\rangle\langle v\rangle) \cdot \mathscr{B}]$ *with $k \in I$;*
- $P \equiv \mathscr{E}[s : (\mathtt{id}' : r', \mathtt{id} : r, l_k\langle \mathscr{I}_k\rangle\langle v\rangle) \cdot \mathscr{B}]$ *implies that* $\mathscr{E}[\mathbf{0}] \longrightarrow^* \mathscr{E}'[s[\mathtt{id} : r]?\langle \mathtt{id}' : r', \{l_i\langle \mathscr{I}_i\rangle(x_i).P_i\}_{i\in I}\rangle]$ *with $k \in I$.*

It is well known [1] that interleaving different services can destroy communication safety also in sessions without roles. In the present calculus also nested joins can destroy communication safety, since joins can fail when one of the required conditions is not satisfied. So we will only consider processes that use a single service and which can be typed with a derivation where:

1. session environments which appear in premises or conclusions of the system $\vdash_{\mathtt{id}}$ contain at most one association between a local type and a channel;
2. in rule $\lfloor \text{SEQ} \rfloor$, if the session environment of the first premise is empty, then the session environment of the second premise must be empty too.

The first condition assures that communications on two different channels can only occur in two parallel threads. The second condition forbids nested joins, since the first condition assures that the session environments for typing joins are empty. It allows instead sequentialisation of joins (when both session environments are empty), sequentialisation of communications on the same channel (when both session environments assign types to this channel), and communications on one channel followed by one join (when the first session environment assigns a type to this channel and the second session environment is empty). We denote by $\vdash^\star$ such kind of derivations.

The calculus of [8] requires a locking/unlocking mechanism to ensure that a service is "well-locked", i.e., that it does not allow a principal to join an ongoing session. Our distinction between services and sessions makes all services well-locked without having to synchronise joins, as hinted previously.

Lemma 1. *Let P be an initial process not containing restrictions. If $a : \langle G \rangle \vdash^{\star} P \rhd \emptyset$ and $P \longrightarrow^{*} P'$, then P' is communication safe.*

In session calculi, progress does not only ask for the absence of service interleaving, but also for the presence of all required participants. In [8] too, progress is assured under the condition that the needed principals can join. In our calculus:

- polls can properly reduce also when no principal satisfies the required condition;
- choices always reduce.

This means that we can avoid to add processes in parallel when defining progress.

The most important peculiarities of our calculus are:

- service registries are permanent and they can always reduce by rule [SessionInit];
- service joins can require conditions which are not satisfied.

The standing availability of rule [SessionInit] implies that reducibility by this rule cannot be considered to assure progress.

Definition 2. *A process P has the* progress property *if $P \longrightarrow^{*} P'$ implies that either P' does not contain runtime channels, or there exists P'' such that $P' \longrightarrow P''$ using a rule different from* [SessionInit] *and P'' has the progress property.*

According to this definition a process with progress can reduce to a parallel composition of service registers and service joins with unsatisfied conditions, which can only reduce by rule [SessionInit] to itself (modulo structural equivalence), since the generated sessions have no participants and so they can be garbage collected.

The progress proof essentially uses communication safety, and the observation that, starting from an initial process with a single service, the required registries and named buffers will be present for sure.

Theorem 2. *Let $P \equiv a\langle G, \phi \rangle \mid P_0$ be an initial process not containing restrictions. If $a : \langle G \rangle \vdash^{\star} P \rhd \emptyset$, then P has the progress property.*

6.3 Local Types for Reputations

We now discuss how to take advantage from local types to predict possible future reputations of principals. To this end, it is handy to define reductions which activate at most one session for each service.

Definition 3. *A reduction is* one-session *if rule* [SessionInit] *can be applied to a session registry for service a only if the current process does not contain $a\langle s, \mathscr{P} \rangle$ for some s, $\mathscr{P}$.*

Note that in [8] a service contains only one session, so all reductions are one-session.

Let h be the history of a principal `id` at the end of the execution of a session in a one-session reduction. Then, in the next session for the same service, principal `id` is allowed to play a role r only if $\phi(h, r)$.

The local type of a role in a service, together with the number of participants in a session, allows us to compute an upper bound to the number of occurrences of a fixed label in the possible histories - of principals playing that role - which can be generated by executing the session, provided the label does not occur under recursion. More precisely, if n_r is the number of principals playing role r in the session, then the number of occurrences of label l in the histories of a role with local type T is bounded by $\#(T,l)$ defined by:

$$\#(!^{\bullet}\langle p,\{l_i\langle\mathscr{I}_i\rangle\langle U_i\rangle.T_i\}_{i\in I}\rangle,l) = \begin{cases} max\{\#(T_{i_0},l)+1,\#(T_i,l) \mid i\in I\setminus\{i_0\}\} & \text{if } l=l_{i_0} \ \& \ i_0\in I, \\ max\{\#(T_i,l) \mid i\in I\} & \text{otherwise.} \end{cases}$$

$$\begin{array}{ll} \#(!\langle p,\{l_i\langle\mathscr{I}_i\rangle\langle U_i\rangle.T_i\}_{i\in I}\rangle,l) = max\{\#(T_i,l) \mid i\in I\} & \#(\mu\mathbf{x}.T,l) = 0 \\ \#(?\langle p,\{l_i\langle\mathscr{I}_i\rangle\langle U_i\rangle.T_i\}_{i\in I}\rangle,l) = max\{\#(T_i,l) \mid i\in I\} & \#(\mathbf{x},l) = 0 \\ \#(\forall\,\iota\notin\mathscr{I}:\mathtt{C}(r,\iota).T,l) = \#(T,l)\times n_r & \#(\varepsilon,l) = 0 \\ \#(\exists\,\iota:\mathtt{B}(r).T,l) = \#(T,l) & \#(\text{end},l) = 0 \\ \#(T_1 \mid T_2,l) = \#(T_1,l)+\#(T_2,l) & \#(T_1\ ;\ T_2,l) = \#(T_1,l)+\#(T_2,l) \end{array}$$

We can exploit this information to choose ϕ bounding the number of occurrences of label l in (part of) the histories, when using one-session reduction. It is enough to set $\phi(h,r)$ to $m+\#(T,l)\leq M$, where m is the number of occurrences of l in the considered part of h, type T is the local type of r and M is the desired bound.

For example, we can modify the *goldBuyer* of Figure 3 by recording in her history the labels BUY and AST. The local type T of the *goldBuyer* then contains

$$!^{\bullet}\langle\iota : goldSeller,\{\mathtt{BUY}\ldots.,\mathtt{AST}\ldots..\}\rangle$$

and $\#(T,\mathtt{AST})$=1. Therefore, if we want to limit to 3 the number of assistance calls in the last 20 transitions, the joining condition for the *goldBuyer* can hold true only if in the last 19 transitions the number of AST is less than or equal to 2.

7 Conclusions and Related Work

In this paper, we studied a role-based multiparty session calculus that takes into account the history of principals, in order to measure their reputation and regulate accordingly their participation in future conversations. Histories are dynamically built by collecting actions performed by principals, in such a way that, if a participant "behaves badly" in a service, this will hinder her further attempts to join the service with particular roles and her possibilities to be chosen by other participants via a poll or a choice operation.

Since in our setting the reputation associated with a principal is *objective* and not subjective (i.e., it is based on real interactions and not on other principals' opinions), one of the major problems arising in reputation systems, *unfair ratings*, is avoided.

We managed to model the regulation of a principal's behaviour depending on her reputation: in Section 2, we showed how a principal's "bad behaviour" may restrict the range of session roles offered by the service to that principal. This is our main result.

However, our solution still suffers from some limitations, in particular we can only type a limited form of delegation, the same as in [8], that does not allow general scenarios to be modelled. The limitation is due to the fact that session environments in the typing rules for poll and choice must contain exactly one channel, while the session environments for typing delegation have at least two channels. Therefore it is impossible to create a channel to be delegated before a poll or a choice. The only way out is to create and discharge it afterwards, unused, by means of a join, right before sending it.

Session calculi were proposed in the mid-nineties to model communication protocols among concurrent and mobile processes. We refer to [9] and [17] for overviews. Since the original proposal of [12], such calculi have been extensively studied and enriched with various features. Initially dealing with binary protocols (often representing an interaction between a user and a server), session calculi have been subsequently extended to *multiparty* sessions [13], involving several principals interacting on an equal footing. More recently, multiparty sessions have been extended with design by contracts [2], dependent types for parametricity [18], upper bounds on buffer sizes [7], exception handling [5], access and information flow control [4] and monitors [3]. The present paper mainly builds on the *role-based* multiparty calculus of [8], as previously discussed.

The study and formalisation of *reputation* has similarly attracted a great deal of interest in recent years. We refer to existing surveys [15,14,11] for a general introduction to *reputation systems*. It is interesting to notice that the reputation system associated with our calculus can be classified, according to [15], as a non-probabilistic experience-based system, where principals are evaluated by inspecting their history, which is built by recording their past interaction with other principals.

As it is grounded on the π-calculus, our proposal may be directly compared with the Calculus for Trust Management (`ctm`) [6], a process calculus for modelling trust based systems. Principals in `ctm` have two components: the protocol and the policy. Protocols are π-calculus style processes. Policies are made of two parts: logic formulae (similar to our single conditions), which describe the rules for taking decisions on the basis of past experiences; experiences (similar to our histories), which collect the messages exchanged in interactions between principals. The treatment of [6] differs from ours in that policies and histories are local and associated with each principal, while we store them in a registry which is global for all participants in a given service. In our calculus, histories are made of sent values and may be checked by both services and other principals involved in the same service; in `ctm`, histories are made of received values and are checked locally before granting access to local resources. Moreover, in `ctm` the focus is on barbed equivalences among principals, while we are mainly concerned with supplying a type system to check communication safety.

Acknowledgments. We would like to thank Nobuko Yoshida and Pierre-Malo Deniélou for useful comments.

References

1. Bettini, L., Coppo, M., D'Antoni, L., De Luca, M., Dezani-Ciancaglini, M., Yoshida, N.: Global Progress in Dynamically Interleaved Multiparty Sessions. In: van Breugel, F., Chechik, M. (eds.) CONCUR 2008. LNCS, vol. 5201, pp. 418–433. Springer, Heidelberg (2008)

2. Bocchi, L., Honda, K., Tuosto, E., Yoshida, N.: A Theory of Design-by-Contract for Distributed Multiparty Interactions. In: Gastin, P., Laroussinie, F. (eds.) CONCUR 2010. LNCS, vol. 6269, pp. 162–176. Springer, Heidelberg (2010)
3. Capecchi, S., Castellani, I., Dezani-Ciancaglini, M.: Information Flow Safety in Multiparty Sessions. In: Luttik, B., Valencia, F. (eds.) EXPRESS 2011. EPTCS, vol. 64, pp. 16–31 (2011)
4. Capecchi, S., Castellani, I., Dezani-Ciancaglini, M., Rezk, T.: Session Types for Access and Information Flow Control. In: Gastin, P., Laroussinie, F. (eds.) CONCUR 2010. LNCS, vol. 6269, pp. 237–252. Springer, Heidelberg (2010)
5. Capecchi, S., Giachino, E., Yoshida, N.: Global Escape in Multiparty Sessions. In: Lodaya, K., Mahajan, M. (eds.) Proc. FSTTCS 2010. LIPIcs, vol. 8, pp. 338–351. Schloss Dagstuhl–Leibniz-Zentrum für Informatik (2010)
6. Carbone, M., Nielsen, M., Sassone, V.: A Calculus for Trust Management. In: Lodaya, K., Mahajan, M. (eds.) FSTTCS 2004. LNCS, vol. 3328, pp. 161–173. Springer, Heidelberg (2004)
7. Deniélou, P.-M., Yoshida, N.: Buffered Communication Analysis in Distributed Multiparty Sessions. In: Gastin, P., Laroussinie, F. (eds.) CONCUR 2010. LNCS, vol. 6269, pp. 343–357. Springer, Heidelberg (2010)
8. Deniélou, P.-M., Yoshida, N.: Dynamic Multirole Session Types. In: Sagiv, M. (ed.) Proc. POPL 2011, pp. 435–446. ACM (2011)
9. Dezani-Ciancaglini, M., de'Liguoro, U.: Sessions and Session Types: An Overview. In: Laneve, C., Su, J. (eds.) WS-FM 2009. LNCS, vol. 6194, pp. 1–28. Springer, Heidelberg (2010)
10. Giachino, E., Sackman, M., Drossopoulou, S., Eisenbach, S.: Softly Safely Spoken: Role Playing for Session Types. Presented at PLACES 2009 (2009)
11. Hoffman, K., Zage, D., Nita-Rotaru, C.: A Survey of Attack and Defence Techniques for Reputation Systems. ACM Computing Surveys 42, 1:1–1:31 (2009)
12. Honda, K.: Types for Dyadic Interaction. In: Best, E. (ed.) CONCUR 1993. LNCS, vol. 715, pp. 509–523. Springer, Heidelberg (1993)
13. Honda, K., Yoshida, N., Carbone, M.: Multiparty Asynchronous Session Types. In: Necula, G.C., Wadler, P. (eds.) Proc. POPL 2008, pp. 273–284. ACM Press (2008)
14. Jøsang, A., Golbeck, J.: Challenges for Robust Trust and Reputation Systems. In: Dimitrakos, T., Martinelli, F. (eds.) Proc. STM 2009. ENTCS, vol. 244. Elsevier (2009)
15. Krukow, K., Nielsen, M., Sassone, V.: Trust Models in Ubiquitous Computing. Philosophical Transactions of the Royal Society 366, 3781–3793 (2008)
16. Milner, R.: Communicating and Mobile Systems: the Pi-Calculus. CUP (1999)
17. Vasconcelos, V.T.: Sessions, from Types to Programming Languages. EATCS Bulletin 103, 53–73 (2011)
18. Yoshida, N., Deniélou, P.-M., Bejleri, A., Hu, R.: Parameterised Multiparty Session Types. In: Ong, L. (ed.) FOSSACS 2010. LNCS, vol. 6014, pp. 128–145. Springer, Heidelberg (2010)

Asynchronous Distributed Monitoring for Multiparty Session Enforcement

Tzu-Chun Chen[1], Laura Bocchi[2], Pierre-Malo Deniélou[3], Kohei Honda[1], and Nobuko Yoshida[3]

[1] Queen Mary, University of London
[2] University of Leicester
[3] Imperial College London

Abstract. We propose a formal model of runtime safety enforcement for large-scale, cross-language distributed applications with possibly untrusted endpoints. The underlying theory is based on multiparty session types with logical assertions (*MPSA*), an expressive protocol specification language that supports runtime validation through monitoring. Our method starts from global specifications based on *MPSA*s which the participants should obey. Distributed monitors use local specifications, projected from global specifications, to detect whether the interactions are well-behaved, and take appropriate actions, such as suppressing illegal messages. We illustrate the design of our model with examples from real-world distributed applications. We prove monitor transparency, communication conformance, and global session fidelity in the presence of possibly unsafe endpoints.

1 Introduction

Communication among distributed components is becoming the norm for building large-scale software, for example in the backend of web services, financial protocols, enterprise applications and cyberinfrastructures. This change is sustained by an accelerating infrastructural support for portable distributed components through technologies such as clouds, messaging middleware and distributed stores. While distribution leads to such virtues as scalability, sharing and resilience [10,22], guaranteeing safety poses new technical challenges. First, endpoints for a distributed application are often managed under multiple administrative domains, making it hard to enforce the use of verified code. Thus, even in a single application, *safe and unsafe components can co-exist*. Secondly, many non-trivial correctness properties of distributed programs rely on reciprocal assurance through cooperating endpoints (for example, a sender multi-casts a message with a type expected by each receiver). Hence a safety property needs be specified as a *global invariant* involving multiple peers. Thirdly, in spite of its global nature, scalable distributed assurance is only feasible through *local validation*: a centralised dynamic validation (validating all distributed interactions in one place) is clearly unrealistic in large-scale distributed systems.

Against these backgrounds, this paper introduces a theory of *runtime* verification for distributed programs, based on distributed endpoint monitoring in which non-trivial global safety assurance results from local runtime verification and enforcement of possibly untrusted endpoints, rather than from static checking. We stipulate that an external

R. Bruni and V. Sassone (Eds.): TGC 2011, LNCS 7173, pp. 25–45, 2012.

monitor is associated with each endpoint participating in a distributed infrastructure (in actual implementations, one or more logical monitors may be realised by (a cluster of) one or more physical monitors). A monitor associated with an endpoint acts for that endpoint as its unique entry point to the infrastructure, and guarantees that its interactions with its environment, which are *globally observable*, never violates a given global specification. The framework hinges on the linkage between local validation and global correctness, and is characterised by asynchrony: each monitor can verify the behaviour of local process only by observing the outgoing or incoming messages and validating that they conform to a given local specification.

For linking the global invariants to local validation, we use the preceding work on *multiparty session types* (*MPST*s) [5,17], which provides a formally founded approach to the local validation of globally specified protocols, assuring communication safety, protocol fidelity and progress. We use its logical extension, called *multiparty session assertions* (*MPSA*s) [3], which further allow, by extending *MPST*s with logical formulae, fine-grained specification of interactional behaviour including message contents, choices of conversation paths and recursion invariants. By projecting a *global assertion* (global protocol specification) onto each *endpoint*, we obtain a local assertion for each endpoint. By all endpoints adhering to their respective local specifications, their interactions satisfy global correctness.

Our theory offers a formal framework to semantically link local behaviour of processes to their global behaviour and to global invariants, through the introduction of a notion of *global observables*. Since, in distributed processes, the sending events and the receiving events are decoupled, and because external monitors can only observe asynchronously exchanged messages, the semantic account of global invariants (hence correctness of runtime verification) should take into account temporary discrepancies of the global view. When a sender sends a message correctly, its local view is updated; however, as the receiver has not yet received the message, we cannot update neither the global view nor the receiver's local view. In other words, to prove the correctness of distributed runtime verification, we cannot simply use the projection from global invariants to endpoints: we need to take into account the time lag between the sending and receiving events. Asynchrony also poses a challenge in the treatment of out-of-order asynchronous message monitoring, which we capture through type-level permutations of actions.

This paper offers an overview of a theory of monitored networks illustrated through many examples. Its main contributions may be summarised as follows.

Contributions. The main contributions of the present paper include:

- A model of distributed monitoring featuring the following elements: (1) endpoint code is possibly ill-behaved; (2) global assertions [3] enable concise global specification of application-level multiparty protocols; and (3) conformance to stipulated global protocols is guaranteed at runtime through local monitoring.
- A multiparty session π-calculus with distributed external monitors, with a new capability passing primitive for fine-grained control of distributed session initialisation. The calculus presents an exact semantic account of monitors' behaviour, offering a foundation of architectural realisations of the proposed framework, with an efficient monitoring mechanism.

- An overview of the fundamental properties of monitored networks, including local and global safety, the latter built on a novel global observational framework. We discuss how local communication conformance leads to global conformance and session fidelity, as well as estalbishing the local and global monitor transparency.

As far as we know, the formal behavioural assurance of global properties for distributed applications with unsafe endpoints against non-trivial logical specifications, built on a rigorous semantic basis, is new. The general ideas of the proposed framework are illustrated in § 2 through a concrete example. An asynchronous distributed calculus with multiparty session primitives and the syntax of endpoint monitors are introduced in § 3. The monitored network and global observable environment (which constructs the global observables) are introduced in § 4. In § 4, we propose a formal framework for *runtime* monitoring, and describe how an endpoint monitor is capable to guide and protect local processes to exactly obey the global specification, and thus assure the safety and correctness of the whole monitored network during runtime. § 5 outlines the resulting properties and theorems, such as local and global safety, local and global transparency, and session fidelity. For further comparisons, see § 6. For full definitions and descriptions of the running example please refer to the online full version [20].

2 Basic Ideas through Examples

2.1 Assumptions and Background

As we discussed in Introduction, we assume that endpoint components of distributed applications may reside in geographically disparate and heterogeneous administrative domains, so that we cannot expect that all programs are pre-verified. This necessitates the use of *runtime* verification and enforcement through trusted monitors. Monitors act as gateways for participating endpoint code: first an endpoint sends a message and other requests to a monitor; then if the monitor finds the message to be valid, it will route it to its designation. If the monitor finds the message to be invalid, it will treat it as an error. Below we illustrate the basic idea of this distributed runtime verification through a concrete use case from a project to build a global distributed infrastructure for ocean science, the Ocean Observatories Initiative (OOI) [23]. The OOI aims to build a distributed network of environmental observatories for ocean sciences, with persistent and interactive capabilities [7]. Its key element is a comprehensive cyberinfrastructure (OOI CI), which offers services to its users through interactions among distributed endpoints in geographically distributed OOI observatories, from seafloor instruments to buoys and on-shore research stations, communicating through a uniform messaging infrastructure. Its usecase scenarios focus on structured conversations among distributed endpoints which may be a thousand miles apart, running under different administrative domains with different degrees of trust. For example, some components of a distributed application may be scripting programs in users' browsers, some may be located in the endpoint cloud of an academic or corporate institution, and some others may be infrastructural components residing in one of the central clouds of the OOI CI.

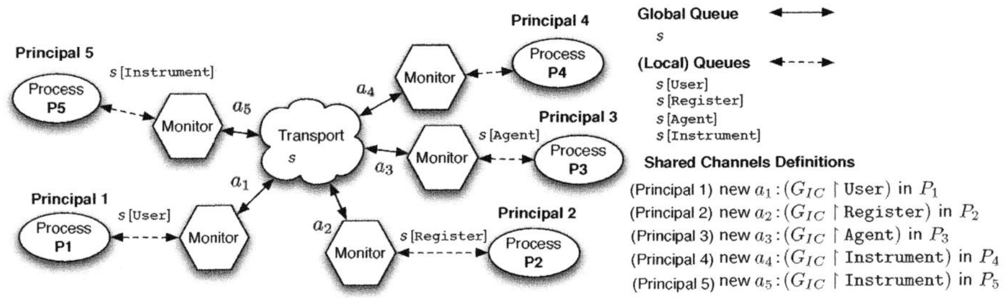

Fig. 1. Monitoring architecture

Because each distributed service in the OOI CI is realised by structured conversations among distributed components, it is essential for its development that protocols for interactions among the participating components are specified with clear semantics. We call these protocols, *application-level protocols*. For example, a scientist may wish to use a remote instrument, say a seabed camera, after being authorised by an agent: the interactions among these three will form a specific application-level protocol. In the OOI CI, the design choice has been made so that these application-level protocols are to be uniformly specified by a common protocol description language. Safety of interactions is validated against these stipulated protocol descriptions.

Since we *cannot* expect either each endpoint code or its environment to be (wholly) trusted, a primary way to ensure a global invariant for such an interactional application is through trusted monitors which enforce correct behaviour for participating programs, a design being considered in the OOI CI. Such monitors need in general to be *external* to these participants, i.e. they are not embedded in their code, because, as already discussed, we may not be able to trust an administrative domain where an endpoint code resides (an endpoint may as well be equipped with its internal monitor). These monitors will check and verify the incoming/outgoing messages to/from distributed components, so that the correctness of global interactions are ensured. Logically, we can stipulate that there is one monitor for each principal, guarding their behaviour.

A particular application-level protocol in the OOI CI is the *instrument command* we shall treat below. It allows a user to perform operations on a remote instrument. This protocol is specified as a global assertion G_{IC}, described later in this section (the formal definition is in § 3.2). G_{IC} models a session which involves roles `User`, `Register`, `Agent` and `Instrument`. Given a global assertion G, we denote its projection on role p as $G \upharpoonright \mathrm{p}$, giving an endpoint assertion which describes the protocol from the perspective of a specific role. We call a participant in one or more distributed applications in the OOI CI, *principal*. A principal executes its local process and interacts with other principals through one or more applications. Its incoming and outgoing messages are validated by a monitor, which is part of the infrastructure. Figure 1 presents a monitored network involving five principals.

We now illustrate, using the instrument command example, some of the features of our formalism, including how the initialisation of conversation is done and how the associated protocol is specified.

2.2 Session Establishment through Distributed Invitations

For a monitor to listen to and check the communications of a principal, it should start by observing the initiation phase of conversations, called *session establishment*. Session establishments are done in two steps:

1. A principal initiates a session by creating a *session channel* for a specific application-level protocol (e.g., G_{IC}); and
2. The principal sends, through shared channels, invitations to other principals to participate in the session in a specified role.

The initiation of a conversation (1) equips the initiator with its *endpoint capabilities*, one for each role, each of which can be passed to another principal (who may in turn pass it to yet another principal). Thus the binding of principals to endpoint roles is incrementally established through capability passing. This fine-grained scheme can represent many real-world examples [6]. Further, the operation can be seen as a asynchronous linear capability passing system, leading to a clear monitor semantics.

As an example, consider the following process P_1 of *Principal*$_1$, from Figure 1, which creates a session s with specification G_{IC} and sends invitations to others.

$$\begin{aligned} P_1 &= \mathsf{new}\, s\!:\!G_{IC}\ \mathsf{in}\ (P_{JOIN} \mid P_{INV}) \\ P_{JOIN} &= \mathsf{join}\ s[\mathtt{User}];P_{\mathtt{user}} \\ P_{INV} &= \overline{a_2}\langle s[\mathtt{Register}]\!:\!G_{IC}\restriction \mathtt{Register}\rangle;\overline{a_3}\langle s[\mathtt{Agent}]\!:\!G_{IC}\restriction \mathtt{Agent}\rangle; \\ &\quad\ \overline{a_4}\langle s[\mathtt{Instrument}]\!:\!G_{IC}\restriction \mathtt{Instrument}\rangle \end{aligned}$$

where the capabilities $s[\mathtt{User}]$, $s[\mathtt{Register}]$, $s[\mathtt{Agent}]$ and $s[\mathtt{Instrument}]$, are either *activated* (i.e. the process has joined the session) or forwarded (i.e. used for inviting others). E.g., P_1 joins the session as `User` (P_{JOIN} above), and sends invitations to the other roles (P_{INV} above). Thus *Principal*$_1$ is inviting other four principals in Figure 1. *Shared channels* $(a_1, a_2, \ldots)$ determine which invitations each process is entitled to receive, e.g. only *Principal*$_4$ and *Principal*$_5$ can accept (by any other process) an invitation $s[\mathtt{Instrument}]$, through a_4 and a_5, respectively.

Below we show *Principal*$_4$, which receives the capability $s[\mathtt{Instrument}]$ and passes it to *Principal*$_5$ who joins the session.

$$\begin{aligned} P_4 &= a_4(y_4[\mathtt{Instrument}]\!:\!G_{IC}\restriction \mathtt{Instrument}).\overline{a_5}\langle y_4[\mathtt{Instrument}]\!:\!G_{IC}\restriction \mathtt{Instrument}\rangle \\ P_5 &= a_5(y_5[\mathtt{Instrument}]\!:\!G_{IC}\restriction \mathtt{Instrument}).\mathsf{join}\ y_5[\mathtt{Instrument}];P_{\mathtt{Instrument}} \end{aligned}$$

Monitors observe the exchange of capabilities between their endpoint and the network. Once a process joins a session, the corresponding monitor is activated and enforces conformance to the conversation scenario prescribed for that session/role for the subsequent interactions. The asynchronous message in transit between a process (as a role in a session) and its monitor is represented as a message in a *local queue*: messages in transit among monitors for a session is called *global queue*. In Figure 1, $s[\mathtt{User}]$, $s[\mathtt{Register}]$, etc., represent local queues, while s is a global queue.

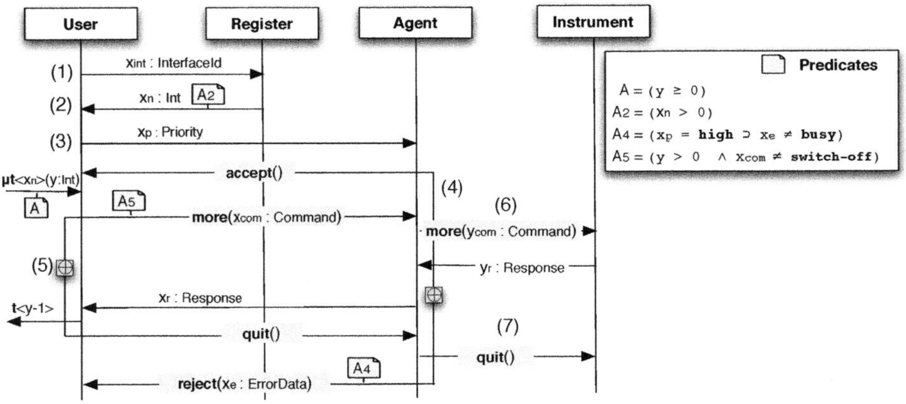

Fig. 2. Illustration of the global assertion for 'OOI Instrument Command'

2.3 Specifying Application-Level Protocols

Monitors dynamically learn about which protocols to enforce during session establishment. Application-level protocols are specified as *MPSA*s [3]. A global *MPSA*, sometimes called global assertion, is an abstract description of the interaction steps taken by the roles in the session. Basic interaction steps are asynchronous message exchanges. Branching and recursion describe potential choices and repeated interactions. Each message exchange/branching is annotated with a predicate specifying a constraint on the message value or the choice of a branch. Recursion is annotated with an invariant.

Figure 2 gives an illustration of global assertion G_{IC} as a message sequence chart, in which `User` performs one or more commands on a remote `Instrument`. `Register` is used to retrieve information on the instrument's usage, e.g., to determine the maximum number of commands allowed in the current session depending on the system load. `Agent` interfaces the communications with the actual `Instrument`.

Full arrows represent interactions where one party sends a branch label and a message value (or just one of the two) to another party. The labels carry information on the branch to follow. Arrows linked by $\oplus$ represent alternative branches.

The conversation proceeds as follows:

(1) `User` sends `Register` a message x_{int} of type InterfaceId.

(2) `Register` replies with an integer x_n which determines the number of commands that `User` will be allowed to perform on the instrument. The predicate annotating this interaction specifies an obligation for `Register` to send a value for x_n satisfying $x_n > 0$; dually `User` can rely on this fact.

(3) `User` sends `Agent` a priority x_p (e.g., *low*, *high*).

(4) `Agent` sends `User` a label which is either `accept` or `reject`. In case of `reject`, `Agent` sends also an error message x_e of type errData and the protocol terminates. The predicate for this branch ensures that a request will not be rejected due to the fact that the instrument is busy if the priority is high. In case of `accept` the protocol continues with a recursion $\mu \mathtt{t}\langle x_n \rangle(y : \mathsf{Int})$ where y is a parameter initialised to x_n,

$y \geq 0$ is an invariant and y is used to enforce User to perform at most x_n commands on the instrument.

(5) User selects either branch more and sends a new command to Agent, or quit and terminates. The predicate $y > 0 \wedge x_{com} \neq$ switch-off is a guard to the branch more: a new command can be sent only if User has not performed already x_n commands in this session and anyway the command must not ask to switch off the instrument.

(6, 7) Finally, either the command (6) or the quit notification (7) is forwarded by Agent to Instrument. In the former case, Instrument responds to Agent (who forwards the message to User).

2.4 Processes for Instrument Command

In the following we present the processes for instrument command used in our later discussions. $Principal_1$ in Figure 1 runs P_1 in § 2.2. P_1 refers to $P_{\texttt{user}}$ which is given as:

$$\begin{aligned} P_{\texttt{user}} &= s[\texttt{User},\texttt{Register}]!\langle v_{int}\rangle; s[\texttt{Register},\texttt{User}]?(x_n).\\ &\quad s[\texttt{User},\texttt{Agent}]!\langle\textsf{High}\rangle; s[\texttt{Agent},\texttt{User}]?\{\texttt{accept}().P^u_{acc},\ \texttt{reject}(x_e)\}\\ P^u_{acc} &= \mu X\langle x_n\rangle(y).\textsf{if}\ needmore() \wedge y > 0\ \textsf{then}\ s[\texttt{User},\texttt{Agent}]!\texttt{more}\langle next()\rangle;\\ &\quad s[\texttt{Agent},\texttt{User}]?(x_r).\textsf{t}\langle y-1\rangle; \textsf{else}\ s[\texttt{User},\texttt{Agent}]!\texttt{quit}\langle\rangle \end{aligned}$$

where $needmore()$ and $next()$ are functions local to $Principal_1$: $needmore()$ returns a boolean (i.e., whether more commands are needed), and $next()$ returns the next command. $Principal_2$ in Figure 1 uses a_2 to receive an invitation, then joins the session as Register. We assume $Principal_2$ returns always 10 allowing all participants to perform at most 10 commands on the instrument. Note any positive value for x_n would satisfy the predicate $x_n > 0$ in **(2)** of §2.2.

$$\begin{aligned} P_2 &= a_2(y_2[\texttt{Register}]:G_{IC}\upharpoonright\texttt{Register}).\textsf{join}\ y_2[\texttt{Register}];P_{register}\\ P_{register} &= y_2[\texttt{User},\texttt{Register}]?(x_{int}).y_2[\texttt{Register},\texttt{User}]!\langle 10\rangle \end{aligned}$$

The next process is for Agent ($Principal_3$ in Figure 1), which, through channel a_3, receives an invitation and joins the session as Agent. We assume $Principal_3$ relies on a local function $error()$ returning an error data. Noticeably, the agent simply forwards the command and the response between the user and the instrument.

$$\begin{aligned} P_3 &= a_3(y_3[\texttt{Agent}]:G_{IC}\upharpoonright\texttt{Agent}).\textsf{join}\ y_3[\texttt{Agent}];P_{agent}\\ P_{agent} &= y_3[\texttt{User},\texttt{Agent}]?(x_p).\textsf{if}\ x_p = \textsf{high then}\ y_3[\texttt{Agent},\texttt{User}]!\texttt{accept}\langle\rangle.P^a_{acc},\\ &\quad \textsf{else}\ y_3[\texttt{Agent},\texttt{User}]!\texttt{reject}\langle error()\rangle\\ P^a_{acc} &= \mu\langle x_n\rangle X(y).y_3[\texttt{User},\texttt{Agent}]?\{\texttt{more}(x_{com}).P^a_{com},\\ &\quad \texttt{quit}().y_3[\texttt{Agent},\texttt{Instrument}]!\texttt{quit}\langle\rangle\}\\ P^a_{com} &= y_3[\texttt{Agent},\texttt{Instrument}]!\texttt{more}\langle x_{com}\rangle; y_3[\texttt{Instrument},\texttt{Agent}]?(y_r).\\ &\quad y_3[\texttt{Agent},\texttt{User}]!\langle y_r\rangle.\textsf{t}\langle y-1\rangle \end{aligned}$$

Finally two instruments, $Principal_4$ and $Principal_5$ in Figure 1, are given below. The first, $Principal_4$, forwards the invitation to $Principal_5$ and terminates. The second, $Principal_5$, joins the session and relies on a local function $response$ that takes a command and returns a response.

$u ::= a,b \mid x,y$	shared channel	$v ::= a \mid \mathsf{true} \mid \mathsf{false} \mid \mathtt{n}$	value
$k ::= s,s' \mid x,y$	sessions	$e ::= v \mid x \mid e+e' \mid e \wedge e' \mid \cdots$	expression
$P ::= \overline{u}\langle k[\mathtt{p}]:T\rangle;P$	request	$\mid k[\mathtt{p}_1,\mathtt{p}_2]!l\langle e\rangle;P$	selection
$\mid u(y[\mathtt{p}]:T).P$	accept	$\mid k[\mathtt{p}_1,\mathtt{p}_2]?\{l_i(x_i).P_i\}_{i\in I}$	branching
$\mid \mathsf{new}\, s{:}G \;\mathsf{in}\; P$	session creation	$\mid P \mid Q$	parallel
$\mid \mathsf{new}\, a{:}T[\mathtt{p}] \;\mathsf{in}\; P$	name creation	$\mid \mathbf{0}$	inact
$\mid \mathsf{join}\; s[\mathtt{p}];P$	join	$\mid \mu\mathsf{t}\langle e\rangle(x).P \mid \mathsf{t}\langle e\rangle$	recursion
$\mid \mathsf{if}\; e \;\mathsf{then}\; P \;\mathsf{else}\; Q$	conditional	$\mid P_{rt}$	runtime process
$P_{rt} ::= (\nu s{:}G)P \mid (\nu a{:}T[\mathtt{p}])P$	hiding	$h ::= \emptyset \mid \langle \mathtt{p},\mathtt{q},l\langle v\rangle\rangle \cdot h$	message queue
$\mid \overline{a}\langle s[\mathtt{p}] : T\rangle$	invitation		
$\mid s[\mathtt{p}] : h$	queue		

Fig. 3. Syntax of processes

$$
\begin{aligned}
P_4 &= a_4(y_4[\mathtt{Instrument}]:G_{IC} \upharpoonright \mathtt{Instrument}).\\
&\quad \overline{a_5}\langle y_4[\mathtt{Instrument}]:G_{IC} \upharpoonright \mathtt{Instrument}\rangle\\
P_5 &= a_5(y_5[\mathtt{Instrument}]:G_{IC} \upharpoonright \mathtt{Instrument}).\mathsf{join}\; y_5[\mathtt{Instrument}];P_{inst}\\
P_{inst} &= \mu\mathsf{t}.y_5[\mathtt{Agent},\mathtt{Instrument}]?\{\\
&\quad \mathtt{more}(y_{com}).y_5[\mathtt{Instrument},\mathtt{Agent}]!\langle response(y_{com})\rangle.\mathsf{t},\\
&\quad \mathtt{quit}()\}
\end{aligned}
$$

This concludes the introduction of processes for the Instrument Command use case.

3 A Calculus for Distributed Monitoring

In this section and the next, we introduce a calculus of distributed monitored processes. The syntax is divided into three parts:

(§ **3.1**) local untyped processes P, with a fine-grained distributed session initiation primitive called *invitation*;
(§ **3.2**) local monitors $\mathcal{M}$ which check the correctness of the incoming and outgoing messages (w.r.t. a set of endpoint assertions) and drop the wrong ones; and
(§ **4.1**) distributed networks N which consist of one or more monitored local processes $\mathcal{M}[P]$ and (global) queues containing pending messages sent by one monitored process but not yet received by another.

3.1 Multiparty Session π-calculus with Distributed Initialisation

This subsection presents the syntax of local processes, extending [5] with fine-grained primitives for session creation and invitation.

Invitations are exchanged through *shared channels* $(a,b,\ldots)$. The session interactions occur through *session channels* $(s,s',\ldots)$ whose names identify session execution instances. Shared channel identifiers ($u, u', \ldots$) denote shared channels or variables; session identifiers ($k, k', \ldots$) denote session channels or variables. We let $\mathtt{p}, \mathtt{q}, \ldots$ range over *participant roles*, given as finite natural numbers. We use x, y for *variables*; v, v' for *values*; and e, e' for natural or boolean expressions.

We let P, P' denote processes. The *request* process asynchronously invites, through a shared channel u, another process to play $\mathtt{p}$ in a session (channel) k and continues as P (T denotes an endpoint assertion, defined later). The *accept* process receives a session invitation for role $\mathtt{p}$ and, after instantiating y with the received session channel, behaves as $\mathtt{p}$ (following endpoint assertion T). Process $\mathsf{new}\, s\!:\!G \text{ in } P$ creates a fresh session s whose protocol obeys a global assertion G, and behaves as P. Similarly for the shared name creation. By *join*, a process joins a session s as $\mathtt{p}$, creating a fresh local queue $s[\mathtt{p}]$.

The *selection* and *branching* represent communications through an established session k. We make the sender $\mathtt{p}_1$ and receiver $\mathtt{p}_2$ explicit by the notation $[\mathtt{p}_1, \mathtt{p}_2]$. The selection sends, in a session k, an expression e with label l from $\mathtt{p}_1$ to $\mathtt{p}_2$. Dually the branching is ready to receive each label l_i, and behaves as $P_i\{e/x\}$. Conditional, parallel composition and inaction are standard. The *recursion* $\mu\mathtt{t}\langle e\rangle(x).P$ defines $\mathtt{t}$ as P with recursion parameter x which is initialised to e; $\mathtt{t}\langle e\rangle$ is the corresponding recursion call.

Once a session is started, we use the runtime syntax P_{rt} (not accessible to the programmer) which includes hiding, asynchronous invitation messages and the queues representing messages in transit between a process and its monitor for a session instance.

For brevity, we often write $k[\mathtt{p}_1, \mathtt{p}_2]?l(x).P$ or $k[\mathtt{p}_1, \mathtt{p}_2]?(x).P$ for a single branch, and omit trailing $\mathbf{0}$ and type annotations. We call *initial* a process which does not contain free variables and runtime syntax.

Figure 4 lists the LTS for processes. Each output is performed in two steps: (1) a local action spawns the message (i.e., invitations remain local and linear messages are inserted in a local queue $s[\mathtt{p}]$) and (2) a visible action sends out the message. Inputs are dual. Whereas local actions are always allowed by monitors, visible actions have to be checked (as it will be clear in § 4.1). The first five rules are for local actions: $\lfloor$ARQ,AAC$\rfloor$ respectively spawn and receive an invitation message through a shared channel; $\lfloor$SEL$\rfloor$ puts a message in a local queue for a session s, after evaluating e to a value v; $\lfloor$BRA$\rfloor$ gets a message from a local queue with label l_j, so that the j-th process P_j receives a value v; $\lfloor$IF$\rfloor$ is standard. The rest models visible actions: $\lfloor$NEW,NEWS$\rfloor$ are for shared channel and session channel creation (it is through these actions that monitors learn about the session specifications to be enforced), $\lfloor$JOIN$\rfloor$ is for session joining using capability $s[\mathtt{p}]$ and creates the corresponding local queue, $\lfloor$OUT$\rfloor$ sends out an invitation, $\lfloor$OUT$\rfloor$ (resp. $\lfloor$IN$\rfloor$) sends out (resp. receives) a message from (resp. into) a local queue.

3.2 Distributed Monitors

To every process is associated a dedicated monitor that manages its interactions with the network (hence with other peers) by inspecting outgoing and incoming messages: the monitor protects the endpoint from bad messages from the environment and the environment from those from the endpoint. The syntax of monitors is presented in Figure 5.

Note that a monitor $\mathcal{M}$ should check two kinds of messages: (1) capability exchanges for invitations via shared channels, and (2) session messages via session channels. Thus

$$\lfloor \text{ARQ,AAC} \rfloor \quad \bar{a}\langle s[\mathrm{p}]\rangle;P \xrightarrow{\tau} \bar{a}\langle s[\mathrm{p}]\rangle \mid P \qquad \bar{a}\langle s[\mathrm{p}]\rangle \mid a(y[\mathrm{p}]).Q \xrightarrow{\tau} Q\{s/y\}$$

$$\lfloor \text{SEL} \rfloor \quad s[\mathrm{p}_1,\mathrm{p}_2]!l\langle e\rangle;P \mid s[\mathrm{p}_1]:h \xrightarrow{\tau} P \mid s[\mathrm{p}_1]:h\cdot\langle \mathrm{p}_1,\mathrm{p}_2,l\langle v\rangle\rangle \qquad (e\downarrow v)$$

$$\lfloor \text{BRA} \rfloor \quad s[\mathrm{p}_1,\mathrm{p}_2]?\{l_i(x_i).P_i\}_{i\in I} \mid s[\mathrm{p}_2]:\langle \mathrm{p}_1,\mathrm{p}_2,l_j\langle v\rangle\rangle\cdot h \xrightarrow{\tau} P_j\{v/x_j\} \mid s[\mathrm{p}_2]:h$$

$$\lfloor \text{IF} \rfloor \quad \mathsf{if\ true\ then}\ P\ \mathsf{else}\ Q \xrightarrow{\tau} P \qquad \mathsf{if\ false\ then}\ P\ \mathsf{else}\ Q \xrightarrow{\tau} Q$$

$$\lfloor \text{NEW,NEWS} \rfloor \quad \mathsf{new}\,a{:}T[\mathrm{p}]\ \mathsf{in}\ P \xrightarrow{\mathsf{new}\ a:T[\mathrm{p}]} P \qquad \mathsf{new}\,s{:}G\ \mathsf{in}\ P \xrightarrow{\mathsf{new}\ s:G} P$$

$$\lfloor \text{JOIN,OUT} \rfloor \quad \mathsf{join}\ s[\mathrm{p}];P \xrightarrow{\mathsf{join}(s[\mathrm{p}])} P \mid s[\mathrm{p}]:\emptyset \qquad s[\mathrm{p}_1]:\langle \mathrm{p}_1,\mathrm{p}_2,l\langle v\rangle\rangle\cdot h \xrightarrow{s[\mathrm{p}_1,\mathrm{p}_2]!l\langle v\rangle} s[\mathrm{p}_1]:h$$

$$\lfloor \text{REQ,IN} \rfloor \quad \bar{a}\langle s[\mathrm{p}]\ :\ T\rangle \xrightarrow{\bar{a}\langle s[\mathrm{p}]\,:\,T\rangle} \mathbf{0} \qquad s[\mathrm{p}_2]:h \xrightarrow{s[\mathrm{p}_1,\mathrm{p}_2]?l\langle v\rangle} s[\mathrm{p}_2]:h\cdot\langle \mathrm{p}_1,\mathrm{p}_2,l\langle v\rangle\rangle$$

We omit standard context/structure congruence rules. Accept $\lfloor \text{ACC} \rfloor$ is defined as a dual of $\lfloor \text{REQ} \rfloor$.

Fig. 4. Labelled transition system for processes

$\mathcal{M} ::= \Gamma,\Delta$	monitor	$\Gamma ::= \emptyset \mid \Gamma, a:T[\mathrm{p}]$		shared env
$\Delta ::= \emptyset \mid \Delta, s[\mathrm{p}]:T \mid \Delta, s[\mathrm{p}]^\bullet:T$	session env	$S ::= \mathsf{nat} \mid \mathsf{bool} \mid T[\mathrm{p}]$		sorts
$G ::= \mathrm{p}\to\mathrm{q}:\{l_i(x_i{:}S_i)\{A_i\}.G_i\}_{i\in I}$	interaction	$T ::= \mathrm{p}!\{l_i(x_i{:}S_i)\{A_i\}.T_i\}_{i\in I}$		selection
$\mid\ G_1 \mid G_2$	parallel	$\mid\ \mathrm{p}?\{l_i(x_i{:}S_i)\{A_i\}.T_i\}_{i\in I}$		branch
$\mid\ \mu\mathsf{t}\langle e\rangle(x{:}S)\{A\}.G \mid \mathsf{t}\langle e\rangle \mid \mathsf{end}$	rec/end	$\mid\ \mu\mathsf{t}\langle e\rangle(x:S)\{A\}.T \mid \mathsf{t}\langle e\rangle \mid \mathsf{end}$		rec/end

Fig. 5. Monitors and global/endpoint assertions (resp. $\mathcal{M}$, G, and T)

the syntax for a monitor above consists of two typing environments, one for shared channels (Γ) and one for sessions (Δ). In Δ, we let $s[\mathrm{p}]:T$ represent a capability which is owned by the local process but is not active yet (i.e., it can still be sent to invite another process); $s[\mathrm{p}]^\bullet : T$ represents an active capability after the monitored process has joined the session as p. The session environment Δ associates each *linear* capability to an endpoint assertion T which describes the behaviour of a specific role in a session.

When a principal creates a session instance $s:G$, the associated monitor learns about its specification from the *global assertion* G, which describes a global scenario among multiple participants annotated with logical formulae. The main construct is a labelled message exchange, where p sends q a label l_i (I is a finite set of integers) and a message x_i with sort S_i. Sorts include base types and shared channel types $T[\mathrm{p}]$. $T[\mathrm{p}]$ is an endpoint assertion T (described later) modelling role p. The global assertion G_i describes the continuation of the session for the selected branch i, and A_i is a predicate on interaction variables specifying what p must guarantee and dually what q can rely on. A_i expresses a constraint on the choice of branch i (e.g., a guard that must hold when selecting label l_i) and on the value of the exchanged message x_i, which we call *interaction variable*. We do not fix a specific logic for A, we only assume it is decidable. Interactions bind each x_i in A_i and in G_i. Parallel composition is written as $G \mid G'$. A recursive assertion is guarded in the standard way and defines a recursion parameter with its initialisation and an invariant predicate A. end ends the session. Below we give an example of a global assertion from the Instrument Command use case.

Example 1 (OOI Instrument Command - Global Assertion). The following is the global assertion for our running example (Figures 1 and 2). A branch without predicate means its accompanying predicate is true. We sometimes omit labels when there is a single branch.

$$
\begin{aligned}
G_{IC} \;=\;& \texttt{User} \to \texttt{Register} : (x_{int} : \mathsf{InterfaceId}).\\
& \texttt{Register} \to \texttt{User} : (x_n : \mathsf{Int})\{x_n > 0\}.\texttt{User} \to \texttt{Agent} : (x_p : \mathsf{Priority}).\\
& \texttt{Agent} \to \texttt{User} : \{\texttt{accept}().G_{acc},\;\; \texttt{reject}(x_E : \mathsf{ErrData})\{x_P = \mathsf{high} \supset x_e \neq \mathsf{busy}\}\}\\
G_{acc} \;=\;& \mu\mathsf{t}\langle x_n\rangle(y)\{y \geq 0\}.\\
& \texttt{User} \to \texttt{Agent} : \{\texttt{more}(x_{com} : \mathsf{Command})\{y > 0 \wedge x_{com} \neq \mathsf{switch\text{-}off}\}.G_{com},\\
& \qquad\qquad \texttt{quit}().\texttt{Agent} \to \texttt{Instrument} : \texttt{quit}()\}\\
G_{com} \;=\;& \texttt{Agent} \to \texttt{Instrument} : (y_{com} : \mathsf{Command}).\\
& \texttt{Instrument} \to \texttt{Agent} : (y_r : \mathsf{Response}).\texttt{Agent} \to \texttt{User} : (x_r : \mathsf{Response}).\;\mathsf{t}\langle y-1\rangle
\end{aligned}
$$

The scenario modelled by G_{IC} has already been described informally in § 2 (Figure 2). We here assume the consistency properties for assertions, the projectability and well-assertedness, from [3,17].[1]

The *endpoint assertions* T are local specification for endpoints, which are used by monitors. They specify which interactions are acceptable for an endpoint: in other words, an endpoint assertion specifies constraints on a session from the perspective of a specific role, rather than globally. In the grammar of Figure 5, selection expresses the transmission to p of a label l_i taken from a set $\{l_i\}_{i \in I}$, together with an interaction variable x_i of sort S_i and that the remaining interaction in the session is T_i. Branching is its dual. Others are similar to their global versions.

An *endpoint projection* or often simply *projection* $G \upharpoonright \mathrm{p}$ projects G onto p returning an endpoint assertion. Projection is defined as in [3] (please see online Appendix [20]). An example follows, projected from global assertions in Example 1.

Example 2 (OOI Instrument Command - Endpoint Assertion for User). Below we show the projections of respectively G_{IC}, G_{acc} and G_{com} onto User.

$$
\begin{aligned}
T_{user} \;=\;& \texttt{Register!}(x_{int} : \mathsf{InterfaceId}).\texttt{Register?}(x_n : \mathsf{Int})\{x_n > 0\}.\texttt{Agent!}(x_p : \mathsf{Priority}).\\
& \texttt{Agent?}\{\texttt{accept}().T^u_{acc},\;\; \texttt{reject}(x_e : \mathsf{ErrData})\{x_p = \mathsf{high} \supset x_e \neq \mathsf{busy}\}\}\\
T_{acc} \;=\;& \mu\mathsf{t}\langle x_n\rangle(y)\{y \geq 0\}.\\
& \texttt{Agent!}\{\texttt{more}(x_{com} : \mathsf{Command})\{y > 0 \wedge x_{com} \neq \mathsf{switch\text{-}off}\}.T^u_{com},\;\; \texttt{quit}()\}\\
T_{com} \;=\;& \texttt{Agent?}(x_r : \mathsf{Response}).\mathsf{t}\langle y-1\rangle
\end{aligned}
$$

3.3 Semantics of Monitors

The semantics of a monitor is given as a LTS following the standard interpretation of typing environments in process calculi. Later, this relation is used to control the

[1] Projectability says that a global assertion is projectable to each endpoint [17] (defined in online Appendix [20]) while well-assertedness says that it is always possible for an endpoint to find a path which satisfies its own obligations [3] (defined in online Appendix [20]). In this paper we only treat global assertions satisfying these properties. See [3,17] for further explanations.

$$[\text{TAU,JOIN}] \qquad \mathcal{M} \xrightarrow{\tau} \mathcal{M} \qquad \mathcal{M}, s[\mathrm{p}]^{\circ}:T \xrightarrow{\mathsf{join}(s[\mathrm{p}])} \mathcal{M}, s[\mathrm{p}]^{\bullet}:T$$

$$[\text{NEW, NEWS}] \qquad \frac{a \notin \mathsf{dom}(\mathcal{M})}{\mathcal{M} \xrightarrow{\mathsf{new}\ a:T[\mathrm{p}]} \mathcal{M}, a:T[\mathrm{p}]} \qquad \frac{s \notin \mathsf{dom}(\mathcal{M})}{\mathcal{M} \xrightarrow{\mathsf{new}\ s:G} \mathcal{M}, \{s[\mathrm{p}_i]^{\circ} : (G \upharpoonright \mathrm{p}_i)\}_{\mathrm{p}_i \in G}}$$

$$[\text{REQ}] \qquad \mathcal{M}, a:T[\mathrm{p}], s[\mathrm{p}]^{\circ}:T \xrightarrow{\overline{a}\langle s[\mathrm{p}]\ :\ T\rangle} \mathcal{M}, a:T[\mathrm{p}]$$

$$[\text{ACC}] \qquad \frac{s \notin \mathsf{dom}(\mathcal{M})}{\mathcal{M}, a:T[\mathrm{p}] \xrightarrow{a\langle s[\mathrm{p}]\ :\ T\rangle} \mathcal{M}, a:T[\mathrm{p}], s[\mathrm{p}]^{\circ}:T}$$

$$[\text{SEL}] \qquad \frac{\mathcal{M} \vdash v:S_j,\ A_j\{v/x_j\} \downarrow \mathsf{true}, T \curvearrowright \mathrm{p}_2!\{(x_i:S_i)\{A_i\}.T_i\}_{i\in I}}{\mathcal{M}, s[\mathrm{p}_1]^{\bullet}:T \xrightarrow{s[\mathrm{p}_1,\mathrm{p}_2]!l_j\langle v\rangle} \mathcal{M}, s[\mathrm{p}_1]^{\bullet}:T_j\{v/x_j\}}$$

$$[\text{BRA}] \qquad \frac{\mathcal{M} \vdash v:S_j,\ A_j\{v/x_j\} \downarrow \mathsf{true}, T \curvearrowright \mathrm{p}_1?\{l_i(x_i:S_i)\{A_i\}.T_i\}_{i\in I}}{\mathcal{M}, s[\mathrm{p}_2]^{\bullet}:T \xrightarrow{s[\mathrm{p}_1,\mathrm{p}_2]?l_j\langle v\rangle} \mathcal{M}, s[\mathrm{p}_2]^{\bullet}:T_j\{v/x_j\}}$$

$$[\text{BRAN}] \qquad \frac{S_j = T[\mathrm{p}],\ a \notin \mathsf{dom}(\mathcal{M}), \forall i\ a \notin A_i,\ A_i \downarrow \mathsf{true},\ T \curvearrowright \mathrm{p}_1?\{l_i(x_i:S_i)\{A_i\}.T_i\}_{i\in I}}{\mathcal{M}, s[\mathrm{p}_2]^{\bullet}:T \xrightarrow{s[\mathrm{p}_1,\mathrm{p}_2]?l_j\langle a\rangle} \mathcal{M}, a:S_j, s[\mathrm{p}_2]^{\bullet}:T_j}$$

Fig. 6. Labelled transition system for monitors

behaviour of processes. $\mathcal{M} \xrightarrow{\ell} \mathcal{M}'$ only if ℓ is a legal action (i.e., that a process should be allowed to perform by the monitor). We use the following labels:

$$\begin{aligned}\ell ::= \tau \mid \overline{a}\langle s[\mathrm{p}] : T\rangle \mid a\langle s[\mathrm{p}] : T\rangle \mid \mathsf{new}\ s:G \mid \mathsf{new}\ a:T[\mathrm{p}] \mid \mathsf{join}(s[\mathrm{p}]) \\ \mid s[\mathrm{p}_1,\mathrm{p}_2]!l\langle v\rangle \mid s[\mathrm{p}_1,\mathrm{p}_2]?l\langle v\rangle\end{aligned}$$

A label can be a τ-action, a session request or reception, the creation of a new session or shared channel, the join of a session, selection or branching. Request and selection (resp. reception and branching) are often collectively called *output* (resp. *input*).

The LTS for monitors is defined in Figure 6. Rule [NEW] allows a shared name creation with type $T[\mathrm{p}]$. Rule [NEWS] is for a new session s with type G, which is always allowed as far as s is fresh; it adds the projections of G at each p_i (denoted by $G \upharpoonright \mathrm{p}_i$), endowing the local process with the capabilities $s[\mathrm{p}_i]$ to play behaviours of all roles in G. Rule [JOIN] activates session $s[\mathrm{p}]$. Rule [REQ] represents that, for invitation at a, if the monitor includes the type of shared channel a as $T[\mathrm{p}]$, and the type of p in session s is exactly T, the monitor approves this invitation and, since this capability has been sent out, relinquishes $s[\mathrm{p}]$; rule [ACC] is its dual.

In [SEL], [BRA] and [BRAN], we use *permutations*, denoted $T \curvearrowright T'$. A sound permutation (called *asynchronous subtyping* in [21]) changes the order of actions to capture the semantics of asynchronously arriving messages without affecting causally related actions. Consider the global assertion $\mathrm{p}_2 \to \mathrm{p}_1 : (x{:}S)\{A\}.\mathrm{p}_3 \to \mathrm{p}_1 : (x'{:}S')\{A'\}.G$ where $\mathrm{p}_1 \neq \mathrm{p}_3$. In an asynchronous network we cannot prevent message x' to reach p_1 *earlier* than x. Hence p_1's monitor needs to accept the messages from p_2 and p_3 in any order. We define $T \curvearrowright T'$ when we can permute up an action in T to the top, and do nothing else, to reach T', via the axioms: $\mathrm{p}_1 \dagger_1 \{l_i(x_i:S_i)\{A_i\}.\mathrm{p}_2 \dagger_2 \{l'_j(x'_j:S'_j)\{A'_j\}.T_{ij}\}_{j\in J}\}_{i\in I} \curvearrowright$

$\mathrm{p}_2 \dagger_2 \{l'_j(x'_j : S'_j)\{A'_j\}.\mathrm{p}_1 \dagger_1 \{l_i(x_i : S_i)\{A_i\}.T_{ij}\}_{i \in I}\}_{j \in I}$ where $\dagger_1 = ?, \dagger_2 = ?$ or $\dagger_1 = !, \dagger_2 = !$ or $\dagger_1 = !, \dagger_2 = ?$. Note that $\dagger_1 = ?, \dagger_2 = !$ is *unsound* since the actions are causally related.

Thus [SEL] says that if the endpoint assertion of $s[\mathrm{p}_1]^\bullet$ at p_1 can be permuted to $\mathrm{p}_2!\{l_i(x_i : S_i)\{A_i\}.T_i\}_{i \in I}$, then the outgoing message with label l_i sent from p_1 to p_2, as far as it satisfies formula $A_j\{v/x_j\}$, is approved by the monitor which prepares the next (incoming or outgoing) message with local specification T_j. Rule [BRA] is its symmetric (input) counterpart, while [BRAN] is one for fresh shared channel a (ensured by $a \notin \mathsf{dom}(\mathscr{M})$ and $a \notin A_i$), so that $a : S_j$ is added to the monitor.

Unmonitored networks are given by erasing the co-domain (types and assertions) from each monitor in a monitored network. The result of such erasure, the monitor which 'switches-off' the monitoring activity, acts simply as a gateway with information on local addresses, including a session endpoint $s[\mathrm{p}]$. We call this stripped-off gateway a *monitor-off* ($\mathscr{M}^\circ, \mathscr{M}_1^\circ, \ldots$), used for routing session messages to the right destinations. The semantics of $\mathscr{M}^\circ$ is obtained by erasing the co-domain from each monitor in each rule in Figure 6. We write $\mathsf{erase}(\mathscr{M})$ for the monitor-off obtained through this erasure of $\mathscr{M}$. Hereafter we denote $\mathsf{erase}(\mathscr{M})$ as $\mathscr{M}^\circ$.

Example 3 ($\mathscr{M}$ **vs** $\mathscr{M}^\circ$). Let $\mathscr{M}_1 \stackrel{\text{def}}{=} s[\mathrm{p}_1]^\bullet : \mathrm{p}_2!(x : \mathsf{Int})\{x > 0\}.T$ and $\ell = s[\mathrm{p}_1,\mathrm{p}_2]!\langle -10 \rangle$. Then $\mathscr{M}_1^\circ \xrightarrow{\ell}$ but $\mathscr{M}_1 \not\xrightarrow{\ell}$ since the value -10 does not satisfy the predicate $x > 0$ in the endpoint assertion for the session monitored by $\mathscr{M}_1$. Similarly, for type violations, if $\mathscr{M}_2 \stackrel{\text{def}}{=} s[\mathrm{p}_1]^\bullet : \mathrm{p}_2!(x{:}\mathsf{String})\{\mathsf{true}\}.T$ and $\ell = s[\mathrm{p}_1,\mathrm{p}_2]!\langle 10 \rangle$ then $\mathscr{M}_2^\circ \xrightarrow{\ell}$ but $\mathscr{M}_2 \not\xrightarrow{\ell}$.

4 Monitored Network and Global Observables

4.1 Monitored Network

Syntax. We write $\mathscr{M}[P]$ for P monitored by $\mathscr{M}$, called *monitored process*. Then a *monitored network* or *network* ($N, N', \ldots$) is given as:

$$N ::= \emptyset \mid \mathscr{M}[P] \mid N_1 \mid N_2 \mid (\nu a{:}T[\mathrm{p}])N \mid (\nu s{:}G)N \mid s : h \mid \overline{a}\langle s[\mathrm{p}] : T \rangle$$

A monitored network represents a network of processes and their monitors, together with messages in transit, which include global message queues for each session ($s : h$ where h is a partial sequence of messages) and an unordered collection of invitations $\overline{a}\langle s[\mathrm{p}] : T \rangle$.

Reduction and Transition. The dynamics of networks, in particular how messages travel from a local configuration through a network to another local configuration, is formalised by the reduction rules in Figure 7. In each rule except ⌊PROC⌋, the ⌊-ERR⌋ case is when the monitor detects a violation of the specification by the current action; we stipulate that $\mathscr{M}$ simply drops such message. Each rule corresponds to a rule for the monitor semantics defined in Figure 6. Rule ⌊NEW⌋ creates a fresh (bound) shared channel, while rule ⌊NEWS⌋ creates a new session channel, together with an empty (global)

⌊PROC⌋
$$\frac{P \xrightarrow{\tau} P'}{\mathcal{M}[P] \to \mathcal{M}[P']}$$

⌊NEW, NEW-ERR⌋
$$\frac{\mathcal{M} \xrightarrow{\mathsf{new}\ a{:}T[\mathrm{p}]} \mathcal{M}'}{\mathcal{M}[\mathsf{new}\,a{:}T[\mathrm{p}]\ \mathsf{in}\ P] \to (\nu a{:}T[\mathrm{p}])(\mathcal{M}'[P])} \qquad \frac{\mathcal{M} \not\xrightarrow{\mathsf{new}\ a{:}T[\mathrm{p}]}}{\mathcal{M}[\mathsf{new}\,a{:}T[\mathrm{p}]\ \mathsf{in}\ P] \to \mathcal{M}[\mathbf{0}]}$$

⌊NEWS, NEWS-ERR⌋
$$\frac{\mathcal{M} \xrightarrow{\mathsf{new}\ s{:}G} \mathcal{M}'}{\mathcal{M}[\mathsf{new}\,s{:}G\ \mathsf{in}\ P] \to (\nu s{:}G)(\mathcal{M}'[P] \mid s:\emptyset)} \qquad \frac{\mathcal{M} \not\xrightarrow{\mathsf{new}\ s{:}G}}{\mathcal{M}[\mathsf{new}\,s{:}G\ \mathsf{in}\ P] \to \mathcal{M}[\mathbf{0}]}$$

⌊JOIN, JOIN-ERR⌋
$$\frac{\mathcal{M} \xrightarrow{\mathsf{join}(s[\mathrm{p}])} \mathcal{M}'}{\mathcal{M}[\mathsf{join}\ s[\mathrm{p}];P] \to \mathcal{M}'[P \mid s[\mathrm{p}]:\emptyset]} \qquad \frac{\mathcal{M} \not\xrightarrow{\mathsf{join}(s[\mathrm{p}])} \mathcal{M}'}{\mathcal{M}[\mathsf{join}\ s[\mathrm{p}];P] \to \mathcal{M}[P]}$$

⌊REQ, REQ-ERR⌋
$$\frac{\mathcal{M} \xrightarrow{\overline{a}\langle s[\mathrm{p}]\,:\,T\rangle} \mathcal{M}'}{\mathcal{M}[\overline{a}\langle s[\mathrm{p}]\ :\ T\rangle] \to \mathcal{M}'[\mathbf{0}] \mid \overline{a}\langle s[\mathrm{p}]\ :\ T\rangle} \qquad \frac{\mathcal{M} \not\xrightarrow{\overline{a}\langle s[\mathrm{p}]\,:\,T\rangle} \mathcal{M}'}{\mathcal{M}[\overline{a}\langle s[\mathrm{p}]\ :\ T\rangle] \to \mathcal{M}[\mathbf{0}]}$$

⌊ACC, ACC-ERR⌋
$$\frac{\mathcal{M} \xrightarrow{a\langle s[\mathrm{p}]\,:\,T\rangle} \mathcal{M}'}{\mathcal{M}[\mathbf{0}] \mid \overline{a}\langle s[\mathrm{p}]\ :\ T\rangle \to \mathcal{M}'[\overline{a}\langle s[\mathrm{p}]\ :\ T\rangle]} \qquad \frac{\mathcal{M} \not\xrightarrow{a\langle s[\mathrm{p}]\,:\,T\rangle} \mathcal{M}'}{\mathcal{M}[\mathbf{0}] \mid \overline{a}\langle s[\mathrm{p}]\ :\ T\rangle \to \mathcal{M}[\mathbf{0}]}$$

⌊OUT⌋
$$\frac{\mathcal{M} \xrightarrow{s[\mathrm{p}_1,\mathrm{p}_2]!l\langle v\rangle} \mathcal{M}'}{\mathcal{M}[s[\mathrm{p}_1] : \langle \mathrm{p}_1,\mathrm{p}_2,l\langle v\rangle\rangle \cdot h] \mid s : h' \to \mathcal{M}'[s[\mathrm{p}_1] : h] \mid s : h' \cdot \langle \mathrm{p}_1,\mathrm{p}_2,l\langle v\rangle\rangle}$$

⌊OUT-ERR⌋
$$\frac{\mathcal{M} \not\xrightarrow{s[\mathrm{p}_1,\mathrm{p}_2]!l\langle v\rangle} \mathcal{M}'}{\mathcal{M}[s[\mathrm{p}_1] : \langle \mathrm{p}_1,\mathrm{p}_2,l\langle v\rangle\rangle \cdot h] \mid s : h' \to \mathcal{M}[s[\mathrm{p}_1] : h] \mid s : h'}$$

⌊IN⌋
$$\frac{\mathcal{M} \xrightarrow{s[\mathrm{p}_1,\mathrm{p}_2]?l\langle v\rangle} \mathcal{M}'}{\mathcal{M}[s[\mathrm{p}_2] : h] \mid s : \langle \mathrm{p}_1,\mathrm{p}_2,l\langle v\rangle\rangle \cdot h' \to \mathcal{M}'[s[\mathrm{p}_2] : h \cdot \langle \mathrm{p}_1,\mathrm{p}_2,l\langle v\rangle\rangle] \mid s : h'}$$

⌊IN-ERR⌋
$$\frac{\mathcal{M} \not\xrightarrow{s[\mathrm{p}_1,\mathrm{p}_2]?l\langle v\rangle} \mathcal{M}'}{\mathcal{M}[s[\mathrm{p}_2] : h] \mid s : \langle \mathrm{p}_1,\mathrm{p}_2,l\langle v\rangle\rangle \cdot h' \to \mathcal{M}[s[\mathrm{p}_2] : h] \mid s : h'}$$

We omit the standard context rules and structural congruence rules.

Fig. 7. Reduction for monitored network

queue used by all processes joining session s. Rule ⌊JOIN⌋ creates a local queue for session s and role p. In rules ⌊REQ,ACC⌋, monitor $\mathcal{M}$ checks outgoing and incoming invitations. Ideally, ⌊REQ⌋ forwards an outgoing invitation, which is still local to a process, to the external environment (dually for ⌊ACC⌋ with an incoming invitation). In ⌊OUT⌋, $\mathcal{M}$ forwards a session message from a local queue $s[\mathrm{p}]$ into the global queue s (dually for ⌊IN⌋). Other rules are standard.

Example 4. Let $P = s[\mathrm{p}_1,\mathrm{p}_2]!\langle 100\rangle;P' \mid s[\mathrm{p}_1] : \emptyset$ be a process with an empty queue playing role p_1 in s. Let also $\mathcal{M}_1 = s[\mathrm{p}_1]^{\bullet} : \mathrm{p}_2!(x : \mathsf{Int})\{x > 0\}.T$ be its local monitor. The communication happens in two steps. First, the message is spawn into the local queue as $P \xrightarrow{\tau} P_2$ with $P_2 = P' \mid s[\mathrm{p}_1] : s[\mathrm{p}_1,\mathrm{p}_2]!\langle 100\rangle$ hence, since $\mathcal{M}_1 \xrightarrow{\tau} \mathcal{M}_1$, then $\mathcal{M}_1[P] \to \mathcal{M}_1[P_2]$. Second, the message is forwarded to the global queue as $P_2 \xrightarrow{\ell} P' \mid s[\mathrm{p}_1] : \emptyset$ with $\ell = s[\mathrm{p}_1,\mathrm{p}_2]!\langle 100\rangle$; hence since $\mathcal{M}_1 \xrightarrow{\ell} s[\mathrm{p}_1]^{\bullet} : T$ then $\mathcal{M}_1[P] \to s[\mathrm{p}_1]^{\bullet} : T[P' \mid s[\mathrm{p}_1] : \emptyset]$.

4.2 The Global Observables

As Figure 7 shows, from the perspective of the global network, all *global-behaviours* of monitored processes become unobservable. To analyse and state properties of monitored networks, the global-behaviours need be observed by linking global assertions to global interactions among monitored networks, neglecting local interactions inside endpoints. We therefore propose a notion of global observables and we define it through two labelled transitions systems: one for networks and one for environments (they represent the abstraction of global specifications and message flows).

First, we formalise the notion of the global observables of *networks* as follows: $N \xrightarrow{\ell}_{\mathrm{g}} N'$ for N without hiding, if any of its monitors of monitored processes has the transition ℓ (by the LTS given Figure 6). Thus global observability is the aggregate of what all monitors observe.

Second, we formalise a global observable environment, ranged over by $\mathscr{E}, \mathscr{E}', \ldots$, in order to witness the legality of all messages in transit. A global observable environment includes pending messages together with global assertions (for ease of defining its LTS, we also include local assertions). The use of pending messages is motivated as follows.

In a monitored network, we expect that all endpoint processes follow exactly what global assertions G define. However, at runtime, monitors at receiver-side can only observe the behaviours of processes through the passing messages, in order to capture whether the incoming message has been sent or not. If this message has not been sent, there should exist a monitor at sender-side specifying this sending action. In this case, these two monitors are coherent. On the other hand, if this message has been sent (so there is no any monitor contains the specification of this sending action), the monitor at receiver-side needs to be compensated not by another monitor specification but by a message in a global queue. This situation is illustrated by the following example.

Example 5. Assume a simple global protocol specifies that:

$$\mathrm{p}_1 \rightarrow \mathrm{p}_2 : (x : \mathsf{int})\{x > 5\}.G_2$$

At the beginning, the specification of sender-side monitor is

$$s[\mathrm{p}_1]^{\bullet} : \mathrm{p}_2!(x : \mathsf{int})\{x > 5\}.G_2 \upharpoonright \mathrm{p}_1$$

and the one of receiver-side is

$$s[\mathrm{p}_2]^{\bullet} : \mathrm{p}_1?(x : \mathsf{int})\{x > 5\}.G_2 \upharpoonright \mathrm{p}_2$$

When the sender-side monitor permits an outgoing message $s : \langle \mathrm{p}_1, \mathrm{p}_2, 10\rangle$, (i.e., a legal sending action), its specification immediately changes to $s[\mathrm{p}_1]^{\bullet} : G_2 \upharpoonright \mathrm{p}_1$ for the next action; however, the specification of receiver-side monitor may not change because it is waiting for the message that is travelling in the global queue $s : h \cdot \langle \mathrm{p}_1, \mathrm{p}_2, 10\rangle$; as long as the message does not arrive, the receiver-side monitor cannot change its specification. In this case, the receiver-side monitor knows the messages will certainly come by looking at the global queue.

Keeping in mind that a global queue (containing assertions of run-time pending messages) is needed as a part of the global observable environment, we define the syntax of global observable environment $\mathscr{E}$ as follows:

$$\mathscr{E} ::= \Gamma, \Delta, \Theta \qquad \Gamma ::= \emptyset \mid \Gamma, a : T[\mathtt{p}] \qquad \Theta ::= \emptyset \mid \Theta, s : G$$
$$\Delta ::= \emptyset \mid \Delta, s[\mathtt{p}] : T \mid \Delta, s[\mathtt{p}]^{\bullet} : T \mid \Delta, s : \vec{mv} \qquad mv ::= \langle \mathtt{p}, \mathtt{q}, l\langle v \rangle \rangle$$

where Γ is a typing environment, Δ is a session environment as the one in Figure 5, to which we add message assertions $s : \vec{mv}$ to model a global queue environment. Each assignment in $s : \vec{mv}$ is of the form $s : mv_1..mv_n$, $n \geq 0$, where mv_i is a message assertion of shape $\langle \mathtt{p}, \mathtt{p}', l\langle v \rangle \rangle$. Θ is a global environment associating sessions to global assertions. Thus $\mathscr{E}$ can use both global specification and pending messages to help monitors and thus ensure that the whole network is in a correct state.

4.3 Labelled Transition Rules for $\mathscr{E}$

In Figure 8 we define $\mathscr{E} \xrightarrow{\ell}_{\mathtt{g}} \mathscr{E}'$, which says: environment $\mathscr{E}$ allows a global observation of ℓ as a valid interaction, and, after the corresponding changes in the assertions and global queues, becomes ready to observe a possible next action as $\mathscr{E}'$.

$$\mathscr{E} \xrightarrow{\tau}_{\mathtt{g}} \mathscr{E} \qquad [\mathscr{E}\text{-TAU}]$$

$$\frac{\mathscr{E} \vdash v : S_j \quad A_j\{v/x_j\} \downarrow \mathsf{true} \quad G \curvearrowright \mathtt{p}_1 \to \mathtt{p}_2 : \{l_i(x_i : S_i)\{A_i\}.G_i\}_{i \in I}}{\mathscr{E}, s : G, s[\mathtt{p}_2]^{\bullet} : T, s : \langle \mathtt{p}_1, \mathtt{p}_2, l_j\langle v \rangle \rangle \cdot \vec{mv} \xrightarrow{s[\mathtt{p}_1,\mathtt{p}_2]?l_j\langle v \rangle}_{\mathtt{g}} \mathscr{E}, s : G_j\{v/x_j\}, s[\mathtt{p}_2]^{\bullet} : T_j, s : \vec{mv}} \qquad [\mathscr{E}\text{-BCH}]$$

$$\frac{\mathscr{E} \vdash v : S_j \quad A_j\{v/x_j\} \downarrow \mathsf{true} \quad T \curvearrowright \mathtt{p}_2!\{l_i(x_i : S_j)\{A_i\}.T_i\}_{i \in I}}{\mathscr{E}, s[\mathtt{p}_1]^{\bullet} : T, s : \vec{mv} \xrightarrow{s[\mathtt{p}_1,\mathtt{p}_2]!l_j\langle v \rangle}_{\mathtt{g}} \mathscr{E}, s[\mathtt{p}_1]^{\bullet} : T_j\{v/x_j\}, s : \vec{mv} \cdot \langle \mathtt{p}_1, \mathtt{p}_2, l_j\langle v \rangle \rangle} \qquad [\mathscr{E}\text{-SEL}]$$

$$\frac{s \notin \mathsf{dom}(\mathscr{E})}{\mathscr{E} \xrightarrow{\mathsf{new}\ s:G}_{\mathtt{g}} \mathscr{E}, s : G, \{s[\mathtt{p}_i] : (G \upharpoonright \mathtt{p}_i)\}_{\mathtt{p}_i \in G}, s : \emptyset} \qquad [\mathscr{E}\text{-NEW S}]$$

$$\frac{a \notin \mathsf{dom}(\mathscr{E})}{\mathscr{E} \xrightarrow{\mathsf{new}\ a:T[\mathtt{p}]}_{\mathtt{g}} \mathscr{E}, a : T[\mathtt{p}]} \qquad [\mathscr{E}\text{-NEW A}]$$

$$\mathscr{E}, s[\mathtt{p}] : T \xrightarrow{\mathsf{join}(s[\mathtt{p}])}_{\mathtt{g}} \mathscr{E}, s[\mathtt{p}]^{\bullet} : T \qquad [\mathscr{E}\text{-JOIN}]$$

$$\mathscr{E}, a : T[\mathtt{p}], s[\mathtt{p}] : T \xrightarrow{\overline{a}\langle s[\mathtt{p}] : T \rangle}_{\mathtt{g}} \mathscr{E}, a : T[\mathtt{p}], s[\mathtt{p}] : T \qquad [\mathscr{E}\text{-REQ}]$$

$$\mathscr{E}, a : T[\mathtt{p}], s[\mathtt{p}] : T \xrightarrow{a\langle s[\mathtt{p}] : T \rangle}_{\mathtt{g}} \mathscr{E}, a : T[\mathtt{p}], s[\mathtt{p}] : T \qquad [\mathscr{E}\text{-ACC}]$$

Fig. 8. Labelled transition system for environments

In [$\mathscr{E}$-BCH], T is obtained by removing all *outputted actions* of p_2 (i.e., $\vec{mv} \upharpoonright \mathrm{p}_2$) from all actions of p_2 (i.e., $G \upharpoonright \mathrm{p}_2$); T_j is, similarly, obtained by removing outputted actions of p_2 from all actions in G_j of p_2 and replacing x_j by v in $G_j \upharpoonright \mathrm{p}_2$. The reason why this is needed, instead of simply applying $G \upharpoonright \mathrm{p}_2$, is to obtain the appropriate endpoint specification considering the asynchrony nature of interactions. We use the following example to show this situation.

Example 6. Given a simple global assertion

$$\mathrm{p}_1 \to \mathrm{q}_1 : (x_1 : \mathsf{int})\{x_1 > 0\}.\mathrm{p}_1 \to \mathrm{q}_2 : (x_2 : \mathsf{int})\{x_2 > 1\}.\mathrm{q}_3 \to \mathrm{p}_1 : (x_3 : \mathsf{int})\{x_3 > 2\}.\mathsf{end} \quad (1)$$

Obviously, as p_1 is active, the local specification of monitor at p_1 is

$$s[\mathrm{p}_1]^\bullet : \mathrm{q}_1!(x_1 : \mathsf{int})\{x_1 > 0\}.\mathrm{q}_2!(x_2 : \mathsf{int})\{x_2 > 1\}.\mathrm{q}_3?(x_3 : \mathsf{int})\{x_3 > 2\}.\mathsf{end} \quad (2)$$

It is possible that participants interact in the following order: (I) q_3 firstly sends message $\langle \mathrm{q}_3, \mathrm{p}_1, \langle 3 \rangle\rangle$ to p_1, (II) then p_1 sends messages to q_1 and q_2 with $\langle \mathrm{p}_1, \mathrm{q}_1, \langle 1 \rangle\rangle$ and $\langle \mathrm{p}_1, \mathrm{q}_2, \langle 2 \rangle\rangle$ respectively. Note that, as the first interaction happens, p_1 may not receive this messages immediately. Assume before this message arrives, p_1 has sent out messages $\langle \mathrm{p}_1, \mathrm{q}_1, \langle 1 \rangle\rangle$ and $\langle \mathrm{p}_1, \mathrm{q}_2, \langle 2 \rangle\rangle$. Therefore, the global queue is

$$\langle \mathrm{q}_3, \mathrm{p}_1, \langle 1 \rangle\rangle \cdot \langle \mathrm{p}_1, \mathrm{q}_1, \langle 1 \rangle\rangle \cdot \langle \mathrm{p}_1, \mathrm{q}_2, \langle 2 \rangle\rangle$$

and the global assertion *maintains* as Equation (1) because no message has been received. However, the current specification of monitor at p_1 is $s[\mathrm{p}_1]^\bullet : \mathrm{q}_3?(x_3 : \mathsf{int})\{x_3 > 2\}.\mathsf{end}$ since it has done two output actions. In such a case, $G \upharpoonright \mathrm{p}_1$, which is still Equation (2), cannot reflect the reality of p_1 that is going to receive a message because of the asynchrony nature.

Continue with rule [$\mathscr{E}$-BCH]. It says that if a value is typed S_j and satisfies A_j, and G has a corresponding interaction up to permutations, it allows $\langle \mathrm{p}_1, \mathrm{p}_2, l_j\langle v \rangle\rangle$ to be received, resulting in the new local/global assertions. The permutation relation $G \curvearrowright G'$ (defined in online Appendix [20]) means that the specification G can be permuted to G', so that what is not *apparently* an active action in G becomes active in G' modulo permutation. For example, if both `Buyer` and `Broker` are sending a message to `Seller`:

$$G \stackrel{\text{def}}{=} \texttt{Buyer} \to \texttt{Seller} : (x : \mathsf{integer}).\texttt{Broker} \to \texttt{Seller} :: (x : \mathsf{string}).\mathsf{end}$$

then `Broker`'s message may as well arrive at `Seller` first, hence we permute this to

$$G' \stackrel{\text{def}}{=} \texttt{Broker} \to \texttt{Seller} : (x : \mathsf{string}).\texttt{Buyer} \to \texttt{Seller} : (x : \mathsf{integer}).\mathsf{end}$$

where $G \curvearrowright G'$ and G' is ready to check an appropriate message from `Broker` to `Seller`. Rule [$\mathscr{E}$-SEL] states that when $\mathscr{E}$ approves an output, its global assertion is unchanged but put a message to the global queue, indicating that an interaction has *partially* happened by an output, but not completed.

[$\mathscr{E}$-NEW s] says if a session s is new to $\mathscr{E}$, $\mathscr{E}$ adds the global assertion of s and the session environments $\{s[\mathrm{p}_i] : (G \upharpoonright \mathrm{p}_i)\}_{\mathrm{p}_i \in G}$ corresponding to s, and the queue $s : \emptyset$ at the same time. [$\mathscr{E}$-NEW A] says if a shared name a is new to $\mathscr{E}$, then $\mathscr{E}$ adds this new shared channel. [$\mathscr{E}$-JOIN] makes the specified session-role $s[\mathrm{p}]$ become active. Finally, since $\mathscr{E}$ watches the global environment (i.e., by watching all endpoint monitors), as request and accept happens at endpoint, it does not affect the global environment. [$\mathscr{E}$-REQ] and [$\mathscr{E}$-ACC] state this fact. Note that, for [$\mathscr{E}$-REQ] (or [$\mathscr{E}$-ACC]), if the left-hand side environment violates the rule, then the rule [$\mathscr{E}$-TAU] is applied; which means that, globally, there is no such a request (or accept) action observed.

5 Transparency, Conformance and Session Fidelity

This section informally outlines the key local and global safety properties that our monitoring mechanism can enforce.

5.1 Local Safety and Transparency

We first list the properties that monitors guarantee for local configurations. Hereafter, we let $\mathscr{L}$, a *located process*, stand for either a monitored process $\mathscr{M}[P]$ or monitor-off process $\mathscr{M}^{\circ}[P]$. *Conformance of a located process to a monitor's specification* means this located process only sends "good" messages (which implies that its monitor always permits those messages) and receive "good" messages (which have been approved by its monitor). In this case we say this process *conforms* to $\mathscr{M}$, (i.e. it behaves well w.r.t. $\mathscr{M}$), represented as $\mathscr{M} \models \mathscr{L}$.

We can then show every monitored process conforms to the specification given by its monitor. Locally speaking, a monitored-process and a monitor-off process behave precisely in the same way if the latter already conforms to its monitor's specification. Therefore $\mathscr{M} \models \mathscr{M}^{\circ}[P]$ implies $\mathscr{M} \models \mathscr{M}^{\circ}[P] \sim \mathscr{M}[P]$, denoting that $\mathscr{M}^{\circ}[P]$ and $\mathscr{M}[P]$ are bisimilar under $\mathscr{M}$ [2] Note that a process P that can be validated by $\Gamma \vdash P \triangleright \Delta$ (in the sense of [3]) is guaranteed to behave correctly and thus satisfies $\mathscr{M} \models \mathscr{M}^{\circ}[P]$ for $\mathscr{M} = \Gamma, \Delta$.

5.2 Global Safety, Fidelity and Transparency

Global Safety and Transparency. Let us say a network is *open* if it has no name restrictions, and *receivable* if all pending messages in global queue can be received by their destinations. Here we state that, *given N is open and receivable, $N \xrightarrow{\ell}_g N'$ implies, for an input ℓ, N' is receivable.*

To describe each party in a network behaves consistently with other parties, *coherence* is defined: an open network N is *coherent* if all of its pending messages are *receivable* up to *permutation* of actions $\curvearrowright$ and, after these messages have been received, the resulting monitors, say $\{\mathscr{M}_i\}_{i \in I}$ with $\mathscr{M}_i = \Gamma_i, \Delta_i$, satisfy the following conditions: **(1)** shared channels carry the same specification; **(2)** no two locations share the same role

[2] Monitored strong bisimulation is defined by: (1) for output or silent actions, if $\mathscr{M}^{\circ}[P]$ allows an action then also the monitor must allow that action; (2) for input actions, if the monitor allows an action then also $\mathscr{M}^{\circ}[P]$ must allow that action.

for a same session and each assertion has its dual; **(3)** for each session channel, the local assertion for each of its roles is the result of projecting from a common global assertion.

Coherence should be preserved by the interactions that can happen in a monitored network. Thus $N \xrightarrow{\ell}_{\mathrm{g}} N'$ with N coherent implies N' is coherent. When N is open, N is *locally conformant* if, for each monitored process $\mathscr{M}_i[P_i]$ in N, we have $\mathscr{M}_i \models \mathsf{erase}(\mathscr{M}_i)[P_i]$. If N is coherent and locally conformant and such that $N \xrightarrow{\ell_1}_{\mathrm{g}} \cdots \xrightarrow{\ell_n}_{\mathrm{g}} N'$, then N' is also coherent and locally conformant. Let $\sim$ be the standard strong bisimilarity defined by $\xrightarrow{\ell}_{\mathrm{g}}$. By the global invariance, we have: *N, which is coherent and locally conformant, implies $N \sim \mathsf{erase}(N)$.*

Session Fidelity. When a new session is generated, it is associated with a global assertion G. This notion is called *session fidelity* [17].

The coherence of $\mathscr{E}$ is defined as the one for network (for the full definition, please see the online Appendix [20]). Given $\mathscr{E}$ and N open, we write $\mathscr{E} \vdash N$ when: $\mathscr{E}$ is coherent, its shared and linear environments come from the *monitors* in N, and its global queue environment comes from the pending messages in N. Whenever N is coherent, we can construct a (coherent) $\mathscr{E}$ such that $\mathscr{E} \vdash N$. Using these results and the exact correspondence between the permutation rules over assertions, we can establish the following result: *$\mathscr{E} \vdash N$ and $N \xrightarrow{\ell}_g N'$ implies $\mathscr{E} \xrightarrow{\ell}_g \mathscr{E}'$ such that $\mathscr{E}' \vdash N'$.* It states that global interactions in a coherent network never violate the expected network-wide global specifications: the former follows the latter step by step.

6 Related Work and Conclusion

Related work. Our previous work [3] uses the static validation of an endpoint process against local (endpoint) assertions for guaranteeing global safety of their behaviour. In other words, the postulated global properties are guaranteed only if the local code of *every* endpoint is statically verified. As discussed in Introduction, this assumption is often not practicable in heterogeneous distributed applications where endpoints are located in multiple administrative domains thus we cannot trust all of the participants to well-behave. The present paper also gives, for the first time, a direct formalisation of the notion of global invariants through global transitions and the induced bisimilarity.

The monitoring mechanism presented in this paper can be seen as a distributed variant of *runtime verification* in the sense of [1,14,15]. We monitor program executions to detect violation of properties and to enforce correct behaviours. The proposed approach is light-weight, concerned only with the observable executions, and does not aim to give a conclusive analysis about all their possible behaviours. Hence it is applicable to real-world systems, where off-line formal verification is intractable or impossible due to incomplete information on system components or the dynamic change in requirements.

In the classification of [8,18], our monitor is *online* (program execution is checked as it takes place) rather than *offline* (only the history of the execution is analysed), and is *outline* (or *external*) (the monitors run as separate processes and analyse the program via its observable events) rather than *inline* (the monitors are embedded in the target programs). This combination is the most effective for specifying and maintaining global correctness and protecting endpoints from illegal interactions (cf. § 2).

Our monitor mechanism respects two important principles: *soundness*, which states that enforcement results in a correct behaviour, and *transparency*, which requires the behaviour of a correct program not to be modified (a principle studied for example in an automata framework [11,25]). Our monitor *suppresses* [19] the illegal actions (as seen in (else) case of $\mathscr{M} \xrightarrow{\ell} \mathscr{M}'$) but neither immediately halts nor inserts the correct actions. Incorporating more elaborate reactions as in edit automata [19,25] is interesting future topics. None of the above work can ensure the fidelity to application-level multiparty global protocols for distributed applications with logical properties.

Our work uses a distributed process calculus to model networks of monitored (possibly unsafe) processes. From this viewpoint, the most closely related formalism is safeDpi [16] (a precursor of [24]) which models filtering for migrating processes, preserving type safety, using channel dependent types. Recently dynamic joining mechanisms are studied in the conversation-calculus [4] (which uses conversation contexts) and [13] (based on roles). Our primitive invites other parties via capability passing through shared channels, while [4,13] formalise joining to the existing session and maintain progress by advanced type checking. The main difference is that our work is about runtime enforcement of global protocol properties rather than static type checking, and that we enforce properties by local runtime checking. Our framework also incorporates logical assertions, offering more fine-grained logical specifications than bare protocols representable by types.

Another recent work [2,9] presents a secure implementation of sequential multiparty sessions. Through the mechanised use of cryptography, the integrity of session executions is protected in the presence of an active attacker controlling the network and some peers. The main differences from [2,9] are our support of a more general class of global specifications based on *MPSA*s and our choice of a framework based on trusted external monitors. We indeed advocate a framework independent from any particular programming language, enabling a greater applicability for large-scale distributed infrastructures. Unifying these two approaches by including active, un-monitored, attackers to the network offers an interesting research opportunity.

Conclusion and On-Going Work. Our formalism aims at providing a reference semantics for efficient and interoperable monitors in order to enforce safe multiparty session executions. A preliminary prototype is running over an advanced messaging middleware, and consists of: a protocol specification language called Scribble [26], the interfaces and runtimes for Scala, Java and Ocaml, and distributed monitors written in Ocaml. Following the monitoring rules in Figure 6, a monitor can be implemented efficiently (incl. the projection algorithm for generating monitors, which is polynomial against the size of global types [12]). Collaborations with OOI and Scribble projects to develop a *MPSA*-based monitor architecture of industrial strength are on-going.

References

1. Barringer, H., Falcone, Y., Finkbeiner, B., Havelund, K., Lee, I., Pace, G., Roşu, G., Sokolsky, O., Tillmann, N. (eds.): RV 2010. LNCS, vol. 6418. Springer, Heidelberg (2010)
2. Bhargavan, K., Corin, R., Deniélou, P.-M., Fournet, C., Leifer, J.: Cryptographic protocol synthesis and verification for multiparty sessions. In: CSF, pp. 124–140 (2009)

3. Bocchi, L., Honda, K., Tuosto, E., Yoshida, N.: A Theory of Design-by-Contract for Distributed Multiparty Interactions. In: Gastin, P., Laroussinie, F. (eds.) CONCUR 2010. LNCS, vol. 6269, pp. 162–176. Springer, Heidelberg (2010)
4. Caires, L., Vieira, H.T.: Conversation Types. In: Castagna, G. (ed.) ESOP 2009. LNCS, vol. 5502, pp. 285–300. Springer, Heidelberg (2009)
5. Carbone, M., Honda, K., Yoshida, N.: Structured Interactional Exceptions in Session Types. In: van Breugel, F., Chechik, M. (eds.) CONCUR 2008. LNCS, vol. 5201, pp. 402–417. Springer, Heidelberg (2008)
6. W3C WS-CDL, `http://www.w3.org/2002/ws/chor/`
7. Chave, M., Arrott, A., Farcas, C., Farcas, E., Krueger, I., Meisinger, M., Orcutt, J., Vernon, F., Peach, C., Schofield, O., Kleinert, J.: Cyberinfrastructure for the US Ocean Observatories Initiative. In: Proc. IEEE OCEANS 2009. IEEE (2009)
8. Chen, F., Rosu, G.: MOP:An Efficient and Generic Runtime Verification Framework. In: OOPSLA, pp. 569–588 (2007)
9. Corin, R., Denielou, P.-M., Fournet, C., Bhargavan, K., Leifer, J.: Secure Implementations for Typed Session Abstractions. In: CSF, pp. 170–186. IEEE Computer Society (2007)
10. Coulouris, G., Dollimore, J., Kindberg, T.: Distributed Systems, Concepts and Design. Addison-Wesley (2001)
11. Dam, M., Jacobs, B., Lundblad, A., Piessens, F.: Security Monitor Inlining for Multithreaded Java. In: Drossopoulou, S. (ed.) ECOOP 2009. LNCS, vol. 5653, pp. 546–569. Springer, Heidelberg (2009)
12. Deniélou, P.-M., Yoshida, N.: Buffered Communication Analysis in Distributed Multiparty Sessions. In: Gastin, P., Laroussinie, F. (eds.) CONCUR 2010. LNCS, vol. 6269, pp. 343–357. Springer, Heidelberg (2010)
13. Deniélou, P.-M., Yoshida, N.: Dynamic multirole session types. In: POPL, pp. 435–446 (2011)
14. Falcone, Y.: You Should Better Enforce Than Verify. In: Barringer, H., Falcone, Y., Finkbeiner, B., Havelund, K., Lee, I., Pace, G., Roşu, G., Sokolsky, O., Tillmann, N. (eds.) RV 2010. LNCS, vol. 6418, pp. 89–105. Springer, Heidelberg (2010)
15. Havelund, K., Goldberg, A.: Verify Your Runs. In: Meyer, B., Woodcock, J. (eds.) VSTTE 2005. LNCS, vol. 4171, pp. 374–383. Springer, Heidelberg (2008)
16. Hennessy, M., Rathke, J., Yoshida, N.: SafeDpi: a language for controlling mobile code. Acta Inf. 42(4-5), 227–290 (2005)
17. Honda, K., Yoshida, N., Carbone, M.: Multiparty Asynchronous Session Types. In: POPL 2008, pp. 273–284. ACM (2008)
18. Leucker, M., Schallhart, C.: A brief account of runtime verification. J. Log. Algebr. Program. 78(5), 293–303 (2009)
19. Ligatti, J., Bauer, L., Walker, D.: Run-time enforcement of nonsafety policies. ACM Trans. Inf. Syst. Secur. 12, 19:1–19:41 (2009)
20. Online Appendix of this paper,
`http://www.eecs.qmul.ac.uk/~tcchen/TGC11/`
21. Mostrous, D., Yoshida, N., Honda, K.: Global Principal Typing in Partially Commutative Asynchronous Sessions. In: Castagna, G. (ed.) ESOP 2009. LNCS, vol. 5502, pp. 316–332. Springer, Heidelberg (2009)
22. Mullender, S. (ed.): Distributed Systems. Addison-Wesley (1993)
23. Ocean Observatories Initiative (OOI),
`http://www.oceanleadership.org/programs-and-partnerships/ocean-observing/ooi/`
24. Riely, J., Hennessy, M.: Trust and partial typing in open systems of mobile agents. In: Proc. POPL 1999 (1999)
25. Schneider, F.B.: Enforceable security policies. ACM Trans. Inf. Syst. Secur. 3, 30–50 (2000)
26. Scribble Project homepage, `http://www.scribble.org`

E-Mobility as a Challenge for New ICT Solutions in the Car Industry

Bernd Werther* and Nicklas Hoch*

Volkswagen AG, Germany

Abstract. Future mobility scenarios show a continuous gain in market shares of electric vehicles (EVs) [1]. However, both speed and magnitude of EV market penetration depend on the evolution of critical success factors. Regulatory policy, e.g. CO2 emission targets, and hard constraints like peak–of–oil are some of the factors positively influencing EV market penetration [1]. In contrary, a partial mismatch of consumer expectations and EV realities exists [2], which negatively influences EV market success. Consumer expectations have been co-created with combustion engine vehicles over 125 years. Mostly price and relative resource shortage of EVs are perceived by consumers as a major entry barrier [3].

Breaking the barrier is a question of resource allocation. The resource shortage can be resolved either physically, e.g. by improving energy density of batteries, or by the means of intelligent services such as smart charging, energy routing, car and ride sharing. Both EV and infrastructure resources such as charging stations can be managed temporally, spatially and energetically so that the consumer does not perceive them as being constraint.

This paper addresses the challenge of intelligent resource coordination both from a formal modelling perspective and a value–added–service perspective. Firstly, it presents a formal ICT [4] based modelling approach, which is developed within the EU–funded project ASCENS [5]. Secondly, it presents an ICT based value–added–service, namely the EV Daily Travel Planning Service, which has been designed for user–centric resource coordination in the EV domain.

1 Introduction

This paper addresses the issue of resource coordination in the electric mobility domain. From a modelling perspective, the entities of the mobility system are heterogeneous, interactions are complex and knowledge is distributed. From a consumer perspective, travel desires need to be met in the best possible way without extensive system interaction, cognitive load and at a minimum price. From an OEM perspective, value is most likely created if products meet consumer requirements, if the personal benefit of the product is communicable and well-perceivable by the user.

* All authors contributed equally.

R. Bruni and V. Sassone (Eds.): TGC 2011, LNCS 7173, pp. 46–57, 2012.

The paper is structured in three parts. **Part one** (section 2) presents the major challenges of e-mobility that are addressed in this paper: Intelligent knowledge distribution, EV travel time and energy prediction and journey planning.

Part two (sections 3, 4) applies the ASCENS modelling framework, which is developed for the generic case, to the particular case of e-mobility. The ASCENS approach is developed for the coordination of large, pervasive, open–ended and self–aware systems [5]. According to ASCENS the mobility system has to be represented by intelligent and self-aware nodes, which group thematically, temporally and spatially in order to reach a goal. In the face of driver-vehicle-infrastructure networks the following questions are answered:

- What are the real world representations of the rather abstract notion of service components within the e-mobility scenario?
- What are the representative service component ensembles?
- When do they reorganize and what are the implications on resources like time, space and energy?

Part three presents a value–added service, which draws upon the ASCENS modelling approach and focuses on user perceivable communication of value–add. The service runs seamlessly on the vehicle backend server, the vehicle infotainment system and the customer's smart phone. Example visualizations of features of the value–added–service are shown in section 5.

2 Challenges

Consumer perceivable mobility parameters — be it driving or charging time, range or parking space — are increasingly constrained. The mobility system is dynamic and heterogeneous and characterized by a high degree of uncertainty. Consumer behaviour, EV conditions, and infrastructure resource availability are mutually dependent. Information about system states — be it traffic, vehicle or energy grid related — are decentrally monitored and made available [6].

This being the situation, three major challenges can be identified. Firstly, intelligent knowledge distribution, secondly, the accurate prediction of EV travel time and energy consumption and thirdly, intelligent journey planning.

Intelligent knowledge distribution: Distribute knowledge about EV requirements, infrastructure states and consumer desires so that information overload is minimized and consumer privacy is guaranteed.

Predicting EV travel time and energy: Use distributed knowledge — e.g. traffic information, route topography, charging station availability/power output — to predict time and energy requirements of EVs.

Journey planning: Manage the consumer's travel desire and the predicted travel limitations in order to render the latter inactive. Possible corrective actions are re-routing, scheduling of alternative charging stations, shifting travel times or changing travel modes.

3 Model Driven Requirement Analysis

3.1 Scenario Description

The model driven requirement analysis differentiates multiple mobility scenarios. Common to all of the scenarios is the aim of finding a travel plan, which is most positively perceived by each individual user.

The basic scenario (S0) considers individual users and privately owned e-vehicles. The daily route sequence is optimized by a daily travel planning service according to the consumer desires such as minimal travel time or minimal waiting time at a charging station. The most suitable charging locations and parking places are identified and booked by the planning service. This is under the assumption that infrastructure services provide availability information of charging stations and car parks.

Assuming that the user is no longer strongly connected to its private vehicle, the S0 scenario is extended to the S1 scenario (car sharing). Car sharing services add a degree of freedom to the planning service by making it possible to flexibly change the car at intermediate destinations. Flexibility however comes at the additional effort of booking vehicles, which in order to gain user acceptance, has to be made as easy as possible and has to be offered together with attractive pricing.

The S1 scenario is further extended to the S2 scenario, namely the carpooling scenario. Dynamic carpooling as a service is used for organizing and executing shared trips with other people in a flexible way. At least two people are using either a private or rented car for travelling together. This extension to the basic scenario significantly improves the utilization of the vehicles, the total cost of ownership (TCO) and it may increase consumer flexibility.

Several multi-modal extensions such as public transport may be included in the future in order to enrich the approach and exploit its full potential.

3.2 Formalization of an e-Mobility Process Model

Coordinating individual entities in the context of global system dynamics is the biggest challenge in the e–mobility scenario. Centrally organized traffic systems controlled by human experts, e.g. rail or air traffic, have common knowledge and more or less precisely defined schedules. The few individually planned entities have a negligible influence on the system. In contrast to the latter in the e–mobility scenario entities only have partial knowledge of the behaviour of other entities and travel schedules are self-managed by individual users. Travel planning systems of users or user groups are decentrally coordinating consumers' desires and the resource-constrained traffic system (e.g. limited set of charging stations).

The mobility scenarios S0-S2 are formally analysed by the use of a Petri-net model. Petri-nets are most useful for representing distributed systems at a microscopic level, at which system interactions are easily describable. Petri-net state space analysis is then used to investigate system behaviour at a global level,

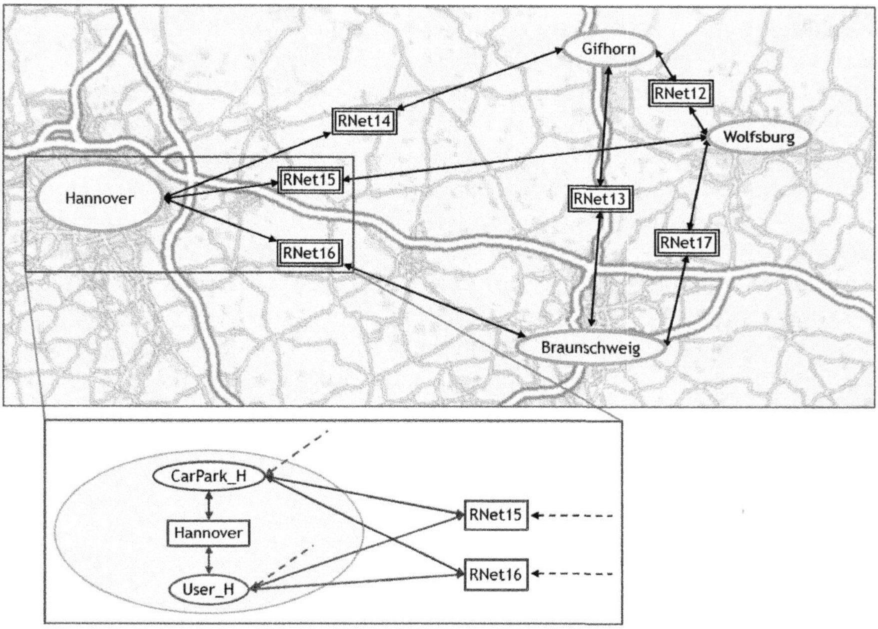

Fig. 1. Formalization of the e-mobility scenario based on a hierarchical Petri net model

at which quality and robustness of resource usage schemes for different mobility service concepts can be evaluated (e.g. car sharing, carpooling).

The e-mobility process model describes several users' travel itineraries, multiple destinations and alternative transportation modes. The model focuses on a detailed description of resource limitations like a limited number of e-vehicles and charging stations. At the destination locations the temporal availability of car parks and charging stations is considered. Between destinations route alternatives are modelled, which are differing in time and energy consumption. Aiming at a simple but comprehensive analysis, the temporal and energetic aspects of the routes only depend on driving behaviour (comfort, eco and sport mode) and route topology.

Figure 1 shows the formal Petri-net representation of a real example scenario that considers four destinations (Wolfsburg, Gifhorn, Braunschweig and Hannover), the road network between the destinations and the processes which are taking place at the destination locations. The road network is described by several transition framed sub nets (e.g. RNet15) [7]. It is assumed that the trips between destinations contain a limited set of variants. Typically three alternative routes and three alternative driving styles are considered, generating a set of maximally 9 variants. Each destination is represented by a transition framed subnet (e.g. Hannover), which models both the vehicle charging process (e.g. CarPark_H) and user specific processes (e.g. User_H) such as appointments.

The charging stations that are connected to the car parks support three different charging modes (normal, fast and ultra-fast charging).

In the ASCENS framework [8] the user and the vehicle are represented as Service Components. Within the Petri net notation, the user and the vehicle behaviour are represented by tokens (active elements in the process). A user token contains the user schedule (appointment location and appointment time window) and his driving behaviour (eco, sport, comfortable). A vehicle token contains the vehicle's energy level and its available seats. The switching of a transition is composed of a set of tokens. In the ASCENS notion this kind of operation represents the temporal orchestration of service components into a service component ensemble. The different types of mobility scenarios that have been introduced in section 3.1 can be modelled by using this kind of token representation. Taking the car pooling service as an example, a group of users that travel together in one car can be described by three user tokens and one vehicle token.

4 Approach and Design

The steps of section 3.2 lead to a formulation of both feasible component models and feasible component interaction models. Interaction models specify the information exchange between components and define when service components assemble temporally in order to form service component ensembles, which plan and support the execution of mobility tasks.

The service component approach is evaluated by comparing the performance of planned vehicles in relation to unplanned vehicles based on a realistic traffic scenario of an urban region [6]. Planned vehicles (fleet) and unplanned vehicles compete for traffic resources, such as parking lots and charging stations.

4.1 Concept Service Centric Car

It has been found that the vehicle is the central service component within the mobility scenarios. During driving operation the vehicle service component interfaces with both the user and the infrastructure service components. During

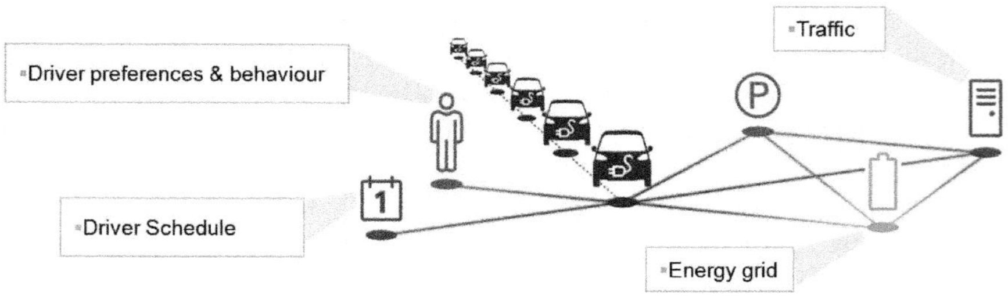

Fig. 2. Service Centric Car concept

charging and non-operation intervals it couples with the infrastructure alone. As shown in Figure 2, services are temporally connecting to the vehicle service component providing travel relevant knowledge in order to fulfil the goals of the mobility task in the best possible way. Each service component is specified by goals, internal knowledge about the environment and the scope of possible actions.

4.2 Level of Mobility Planning

Information that is provided to a vehicle by a service differ in temporal and thematic relevance. Temporally, a strategical and tactical time horizon are distinguished. Thematically, it is advisable to discern four different mobility planning levels [9].

The **Component Level** refers to individual component behaviour. Relevant information is input to component models, which output component behaviour. A typical example could be the drive train subcomponent of the vehicle component, which outputs velocity, acceleration and vehicle consumption information for a specific user input and environmental model.

On the next level of complexity, namely the **Trip Level**, trip relevant information is aggregated and used for optimization. A typical example of trip relevant information is the trip's total energy consumption, which is the integrated output of the vehicle component over the trip length, more specifically the integrated output of both the drive-train and the auxiliary consumer subcomponents. As a general rule, higher levels of mobility planning integrate lower level information. A typical example of trip level relevant optimization is energy- and time-optimal route calculation.

On the **Journey Level**, sequences of trips are combined to form a journey. Again trip level information is integrated to form journey level information. A journey optimization is performed, which examines the coupled, directed sequence of trip level data. For example, charging is mostly relevant on the journey level. Charging is optimized over the coupled and directed trip sequence under consideration of driving styles, appointment durations and charging locations. Treating the charging problem on the journey level fosters results, which are most likely superior to a treatment of the problem on the trip level.

The **Mobility Level** represents the highest level of complexity. At this level, user and vehicle groups (e.g. fleets) are coordinated and supervised. Examples of these kinds of mobility services are fleet manager, car sharing or carpooling services.

4.3 Service Components in a User-Vehicle-Infrastructure Network

In this section a detailed description of the service components is provided. The **Vehicle Service Component**(see also Figure 3) represents the e-vehicle. The user service component or any other service (e.g. car sharing provider) provides the travel input to the vehicle service component. The vehicle service component monitors internal vehicle states (e.g. state of charge), manages current and future trips (e.g route calculation) and plans the vehicle resource usage (e.g. scheduling of charging and parking events). Its high–level task is to plan a sequence of coupled trips. The goal is to find a feasible sequence, which is not violating any constraints and at best maximizes the vehicle's cost functions. Table 1 gives an overview of the main properties. Vehicle service components are allocated to the journey level.

Table 1. Properties of the Vehicle Service Component

Goal	Optimal travel sequence without violating constraints
Awareness issues	1: Current and predicted internal vehicle states 2: Current and future trips
Task	Planning of the vehicle journeys
Actions	1: Acquire and distribute information 2: Planning individual vehicle trips 3: Planning resource usage

The **User Service Component** (see also Figure 3) plans the user's journey based on knowledge about the user schedule and its preferences. The user schedule typically contains appointment information, whilst preferences describe, inter alia, driving profiles and climate comfort requirements of the user. The user service component manages temporal conflicts (e.g. shifting an appointment in case it cannot be reached in time) and travel modalities (e.g. participating in a ride sharing scheme). The goal is to reach the destinations in time and at a maximum fulfilment rate of the user preferences (e.g. minimal travel time). Table 2 contains the properties of the user service component. User service components are assigned to the journey level.

Table 2. Properties of the User Service Component

Goals	1: Guarantee to reach each user destination in time 2: Maximize the fulfilment rate of the user preferences
Awareness issues	1: User schedule 2: User preferences
Task	Planning the user's journey
Actions	1: Acquire and distribute information 2: Manage temporal conflicts of the user schedule 3: Manage travel modalities

The **Infrastructure Service Component** (see also Figure 3) manages infrastructure resources (e.g. roads, charging stations, parking space). It manages pricing and booking of resources on the basis of supply and demand information and maximizes both the capacity usage of the infrastructure resource and the quality of service (e.g. guarantee availability of booked charging stations). Table 3 shows the properties of the Infrastructure Service Component, which is assigned to the component level.

Table 3. Properties of the Infrastructure Service Component

Goal	1: Optimal capacity usage of the infrastructure resource 2: Guarantee quality-of-service
Awareness issues	1: Bookings 2: Availability estimate 3: Price-sales-function for infrastructure demand
Task	Supply and demand management
Actions	1: Acquire and distribute information 2: Manage bookings 3: Manage pricing

4.4 Composition of Service Component Ensembles

In Figure 3, a user journey is presented which is composed of 3 trips (A, B, C). It serves the purpose of illustrating the temporal orchestration of service components and gives a feel for the real world representation of service components and service component ensembles.

Person 1 (dark blue user SC) starts at position 1 and travels to destination 2 where he has scheduled an appointment. After the appointment has finished, person 1 proceeds to destination 3 where he has to pick up a parcel that has to be delivered to destination 4. The user service component monitors all temporal travel aspects of person 1. Based on the knowledge about the daily events, the SC starts to organize the journey. Going from destination 1 to destination 2 the user service component autonomously books an available vehicle from a car sharing provider (brown vehicle SC). The vehicle's range is not sufficient to complete

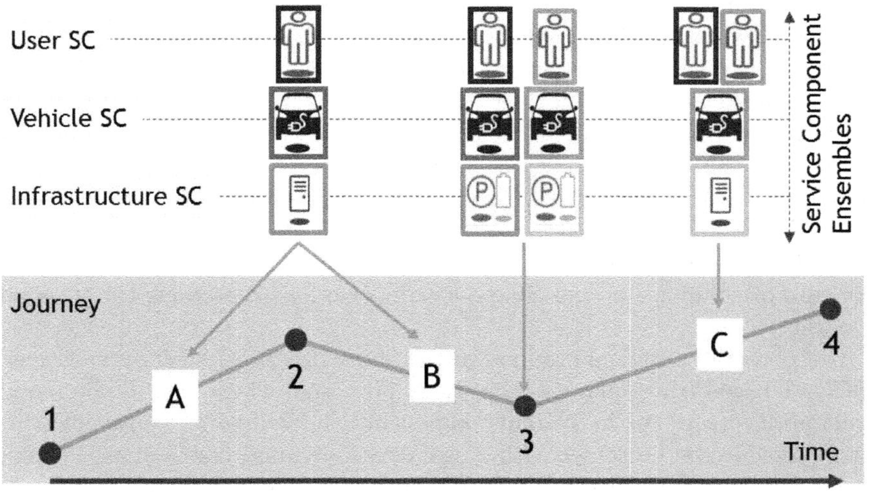

Fig. 3. Concept of Service Component Ensemble composition

the entire journey without recharging. The vehicle service component books a charging station at a car park in the vicinity of destination 3 by requesting the corresponding infrastructure service component (dark green infrastructure SC). At destination 3 the time necessary for recharging the car would exceed the duration of the user's appointment resulting in a delay of the user's journey. Within this time window alternative car sharing vehicles are not available. The user service component checks alternative mobility services. A carpooling service provides a trip from destination 3 to destination 4. The user service component negotiates the trip with the other service components (vehicle and user service components). Together with the second person (light blue user SC) person 1 travels to destination 4 in order to deliver the parcel and end his day.

The example describes a decentralized approach for organizing trips and journeys. The responsibilities are divided between service components. The user service components are responsible for reaching the destinations in time. Vehicle service components have to guarantee that the vehicles have sufficient energy for reaching the destinations. Infrastructure service components have to guarantee that the required infrastructure resources are available.

5 Practical Usage of Service Component Ensembles for Mobility Planning

As an example, consider a business customer within a heavily resource–constrained environment as it holds for e-mobility in mega-cities: crowded roads, lack of parking space and charging stations, tight customer schedules, limited driving range and extended charging times [10]. The customer desires to travel seamlessly through the environment. The customer is always connected. He bases his travel decisions upon the limited knowledge available and without considering how his personal travel decisions influence the traffic system such as road traffic, the availability of parking places, charging stations and possibly car sharing vehicles. Now, the question is how can ASCENS help the customer to improve his personal travel plan and what should the application look like?

As has been described in former sections, the entities of the e-mobility system are represented by service components or service component ensembles: The user is represented by a user service component, the vehicle by a vehicle service component, some parking places by individual infrastructure service components and other parking places (e.g. car parks) by infrastructure service component ensembles. The same holds for charging stations, roads and the energy net. The sum of components and component interactions represents the e–mobility scenario.

As a potential practical product for the above described business customer an ASCENS based travel planning service is proposed, which acts at the mobility level and leverages the individual components and component ensembles in order to provide the customer with a seamless individual travel plan. The travel planning service runs seamlessly on the customer's mobile phone, in his vehicle navigation unit and as a web portal service on the backend. Pre–trip, the customer uses either the web portal application or his mobile phone application of

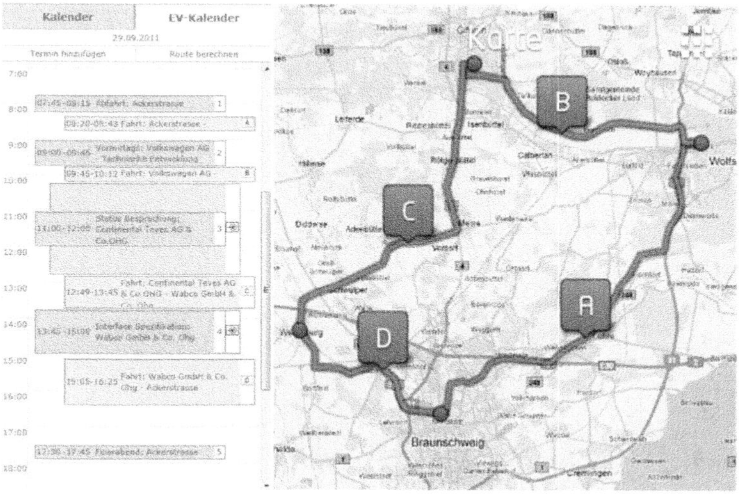

Fig. 4. Journey planning via the web portal service

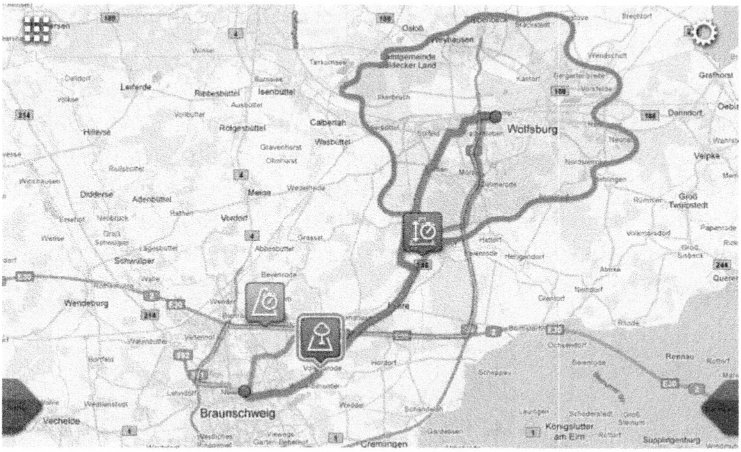

Fig. 5. E-vehicle HMI visualization of alternative routes (sport=yellow, comfortable=blue, eco=green) and the residual range prediction of the activated green route

the travel planning service to organize his journey. The travel planning service requests from the user service component the customer's appointment sequence, his travel preferences and travel modalities. The vehicle service component manages the respective trips by communicating with infrastructure service components. Service component interaction results in a customer journey, which is composed of customer appointments, trips between the appointment locations (including parking places and charging stations) and charging events. A visualisation of the portal application can be seen in Figure 4. The left side of Figure 4 displays the

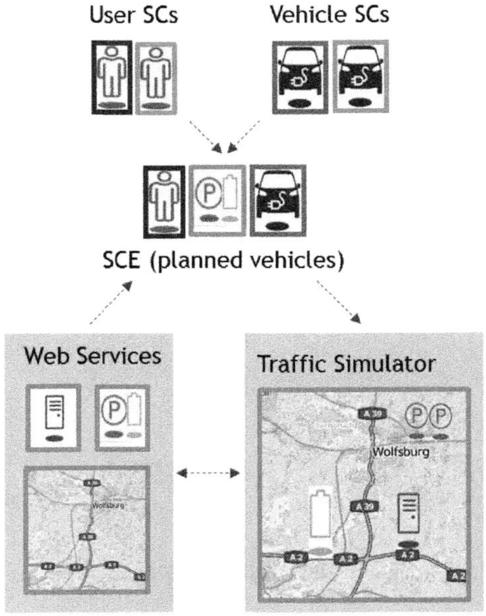

Fig. 6. Integration of the ASCENS approach and the traffic simulation [11]

customer journey as a timed sequence of events in a calender-like format. The right side displays the events as a geographical sequence of locations.

The on–trip relevant journey information becomes accessible in the vehicle's navigation unit. Figure 5 presents an example of a range visualisation for an individual trip of the customer's journey on the e–vehicle HMI. Changes of service component states throughout the execution of the trip will trigger a recalculation and adaptation to the needs.

6 Future Work

The model will be integrated into a traffic simulation in order to evaluate the suitability of the ASCENS framework for electric mobility. The mobility services will be validated in a realistic traffic simulation [11]. Figure 6 shows the integration of the envisioned simulation framework into the ASCENS context. Service components dynamically collect availability information of the infrastructure components from the simulation (road throughput, charging stations, car parks, etc.) in order to schedule daily journeys for the user. Service components orchestrate into service component ensembles. Amongst others the simulation will be used to quantify the performance of planned vehicles in relation to unplanned vehicles based on a realistic traffic scenario of an urban region.

References

1. McKinsey: Transforming the powertrain value chain - a portfolio challenge (January 2011)
2. Deloitte: Unplugged: Electric vehicle realities versus consumer expectations (September 2011)
3. Krebs-Hartmann, C.: Zukünftige Mobilität: Was Frauen und Männer erwarten. Konzern Zukunftsforschung und Trendtransfer, Volkswagen Aktiengesellschaft - nur zum internen Gebrauch (2011)
4. Information and Communications Technology (ICT) as an Engine for the Electromobility of the Future, `http://orion.fortiss.org/download/ikt2030/ikt2030de-gesamt.pdf`
5. ASCENS Autonomous Service-Component Ensembles, `http://www.ascens-ist.eu/`
6. Hoch, N., Werther, B., Bensler, H.-P., Masuch, N., Lützenberger, M., Hessler, A., Albayrak, S., Siegwart, R.Y.: A User-Centric Approach for Efficient Daily Mobility Planning in E-Vehicle Infrastructure Networks. In: Advanced Microsystems for Automotive Applications 2011 (2011)
7. CPN Tools, `http://cpntools.org/`
8. ASCENS White paper (2011), `http://www.ascens-ist.eu/whitepaper`
9. Axhausen, K.W., Zimmermann, A., Schönfelder, S., Rindsfüser, G., Haupt, T.: Observing the rhythms of daily life: A six-week travel diary 29(2). Transportation 29(2), 95-124 (2002)
10. Second interim Report of the National Platform for Electric Mobility (2011), `http://www.bmu.de/files/pdfs/allgemein/application/pdf/bericht_emob_2.pdf`
11. MatSim - Multi-Agent Transport Simulation Toolkit, `http://www.matsim.org/`

On the Existence of Nash Equilibria in Strategic Search Games*

Carme Àlvarez[1], Amalia Duch[1], Maria Serna[1], and Dimitrios Thilikos[2]

[1] ALBCOM Research Group. Technical University of Catalonia
[2] Department of Mathematics. National and Kapodistrian University of Athens

Abstract. We consider a general multi-agent framework in which a set of n agents are roaming a network where m valuable and sharable goods (resources, services, information ....) are hidden in m different vertices of the network. We analyze several strategic situations that arise in this setting by means of game theory. To do so, we introduce a class of strategic games that we call strategic search games. In those games agents have to select a simple path in the network that starts from a predetermined set of initial vertices. Depending on how the value of the retrieved goods is splitted among the agents, we consider two game types: *finders-share* in which the agents that find a good split among them the corresponding benefit and *firsts-share* in which only the agents that first find a good share the corresponding benefit. We show that finders-share games always have pure Nash equilibria (PNE). For obtaining this result, we introduce the notion of *Nash-preserving reduction* between strategic games. We show that finders-share games are Nash-reducible to single-source network congestion games. This is done through a series of Nash-preserving reductions. For firsts-share games we show the existence of games with and without PNE. Furthermore, we identify some graph families in which the firsts-share game has always a PNE that is computable in polynomial time.

1 Introduction

The aim of this paper is the study of resource discovery in distributed networks from a game theoretical perspective. We are interested in analyzing the strategic situation that arises when a set of hiders do not move and a set of searchers set their strategies in a selfish way considering economical benefits and rewards. We consider a general framework of strategic search in which a set of n mobile agents are roaming a network where m valuable items are hidden in m different vertices. We want to take into consideration different aspects that affect the agents decisions as well as their rewards in order to analyze the existence of Nash

* The first and third authors were partially supported by TIN-2007-66523 (FORMALISM). The second author was supported by TIN-2010-17254 (FRADA). The fourth author was supported by the project "Kapodistrias" (AΠ 02839/28.07.2008) of the National and Kapodistrian University of Athens (project code: 70/4/8757).

R. Bruni and V. Sassone (Eds.): TGC 2011, LNCS 7173, pp. 58–72, 2012.

equilibria. This framework differs from other resource sharing strategic games considered in the literature and, in particular, from the well known framework of *congestion games* [11,8] and classical search games [4,3]. In their classical setting, search games are intended to look upon the situation as a game between a searcher and a hider and the aim of the analysis is to provide optimal strategies for the participants. That is strategies that allow the searcher to find the hider and the hider to avoid the searchers.

In this initial work we concentrate in analyzing the existence or not of pure Nash equilibria in a static draw of the proposed games.

Before defining the games, we consider the main parameters and take some initial decision for the model.

Benefit? Benefit depends, on one side, on the cost that the agents have to pay for traversing network links and, on the other, in the way in which the rewards or the value of the goods found by the agent are distributed among the agents that discover the same good. We consider two natural reward models. When the good is non portable, any agent that discovers it will get some benefit. When the good is portable, only agents that arrive first can benefit from the discovery. We consider two game variants: The *finders-share game* in which the item value is split equitably among all the players that discover it at some moment and the *firsts-share game* in which the item value is shared only among all the agents that discover the item first (all of them at the same time).

Where do the agents start their roaming? We consider two different possibilities: Either players start their roaming at one initial vertex or they can choose one from a set of initial vertices. In both cases we consider that the initial vertex (or set of vertices) is the same for all the players.

What is the cost for the agents? It seems natural that they have to incur some cost in traversing a link due to communication or movement. We assume that each link in the network has associated a non negative cost. To any agent's trajectory, we associate as cost the sum of the cost of the edges present in it.

How the agents move? We consider different kinds of trajectories. Initially we study the problems assuming that the players strategy is formed by the selection of a simple path (without repeated nodes) in the network. We also analyze finders-share games under two other trajectories: paths, where nodes can be repeated but edges can not appear twice, and trees. When the trajectory is a path, a player can pass more than once through one edge in order to access additional valuable resources. The tree trajectory arises naturally assuming that the agents are buying links, so that they can cross them as many times as they wish without additional payment.

We show that finders-share games in which the players are restricted to select a simple path always have pure Nash equilibria (PNE). This result is independent of the type of initial location or on whether the network is directed or undirected. For doing so, we introduce the notion of *Nash-preserving reduction* between strategic games. This is an appropriate extension of traditional reducibility among problems. Those reductions preserve the existence of PNE and the fact that a PNE can be computed in polynomial time. We show that finders-share games are Nash-reducible to single-source network congestion games. This is done through a series of Nash-preserving reductions. First, by a series of transformations, we reduce the general case to the single-source finders-share game. Finally, the single-source finders-share game is reduced to the single-source network congestion game. These reductions guarantee also the property that a PNE can be computed in polynomial time.

For the firsts-share games in which the players are restricted to select a simple path, we show the existence of games with and without PNE, for different variations of the type of game. Furthermore, we identify some graph families in which the firsts-share game has always a PNE. In those cases we provide algorithms for computing a PNE in polynomial time.

Finally, we consider two variations on the trajectories, one allowing paths with repeated nodes and the other allowing trees. We show that in both cases the finders-share games can be Nash-reduced to congestion games. This reduction shows the existence of PNE but leaves open the existence or not of a polynomial time algorithm for computing a PNE for such games.

2 Definitions and Preliminaries

Throughout the paper we use the standard graph notation and in particular we consider that for an undirected graph: A *walk* is a sequence of vertices such that for each pair of consecutive vertices the corresponding edge is present in the graph. A *path* is a walk in which *none of the edges* appears twice. A *simple path* is a walk in which none of the vertices appears twice.

In the case of considering arcs instead of edges we add to the name of these sequences the adjective *directed* (*directed* walk, *directed* path and *directed* simple path, respectively).

A *strategic game* $\Gamma = (N, (\Pi_i)_{i\in N}, (u_i)_{i\in N})$ is defined by a finite set of *players or agents* $N = \{1, \dots, n\}$, a finite set of *strategies* (or actions) Π_i, for each agent $i \in N$, and a *payoff function* $u_i : \Pi \to \mathbb{R}$, for each player $i \in N$, where $\Pi = \times_{i\in N}\Pi_i$. Every element $(p_1, \dots, p_n) \in \Pi$ is known as a *pure strategy profile* or *configuration* and represents a possible outcome of the game. We also denote Π of Γ by $\Pi(\Gamma)$.

Given a profile $\pi = (p_1, \dots, p_n)$, p_i represents the strategy followed by agent $i \in N$. In addition, it is usual to denote by (π_{-i}, p), with $i \in N$, the profile that we obtain substituting the i-th element of π (p_i) by p. A *Pure Nash Equilibrium* (PNE, for short) is a configuration $\pi = (\pi_1, \dots, \pi_n)$ such that for each agent $i \in N$ $u_i(\pi) \geq u_i((\pi_{-i}, p))$ for any $p \in \Pi_i$. We denote as PNE(Γ) the set of pure Nash equilibria of game Γ.

A *congestion game* is defined by a tuple $\Gamma = (N, E, (\Pi_i)_{i\in N}, (d_e)_{e\in E})$ where $N = \{1, \dots, n\}$ is the set of players, E is a finite set of resources, $\Pi_i \subset \mathcal{P}(E)$ is the set of allowed actions for each player $i \in N$, and $d_e : \mathbb{N} \to \mathbb{R}$ is the delay function of each resource $e \in E$, which is assumed to be polynomial-time computable and models the delay $d_e(k)$ provoked by resource e under a congestion $k \in \{1, \dots, n\}$. $d_e(k)$ is non-decreasing in k. Let $\Pi = \times_{i\in N}\Pi_i$. For all $\pi = (p_1, \dots, p_n) \in \Pi$ and for every $e \in E$, let $\omega_e(\pi)$ be the number of users of resource e according to the configuration π, $\omega_e(\pi) = |\{i \in N : e \in p_i\}|$. Each player $i \in N$ has associated a cost function $c_i : \Pi \to \mathbb{R}$ defined by

$$c_i(\pi) = \sum_{e \in p_i} d_e(\omega_e(\pi)).$$

We can also say that each player i has a payoff function u_i and it is defined in terms of the cost function, as usual, as $u_i(\pi) = -c_i(\pi)$.

Using the definition coming from [1], a *network congestion game* Γ is a congestion game defined in a directed graph using the arcs as resources. Formally, it is defined by a tuple $\Gamma = (N, G, (s_i, t_i)_{i \in N}, (d_e)_{e \in E(G)})$ where $N = \{1, \dots, n\}$ is the set of players, $G = (V, E)$ is a directed graph, $(s_i, t_i) \in V \times V$ is the pair of origin and destination nodes (or source and target nodes) for each player $i \in N$, and $d_e : \mathbb{N} \to \mathbb{R}$ is the delay function of every edge $e \in E$, which is assumed to be polynomial-time computable.

The strategy set of player i consists of simple paths in the directed graph G. In fact, Π_i is the set of all simple paths from s_i to t_i, denoted as all $(s_i\text{-}t_i)$ paths, where the notation $(s\text{-}t)$ path refers to a simple path between the nodes s and t. Since only simple paths are considered, the set formed by all the $(s_i\text{-}t_i)$ paths is finite. In the case in which all the pairs (s_i, t_i) coincide with a unique pair (s, t), the game is said to be a *single-commodity network congestion game*, (otherwise it is called *multi-commodity*) and since all players share the same strategy-set the game is said to be symmetric.

There is a rich literature on congestion games [11,7,6,10,1,9,5,2,8], here are some results concerning PNE that we use.

Theorem 1 (Rosenthal [11]). *Every congestion game has a* PNE.

Theorem 2 (Fabrikant, Papadimitriou, Talwar [1]). *There is a polynomial time algorithm to compute a* PNE *in symmetric network congestion games (single-commodity network congestion games).*

It is useful to define a suitable notion of reduction among strategic games that preserves the existence of PNE and, if this is the case, the complexity of finding a PNE.

Let $\mathcal{G}_1, \mathcal{G}_2$ be two classes of strategic games. We say that $\mathcal{G}_1$ is *Nash-preserving reducible* or *reducible* to $\mathcal{G}_2$ (in polynomial-time) if there exist two (polynomial-time) computable functions f and g such that for any strategic game Γ, if $\Gamma \in \mathcal{G}_1$ then

i) $f(\Gamma) \in \mathcal{G}_2$,
ii) if π is a strategy profile of the game $f(\Gamma)$ then $g(\pi)$ is a strategy profile of Γ, and
iii) if π is a PNE of $f(\Gamma)$ then $g(\pi)$ also is a PNE of Γ.

The following result follows from the definition.

Theorem 3. *Let $\mathcal{G}_1$, $\mathcal{G}_2$ be two classes of strategic games. If any game in $\mathcal{G}_2$ has a pure Nash equilibrium and $\mathcal{G}_1$ is reducible to $\mathcal{G}_2$ then any game in $\mathcal{G}_1$ has a pure Nash equilibrium. If any game in $\mathcal{G}_2$ has a pure Nash equilibrium computable in polynomial time and $\mathcal{G}_1$ is reducible to $\mathcal{G}_2$ in polynomial time then any game in $\mathcal{G}_1$ has a pure Nash equilibrium computable in polynomial time.*

In what follows we consider that a *network* $\mathcal{N}$ is a tuple consisting of a weighted graph $G = (V, E)$ with non-negative weights a_e associated to each edge $e \in E(G)$ (the toll of traversing edge e) and non-negative weights b_v associated to each vertex $v \in V(G)$ (the value of the hidden item), this is, $\mathcal{N} = (G, (a_e)_{e \in E(G)}, (b_v)_{v \in V(G)})$. In the case that the graph is directed, we use the term *directed network* and for undirected graphs the term *undirected network*.

3 Finders-Share Games

We start introducing the first family of strategic search games in which the benefit obtained from a node is split evenly among all the agents that have discovered the node.

A finders-share game is a tuple $\Gamma = (N, \mathcal{N}, (s_i)_{i \in N})$ representing the strategic game in which N is a set of n players and $\mathcal{N} = (G, (a_e)_{e \in E(G)}, (b_v)_{v \in V(G)})$ is a network. For each player i there is a special vertex s_i of the graph which is its *starting point* (its source or origin). The strategies Π_i for player i are the set of simple paths in G starting at s_i.

Given a configuration $\pi = (p_1, \ldots, p_n)$, the payoff or utility function u_i for player i is defined as follows.

$$u_i(\pi) = \sum_{v \in p_i} \frac{b_v}{l_v(\pi)} - \sum_{e \in p_i} a_e.$$

where $l_v(\pi) = |\{i | v \in p_i\}|$ is the number of players whose strategy contains vertex v.

Without lost of generality, throughout this article, we consider that the weight associated to each starting point is zero. This fact does not affect any of the results as we can consider the following transformation of the graph. We add an additional vertex per each source. The new source is connected only to the original source. Assigning weight zero to the new sources and to the connecting links we have a polynomial reduction to the variant in which the sources have always zero weight.

In the case in which all the s_i coincide with a unique vertex s the game is said to be a *single-source*, denoted as $\Gamma = (N, \mathcal{N}, s)$. Otherwise the game is *multi-source*.

In the case of strategic search games in which the source point for a player is a set of vertices instead of a single vertex, the game is said to be *multi-start* and can be single or multi-source, depending on whether the starting set is common or not for all the players. Observe that, the most general class is formed by the multi-start multi-source games that include all the other classes.

Given an undirected network with associated graph G, we consider the directed network with associated graph G^d. G^d is obtained by transforming every edge $\{u, v\} \in V(G)$ with the same associated weight $a_{\{u,v\}}$ to the two arcs (u, v), (v, u) each with associated weight $a_{\{u,v\}}$. Observe that there is a one-to-one correspondence between the set of simple paths in G and the set of simple paths in G^d. Using this argument and taking into account that the node and edge weights do not change, we obtain the following result.

Lemma 1. *For undirected networks, the class of finders-share games is polynomial time reducible to the class of finders-share games for directed networks.*

Now we show the reduction from multi-start to multi-source finders-share games.

Lemma 2. *For directed networks, the class of multi-start multi-source finders-share games is polynomial time reducible to the class of multi-source finders-share games.*

Proof. Given $\Gamma = (N, \mathcal{N}, (S_i)_{i\in N})$ a multi-start multi-source finders-share game, we define the corresponding multi-source finders-share game $\Gamma' = f(\Gamma)$ as follows. Assume that $\mathcal{N} = (G(V, E), (b_v)_{v\in V}, (a_e)_{e\in E})$. Then $\Gamma' = (N, \mathcal{N}', (s_i)_{i\in N})$ where $\mathcal{N}' = (G(V', E'), (b'_v)_{v\in V}, (a'_e)_{e\in E})$ with:

- $V' = V \cup \{s_i | i \in N\}$, where s_i is a new vertex for player i. For each vertex $v \in V$, $b'_v = b_v$ and, $\forall i \in N, b'_{s_i} = 0$.
- $E' = E \cup \{(s_i, u) | i \in N \wedge u \in S_i\}$ where for each player i we add one edge from s_i to each different starting node $u \in S_i$. For each $e \in E, a'_e = a_e$ and $\forall i \in N, u \in S_i, a'_{(s_i,u)} = 0$.

Finally, $(s_i)_{i\in N}$ is the set of added vertices and s_i is the source of each player $i \in N$.

In order to distinguish the utility functions of both games, let us denote by u_i (u'_i) the utility function of player i in Γ (Γ').

Additionally, for any simple path p' of $G(V', E')$ starting at a source node of s_i, we define its corresponding simple path p of $G(V, E)$ as follows:

i) If $p' = s_i, v_0, \ldots, v_m$ then $p = v_0, \ldots, v_m$. Notice that s_i is a new node of Γ' and $p' = s_i, p$ where p is a simple path in $G(V, E)$ starting at $v_0 \in S_i$.
ii) If $p' = s_i$ then $p = v$ for some arbitrary node $v \in S_i$

We define a mapping $g : \Pi(\Gamma') \to \Pi(\Gamma)$ such that for every strategy profile $\pi' = (p'_1, \ldots, p'_n) \in \Pi(\Gamma')$, $g(\pi') = \pi$ where $\pi = (p_1, \ldots, p_n)$. Note that $g(\pi'_{-i}, p'_i) = (\pi_{-i}, p_i)$. If we consider the load of each $v \in V - \bigcup_{1\le i\le n} S_i$ in both profiles π' and $\pi = g(\pi')$ we have that $l_v(\pi')$ in Γ' coincides with $l_v(\pi)$ in Γ. The load of the source nodes $v \in \bigcup_{1\le i\le n} S_i$ in Γ may be different from the load in Γ' but in both games the benefit $b_v = 0$ as well as $b_{s_i} = 0$ for each new s_i. Finally, note that for the new added edges $a_{(s_i,u)} = 0$. Hence, for each player i, $u'_i(\pi') = u_i(g(\pi')) = u_i(\pi)$.

Therefore, if $\pi' = (p'_1, \ldots, p'_n)$ is in PNE(Γ') then for every player i and every p' starting at s_i $u'_i(\pi') = u_i(\pi) \geq u'_i((\pi'_{-i}, p')) = u_i((\pi_{-i}, p))$ implying that $\pi = g(\pi')$ is in PNE(Γ).

Since f and g are polynomial-time computable, the result follows. □

Finally we reduce to the class of single-source finders-share games.

Lemma 3. *For directed networks, the class of multi-source finders-share games is polynomial time reducible to the class of single-source finders-share games.*

Proof. Given a multi-source finders-share game $\Gamma = (N, \mathcal{N}, (s_i)_{i \in N})$ we define the corresponding single-source finders-share game $f(\Gamma) = \Gamma' = (N, \mathcal{N}', s)$ as follows:

Assume that $\mathcal{N} = (G(V, E), (a_e)_{e \in E}, (b_v)_{v \in V})$ and that s_i is the starting vertex of k_i players. Let $b = \sum_{v \in V(G)} b_v$, $k = \max\{k_i | i \in N\}$ and $a = (k+1)b$. Then we define $\mathcal{N}' = (G(V', E'), (b'_v)_{v \in V}, (a'_e)_{e \in E})$ where $V' = V \cup \{s\}$ and $E' = E \cup \{(s, s_i) | i \in N\}$. The weights are defined as:

- $b'_s = 0$, for each player i, $b'_{s_i} = k_i a$, and for each v in $V \setminus \{(s_i)_{i \in N}\}$, $b'_v = b_v$.
- For each player i, $a'_{(s,s_i)} = a$ and, for each $e \in E$, $a'_e = a_e$.

Let us denote by u_i the utility function of player i in Γ and by u'_i the utility function of player i in Γ'. Notice that, by the definition of Γ', each simple path p' in Γ' starts at s and then continues visiting some of the original source nodes s_i of Γ. Hence $p' = s, p$ where p is a simple path of Γ. By definition of a and b, in any strategy profile π' of Γ', if a node s_i in V' is visited by more than k_i players then $u'_i(\pi') < 0$. Hence it can not be a PNE since $u'_i(\pi'_{-i}, s) = 0$.

We define a mapping $g : \Pi(\Gamma') \longrightarrow \Pi(\Gamma)$ such that, for every strategy profile $\pi' = (p'_1, \ldots, p'_n) \in \Pi$, $g(\pi') = \pi$ where $\pi = (p_1, \ldots, p_n)$ where

i) If $p'_i = s, s_i, p$ (p may be empty), then $p_i = s_i, p$, and
ii) If $p'_i = s, s_j, p$ (p may be empty) and $j \neq i$, then $p_i = s_i$.

Notice that $\forall i \in N$,

$$u_i(\pi) = \begin{cases} u'_i(\pi') & \text{if } p'_i = s, s_i, p, \\ 0 & \text{otherwise } (u'_i(\pi') < 0 \text{ and then } \pi' \text{ is not a PNE.}) \end{cases}$$

Therefore, if π' is in PNE(Γ') we have that $u'_i(\pi') = u_i(\pi) \geq u'_i((\pi'_{-i}, p)) = u_i(g(\pi'_{-i}, p))$ for any strategy p of player $i \in N$ of Γ', implying that π is in PNE(Γ).

Since f and g are polynomial-time computable, the result follows. □

Next result shows the reduction to single-commodity network congestion games.

Lemma 4. *For directed networks, the class of single-source finders-share games is polynomial time reducible to the class of single-commodity network congestion games.*

Proof. Given a single-source finders-share game $\Gamma = (N, \mathcal{N}, s)$, we define the corresponding network congestion game $\Gamma' = f(\Gamma)$ as follows. Assume that $\mathcal{N} = (G(V,E), (a_e)_{e \in E}, (b_v)_{v \in V})$. $G' = (V', E')$ where:

- $V' = V \cup \{t\} \cup \{u' | u \in V \setminus \{s\}\}$.
- $E' = E \cup \{(u, u') | u \in V \setminus \{s\}\} \cup \{(u', t) | u' \in V' \setminus \{V \cup \{t\}\}\}$
  $\cup \{(u', v) | (u, v) \in E\}$.
- We define the non-decreasing delay function $d_e(x)$ as follows.

$$d_e(x) = \begin{cases} a_e & \text{if } e \in E \\ -\frac{b_u}{x} & \text{if } e = (u, u') \\ 0 & \text{if } e = (u', t), \\ a_{(u,v)} & \text{if } e = (u', v) \end{cases}$$

Finally, $\Gamma' = (N, G', (s,t), (d_e)_{e \in E(G)})$.

Additionally, for every strategy profile $\pi' = (p'_1, \dots, p'_n)$ in $\Pi(\Gamma')$ such that $p'_i = s, v_0, v'_0, \dots, v_k, v'_k, t$ is a simple path, we define $\pi = g(\pi')$ of $\Pi(\Gamma)$ as $\pi = (p_1, \dots, p_n)$ with $p_i = s, v_0, \dots, v_k$. Notice that $\forall i \in N$, p_i is a simple path and that $c_i(\pi') = u_i(\pi)$. Therefore, if π' is in PNE(Γ') we have that $c_i(\pi') = u_i(\pi) \geq c_i((\pi'_{-i}, p)) = u_i(g(\pi'_{-i}, p))$ for any strategy p of player $i \in N$ of Γ', implying that π is in PNE(Γ).

Since f and g are polynomial-time computable, the result follows. □

As a consequence of the previous results and Theorems 1 and 2 we can state the following.

Theorem 4. *Every multi-start multi-source finders-share game on a directed or undirected network has a* PNE *that can be computed in polynomial time.*

Recall that multi-start multi-source finders-share game includes all the subclasses of finders-share games considered in this section.

4 Firsts-Share Games

Now we introduce the second family of strategic search games in which the benefit obtained from a node is split evenly only among all the agents that discover it for the first time. We assume uniformity on the time to traverse a link and measure time by the number of traversed links.

A firsts-share game is a tuple $\Gamma = (N, \mathcal{N}, (s_i)_{i \in N})$ representing the strategic game in which strategies are the same as for the finders-share games, but given a configuration $\pi = (p_1, \dots, p_n)$, the utility function u_i for player i is defined as:

$$u_i(\pi) = \sum_{\substack{v \in p_i \\ \mathbf{dist}(v, p_i) = d_{min}(v, \pi)}} \frac{b_v}{l_v(\pi)} - \sum_{e \in p_i} a_e$$

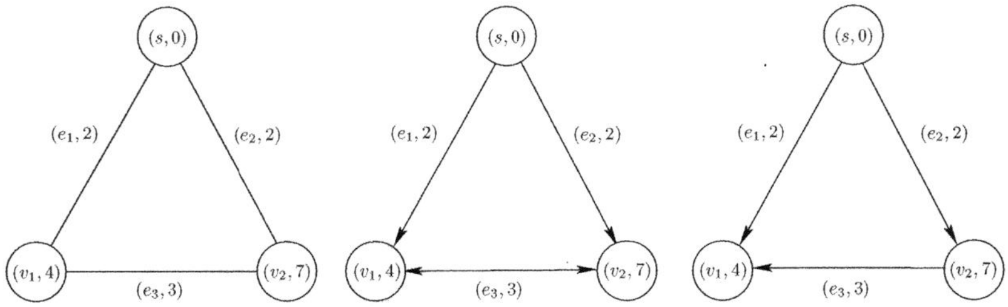

Fig. 1. Examples of firsts-share games for 2 players that do not have PNE

where, $\mathbf{dist}(v, p_i)$ denotes the distance from the source to v in p_i (and it is defined as the length of the path from the source to v if v is in p_i and as ∞ otherwise), $d_{min}(v, \pi) = \min\{\mathbf{dist}(v, p_i) \mid p_i \in \pi\})$ is the minimum distance of v over every p_i in the strategic profile π and, $l_v(\pi) = |\{i \in N | \mathbf{dist}(v, p_i) = d_{min}(v, \pi)\}|$ is the number of players whose strategy contains vertex v with minimal distance to the source.

Let us observe that the difference between firsts-share games and finders-share games relies on the definition of $l_v(\pi)$. As we shall see in what follows, this difference in the splitting of discoveries has relevant implications on the existence of PNE as the games have very different properties.

Theorem 5. *In the class of firsts-share games there are games with* PNE *and games without* PNE.

Proof. The games with two players associated to the graphs in Fig. 1 do not have a PNE. Examples of firsts-share game with PNE can be obtained from the graphs in Figure 1 changing the weights of vertices v_1 and v_2 to 2, of edges e_1 and e_2 to 1 and of edge e_3 to 0. In all the cases, the proof of existence or not of PNE is by inspection of all the possible strategy profiles for the two players. □

Using a construction inspired in the examples in Fig. 1 we can state conditions under which the family of search games that are played on a fixed graph does not always have a PNE.

Theorem 6. *Let G be a graph in which there are vertices $s, v \in V(G)$ with two paths of different length from s to v. There is a weight assignment to G such that the firsts-share game on G with at least two players and source s has no* PNE.

Now we identify some subfamilies of games, defined by properties of the network, with PNE. According to the previous results we have to restrict our subfamilies to guarantee some equidistance properties for the sources. Observe that the reduction from the multi-source to the single-source version of the finders-share game given in Lemma 3 is not valid anymore as this reduction might generate paths of different lengths from the new source.

Observe that an undirected graph that contains a cycle accessible from a source verifies the conditions of Theorem 6. Therefore, for having always a PNE, independently of the weights, we must restrict to acyclic undirected graphs. In such a case the graph is a forest and therefore there is a unique simple path from every potential source to any other vertex of the same tree. Therefore, firsts-share and finders-share benefits are the same and, according to Theorem 4, we have the following result.

Theorem 7. *Every multi-source firsts-share game played in a forest with at most one source per tree has a* PNE *that can be computed in polynomial time.*

For the case of directed graphs we introduce three graph families: equidistant graphs, hierarchical-equidistant graphs and asymmetric tree coupling, and show the existence of PNE for their associated firsts-share games.

An *equidistant graph* is a directed network with a set of $k \geq 1$ sources $s_1, \ldots, s_k$ in which: (a) For any vertex u and any source s_i all the simple paths from s_i to u have the same length. (b) For any vertex u and any two sources s_i and s_j such that there is a path from s_i to u and from s_j to u, both paths have the same length.

Observe that, in such a graph, the distances from any source are equal. In consequence the utility function for every player is the same for firsts-share game as for finders-share game and we obtain the following result.

Theorem 8. *Every single and multi-source firsts-share game played in an equidistant graph has a* PNE *that can be computed in polynomial time.*

A *hierarchical-equidistant graph* is a directed network with set of vertices V and set of sources S, such that, for some k there are subsets $V_1, \ldots, V_k$, $V = \cup_{1 \leq i \leq k} V_i$, and $S_1, \ldots, S_k$, $S = \cup_{1 \leq i \leq k} S_i$, in such a way that:

(a) The subgraph of G restricted to V_i and S_i, for every $1 \leq i \leq k$, is an equidistant graph.
(b) For all i, j with $1 \leq i < j \leq k$ and every vertex $u \in V$, if there is a path from a source $s_i \in S_i$ to u and a path from a source $s_j \in S_j$ to u then it follows that the path from s_i to u is shorter than the path from s_j to u.

We provide a polynomial time algorithm for computing a PNE for firsts-share games on hierarchical-equidistant graphs. The algorithm uses self-reducibility and the polynomial time algorithm for equidistant graph. The recursion relies on the hierarchical structure of the sources.

Theorem 9. *Every single and multi-source firsts-share game played in a hierarchical-equidistant graph has a* PNE *that can be computed in polynomial time.*

Proof. Consider the following algorithm in which players from different sources play among them on a particular subgraph that is determined by the strategies of the previously considered players.

In round 1 the players whose source is in S_1 select their strategy according to a PNE π_1 in the graph induced by V_1. This Nash equilibrium is computed in polynomial time using the algorithm in Theorem 8. Since all the players whose source is not in S_1 arrive later to nodes in V_1, there is no conflict with the hidden items in these nodes and therefore players starting in S_1 won't have any incentive to change their strategy. Players starting from other sources cannot get any benefit from the discovered places. Therefore the selections of the players in S_1 remain fixed for forthcoming rounds. For doing so we modify the node weights of the nodes in the paths selected in π_1 to zero. The same procedure is repeated for rounds 2 to k. At round i the players in S_i compute a pure Nash equilibrium π_i on the graph modified according to the selected strategies $\pi_1, \ldots, \pi_{i-1}$.

Since, for every round, the selection of strategies is performed in polynomial time and there are k such rounds, the PNE is computed in polynomial time. □

An *asymmetric tree coupling* is a directed network composed by two rooted trees which intersect only on the set of leaves, oriented from the root to the leaves, such that each common leaf has a different distance from the two roots. We provide a polynomial time algorithm based on a *conquer and retreat* paradigm combined with a greedy algorithm for computing a PNE in a single-source firsts-share game played on a tree.

Theorem 10. *Every 2-source firsts-share game played in an asymmetric tree coupling has a* PNE *that can be computed in polynomial time.*

Proof. Our algorithm for computing an equilibrium is based on a conquer and retreat paradigm. Initially the players with source s_i $(i = 1, 2)$ play the search game on a subtree that contains only those leaves that are closer to their source. Along the algorithm players in turn reconsider whether it its convenient for them to change their strategy. They can use paths that lead to leaves that were not used by the players that start in the other source. Before describing the algorithm we need a procedure that solves the problem of recomputing a PNE on a single-source tree with additional accessible leaves.

Assume that we have a tree T. Assume also that we have a strategy profile π which is a PNE in the subtree in which a subset of the leaves L is removed. The following greedy rule computes a PNE for T.

> GreedyNash(T, π) Select a path p_m in π with minimum benefit. Let i be one of the players selecting p_m. Compute the path p_M which is the best response of i to π_{-i}. If the benefit obtained in p_m is strictly smaller than that of p_M, set $\pi = (\pi_{-i}; p_M)$. Repeat the process until no changes can be made any more.

Observe that the algorithm finalizes in polynomial time. The number of considered paths is polynomial, as the graph is a tree. Besides the minimum and strictly increasing rule guarantees that an abandoned path will provide benefit below the minimum path benefit on the new profile and, therefore, will never be reconsidered again. At the end of the algorithm we have that all the non used paths have a benefit of at most the minimum over the selected paths, so the resulting strategy is a PNE.

Let $G = (V, E)$ be an asymmetric tree coupling formed by the two trees $T_1 = (V_1, E_1)$ and $T_2 = (V_2, E_2)$. Let L_1 be the set of leaves whose distance to the root of T_1 is smaller than their distance to the root of T_2 and L_2 be the set of leaves in which this distance is greater. For a set of leaves A, let $T \setminus A$ denote the subtree in which the vertices in A are removed.

Consider the following algorithm in which initially we compute separately PNEs for the two firsts-share games in which the two trees are separated and the players have access only to the leaves at shortest distance to their source. The algorithm will refine this situation by allowing the conquest of the leaves that do not appear in the paths selected by the players starting on the other source.

```
Set A1 = L1 and A2 = L2.
Compute π1, that is a PNE for the game played on the tree T1 \ A2.
Compute π2, that is a PNE for the game played on the tree T2 \ A1.
Let A'1 be the set of leaves occupied by π1
Let A'2 be the set of leaves occupied by π2
found = (A1 = A'1 or A2 = A'2).
while not found do
    A1 = A'1; A2 = A'2.
    π1 = GreedyNash(T1 \ A2, π1).
    Let A'1 be the set of leaves occupied by π1
    If A1 = A'1, found = true
    otherwise,
        π2 = GreedyNash(T2 \ A'1, π2).
        Let A'2 be the set of leaves occupied by π2
        If A2 = A'2, found = true
    endif
endwhile
return (π1, π2).
```

In the first steps the algorithm computes a PNE for the set of players with source s_i, in the graph formed by the subtree of T_i that results from subtracting the set of leaves closed to the other source. Observe that, if either π_1 or π_2 occupy the whole sets L_1 or L_2 respectively, then the strategic profile $\pi = (\pi_1, \pi_2)$, is a PNE for the game in which the whole network G is considered.

In the forthcoming rounds, the algorithm starts with a set of leaves L'_i, for each player i, that has been occupied by the PNE computed in the previous step. In the next round, we allow, first, players from s_1 to play in the tree with their closest leaves and the other source players unused leaves. Let π'_1 be the resulting PNE that doesn't occupy the set of leaves $E'_1 \subseteq L_1$. Then, either $E'_1 = L'_1$ and, in this case, $\pi = (\pi_1, \pi_2)$ is a PNE, or $E'_1 \supset L'_1$ since the unique way a player from s_1 can ameliorate their strategy is by means of a new path, one not considered in previous round, and therefore using at least an additional leaf closer to s_2. Observe that either we found a PNE or the subset of leaves used by players from source s_1 in L_2 has increased at least by one.

The process continues in alternative rounds until the set of occupied leaves doesn't change. The final strategic profiles of the two set of players will conform then a PNE for the game in the whole network G.

Since the size of the sets of conquered leaves from s_1 in L_2 and from s_2 in L_1 increases at each complete round, the maximum number of possible rounds is $O(|L_1| + |L_2|)$ and therefore a PNE can be computed in polynomial time. □

All along this section we have taken the number of edges as the measure of the length of a path. The results in this section also hold when we associate to each edge a positive integer distance of polynomial length.

5 Finders-Share Games under other Strategy Definitions

We consider now the case in which the strategy for each player is selected from the set of all paths (instead of the set of all simple-paths) of the network starting at the designated origins. Recall that in a path the agent can pass more than once through a node but cannot use twice the same link (edge or arc). We have the following result.

Theorem 11. *Every finders-share game played in a directed or undirected network, where the set of strategies consists of paths, always has a* PNE.

Proof. We show that when the set of possible strategies Π consists of a set of paths of a directed or undirected network, every finders-share game can be reduced to a congestion game. Thus, as a consequence of Theorem 1, we get the claimed result.

Consider a finders-share game $\Gamma = (N, \mathcal{N}, (S_i)_{i \in N})$ on an undirected network $\mathcal{N}$, where agent $i \in N$ is allowed to follow any path starting at some vertex in the set S_i. For any agent $i \in N$, set $\mathcal{P}(i)$ to be the set of allowed trajectories for i, that is all paths in $\mathcal{N}$ that start in a vertex in S_i. For any path p in $\mathcal{N}$ define $R(p)$ to be the set formed by all the nodes and edges that appear in p. We define the corresponding congestion game $\Gamma' = f(\Gamma) = (N, \mathcal{R}, (\Pi_i)_{i \in N}, (d_e)_{e \in \mathcal{R}})$ as follows. Assume that $\mathcal{N} = (G(V,E), (a_e)_{e \in E}, (b_v)_{v \in V})$, an then set $\mathcal{R} = V \cup E$. For any $i \in N$, set $\Pi_i = \{R(p) \mid p \in \mathcal{P}(i)\}$. For any $r \in \mathcal{R}$, we define the non-decreasing delay function $d_r(x)$ as follows.

$$d_r(x) = \begin{cases} a_r & \text{if } r \in E \\ -\frac{b_r}{x} & \text{if } e \in V \end{cases}$$

For every strategy for agent i in Γ', we associate, in a unique way, a valid path for agent i in $\mathcal{N}$. Observe that when the set of edges form a cycle, there might be more that one path giving raise to this set. To break ties we will use the lexicographic order of edges going out of a node. In a cycle of an undirected graph we select the first edge in lexicographic order to start traversing the cycle. When the trajectory have more than one cycle, we traverse cycles in lexicographic order. In this way we define, for any strategy profile, $\pi' \in \Pi(\Gamma')$ a strategy profile $g(\pi') \in \Pi(\Gamma)$. Observe that f and g can be computed in polynomial time and that $c_i(\pi') = u_i(g(\pi'))$ and the result follows for undirected networks.

For the case of a directed network, the proof follows the same lines but we have to consider as resources in the congestion game the union of nodes and arcs. □

We can also consider the case in which the cost per edge corresponds to buying the right to traverse the edge as many times as wished. It is easy to show that, under such cost interpretation for the finders-share search game PNE happens on strategies that correspond to a subtree rooted at the associated starting vertex of the graph. The proof of the following result is similar to the one for path strategies.

Theorem 12. *Every finders-share game played in a directed or undirected search network where the set of trajectories consists of trees always has a* PNE.

Proof. Consider a finders-share strategic search game $\Gamma = (N, \mathcal{N}, (S_i)_{i \in N})$ on an undirected network $\mathcal{N}$, where agent $i \in N$ is allowed to select any tree rooted at some vertex in the set S_i. For any agent $i \in N$, set $\mathcal{T}(i)$ to be the set of allowed trajectories for i, that is all trees in $\mathcal{N}$ rooted in a vertex in S_i. For any tree t in $\mathcal{N}$, define $R(t)$ to be the set formed by all the nodes and edges that appear in t. We define the corresponding congestion game $\Gamma' = f(\Gamma) = (N, \mathcal{R}, (\Pi_i)_{i \in N}, (d_e)_{e \in \mathcal{R}})$ as follows. Assume that $\mathcal{N} = (G(V, E), (a_e)_{e \in E}, (b_v)_{v \in V})$, then $\mathcal{R} = V \cup E$. For any $i \in N$, set $\Pi_i = \{R(p) \mid p \in \mathcal{P}(i)\}$. For any $r \in \mathcal{R}$ we define the non-decreasing delay function $d_r(x)$ as follows.

$$d_r(x) = \begin{cases} a_r & \text{if } r \in E \\ -\frac{b_r}{x} & \text{if } e \in V. \end{cases}$$

Observe that for every strategy for agent i in Γ', we can associate, in a unique way, a valid tree for agent i in $\mathcal{N}$. In this way we define, for any strategy profile, $\pi' \in \Pi(\Gamma')$ a strategy profile $g(\pi') \in \Pi(\Gamma)$ with $c_i(\pi') = u_i(g(\pi'))$. Since f and g are polynomial-time computable, the result for undirected networks follows.

For the case of a directed network, the proof is the same, considering as set of resources the union of the set of nodes and arcs. □

The previous results guarantee only the existence of PNE but it remains open whether a polynomial time algorithm for computing one PNE exists in those particular cases.

6 Conclusions and Open Problems

We have defined a new class of strategic games, those games have been motivated by the study of resource discovery in distributed networks. We believe that this framework is general enough to incorporate other mechanisms for splitting benefits and costs in other settings. We have also introduced the notion of Nash-preserving reduction that could be used to derive further results in the study of other strategic games. Our results show a close connection between network congestion games and finders-share games while the class of firsts-share games behaves differently from the point of view of the existence of a PNE.

There are still many open problems concerning the firsts-share model. It will be of interest to obtain a characterization of the networks on which firsts-search games have always a PNE. Observe that in some cases this might be difficult as the existence of a PNE depends on the edge and node weights. Another problem of interest is to determine whether the existence of PNE can be solved in polynomial time for non-equidistant networks. Finally, we point out that in the asymmetric tree coupling, all the common leaves are dominated by exactly one of the two sources, but we do not know whether the existence of PNE can be established for a tree coupling in which a subset of the common leaves are at the same distance from the two sources.

For the finders-share cost model we have shown the existence of PNE equilibria and that a PNE can be obtained in polynomial time, independently of the number of sources. It will be of interest to analyze further properties on the structure of the PNE in regard to some topological graph property.

There are many ways of defining a social cost in this context, some of them clearly contradictory with the player utility functions, as for example trying to maximize the total value of the recovered items or trying to get the maximum benefit due to the toll paid by the agents. For those two cases it is straightforward to show that the price of anarchy is unbounded. It is of interest to find an adequate and natural definition of the social benefit that provides bounded anarchy price.

References

1. Fabrikant, A., Papadimitriou, C., Talwar, K.: The complexity of pure Nash equilibria. In: Proceedings of the Thirty-Sixth Annual ACM Symposium on Theory of Computing (STOC), pp. 604–612 (2004)
2. Fotakis, D., Kontogiannis, S., Spirakis, P.: Symmetry in Network Congestion Games: Pure Equilibria and Anarchy Cost. In: Erlebach, T., Persinao, G. (eds.) WAOA 2005. LNCS, vol. 3879, pp. 161–175. Springer, Heidelberg (2006)
3. Gal, S.: Search Games. Academic Press (1980)
4. Isaacs, R.: Differential Games. John Wiley and Sons (1965)
5. Kontogiannis, S., Spirakis, P.: Atomic Selfish Routing in Networks: A Survey. In: Deng, X., Ye, Y. (eds.) WINE 2005. LNCS, vol. 3828, pp. 989–1002. Springer, Heidelberg (2005)
6. Koutsoupias, E., Papadimitriou, C.: Worst-Case Equilibria. In: Meinel, C., Tison, S. (eds.) STACS 1999. LNCS, vol. 1563, pp. 404–413. Springer, Heidelberg (1999)
7. Milchtaich, I.: Congestion games with player-specific payoff functions. Games and Economic Behavior 13(1), 111–124 (1996)
8. Nisan, N., Roughgarden, T., Tardos, E., Vazirani, V. (eds.): Algorithmic Game Theory. Cambridge University Press, New York (2007)
9. Panagopoulou, P.N., Spirakis, P.G.: Efficient Convergence to Pure Nash Equilibria in Weighted Network Congestion Games. In: Nikoletseas, S.E. (ed.) WEA 2005. LNCS, vol. 3503, pp. 203–215. Springer, Heidelberg (2005)
10. Papadimitriou, C.: Algorithms, games, and the internet. In: STOC 2001: Proceedings of the Thirty-Third Annual ACM Symposium on Theory of Computing, pp. 749–753. ACM Press, New York (2001)
11. Rosenthal, R.W.: A class of games possessing pure-strategy Nash equilibria. International Journal of Game Theory (2), 65–67 (1973)

Static Enforcement of Information Flow Policies for a Concurrent JVM-like Language*

Gilles Barthe and Exequiel Rivas

IMDEA Software Institute, Madrid, Spain

Abstract. An essential security goal of mobile code platforms is to protect confidential data against untrusted third-party applications; yet, prevailing mechanisms for ensuring confidentiality of mobile code are limited to sequential programs, whereas existing applications are generally concurrent. To bridge this gap, we develop a sound information-flow type system for a JVM-like, low-level concurrent object-oriented language. The type system builds upon existing solutions for object-oriented languages and concurrency, solving a number of intricate issues in their combination. Moreover, we connect the type system for bytecode programs to a type system for Java programs, extending the results of type-preserving compilation developed in earlier works.

1 Introduction

Non-interference is a baseline information flow policy which provides strong end-to-end security guarantees about programs, ensuring that they do not reveal confidential data throughout execution. Because information flow policies focus on program behavior rather than program origin, they are suitable for mobile code security, where confidential data must be protected against applications originating from untrusted third parties. Hence, there have been efforts to enhance the Java bytecode verifier, one of the two main security mechanisms of the Java Virtual Machine, so that it provides a type-based enforcement mechanism for non-interference. For instance, Barthe, Pichardie and Rezk [4] give a sound information flow type system for a large fragment of the Java Virtual Machine, including objects and arrays, methods, and exceptions. One important limitation of [4] is that it is restricted to sequential programs. Indeed, mobile code applications are generally concurrent, and hence cannot be handled by the type system.

Developing flexible information flow type systems for concurrent languages is notoriously difficult. Indeed, the concurrent execution of two secure programs may be insecure [14], and hence information flow type systems impose stringent restrictions on programs. In [12,13], Russo and Sabefeld introduce the notion of secure scheduler to provide a more flexible (and yet sound) approach to handle concurrency. Building on their idea, Barthe, Rezk, Russo and Sabelfeld [5] give a modular method for extending an information flow type system for a sequential low-level language into an information flow type system for a concurrent low-level language, and instantiate their method to

* Partially funded by European Projects FP7-231620 HATS and FP7-256980 NESSoS, Spanish project TIN2009-14599 DESAFIOS 10, Madrid Regional project S2009TIC-1465 PROMETIDOS.

R. Bruni and V. Sassone (Eds.): TGC 2011, LNCS 7173, pp. 73–88, 2012.

a minimal stack-based language that can serve as a target for compiling WHILE programs; the crux of the method is to make schedulers aware of the security environment that maps program points to a security level that lowers bound their effect, and to require that schedulers do not leak information through internal timing. Although the method is modular, its application to the type system of [4] raises a significant difficulty, because the soundness of the latter is based on a mix-step semantics, in which method calls are performed in one step. While the mix-step semantics makes soundness proofs considerably simpler, it is inappropriate for reasoning about concurrent programs, since the execution of separate threads might be interleaved. In this paper, we address this problem by enhancing the proof method of [4] so that all reasoning about program executions is performed directly with respect to a small-step semantics. This requires substantial generalizations in the notions of state equivalence, and substantial adaptations in the unwinding lemmas. Moreover, we provide a more realistic treatment of thread creation, so that it matches more closely the operational semantics of the JVM, and recast one technical hypothesis of [5] in terms of control dependence regions, making its verification simpler.

Moreover, we consider the issue of type-preserving compilation: we define an information flow type system for a concurrent fragment of Java and show that non-optimizing compilation preserves typability of programs, thereby generalizing [3,5]. Besides establishing that developers and consumers views on secure information flow (respectively embodied in the Java and JVM type systems) coincide, our result allows us to derive that the source type system is sound, i.e. enforces non-interference. To our best knowledge, this is the first proof of non-interference for a concurrent fragment of Java.

In summary, the main contributions of this article are:

- we provide the first sound information-flow type system for low-level, concurrent, object-oriented language;
- we define an information flow type system for a concurrent fragment of Java, prove type-preserving compilation, and derive soundness of the type system;
- we simplify one technical hypothesis in [5] that was extremely difficult to establish, even for a simple language.

2 A Concurrent JVM Language

We consider a concurrent JVM-like language, but omit some features most notably locks and exceptions.

Programs. Figure 2 gives the definition of programs. Informally, a program P is given by: i) a set $\mathcal{C}$ of classes, including a **main** class; ii) a set $\mathcal{F}$ of fields, and a function $\mathsf{fieldsof} : \mathcal{C} \to \wp(\mathcal{F})$ that yields a partition of $\mathcal{F}$; iii) a set $\mathcal{M}_{id}$ of method identifiers; iv) a set $\mathcal{M}_{vt}$ of virtual method identifiers, including an identifier run reserved for methods that run as new threads; v) a set $\mathcal{M}$ of methods, including a method identifier, a virtual method identifier, an argument table that maps argument positions to local variable names, and a sequence of instructions from Figure 1; vi) a function lookup attached to each program that takes a method identifier and a class name and returns the

$$\begin{array}{rl}\textsf{Instr} ::= & \textsf{binop}\ op \mid \textsf{push}\ n \mid \textsf{load}\ x \mid \textsf{store}\ x \mid \textsf{ifeq}\ j \mid \\ & \textsf{goto}\ j \mid \textsf{invokevirtual}\ m_{ID} \mid \textsf{return} \mid \textsf{start}\end{array}$$

where op is a binary operation, n is an integer, i and j are natural numbers, and x is an identifier.

Fig. 1. Instruction set

$$\begin{array}{rll}
\mathcal{C} \ni C & & \text{(classes)} \\
\mathcal{F} \ni f & & \text{(fields)} \\
\mathcal{C} \to \wp(\mathcal{F}) \ni \textsf{fieldsof} & & \text{(class description)} \\
\mathcal{M}_{id} \ni m_{id} & & \text{(method ids.)} \\
\mathcal{M}_{vt} \ni m_{vt} & & \text{(virt. method ids.)} \\
\textsf{Instr} \ni ins & & \text{(instruction)} \\
\textsf{List} \ni lis ::= ins :: lis \mid ins & & \text{(instruction listing)} \\
\mathbb{N} \rightharpoonup \mathcal{I} \ni \textsf{arg} & & \text{(argument table)} \\
\mathcal{M} \ni m ::= \langle m_{vt}, m_{id}, \textsf{arg}, lis \rangle & & \text{(methods)} \\
\mathcal{M}_{id} \times \mathcal{C} \to \mathcal{M} \ni \textsf{lookup} & & \text{(class lookup)} \\
\mathcal{P} \ni i ::= \langle n, m_{id} \rangle & & \text{(program points)} \\
\textsf{Program} \ni P ::= \langle \mathcal{C}, \mathcal{F}, \textsf{fieldsof}, \mathcal{M}, \mathcal{M}_{id}, \mathcal{M}_{vt}, \textsf{lookup} \rangle & & \text{(programs)}
\end{array}$$

Fig. 2. Programs

method to be executed. A program point consists of a method m, and an integer i that is smaller than the length of the list of instructions attached to m, and only i is used if the method is understood from context. We let $P_m[i]$ denote the instruction at index i of method m and let $\mathcal{P}$ denote the set of program points. We write $\textsf{arg}_m$ for the argument table corresponding to method m, and assume a set $\mathcal{I}$ of variable identifiers.

States. Figure 2 introduces the semantic domains used to interpret the program behavior. Informally, a state is a set of threads indexed by thread identifiers together with a heap. The local state of a thread is given by a stack of frames, where each frame contains some local state used to execute a method invocation. The heap is modeled as partial maps from locations to objects; objects are themselves modeled as pairs, consisting of a class and of a partial map from fields to values. We assume heaps satisfy standard well-formedness constraints, e.g the domain of p include the fields of C, and o maps fields to values of the correct type. Values can be either integer numbers or locations, i.e. $\mathcal{V} = \mathbb{Z} \cup \mathcal{L} \cup \{\textsf{null}\}$, where $\mathcal{L}$ is an (infinite) set of locations used to store the address of an object in the heap and null denotes the null pointer. Following [4], we avoid pointer arithmetic by making a distinction between locations and integer values. A set of accessors that we use to extract information from frames and states is defined.

Thread-local semantics. The operational semantics of JVM programs is defined in two steps: we first define a thread-local semantics that characterize the effect of executing

$$
\begin{array}{rll}
\mathcal{L} \ni \ell & & \text{(locations)} \\
\mathcal{V} \ni v ::= \mathbb{Z} \cup \mathcal{L} \cup \{\mathsf{null}\} & & \text{(values)} \\
\mathcal{V}^* \ni s ::= v :: s \mid \epsilon & & \text{(operand stacks)} \\
\mathcal{F} \rightharpoonup \mathcal{V} \ni p & & \text{(properties)} \\
\mathcal{O} \ni o ::= \langle C, p \rangle & & \text{(objects)} \\
\mathbb{N} \rightharpoonup \mathcal{V} \ni \rho & & \text{(environments)} \\
\mathsf{Frame} \ni f ::= \langle m_{id}, i, \rho, s \rangle & & \text{(frames)} \\
\mathsf{Thread} \ni t ::= f :: t \mid f & & \text{(threads)} \\
\mathcal{T} \rightharpoonup \mathsf{Thread} \ni ts & & \text{(thread set)} \\
\mathsf{Mem} = \mathcal{L} \to \mathcal{O} \ni \mu & & \text{(heaps)} \\
\mathsf{State} \ni s ::= \langle ts, \mu \rangle & & \text{(states)}
\end{array}
$$

$$
\begin{array}{lll}
f.\mathsf{m} \Rightarrow m_{id} & f.\mathsf{s} \Rightarrow s & s.\mathsf{ts} \Rightarrow ts \\
f.\mathsf{pc} \Rightarrow i & t.\mathsf{s} \Rightarrow \mathsf{hd}(t).\mathsf{s} & s.\mathsf{act} \Rightarrow \mathsf{dom}(ts) \\
f.\mathsf{env} \Rightarrow \rho & t.\mathsf{pc} \Rightarrow \mathsf{hd}(t).\mathsf{pc} & s.\mathsf{mem} \Rightarrow \mu
\end{array}
$$

Fig. 3. Semantic domains and accessors

an instruction on a thread. We omit its definition, which is totally standard, and can be found in the full version of the paper. The thread-local semantics is defined as a relation $\leadsto_{\mathsf{s}} \subseteq \mathsf{Thread} \times \mathsf{Mem} \times \mathsf{Thread}_\perp \times \mathsf{Mem}$: we write $\langle t, \mu \rangle \leadsto_{\mathsf{s}} \langle t', \mu' \rangle$ instead of $\langle t, \mu, t', \mu' \rangle \in \leadsto_{\mathsf{s}}$ as is standard. Note that termination of a thread corresponds to $t' = \perp$. The semantics is parametrized by a function $\mathsf{default} : \mathcal{C} \to \mathcal{O}$ that returns a default object of the corresponding class and it is used to create the new objects.

Global semantics. The semantics of programs is parametrized by a scheduler, that picks a thread to be executed, according to the current state, and a history h. A history is defined as a sequence of thread identifiers; we let $\mathcal{H}$ denote the set of histories, and let ϵ denote the initial history. We model a scheduler as a function $\mathsf{pickt} : \mathsf{State} \times \mathcal{H} \to \mathcal{T}$ that picks the next instruction to be executed. Moreover, we assume given a function $\mathsf{updh} : \mathsf{State} \times \mathcal{H} \to \mathcal{H}$ that updates the history after program execution. Formally, one-step execution is defined as a relation between pairs of states and histories. We write $\langle s, h \rangle \leadsto \langle s', h' \rangle$ when executing s with history h leads to state s' with history h'; the rules for the semantics are given in Figure 4. The semantics considers three cases: i) the instruction to be executed spawns a new thread; ii) it terminates the execution of a thread (in case the instruction is a return instruction and the thread has a single frame); iii) otherwise, the thread-local effect of the instruction is propagated to the active thread. We assume given a function fresht that takes as input a set of thread identifiers and generates a new thread identifier. Finally, we define the evaluation semantics.

Definition 1 (Evaluation semantics). *The evaluation relation* $\Downarrow \subseteq (\mathsf{State} \times \mathcal{H}) \times \mathsf{Mem}$ *is defined as:* $s, h \Downarrow \mu'$ *iff there is a pair* s', h' *such that* $s, h \leadsto^* s', h'$ *and* $s'.\mathsf{act} = \emptyset$ *and* $s'.\mathsf{mem} = \mu$. *We write* $P, \mu \Downarrow \mu'$ *as a shorthand for* $s_{init}(\mu), \epsilon \Downarrow \mu'$*, where* $s_{init}(\mu)$ *stands for* $\langle \{\mathsf{fresht}(\emptyset) \mapsto \langle 1_{\mathsf{main.run}}, \rho, \epsilon \rangle\}, \mu \rangle$ *where* ρ *is an empty environment.*

$$\frac{\begin{array}{c}\mathsf{pickt}(s,h)=ctid \quad \mathsf{updh}(s,h)=h' \quad s_{ctid}.\mathsf{pc}=i \quad P_m[i]=\mathsf{start} \quad s_{ctid}.\mathsf{os}=o::os\\ \mathsf{fresht}(s)=ntid \quad r=\mathsf{lookup}(\mathsf{run},\mathsf{class}(s.\mathsf{mem}(o))) \quad s_{ctid}.[\mathsf{pc}:=i+1]=\sigma'\end{array}}{s,h \leadsto s.[\mathsf{lst}(ctid).\mathsf{lst}:=\sigma', \mathsf{lst}(ntid):=\langle\langle 1,\{this\mapsto o\},\epsilon\rangle\rangle],h'}\ (\mathrm{Spawn})$$

$$\frac{\mathsf{pickt}(s,h)=ctid \quad \mathsf{updh}(s,h)=h' \quad s_{ctid}.\mathsf{pc}=i \quad P_m[i]=\mathsf{return} \quad \langle s_{ctid}.\mathsf{ts}, s.\mathsf{mem}\rangle \leadsto_{\mathrm{s}} \langle\bot,\mu\rangle}{s,h \leadsto s.[\mathsf{lst}:=\mathsf{lst}\setminus ctid, \mathsf{mem}:=\mu],h'}\ (\mathrm{Kill})$$

$$\frac{\mathsf{pickt}(s,h)=ctid \quad \mathsf{updh}(s,h)=h' \quad s_{ctid}.\mathsf{pc}=i \quad P_m[i]\neq\mathsf{start} \quad \langle s(ctid).\mathsf{ts}, s.\mathsf{mem}\rangle \leadsto_{\mathrm{s}} \langle\sigma,\mu\rangle}{s,h \leadsto s.[\mathsf{lst}(ctid):=\sigma, \mathsf{mem}:=\mu],h'}\ (\mathrm{Seq})$$

Fig. 4. Semantics of multithreaded programs

Next, we define non-interference using the evaluation semantics, and characterize the class of schedulers for which our type system enforces non-interference.

3 Policy, Schedulers and Type System

This section presents an information flow type system for the concurrent language described in the previous section. The type system, and the policy it enforces, rely on security annotations on programs. The annotations use security levels, drawn from the set $\mathcal{S}=\{L,H\}$; the set $\mathcal{S}$ is given a lattice structure by declaring $L\sqsubseteq H$. Figure 5 gives a summary of the security annotations for each program. They include: i) a function ft that assigns security levels to fields; ii) a security environment that assigns security levels to program points, and is used to track implicit flows, and; iii) a method signature table, that assigns to each virtual method a security signature; a signature for a virtual method identifier m consists of a function k_v that gives the security levels describing the security level for each of its local variables, a level k_h that gives the effect of the method on the heap (in the sequel we write $\mathsf{eff}(m)$ for k_h), and a security level k_r for the value returned.

3.1 Policy

The definition of non-interference relies on memory indistinguishability. Following [1,4], we allow the allocator to be non-deterministic and use a partial bijection β on locations to accommodate dynamic creation of low objects. More precisely, the partial bijection β is used to track the relation between low objects, since, given two identical states,

$$\begin{array}{rll}\mathcal{S}\ni s ::= L \mid H & & \text{(security levels)}\\ \mathcal{F}\to\mathcal{S}\ni \mathsf{ft} & & \text{(security level of fields)}\\ \mathcal{I}\rightharpoonup\mathcal{S}\ni\Gamma & & \text{(local variables security levels)}\\ \mathsf{SE}=\mathcal{P}\to\mathcal{S}\ni se & & \text{(security environments)}\\ \mathsf{Sig}\ni sig ::= \Gamma\xrightarrow{s} s & & \text{(signatures)}\\ \mathcal{M}_{vt}\to\mathsf{Sig}\ni\mathsf{mt} & & \text{(method table)}\end{array}$$

Fig. 5. Security setting

a non-deterministic allocator may allocate objects in different locations. High objects (i.e. objects created in a high state) are considered indistinguishable, and the partial bijection β needs not track them.

Definition 2. *Let β be a partial bijection between locations.*

- *Value indistinguishability is defined by the clauses:*

$$\frac{}{\mathsf{null} \overset{v}{\sim}_{\beta,L} \mathsf{null}} \qquad \frac{}{v \overset{v}{\sim}_{\beta,H} v'} \qquad \frac{v \in \mathbb{Z}}{v \overset{v}{\sim}_{\beta,L} v} \qquad \frac{v, v' \in \mathcal{L} \quad \beta(v) = v'}{v \overset{v}{\sim}_{\beta,L} v'}$$

- *Two objects $o_1, o_2 \in \mathcal{O}$ are indistinguishable, written $o_1 \overset{o}{\sim}_\beta o_2$, iff o_1 and o_2 are of the same class, and $o_1.f \overset{v}{\sim}_{\beta,\mathsf{ft}(f)} o_2.f$ for all fields f in o_1.*
- *Two memories μ_1 and μ_2 are indistinguishable w.r.t. β, written $\mu_1 \overset{\mu}{\sim}_\beta \mu_2$, iff $\mathsf{dom}(\beta) \subseteq \mathsf{dom}(\mu_1)$, $\mathsf{rng}(\beta) \subseteq \mathsf{dom}(\mu_2)$ and for every $l \in \mathsf{dom}(\beta)$, we have $\mu_1(l) \overset{o}{\sim}_\beta \mu_2(\beta(l))$.*

We can now define our policy: following [4,5], we consider termination-insensitive non-interference. This policy is more permissive than bisimulation-based properties, which are overly conservative for most purposes.

Definition 3 (Non-interfering program). *A program P is non-interfering if for all memories $\mu_1, \mu_2, \mu_1', \mu_2'$, and partial bijection β, there exists a partial bijection $\beta' \supseteq \beta$ s.t.*

$$\mu_1 \overset{\mu}{\sim}_\beta \mu_2 \text{ and } P, \mu_1 \Downarrow \mu_1' \text{ and } P, \mu_2 \Downarrow \mu_2' \text{ implies } \mu_1' \overset{\mu}{\sim}_{\beta'} \mu_2'$$

3.2 Schedulers

Execution of a concurrent JVM program proceeds by invoking the scheduler to select an active thread, and executing the current instruction for the selected thread. Following [12,13,5], we prevent internal timing leaks by instrumenting the state with security-relevant information, and making the scheduler aware of the security levels at which threads are executing. To this end, we separate thread identifiers in two sets $\mathcal{T}_H$ of high threads and $\mathcal{T}_L$ of low threads; moreover, we assume that $\mathsf{fresht}(\emptyset)$ is a low thread.

The critical property of a secure scheduler is that it always executes critical threads whenever they arise. A low thread becomes critical when it branches over a high value or it performs a method call on a high object. When it happens, we require that the scheduler executes the critical thread, until it terminates the execution of the conditional branch, or it returns from the high method. Formally, we say that a frame f is low, written $\mathsf{L}(f)$, if $se(f.\mathsf{pc}) = L$ and $\mathsf{eff}(f.\mathsf{m}) = L$, and that a thread t is low, written $\mathsf{L}(t)$, if all its frames are. The set of non-critical and critical threads of a state are defined as:

$$s.\mathsf{lowT} = \{tid \in s.\mathsf{act} \cap \mathcal{T}_L \mid \mathsf{L}(s_{tid})\} \qquad s.\mathsf{critT} = (s.\mathsf{act} \cap \mathcal{T}_L) \setminus s.\mathsf{lowT}$$

Note that, in comparison to [5], we omit the definition of always high threads, since such an analysis breaks modularity for languages with method calls.

The other essential property of a secure scheduler is that, whenever it chooses a low thread, its choice only depends on the low part of the history. To formalize the latter notion, we must taint in histories the instances of thread identifiers that correspond to the execution of critical threads. Then, we define the low part $h_{|L}$ of a history h as the subsequence of h where high thread identifiers and tainted instances of thread identifiers are removed.

Definition 4 (Secure scheduler). *A function* $\mathsf{pickt} : \mathsf{State} \times \mathcal{H} \to \mathcal{T}$ *is a secure scheduler iff for all states* s *and* s' *and for all histories* h *and* h'*:*

1. $\mathsf{pickt}(\langle s, h\rangle) \in s.\mathsf{act}$
2. *if* $s.\mathsf{crit} \neq \emptyset$, *then* $\mathsf{pickt}(\langle s, h\rangle) \in s.\mathsf{crit}$;
3. *if* $\mathsf{pickt}(s, h) \in s.\mathsf{lowT}$ *and* $s'.\mathsf{crit} = \emptyset$ *and* $s'.\mathsf{act} \neq \emptyset$, *and* $s.\mathsf{lowT} = s'.\mathsf{lowT}$, *and* $h_{|L} = h'_{|L}$, *then* $\mathsf{pickt}(s, h) = \mathsf{pickt}(s', h')$.

Examples of secure schedulers include (mildly adapted) round robin schedulers [5].

3.3 Control Dependence Regions

The definition of the type system is parametrized by an approximation of control dependence regions. This approximation is used in the typing rule for branching statements to prevent implicit flows.

Control dependence regions are formulated in terms of the successor relation $\mapsto$, which is defined by the clauses: i) $i \mapsto i + 1$ if $P_m[i]$ is of the form binop *op*, push n, load x, store x, invokevirtual m_{ID}, start, ifeq j, getfield f, putfield f, or new C; ii) $i \mapsto j$ if $P_m[i]$ is of the form goto j, or ifeq j; iii) $i \mapsto$, i.e. i does not have a successor if $P_m[i]$ is a return instruction. We let $\mapsto^*$ denote the reflexive-transitive closure of $\mapsto$. Moreover, we say that i is a branching point iff there exists program points j and k such that $j \neq k$, $i \mapsto j$ and $i \mapsto k$. We let $\mathcal{P}^\sharp$ be the set of branching points.

In the sequel, we consider that programs come equipped with a CDR structure $\langle \mathsf{region}, \mathsf{jun}\rangle$, where region is a function from branching points to sets of program points and jun is a partial function from branching points to program points, such that for all program points i, j and k:

CDR1 if $i \mapsto j$ then $j \in \mathsf{region}(i)$ or $j = \mathsf{jun}(i)$;
CDR2 if $j \in \mathsf{region}(i)$ and $j \mapsto k$, then either $k \in \mathsf{region}(i)$ or $k = \mathsf{jun}(i)$;
CDR3 if $j \in \mathsf{region}(i)$ and $j \mapsto$ then $\mathsf{jun}(i)$ is undefined;
CDR4 if $j \in \mathsf{region}(k)$ and $i \mapsto j$ then $i \in \mathsf{region}(k)$ or $k = i$;
CDR5 if $\mathsf{jun}(i) \in \mathsf{region}(j)$ then $\mathsf{region}(i) \subseteq \mathsf{region}(j)$;
CDR6 if $\mathsf{region}(i) \cap \mathsf{region}(j) \neq \emptyset$ then $\mathsf{region}(i) \subseteq \mathsf{region}(j)$ or $\mathsf{region}(j) \subseteq \mathsf{region}(i)$;
CDR7 if $i \in \mathsf{region}(j)$, then $j \mapsto^* i$.

In comparison with earlier works, e.g. [4], the last four CDR assumptions are new. These additional assumptions have a limited impact in our development: we briefly comment on two key points. On the one hand, our infrastructure requires that a CDR checker is executed prior to type checking. In order to ensure soundness of our verification method, the CDR checker must therefore be enhanced to verify these additional properties; fortunately, the additional verifications can be performed without increasing the complexity of the algorithm. On the other hand, type-preserving compilation also requires showing that source programs are compiled into JVM programs and CDR structures that are accepted by the checker. Thus, we must verify for each compiler that the CDR structures it outputs verify the additional assumptions. This is the purpose of Proposition 2.

On the other hand, these additional assumptions allow a direct proof of the existence of a function next that returns the next (relative to the successor relation) junction point that is not inside a high region. Before we proceed with the definition of the next function, we observe that extending CDR checkers so that they verify the above hypotheses, allows us to define a security environment that respects the CDR structure. It is assumed a function ise that each branching point is mapped to the security level of the value over which the branch is done.

Proposition 1 (Next function). *Let* $\langle \mathsf{region}, \mathsf{jun} \rangle$ *be a CDR structure. Moreover, let* $ise : \mathcal{P}^\sharp \to \mathcal{S}$ *and for all* $i \in \mathcal{P}$, *let* $\bar{i} = \{k \in \mathcal{P}^\# : i \in \mathsf{region}(k) \land ise(k) = H\}$. *Set the security environment* se *as follows:*

$$se(i) = \begin{cases} H \ \mathit{if}\ \bar{i} \neq \emptyset \\ L \ \ \mathit{if}\ \bar{i} = \emptyset \end{cases}$$

Then there exists a function $\mathsf{next} : \mathcal{P} \rightharpoonup \mathcal{P}$ *such that the following properties hold:*

NePd $\mathsf{dom}(\mathsf{next}) = \{i \in \mathcal{P} : se(i) = H\}$
NeP1 $i, j \in \mathsf{dom}(\mathsf{next}) \land i \mapsto j \Rightarrow \mathsf{next}(i) = \mathsf{next}(j)$
NeP2 $i \in \mathsf{dom}(\mathsf{next}) \land j \notin \mathsf{dom}(\mathsf{next}) \land i \mapsto j \Rightarrow \mathsf{next}(i) = j$
NeP3 $j, k \in \mathsf{dom}(\mathsf{next}) \land i \notin \mathsf{dom}(\mathsf{next}) \land i \mapsto j \land i \mapsto k \land j \neq k \Rightarrow \mathsf{next}(j) = \mathsf{next}(k)$
NeP4 $i, j \in \mathsf{dom}(\mathsf{next}) \land k \notin \mathsf{dom}(\mathsf{next}) \land i \mapsto j \land i \mapsto k \land j \neq k \Rightarrow \mathsf{next}(j) = k$

The proof of soundness makes use of the existence of the next function.

3.4 Type System

The type system adopts the principles of bytecode verification. It performs a modular (method-wise) data flow analysis that operates on stack of security levels, known as security stacks, and outputs a security type, i.e. a mapping from program points to security stacks:

$$\begin{array}{rll} \mathcal{ST} \ni st ::= s :: st \mid \epsilon & \text{(security stacks)} \\ \mathsf{Type} = \mathcal{P} \to \mathcal{ST} \ni S & \text{(security types)} \end{array}$$

More specifically, the type system is defined by a set of transfer rules that relate the stack type at a given program point to the stack type of its successors. The transfer rules are given in Figure 6. Their judgments are of the form $\mathsf{mt}, \mathsf{region}, se, i \vdash st \Rightarrow st'$, where st and st' are stack types; we simply write $i \vdash st \Rightarrow st'$ when the other components are understood from the context.

Definition 5 (Typable program). *A program* P *is typable w. type* S, *written* $S \vdash P$, *if*

1. $S(\langle 1, m_{id} \rangle) = \epsilon$, *for all methods* m_{id}; *and*
2. $\mathsf{mt}, \mathsf{region}, i, se \vdash S(i) \Rightarrow st$ *where* $st \sqsubseteq S(j)$, *for all program points* i *and* j *such that* $i \mapsto j$; *and*
3. $\mathsf{mt}, \mathsf{region}, i, se \vdash S(i) \Rightarrow$, *for all program point* i *such that* $P_m[i] = \mathsf{return}$.

$$\frac{P_m[i] = \mathsf{push}\ n}{\mathsf{mt}, \mathsf{region}, i, se \vdash st \Rightarrow se(i) :: st} \qquad \frac{P_m[i] = \mathsf{load}\ x \quad \mathsf{mt}(m) = k_v \xrightarrow{k_h} k_r}{\mathsf{mt}, \mathsf{region}, i, se \vdash st \Rightarrow (se(i) \sqcup k_v(x)) :: st}$$

$$\frac{P_m[i] = \mathsf{goto}\ j}{\mathsf{mt}, \mathsf{region}, i, se \vdash st \Rightarrow st} \qquad \frac{P_m[i] = \mathsf{binop}\ op}{\mathsf{mt}, \mathsf{region}, i, se \vdash k_1 :: k_2 :: st \Rightarrow (se(i) \sqcup k_1 \sqcup k_2) :: st}$$

$$\frac{\begin{array}{c}P_m[i] = \mathsf{store}\ x \quad \mathsf{mt}(m) = k_v \xrightarrow{k_h} k_r \\ se(i) \sqcup k \sqsubseteq k_v(x)\end{array}}{\mathsf{mt}, \mathsf{region}, i, se \vdash k :: st \Rightarrow st} \qquad \frac{\begin{array}{c}P_m[i] = \mathsf{invokevirtual}\ m_{vt} \quad \mathsf{mt}(m_{ID}) = k_v \xrightarrow{k_h} k_r \\ k :: \vec{k} \sqsubseteq k_v.\mathsf{arg}_{m_{vt}} \quad k \sqcup se(i) \sqcup \mathsf{eff}(m) \sqsubseteq k_h\end{array}}{\mathsf{mt}, \mathsf{region}, i, se \vdash \vec{k} :: k :: st \Rightarrow (k_r \sqcup k_h) :: st}$$

$$\frac{P_m[i] = \mathsf{ifeq}\ j \quad \forall j' \in \mathsf{region}(i), k \sqsubseteq se(j')}{\mathsf{mt}, \mathsf{region}, i, se \vdash k :: st \Rightarrow \mathsf{lift}_k(st)} \qquad \frac{P_m[i] = \mathsf{return} \quad se(i) \sqcup k \sqsubseteq k_r \quad se(i) \sqsubseteq \mathsf{eff}(m)}{\mathsf{mt}, \mathsf{region}, i, se \vdash k :: st \Rightarrow}$$

$$\frac{P_m[i] = \mathsf{start} \quad k \sqcup se(i) \sqcup \mathsf{eff}(m) \sqsubseteq \mathsf{eff}(\mathsf{run})}{\mathsf{mt}, \mathsf{region}, i, se \vdash k :: st \Rightarrow st} \qquad \frac{P_m[i] = \mathsf{getfield}\ f}{\mathsf{mt}, \mathsf{region}, i, se \vdash k :: st \Rightarrow (k \sqcup \mathsf{ft}(f) \sqcup se(i)) :: st}$$

$$\frac{P_m[i] = \mathsf{putfield}\ f \quad k_1 \sqcup se(i) \sqcup k_2 \sqsubseteq \mathsf{ft}(f) \quad \mathsf{eff}(m) \sqsubseteq \mathsf{ft}(f)}{\mathsf{mt}, \mathsf{region}, i, se \vdash k_1 :: k_2 :: st \Rightarrow st}$$

Fig. 6. Transfer rules

4 Soundness

This section establishes the soundness property for the type system presented in the previous section: we prove that typable programs are non-interfering. The overall structure of the proof is similar to [4,5]: one first proves locally-respects and step-consistent unwinding lemmas, and then one derives a locally-respects unwinding lemma for a notion of visible execution; finally, one proves non-interference by an argument on traces. The former critically relies on an appropriate notion of state indistinguishability, whereas the latter relies on properties of the control dependence regions and the security environment. In both cases, significant extensions to [4,5] are required. In particular, the notion of state equivalence must be extended to accommodate threads, i.e. stacks of frames, rather than a single frame. The intuition is that two threads are indistinguishable if their frames are in one-to-one correspondence[1] until there is a call to a high method in both threads, or one of the threads enters in a high branch. Throughout this section, we assume that P is typable program whose type is S, i.e. $S \vdash P$.

We first define state equivalence. As the high threads cannot modify the low part of the heap, state equivalence only depends on low threads, and the heap.

Definition 6 (State equivalence). *Let β be a partial bijection on locations.*

– *Operand stack equivalence is defined inductively by the clauses:*

$$\frac{\mathsf{highos}(os, st) \quad \mathsf{highos}(os', st')}{os : s \overset{\mathsf{os}}{\sim}_\beta os' : st'} \qquad \frac{os : st \overset{\mathsf{os}}{\sim}_\beta os' : st' \quad v \overset{v}{\sim}_{\beta,k} v'}{v :: os : k :: st \overset{\mathsf{os}}{\sim}_\beta v' :: os' : k :: st'}$$

where $\mathsf{highos}(os, st)$ *iff* $|os| = |st|$ *and* $st(i) = H$ *for all* $1 \leq i \leq |st|$.

[1] This correspondence is expressed below by the auxiliary relation $\overset{\ell}{\sim}$.

– *Frame equivalence is defined by the clause:*

$$f \overset{\mathsf{s}}{\sim}_\beta f' \text{ iff } f.\mathsf{os} : S(f.\mathsf{pc}) \overset{\mathsf{os}}{\sim}_\beta f'.\mathsf{os} : S(f'.\mathsf{pc}) \text{ and}$$
$$f.\mathsf{m} = f'.\mathsf{m} \text{ and}$$
$$f.\mathsf{env} \overset{\mathsf{env}}{\sim}_{\beta, f.\mathsf{m}} f'.\mathsf{env}$$

where $\rho \overset{\mathsf{env}}{\sim}_{\beta,m} \rho'$ *iff* $\rho(x) \overset{v}{\sim}_{\beta,k_v(x)} \rho'(x)$ *and* $\mathsf{mt}(m) = k_v \xrightarrow{k_h} k_r$.

– *Thread equivalence is defined inductively by the clauses:*

$$\frac{}{\epsilon \overset{\ell}{\sim}_\beta \epsilon} \qquad \frac{\mathsf{high}(fs_0) \quad \mathsf{high}(fs'_0) \quad fs \overset{\ell}{\sim}_\beta fs'}{fs_0 :: fs \overset{t}{\sim}_\beta fs'_0 :: fs'}$$

$$\frac{f \overset{\mathsf{s}}{\sim}_\beta f' \quad \mathsf{eff}(f.\mathsf{m}) = L \quad fs \overset{\ell}{\sim}_\beta fs' \quad \mathsf{L}(f) \wedge \mathsf{L}(f') \Rightarrow f.\mathsf{pc} = f'.\mathsf{pc}}{f :: fs \overset{\ell}{\sim}_\beta f' :: fs'}$$

where $\mathsf{high}(fs)$ *means that* $\mathsf{eff}(fs[i].\mathsf{m}) = H$ *for all* $1 \leq i \leq |fs|$.

– *State equivalence is defined by the clause:*

$$s \overset{\mathsf{c}}{\sim}_\beta s' \text{ iff } s.\mathsf{mem} \overset{\mu}{\sim}_\beta s'.\mathsf{mem} \wedge \forall t \in s.\mathsf{act} \cap \mathcal{T}_L.s_t \overset{t}{\sim}_\beta s'_t$$

The proof of the soundness theorem introduces three new execution relations, including a notion of visible step; the formal definitions are given in Figure 7. An intuition for these execution relations is: $s, h \leadsto_{\text{vis}} s', h'$ iff neither s or s' have a critical thread, and $s, h \leadsto s', h'$ or $s, h \leadsto^* s', h'$ and all intermediate states have a critical thread. For the proofs, it is convenient to divide this relation into two disjoint ones, corresponding to the reasons under which a thread can be made critical. Specifically, we define $s, h \leadsto_{\text{method}} s', h'$ iff $s, h \leadsto^* s', h'$ and s, s' and all the intermediate states have a critical thread caused by a method call on a high object; and $s, h \leadsto_{\text{branch}} s', h'$ iff $s, h \leadsto^* s', h'$ and s, s' and all the intermediate states have a critical thread caused by a branching over a high value. The predicates $\mathsf{C_m}$ and $\mathsf{C_b}$ determine whether a thread is high because of a branch or a method call, and NCT, $\mathsf{CT_b}$ and $\mathsf{CT_m}$ respectively indicate that the state has no critical thread; or a critical thread because of a branch; or a critical thread because of a method call. VS predicate is used to ensure threads with high identifiers do actually correspond to high threads.

Then, we prove unwinding lemmas for the newly introduced execution relations. The first two have the form of step-consistent lemmas, while the third has the form of a locally-respect lemma. For the sake of readability, we extend the next function to (critical) threads and (critical) states. For a critical thread t, $\mathsf{next}(t)$ is defined as $\mathsf{next}(i)$ where i is the program point that caused the thread to become critical. Formally,

$$\mathsf{next}(t) = \begin{cases} \mathsf{next}(\mathsf{hd}(t).\mathsf{pc}) \text{ if } se(\mathsf{hd}(t).\mathsf{pc}) = H \wedge \mathsf{eff}(\mathsf{hd}(t).\mathsf{m}) = L \wedge \mathsf{L}(\mathsf{tl}(t)) \\ \mathsf{next}(\mathsf{tl}(t)) \qquad \text{otherwise} \end{cases}$$

Since the current thread (the one picked by the scheduler) can be deduced from the context, we further write $\mathsf{next}(s)$ for $\mathsf{next}(s_{ctid})$ where $ctid$ is the current thread.

$$
\begin{array}{llll}
\mathsf{C_m}(f) & \equiv \mathsf{eff}(f.\mathsf{m}) = H \wedge \mathsf{highos}(f.\mathsf{pc}, S(f.\mathsf{pc})) & \mathsf{C_m}(t) & \equiv \exists i.\mathsf{C_m}(t[i]) \wedge \forall j < i.\mathsf{L}(t[j]) \\
\mathsf{C_b}(f) & \equiv se(f.\mathsf{pc}) = H \wedge \mathsf{eff}(f.\mathsf{m}) = L & \mathsf{C_b}(t) & \equiv \exists i.\mathsf{C_b}(t[i]) \wedge \forall j < i.\mathsf{L}(t[j]) \\
\mathsf{CT_b}(s) & \equiv s.\mathsf{critT} = \{tid\} \wedge \mathsf{C_b}(s_{tid}) \wedge \mathsf{VS}(s) & \mathsf{VS}(s) & \equiv \forall tid \in s.\mathsf{act} \cap \mathcal{T}_H.\mathsf{C_m}(s_{tid}) \\
\mathsf{CT_m}(s) & \equiv s.\mathsf{critT} = \{tid\} \wedge \mathsf{C_m}(s_{tid}) \wedge \mathsf{VS}(s) & \mathsf{NCT}(s) & \equiv s.\mathsf{critT} = \emptyset \wedge \mathsf{VS}(s)
\end{array}
$$

$$
\frac{\mathsf{NCT}(s) \quad \mathsf{NCT}(s') \quad s, h \rightsquigarrow s', h'}{s, h \rightsquigarrow_{\mathrm{vis}} s', h'}
$$

$$
\frac{\mathsf{CT_b}(s) \quad \mathsf{CT_b}(s') \quad s, h \rightsquigarrow s', h'}{s, h \rightsquigarrow_{\mathrm{branch}} s', h'}
\qquad
\frac{\mathsf{CT_m}(s) \quad \mathsf{CT_m}(s') \quad s, h \rightsquigarrow s', h'}{s, h \rightsquigarrow_{\mathrm{method}} s', h'}
$$

$$
\frac{s, h \rightsquigarrow_{\mathrm{branch}} s', h' \quad s', h' \rightsquigarrow_{\mathrm{branch}} s'', h''}{s, h \rightsquigarrow_{\mathrm{branch}} s'', h''}
\qquad
\frac{s, h \rightsquigarrow_{\mathrm{method}} s', h' \quad s', h' \rightsquigarrow_{\mathrm{method}} s'', h''}{s, h \rightsquigarrow_{\mathrm{method}} s'', h''}
$$

$$
\frac{s, h \rightsquigarrow s', h' \quad s', h' \rightsquigarrow_{\mathrm{branch}} s'', h'' \quad s'', h'' \rightsquigarrow s''', h'''}{s, h \rightsquigarrow_{\mathrm{vis}} s''', h'''}
$$

$$
\frac{s, h \rightsquigarrow s', h' \quad s', h' \rightsquigarrow_{\mathrm{method}} s'', h'' \quad s'', h'' \rightsquigarrow s''', h'''}{s, h \rightsquigarrow_{\mathrm{vis}} s''', h'''}
$$

Fig. 7. Auxiliary execution relations

Lemma 1. *If* $s, h_s \rightsquigarrow_{\mathrm{branch}} s', h_{s'}$ *and* $s \overset{c}{\sim}_\beta t$ *then we have* $s' \overset{c}{\sim}_\beta t$, $h_s \overset{h}{\sim} h_{s'}$, *and* $\mathsf{next}(s) = \mathsf{next}(s')$.

Lemma 2. *If* $s, h_s \rightsquigarrow_{\mathrm{method}} s', h_{s'}$ *and* $s \overset{c}{\sim}_\beta t$ *then we have* $s' \overset{c}{\sim}_\beta t$, *and* $h_s \overset{h}{\sim} h_{s'}$.

Lemma 3. *If* $s, h_s \rightsquigarrow_{\mathrm{vis}} s', h_{s'}$ *and* $t, h_t \rightsquigarrow_{\mathrm{vis}} t', h_{t'}$ *and* $s \overset{c}{\sim}_\beta t$ *and* $h_s \overset{h}{\sim} h_t$ *then we have* $s' \overset{c}{\sim}_{\beta'} t'$ *and* $h_{s'} \overset{h}{\sim} h_{t'}$ *for some* β' *such that* $\beta \subseteq \beta'$.

Theorem 1 (Soundness). *If P is typable with respect to a CDR structure* $\langle \mathsf{region}, \mathsf{jun} \rangle$, *then P is non-interfering.*

Proof (Sketch of proof). Suppose that $\mu_1 \overset{\mu}{\sim}_\beta \mu_2$, $P, \mu_1 \Downarrow \mu_1'$ and $P, \mu_2 \Downarrow \mu_2'$. Note that if $P, \mu_1 \Downarrow \mu_1'$ then $s_{init}(\mu_1), \epsilon\ (\rightsquigarrow_{\mathrm{vis}})^*\ s_1, h_{s_1}$ with $s_1.\mathsf{lowT} = \emptyset$ and $s_1.\mathsf{mem} = \mu_1'$. Analogously, $s_{init}(\mu_2), \epsilon\ (\rightsquigarrow_{\mathrm{vis}})^*\ s_2, h_{s_2}$ with $s_2.\mathsf{lowT} = \emptyset$ and $s_2.\mathsf{mem} = \mu_2'$. Moreover, as the $\rightsquigarrow_{\mathrm{vis}}$ relation "steps over" the critical execution steps both executions take the same number of $\rightsquigarrow_{\mathrm{vis}}$ steps. By lemma 3, we conclude.

5 Type-Preserving Compilation

The purpose of this section is to define an information flow type system for a concurrent fragment of Java, and to show that compilation transforms typable programs into typable programs.

5.1 Source Language and Compiler

The expressions and commands of the source language are defined in Figure 8; the overall structure of a program remains identical. The compiler must produce, in addition to

$$e ::= n \mid x \mid e\ op\ e \mid \mathsf{new}\ C$$

$$c ::= x = e \mid c\,;c \mid \mathsf{if}\ e\ \mathsf{then}\ c\ \mathsf{else}\ c \mid \mathsf{while}\ e\ \mathsf{do}\ c \mid e.f = e \mid \\ \mathsf{return}\ e \mid e.\mathsf{start}() \mid x = e.f \mid x = e.m(\bar{e})$$

$$p ::= [\mathsf{m}(\bar{e})\{c\,;\mathsf{return}\ e\}]$$

Fig. 8. Source language

the JVM program, a CDR structure. It is convenient for constructing the latter to consider a labeled version of the commands, and to define a mapping $\mathcal{A}$ that automatically give the commands of the source program labels such that there are no two commands in the source that have the same label; the syntax of the labeled commands in Figure 9. The definition of $\mathcal{A}$ can be found in the full version of the paper. The function $\mathcal{A}$ takes an integer, the number from where it starts to label the subcommands, and a command to be labeled, and returns a labeled command. To label a program, we use $\mathcal{A}$ in each method using as integer the length of the previous method compiled plus one and one for the first method to be compiled.

$$c ::= [x = e]^n \mid c\,;c \mid [\mathsf{if}\ e\ \mathsf{then}\ c\ \mathsf{else}\ c]^n \mid [\mathsf{while}\ e\ \mathsf{do}\ c]^n \mid [e.f = e]^n \mid \\ [\mathsf{return}\ e]^n \mid [e.\mathsf{start}()]^n \mid [x = e.f]^n \mid [x = e.m(\bar{e})]^n$$

Fig. 9. Labeled syntax

The compiler functions $[\![-]\!]$ transform expressions and commands of the source language as lists of JVM instructions; their definition is given in Figure 10. As in [3], we define for each branching command of the source language a *main instruction* in the target code. This instruction is a branching program point in the target program, and hence a program point for which we need to define the region and the junction point. Finally, programs are compiled by applying $[\![-]\!]$ to each method body.

5.2 Source Type System

The type system for the source language is defined in Figure 11. As for the JVM, the type system assumes that the program comes equipped with a mapping of fields to security levels, and a security signature for each method. Following the standard approach for source type system, we first type the expressions and then the commands. A method is well-typed if its command is typed with a type that is compatible with the method signature. A program is well-typed if all its methods are well-typed.

$$
\begin{aligned}
[\![x]\!] &= \mathsf{load}\ x \\
[\![n]\!] &= \mathsf{push}\ n \\
[\![e\ op\ e]\!] &= [\![e]\!] :: [\![e']\!] :: \mathsf{binop}\ op \\
[\![\mathsf{new}\ C]\!] &= \mathsf{new}\ C \\
[\![x = e]\!] &= [\![e]\!] :: \mathsf{store}\ x \\
[\![c_1 \,; c_2]\!] &= [\![c_1]\!] :: [\![c_2]\!] \\
[\![e.f = e']\!] &= [\![e']\!] :: [\![e]\!] :: \mathsf{putfield}\ f \\
[\![\mathsf{return}\ e]\!] &= [\![e]\!] :: \mathsf{return} \\
[\![\mathsf{while}\ e\ \mathsf{do}\ c]\!] &= \mathsf{goto}\ (pc + \#lc + 1) :: lc :: le :: \underline{\mathsf{ifeq}\ (pc - \#lc - \#le)} \\
&\quad \text{where } le = [\![e]\!], lc = [\![c]\!] \\
[\![\mathsf{if}\ e\ \mathsf{then}\ c_1\ \mathsf{else}\ c_2]\!] &= le :: \underline{\mathsf{ifeq}\ (pc + \#lc_2 + 2)} :: lc_2 :: \mathsf{goto}\ (pc + \#lc_1 + 1) :: lc_1 \\
&\quad \text{where } le = [\![e]\!], lc_1 = [\![c_1]\!], lc_2 = [\![c_2]\!] \\
[\![e.\mathsf{start}()]\!] &= [\![e]\!] :: \mathsf{start} \\
[\![x = e.f]\!] &= [\![e]\!] :: \mathsf{getfield}\ f :: \mathsf{store}\ x \\
[\![x = e.m(\bar{e})]\!] &= [\![\bar{e}]\!] :: [\![e]\!] :: \mathsf{invokevirtual}\ m :: \mathsf{store}\ x
\end{aligned}
$$

Fig. 10. Compilation

5.3 Preservation Proof

As in [3], the preservation proof preserves in three steps: first, we define a function sregion for the source language, which is used later to obtain a CDR structure for the compiled program. Then, we define an intermediate type system for the source language, and prove its equivalence with the original type system; the intermediate type system is defined with help of the sregion function, and facilitates the third and final step, which is the proof of type-preserving compilation itself. We highlight some critical steps below.

We first define the sregion function, which is the equivalent of a CDR structure for the source language: for each branching command $[c]^n$, we let $\mathsf{sregion}(n)$ be the set of labels that appear in c, i.e. that label the subcommands of c.

Proposition 2. *For every program P, $\langle \mathsf{tregion}, \mathsf{tjun}\rangle$ is a CDR structure for the program $[\![P]\!]$, where for every branching instruction $[c]^n$ in the source code,* $\mathsf{tregion}(n)$ *is defined as the set of instructions obtained by compiling commands $[c']^{n'}$, where $n' \in \mathsf{sregion}(n)$, and $\mathsf{tjun}(n) = \max\{i : i \in \mathsf{tregion}(n)\} + 1$.*

The proof involves showing that every branching program point in the target language is the image of a branching program point in the source language, and derive the CDR properties from the definition of the compiler.

We now define a function ise that associates to each branching point in the compiled program the security level of the corresponding guard in the source language. Proposition 1 yields the existence of a function next that satisfies the **NeP** hypotheses w.r.t. the security environment built from ise.

The proof of type-preserving compilation between the source and target type systems is performed first on expressions, then on commands. Finally, we conclude that

$$\frac{k_v \vdash \mathsf{e} : k \quad k \sqsubseteq k_v(x)}{k_v \xrightarrow{k_h} k_r \vdash x = \mathsf{e} : k_v(x)} \qquad \frac{k_v \vdash \mathsf{e} : k \quad k_v \xrightarrow{k_h} k_r \vdash \mathsf{c} : k}{k_v \xrightarrow{k_h} k_r \vdash \mathsf{while\ e\ do\ c} : k} \qquad \frac{k_v \vdash \mathsf{e} : k \quad k_v \xrightarrow{k_h} k_r \vdash \mathsf{c} : k \quad k_v \xrightarrow{k_h} k_r \vdash \mathsf{c}' : k}{k_v \xrightarrow{k_h} k_r \vdash \mathsf{if\ e\ then\ c\ else\ c}' : k}$$

$$\frac{k_v \vdash \mathsf{e} : k \quad k \sqsubseteq k_r \sqcap k_h}{k_v \xrightarrow{k_h} k_r \vdash \mathsf{return\ e} : k} \qquad \frac{k_v \vdash \mathsf{e} : k \quad k \sqcup \mathsf{ft}(f) \sqsubseteq k_v(x)}{k_v \xrightarrow{k_h} k_r \vdash x = e.f : k_v(x)} \qquad \frac{k_v \vdash \mathsf{e} : k \; k_v \vdash \mathsf{e}' : k' \; k \sqcup k' \sqcup k_h \sqsubseteq \mathsf{ft}(f)}{k_v \xrightarrow{k_h} k_r \vdash e.f = e' : \mathsf{ft}(f)}$$

$$\frac{k_v \xrightarrow{k_h} k_r \vdash \mathsf{c} : k \quad k' \sqsubseteq k}{k_v \xrightarrow{k_h} k_r \vdash \mathsf{c} : k'} \qquad \frac{k_v \vdash \mathsf{e} : k \quad k \sqcup k_h \sqsubseteq \mathsf{eff(run)}}{k_v \xrightarrow{k_h} k_r \vdash \mathsf{e.start()} : \mathsf{eff(run)}} \qquad \frac{k_v \xrightarrow{k_h} k_r \vdash \mathsf{c} : k \quad k_v \xrightarrow{k_h} k_r \vdash \mathsf{c}' : {}'k}{k_v \xrightarrow{k_h} k_r \vdash \mathsf{c} ; \mathsf{c}' : k \sqcap k'}$$

$$\frac{\forall i. k_v \vdash \mathsf{e}[i] : k_v(\bar{\mathsf{e}}[i]) \quad k \sqcup k_h \sqsubseteq k'_h \quad k_v \vdash \mathsf{e} : k \quad \mathsf{mt}(m) = k'_v \xrightarrow{k'_h} k'_r \quad k_r \sqsubseteq k'_v(x)}{k_v \xrightarrow{k_h} k_r \vdash x = e.m(\bar{e}) : k_v(x) \sqcap \mathsf{eff}(m)}$$

Fig. 11. A high-level type system for the source language

a typable source program is transformed into a JVM program that is typable w.r.t. the same policy as the source program, the CDR structure generated by the compiler, and the security environment built from ise.

Theorem 2. *Suppose we have a* $\vdash SP$*, then* $\vdash [\![SP]\!]$.

6 A Toy Example

To explore and concretise some details of the type system, we introduce a toy example. Three classes are defined: A, B, and C, with fields defined fieldsof(A) $=$ {varA}, fieldsof(B) $=$ {varB}, fieldsof(C) $=$ {varL, varH}, and ft defined by the rules ft(varL) $= L$, and ft(varH) $=$ ft(varA) $=$ ft(varB) $= H$. The methods are defined in Fig. 12.

From the type system, o is high as it is set inside a high-branch. Also, as o is high, from the start typing rule, we conclude that eff(run) must be high as well. This is consistent with the typing rule for assignment, as the fields varA and varB are high too.

A small change would make the program become insecure and untypable. If we force one of varA or varB to be a low field, then the type system would reject the code as the value of varH could be determined by inspecting varA or varB.

From this example, we can learn that if a method implementing run is high, then all other instances are forced to be high too. While it seems that this could be fixed in part by considering whether start is launched from a high or low region/object, the problem

```
void A.run() {
  this.varA = 0;
}
void B.run() {
  this.varB = 1;
}
void C.run() {
  if (this.varH)
    o = new A();
  else
    o = new B();
  o.start();
  ...
}
```

Fig. 12. Code of example

is actually harder than this: we can arrive to a start instruction from different methods with different security levels.

7 Related Work

The prevalence of Java in mobile code applications makes it a natural target for information flow analysis, and there is a substantial body of literature on enforcement mechanisms for Java or JVM programs. In particular, Myers *et al* [9] have developed the Jif language, an information flow aware extension of (sequential) Java; Jif has been used for developing significant examples of secure applications, including the Civitas voting system. While there is no soundness proof for the whole Jif type system, Banerjee and Naumann [1] have developed a sound information flow type system for a significant fragment of Java. Barthe, Naumann and Rezk [3] extend the type system and soundness proof to a simplified form of exception. Our work adopts many notions and techniques from [1,9] for object-oriented programs, and [4,8] for bytecode languages. All these works are confined to sequential fragments of Java.

More recently, there have been many proposals for a dynamic approach to information flow, as developed by Le Guernic *et al* for a core imperative [7] and concurrent [6] languages. Nair *et al* [10] report on the implementation of the Trishul system, which dynamically tracks information flow in Java applications; however, no formal guarantee is established.

8 Conclusion

Developing sound and flexible information flow type systems for mobile code is an important goal for language-based security. This article leverages previous works on concurrent bytecode languages and on the sequential JVM to propose for the first time a sound information flow type system for a concurrent low-level object-oriented language. Our work, and in particular the notions of program equivalence we use, lay the foundations for designing flexible type systems for the full JVM. In the future, it would be interesting to extend the type system to exceptions (which are treated in [11]), declassification (in the style of [2]), and locks.

References

1. Banerjee, A., Naumann, D.: Stack-based access control for secure information flow. Journal of Functional Programming 15, 131–177 (2005); Special Issue on Language-Based Security
2. Barthe, G., Cavadini, S., Rezk, T.: Tractable enforcement of declassification policies. In: IEEE Computer Security Foundations Symposium (June 2008)
3. Barthe, G., Naumann, D., Rezk, T.: Deriving an information flow checker and certifying compiler for Java. In: Symposium on Security and Privacy. IEEE Press (2006)
4. Barthe, G., Pichardie, D., Rezk, T.: A Certified Lightweight Non-interference Java Bytecode Verifier. In: De Nicola, R. (ed.) ESOP 2007. LNCS, vol. 4421, pp. 125–140. Springer, Heidelberg (2007)

5. Barthe, G., Rezk, T., Russo, A., Sabelfeld, A.: Security of multithreaded programs by compilation. ACM Trans. Inf. Syst. Secur. 13(3) (2010)
6. Le Guernic, G.: Automaton-based confidentiality monitoring of concurrent programs. In: CSF, pp. 218–232. IEEE Computer Society (2007)
7. Le Guernic, G., Banerjee, A., Jensen, T., Schmidt, D.A.: Automata-Based Confidentiality Monitoring. In: Okada, M., Satoh, I. (eds.) ASIAN 2006. LNCS, vol. 4435, pp. 75–89. Springer, Heidelberg (2007)
8. Kobayashi, N., Shirane, K.: Type-based information analysis for low-level languages. In: Asian Programming Languages and Systems Symposium, pp. 302–316 (2002)
9. Myers, A.C.: JFlow: Practical mostly-static information flow control. In: Principles of Programming Languages, pp. 228–241. ACM Press (1999), Ongoing development at `http://www.cs.cornell.edu/jif/`
10. Nair, S.K., Simpson, P.N.D., Crispo, B., Tanenbaum, A.S.: A virtual machine based information flow control system for policy enforcement. Electr. Notes Theor. Comput. Sci. 197(1), 3–16 (2008)
11. Rezk, T.: Verification of confidentiality policies for mobile code. PhD thesis, Université de Nice Sophia-Antipolis (2006)
12. Russo, A., Sabelfeld, A.: Securing interaction between threads and the scheduler. In: Computer Security Foundations Workshop, pp. 177–189 (2006)
13. Russo, A., Sabelfeld, A.: Security for Multithreaded Programs Under Cooperative Scheduling. In: Virbitskaite, I., Voronkov, A. (eds.) PSI 2006. LNCS, vol. 4378, pp. 474–480. Springer, Heidelberg (2007)
14. Smith, G., Volpano, D.: Secure Information Flow in a Multi-threaded Imperative Language. In: Principles of Programming Languages, pp. 355–364 (1998)

Weak Markovian Bisimulation Congruences and Exact CTMC-Level Aggregations for Sequential Processes

Marco Bernardo

Dipartimento di Scienze di Base e Fondamenti, Università di Urbino, Italy

Abstract. The Markovian behavioral equivalences defined so far treat exponentially timed internal actions like any other action. Since an exponentially timed internal action has a nonzero duration, it can be observed whenever it is executed between a pair of exponentially timed noninternal actions. However, no difference may be noted at steady state between a sequence of exponentially timed internal actions and a single exponentially timed internal action as long as their average durations coincide. We show that Milner's construction to derive a weak bisimulation congruence for nondeterministic processes can be extended to sequential Markovian processes in a way that captures the above situation. The resulting weak Markovian bisimulation congruence admits a sound and complete axiomatization, induces an exact CTMC-level aggregation at steady state, and is decidable in polynomial time for finite-state processes having no cycles of exponentially timed internal actions.

1 Introduction

System models with an underlying continuous-time Markov chain (CTMC) [23] semantics can be compared and manipulated by means of Markovian behavioral equivalences. Several of them have appeared in the literature – see [1] and the references therein – which are extensions of the traditional approaches to the definition of behavioral equivalences that take into account performance aspects too. A feature shared by relations like Markovian bisimilarity, Markovian testing equivalence, and Markovian trace equivalence is that of being strong. Only a few variants investigated in [12,21,17,6] are capable of abstracting from internal immediate actions and/or purely probabilistic branchings.

Let us denote by τ the invisible or silent action. In a nondeterministic setting, a process that can perform action a followed by τ and action b and then terminates – written $a \,.\, \tau \,.\, b \,.\, \underline{0}$ – is weakly equivalent to a process that can perform action a followed by action b and then terminates – written $a \,.\, b \,.\, \underline{0}$. By contrast, in a setting where actions have exponentially distributed durations – uniquely identified by positive real numbers called rates – it is not necessarily the case that simplifications like the one above can be made.

For instance, if a has rate λ, b has rate μ, and τ has rate γ, the two resulting processes $<a, \lambda>.<\tau, \gamma>.<b, \mu>.\underline{0}$ and $<a, \lambda>.<b, \mu>.\underline{0}$ are not weakly equivalent. In fact, recalling that the average (i.e., expected) duration of an action

R. Bruni and V. Sassone (Eds.): TGC 2011, LNCS 7173, pp. 89–103, 2012.

coincides with the reciprocal of the rate of the action, the former process has a maximal computation whose average duration is $\frac{1}{\lambda} + \frac{1}{\gamma} + \frac{1}{\mu}$, whereas the latter process has a maximal computation whose average duration is $\frac{1}{\lambda} + \frac{1}{\mu}$. From another viewpoint, in the former case an external observer would see an a-action for an amount of time t_λ and a b-action for an amount of time t_μ with a delay t_γ in between, while in the latter case the external observer would not see any delay between the execution of a and the execution of b. Therefore, in a Markovian setting a τ-action executed between a pair of non-τ-actions cannot be abstracted away because it has a nonzero duration and hence can be observed.

As a different example, take now a process that can perform action a at rate λ followed by two τ-actions with rates γ_1 and γ_2, respectively, and then behaves as process P, i.e., $<a, \lambda>.<\tau, \gamma_1>.<\tau, \gamma_2>.P$. In this case, an observer may not be able to distinguish between the execution of the two τ-actions above and the execution of a single τ-action whose average duration is the sum of the average durations of the two original τ-actions, i.e., $\frac{1}{\gamma_1} + \frac{1}{\gamma_2} = \frac{\gamma_1 + \gamma_2}{\gamma_1 \cdot \gamma_2}$. In other words, the process may be viewed as being weakly equivalent to $<a, \lambda>.<\tau, \frac{\gamma_1 \cdot \gamma_2}{\gamma_1 + \gamma_2}>.P$.

The two processes above are weakly equivalent from a functional standpoint. However, since the sum of the two exponential random variables quantifying the durations of the two original τ-actions has been approximated with a single average-preserving exponential random variable, it is not necessarily the case that the two processes have the same performance characteristics. This would be true if the equivalence induced an exact CTMC-level aggregation, i.e., an aggregation such that the transient/stationary probability of being in a macrostate of a reduced CTMC is the sum of the transient/stationary probabilities of being in one of the constituent microstates of the CTMC from which the reduced one has been obtained. This is the case with Markovian bisimilarity, which is in agreement with an exact CTMC-level aggregation called ordinary lumpability [14,10], and Markovian testing and trace equivalences, which are consistent with a coarser exact CTMC-level aggregation called T-lumpability [4].

In this paper, we show that the construction used in [18] to derive a weak bisimulation congruence for nondeterministic processes can be extended to sequential Markovian processes. The resulting equivalence is weak in the sense that it is capable of abstracting from the number of consecutive exponentially timed τ-actions in a computation. It reduces any such sequence to a single exponentially timed τ-action preserving both the average duration and the execution probability of the original action sequence, which turns out to induce an exact CTMC-level aggregation at steady state. We also prove that the weak Markovian bisimulation congruence admits a sound and complete axiomatization and – in the absence of cycles of exponentially timed internal actions – is decidable in polynomial time for finite-state processes.

This paper is organized as follows. In Sect. 2, we introduce a process calculus for sequential Markovian processes with abstraction and we recall Markovian bisimilarity. In Sect. 3, we develop the weak variant of Markovian bisimilarity and we investigate its congruence, axiomatizatibility, exactness, and decidability properties. Finally, in Sect. 4 we conclude with related and future work.

2 Sequential Markovian Processes and Bisimilarity

In order to study properties like congruence and axiomatizability of the weak variant of Markovian bisimilarity, we need to define a Markovian process calculus (MPC for short). In particular, we introduce a calculus that generates all the CTMCs with as few operators as possible: the inactive process, exponentially timed action prefix, alternative composition, and recursion. Therefore, the resulting processes will be sequential Markovian processes governed by the race policy: if several exponentially timed actions are simultaneously enabled, the action that is executed is the one sampling the least duration. In addition to those operators, we include hiding because the behavioral equivalence we are going to propose is weak and hence we need a way for causing actions to become the internal action τ.

Definition 1. *Let* $Act_{\mathrm{M}} = Name \times \mathbb{R}_{>0}$ *be a set of actions, where* $Name = Name_{\mathrm{v}} \cup \{\tau\}$ *is a set of action names – ranged over by* a, b *– and* $\mathbb{R}_{>0}$ *is a set of action rates – ranged over by* λ, μ, γ. *Let Var be a set of process variables ranged over by* X, Y. *The process language* $\mathcal{PL}_{\mathrm{M}}$ *is generated by the following syntax:*

$P ::= \underline{0}$	*inactive process*
$\mid\ <a, \lambda>.P$	*exponentially timed action prefix*
$\mid\ P + P$	*alternative composition*
$\mid\ X$	*process variable*
$\mid\ \mathrm{rec}\, X : P$	*recursion*
$\mid\ P/H$	*hiding*

where $a \in Name$, $\lambda \in \mathbb{R}_{>0}$, $X \in Var$, *and* $H \subseteq Name_{\mathrm{v}}$. *We denote by* $\mathbb{P}_{\mathrm{M}}$ *the set of closed and guarded process terms of* $\mathcal{PL}_{\mathrm{M}}$ *– ranged over by* P, Q. ■

In order to distinguish between process terms like $<a, \lambda>.\underline{0} + <a, \lambda>.\underline{0}$ and $<a, \lambda>.\underline{0}$, the semantic model $[\![P]\!]_{\mathrm{M}}$ for a process term $P \in \mathbb{P}_{\mathrm{M}}$ is a labeled multitransition system that takes into account the multiplicity of each transition, intended as the number of different proofs for the transition derivation. The multitransition relation of $[\![P]\!]_{\mathrm{M}}$ is contained in the smallest multiset of elements of $\mathbb{P}_{\mathrm{M}} \times Act_{\mathrm{M}} \times \mathbb{P}_{\mathrm{M}}$ that satisfies the operational semantic rules below – where $\{\_ \hookrightarrow \_\}$ denotes syntactical replacement – and keeps track of all the possible ways of deriving each of its transitions:

$$(\textsc{Pre}_{\mathrm{M}})\quad \frac{}{<a, \lambda>.P \xrightarrow{a,\lambda}_{\mathrm{M}} P} \qquad (\textsc{Rec}_{\mathrm{M}})\quad \frac{P\{\mathrm{rec}\, X : P \hookrightarrow X\} \xrightarrow{a,\lambda}_{\mathrm{M}} P'}{\mathrm{rec}\, X : P \xrightarrow{a,\lambda}_{\mathrm{M}} P'}$$

$$(\textsc{Alt}_{\mathrm{M},1})\quad \frac{P_1 \xrightarrow{a,\lambda}_{\mathrm{M}} P'}{P_1 + P_2 \xrightarrow{a,\lambda}_{\mathrm{M}} P'} \qquad (\textsc{Alt}_{\mathrm{M},2})\quad \frac{P_2 \xrightarrow{a,\lambda}_{\mathrm{M}} P'}{P_1 + P_2 \xrightarrow{a,\lambda}_{\mathrm{M}} P'}$$

$$(\textsc{Hid}_{\mathrm{M},1})\quad \frac{P \xrightarrow{a,\lambda}_{\mathrm{M}} P' \quad a \notin H}{P/H \xrightarrow{a,\lambda}_{\mathrm{M}} P'/H} \qquad (\textsc{Hid}_{\mathrm{M},2})\quad \frac{P \xrightarrow{a,\lambda}_{\mathrm{M}} P' \quad a \in H}{P/H \xrightarrow{\tau,\lambda}_{\mathrm{M}} P'/H}$$

Bisimilarity for MPC is based on the comparison of exit rates [14,13]. The exit rate of $P \in \mathbb{P}_{\rm M}$ with respect to action name $a \in Name$ and destination $D \subseteq \mathbb{P}_{\rm M}$ is the rate at which P can execute actions of name a that lead to D:

$$\boxed{rate(P, a, D) \; = \; \sum \{\!| \, \lambda \in \mathbb{R}_{>0} \mid \exists P' \in D. \, P \xrightarrow{a,\lambda}_{\rm M} P' \, |\!\}}$$

where $\{\!|$ and $|\!\}$ are multiset delimiters and the summation is taken to be zero if its multiset is empty. By summing up the rates of all the actions of P, we obtain the total exit rate of P, i.e., $rate_{\rm t}(P) = \sum_{a \in Name} rate(P, a, \mathbb{P}_{\rm M})$, which is the reciprocal of the average (i.e., expected) sojourn time associated with P.

Definition 2. *An equivalence relation $\mathcal{B}$ over $\mathbb{P}_{\rm M}$ is a Markovian bisimulation iff, whenever $(P_1, P_2) \in \mathcal{B}$, then for all action names $a \in Name$ and equivalence classes $D \in \mathbb{P}_{\rm M}/\mathcal{B}$:*

$$rate(P_1, a, D) \; = \; rate(P_2, a, D)$$

Markovian bisimilarity $\sim_{\rm MB}$ is the union of all the Markovian bisimulations. ■

3 Abstracting from Exponentially Timed τ-Actions

In this section, we weaken the distinguishing power of $\sim_{\rm MB}$ in order to be able to abstract from sequences of exponentially timed τ-actions. As noted in Sect. 1, while it is not possible to get rid of an exponentially timed τ-action executed between a pair of exponentially timed non-τ-actions, a sequence of exponentially timed τ-actions may be indistinguishable at steady state from a single exponentially timed τ-action having the same average duration as the sequence.

We say that $P \in \mathbb{P}_{\rm M}$ is stable if $P \stackrel{\tau,\lambda}{\not\longrightarrow}_{\rm M} P'$ for all λ and P', otherwise we say that P is unstable. In the latter case, we say that P is fully unstable iff, whenever $P \xrightarrow{a,\lambda}_{\rm M} P'$, then $a = \tau$. We denote by $\mathbb{P}_{\rm M,fu}$ and $\mathbb{P}_{\rm M,nfu}$ the sets of process terms of $\mathbb{P}_{\rm M}$ that are fully unstable and not fully unstable, respectively.

The most natural candidates as sequences of exponentially timed τ-actions to abstract are those labeling computations that traverse fully unstable states.

Definition 3. *Let $n \in \mathbb{N}_{>0}$ and $P_1, P_2, \ldots, P_{n+1} \in \mathbb{P}_{\rm M}$. A computation c of length n from P_1 to P_{n+1} having the form $P_1 \xrightarrow{\tau,\lambda_1}_{\rm M} P_2 \xrightarrow{\tau,\lambda_2}_{\rm M} \ldots \xrightarrow{\tau,\lambda_n}_{\rm M} P_{n+1}$ is reducible iff $P_i \in \mathbb{P}_{\rm M,fu}$ for all $i = 1, \ldots, n$.* ■

If reducible, the computation c above can be reduced to a single exponentially timed τ-transition whose rate is obtained from the positive real value below:

$$\boxed{probtime(c) \; = \; \left(\prod_{i=1}^{n} \frac{\lambda_i}{rate(P_i, \tau, \mathbb{P}_{\rm M})} \right) \cdot \left(\sum_{i=1}^{n} \frac{1}{rate(P_i, \tau, \mathbb{P}_{\rm M})} \right)}$$

by leaving its first factor unchanged and taking the reciprocal of the second one. This value is a measure of the execution probability of c (first factor: product of the execution probabilities of the transitions of c) and the average duration of c (second factor: sum of the average sojourn times in the states traversed by c).

Notice that we consider only reducible computations of finite length. This will be enough to distinguish between fully unstable process terms that must be told apart. In fact, assuming $\lambda_1 \neq \lambda_2$, it makes sense to discriminate between $<\tau, \lambda_1>.P$ and $<\tau, \lambda_2>.P$ if P can reach a non-fully-unstable process term. By contrast, an external observer cannot see any difference between two divergent process terms like $\mathrm{rec}\, X : <\tau, \lambda_1>.X$ and $\mathrm{rec}\, X : <\tau, \lambda_2>.X$.

We are now ready to define a weak variant of $\sim_{\rm MB}$ such that (i) processes in $\mathbb{P}_{\rm M,nfu}$ are dealt with as in $\sim_{\rm MB}$ and (ii) the length of reducible computations from processes in $\mathbb{P}_{\rm M,fu}$ to processes in $\mathbb{P}_{\rm M,nfu}$ is abstracted away while preserving their execution probability and average duration. In the latter case, we need to lift measure *probtime* from individual reducible computations to multisets of reducible computations. More precisely, denoting by $\mathit{reducomp}(P, D, t)$ the multiset of reducible computations from $P \in \mathbb{P}_{\rm M,fu}$ to some P' in $D \subseteq \mathbb{P}_{\rm M}$ whose average duration is $t \in \mathbb{R}_{>0}$, we consider the following t-indexed multiset of sums of *probtime* measures:

$$\boxed{\mathit{pbtm}(P, D) \;=\; \bigcup_{t \in \mathbb{R}_{>0} \text{ s.t. } \mathit{reducomp}(P,D,t) \neq \emptyset} \{\!|\; \sum_{c \in \mathit{reducomp}(P,D,t)} \mathit{probtime}(c) \;|\!\}}$$

Notice that *pbtm* is not simply the multiset of the *probtime* measures of the various reducible computations from P to D. In that case, for example we would have $\mathit{pbtm}(<\tau, \lambda_1>.\underline{0} + <\tau, \lambda_2>.\underline{0}, \{\underline{0}\}) = \{\!| \frac{\lambda_1}{\lambda_1+\lambda_2} \cdot \frac{1}{\lambda_1+\lambda_2}, \frac{\lambda_2}{\lambda_1+\lambda_2} \cdot \frac{1}{\lambda_1+\lambda_2} |\!\}$ while $\mathit{pbtm}(<\tau, \lambda_1 + \lambda_2>.\underline{0}, \{\underline{0}\}) = \{\!| \frac{1}{\lambda_1+\lambda_2} |\!\}$, thus obtaining a behavioral equivalence that is not a conservative extension of $\sim_{\rm MB}$. On the other hand, *probtime* measures should be summed up only over reducible computations from P to D having the same average duration t. If this were not the case, then for instance we would have $\mathit{pbtm}(<\tau, \mu>.\underline{0}, \{\underline{0}\}) = \mathit{pbtm}(<\tau, \mu_1>.\underline{0} + <\tau, \mu_2>.<\tau, \gamma>.\underline{0})$ when $\frac{1}{\mu} = \frac{\mu_1}{\mu_1+\mu_2} \cdot \left(\frac{1}{\mu_1+\mu_2}\right) + \frac{\mu_2}{\mu_1+\mu_2} \cdot \left(\frac{1}{\mu_1+\mu_2} + \frac{1}{\gamma}\right)$, which would not be meaningful on the performance side as it would not induce an exact CTMC-level aggregation.

Definition 4. *An equivalence relation* $\mathcal{B} \subseteq (\mathbb{P}_{\rm M,nfu} \times \mathbb{P}_{\rm M,nfu}) \cup (\mathbb{P}_{\rm M,fu} \times \mathbb{P}_{\rm M,fu})$ *is a weak Markovian bisimulation iff for all* $(P_1, P_2) \in \mathcal{B}$*:*

- *If* $P_1, P_2 \in \mathbb{P}_{\rm M,nfu}$*, then for all* $a \in \mathit{Name}$ *and equivalence classes* $D \in \mathbb{P}_{\rm M}/\mathcal{B}$*:*
$$\mathit{rate}(P_1, a, D) \;=\; \mathit{rate}(P_2, a, D)$$
- *If* $P_1, P_2 \in \mathbb{P}_{\rm M,fu}$*, then for all equivalence classes* $D \in \mathbb{P}_{\rm M,nfu}/\mathcal{B}$*:*
$$\mathit{pbtm}(P_1, D) \;=\; \mathit{pbtm}(P_2, D)$$

Weak Markovian bisimilarity $\approx_{\rm MB}$ *is the union of all the weak Markovian bisimulations.* ■

Example 1. Consider the following two process terms:

$$\bar{P}_1 \;\equiv\; <\tau, \mu>.<\tau, \gamma>.Q \qquad (\text{or } \bar{P}_1 \;\equiv\; <\tau, \gamma>.<\tau, \mu>.Q)$$
$$\bar{P}_2 \;\equiv\; <\tau, \tfrac{\mu \cdot \gamma}{\mu + \gamma}>.Q$$

with $Q \in \mathbb{P}_{\rm M,nfu}$. As anticipated in Sect. 1, it turns out that $\bar{P}_1 \approx_{\rm MB} \bar{P}_2$ because:

$$\mathit{pbtm}(\bar{P}_1, [Q]_{\approx_{\rm MB}}) \;=\; \{\!|\, (1 \cdot 1) \cdot (\tfrac{1}{\mu} + \tfrac{1}{\gamma}) \,|\!\} \;=\; \{\!|\, 1 \cdot \tfrac{\mu+\gamma}{\mu \cdot \gamma} \,|\!\} \;=\; \mathit{pbtm}(\bar{P}_2, [Q]_{\approx_{\rm MB}})$$

where $[Q]_{\approx_{\rm MB}}$ is the equivalence class of Q with respect to $\approx_{\rm MB}$.

In general, for $l \in \mathbb{N}_{>0}$ we have that $<\tau, \mu>.<\tau, \gamma_1>. \dots .<\tau, \gamma_l>.Q$ is weakly Markovian bisimilar to $<\tau, \left(\frac{1}{\mu} + \frac{1}{\gamma_1} + \dots + \frac{1}{\gamma_l}\right)^{-1}>.Q$. ■

Example 2. Consider the following two process terms:

$$\bar{P}_3 \equiv <\tau, \mu>.(<\tau, \gamma_1>.Q_1 + <\tau, \gamma_2>.Q_2)$$

$$\bar{P}_4 \equiv <\tau, \frac{\gamma_1}{\gamma_1+\gamma_2} \cdot \left(\frac{1}{\mu} + \frac{1}{\gamma_1+\gamma_2}\right)^{-1}>.Q_1 + <\tau, \frac{\gamma_2}{\gamma_1+\gamma_2} \cdot \left(\frac{1}{\mu} + \frac{1}{\gamma_1+\gamma_2}\right)^{-1}>.Q_2$$

with $Q_1, Q_2 \in \mathbb{P}_{\mathrm{M,nfu}}$ and $Q_1 \not\approx_{\mathrm{MB}} Q_2$. Unlike action $<\tau, \mu>$ of $\bar{P}_1$ in the previous example, action $<\tau, \mu>$ of $\bar{P}_3$ is followed by a choice between two exponentially timed τ-actions. It turns out that $\bar{P}_3 \approx_{\mathrm{MB}} \bar{P}_4$ because:

$$pbtm(\bar{P}_3, [Q_1]_{\approx_{\mathrm{MB}}}) = \{\!| \frac{\gamma_1}{\gamma_1+\gamma_2} \cdot \left(\frac{1}{\mu} + \frac{1}{\gamma_1+\gamma_2}\right) |\!\} = pbtm(\bar{P}_4, [Q_1]_{\approx_{\mathrm{MB}}})$$

$$pbtm(\bar{P}_3, [Q_2]_{\approx_{\mathrm{MB}}}) = \{\!| \frac{\gamma_2}{\gamma_1+\gamma_2} \cdot \left(\frac{1}{\mu} + \frac{1}{\gamma_1+\gamma_2}\right) |\!\} = pbtm(\bar{P}_4, [Q_2]_{\approx_{\mathrm{MB}}})$$

In general, for $n \in \mathbb{N}_{>0}$ we have that $<\tau, \mu>.(<\tau, \gamma_1>.Q_1 + \dots + <\tau, \gamma_n>.Q_n)$ is weakly Markovian bisimilar to $<\tau, \frac{\gamma_1}{\gamma_1+\dots+\gamma_n} \cdot \left(\frac{1}{\mu} + \frac{1}{\gamma_1+\dots+\gamma_n}\right)^{-1}>.Q_1 + \dots +$ $<\tau, \frac{\gamma_n}{\gamma_1+\dots+\gamma_n} \cdot \left(\frac{1}{\mu} + \frac{1}{\gamma_1+\dots+\gamma_n}\right)^{-1}>.Q_n$. ■

Example 3. Consider the following two process terms:

$$\bar{P}_5 \equiv <\tau, \mu_1>.<\tau, \gamma>.Q_1 + <\tau, \mu_2>.<\tau, \gamma>.Q_2$$

$$\bar{P}_6 \equiv <\tau, \frac{\mu_1}{\mu_1+\mu_2} \cdot \left(\frac{1}{\mu_1+\mu_2} + \frac{1}{\gamma}\right)^{-1}>.Q_1 + <\tau, \frac{\mu_2}{\mu_1+\mu_2} \cdot \left(\frac{1}{\mu_1+\mu_2} + \frac{1}{\gamma}\right)^{-1}>.Q_2$$

with $Q_1, Q_2 \in \mathbb{P}_{\mathrm{M,nfu}}$ and $Q_1 \not\approx_{\mathrm{MB}} Q_2$ as before. Unlike $\bar{P}_1$ and $\bar{P}_3$ in the previous two examples, $\bar{P}_5$ starts with a choice between two exponentially timed τ-actions, each of which is followed by the same action $<\tau, \gamma>$. It turns out that $\bar{P}_5 \approx_{\mathrm{MB}} \bar{P}_6$ because:

$$pbtm(\bar{P}_5, [Q_1]_{\approx_{\mathrm{MB}}}) = \{\!| \frac{\mu_1}{\mu_1+\mu_2} \cdot \left(\frac{1}{\mu_1+\mu_2} + \frac{1}{\gamma}\right) |\!\} = pbtm(\bar{P}_6, [Q_1]_{\approx_{\mathrm{MB}}})$$

$$pbtm(\bar{P}_5, [Q_2]_{\approx_{\mathrm{MB}}}) = \{\!| \frac{\mu_2}{\mu_1+\mu_2} \cdot \left(\frac{1}{\mu_1+\mu_2} + \frac{1}{\gamma}\right) |\!\} = pbtm(\bar{P}_6, [Q_2]_{\approx_{\mathrm{MB}}})$$

In general, for $n \in \mathbb{N}_{>0}$ we have that $<\tau, \mu_1>.<\tau, \gamma>.Q_1 + .. + <\tau, \mu_n>.<\tau, \gamma>.Q_n$ is weakly Markovian bisimilar to $<\tau, \frac{\mu_1}{\mu_1+\dots+\mu_n} \cdot \left(\frac{1}{\mu_1+\dots+\mu_n} + \frac{1}{\gamma}\right)^{-1}>.Q_1 + \dots +$ $<\tau, \frac{\mu_n}{\mu_1+\dots+\mu_n} \cdot \left(\frac{1}{\mu_1+\dots+\mu_n} + \frac{1}{\gamma}\right)^{-1}>.Q_n$. The equivalence holds even if the derivative terms of actions $<\tau, \mu_i>$, $1 \leq i \leq n$, start with a choice among several exponentially timed τ-actions instead of a single exponentially timed τ-action, provided that all these derivative terms have the same total exit rate γ. ■

Example 4. We now examine all possible variants of $\bar{P}_5$ related to actions $<\tau, \gamma>$ and we show that none of these variants allows for any reduction because it is not possible to preserve execution probabilities or average durations.
Firstly, consider the following two process terms:

$$\bar{P}_7 \equiv <\tau, \mu_1>.<\tau, \gamma_1>.Q_1 + <\tau, \mu_2>.<\tau, \gamma_2>.Q_2$$

$$\bar{P}_8 \equiv <\tau, \frac{\mu_1}{\mu_1+\mu_2} \cdot \left(\frac{1}{\mu_1+\mu_2} + \frac{1}{\gamma_1}\right)^{-1}>.Q_1 + <\tau, \frac{\mu_2}{\mu_1+\mu_2} \cdot \left(\frac{1}{\mu_1+\mu_2} + \frac{1}{\gamma_2}\right)^{-1}>.Q_2$$

with $\gamma_1 \neq \gamma_2$. Then $\bar{P}_7 \not\approx_{\mathrm{MB}} \bar{P}_8$ because for instance:

$$pbtm(\bar{P}_7, [Q_1]_{\approx_{\rm MB}}) = \{\!|\ \frac{\mu_1}{\mu_1+\mu_2} \cdot \left(\frac{1}{\mu_1+\mu_2} + \frac{1}{\gamma_1}\right)\ |\!\}$$

$$pbtm(\bar{P}_8, [Q_1]_{\approx_{\rm MB}}) = \{\!|\ \frac{\frac{\mu_1}{\mu_1+\mu_2} \cdot \left(\frac{1}{\mu_1+\mu_2} + \frac{1}{\gamma_1}\right)^{-1}}{\frac{\mu_1}{\mu_1+\mu_2} \cdot \left(\frac{1}{\mu_1+\mu_2} + \frac{1}{\gamma_1}\right)^{-1} + \frac{\mu_2}{\mu_1+\mu_2} \cdot \left(\frac{1}{\mu_1+\mu_2} + \frac{1}{\gamma_2}\right)^{-1}} \cdot \frac{1}{\frac{\mu_1}{\mu_1+\mu_2} \cdot \left(\frac{1}{\mu_1+\mu_2} + \frac{1}{\gamma_1}\right)^{-1} + \frac{\mu_2}{\mu_1+\mu_2} \cdot \left(\frac{1}{\mu_1+\mu_2} + \frac{1}{\gamma_2}\right)^{-1}}\ |\!\}$$

Secondly, consider the following two process terms:

$$\bar{P}_9 \equiv <\tau, \mu_1>.<\tau, \gamma>.Q_1 + <\tau, \mu_2>.Q_2$$

$$\bar{P}_{10} \equiv <\tau, \frac{\mu_1}{\mu_1+\mu_2} \cdot \left(\frac{1}{\mu_1+\mu_2} + \frac{1}{\gamma}\right)^{-1}>.Q_1 + <\tau, \mu_2>.Q_2$$

Then $\bar{P}_9 \not\approx_{\rm MB} \bar{P}_{10}$ because for instance:

$$pbtm(\bar{P}_9, [Q_2]_{\approx_{\rm MB}}) = \{\!|\ \frac{\mu_2}{\mu_1+\mu_2} \cdot \frac{1}{\mu_1+\mu_2}\ |\!\}$$

$$pbtm(\bar{P}_{10}, [Q_2]_{\approx_{\rm MB}}) = \{\!|\ \frac{\mu_2}{\frac{\mu_1}{\mu_1+\mu_2} \cdot \left(\frac{1}{\mu_1+\mu_2} + \frac{1}{\gamma}\right)^{-1} + \mu_2} \cdot \frac{1}{\frac{\mu_1}{\mu_1+\mu_2} \cdot \left(\frac{1}{\mu_1+\mu_2} + \frac{1}{\gamma}\right)^{-1} + \mu_2}\ |\!\} \quad \blacksquare$$

Proposition 1. *Let $I \neq \emptyset$ be a finite set, $J_i \neq \emptyset$ be a finite set for all $i \in I$, and $P_{i,j} \in \mathbb{P}_{\rm M}$ for all $i \in I$ and $j \in J_i$. Then:*

$$\sum_{i \in I} <\tau, \mu_i>. \sum_{j \in J_i} <\tau, \gamma_{i,j}>.P_{i,j} \approx_{\rm MB} \sum_{i \in I} \sum_{j \in J_i} <\tau, \frac{\mu_i}{\sum_{k \in I} \mu_k} \cdot \frac{\gamma_{i,j}}{\sum_{h \in J_i} \gamma_{i,h}} \cdot \left(\frac{1}{\sum_{k \in I} \mu_k} + \frac{1}{\sum_{h \in J_i} \gamma_{i,h}}\right)^{-1}>.P_{i,j}$$

whenever $\sum_{j \in J_{i_1}} \gamma_{i_1,j} = \sum_{j \in J_{i_2}} \gamma_{i_2,j}$ for all $i_1, i_2 \in I$. ■

3.1 Congruence Property

Let us investigate the compositionality of $\approx_{\rm MB}$ with respect to MPC operators.

Proposition 2. *Let $P_1, P_2 \in \mathbb{P}_{\rm M}$. Whenever $P_1 \approx_{\rm MB} P_2$, then:*

1. *$<a, \lambda>.P_1 \approx_{\rm MB} <a, \lambda>.P_2$ for all $<a, \lambda> \in Act_{\rm M}$.*
2. *$P_1/H \approx_{\rm MB} P_2/H$ for all $H \subseteq Name_{\rm v}$.* ■

Similar to weak bisimilarity for nondeterministic processes, $\approx_{\rm MB}$ is not a congruence with respect to the alternative composition operator. The problem has to do with fully unstable process terms: e.g., $<\tau, \mu>.<\tau, \gamma>.\underline{0} \approx_{\rm MB} <\tau, \frac{\mu \cdot \gamma}{\mu+\gamma}>.\underline{0}$ but $<\tau, \mu>.<\tau, \gamma>.\underline{0} + <a, \lambda>.\underline{0} \not\approx_{\rm MB} <\tau, \frac{\mu \cdot \gamma}{\mu+\gamma}>.\underline{0} + <a, \lambda>.\underline{0}$. In fact, if it were $a \neq \tau$ then we would have:

$$rate(<\tau, \mu>.<\tau, \gamma>.\underline{0} + <a, \lambda>.\underline{0}, \tau, [\underline{0}]_{\approx_{\rm MB}}) = 0$$

$$rate(<\tau, \frac{\mu \cdot \gamma}{\mu+\gamma}>.\underline{0} + <a, \lambda>.\underline{0}, \tau, [\underline{0}]_{\approx_{\rm MB}}) = \frac{\mu \cdot \gamma}{\mu+\gamma}$$

otherwise for $a = \tau$ we would have:

$$pbtm(<\tau, \mu>.<\tau, \gamma>.\underline{0} + <a, \lambda>.\underline{0}, [\underline{0}]_{\approx_{\rm MB}}) = \{\!|\ \frac{\mu}{\mu+\lambda} \cdot \left(\frac{1}{\mu+\lambda} + \frac{1}{\gamma}\right), \frac{\lambda}{\mu+\lambda} \cdot \frac{1}{\mu+\lambda}\ |\!\}$$

$$pbtm(<\tau, \frac{\mu \cdot \gamma}{\mu+\gamma}>.\underline{0} + <a, \lambda>.\underline{0}, [\underline{0}]_{\approx_{\rm MB}}) = \{\!|\ \frac{1}{\frac{\mu \cdot \gamma}{\mu+\gamma} + \lambda}\ |\!\}$$

The congruence violation with respect to the alternative composition operator can be prevented by adopting a construction analogous to the one used in [18] for weak bisimilarity over nondeterministic process terms. In other words, we have to apply the exit rate equality check also to fully unstable process terms, with the equivalence classes to consider being the ones with respect to $\approx_{\rm MB}$.

Definition 5. *Let $P_1, P_2 \in \mathbb{P}_{\mathrm{M}}$. We say that P_1 is weakly Markovian bisimulation congruent to P_2, written $P_1 \simeq_{\mathrm{MB}} P_2$, iff for all action names $a \in Name$ and equivalence classes $D \in \mathbb{P}_{\mathrm{M}} / \approx_{\mathrm{MB}}$:*

$$rate(P_1, a, D) \; = \; rate(P_2, a, D)$$ ■

Proposition 3. $\sim_{\mathrm{MB}} \subset \simeq_{\mathrm{MB}} \subset \approx_{\mathrm{MB}}$*, with* $\simeq_{\mathrm{MB}} = \approx_{\mathrm{MB}}$ *over* $\mathbb{P}_{\mathrm{M,nfu}}$. ■

Proposition 4. *Let $P_1, P_2 \in \mathbb{P}_{\mathrm{M}}$ and $<a, \lambda> \in Act_{\mathrm{M}}$. Then $<a, \lambda>.P_1 \simeq_{\mathrm{MB}} <a, \lambda>.P_2$ iff $P_1 \approx_{\mathrm{MB}} P_2$.* ■

It turns out that $\simeq_{\mathrm{MB}}$ is the coarsest congruence – with respect to all the operators of MPC as well as recursion – contained in $\approx_{\mathrm{MB}}$.

Theorem 1. *Let $P_1, P_2 \in \mathbb{P}_{\mathrm{M}}$. Whenever $P_1 \simeq_{\mathrm{MB}} P_2$, then:*

1. $<a, \lambda>.P_1 \simeq_{\mathrm{MB}} <a, \lambda>.P_2$ *for all* $<a, \lambda> \in Act_{\mathrm{M}}$.
2. $P_1 + P \simeq_{\mathrm{MB}} P_2 + P$ *and* $P + P_1 \simeq_{\mathrm{MB}} P + P_2$ *for all* $P \in \mathbb{P}_{\mathrm{M}}$.
3. $P_1 / H \simeq_{\mathrm{MB}} P_2 / H$ *for all* $H \subseteq Name_{\mathrm{v}}$. ■

Theorem 2. *Let $P_1, P_2 \in \mathbb{P}_{\mathrm{M}}$. Then $P_1 \simeq_{\mathrm{MB}} P_2$ iff $P_1 + P \approx_{\mathrm{MB}} P_2 + P$ for all $P \in \mathbb{P}_{\mathrm{M}}$.* ■

With regard to recursion, we need to extend $\simeq_{\mathrm{MB}}$ to open process terms in the usual way. The congruence proof is based on a notion of weak Markovian bisimulation up to $\approx_{\mathrm{MB}}$ inspired by the notion of Markovian bisimulation up to $\sim_{\mathrm{MB}}$ of [9]. It differs from its nondeterministic counterpart [18] due to the necessity of working with equivalence classes in this Markovian setting.

Definition 6. *Let $P_1, P_2 \in \mathcal{PL}_{\mathrm{M}}$ be process terms containing free occurrences of $k \in \mathbb{N}$ process variables $X_1, \ldots, X_k \in Var$ at most. We define $P_1 \simeq_{\mathrm{MB}} P_2$ iff $P_1\{Q_i \hookrightarrow X_i \mid 1 \le i \le k\} \simeq_{\mathrm{MB}} P_2\{Q_i \hookrightarrow X_i \mid 1 \le i \le k\}$ for all $Q_1, \ldots, Q_k \in \mathcal{PL}_{\mathrm{M}}$ containing no free occurrences of process variables.* ■

Definition 7. *Let $^+$ denote the operation of transitive closure for relations. A binary relation $\mathcal{B} \subseteq (\mathbb{P}_{\mathrm{M,nfu}} \times \mathbb{P}_{\mathrm{M,nfu}}) \cup (\mathbb{P}_{\mathrm{M,fu}} \times \mathbb{P}_{\mathrm{M,fu}})$ is a weak Markovian bisimulation up to $\approx_{\mathrm{MB}}$ iff for all $(P_1, P_2) \in \mathcal{B}$:*

– *If $P_1, P_2 \in \mathbb{P}_{\mathrm{M,nfu}}$, then for all $a \in Name$ and $D \in \mathbb{P}_{\mathrm{M}} / (\mathcal{B} \cup \mathcal{B}^{-1} \cup \approx_{\mathrm{MB}})^+$:*
$$rate(P_1, a, D) \; = \; rate(P_2, a, D)$$
– *If $P_1, P_2 \in \mathbb{P}_{\mathrm{M,fu}}$, then for all $D \in \mathbb{P}_{\mathrm{M,nfu}} / (\mathcal{B} \cup \mathcal{B}^{-1} \cup \approx_{\mathrm{MB}})^+$:*
$$pbtm(P_1, D) \; = \; pbtm(P_2, D)$$ ■

Proposition 5. *Let $\mathcal{B} \subseteq (\mathbb{P}_{\mathrm{M,nfu}} \times \mathbb{P}_{\mathrm{M,nfu}}) \cup (\mathbb{P}_{\mathrm{M,fu}} \times \mathbb{P}_{\mathrm{M,fu}})$. If $\mathcal{B}$ is a weak Markovian bisimulation up to $\approx_{\mathrm{MB}}$, then $(P_1, P_2) \in \mathcal{B}$ implies $P_1 \approx_{\mathrm{MB}} P_2$ for all $P_1, P_2 \in \mathbb{P}_{\mathrm{M}}$. Moreover $(\mathcal{B} \cup \mathcal{B}^{-1} \cup \approx_{\mathrm{MB}})^+ = \approx_{\mathrm{MB}}$.* ■

Theorem 3. *Let $P_1, P_2 \in \mathcal{PL}_{\mathrm{M}}$ be process terms containing free occurrences of $k \in \mathbb{N}$ process variables $X_1, \ldots, X_k \in Var$ at most. Whenever $P_1 \simeq_{\mathrm{MB}} P_2$, then* $\mathrm{rec}\, X_1 : \ldots : \mathrm{rec}\, X_k : P_1 \simeq_{\mathrm{MB}} \mathrm{rec}\, X_1 : \ldots : \mathrm{rec}\, X_k : P_2$. ■

3.2 Sound and Complete Axiomatization

$\simeq_{\rm MB}$ has a sound and complete axiomatization over the set $\mathbb{P}_{\rm M,nr}$ of nonrecursive process terms of $\mathbb{P}_{\rm M}$, which is shown below. The first four axioms are inherited from $\sim_{\rm MB}$. They are valid for $\simeq_{\rm MB}$ too because $\sim_{\rm MB} \subset \simeq_{\rm MB}$ as stated by Prop. 3. The fifth axiom characterizes $\simeq_{\rm MB}$. Its validity comes from Props. 1 and 4. The last four axioms are the usual distributive laws for the hiding operator.

$(\mathcal{A}_{\rm MB,1})$	$P_1 + P_2$	$=$	$P_2 + P_1$	
$(\mathcal{A}_{\rm MB,2})$	$(P_1 + P_2) + P_3$	$=$	$P_1 + (P_2 + P_3)$	
$(\mathcal{A}_{\rm MB,3})$	$P + \underline{0}$	$=$	P	
$(\mathcal{A}_{\rm MB,4})$	$<a, \lambda_1>.P + <a, \lambda_2>.P$	$=$	$<a, \lambda_1 + \lambda_2>.P$	

$(\mathcal{A}_{\rm MB,5})$

$$<a, \lambda>. \sum_{i \in I} <\tau, \mu_i>. \sum_{j \in J_i} <\tau, \gamma_{i,j}>.P_{i,j} = <a, \lambda>. \sum_{i \in I} \sum_{j \in J_i} <\tau, \frac{\mu_i}{\mu} \cdot \frac{\gamma_{i,j}}{\gamma} \cdot \left(\frac{1}{\mu} + \frac{1}{\gamma}\right)^{-1}>.P_{i,j}$$

if: $I \neq \emptyset$ is a finite index set
$J_i \neq \emptyset$ is a finite index set for all $i \in I$
$\mu = \sum_{i \in I} \mu_i$
$\gamma = \sum_{j \in J_i} \gamma_{i,j}$ for all $i \in I$

$(\mathcal{A}_{\rm MB,6})$	$\underline{0}/H$	$=$	$\underline{0}$	
$(\mathcal{A}_{\rm MB,7})$	$(<a, \lambda>.P)/H$	$=$	$<a, \lambda>.(P/H)$	if $a \notin H$
$(\mathcal{A}_{\rm MB,8})$	$(<a, \lambda>.P)/H$	$=$	$<\tau, \lambda>.(P/H)$	if $a \in H$
$(\mathcal{A}_{\rm MB,9})$	$(P_1 + P_2)/H$	$=$	$P_1/H + P_2/H$	

Regarding completeness, we show that every nonrecursive process term can be transformed into a normal form that abstracts from the order of summands (consistent with the first two axioms), rules out all null summands and occurrences of the hiding operator (consistent with the third and the last four axioms), and does not allow for simplifications based on the fourth and fifth axioms.

Unlike the nondeterministic case, we cannot encode any saturation [18] in the normal form, as this would alter the quantitative behavior. In contrast, we elaborate on the result of Prop. 1 so as to discover that pairs of terms related by $\approx_{\rm MB}$ but not by $\simeq_{\rm MB}$ enjoy properties concerned with $\mathcal{A}_{\rm MB,4}$ and $\mathcal{A}_{\rm MB,5}$.

Lemma 1. *Let $P_1, P_2 \in \mathbb{P}_{\rm M,nr}$. If $P_1 \approx_{\rm MB} P_2$ but $P_1 \not\simeq_{\rm MB} P_2$, then P_1 and P_2 are respectively of the form:*

$$\sum_{i \in I_1} <\tau, \mu_{1,i}>.P_{1,i} \quad \text{and} \quad \sum_{i \in I_2} <\tau, \mu_{2,i}>.P_{2,i}$$

where $I_1 \neq \emptyset, I_2 \neq \emptyset$ are finite index sets and at least one process term in $\{P_{1,i} \mid i \in I_1\} \cup \{P_{2,i} \mid i \in I_2\}$ is fully unstable. Moreover:

$$\{D \in \mathbb{P}_{\rm M}/\approx_{\rm MB} \mid \exists i \in I_1.\, P_{1,i} \in D\} \neq \{D \in \mathbb{P}_{\rm M}/\approx_{\rm MB} \mid \exists i \in I_2.\, P_{2,i} \in D\} \quad \blacksquare$$

Proposition 6. *Let $P_1, P_2 \in \mathbb{P}_{\rm M,nr}$. If $P_1 \approx_{\rm MB} P_2$ but $P_1 \not\simeq_{\rm MB} P_2$, then at least one between P_1 and P_2 is of the form:*

$$\sum_{i \in I} <\tau, \mu_i>. \sum_{j \in J_i} <\tau, \gamma_{i,j}>.P_{i,j}$$

where $I \neq \emptyset$ is a finite index set, $J_i \neq \emptyset$ is a finite index set for all $i \in I$, and one of the following two properties holds:

– $\sum_{j \in J_{i_1}} <\tau, \gamma_{i_1,j}>.P_{i_1,j} \approx_{\rm MB} \sum_{j \in J_{i_2}} <\tau, \gamma_{i_2,j}>.P_{i_2,j}$ *for all* $i_1, i_2 \in I$.
– $\sum_{j \in J_{i_1}} \gamma_{i_1,j} = \sum_{j \in J_{i_2}} \gamma_{i_2,j}$ *for all* $i_1, i_2 \in I$. ■

Definition 8. *We say that* $P \in \mathbb{P}_{\rm M,nr}$ *is in* $\simeq_{\rm MB}$*-normal-form iff either* P *is* $\underline{0}$ *or* P *is of the form* $\sum_{i \in I} <a_i, \lambda_i>.P_i$ *with* I *finite and nonempty,* P *initially minimal with respect to* $\mathcal{A}_{\rm MB,4}$*,* $<a_i, \lambda_i>.P_i$ *initially minimal with respect to* $\mathcal{A}_{\rm MB,5}$ *for all* $i \in I$*, and* P_i *in* $\simeq_{\rm MB}$*-normal-form for all* $i \in I$. ■

In the definition above, by P initially minimal with respect to $\mathcal{A}_{\rm MB,4}$ we mean that P does not contain any two summands like the ones on the left-hand side of $\mathcal{A}_{\rm MB,4}$. Likewise, by $<a_i, \lambda_i>.P_i$ initially minimal with respect to $\mathcal{A}_{\rm MB,5}$ we mean that $<a_i, \lambda_i>.P_i$ does not match the left-hand side of $\mathcal{A}_{\rm MB,5}$.

It is worth noting that by virtue of Prop. 6, whenever it holds $P_1 \approx_{\rm MB} P_2$ but $P_1 \not\simeq_{\rm MB} P_2$, then at least one between P_1 and P_2 is not in $\simeq_{\rm MB}$-normal-form because of a violation of initial minimality with respect to $\mathcal{A}_{\rm MB,4}$ or $\mathcal{A}_{\rm MB,5}$. This fact will be exploited in the proof of the completeness part of Thm. 4 below.

Lemma 2. *For all* $P \in \mathbb{P}_{\rm M,nr}$ *there exists* $Q \in \mathbb{P}_{\rm M,nr}$ *in* $\simeq_{\rm MB}$*-normal-form such that* $\mathcal{A}_{\rm MB} \vdash P = Q$. ■

Theorem 4. *Let* $P_1, P_2 \in \mathbb{P}_{\rm M,nr}$*. Then* $\mathcal{A}_{\rm MB} \vdash P_1 = P_2 \iff P_1 \simeq_{\rm MB} P_2$. ■

3.3 Exactness at Steady State

Weak Markovian bisimulation equivalence and the coarsest congruence contained in it are more liberal than Markovian bisimilarity, because they allow every sequence of exponentially timed τ-actions to be considered equivalent to a single exponentially timed τ-action having the same average duration. From a stochastic viewpoint, this amounts to approximating a hypoexponentially or Erlang distributed random variable with an exponentially distributed random variable having the same expected value. From a performance evaluation viewpoint, this can be exploited to assess more quickly properties expressed in terms of the mean time to certain events by working on an aggregated CTMC. [1]

However, it is not necessarily the case that those properties are the only ones preserved by the two weak Markovian behavioral equivalences that we have introduced. This can be investigated by examining the CTMC-level aggregation induced by such equivalences. If it turns out to be an exact CTMC-level aggregation, then the two weak Markovian behavioral equivalences preserve all the performance characteristics. This means that they can be used for reducing the size of models with an underlying CTMC-based semantics without altering the value of any performance measure. [2]

[1] To be precise, since the Markov property of the original CTMC is not preserved but the aggregated stochastic process is still assumed to be a CTMC, it would be more appropriate to call the aggregation a pseudo-aggregation [22].

[2] To be precise, this is true as long as rewards [15,7] are not associated with fully unstable states and exponentially timed τ-transitions, which is quite reasonable.

Since $\sim_{\mathrm{MB}}$ is consistent with ordinary lumpability and the axiomatization of $\simeq_{\mathrm{MB}}$ differs from the one of $\sim_{\mathrm{MB}}$ only for $\mathcal{A}_{\mathrm{MB},5}$, we can concentrate on this axiom when studying the CTMC-level aggregation induced by $\approx_{\mathrm{MB}}$ and $\simeq_{\mathrm{MB}}$. If we view $\mathcal{A}_{\mathrm{MB},5}$ without its two $<a, \lambda>$ actions as the following rewriting rule:

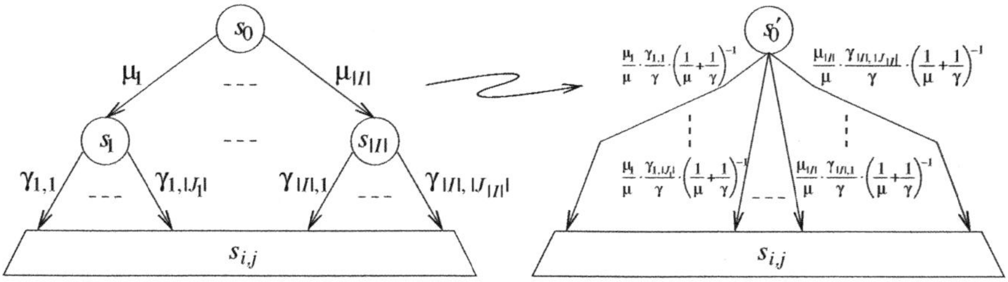

then we say that a CTMC is W-lumpable iff a portion of its state space matches the left-hand side of the rewriting rule, in which case it is replaced by the right-hand side where the topmost $1 + |I|$ states have been merged into a single one.

Theorem 5. *W-lumpability is exact at steady state, i.e., the stationary probability of being in a macrostate of a CTMC obtained via W-lumpability is the sum of the stationary probabilities of being in one of the constituent microstates of the CTMC from which the reduced one has been obtained.* ■

Unlike ordinary lumpability and T-lumpability, W-lumpability is not exact at transient state, which means that properties expressed in terms of transient state probabilities may not be preserved. A counterexample is provided by process terms $\bar{P}_1$ and $\bar{P}_2$ of Ex. 1, because the sum of the probabilities of being in one of the first two states of $[\![\bar{P}_1]\!]_{\mathrm{M}}$ at time $t \in \mathbb{R}_{>0}$ is different from the probability of being in the first state of $[\![\bar{P}_2]\!]_{\mathrm{M}}$ at the same time instant.

In fact, the probability of being in that state of $[\![\bar{P}_2]\!]_{\mathrm{M}}$ at that time is the probability that the exponentially distributed duration of its outgoing transition is greater than t, which is $1 - (1 - \mathrm{e}^{-\frac{\mu \cdot \gamma}{\mu + \gamma} \cdot t}) = \mathrm{e}^{-\frac{\mu \cdot \gamma}{\mu + \gamma} \cdot t}$ and reduces to $\mathrm{e}^{-\frac{\mu}{2} \cdot t}$ when $\mu = \gamma$. In contrast, the probability of being in one of those states of $[\![\bar{P}_1]\!]_{\mathrm{M}}$ at that time is the probability that the hypoexponentially (for $\mu \neq \gamma$) or Erlang (for $\mu = \gamma$) distributed duration of their two consecutive outgoing transitions is greater than t, which is $1 - (1 - \frac{\gamma}{\gamma - \mu} \cdot \mathrm{e}^{-\mu \cdot t} + \frac{\mu}{\gamma - \mu} \cdot \mathrm{e}^{-\gamma \cdot t}) = \frac{\gamma}{\gamma - \mu} \cdot \mathrm{e}^{-\mu \cdot t} - \frac{\mu}{\gamma - \mu} \cdot \mathrm{e}^{-\gamma \cdot t}$ or $1 - (1 - (1 + \mu \cdot t) \cdot \mathrm{e}^{-\mu \cdot t}) = (1 + \mu \cdot t) \cdot \mathrm{e}^{-\mu \cdot t}$, respectively.

3.4 Decidability in Polynomial Time

In order to check whether $P_1 \approx_{\mathrm{MB}} P_2$ or $P_1 \simeq_{\mathrm{MB}} P_2$ for any two finite-state processes $P_1, P_2 \in \mathbb{P}_{\mathrm{M}}$, similar to other bisimulation equivalences we can employ a partition refinement algorithm based on [20] that:

- Starts with a partition containing one equivalence class for all the non-fully-unstable states of $[\![P_1]\!]_{\mathrm{M}}$ and $[\![P_2]\!]_{\mathrm{M}}$ and one equivalence class for all the fully unstable states of $[\![P_1]\!]_{\mathrm{M}}$ and $[\![P_2]\!]_{\mathrm{M}}$.

- Refines the partition until a fixed point is reached, by applying the *rate*-based equality check for splitting the classes of non-fully-unstable states and the *pbtm*-based equality check for splitting the classes of fully unstable states.
- In the case of $\approx_{\mathrm{MB}}$, returns yes or no depending on whether P_1 and P_2 belong to the same equivalence class.
- In the case of $\simeq_{\mathrm{MB}}$, returns yes or no depending on whether P_1 and P_2 belong to the same equivalence class and satisfy the *rate*-based equality check with respect to all action names and equivalence classes.

Unlike weak bisimulation equivalences for nondeterministic processes and probabilistic processes – which can be decided in polynomial time for all pairs of finite-state processes with analogous partition refinement algorithms [16,2] – the above algorithm executes in polynomial time only when $[\![P_1]\!]_{\mathrm{M}}$ and $[\![P_2]\!]_{\mathrm{M}}$ have no cycles of exponentially timed internal transitions.

In fact, while cycles of nondeterministic internal transitions are unimportant from a quantitative viewpoint and cycles of probabilistic internal transitions can be left in the long run with probability 1 (if admitting a way out) or 0 (if connecting an absorbing set of states), cycles of exponentially timed internal transitions cause time to progress and hence cannot be ignored. In particular, their presence causes *pbtm* multisets to be infinite.

For instance, consider $P \equiv \, <\tau, \mu>. \mathrm{rec}\, X : (<\tau, \delta>.X + <\tau, \gamma>.Q)$ where $Q \in \mathbb{P}_{\mathrm{M,nfu}}$. Due to the presence in $[\![P]\!]_{\mathrm{M}}$ of the exponentially timed internal selfloop labeled with $<\tau, \delta>$, we have that $pbtm(P, [Q]_{\approx_{\mathrm{MB}}})$ contains infinitely many *probtime* values of the form $(\frac{\delta}{\delta+\gamma})^n \cdot \frac{\gamma}{\delta+\gamma} \cdot (\frac{1}{\mu} + (n+1) \cdot \frac{1}{\delta+\gamma})$ where $n \in \mathbb{N}$. If the selfloop were ignored, then P would erroneously be considered to be weakly Markovian bisimilar to $<\tau, \frac{\mu \cdot \gamma}{\mu+\gamma}>.Q$. Likewise, if only a finite number of *probtime* values were taken into account, then P would erroneously be considered to be weakly Markovian bisimilar to some process such that the average duration of all the reducible computations starting from that process is bounded.

4 Conclusion

In this paper, we have introduced a weak variant $\approx_{\mathrm{MB}}$ of Markovian bisimilarity for sequential processes with abstraction, which reduces any sequence of at least two exponentially timed τ-actions to a single exponentially timed τ-action whenever it is possible to preserve the average duration and the execution probability of the sequence. Then, we have characterized the coarsest congruence $\simeq_{\mathrm{MB}}$ contained in $\approx_{\mathrm{MB}}$ and we have found a sound and complete axiomatization for it, which has been exploited to prove the exactness at steady state of the induced CTMC-level aggregation for all the considered processes. Finally, we have established the decidability in polynomial time of $\approx_{\mathrm{MB}}$ and $\simeq_{\mathrm{MB}}$ over finite-state processes without cycles of exponentially timed internal actions.

From a different viewpoint, this paper confirms in a Markovian setting the adequacy of the construction used in [18] to single out the coarsest congruence included in a weak bisimulation equivalence for nondeterministic processes that is not closed with respect to alternative composition. It is worth noting that different approaches to the definition of a weak bisimulation equivalence like branching bisimulation [11] and dynamic/progressing bisimulation [19] are no longer suitable in a Markovian setting, as they are too demanding about matching exponentially timed internal actions.

On the stochastic side, we have assumed in this paper that an external observer can see the names of the actions that are performed by the processes as well as the average durations of those actions. Consequently, the external observer is not able to distinguish between an arbitrarily long sequence of exponentially timed τ-actions and a single exponentially timed τ-action having the same average duration. This leads to a state space reduction that preserves steady-state performance measures, but not transient-state performance measures except those that are expressed in terms of mean time to certain events. We point out that considering higher moments – e.g., the variance – of the duration of the actions in addition to its expectation may bring some advantage in terms of transient measure preservation. However, we would end up with a much finer Markovian behavioral equivalence, because the two random variables respectively quantifying the duration of a sequence of exponentially timed τ-actions and the duration of a single exponentially timed τ-action do not necessarily have the same variance when their expected values coincide.

4.1 Related Work

The idea of reducing a sequence of exponentially timed τ-actions to a single exponentially timed τ-action preserving the average duration of the action sequence was originally proposed in [14] through a relation called weak (Markovian) isomorphism. This was shown to be a congruence for both sequential and concurrent processes and to be exact at steady state only for a class of processes satisfying certain constraints on action synchronization. However, unlike $\approx_{\rm MB}$ and $\simeq_{\rm MB}$, no axiomatization was provided.

In this paper, we have revisited the idea at the basis of weak (Markovian) isomorphism in the less restrictive bisimulation framework. An important extension with respect to [14] is that we have considered not only individual sequences of exponentially timed τ-actions. In fact, we have addressed trees of exponentially timed τ-actions and we have established the conditions under which such trees can be reduced by preserving both the average duration and the execution probability of their branches. For instance, the pairs of process terms compared in Exs. 2 and 3 are not related by weak (Markovian) isomorphism. A further difference with respect to [14] is that W-lumpability is exact at steady state for all processes even if we consider a Markovian process calculus including parallel composition – as the memoryless property of exponential distributions allows us to take an interleaving view of concurrent process terms – without having to respect any constraint on action synchronization.

Another approach to abstracting from τ-actions in an exponentially timed setting comes from [8], where a variant of Markovian bisimilarity was defined that checks for exit rate equality with respect to all equivalence classes apart from the one including the processes under examination. Congruence and axiomatization results were provided for the proposed equivalence, and a logical characterization based on CSL was illustrated in [3]. However, unlike $\approx_{\mathrm{MB}}$ and $\simeq_{\mathrm{MB}}$, nothing was said about exactness.

4.2 Future Work

A drawback of $\simeq_{\mathrm{MB}}$ is that – unlike weak (Markovian) isomorphism – it is not a congruence with respect to parallel composition, a fact that limits its usefulness for compositional state space reduction purposes. We are currently working on a generalization of $\simeq_{\mathrm{MB}}$ inspired by [14] that exploits context-related information when traversing trees of exponentially timed τ-actions of concurrent processes. The idea is to allow for reductions also in the case of replicas of computations originated from a single process whose local states are fully unstable but are part of global states (due to parallel composition) that are not fully unstable [5].

Having two distinct weak Markovian bisimulation congruences – $\simeq_{\mathrm{MB}}$ and its generalization to concurrent processes – seems to be justified by the tradeoff that exists between achieving compositionality also over concurrent processes and ensuring exactness at steady state for all the considered processes without imposing any constraint.

Acknowledgment. This work has been funded by MIUR-PRIN project *PaCo – Performability-Aware Computing: Logics, Models, and Languages.*

References

1. Aldini, A., Bernardo, M., Corradini, F.: A Process Algebraic Approach to Software Architecture Design. Springer, Heidelberg (2010)
2. Baier, C., Hermanns, H.: Weak Bisimulation for Fully Probabilistic Processes. In: Grumberg, O. (ed.) CAV 1997. LNCS, vol. 1254, pp. 119–130. Springer, Heidelberg (1997)
3. Baier, C., Katoen, J.-P., Hermanns, H., Wolf, V.: Comparative Branching-Time Semantics for Markov Chains. Information and Computation 200, 149–214 (2005)
4. Bernardo, M.: Non-Bisimulation-Based Markovian Behavioral Equivalences. Journal of Logic and Algebraic Programming 72, 3–49 (2007)
5. Bernardo, M.: Weak Markovian Bisimulation Congruences and Exact CTMC-Level Aggregations for Concurrent Processes (in preparation)
6. Bernardo, M., Aldini, A.: Weak Markovian Bisimilarity: Abstracting from Prioritized/Weighted Internal Immediate Actions. In: Proc. of the 10th Italian Conf. on Theoretical Computer Science (ICTCS 2007), Rome, Italy, pp. 39–56. World Scientific (2007)
7. Bernardo, M., Bravetti, M.: Performance Measure Sensitive Congruences for Markovian Process Algebras. In: Theoretical Computer Science 290, 117–160 (2003)
8. Bravetti, M.: Revisiting Interactive Markov Chains. In: Proc. of the 3rd Int. Workshop on Models for Time-Critical Systems (MTCS 2002), Brno, Czech Republic. ENTCS, vol. 68(5), pp. 1–20. Elsevier (2002)

9. Bravetti, M., Bernardo, M., Gorrieri, R.: A Note on the Congruence Proof for Recursion in Markovian Bisimulation Equivalence. In: Proc. of the 6th Int. Workshop on Process Algebra and Performance Modelling (PAPM 1998), Nice, France, pp. 153–164 (1998)
10. Buchholz, P.: Exact and Ordinary Lumpability in Finite Markov Chains. Journal of Applied Probability 31, 59–75 (1994)
11. van Glabbeek, R.J., Weijland, W.P.: Branching Time and Abstraction in Bisimulation Semantics. Journal of the ACM 43, 555–600 (1996)
12. Hermanns, H. (ed.): Interactive Markov Chains. LNCS, vol. 2428. Springer, Heidelberg (2002)
13. Hermanns, H., Rettelbach, M.: Syntax, Semantics, Equivalences, and Axioms for MTIPP. In: Proc. of the 2nd Int. Workshop on Process Algebra and Performance Modelling (PAPM 1994), Technical Report 27-4, Erlangen, Germany, pp. 71–87 (1994)
14. Hillston, J.: A Compositional Approach to Performance Modelling. Cambridge University Press (1996)
15. Howard, R.A.: Dynamic Probabilistic Systems. John Wiley & Sons (1971)
16. Kanellakis, P.C., Smolka, S.A.: CCS Expressions, Finite State Processes, and Three Problems of Equivalence. Information and Computation 86, 43–68 (1990)
17. Markovski, J., Trcka, N.: Lumping Markov Chains with Silent Steps. In: Proc. of the 3rd Int. Conf. on Quantitative Evaluation of Systems (QEST 2006), Riverside, CA, pp. 221–230. IEEE-CS Press (2006)
18. Milner, R.: Communication and Concurrency. Prentice Hall (1989)
19. Montanari, U., Sassone, V.: Dynamic Congruence vs. Progressing Bisimulation for CCS. Fundamenta Informaticae 16, 171–199 (1992)
20. Paige, R., Tarjan, R.E.: Three Partition Refinement Algorithms. SIAM Journal on Computing 16, 973–989 (1987)
21. Rettelbach, M.: Probabilistic Branching in Markovian Process Algebras. Computer Journal 38, 590–599 (1995)
22. Rubino, G., Sericola, B.: Sojourn Times in Finite Markov Processes. Journal of Applied Probability 27, 744–756 (1989)
23. Stewart, W.J.: Introduction to the Numerical Solution of Markov Chains. Princeton University Press (1994)

Constraints for Service Contracts*

Maria Grazia Buscemi[1], Mario Coppo[2],
Mariangiola Dezani-Ciancaglini[2], and Ugo Montanari[3]

[1] IMT Institute for Advanced Studies, Lucca, Italy
[2] Dipartimento di Informatica, Università di Torino, Italy
[3] Dipartimento di Informatica, Università di Pisa, Italy

Abstract. This paper focuses on client-service interactions distinguishing between three phases: negotiate, commit and execute. The participants negotiate their behaviours, and if an agreement is reached they commit and start an execution which is guaranteed to respect the interaction scheme agreed upon. These ideas are materialised through a calculus of contracts enriched with semiring-based constraints, which allow clients to choose services and to interact with them in a safe way. A concrete representation of these constraints with logic programs is straightforward, thus reducing constraint solution (and consequently the establishment of a contract) to the execution of a logic program.

1 Introduction

Communicating systems have attracted a lot of interest since the eighties in several areas of computer science. In particular, verification methods have been studied in depth, given the difficulty of correctly designing communication protocols. Very successful has been the decision to abstract out from the actual data and their algorithmic complexity, and to focus on communication properties. Typically, the number of states of a system becomes finite (while possibly very large) and verification techniques based on model checking static analysis become feasible, and quite effective. The need of programming and maintaining *eternal*, highly decentralised systems (e.g. those considered by the FP7-FET initiative *Forever Yours*) has emphasised the need to extend to run time as much as possible the verification activity. The expected scenario shows the interacting partners to undergo a verification step: if it succeeds the interaction will be correct. The typical property to check is lack of deadlock, more precisely, stuck-freedom [20]: there are no messages waiting forever to be sent or sent messages which are never received, thus assuring that the interaction between partners will successfully end.

The key idea is to associate to a process an abstract description of its behaviour, and to check if the pairs[1] of processes which are expected to communicate do match. The extended version of [9] discusses several different approaches to the global and local descriptions of communication protocols. The most common styles used to model abstract process behaviour are session types and behavioural contracts.

* Work partially funded by the MIUR Project IPODS and by the EU IST Project ASCENS.

[1] The most common arrangement consists of pair of processes, but multi-party communication is also considered.

R. Bruni and V. Sassone (Eds.): TGC 2011, LNCS 7173, pp. 104–120, 2012.

Sessions and session types (first introduced in [22]) are built on pi-calculus [18]: the key idea is that types include information about the sequences of messages sent and received, and that type correctness, as defined by suitable type checking rules, assures stuck-freedom. We refer to [12] and [23] for overviews.

Behavioural contracts are CCS-like processes which describe the communications between clients and services. Many recent papers focus on the compatibility between clients and services and the safe replacements of services. The necessary control on communications is achieved by explicit interfaces [15] and message filtering [10]. Also suitable centralised or decentralised coordination strategies like orchestration [19] or choreography [6] are employed to guarantee safe communication.

There is a large literature on conditions for assuring stuck freedom in process calculi, see [14] and the references there. In particular [13,1] deal with the case of sessions.

We criticise the existing approaches on two grounds: (i) the result of the static analysis is on-off: either the interaction is acceptable or not. In most cases, an acceptable communication could be achieved, even if less appealing, by restricting partner behaviours. Ideally, the behaviour should be restricted the least, compatibly with stuck-freedom. Also, the execution should be monitored in such a way that only the harmless alternatives are left open; (ii) the verification process must be repeated for every pair of partners. It would be more convenient to split it into two parts: a *compilation* step, to be executed at deployment time, where the abstract behaviour is determined, and a *matching* step to be executed at run time, for every pair of partners willing to communicate.

We believe that an approach based on constraints would be able to overcome these difficulties: (i) the compilation step should generate a constraint modelling the behaviour; (ii) the matching step should be simply constraint composition, successful only if the resulting constraint is satisfiable; (iii) the actual execution should be monitored by ask-like guards, reminiscent of concurrent constraint programming [21]. The advantage of a constraint based approach is clear: the necessary constraints can be built inductively at compile time, composed at matching time and tested at run time taking advantage of concepts well-studied in the area of constraint programming.

To the best of our knowledge, the idea of using constraints for negotiating which interactions to choose, hence avoiding deadlocks and assuring success, is novel. Note that the kind of constraints we need is by no means peculiar: a constraint is essentially a set of computed answer substitutions of logic programming, once the Herbrand signature is suitably chosen. Similar constraints are used in [11] to assure quality of services.

We present our constraint system as an instantiation of the class of *named constraint semirings* [7], which have been originally proposed by two of the authors as the underlying structure of the cc-pi calculus [7], a process calculus for modelling agreements on non-functional parameters in a service oriented scenario. The target calculus we propose is close in spirit to the cc-pi calculus, except for the fact that the primitives of our target calculus are meant to model two-party interactions. [8] presents a prioritised version of cc-pi calculus, in which the non-deterministic choice is replaced by an operation that allows selecting an action if the corresponding constraint has a priority over the constraints of the alternative branches. Though priorities are assigned following different criteria, our optimised semantics is inspired by the prioritised cc-pi calculus.

Constraint semirings [3] are semirings with an idempotent additive operation and a commutative multiplicative operation. They generalise boolean algebra and are equipped with a partial ordering with 1 as maximal and 0 as minimal element. Semiring values model constraints: larger values are less constraining, multiplication means combination of constraints, sum returns the least upper bound. Constraint semirings are meant to define *soft* constraints, namely constraints which do not return only true or false, but more informative values instead (e.g., degree of preference, cost), thus allowing to extend paradigms such as concurrent constraint programming and constraint logic programming. In [5] a version of the soft concurrent constraint programming has been proposed for specification of SLA negotiations, basically with the same goal of the cc-pi calculus. *Named* constraint semirings in addition come equipped with an algebra of name permutations, which allows characterising the set of relevant names of a constraint as the support of a permutation, that is basically the minimum set of names that are changed by the permutation. Named constraint semirings inherit from ordinary constraints on the boolean semiring properties and efficient algorithms, like constraint propagation and dynamic programming.

As mentioned above, here we take advantage of a quite simple and standard named constraint semiring: the one employed by logic programming, where the Herbrand signature contains as many unary operations as actions and a constant to model termination. In the context of this paper we will use the term 'variable' rather than 'name' in conformance with the standard notation of logic programming. The semiring values are sets of assignments with Herbrand terms to all the variables. However, only the assignments to the tuples of variables forming the support are relevant. Existential quantification adds all the assignments where the restricted variable is assigned in all possible ways. The correspondence with logic programming is quite simple: given a set of clauses and a goal $P(x_1,\ldots,x_n)$, its semantics in terms of our constraint system is the set of all the ground instantiations of the goal which satisfy the clauses. The support is the set $\{x_1,\ldots,x_n\}$ or smaller. Goal composition is multiplication, while multiple clauses for the same goal model sum. Variables appearing in the body but not in the head of a clause are existentially quantified. In our notation, the effect of recursive clauses is obtained by an explicit fixpoint operator.

Our approach distinguishes three phases: NCE, Negotiate, Commit, Execute, where agents negotiate certain desired behaviours, but without any guarantee of success. However, if and when an agreement is reached (commit), under certain conditions a coordinated computation of the involved agents can start, which is guaranteed to have the properties agreed upon in the negotiation phase. We present a simple source calculus with client and service processes and with a semantics given in terms of labelled transition systems: the clients are recursive and can place nested service calls, while services are permanent (namely a service is not consumed by a call) and nonrecursive. The calculus is nondeterministic, with external choices (à la Milner [17] or, similarly, in the style of nondeterministic choices in logic programming), and a client-service behaviour which allows for more choices is considered better, provided they are stuck-free. A target calculus is then defined, where clients and services are compiled to, augmenting them with named constraint semirings, which encode their behaviour.

To understand our approach, let us first consider the case of a client without nested calls and with a single service. The source client is then compiled into a target client combined with a constraint with just one variable in its support, say x. The constraint is thus just a set of traces, representing the behaviour of the client. The compiled code is very similar to the source, except that its choices are guarded by *check* constructs, similar to the *ask* constructs of concurrent constraint programming, which enable the corresponding continuations only if the global constraint allows it. The source service is also compiled, yielding a constraint on y which represents its behaviour, but no check guards are included. The negotiation phase consists of multiplying the two constraints, and their result with the constraint[2] $x = y$. The resulting constraint contains exactly all the executions of the source client-service system which are not stuck. If the constraint is not 0, i.e. if it is not the empty set, the commit takes place, and the execution phase can start. Thanks to the check guards, the traces possible for the target client-service system are exactly those satisfying the constraint. Notice that while the client (service) compilation is static, and thus it does not fit in the NCE scheme, it does not depend on the particular service (client) partner it will be matched to. Thus the open endless requirement is here satisfied by the possibility of deploying new services (clients) without the need of any further modification of the existing services (clients).

For instance, let T be a client which offers the choice between co-actions $\overline{\alpha}$ and $\overline{\beta}$, and S be a service which offers the choice between actions α and γ, and only co-actions and actions interact successfully. Therefore T and S can safely interact only choosing $\overline{\alpha}$ and α, respectively. In our calculus we represent them as $T = \overline{\square}.\overline{\alpha}.\overline{\boxtimes}.\mathbf{0} + \overline{\beta}.\overline{\boxtimes}.\mathbf{0}$ and $S = \square.\alpha.\boxtimes + \gamma.\boxtimes$, where $\overline{\square}$ is service call, $\overline{\boxtimes}$ is call end, and $\square$, $\boxtimes$ are service and end acceptance. The interactions offered by T and S are represented, respectively, by the constraints $c = (x = \alpha(end)) \oplus (x = \beta(end))$ and $d = (y = \alpha(end)) \oplus (y = \gamma(end))$ (noting that we write constraints using only actions). It holds that $c \otimes d \otimes (x = y) = (x = \alpha(end)) \otimes (y = \alpha(end)) \otimes (x = y) \neq 0$, which reflects the fact that the only successful interaction between T and S is (over) α.

Let us now consider the general case of a client with nested calls and several services. Services are compiled in the usual way. The behaviour of the client, instead, must be represented by a constraint with several variables in the support. In fact, different service calls may not be independent: imagine that the client makes a choice in an inner call which must be matched by the corresponding service. Then the client returns to the outer level and makes another choice which must be matched this time by the service corresponding to the outer call. The two choices may be dependent, and this requirement is represented by a constraint with a two-variable support. Thus the ability of the constraint system of representing sets of tuples of traces allows us to guarantee stuck-freedom for complex client-service pairs, which at the best of our knowledge have not been considered in the literature by now.

An example of this kind of clients is $\overline{\square}.\overline{\alpha}.\overline{\square}.\overline{\beta}.(\overline{\gamma}.\overline{\boxtimes}.\overline{\delta}.\overline{\boxtimes}.\mathbf{0} + \overline{\mu}.\overline{\boxtimes}.\overline{\rho}.\overline{\boxtimes}.\mathbf{0})$, where the choices made by the two nested calls depend on each other. Such a dependency can arise, for instance, when modelling a traveller who asks both for a flight ($\overline{\alpha}$) to an airline company and for a room ($\overline{\beta}$) to a hotel in two alternative different dates. The

[2] Constraint $x = y$ has support $\{x, y\}$ and contains all assignments with the same term for x and y. In logic programming it is specified by the goal $eq(x, y)$ with the clause eq(x,x):-.

client request (room, flight) are represented respectively by actions $\bar{\gamma}$, $\bar{\delta}$ for one date and $\bar{\mu}$, $\bar{\rho}$ for the other date. This client offers then the choice between the pairs of traces $< \alpha(\delta(end)), \beta(\gamma(end)) >$ and $< \alpha(\rho(end)), \beta(\mu(end)) >$. The resulting constraint

$$(x_1 = \alpha(\delta(end))) \otimes (x_2 = \beta(\gamma(end))) \oplus (x_1 = \alpha(\rho(end))) \otimes (x_2 = \beta(\mu(end))),$$

with support $\{x_1, x_2\}$, obliges the run of related service call to be coherent.

Paper Summary. In the paper, the source and the target calculus are the content of §2 and §3, respectively. §4 presents the compilation from the first to the second calculus and states its soundness and completeness. §5 shows how to use the constraints in order to get most liberal interactions. Lastly §6 discuss some future developments.

2 Source Calculus

In choosing the source calculus we were guided by the requirement of having a minimal number of process operators to represent one client with (nested) service calls and a set of available services offering finite interactions. For this reason communications are atomic actions, all choices are external, client processes are recursive and can do nested calls, services are permanent, non recursive and each instance of a service can accept exactly one call. Let $\mathcal{A}$ be an infinite set of actions (ranged over by $\alpha, \beta, \ldots$) and

Table 1. Syntax of source client and service processes

Source client processes

$$P := \overline{\square}.P \;\Big|\; \bar{\alpha}.P \;\Big|\; P+P \;\Big|\; rec\, p.P \;\Big|\; \overline{\boxtimes}.P \;\Big|\; p \;\Big|\; \mathbf{0}$$

Source service processes

$$Q := \alpha.Q \;\Big|\; Q+Q \;\Big|\; \boxtimes$$

$\bar{\mathcal{A}}$ be an infinite set of disjoint co-actions (ranged over by $\bar{\alpha}, \bar{\beta}, \ldots$), with as usual $\bar{\bar{\alpha}} = \alpha$. The syntax of client and service processes is the content of Table 1. For the sake of readability we assume that client processes offer co-actions and service processes offer actions, $+$ is the external choice, $\overline{\square}$ is service call and $\overline{\boxtimes}, \boxtimes$ are end of call for client and service processes, respectively.

Table 2. LTS for the source calculus

$$\frac{\square.Q \in \mathbb{S}_s}{\overline{\square}.P \xrightarrow{[} [P \mid Q]} \;(s\text{-}call) \qquad \lambda.W \xrightarrow{\lambda} W \;(s\text{-}action) \qquad \overline{\boxtimes}.P \xrightarrow{\overline{\boxtimes}} P \;(s\text{-}end)$$

$$\frac{W \xrightarrow{\phi} W'}{W + W_1 \xrightarrow{\phi} W'} \;(s\text{-}choice) \qquad \frac{P \xrightarrow{\bar{\alpha}} P' \quad Q \xrightarrow{\alpha} Q'}{P \mid Q \xrightarrow{\alpha} P' \mid Q'} \;(s\text{-}interaction)$$

$$\frac{P \xrightarrow{\overline{\boxtimes}} P' \quad Q \downarrow_{\boxtimes}}{[P \mid Q] \xrightarrow{]} P'} \;(s\text{-}up) \qquad \frac{U \xrightarrow{\psi} U'}{[U] \xrightarrow{\psi} [U']} \;(s\text{-}box) \qquad \frac{V \xrightarrow{\psi} V'}{V \mid Q \xrightarrow{\psi} V' \mid Q} \;(s\text{-}parallel)$$

Recursive processes cannot have nested calls (namely, service calls cannot occur under the scope of the *rec* operator). We will consider recursive processes modulo fold/unfold, i.e. we identify the processes $rec\,p.P$ and $P[^{rec\,p.P}/_p]$.

A *client* is a client process of the shape $\overline{\square}.P$. A client is *balanced* if each $\overline{\square}$ is followed by exactly one corresponding $\overline{\boxtimes}$ in each branch. We use T to range over balanced clients.

A *service* is a service process prefixed by $\square$ (representing call acceptance), i.e. it has the shape $\square.Q$. We use S to range over services.

We consider *systems* formed by one balanced client and a set $\mathbb{S}_s$ of available services. The interaction between a client and a service is represented by boxing, i.e. enclosing in square brackets, the parallel composition of the client process which follows the call with the interacting service process (see rule (*s-call*) in Table 2). A client is always interacting with the "copy" of a service in the innermost "box" and outermost instances of services have to wait until an (*s-up*) rule is applied. Therefore by reducing a balanced client we will get a box containing either the parallel composition of a client process and a service process or the parallel composition of a box and a service process. We get then the following syntax for systems V:

$$V ::= T \;\big|\; [U] \;\big|\; \mathbf{0} \qquad\qquad U ::= P \mid Q \;\big|\; [U] \mid Q$$

Since we want to compare reductions in the source and in the target calculus we give the operational semantics of both calculi via labelled transition systems (LTSs). We say that the process Q *exhibits the service end* (notation $Q\downarrow_{\boxtimes}$) if either Q is $\boxtimes$ or Q is the sum of two processes one of which exhibits the service end.
Table 2 gives the reduction rules for the source calculus, where W denotes a client process or a service process, $\lambda \in \mathcal{A} \cup \overline{\mathcal{A}}$, $\phi \in \{[,\overline{\boxtimes}\} \cup \mathcal{A} \cup \overline{\mathcal{A}}$ and $\psi \in \{[,]\} \cup \mathcal{A}$. The symmetric rule with respect to $+$ has been omitted. Rule (*s-interaction*) is non standard since α labels the transition in the conclusion, but this does not harm the intended semantics of the calculus. In fact processes do not compose in parallel, systems do not emit outputs, hence no further synchronisation on α is possible. Rule (*s-up*) terminates the execution of a call leaving the client process which follows this call one nesting level up.
Let σ be a strings on $\{[,]\} \cup \mathcal{A}$. We define $V \stackrel{\sigma}{\Longrightarrow} V'$ if
- either $\sigma = \varepsilon$ and $V = V'$
- or $\sigma = \psi\sigma'$ and $V \stackrel{\psi}{\longrightarrow}\stackrel{\sigma'}{\Longrightarrow} V'$.

We write $V \Downarrow^{may}$ if $\exists\sigma$ such that $V \stackrel{\sigma}{\Longrightarrow} \mathbf{0}$, i.e. if the system V can reduce to the inert client $\mathbf{0}$.
Example 1. A possible reduction of the client $T = \overline{\square}.\overline{\alpha}.\overline{\square}.\overline{\beta}.(\overline{\gamma}.\overline{\boxtimes}.\overline{\delta}.\overline{\boxtimes}.\mathbf{0} + \overline{\mu}.\overline{\boxtimes}.\overline{\rho}.\overline{\boxtimes}.\mathbf{0})$ with a set of services including $\{\square.\alpha.\delta.\boxtimes,\ \square.\beta.(\gamma.\boxtimes + \nu.\boxtimes)\}$ is:

$$\begin{aligned}
T &\stackrel{[}{\longrightarrow} [\overline{\alpha}.\overline{\square}.\overline{\beta}.(\overline{\gamma}.\overline{\boxtimes}.\overline{\delta}.\overline{\boxtimes}.\mathbf{0} + \overline{\mu}.\overline{\boxtimes}.\overline{\rho}.\overline{\boxtimes}.\mathbf{0}) \mid \alpha.\delta.\boxtimes]\\
&\stackrel{\alpha}{\longrightarrow} [\overline{\square}.\overline{\beta}.(\overline{\gamma}.\overline{\boxtimes}.\overline{\delta}.\overline{\boxtimes}.\mathbf{0} + \overline{\mu}.\overline{\boxtimes}.\overline{\rho}.\overline{\boxtimes}.\mathbf{0}) \mid \delta.\boxtimes]\\
&\stackrel{[}{\longrightarrow} [[\overline{\beta}.(\overline{\gamma}.\overline{\boxtimes}.\overline{\delta}.\overline{\boxtimes}.\mathbf{0} + \overline{\mu}.\overline{\boxtimes}.\overline{\rho}.\overline{\boxtimes}.\mathbf{0}) \mid \beta.(\gamma.\boxtimes + \nu.\boxtimes)] \mid \delta.\boxtimes]\\
&\stackrel{\beta}{\longrightarrow} [[(\overline{\gamma}.\overline{\boxtimes}.\overline{\delta}.\overline{\boxtimes}.\mathbf{0} + \overline{\mu}.\overline{\boxtimes}.\overline{\rho}.\overline{\boxtimes}.\mathbf{0}) \mid (\gamma.\boxtimes + \nu.\boxtimes)] \mid \delta.\boxtimes]\\
&\stackrel{\gamma}{\longrightarrow} [[\overline{\boxtimes}.\overline{\delta}.\overline{\boxtimes}.\mathbf{0} \mid \boxtimes] \mid \delta.\boxtimes] \stackrel{]}{\longrightarrow} [\overline{\delta}.\overline{\boxtimes}.\mathbf{0} \mid \delta.\boxtimes] \stackrel{\delta}{\longrightarrow} [\overline{\boxtimes}.\mathbf{0} \mid \boxtimes] \stackrel{]}{\longrightarrow} \mathbf{0}
\end{aligned}$$

3 Target Calculus

The target calculus enriches the source calculus by introducing constraints, which are meant to prevent clients and services from initiating interactions that will eventually lead to deadlocks. The constraints we adopt coincide with those used in logic programming and form a *named constraint semiring* [7], which is a constraint semiring [3] with a notion of relevant names (here represented by variables) that allows plugging constraints into languages with an explicit concept of names. Below we recall some concepts that are used in the paper. We refer to [7,3,2] for a complete treatment.

3.1 Constraints

Assume a set of variables $\mathcal{V}$, ranged over by $x, y, \ldots$ Let Σ be a signature consisting of monadic functions representing actions plus a constant *end* (expressing successful end):

$$\Sigma = \{\alpha(\_), end \mid \alpha \in \mathcal{A}\}$$

A term is any expression that can be obtained from $\mathcal{V}$ and Σ; a ground term is a term that does not contain variables. The Herbrand Universe $\mathcal{H}$, ranged over by h, is the set of ground terms over Σ. A ground assignment is a total function s that maps variables to ground terms, namely $s : \mathcal{V} \to \mathcal{H}$. We define $s[h/x]$ by $s[h/x](x) = h$ and $s[h/x](y) = s(y)$ if $y \neq x$.

A *constraint* is a set of ground assignments and we let C, ranged over by c, be the set of all constraints. The operator $\exists x$ over a constraint c makes a variable x local in c, and is defined as $\exists x.c = \{s[h/x] \mid h \in \mathcal{H}, s \in c\}$. Of course, the ordering of $\exists x$'s in a constraint is irrelevant. Thus, we can conveniently write $\exists X$ in place of $\exists x_1, \ldots, \exists x_n$, for $X = \{x_1, \ldots, x_n\}$. The *support* of a constraint supp(c) is the minimum set $\mathcal{W}$ of variables such that $x \in \mathcal{W}$ implies that $\exists x.c \neq c$. Intuitively, the support of a constraint c contains all the variables which are *relevant* for c. The notion of support corresponds to the concept of set of free variables in process calculi. We abbreviate the notation for constraints by disregarding variables which are not in the support. Hence, by $(x = y)$ we write the constraint c with support $\{x, y\}$ that contains all assignments to the same ground term for x and y, namely $c = \{s_1, s_2, \ldots\}$ such that $s_i = [h_i/x, h_i/y, h_i'/z, \ldots]$, where $z \in \mathcal{V} \setminus \{x, y\}$. Similarly, by $(x = end)$ we denote the constraint consisting of all the assignments that map x to *end*. The set C can be proved to be a named constraint semiring [7] by taking product $\otimes$, sum $\oplus$, 0, and 1 as follows:

- $c \oplus d = c \cup d$;
- $c \otimes d = c \cap d$;
- The bottom element 0 is the empty set;
- The top element 1 is the constraint with empty support, i.e. the set of all ground assignments.

We also define a recursive operator $rec_x\mathsf{c}$ over constraints. Recursive constraint variables c_y contain (except for the binding construct) an extra variable that is used when unfolding the constraint. All occurrences of a c_y in c are bound by $rec_x\mathsf{c}$ in $rec_x\mathsf{c}.c$, independently of the variable appearing in the subscript. Recursive constraints are folded/unfolded using the following equation:

$$rec_x \mathsf{c}.\exists X.c = \exists X.c[{}^{c_i}/_{\mathsf{c}_{y_i}} \mid i \in I]$$

with $c_i = rec_{y_i} \mathsf{c}.\exists X.c[{}^{y_i}/_x]$ and y_i for $i \in I$ the variables occurring as indexes of c in c. The (solution of the) recursive constraint $rec_x\mathsf{c}.c$ can be defined as the least fixpoint associated to the above recursive equation, which exists because the operations on constraints are continuous and are defined over a domain that is a lattice.

It can be proved that finitary constraints like those ones generated by the compilation in §4 have a corresponding logic program [16]. As an example, consider a recursive constraint that amounts to assigning to a variable z an arbitrary number of α's followed by β and, subsequently, by *end*. Namely:

$$\begin{aligned} c = rec_z\mathsf{c}.\exists x_1, x_2, y_1, y_2.((z = x_1) \oplus (z = y_1))\otimes \\ (x_1 = \beta(x_2)) \otimes (x_2 = end) \otimes (y_1 = \alpha(y_2)) \otimes \mathsf{c}_{y_2} \end{aligned}$$

The logic program corresponding to c is given by the clauses below plus the goal `F(z)`:

F(x1) :- G1(x1)
F(y1) :- H1(y1)
G1(β(x2)) :- G2(x2)
G2(*end*).
H1(α(y2)) :- H2(y2)
H2(y2):- F(y2)

Note that the constraint c is generated by compiling the process of Example 4 in §4.

3.2 Syntax and Semantics

The syntax of target calculus (see Table 3) is analogous to the syntax of the source calculus apart for the introduction in the target processes of constraints $c \in \mathcal{C}$, as defined in §3.1, over possibly restricted variables. A service calls $\overline{\Box}\langle x\rangle$ includes the 'root' variable x of the constraint representing the interaction offered by the client to the invoked service. The process check $c_1.\mathsf{P}_1$, check $c_2.\mathsf{P}_2$ generalises the external choice by evolving to the process P_i if $c_i \otimes c \neq 0$, with c the current constraint and $i = 1,2$.

We use (X) where $X = \{x_1, \ldots, x_n\}$ to denote the restriction of the variables $x_1, \ldots, x_n$. We also write $(x_1, \ldots, x_n)$ for $(\{x_1, \ldots, x_n\})$. Throughout the paper, we simplify constraints by implicitly assuming that restriction on constraints coincides with existential operator (namely, $(x)\mathsf{P} \mid c$ has the same meaning of $\mathsf{P} \mid \exists x.c$, if x does not belong to the free variables of P), that restriction can be moved in and out of boxes, and that restrictions of variables not occurring in a term can be erased.

Akin to recursive constraints, recursive processes are also decorated with a source process recursion variable p. All occurrences of p^p_x in R are bound by $rec_y\mathsf{p}^p$ in $rec_y\mathsf{p}^p.\mathsf{R}$. We identify recursive processes via the following fold/unfold equation

$$rec_x \mathsf{p}^p.(X)c \mid \mathsf{P} = (X)c \mid \mathsf{P}[{}^{\mathsf{P}_i}/_{\mathsf{p}^p_{y_i}} \mid i \in I]$$

where $\mathsf{P}_i = rec_{y_i} p.(X)c[{}^{y_i}/_x] \mid \mathsf{P}[{}^{y_i}/_x]$ and y_i for $i \in I$ are all the variables occurring as indexes of p^p in P.

A *target client* has the shape $(X)c \mid \overline{\Box}\langle x\rangle.\mathsf{P}$. We use T to range over target clients. A *target service* has the shape $(X)c \mid \Box\langle x\rangle.\mathsf{Q}$. We use S to range over target services. *Target systems* V are the same as source systems apart for the fact that the parallel

Table 3. Syntax of target client and service processes

Target client processes
$\mathsf{P} := \overline{\Box}\langle x\rangle.\mathsf{P} \mid \overline{\alpha}.\mathsf{P} \mid (\mathtt{check}\ c_1.\mathsf{P}_1, \mathtt{check}\ c_2.\mathsf{P}_2) \mid \mathsf{p}^p_x \mid rec_x \mathsf{p}^p.\mathsf{R} \mid \mathsf{R} \mid \boxtimes.\mathsf{P} \mid \mathbf{0}$ $\quad \mathsf{R} := (X)c \mid \mathsf{P}$
Target service processes
$\mathsf{Q} := \alpha.\mathsf{Q} \mid \mathsf{Q}+\mathsf{Q} \mid \boxtimes$

composition of a client and a service includes a constraint and that a set X of variables can be restricted in a box (where restricted variables are bound in their scope):

$$\mathsf{U} ::= c \mid \mathsf{P} \mid \mathsf{Q} \;\Big|\; (X)[\mathsf{U}] \mid \mathsf{Q} \qquad \mathsf{V} ::= \mathsf{T} \;\Big|\; (X)[\mathsf{U}] \;\Big|\; (X)c \mid \mathbf{0}$$

Assume a set of available target services $\mathbb{S}_t$. We start by characterising the shape of the initial state of the LTS, which plays a key role in our theory as the existence of the initial state is meant to guarantee absence of deadlocks. To this purpose, we first define a function $I(\_)$ that applied to a target client gives the set Y of sets of variables which start the service calls. Each set of Y contains the variables corresponding to a different execution path. Note that Y cannot be infinite because recursive clients cannot have nested calls. For Y a collection of sets, we let $\{x\} \uplus Y = \{\{x\} \cup Z \,|\, Z \in Y\}$.

$$I(\overline{\Box}\langle x\rangle.\mathsf{P}) = \{x\} \uplus I(\mathsf{P}) \qquad I(\overline{\alpha}.\mathsf{P}) = I(\mathsf{P}) \qquad I(\mathbf{0}) = \{\emptyset\} \qquad I(\boxtimes.\mathsf{P}) = I(\mathsf{P})$$
$$I((\mathtt{check}\ c_1.\mathsf{P}_1, \mathtt{check}\ c_2.\mathsf{P}_2)) = I(\mathsf{P}_1) \cup I(\mathsf{P}_2) \quad I(\mathsf{p}^p_x) = \{\emptyset\} \quad I(rec_x \mathsf{p}^p.\mathsf{R}) = \{\emptyset\}$$

Assume a client T and a set of available services $\mathbb{S}_t$. Suppose

$$\mathsf{T} = (X)c_0 \mid \overline{\Box}\langle x\rangle.\mathsf{P} \qquad \mathbb{S}_t = \{(X_i)\ c_i \mid \Box\langle x_i\rangle.\mathsf{Q}_i \mid i \in I\}$$
$$I(\overline{\Box}\langle x\rangle.\mathsf{P}) = Y \qquad d_Y = \bigoplus_{Z \in Y} \bigotimes_{z \in Z} \bigoplus_{i \in I} \exists X_i.c_i \otimes (z = x_i)$$

If $c_0 \otimes d_Y \neq 0$ then $\mathtt{start}(\mathsf{T}, \mathbb{S}_t) = (X \cup \bigcup_{Z \in Y} Z)c_0 \otimes d_Y \mid \overline{\Box}\langle x\rangle.\mathsf{P}$ is the *initial state* of the LTS in Table 4.

Table 4. LTS for the target calculus

$$\frac{(X)d \mid \Box\langle x\rangle.\mathsf{Q} \in \mathbb{S}_t \quad c \otimes d \neq 0}{c \mid \overline{\Box}\langle x\rangle.\mathsf{P} \xrightarrow{[} (X)[c \otimes d \mid \mathsf{P} \mid \mathsf{Q}]}\ (t\text{-}call) \qquad c \mid \boxtimes.\mathsf{P} \xrightarrow{\boxtimes} c \mid \mathsf{P}\ (t\text{-}end)$$

$$c \mid \overline{\alpha}.\mathsf{P} \xrightarrow{\overline{\alpha}} c \mid \mathsf{P}\ (t\text{-}action_C) \qquad \alpha.\mathsf{Q} \xrightarrow{\alpha} \mathsf{Q}\ (t\text{-}action_S)$$

$$\frac{c \mid \mathsf{P}_i \xrightarrow{\varphi} \mathsf{W} \qquad c \otimes c_i \neq 0}{c \mid \mathtt{check}\ c_1.\mathsf{P}_1, \mathtt{check}\ c_2.\mathsf{P}_2 \xrightarrow{\varphi} \mathsf{W}}\ (t\text{-}check) \qquad \frac{\mathsf{Q} \xrightarrow{\alpha} \mathsf{Q}'}{\mathsf{Q}+\mathsf{Q}_1 \xrightarrow{\alpha} \mathsf{Q}'}\ (t\text{-}choice)$$

$$\frac{c \mid \mathsf{P} \xrightarrow{\overline{\alpha}} c \mid \mathsf{P}' \quad \mathsf{Q} \xrightarrow{\alpha} \mathsf{Q}'}{c \mid \mathsf{P} \mid \mathsf{Q} \xrightarrow{\alpha} c \mid \mathsf{P}' \mid \mathsf{Q}'}\ (t\text{-}interaction) \qquad \frac{c \mid \mathsf{P} \xrightarrow{\boxtimes} c \mid \mathsf{P}' \quad \mathsf{Q} \downarrow_{\boxtimes}}{[c \mid \mathsf{P} \mid \mathsf{Q}] \xrightarrow{]} c \mid \mathsf{P}'}\ (t\text{-}up)$$

$$\frac{\mathsf{U} \xrightarrow{\psi} \mathsf{U}'}{[\mathsf{U}] \xrightarrow{\psi} [\mathsf{U}']}\ (t\text{-}box) \qquad \frac{\mathsf{V} \xrightarrow{\psi} \mathsf{V}'}{\mathsf{V} \mid \mathsf{Q} \xrightarrow{\psi} \mathsf{V}' \mid \mathsf{Q}}\ (t\text{-}parallel) \qquad \frac{\mathsf{V} \xrightarrow{\psi} \mathsf{V}'}{(X)\mathsf{V} \xrightarrow{\psi} (X)\mathsf{V}'}\ (t\text{-}restr)$$

The consistency check $c_0 \otimes d_Y$ amounts to say that for at least one set $Z \in Y$, every service call corresponding to a $z \in Z$ can successfully interact with a service in $\mathbb{S}_t$. Remark that rule (*t-call*) is applied with c being the product of c_0, the constraint of the client, and the constraints d_Y of services interacting with service calls. Hence, the condition $c \otimes d \neq 0$ not only ensures that the interaction with the actual service will be successful, but also that any subsequent service call will find a suitable service.

In Table 4, $\varphi \in \{[, \boxtimes\} \cup \overline{\mathcal{A}}$, $\psi \in \{[,]\} \cup \mathcal{A}$, $\mathsf{Q} \downarrow_{\boxtimes}$ is defined as for source processes, W stands for $c \mid \mathsf{P}$ or $(X)[\mathsf{U}]$, and the symmetric rule with respect to $+$ has been omitted. The rules are the same as their homologous ones in the source calculus, taking into account that systems contain constraints. Rule (*t-check*) activates a process continuation P_i only if the corresponding guard is consistent with the constraint store (condition $c \otimes c_i \neq 0$).

Notably, recursion of target clients is useful also if initial states choose finite sets of finite services, since the target calculus mimics all reductions of the source calculus (Theorem 4).

We define $\mathsf{V} \stackrel{\sigma}{\Longrightarrow}$ as expected. A system V is *satisfied* if it is of the shape $(X)c \mid \mathbf{0}$ for some X, c. We define $\mathsf{V} \Downarrow^{must}$ if either V is satisfied or for all σ, V' such that $\mathsf{V} \stackrel{\sigma}{\Longrightarrow} \mathsf{V}'$ we have $\mathsf{V}' \Downarrow^{must}$, i.e. all computations terminate with a satisfied system.

Example 2. Take the client $\mathsf{T} = (x_0)c_0 \mid \overline{\square}\langle x_1 \rangle.\mathsf{P}$ with

$$c_0 = (x_1 = \alpha(x_0)) \otimes ((x_0 = \delta(end)) \oplus (x_0 = \rho(end)))$$

and

$$\mathsf{P} = \overline{\alpha}.(\texttt{check}\ (x_0 = \delta(end)).\overline{\delta}.\overline{\boxtimes}.\mathbf{0}, \texttt{check}\ (x_0 = \rho(end)).\overline{\rho}.\overline{\boxtimes}.\mathbf{0})$$

and the service

$$\mathsf{Q} = (y_0, y_1)d \mid \square\langle y_1 \rangle.\alpha.\delta.\boxtimes \text{ with } d = (y_1 = \alpha(y_0)) \otimes (y_0 = \delta(end))$$

Then we get $I(\overline{\square}\langle x_1 \rangle.\mathsf{P}) = \{\{x_1\}\} = Y$ and $d_Y = \exists y_0, y_1.d \otimes (x_1 = y_1)$.
The initial state of the client T for the set of services $\{\mathsf{Q}\}$ is

$$\texttt{start}(\mathsf{T}, \{\mathsf{Q}\}) = (x_0, x_1)c \mid \overline{\square}\langle x_1 \rangle.\mathsf{P}$$

where $c = c_0 \otimes \exists y_0, y_1.d \otimes (x_1 = y_1)$. It can reduce as follows:

$$\begin{aligned}
(x_0, x_1)c \mid \overline{\square}\langle x_1 \rangle.\mathsf{P} &\stackrel{[}{\longrightarrow} (x_0, x_1, y_0, y_1)[c \otimes d \mid \mathsf{P} \mid \alpha.\delta.\boxtimes] \\
&\stackrel{\alpha}{\longrightarrow} (x_0, x_1, y_0, y_1)[c \otimes d \mid \\
&\qquad \texttt{check}\ (x_0 = \delta(end)).\overline{\delta}.\overline{\boxtimes}.\mathbf{0}, \texttt{check}\ (x_0 = \rho(end)).\overline{\rho}.\overline{\boxtimes}.\mathbf{0} \mid \delta.\boxtimes] \\
&\stackrel{\delta}{\longrightarrow} (x_0, x_1, y_0, y_1)[c \otimes d \mid \overline{\boxtimes}.\mathbf{0} \mid \boxtimes] \\
&\stackrel{]}{\longrightarrow} (x_0, x_1, y_0, y_1)c \otimes d \mid \mathbf{0}
\end{aligned}$$

4 Compilation

We map the source calculus into the target calculus by adding constraints which take into account the interactions offered by the processes. This allows us to model the negotiation phase which precedes the choice of a service.

The compilation of services (Table 5) is simple, since the syntax of source and target processes is the same, when forgetting constraints and restrictions. This compilation adds an appropriate constraint for each process constructor by introducing a fresh variable x which is equated to *end* for $\boxtimes$, to $\alpha(y)$ for $\alpha.Q$ (where y is the variable introduced

Table 5. Compilation of services

$$\{[\boxtimes]\}_x = (x = end) \mid \boxtimes$$

$$\{[Q]\}_y = (X)c \mid \mathsf{Q} \text{ implies } \{[\alpha.Q]\}_x = (X \cup \{y\})c \otimes eq(x, \alpha(y)) \mid \alpha.\mathsf{Q}$$

$$\{[Q_1]\}_{x_1} = (X_1)c_1 \mid \mathsf{Q}_1 \text{ and } \{[Q_2]\}_{x_2} = (X_2)c_2 \mid \mathsf{Q}_2 \text{ imply } \{[Q_1 + Q_2]\}_x = (X_1 \cup X_2 \cup \{x_1\} \cup \{x_2\})c_1 \otimes c_2 \otimes ((x = x_1) \oplus (x = x_2)) \mid \mathsf{Q}_1 + \mathsf{Q}_2$$

$$\{[Q]\}_x = (X)c \mid \mathsf{Q} \text{ implies } \{[\Box.Q]\} = (X \cup \{x\})c \mid \Box\langle x\rangle.\mathsf{Q}$$

by the compilation of Q), to x_1 or x_2 for $Q_1 + Q_2$ (where x_1, x_2 are the variables introduced by the compilation of Q_1, Q_2, respectively). Lastly the compilation of a service $\Box.Q$ uses the variable x introduced by the compilation of Q to get $\Box\langle x\rangle.\mathsf{Q}$, where Q is the process obtained by compiling Q. All variables occurring in constraints are restricted in the resulting target service.

The compilation of clients (Table 6) is more complex, since client processes have nested calls, recursion and check expressions.

In order to deal with nested service calls we use a stack, represented as a list (*nesting list*), recording the variables which are the roots of the constraints in the encoding of the nested service calls which are still open and suspended (and then need to be closed); the head of this list contains the variable corresponding to the constraint root of the current call. We denote by `nil` the empty list, by ℓ an arbitrary list of variables or $\star$ and by $\texttt{cons}(x, \ell)$ the list with head x and tail ℓ. The nesting list of $\mathbf{0}$ is `nil`. For an interaction $\overline{\alpha}.P$ the nesting list is obtained just replacing the fresh variable x to the variable y which is the head of the nesting list in the compilation of process P. The compilation of the end $\boxtimes$ of a service call corresponds (being the compilation bottom-up) to the resumption of the interaction with a service after the end of the nested interaction. Then we push a new fresh variable on the nesting list corresponding to the last action of the nested call.

When compiling a recursion variable the list of nested service is not yet known (being the compilation one-step) and so is replaced by the placeholder $\star$. Going on in the compilation process, however, we check (via the function EQ defined in in Table 7) that the nesting lists of the suspended services in all branches of the recursive client are consistent (recall that no new service can be opened inside a recursive processes).

In the compilation of a choice we must assure that the suspended service calls will be resumed safely in the different branches (which could require different choices also in the paired services). This check is performed using the function $\mathcal{F}$ (see Table 7) which creates a new fresh nesting list starting from the nesting lists in the compilation of the two branches. The application of $\mathcal{F}$ to the lists ℓ_1, ℓ_2 is defined only if either ℓ_1, ℓ_2 have the same length or the shorter list terminates with $\star$. When defined the value of $\mathcal{F}(\ell_1, \ell_2)$ is a list of n fresh variables, where n is the maximum of the lengths of ℓ_1, ℓ_2, terminating with $\star$ if both ℓ_1, ℓ_2 terminate with $\star$ and with `nil` otherwise. Note that in a recursive process no $\boxtimes$ can occur along a path ending in a recursion variable.

The compilation of a service call uses the head variable of the nesting list to compile the call and continues with the tail of the nesting list going then one level up in the call nesting. Note that the compilation of a balanced client has `nil` as final nesting list.

Table 6. Compilation of balanced clients

$$[\![\mathbf{0}]\!]_{\mathtt{nil}} = \mathbf{0}$$

$$[\![p]\!]_{\mathtt{cons}(x,\star)} = \mathsf{c}^p_x \mid \mathsf{p}^p_x$$

$$[\![P]\!]_\ell = (X)c \mid \mathsf{P} \text{ implies } [\![\boxtimes.P]\!]_{\mathtt{cons}(x,\ell)} = (X)c \otimes eq(x, end) \mid \boxtimes.\mathsf{P}$$

$$[\![P]\!]_{\mathtt{cons}(y,\ell)} = (X)c \mid \mathsf{P} \text{ implies } [\![\overline{\alpha}.P]\!]_{\mathtt{cons}(x,\ell)} = (X \cup \{y\})c \otimes eq(x, \alpha(y)) \mid \overline{\alpha}.\mathsf{P}$$

$$[\![P]\!]_{\mathtt{cons}(x,\ell)} = (X)c \mid \mathsf{P} \text{ implies}$$
$$[\![rec\,p.P]\!]_{\mathtt{cons}(x,\ell)} = rec_x\, \mathsf{c}^p.(\exists X.c) \mid rec_x \mathsf{p}^p.((X)c[{}^1/_{\mathsf{c}^p_{y_i}} \mid i \in I] \mid \mathsf{P})$$

where y_i for $i \in I$ are all the variables occurring as indexes of c^p in c.

$$[\![P_1]\!]_{\ell_1} = (X_1)c_1 \mid \mathsf{P}_1 \text{ and } [\![P_2]\!]_{\ell_2} = (X_2)c_2 \mid \mathsf{P}_2 \text{ imply}$$
$$[\![P_1 + P_2]\!]_\ell =$$
$$(X_1 \cup X_2 \cup \mathcal{X}(\ell_1) \cup \mathcal{X}(\ell_2)\})c_1 \otimes c_2 \otimes (EQ(\ell,\ell_1) \oplus EQ(\ell,\ell_2)) \mid$$
$$(\mathtt{check}\ EQ(\ell,\ell_1).\mathsf{P}_1, \mathtt{check}\ EQ(\ell,\ell_2).\mathsf{P}_2)$$

where $\ell = \mathcal{F}(\ell_1, \ell_2)$

$$[\![P]\!]_{\mathtt{cons}(x,\ell)} = (X)c \mid \mathsf{P} \text{ implies } [\![\overline{\Box}.P]\!]_\ell = (X)c \mid \overline{\Box}\langle x\rangle.\mathsf{P}$$

The process resulting from the compilation of a recursion variable is the parallel of a constraint variable and a process variable. This is so since in compiling recursive processes we need to generate both a recursive "global" constraint (taking into account all possible unfoldings of the process) and a recursive process including a "local" copy of its constraint (associated to each specific unfolding). The global recursive constraint characterises the process behaviour and is used in searching for a contract of one available service. The local copy of the constraints in each recursive call is used instead to keep track of the overall solution in the `check` branches. In the local copy of the constraint the occurrences of the recursion constraint variable (which are free) can be replaced by 1 since the consistency with the global solution is assured by the replacements of the process variables.

The compilation of a choice needs to check if one or both of the two branches agree with the interactions offered by services. This is accomplished by requiring that the list $\mathcal{F}(\ell_1, \ell_2)$ can be equated to ℓ_1 or to ℓ_2 considering that $\star$ can be equated to any list (see the definition of EQ in Table 7).

All fresh variables which are introduced by the compilation are restricted in the resulting process, but for the variables occurring in the service calls. We use the function $\mathcal{X}$ defined in Table 7 to restrict the variables of nesting lists in the compilation of choices.

It is easy to verify that all consistency checks in the premises of the rules of Table 4 are decidable when the target processes are obtained by compiling source processes. Indeed, recursive clients cannot have nested calls and the unfolding of the recursive constraints generated by the compilation of clients can be *bounded* by the maximum depth of the constraints generated by compiling the services, which are finite.

Example 3. The compilation of the source client $\overline{\Box}.\alpha.\overline{\Box}.\beta.(\overline{\gamma}.\boxtimes.\overline{\delta}.\boxtimes.\mathbf{0} + \overline{\mu}.\boxtimes.\overline{\rho}.\boxtimes.\mathbf{0})$, which is introduced in Example 1, is the following target client:

$$
\begin{array}{l}
(x_0,y_0,t_1,t_0,v_1,v_0,w_1,w_0,z_1,z_0)(x_1 = \alpha(x_0)) \otimes (y_1 = \beta(y_0)) \otimes \\
((x_0 = t_1) \otimes (y_0 = v_1) \oplus (x_0 = w_1) \otimes (y_0 = z_1)) \otimes (v_1 = \gamma(v_0)) \otimes (v_0 = end) \otimes \\
(t_1 = \delta(t_0)) \otimes (t_0 = end) \otimes (z_1 = \mu(z_0)) \otimes (z_0 = end) \otimes (w_1 = \rho(w_0)) \otimes (w_0 = end) \mid \\
\overline{\Box}\langle x_1\rangle.\overline{\alpha}.\overline{\Box}\langle y_1\rangle.\overline{\beta}.(\texttt{check}\ (x_0 = t_1) \otimes (y_0 = v_1).\overline{\gamma}.\boxtimes.\overline{\delta}.\boxtimes.\mathbf{0}, \\
\qquad \texttt{check}\ (x_0 = w_1) \otimes (y_0 = z_1).\overline{\mu}.\boxtimes.\overline{\rho}.\boxtimes.\mathbf{0})
\end{array}
$$

which can be simplified to

$$
\begin{array}{l}
(x_0,y_0)(x_1 = \alpha(x_0)) \otimes (y_1 = \beta(y_0)) \otimes \\
((x_0 = \delta(end)) \otimes (y_0 = \gamma(end)) \oplus (x_0 = \rho(end)) \otimes (y_0 = \mu(end))) \mid \\
\overline{\Box}\langle x_1\rangle.\overline{\alpha}.\overline{\Box}\langle y_1\rangle.\overline{\beta}.(\texttt{check}\ (x_0 = \delta(end)) \otimes (y_0 = \gamma(end)).\overline{\gamma}.\boxtimes.\overline{\delta}.\boxtimes.\mathbf{0}, \\
\qquad \texttt{check}\ (x_0 = \rho(end)) \otimes (y_0 = \mu(end)).\overline{\mu}.\boxtimes.\overline{\rho}.\boxtimes.\mathbf{0})
\end{array}
$$

Note that this client can safely interact, for instance, with a set of (source) services including $\{\Box.\alpha.\delta.\boxtimes,\ \Box.\beta.(\gamma.\boxtimes + \nu.\boxtimes)\}$, while he is stuck when the set of services is $\{\Box.\alpha.\delta.\boxtimes,\ \Box.\beta.\mu.\boxtimes\}$.

Example 4. Compiling the recursive process $\overline{\Box}.rec\,p.(\overline{\alpha}.p + \overline{\beta}.\boxtimes.\mathbf{0})$ we get, after some simplifications:

$$
\begin{array}{l}
rec_x \mathsf{c}^p.\exists z.((x = \alpha(z)) \oplus (x = \beta(end))) \otimes \mathsf{c}^p_z \mid \\
\overline{\Box}\langle x\rangle.rec_x \mathsf{p}^p.(z)((x = \alpha(z)) \oplus (x = \beta(end))) \mid \\
\quad (\texttt{check}\ (x = \alpha(z)).\overline{\alpha}.\mathsf{p}^p_z, \texttt{check}\ (x = \beta(end)).\overline{\beta}.\mathbf{0})
\end{array}
$$

The recursive constraint after two unfoldings and some simplifications becomes:

$$
\begin{array}{l}
c = \exists z,z'.((x = \alpha(z)) \oplus (x = \beta(end))) \otimes ((z = \alpha(z')) \oplus (z = \beta(end))) \otimes \\
\qquad rec_{z'} \mathsf{c}^p.(z'')(((z' = \alpha(z'')) \oplus (z' = \beta(end))) \otimes \mathsf{c}^p_{z''})
\end{array}
$$

and the corresponding process:

$$
\begin{array}{l}
\overline{\Box}\langle x\rangle.(z)((x = \alpha(z)) \oplus (x = \beta(end))) \mid \\
(\texttt{check}\ (x = \alpha(z)).\overline{\alpha}.(z')((z = \alpha(z')) \oplus (z = \beta(end))) \mid \\
(\texttt{check}\ (z = \alpha(z')).\overline{\alpha}.rec_{z''}\mathsf{p}^p....., \texttt{check}\ (z = \beta(end)).\overline{\beta}.\mathbf{0}), \texttt{check}\ (x = \beta(end)).\overline{\beta}.\mathbf{0})
\end{array}
$$

If the service $(y)d \mid \Box\langle y\rangle.\alpha.\beta.\boxtimes$, where

$$
d = \exists w_0, w_1.\ (y = \alpha(w_0)) \otimes (w_0 = \beta(w_1)) \otimes (w_1 = end)
$$

is available, then the constraint $\exists y.c \otimes d \otimes (x = y)$ is equal to $(x = \alpha(\beta(end)))$. This solution is determined only by the (proper) unfolding of the recursive constraint of the client and the constraint of the service. Once the solution is determined the constraint of each unfolding is used only to assure the correct choices in the `check` branches. These constraints are propagated via the unfolding of the recursive process and so no unfolding of the outermost recursive constraint is needed in the process reduction.

It is easy to verify that our compilation is successful for all source clients and processes, but for the case of unbalanced clients.

Theorem 1. *Each balanced client and each service can be compiled.*

More interesting (and more complex to prove) is the fact that given a compiled client T and a set of available services $\mathbb{S}_t$, either $\texttt{start}(\mathsf{T},\mathbb{S}_t)$ is stuck or it always terminates.

Theorem 2. *If* T *is obtained by compiling a source client and* $\texttt{start}(\mathsf{T},\mathbb{S}_t) \stackrel{\sigma}{\Longrightarrow} \mathsf{V}$, *then* $\mathsf{V} \Downarrow^{must}$.

Table 7. Auxiliary functions for the compilation of client choices

$$\mathcal{F}(\ell_1,\ell_2)=\begin{cases}\mathtt{cons}(x,\mathcal{F}(\ell_1',\ell_2')) & \text{if } \ell_i=\mathtt{cons}(x_i,\ell_i') \quad i=1,2\\ \mathtt{cons}(x,\mathcal{F}(\ell_1',\star)) & \text{if } \ell_1=\mathtt{cons}(x_1,\ell_1') \text{ and } \ell_2=\star\\ \mathtt{cons}(x,\mathcal{F}(\ell_2',\star)) & \text{if } \ell_2=\mathtt{cons}(x_2,\ell_2') \text{ and } \ell_1=\star\\ \mathtt{nil} & \text{if } \ell_1=\ell_2=\mathtt{nil} \text{ or } \ell_1=\mathtt{nil} \text{ and } \ell_2=\star\\ & \text{or } \ell_2=\mathtt{nil} \text{ and } \ell_1=\star\\ \star & \text{if } \ell_1=\ell_2=\star\\ \text{undefined} & \text{otherwise.}\end{cases} \quad \text{where } x \text{ is fresh}$$

$$EQ(\ell_1,\ell_2)=\begin{cases}(x_1=x_2)\otimes EQ(\ell_1',\ell_2') & \text{if } \ell_i=\mathtt{cons}(x_i,\ell_i') \quad i=1,2\\ 1 & \text{if } \ell_1=\ell_2=\mathtt{nil} \text{ or } \ell_1=\star \text{ or } \ell_2=\star,\\ \text{undefined} & \text{otherwise.}\end{cases}$$

$$\begin{aligned}\mathcal{X}(\mathtt{nil}) &= \emptyset\\ \mathcal{X}(\star) &= \emptyset\\ \mathcal{X}(\mathtt{cons}(x,\ell)) &= \{x\}\cup\mathcal{X}(\ell)\end{aligned}$$

Comparing the reduction rules in Tables 2 and 4 it is easy to verify that the reductions of a target client obtained by compiling a source client correspond to reductions of the source client itself. We denote by $|\mathsf{V}|$ the source system obtained from the target system V by erasing all constraints and restrictions and by replacing checks by sums.

Theorem 3. *(Soundness) If $\mathbb{S}_t$ is obtained by compiling the source services of $\mathbb{S}_s$ and $\mathtt{start}([\![T]\!],\mathbb{S}_t)\stackrel{\sigma}{\Longrightarrow}\mathsf{V}$, then $T\stackrel{\sigma}{\Longrightarrow}|\mathsf{V}|$.*

The aim of the compilation is to avoid deadlocks, but also to preserve all successful interactions. This is the content of the following theorem, whose proof requires a precise analysis of the relations between the reduct of a target system and the compilation of the reduct of a source system.

Theorem 4. *(Completeness) If $\mathbb{S}_t$ is obtained by compiling the source services of $\mathbb{S}_s$ and $T\stackrel{\sigma}{\Longrightarrow}V$ and $V\Downarrow^{may}$, then there is V such that $\mathtt{start}([\![T]\!],\mathbb{S}_t)\stackrel{\sigma}{\Longrightarrow}\mathsf{V}$ and $|\mathsf{V}|=V$.*

5 Optimised Semantics

In the previous Section we have shown that the semantics of the target calculus ensures stuck-freedom provided that for each service call of a client there is a service which is able to complete an interaction with the client successfully. Nevertheless, during a client-service negotiation, it is desirable to have a mean to select the services that offer more choices to the client (considering all choices equally satisfactory), among all services which can successfully complete an interaction. This property holds for the target LTS only if there is a single service. By contrast, in the general case in which there is more than a 'complying' service available, the target LTS gives no guarantee on this respect. For instance, let $T=\overline{\square}.(\overline{\alpha}.\overline{\boxtimes}.\mathbf{0}+\overline{\beta}.\overline{\boxtimes}.\mathbf{0})$ be a client and $S_1=\square.(\alpha.\boxtimes+\beta.\boxtimes)$ and $S_2=\square.(\alpha.\boxtimes+\gamma.\boxtimes)$ be two services. According to the target semantics both S_1 and S_2 can be selected, as none of them would lead to a deadlock. Nevertheless, S_1 is somehow preferable as it additionally allows T to exhibit action $\overline{\beta}$. Clearly for the client $\overline{\Box}.(\overline{\alpha}.\boxtimes.\mathbf{0}+\overline{\gamma}.\boxtimes.\mathbf{0})$ the service S_2 is better.

We define an *optimised* LTS that is obtained from the LTS given in Table 4 by replacing rule (*t-call*) by the following rule:

$$\frac{(X)\,d \mid \Box\langle x\rangle.\mathsf{Q} \in \mathbb{S}_t \qquad \begin{array}{l} c\otimes d \neq 0 \text{ and } \nexists (X')\,d' \mid \Box\langle x\rangle.\mathsf{Q}' \in \mathbb{S}_t \text{ s.t.} \\ c\otimes d \subset c\otimes d' \end{array}}{c \mid \overline{\Box}\langle x\rangle.\mathsf{P} \xrightarrow{\lceil} (X)[c\otimes d \mid \mathsf{P} \mid \mathsf{Q}]} \quad (t\text{-}call')$$

Recall that constraints are sets of ground assignments, so they can be compared by inclusion. We denote by $\overset{\sigma}{\Longmapsto}$ reductions in the optimised LTS. Rule (*t-call'*) ensures that a service S is selected if it is *one of the best* possible services, namely such that there is no other service which offers the *same* successful interaction paths of S and some more. Clearly in general we can get incomparable constraints, like for example for the client $T' = \overline{\Box}.(\overline{\alpha}.(\overline{\mu}.\boxtimes.\mathbf{0}+\overline{\rho}.\boxtimes.\mathbf{0})+\overline{\beta}.\boxtimes.\mathbf{0}+\overline{\gamma}.\boxtimes.\mathbf{0})$ and the services $S_3 = \Box.(\alpha.\mu.\boxtimes + \beta.\boxtimes + \gamma.\boxtimes)$ and $S_4 = \Box.\alpha.(\mu.\boxtimes + \rho.\boxtimes)$. Note that the client T' has 3 successful paths choosing service S_3 and only 2 successful paths choosing service S_4, but these paths are incomparable. In such cases rule (*t-call'*) chooses in a non deterministic way.

We prove that the new target semantics is *optimal*, in the sense that by choosing one of best services at each service call we obtain a set of services that guarantee the same interactions with more choices to a client. For simplicity we consider only *unambiguous* source processes, i.e. processes whose sums start with two different actions (modulo commutativity and associativity of sums). In order to formally state our result we note that each target system V which is obtained by reducing the compilation of a client and it is not satisfied has the shape $\mathsf{V} = (X_n)[(X_{n-1})\ldots[(X_0)[c \mid \mathsf{P} \mid \mathsf{Q}_0]|\mathsf{Q}_1]\ldots\mathsf{Q}_n]$. This justifies the following definition.

Definition 1. *The constraint of the target system* V *(notation* $\mathtt{constr}(\mathsf{V})$*) is inductively defined by:*

$$\begin{array}{r} \mathtt{constr}((X)c \mid \mathbf{0}) = \mathtt{constr}(c \mid \mathsf{P} \mid \mathsf{Q}) = c \\ \mathtt{constr}((X)[\mathsf{U}] \mid \mathsf{Q}) = \mathtt{constr}((X)[\mathsf{U}]) = \mathtt{constr}(\mathsf{U}) \end{array}$$

Theorem 5. *If* T *is obtained by compiling a source client and* $\mathtt{start}(\mathsf{T},\mathbb{S}_t) \overset{\sigma}{\Longmapsto} \mathsf{V}$, *then there is no* V' *such that* $\mathtt{start}(\mathsf{T},\mathbb{S}_t) \overset{\sigma}{\Longrightarrow} \mathsf{V}'$ *and* $\mathtt{constr}(\mathsf{V}) \subset \mathtt{constr}(\mathsf{V}')$.

6 Conclusion and Future Work

In the paper we have augmented a client-service calculus with suitable constraints. A run time combination (multiplication in the simple cases) of client and service constraints guarantees that all and only the stuck-free interactions are possible. The constraints are exactly those of logic programming, and in fact a concrete representation of our constraints with logic programs and logic program combinations is straightforward. This property is comfortable from a theoretical point of view, since logic programs are well understood, but it is now appropriate to ask if it might be useful also from a practical point of view. We did not study the issue, which is outside the scope of this paper, but we can say that asking for satisfaction of the combined client-service constraint would be perfectly possible in any logic programming implementation, which would return an example of stuck-free interaction. Efficiency might depend on the exact way in which clauses are listed and parallel goals expanded. However it might be possible to devise an efficient algorithm (e.g. factorizing constraints and matching them top down breadth first) and to build a metainterpreter implementing the algorithm.

In the future, we plan to generalise the current target calculus by exploiting the formalism of Soft Constraint Logic Programming by Bistarelli, Montanari and Rossi [4]. In that paper, the ground semantics of a logic program (a goal and set of clauses) is not a set of ground assignments of the free variables of its goal, but rather a function from ground assignments to values of (another) constraint semiring. These values could give a measure of how acceptable the assignments are. Such functions, computed pointwise, form again a constraint semiring, and thus the formal treatment turns out simple and elegant. In particular the three semantics of logic programming (operational, denotational and model theoretical) can be defined also for soft constraint logic programming and proved equivalent. Specifically, in the context of the present paper a particular client-service computation would not be only possible or impossible, but it could be assigned an acceptance weight, which might itself be structured by measuring the quality of service obtained in the interaction. For instance these weights could be taken into account in the reduction rules (*t-call*) and (*t-choice*) in order to allow only executions which maximise client's satisfaction.

In a different direction we will extend both source and target calculi with internal choices in order to model interactions in which one participant takes one branch independently from what is offered by the other participant.

References

1. Bettini, L., Coppo, M., D'Antoni, L., De Luca, M., Dezani-Ciancaglini, M., Yoshida, N.: Global Progress in Dynamically Interleaved Multiparty Sessions. In: van Breugel, F., Chechik, M. (eds.) CONCUR 2008. LNCS, vol. 5201, pp. 418–433. Springer, Heidelberg (2008)
2. Bistarelli, S., Gadducci, F.: Enhancing constraints manipulation in semiring-based formalisms. In: Brewka, G., Coradeschi, S., Perini, A., Traverso, P. (eds.) ECAI 2006. FAIA, vol. 141, pp. 63–67. IOS Press (2006)
3. Bistarelli, S., Montanari, U., Rossi, F.: Semiring-based constraint satisfaction and optimization. Journal of the ACM 44(2), 201–236 (1997)
4. Bistarelli, S., Montanari, U., Rossi, F.: Semiring-based constraint logic programming: syntax and semantics. ACM Transactions on Programming Languages and Systems 23(1), 1–29 (2001)
5. Bistarelli, S., Santini, F.: A nonmonotonic soft concurrent constraint language for SLA negotiation. In: Aldini, A., ter Beek, M., Gadducci, F. (eds.) CILC 2008. ENTCS, vol. 236, pp. 147–162. Elsevier (2009)
6. Bravetti, M., Zavattaro, G.: A theory of contracts for strong service compliance. Mathematical Structures in Computer Science 19, 601–638 (2009)
7. Buscemi, M.G., Montanari, U.: CC-Pi: A Constraint-Based Language for Specifying Service Level Agreements. In: De Nicola, R. (ed.) ESOP 2007. LNCS, vol. 4421, pp. 18–32. Springer, Heidelberg (2007)

8. Buscemi, M.G., Montanari, U.: Qos negotiation in service composition. Journal of Logic and Algebraic Programming 80(1), 13–24 (2011)
9. Castagna, G., Dezani-Ciancaglini, M., Padovani, L.: On Global Types and Multi-party Sessions. In: Bruni, R., Dingel, J. (eds.) FMOODS/FORTE 2011. LNCS, vol. 6722, pp. 1–28. Springer, Heidelberg (2011)
10. Castagna, G., Gesbert, N., Padovani, L.: A theory of contracts for web services. ACM Transactions on Programming Languages and Systems 31, article n.19, 51 (2009)
11. Coppo, M., Dezani-Ciancaglini, M.: Structured Communications with Concurrent Constraints. In: Kaklamanis, C., Nielson, F. (eds.) TGC 2008. LNCS, vol. 5474, pp. 104–125. Springer, Heidelberg (2009)
12. Dezani-Ciancaglini, M., de'Liguoro, U.: Sessions and Session Types: An Overview. In: Laneve, C., Su, J. (eds.) WS-FM 2009. LNCS, vol. 6194, pp. 1–28. Springer, Heidelberg (2010)
13. Dezani-Ciancaglini, M., de'Liguoro, U., Yoshida, N.: On Progress for Structured Communications. In: Barthe, G., Fournet, C. (eds.) TGC 2007. LNCS, vol. 4912, pp. 257–275. Springer, Heidelberg (2008)
14. Kobayashi, N.: Type-Based Information Flow Analysis for the Pi-Calculus. Acta Informatica 42(4-5), 291–347 (2005)
15. Laneve, C., Padovani, L.: The Must Preorder Revisited: An Algebraic Theory for Web Services Contracts. In: Caires, L., Vasconcelos, V.T. (eds.) CONCUR 2007. LNCS, vol. 4703, pp. 212–225. Springer, Heidelberg (2007)
16. Lloyd, J.W.: Foundations of Logic Programming, 2nd Edition. Springer, Heidelberg (1987)
17. Milner, R.: A Calculus of Communicating Systems. Springer, Heidelberg (1980)
18. Milner, R.: Communicating and Mobile Systems: the Pi-Calculus. CUP (1999)
19. Padovani, L.: Contract-Directed Synthesis of Simple Orchestrators. In: van Breugel, F., Chechik, M. (eds.) CONCUR 2008. LNCS, vol. 5201, pp. 131–146. Springer, Heidelberg (2008)
20. Rajamani, S.K., Rehof, J.: Conformance Checking for Models of Asynchronous Message Passing Software. In: Brinksma, E., Larsen, K.G. (eds.) CAV 2002. LNCS, vol. 2404, pp. 166–179. Springer, Heidelberg (2002)
21. Saraswat, V.A., Rinard, M.C.: Concurrent constraint programming. In: Allen, F.E. (ed.) POPL 1990, pp. 232–245. ACM (1990)
22. Takeuchi, K., Honda, K., Kubo, M.: An Interaction-Based Language and Its Typing System. In: Halatsis, C., Philokyprou, G., Maritsas, D., Theodoridis, S. (eds.) PARLE 1994. LNCS, vol. 817, pp. 398–413. Springer, Heidelberg (1994)
23. Vasconcelos, V.T.: Sessions, from types to programming languages. EATCS Bulletin 103, 53–73 (2011)

Security of the Enhanced TCG Privacy-CA Solution

Liqun Chen[1], Ming-Feng Lee[2], and Bogdan Warinschi[2]

[1] HP Labs
liqun.chen@hp.com
[2] University of Bristol
{lee,bogdan}@cs.bris.ac.uk

Abstract. The privacy-CA solution (PCAS) designed by the Trusted Computing Group (TCG) was specified in TCG Trusted Platform Module (TPM) Specification Version 1.2 in 2003 and allows a TPM to obtain from a certification authority (CA) certificates on short term keys. The PCAS protocol is a lighter alternative to the Direct Anonymous Attestation (DAA) scheme for anonymous platform authentication.

The first rigorous analysis of PCAS was recently performed by Chen and Warinschi who focus on an unforgeability property (a TPM cannot obtain a certificate without the CA knowing its identity). The analysis in that paper holds only when no TPM is corrupt as, otherwise, an attack can be easily mounted. The authors also propose a stronger protocol (which we refer to as the enhanced PCAS or ePCAS) intended to withstand attacks of corrupt TPMs, but the protocol had never been formally analyzed.

The contribution of this paper is two-fold. We formalize three security properties desired from the ePCAS protocol. *Unforgeability* refines the earlier model for the case where TPMs may be corrupted. *Deniability* is the property that a CA cannot prove to a third party that he engaged in a run of the protocol with a certain TPM. Finally, *anonymity* is the property that third parties cannot tell the identity of TPMs based on the certificates that the TPM uses. The second contribution are proofs that the ePCAS protocol does indeed satisfy the security requirements that we formalize in this paper.

Keywords: Privacy-CA Solution, PCAS, TPM, Platform Attestation.

1 Introduction

The Trusted Platform Module (TPM) introduced by the industrial standard body Trusted Computing Group (TCG) [11], is a tamper-resistant hardware chip designed to enable computing to achieve better security than was previously possible. One of the main functionalities of TPMs is platform attestation. This property enables a platform to attest to certain statements about the configuration of the platform to a remote verifier. For the purpose of the attestation

R. Bruni and V. Sassone (Eds.): TGC 2011, LNCS 7173, pp. 121–141, 2012.

application, each TPM holds a unique long-term asymmetric key pair called Endorsement Key (EK) which is generated and certified by the TPM manufacturer.

This long-term asymmetric key cannot be directly and repeatedly used in the attestation process without raising serious privacy issues for the owner of the platform. For example, it may be possible for any third party to identify a communication as belonging to the particular TPM that owns EK, or link two different communications as pertaining to the same TPM. Both scenarios are undesirable: the key requirement of platform attestation is that it preserves the privacy (i.e. anonymity and unlinkability of the communications) of the platform.

The privacy-CA solution (PCAS for short) was one of the protocols specified in the TCG TPM specification version 1.2 [10]. This specification has been adopted by ISO/IEC as an international standard [9]. PCAS is a special type of public key certification services using a privacy-preserving Certificate Authority (privacy-CA or CA for short). The protocol enables a TPM to create a number of short-term signature/verification key pairs, called Attestation Identity Keys (AIKs) and obtain certificates on AIKs which are issued by a certificate authority. An AIK can later be used as attestation keys (by, for example, signing statements regarding the state of the TPM). Through the use of these short-term keys, the privacy of TPM is therefore maitained: anonymity holds since an AIK does not reveal the real identity of the TPM; unlinkability holds if each AIK is used once only. Authentication but link between EK and AIK is achieved by introducing a privacy-preserving Certificate Authority whose responsibility is to issue a certificate on an AIK provided by a TPM as long as the TPM is in possession of a valid EK.

The difference between a conventional public key certificate and the PCAS certificate is that the certificate on AIK only provides the assurance that this AIK belongs to a valid TPM but does not reveal which TPM. The CA is required to maintain the link between the EK and AIK privately, and PCAS does not provide any cryptographic evidence, which enables the CA to convince a third party that a certain pair (EK,AIK) belongs to the same TPM. In a typical conventional service, a CA issues a certificate on a new public key after checking a signature of the key under an already known public key and also checking a possession proof of the corresponding secret key. In PCAS the CA is given neither a cryptographic binding between the EK and AIK nor the standard proof of possession of the secret part of the AIK. However, by using an encryption/decryption algorithm and a challenge-response protocol based on encryption, the CA authenticates the TPM. A genuine TPM is responsible for using its AIKs correctly. In order to ensure this, the EK is restricted to be an encryption/decryption key pair rather than a signature/verification key pair.

PCAS is an alternative to the Direct Anonymous Attestation (DAA) protocol [2]. DAA achieves a group signature-like functionality: it allows parties (TPMs) to join a group of signers and produce signatures on behalf of the group. The signatures cannot be linked to the parties (not even by the group manager) . From this perspective DAA achieves stronger anonymity guarantees than PCAS:

the protocol allows CAs to essentially sign AIKs of TPMs in a way that hides the individual TPM's identity.

Although PCAS does not achieve the same security level as a DAA scheme does, PCAS is suitable for many applications, particularly those that naturally involve privacy-CAs. One important merit of PCAS, in contrast with DAA, is that its design idea is simple and easily understandable by non-cryptographers. Moreover, there is also a sort of platform attestation protocols which combine DAA and privacy-CA certificate [6]. Such protocols provide trusted privacy-CA certificate and security level of DAA.

Due to their relevance to practice many of the protocols used in the context of TPMs have been thoroughly analyzed using the methods of modern provable security. For example, the standard security notions for group signatures were developed in [4,5], the standard security notions and analysis for DAA schemes were addressed in multiple papers, e.g. [2,3,7]. However, the security of PCAS protocol was never rigourously analyzed till recently [8]. The authors propose a security model where they define a notion of unforgeability for the certificate issued by the CA and show that the PCAS protocol meets the security notion if the underlying primitives meet standard security requirements. Importantly, the model proposed in that paper only considers the case where all TPMs are honest and the authors describe an attack against unforgeability if even one TPM is corrupt.

To cope with this scenario, the authors propose a new protocol, to which we refer to as the enhanced PCAS protocol, or the ePCAS protocol. The protocol is significantly simpler than the DAA protocol, can be implemented with no modifications to the existing TPM functionalities but its security guarantees have not been properly investigated.

Contributions. The focus of this paper is on the ePCAS protocol. We start with a refinement of the security model of [8] which we adapt to account for the setting specific to ePCAS (as opposed to PCAS) and allow for corrupt TPMs. As far as security models are concerned, we also formulate two additional important security properties identified by the TCG as important for TPMs. Third-party anonymity captures the idea that i) the AIKs certified by the CA cannot be linked to the TPM by third parties (the CA learns the AIKs associated to the different TPMs) ii) the use of two different AIKs by the same TPM cannot be linked by third parties. To model third-party anonymity, we consider an experiment that involves an adversary who interacts with multiple TPMs and CAs and has absolute control of the communication. We model in this way the conservative assumption that the hosts of the TPMs may act completely maliciously. Furthermore, we allow the adversary to corrupt as many CAs and TPMs as it wants. The adversary has then to distinguish between certificates produced for one out of two TPMs. The next security notion is deniability. Informally, deniability in this context requires that it should not be possible for the a CA to convince a third-party that a certain TPM was involved in a run of the protocol with that CA. Here, we propose two variants. In strong deniability we consider an active adversary who controls all of the communication between

CAs and TPMs. In weak deniability we consider a passive adversary who can only obtain transcripts of the communication. Moreover, in both games, we allow the adversary to collude with all CAs. Deniability (in each of the two scenarios) requires the existence of a simulator that can emulate the behaviour of the adversary without access to TPMs. The main result of the paper are security proofs that demonstrate that the ePCAS protocol is unforgeable, third-party anonymous, and strongly deniable.

The rest of this paper is organized as follows. We give an overview of the ePCAS in Section 2. The formalization of the security properties that we consider is given in Section 3, and the proof that ePCAS meets these requirements is in Section 4. We conclude in Section 5.

2 The Enhanced PCAS Protocol

In this section we recall the ePCAS protocol and motivate its design. We start with an outline of the attack against the PCAS protocol. The attack was already known, but we give it here since it is important to understand the design idea behind ePCAS.

CHOSEN COMPROMISED TPM ATTACK OF THE TCG PCAS PROTOCOL. In the TCG PCAS protocol (see Appendix A for details), from the CA's point of view, the possession of the TPM t_l's secret key esk_l is proved by using a challenge-response protocol based on the asymmetric encryption scheme AENC. Roughly, the CA sends a random nonce together with a short term public key pk_{li} encrypted under the endorsement key of the TPM and expects to receive the nonce. Notice that this part of the protocol somehow guarantees that the CA talks to the TPM that knows esk_l, but does not guarantee that the TPM knows the secret key associated to the short term public key pk_{li}. The CA accepts the statement that the owner of epk_l also owns pk_{li} relying on the fact that the TPM with the key esk_l should follow the protocol properly, since the TPM is a tamper-resistant chip. However, if any TPM is compromised (and attacks against the TPMs are nowadays a reality), this fact will no longer be true. If a compromised TPM's epk is still in the list Valid (the list of TPMs which the CA considers valid, and for which he is willing to provide certificates) then the corrupt TPM can obtain a certificate on any honest TPM's pk. This should be considered an attack against the PCAS. The attack requires however a corrupt TPM and is outside the security model used for analysis in [8]. Stronger protocols are however needed as attacks that bypass tamper-resistance of TPMs are already known.

The ePCAS protocol proposed in [8] supposedly tolerates this type of stronger attacks. The idea is that a successful run of the protocol should ensure that the TPM knows both the secret key corresponding to the endorsement key used in the run, but also the secret key corresponding to the short term public key which is certified in that run. We detail the protocol next. Here, and in the remainder of the paper we use the following notation. If S is a set, we denote the act of sampling from S uniformly at random and assigning the result to the variable x by $x \leftarrow S$. We let $\{0,1\}^*$ and $\{0,1\}^t$ denote the set of binary strings of arbitrary length and length t respectively. If A is an algorithm, we write $x \leftarrow A(y_1, \ldots, y_n)$ to indicate that x is obtained by invoking A on inputs $y_1, \ldots, y_n$. The algorithms that we consider may have access to oracles. We write $\mathcal{A}^{\mathcal{O}}$ to indicate that adversary $\mathcal{A}$ has access to oracle $\mathcal{O}$. We denote concatenation of two date strings x and y as $x \| y$.

PARTIES. The ePCAS is a protocol that involves a TPM, the host platform (host for short) that contains the TPM, and a privacy-CA (CA for short). The general setting that we analyze in this paper considers sets $\mathcal{C}$, $\mathcal{T}$ and $\mathcal{H}$ of CAs, TPMs, and Host entities. The latter set is in some sense irrelevant; it plays no role in our analysis as we assume that of all hosts are compromised in the unforgeability experiment. So, from the point of view of our analysis, the ePCAS is a two party protocol between a CA and a TPM.

CRYPTOGRAPHIC PRIMITIVES. Each CA $c_j \in \mathcal{C}$ has a public/private key pair $(\mathsf{cpk}_j, \mathsf{csk}_j)$ for a digital signature scheme $\mathsf{DSIG} = (\mathsf{KG}, \mathsf{SIG}, \mathsf{VER})$. Each TPM $t_l \in \mathcal{T}$ has a encryption/decryption key pair $(\mathsf{epk}_l, \mathsf{esk}_l)$ for an asymmetric encryption scheme $\mathsf{AENC} = (\mathsf{A.KG}, \mathsf{A.ENC}, \mathsf{A.DEC})$. Recall that the key pair $(\mathsf{epk}_l, \mathsf{esk}_l)$ is the TPM unique and long-term Endorsement Key (EK). Often in this paper, we identify CA c_j and TPM t_l via their public keys, cpk_j and epk_l, respectively. The protocol also uses a symmetric encryption scheme $\mathsf{SENC} = (\mathsf{S.KG}, \mathsf{S.ENC}, \mathsf{S.DEC})$.

PROTOCOL DESCRIPTION. The ePCAS protocol is shown in Figure 1. The description of the protocol intertwines the real execution with some modelling aspects. We put square brackets around the parts that pertain to the model and outside square brackets the parts that pertain to the actual protocol.

We next give the steps of the protocol and describe the intuition behind their design.

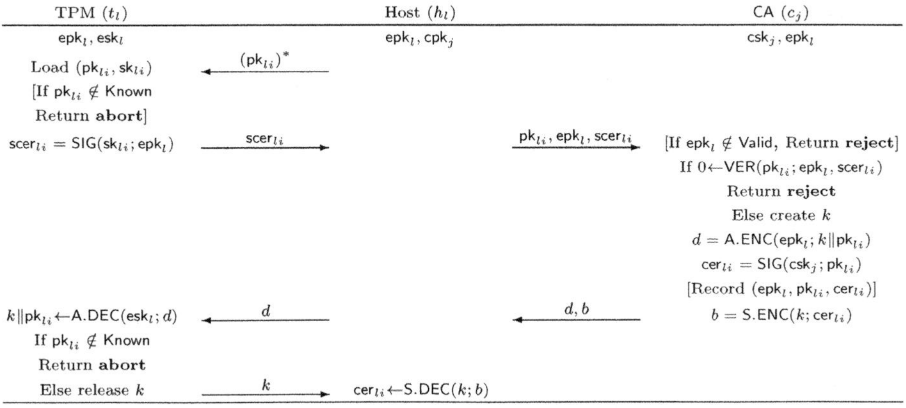

Fig. 1. The ePCAS protocol

1. h_l initiates the protocol by sending to t_l a data pack $(\mathsf{pk}_{li})^*$. t_l loads the key pair $(\mathsf{pk}_{li}, \mathsf{sk}_{li})$ and verifies that the key is in the list Known. The list Known maintains these keys created by t_l and has been loaded to t_l. We are not concerned with how this verification takes place, but we require, that if the verification passes then the TPM knows the secret key associated to pk_{li}. If this is the case, t_l signs its endorsement public key epk_l under sk_{li} and returns the signature scer_{li} back to h_l, who then sends pk_{li}, epk_l and scer_{li} to c_j. The rationale of this step is that the TPM shows to the CA that he knows the secret key associated to the public key for which it desires a certificate.
2. Next, c_j checks that epk_l is in the list Valid. This list is part of our modelling and records which epk's are valid from the point of view of the CA c_j. For these TPMs the CA is willing to produce certificates on short term keys. c_j also checks whether scer_{li} is a valid signature of epk_l. If both checks pass, c_j creates a fresh symmetric key k, a certificate on pk_{li}, say cer_{li}, and encrypts the value $k \| \mathsf{pk}_{li}$ under epk_l by using AENC to get the ciphertext d. In addition, c_j encrypts cer_{li} under k by using SENC to get the ciphertext b, and then sends both d and b to h_l. In the end, c_j records the triple $(\mathsf{epk}_l, \mathsf{pk}_{li}, \mathsf{cer}_{li})$ into a list Record to maintain certificated keys with epk's.
3. After receiving the values d from h_l, t_l decrypts d by using esk_l and then checks whether pk_{li} is in the list Known. If the checks succeed, t_l releases the value k to h_l.
4. h_l decrypts b under k to obtain cer_{li}.

Remark 1. Importantly, the ePCAS protocol can be implemented with not changes to the existing functionality of TPMs. The execution on the TPMs side corresponds essentially to TPM commands TPM_CertifyKey and TPM_ActivateIdentity.

3 Security Model for Enhanced PCAS Protocol

In this section we detail the security model that we use to study the ePCAS protocol. We have the following three security properties of the PCAS protocol and ePCAS protocol: third-part anonymity, unforgeability and deniability.

3.1 Oracles Needed in the Security Games

Our security definitions use oracles that model the different abilities of an adversary against the ePCAS protocol.

- TPM$(\mathsf{epk}_l, \mathsf{pk})$: The adversary can use this oracle to interact with TPM t_l.
- CA$(\mathsf{cpk}_j, \mathsf{epk}_l, \mathsf{pk})$: The adversary can use this oracle to interact with CA c_j.
- $\mathrm{CH}_\mathrm{b}(\mathsf{epk}_{l_0}, \mathsf{epk}_{l_1}, \mathsf{cpk}_j)$: This oracle is a left-right oracle for defining third-party anonymity. The adversary sends a tuple $(\mathsf{epk}_{l_0}, \mathsf{epk}_{l_1}, \mathsf{cpk}_j)$ to the oracle and gets back $(\mathsf{pk}, \mathsf{cer})$ of the ePCAS protocol executed by TMP t_{l_b} and CA c_j.

- $\mathsf{TRAN}(\mathsf{epk}_l, \mathsf{cpk}_j)$: The oracle returns a public transcript between TPM and CA in a transaction.
- $\mathsf{CorrCA}(j)$: This oracle allows the adversary to access the secret signing key of CA c_j.
- $\mathsf{CorrTPM}(l)$: This oracle allows the adversary to access the secret decryption key of TPM t_l.

Each TPM oracle is parametrized by a pair of encryption/decryption keys $(\mathsf{epk}, \mathsf{esk})$. All of these oracles share a global variable $\mathsf{ValidKey}$. This variable maintains a list of pairs $(\mathsf{epk}, \mathsf{pk})$ with the meaning that the key pk is valid for the TPM with the public key epk. We also write $\mathsf{ValidKey}(\mathsf{epk}, \mathsf{pk}) = 1$ to indicate that $(\mathsf{epk}, \mathsf{pk})$ occurs in $\mathsf{ValidKey}$. The oracle expects to receive as input a pair of key $(\mathsf{epk}_l, \mathsf{pk})$ where pk should be one of the short-term keys which the TPM owns. If this is not the case, the execution is aborted. Otherwise, the TPM signs its long-term public key epk under the short-term signing key sk and returns the self certificate scer. Later the oracle expects to receive the encryption of a plaintext $k||\mathsf{pk}$ under epk_l, in which case it returns k; otherwise the oracle aborts the execution.

The CA oracle is parametrized by verification and signing keys $(\mathsf{cpk}, \mathsf{csk})$. All of the CA oracles share a global variable $\mathsf{ValidTPM}$. This variable maintains a list of pairs $(\mathsf{cpk}, \mathsf{epk})$; each such pair indicates that CA with the public key cpk knows the TPM with the public key epk. We also write $\mathsf{ValidTPM}(\mathsf{cpk}, \mathsf{epk}) = 1$ to indicate that $(\mathsf{cpk}, \mathsf{epk})$ occurs in $\mathsf{ValidTPM}$. The CA oracle is activated by a CA public key cpk. The oracle expects to receive as input tuple $(\mathsf{pk}, \mathsf{epk}, \mathsf{scer})$. If epk_l is not the public key of a valid TPM that CA c_j knows, the oracle aborts its execution. If the self certificate is not a valid signature on epk under sk the oracle also aborts. Otherwise, the oracle sends out a symmetric encryption of cer under a freshly generated key k, together with an asymmetric encryption of $k||\mathsf{pk}$ under epk_l.

The $\mathrm{CH_b}$ oracle is activated by a tuple $(\mathsf{epk}_{l_0}, \mathsf{epk}_{l_1}, \mathsf{cpk}_j)$ where epk_{l_0} and epk_{l_1} are two different TPM public keys and cpk_j is a CA public key. The $\mathrm{CH_b}$ oracle maintains the global variables $\mathsf{ValidTPM}$ and $\mathsf{ValidKey}$. If $\mathsf{ValidTPM}(\mathsf{cpk}_j, \mathsf{epk}_{l_0}) \oplus \mathsf{ValidTPM}(\mathsf{cpk}_j, \mathsf{epk}_{l_1}) = 1$, then the oracle aborts. If csk_j, esk_0 or esk_1 is corrupt then the oracle aborts the execution. Otherwise, the oracle first generates a new key pair $(\mathsf{sk}, \mathsf{pk})$. Then the oracle randomly selects a bit $b \in \{0, 1\}$ and assigns pk to TPM t_{lb}. The oracle also updates the variable $\mathsf{ValidKey}$. Next, the oracle runs $\mathrm{TPM}(\mathsf{epk}_{l_b}, \mathsf{pk})$ and $\mathrm{CA}(\mathsf{cpk}_j)$. The $\mathrm{CH_b}$ oracle computes the certificate cer on pk according the results of CA and TPM oracles and finally outputs $(\mathsf{pk}, \mathsf{cer})$.

The TRAN oracle maintains the variable $\mathsf{ValidKey}$ and takes as input a tuple $(\mathsf{epk}_l, \mathsf{cpk}_j)$. Next, the TRAN oracle runs CA and TPM oracles to obtain a public transcript τ in a transaction between TPM t_l and CA c_j.

The behaviour of the above four types of oracles is summarized in Figure 2 respectively. In addition, the adversary is given access to CA and TPM corruption oracle.

The CA corruption oracle, CorrCA has access to the secret signing keys of the CAs. On an input $1 \leq j \leq p(\eta)$ the oracle returns csk_j. If the adversary sends j to this corruption oracle, then we say that its secret key csk_j is corrupt. The TPM corruption oracle, CorrTPM has access to the secret signing keys of the TPMs. On an input $1 \leq l \leq p(\eta)$ the oracle returns esk_l. If the adversary sends l to this corruption oracle, then we say that its secret key esk_l is corrupt.

TPM($\mathsf{epk}_l, \mathsf{pk}$)

- if $\mathsf{ValidKey}(\mathsf{epk}_l, \mathsf{pk}) = 0$ then **abort**
  - $\mathsf{scer} \leftarrow \mathsf{SIG}(\mathsf{sk}, \mathsf{epk}_l)$
  - send scer
- receive d
  - if $\mathsf{A.DEC}(\mathsf{esk}_l, d) \neq k||\mathsf{pk}$ for some k then **abort**
- send k

CA($\mathsf{cpk}_j, \mathsf{epk}_l, \mathsf{pk}$)

- receive scer
  - if $\mathsf{ValidTPM}(\mathsf{cpk}_j, \mathsf{epk}_l) = 0$ then **abort**
  - $0 \leftarrow \mathsf{VER}(\mathsf{pk}, \mathsf{epk}_l, \mathsf{scer})$ then **abort**
  - $k \leftarrow \mathsf{A.KG}(\eta)$
  - $d \leftarrow \mathsf{A.ENC}(\mathsf{epk}, k||\mathsf{pk})$
  - $\mathsf{cer} \leftarrow \mathsf{SIG}(\mathsf{csk}, \mathsf{pk})$
  - append $(\mathsf{epk}, \mathsf{cpk}, \mathsf{pk}, \mathsf{cer})$ to RegList
  - $b \leftarrow \mathsf{S.ENC}(k, \mathsf{cer})$
- send d, b

CH$_b$($\mathsf{epk}_{l_0}, \mathsf{epk}_{l_1}, \mathsf{cpk}_j$)

- if $\mathsf{ValidTPM}(\mathsf{cpk}_j, \mathsf{epk}_{l_0}) \oplus \mathsf{ValidTPM}(\mathsf{cpk}_j, \mathsf{epk}_{l_1}) = 1$ then **abort**
- if csk_j is corrupt then **abort**
- if esk_0 or esk_1 is corrupt then **abort**
- $(\mathsf{pk}, \mathsf{sk}) \leftarrow \mathsf{KG}(\eta)$
- $(D, B) \leftarrow \mathrm{CA}(\mathsf{cpk}_j, \mathsf{epk}_{l_b}, \mathsf{pk})$
- $(\mathsf{scer}, K) \leftarrow \mathrm{TPM}(\mathsf{epk}_{l_b}, \mathsf{pk})$
- $\mathsf{cer} \leftarrow \mathsf{S.DEC}(K, B)$
- return $(\mathsf{pk}, \mathsf{cer})$

TRAN($\mathsf{epk}_l, \mathsf{cpk}_j$)

- $(\mathsf{pk}, \mathsf{sk}) \leftarrow \mathsf{KG}(\eta)$
- $(d, b) \leftarrow \mathrm{CA}(\mathsf{cpk}_j, \mathsf{epk}_l, \mathsf{pk})$
- $(\mathsf{scer}, k) \leftarrow \mathrm{TPM}(\mathsf{epk}_l, \mathsf{pk})$
- $\tau \leftarrow (\mathsf{scer}, d, b)$
- return τ

Fig. 2. Oracles defining security for ePCAS protocol

3.2 Security Games

Third-Party Anonymity. Intuitively, we say the ePCAS protocol is third-party anonymous if no third party can determine which TPM is issued a certificate on its short-term public key from a pair $(\mathsf{cer}, \mathsf{pk})$ except the engaged TPM and CA. The experiment of third-party anonymity, which we specify in detail in Figure 3, proceeds as follows. First, keys are generated for the TPMs and for the CAs. We write **cpk** for the set $\{\mathsf{cpk}_1, \mathsf{cpk}_2, \ldots\}$ of all public keys of the CAs, and **epk** for the set $\{\mathsf{epk}_1, \mathsf{epk}_2, \ldots\}$ of all public keys of the TPMs. The adversary is given all of the public keys. The adversary then specifies some arbitrary initial configurations. In this experiment, we assume the adversary can collude with any malicious CAs or TPMs except the two challenge TPMs and corresponding CA which issues certificate to the challenge TPMs. Therefore, we allow the adversary to know which CAs know which TPMs and which TPMs own which public keys. In particular, the adversary decides which CAs know which TPMs, by specifying a list $\mathsf{ValidTPM} \subset \mathbf{cpk} \times \mathbf{epk}$. The adversary also decides for each TPM what are the list of short-term keys that the TPM knows by specifying the list $\mathsf{ValidKey} \subset \{\mathsf{epk}_1, \mathsf{epk}_2, \ldots, \} \times \{0,1\}^*$. We require that ValidKey satisfies that for any $\mathsf{pk} \in \{0,1\}^*$, $\mathsf{ValidKey}(\mathsf{epk}_i, \mathsf{pk}) = 1$ then $\mathsf{ValidKey}(\mathsf{epk}_j, \mathsf{pk}) = 0$ for any $j \neq i$. This reflects the idea that the short-term keys valid for the TPM are disjoint. Notice that we do not impose any conditions on how the short-term keys are generated; the adversary is allowed to select arbitrary bit-strings for these keys.

The adversary first queries some TPM, CA, CorrTPM and CorrCA oracles, and then outputs a tuple $(\mathsf{epk}_{l_0}, \mathsf{epk}_{l_1}, \mathsf{cpk}_j)$ where epk_{l_0} and epk_{l_1} are two different TPM public keys and cpk_j is a CA public key. Note that the short-term key generation algorithms of TPMs t_{l_0} and t_{l_1} should be the same, for example, both are RSA keys or discrete logarithm keys. If the short-term keys are of different key generation algorithms, the adversary may know a short-term public key belonging to which of the two TPMs. After generating the tuple $(\mathsf{epk}_{l_0}, \mathsf{epk}_{l_1}, \mathsf{cpk}_j)$, the adversary then queries a $\mathrm{CH_b}$ oracle (this oracle can be queried just once in a experiment) and some TPM, CA and CorrCA oracles. The adversary is not allowed to query the challenge short-term public key pk to CA or TPM oracle or access the variable ValidKey after the $\mathrm{CH_b}$ oracle query. At the end of the execution, the adversary outputs a decision bit $\hat{b}$

$\mathbf{Exp}^{anon\text{-}b}_{\mathsf{ePCAS},\mathcal{A}}(\eta)$
  for each CA c_j do $(\mathsf{cpk}_j, \mathsf{csk}_j) \leftarrow \mathsf{KG}(\eta)$
  for each TPM t_l do $(\mathsf{epk}_l, \mathsf{esk}_l) \leftarrow \mathsf{A.KG}(\eta)$
  $\mathsf{ValidTPM}, \mathsf{ValidKey} \leftarrow \mathcal{A}(\mathbf{cpk}, \mathbf{epk})$
  $(\mathsf{epk}_{l_0}, \mathsf{epk}_{l_1}, \mathsf{cpk}_j) \leftarrow \mathcal{A}^{\mathrm{TPM,CA,CorrCA,CorrTPM}}(\mathbf{epk}, \mathbf{cpk}, \mathsf{ValidTPM}, \mathsf{ValidKey})$
  $\hat{b} \leftarrow \mathcal{A}^{\mathrm{CH_b,TPM,CA,CorrCA,CorrTPM}}(\mathbf{epk}, \mathbf{cpk}, \mathsf{ValidTPM})$
  return $\hat{b}$

Fig. 3. Experiment that defines the security of third-party anonymity

Definition 1. Third-Party Anonymity: *We define*

$$\mathbf{Adv}^{anon}_{\mathsf{ePCAS},\mathcal{A}}(\eta) = \left|\Pr[\mathbf{Exp}^{anon\text{-}0}_{\mathsf{ePCAS},\mathcal{A}}(\eta) = 1] - \Pr[\mathbf{Exp}^{anon\text{-}1}_{\mathsf{ePCAS},\mathcal{A}}(\eta) = 1]\right|,$$

and we say the protocol is third-party anonymous *if* $\mathbf{Adv}^{anon}_{\mathsf{ePCAS},\mathcal{A}}(\eta)$ *is a negligible function of* η *for all polynomial time adversaries* $\mathcal{A}$.

Unforgeability. Intuitively, we say the ePCAS protocol is unforgeable if no adversary can forge a certificate on a short-term public key of TPM. The major difference between our unforgeability experiment for ePCAS and the unforgeability experiment for PCAS [8] is our unforgeability experiment allows the adversary to corrupt some TPMs (i.e. we consider the chosen corrupted TPM attack). Another difference is that the adversary against ePCAS is only given the variables ValidKey and ValidTPM whereas the adversary against PCAS in

Chen-Warinshi model [8] can specify these variables. Why our unforgeability experiment does not allow the adversary to specify these variables is because this will make the security proof derive an uncertain probability of EU-CMA security for digital signatures. Although the adversary cannot specify $\mathsf{ValidKey}$ and $\mathsf{ValidTPM}$ in our model, it is still mightier than the attackers in realistic situation. The experiment of unforgeability, which we specify in detail in Figure 4, proceeds as follows. First, keys are generated for the TPMs and for the CAs. We write $\mathbf{cpk}$ for the set $\{\mathsf{cpk}_1, \mathsf{cpk}_2, \ldots\}$ of all public keys of the CAs, and $\mathbf{epk}$ for the set $\{\mathsf{epk}_1, \mathsf{epk}_2, \ldots\}$ of all public keys of the TPMs. The adversary is given all of the public keys. The variables $\mathsf{ValidTPM} \subset \mathbf{cpk} \times \mathbf{epk}$ and $\mathsf{ValidKey} \subset \{\mathsf{epk}_1, \mathsf{epk}_2, \ldots, \} \times \{0,1\}^*$ is also specified by an authority Auth. We require that $\mathsf{ValidKey}$ satisfies that for any $\mathsf{pk} \in \{0,1\}^*$, $\mathsf{ValidKey}(\mathsf{epk}_i, \mathsf{pk}) = 1$ then $\mathsf{ValidKey}(\mathsf{epk}_j, \mathsf{pk}) = 0$ for any $j \neq i$. This reflects the idea that the short-term keys valid for the TPM are disjoint. Notice that we do not impose any conditions on how the short-term keys are generated. The adversary is initially given $(\mathbf{epk}, \mathbf{cpk}, \mathsf{ValidTPM}, \mathsf{ValidKey})$. We also write TPM_l^n for the n-th instance of the TPM oracle initialized with keys $\mathsf{epk}_l, \mathsf{esk}_l$. Similarly, we write CA_j^m for the m-th instance of the CA oracle initialized with keys $\mathsf{cpk}_j, \mathsf{csk}_j$. The adversary is given access to some CorrCA and $\mathsf{CorrTPM}$ oracles multiple instances of the TPM and CA oracles At the end of the execution, the adversary outputs a tuple $(\mathsf{epk}_{i^*}, \mathsf{cpk}_{j*}, \mathsf{pk}^*, \mathsf{cer}^*)$ with $\mathsf{epk}_{l^*} \in \mathbf{epk}$, $\mathsf{cpk}_{j^*} \in \mathbf{cpk}$ and $\mathsf{pk}^*, \mathsf{cer}^* \in \{0,1\}^*$. The outcome of the experiment is determined as follows.

If cer^* is not a valid signature on pk^* under cpk_{j^*} or the key csk_{j^*} has been corrupted then the experiment returns 0. Otherwise, if either c_{j^*} (with associated verification key cpk_{j^*}) never certified key pk so a tuple of the form $(\mathsf{epk}, \mathsf{cpk}_{j^*}, \mathsf{pk}^*, \mathsf{cer})$ does not occur in $\mathsf{RegList}$ (in the formulation of the experiment we indicate using a "don't care" on the first position of the tuple), or if a tuple of the form $(\mathsf{epk}_l, \mathsf{cpk}_{j^*}, \mathsf{pk}^*, \mathsf{cer}^*)$ does occur in $\mathsf{RegList}$ (for some TPM public key TPM_l), then the key pk^* does not belong to TPM t_l, so $\mathsf{ValidKey}(\mathsf{epk}_l, \mathsf{pk}^*) = 0$ the experiment returns 1. If neither condition is satisfied, then the experiment returns 0.

Definition 2. Unforgeability: *We define*

$$\mathbf{Adv}^{unforge}_{\mathsf{ePCAS},\mathcal{A}}(\eta) = \Pr[\mathbf{Exp}^{unforge}_{\mathsf{ePCAS},\mathcal{A}}(\eta) = 1],$$

and we say the protocol is unforgeable *if* $\mathbf{Adv}^{unforge}_{\mathsf{ePCAS},\mathcal{A}}(\eta)$ *is a negligible function of* η *for all polynomial time adversaries* $\mathcal{A}$.

Deniability. Intuitively, we say the ePCAS protocol is deniable if a TPM can deny that it was engaged in a transaction with a CA even if this transaction actually took place. We define two kinds of deniability: strong deniability and weak deniability which both catch this security requirement. We say the scheme is *strongly/weakly deniable* if for each adversary $\mathcal{A}$ that produces τ_0 (the output in interaction in real transaction), there exists a simulator $\mathcal{S}$ that can produce τ_1 (the output in simulation) which is indistinguishable from τ_0, i.e. no ppt

$\mathbf{Exp}^{unforge}_{\mathsf{ePCAS},\mathcal{A}}(\eta)$
for each CA c_j do $(\mathsf{cpk}_j, \mathsf{csk}_j) \leftarrow \mathsf{KG}(\eta)$
for each TPM t_l do $(\mathsf{epk}_l, \mathsf{esk}_l) \leftarrow \mathsf{A.KG}(\eta)$
$\mathsf{ValidTPM}, \mathsf{ValidKey} \leftarrow \mathsf{Auth}(\mathbf{cpk}, \mathbf{epk})$
$\mathsf{RegList} \leftarrow \emptyset$
$(\mathsf{epk}_{l^*}, \mathsf{cpk}_{j^*}, \mathsf{pk}^*, \mathsf{cer}^*) \leftarrow \mathcal{A}^{\mathrm{TPM}_l^n, \mathrm{CA}_j^m, \mathsf{CorrCA}, \mathsf{CorrTPM}}(\mathbf{epk}, \mathbf{cpk}, \mathsf{ValidTPM}, \mathsf{ValidKey})$
if $\mathsf{VER}(\mathsf{cpk}_{j^*}, (\mathsf{pk}^*, \mathsf{cer}^*)) = 0$ return 0
if csk_{j^*} is corrupt return 0
if $(*, \mathsf{cpk}_{j^*}, \mathsf{pk}^*, \mathsf{cer}^*) \notin \mathsf{RegList}$ return 1
if $(\mathsf{epk}_{l^*}, \mathsf{cpk}_{j^*}, \mathsf{pk}^*, \mathsf{cer}^*) \in \mathsf{RegList}$ and
$\mathsf{ValidKey}(\mathsf{epk}_{l^*}, \mathsf{pk}^*) = 0$ return 1
return 0

Fig. 4. Experiment that defines the security of unforgeability

algorithm $\mathcal{D}$ can distinguish them with non-negligible probability. We consider the scenario that the TPMs and hosts are honest, but all CAs are malicious. The experiment of deniability is specified in Figure 6. Let *x-deni* be *s-deni* (strong deniability) or *w-deni* (weak deniability). First, keys are generated for the TPMs and for the CAs. We write $\mathbf{cpk}$ for the set $\{\mathsf{cpk}_1, \mathsf{cpk}_2, \ldots\}$ of all public keys of the CAs, $\mathbf{csk}$ for the set $\{\mathsf{csk}_1, \mathsf{csk}_2, \ldots\}$ of all secret keys of the CAs, and $\mathbf{epk}$ for the set $\{\mathsf{epk}_1, \mathsf{epk}_2, \ldots\}$ of all public keys of the TPMs. $\{\mathsf{epk}_1, \mathsf{epk}_2, \ldots\}$ of all public keys of the TPMs. The variables $\mathsf{ValidTPM} \subset \mathbf{cpk} \times \mathbf{epk}$ and $\mathsf{ValidKey} \subset \{\mathsf{epk}_1, \mathsf{epk}_2, \ldots,\} \times \{0,1\}^*$ is also specified by an authority Auth. We require that $\mathsf{ValidKey}$ satisfies that for any $\mathsf{pk} \in \{0,1\}^*$ $\mathsf{ValidKey}(\mathsf{epk}_i, \mathsf{pk}) = 1$ then $\mathsf{ValidKey}(\mathsf{epk}_j, \mathsf{pk}) = 0$ for any $j \neq i$. This reflects the idea that the short-term keys valid for the TPM are disjoint. The adversary $\mathcal{A}$ and the simulator $\mathcal{S}$ are given the same information $(\mathbf{epk}, \mathbf{cpk}, \mathbf{csk}, \mathsf{ValidTPM})$ initially. This reflects that the adversary can collude with all CAs. Note we do not give $\mathsf{ValidKey}$ to the adversary since we assume the TPMs and hosts are honest in this experiment.

If $x = s$ (i.e. strong deniability), then the active adversary $\mathcal{A}$ accesses some TPM′ oracles and outputs τ_0 (a transcript or an arbitrary string). We do not give the adversary CA oracle since the adversary has been given $\mathbf{csk}$, he can naturally do the same thing that CA oracle does. Note that we assume the hosts are honest, thus the adversary cannot obtain the final stage output k from the original TPM oracle, he is just given $(\mathsf{pk}, \mathsf{epk}, \mathsf{scer})$. Therefore, in this experiment the adversary accesses a modified TPM′ oracle which is specified in Figure 5. If $x = w$,(i.e. weak deniability) then the passive adversary $\mathcal{A}$ accesses TRAN oracle and outputs τ_0 (a transcript or an arbitrary string). The simulator that can access all the secret signing keys of all CAs runs $\mathcal{A}$ as a black-box and outputs τ_1 (a transcript or an arbitrary string). A distinguisher $\mathcal{D}$ is given $\tau_b \in \{\tau_0, \tau_1\}$ and finally outputs a decision bit $\hat{b}$.

$\text{TPM}'(\mathsf{epk}_l, \mathsf{pk})$
1 if $\mathsf{ValidKey}(\mathsf{epk}_l, \mathsf{pk}) = 0$ then **abort**
$\mathsf{scer} \leftarrow \mathsf{SIG}(\mathsf{sk}, \mathsf{epk}_l)$
send scer
2 receive d
$k||\mathsf{pk} \leftarrow \mathsf{A.DEC}(\mathsf{esk}_l, d)$

Fig. 5. The TPM′ oracle

$\mathbf{Exp}^{x\text{-}deni\text{-}b}_{\mathsf{ePCAS},\mathcal{D}}(\eta)$
for each CA c_j do $(\mathsf{cpk}_j, \mathsf{csk}_j) \leftarrow \mathsf{KG}(\eta)$
for each TPM t_l do $(\mathsf{epk}_l, \mathsf{esk}_l) \leftarrow \mathsf{A.KG}(\eta)$
$\mathsf{ValidTPM}, \mathsf{ValidKey} \leftarrow \mathsf{Auth}(\mathbf{cpk}, \mathbf{epk})$
$\tau_0 \leftarrow \mathcal{A}^{\mathcal{O}_x}(\mathbf{epk}, \mathbf{cpk}, \mathbf{csk}, \mathsf{ValidTPM})$
(if $x = s$ then $\mathcal{O}_x = \text{TPM}'$; if $x = w$ then $\mathcal{O}_x = \text{TRAN}$)
$\tau_1 \leftarrow \mathcal{S}^{\mathcal{A}}(\mathbf{epk}, \mathbf{cpk}, \mathbf{csk}, \mathsf{ValidTPM})$
$\hat{b} \leftarrow \mathcal{D}(\tau_b)$
return $\hat{b}$

Fig. 6. Experiment that defines the security of strong/weak deniability

Definition 3. *We define*

$$\mathbf{Adv}^{x\text{-}deni}_{\mathsf{ePCAS},\mathcal{D}}(\eta) = \left|\Pr[\mathbf{Exp}^{x\text{-}deni\text{-}0}_{\mathsf{ePCAS},\mathcal{D}}(\eta) = 1] - \Pr[\mathbf{Exp}^{x\text{-}deni\text{-}1}_{\mathsf{ePCAS},\mathcal{D}}(\eta) = 1]\right|,$$

and we say the protocol is strongly/weakly deniable *if* $\mathbf{Adv}^{x\text{-}deni}_{\mathsf{ePCAS},\mathcal{D}}(\eta)$ *is a negligible function of* η *for all polynomial time distinguishers* $\mathcal{D}$.

Remark 2. Although the behaviour of the oracles of the PCAS protocol is different from that of the ePCAS protocol, the original TCG PCAS protocol should also offer the same security requirements (i.e. third-party anonymity, unforgeabilily, deniability) and its experiments are similar to that of the ePCAS protocol.

4 Security Analysis

In this section, we show that the ePCAS protocol has the properties of third-party anonymity, unforgeability and stronger deniability. Due to the page limitation, the full proofs are given in Appendix C, and here we only outline the proof strategies that we use.

Theorem 1. *The* ePCAS *protocol is third-party anonymous.*

The intuition why this property holds is quite simple. Clearly, ePCAS does not satisfy full anonymity as a CA can tell to which TPM certificates that it issues belong. However, as long as short term keys for the TPMs are selected from the same distribution there is no relation between the long term key of a TPM and its short term keys, as far as parties (different from the CA that signs the short term keys) are concerned. Security in this case is information theoretic (and does not rely on any security property of the underlying primitives). The formal statement, and the argument that it holds are in Appendix C.1.

Theorem 2. *If the signature scheme used in* ePCAS *is* EU-CMA *secure, then the* ePCAS *protocol is unforgeable.*

The security of the digital signature scheme is used here in two distinct ways. It prevents an adversary to simply create certificates for whatever keys it wants; in this case a forgery is straightforward. Secondly, it prevents an adversary to impersonate a TPM by producing signatures that verify under the short term key of some other TPM. In terms of our security experiment, a successful adversary $\mathcal{A}$ wins the unforgeability game either $\mathcal{A}$ produces a certificate on some public key pk that had not been involved in an execution with the CA (i.e. $\mathcal{A}$ produced the certificate on his own) or $\mathcal{A}$ managed to produce a self certificate which is a signature on epk_l under sk however the short-term key pair $(\mathsf{pk}, \mathsf{sk})$ does not belong to the TPM t_l. For each of the two cases we show how to construct an adversary that breaks the digital signature scheme. Technically, we show that for any adversary $\mathcal{A}$ against the ePCAS protocol, there exists adversaries $\mathcal{B}$ and $\mathcal{C}$ against the signature scheme such that:

$$\mathbf{Adv}^{unforge}_{\mathsf{ePCAS},\mathcal{A}}(\eta) \leq \frac{1}{p(\eta)} \cdot \mathbf{Adv}^{\mathsf{eucma}}_{\mathsf{DSIG},\mathcal{B}}(\eta) + \frac{1}{p'(\eta)} \mathbf{Adv}^{\mathsf{eucma}}_{\mathsf{DSIG},\mathcal{C}} \tag{1}$$

The adversaries $\mathcal{B}$ and $\mathcal{C}$ correspond to the two potential forgeries described above. The detailed proof of this theorem is in Appendix C.2.

Theorem 3. *The* ePCAS *protocol satisfies strong deniability.*

Deniability holds also information-theoretically. A simulator needs to simulate the behaviour of honest TPMs. This is however trivial: the only operation that the TPM executes (from the point of view of a CA) is to sign its endorsement key using a short term key. This can however be easily simulated, provided that the distribution from which the short term keys are generated is known. This argument is formalized in Appendix C.3.

5 Conclusion

In this paper we analyse the security of the ePCAS protocol. We present security models for three desirable properties (unforgeability of certificates, third-party anonymity of TPMs, and deniability of the certification protocol), and formally prove that the ePCAS protocol meets these requirements based on standard security assumptions on the underlying primitives.

As we explain unforgeability for the original PCAS protocol only holds when no TPM is ever corrupt. It is interesting to also investigate to what extent PCAS meets the two new properties that we put forth here, anonymity and deniability. Third-party anonymity should hold via a similar argument as the one for ePCAS: the short term keys are independent of the long term keys so certificates on different keys (even belonging to the same TPM) cannot be linked with one another. Deniability seems to be trickier: it is difficult to envision a simulator that can behave as an active adversary does (as the latter has access to TPM oracles whereas a passive one does not). It may be possible that PCAS satisfies however the weaker version of deniability that we put forth in this paper, but a careful analysis is left for future work.

Our findings should inform the ongoing work of the TCG group in devising the standard for the next generation of TPMs.

Acknowledgement. This work has been supported in part by the European Commission through the ICT Programme under Contract ICTV2007V216676 ECRYPT II.

References

1. Bellare, M., Boldyreva, A., Micali, S.: Public-Key Encryption in a Multi-user Setting: Security Proofs and Improvements. In: Preneel, B. (ed.) EUROCRYPT 2000. LNCS, vol. 1807, pp. 259–274. Springer, Heidelberg (2000)
2. Brickell, E., Camenisch, J., Chen, L.: Direct anonymous attestation. In: The 11th ACM Conference on Computer and Communications Security, pp. 132–145. ACM Press (2004)
3. Brickell, E., Chen, L., Li, J.: Simplified security notions for direct anonymous attestation and a concrete scheme from pairings. Int. Journal of Information Security 8, 315–330 (2009)
4. Bellare, M., Micciancio, D., Warinschi, B.: Foundations of Group Signatures: Formal Definitions, Simplified Requirements, and a Construction Based on General Assumptions. In: Biham, E. (ed.) EUROCRYPT 2003. LNCS, vol. 2656, pp. 614–629. Springer, Heidelberg (2003)
5. Bellare, M., Shi, H., Zhang, C.: Foundations of Group Signatures: The Case of Dynamic Groups. In: Menezes, A. (ed.) CT-RSA 2005. LNCS, vol. 3376, pp. 136–153. Springer, Heidelberg (2005)
6. Camenisch, J.: Better Privacy for Trusted Computing Platforms. In: Samarati, P., Ryan, P.Y.A., Gollmann, D., Molva, R. (eds.) ESORICS 2004. LNCS, vol. 3193, pp. 73–88. Springer, Heidelberg (2004)
7. Chen, L., Morrissey, P., Smart, N.P.: DAA: Fixing the pairing based protocols. Cryptology ePrint Archive. Report 2009/198, `http://eprint.iacr.org/2009/198`
8. Chen, L., Warinschi, B.: Security of the TCG privacy-CA solution. In: Proceedings of IEEE TrustCom 2010 (December 2010)
9. ISO/IEC 11889:2009 Information technology – Security techniques – Trusted Platform Module
10. Trusted Computing Group. TCG TPM specification 1.2 (2003), `http://www.trustedcomputinggroup.org`
11. Trusted Computing Group, `http://www.trustedcomputinggroup.org` (last accessed on June 30, 2010)

A   The TCG PCAS Protocol

TPM (t_l)	Host (h_l)	CA (c_j)
esk_l	$\mathsf{epk}_l, \mathsf{cpk}_j$	$\mathsf{csk}_j, \mathsf{epk}_l$
Load $(\mathsf{pk}_{l_i}\mathsf{sk}_{l_i})$ $\quad\xleftarrow{\;(\mathsf{pk}_{l_i})^*\;}$	$\quad\xrightarrow{\;\mathsf{pk}_{l_i}, \mathsf{epk}_l\;}$	If $\mathsf{epk}_l \notin$ Valid
		Return **reject**
		Else $c \leftarrow \{0,1\}^n$
$c\|\mathsf{pk}_{l_i}\leftarrow\mathsf{A.DEC}(\mathsf{esk}_l; a)$ $\xleftarrow{\;a\;}$	$\xleftarrow{\;a\;}$	$a = \mathsf{A.ENC}(\mathsf{epk}_l; c\|\mathsf{pk}_{l_i})$
If $\mathsf{pk}_{l_i} \notin$ Known		
Reture **abort**		
Else release c $\xrightarrow{\;c\;}$	$\xrightarrow{\;c\;}$	If c is not valid
		Return **reject**
		Else create k
		$d = \mathsf{A.ENC}(\mathsf{epk}_l; k\|\mathsf{pk}_{l_i})$
		$\mathsf{cer}_{l_i} = \mathsf{SIG}(\mathsf{csk}_j; \mathsf{pk}_{l_i})$
		Record $(\mathsf{epk}_l, \mathsf{pk}_{l_i}, \mathsf{cer}_{l_i})$
$k\|\mathsf{pk}_{l_i}\leftarrow\mathsf{A.DEC}(\mathsf{esk}_l; d)$ $\xleftarrow{\;d\;}$	$\xleftarrow{\;d, b\;}$	$b = \mathsf{S.ENC}(k; \mathsf{cer}_{l_i})$
If $\mathsf{pk}_{l_i} \notin$ Known		
Return **abort**		
Else release k $\xrightarrow{\;k\;}$	$\mathsf{cer}_{l_i}\leftarrow\mathsf{S.DEC}(k; b)$	

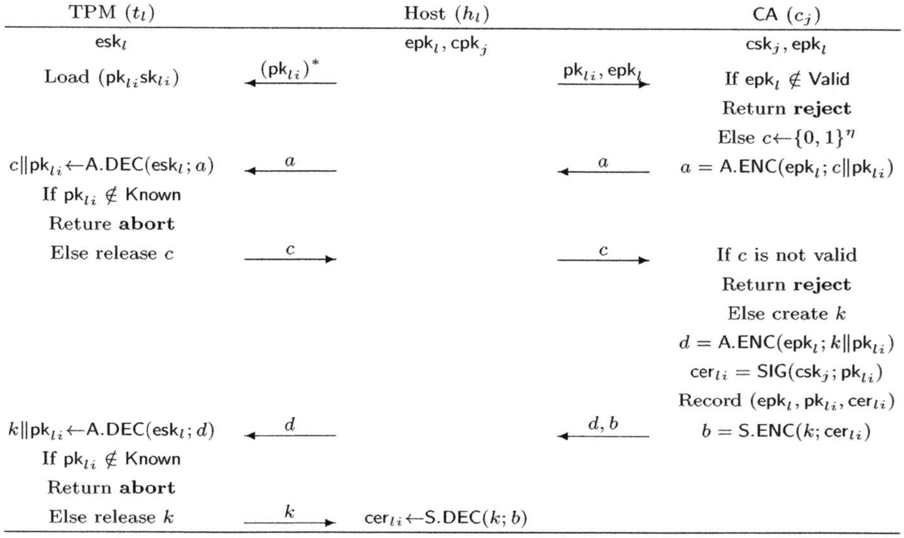

Fig. 7. The TCG PCAS protocol

PARTIES. The TCG PCAS is a protocol that involves a TPM, the host platform (host for short) that contains the TPM, and a privacy-CA (CA for short). The general setting that we analyze in this paper considers sets $\mathcal{C}$, $\mathcal{T}$ and $\mathcal{H}$ of CAs, TPMs, and Host entities. The latter set is in some sense irrelevant; it plays no role in the analysis. So, strictly speaking, PCAS is a two party protocol between a CA and a TPM.

CRYPTOGRAPHIC PRIMITIVES. Each CA $c_j \in \mathcal{C}$ has a public/private key pair $(\mathsf{cpk}_j, \mathsf{csk}_j)$ for a digital signature scheme $\mathsf{DSIG} = (\mathsf{KG}, \mathsf{SIG}, \mathsf{VER})$. Each TPM $t_l \in \mathcal{T}$ has a encryption/decryption key pair $(\mathsf{epk}_l, \mathsf{esk}_l)$ for an asymmetric encryption scheme $\mathsf{AENC} = (\mathsf{A.KG}, \mathsf{A.ENC}, \mathsf{A.DEC})$. Recall that the key pair $(\mathsf{epk}_l, \mathsf{esk}_l)$ is the TPM unique and long-term Endorsement Key (EK). Often in this paper, we identify CA c_j and TPM t_l via their public keys, cpk_j and epk_l, respectively. The protocol also uses a symmetric encryption scheme $\mathsf{SENC} = (\mathsf{S.KG}, \mathsf{S.ENC}, \mathsf{S.DEC})$.

EXECUTION. The goal of the PCAS protocol is two-fold. On the one hand the CA wants to ensure that it interacts with a legitimate TPM, and on the other hand the TPM wants to obtain a certificate (i.e. a signature of the CA) on some short-term public keys (i.e. Attestation Identity Keys (AIKs)) known by the TPM. Notice that for the purposes of this paper it is irrelevant how these keys are generated and for what particular communication applications they are intended. All that matters is that the TPM knows somehow these keys (and the associated secret keys) and that the TPM is able to verify its ownership of these keys. To have an easy mnemonic, we assume that $(\mathsf{pk}_{l1}, \mathsf{sk}_{l1}), (\mathsf{pk}_{l2}, \mathsf{sk}_{l2}), \ldots$ are the keys known by the TPM t_l. We also reflect this association via a list Known that maintains pairs of the form $(\mathsf{epk}, \mathsf{pk})$ with the meaning that a TPM with the public key epk had generated the short-term key pk. In addition, each CA knows the public key of some of the TPMs. We model this knowledge through a list Valid that maintains pairs of the form $(\mathsf{cpk}_j, \mathsf{epk}_l)$ to indicate that CA c_j knows the long-term public key of TPM t_l, that enables c_j to verify the legitimacy and attendance of t_l.

The PCAS protocol as shown in Figure 7, proceeds the following steps amongst the TPM t_l, the corresponding host h_l and the CA c_j:

1. h_l initiates the protocol by sending t_l a data pack denoted by $(\mathsf{pk}_{li})^*$ that asks t_l to load the key pair $(\mathsf{pk}_{li}, \mathsf{sk}_{li})$, and meanwhile, h_l sends $(\mathsf{pk}_{li}, \mathsf{epk}_l)$ to c_j.
2. c_j checks whether epk_l is in the list Valid. If the entry is found, c_j chooses a random challenge nonce c and encrypts $c \| \mathsf{pk}_{li}$ under epk_l by using AENC, and sends the ciphertext a back to h_l, who then forwards it to t_l.
3. t_l decrypts a using esk_l to get $c \| \mathsf{pk}_{li}$, and checks that pk_{li} is in the list Known and that the key pair $(\mathsf{pk}_{li}, \mathsf{sk}_{li})$ has been loaded; if the check passes, t_l releases c to h_l, who then forwards it to c_j.
4. c_j checks whether the received c matches with his challenge. If it does, c_j creates a fresh symmetric key k, a certificate on pk_{li}, say cer_{li}, and encrypts the value $k \| \mathsf{pk}_{li}$ again under epk_l by using AENC to get the ciphertext d. Meanwhile c_j encrypts cer_{li} under k by using SENC to get the ciphertext b, and then sends both d and b to h_l. In the end, c_j records the triple $(\mathsf{epk}_l, \mathsf{pk}_{li}, \mathsf{cer}_{li})$ into a list Record to maintain certificated keys with epk's.
5. After receiving the value d from h_l, t_l takes the same action as in the item 3), checks pk_{li} is in the list Known and $(\mathsf{pk}_{li}, \mathsf{sk}_{li})$ has been loaded and then, if the checks succeed, releases the value k to h_l.
6. h_l decrypts b under k to obtain cer_{li}.

Remark 3. The TPM functionality in the PCAS protocol is achieved by running two TPM commands: the item 1) is done with the command TPM_LoadKey2; the items 3) and 5) are done with the command TPM_ActivateIdentity. The details of these two commands are specified in [9,10].

B EU-CMA for Digital Signature Schemes

The security of a signature scheme $\mathsf{DSIG} = (\mathsf{KG}, \mathsf{SIG}, \mathsf{VER})$ is defined through game $\mathbf{Exp}^{\mathsf{eucma}}_{\mathsf{DSIG},\mathcal{A}}(\eta)$. In this game a pair of signing and verification keys (sk, pk) is generated by running the key generation algorithm of the digital signature scheme. Then, adversary $\mathcal{A}$ is given the verification key pk is provided with access to an oracle $\mathsf{SIG}(\mathsf{sk}, \cdot)$. For each message m that the adversary sends to the oracle, the oracle responds with a signature σ on m. Eventually, the adversary terminates its execution and outputs a message signature pair (m^*, σ^*). The experiment returns 1 if σ^* is a valid signature on m^* under pk^* and the message m^* was never queried to the oracle. The experiment returns 0 otherwise. The advantage of the adversary in breaking existential-unforgeability under chosen message attack for the scheme DSIG is defined as:

$$\mathbf{Adv}^{\mathsf{eucma}}_{\mathsf{DSIG},\mathcal{A}}(\eta) = \Pr[\mathbf{Exp}^{\mathsf{eucma}}_{\mathsf{DSIG},\mathcal{A}}(\eta) = 1]$$

The scheme DSIG is EU-CMA secure if for any probabilitisc polynomial time adversary $\mathcal{A}$, its advantage $\mathbf{Adv}^{\mathsf{eucma}}_{\mathsf{DSIG},\mathcal{A}}(\eta)$ is a negligible function.

C Security Proof

Here, we prove that the ePCAS protocol has the properties of third-party anonymity, unforgeability and strongly deniability.

C.1 Proof of Theorem 1

Proof. Assume $\mathcal{A}$ is an adversary against third-party anonymity of the ePCAS protocol in the $\mathbf{Exp}^{anon\text{-}b}_{\mathsf{ePCAS},\mathcal{A}}(\eta)$. Now, we claim that $\mathbf{Adv}^{anon}_{\mathsf{ePCAS},\mathcal{A}}(\eta)$ is negligible with the following observation. In the $\mathrm{CH_b}$ oracle, after randomly selecting a bit b, the oracle assigns a public key pk to TMP t_{l_b} , activates CA and TPM oracles with $(\mathsf{epk}_{l_b}, \mathsf{pk})$ and finally outputs a certificate cer. However, no matter the identity of TPM t_{l_b} is, the CA always creates the certificate according to the following equation: $\mathsf{cer} = \mathsf{SIG}(\mathsf{csk}_j, \mathsf{pk})$ without any inference of identity or long term public key of TPM t_{l_b}. This certificate cer on the uniform chosen pk is exactly the output of the $\mathrm{CH_b}$ oracle. Because the adversary obtains no information about the selected TPM from the outputting pair $(\mathsf{cer}, \mathsf{pk})$, the adversary always outputs decision bit b by guessing. It is essential that the outputs of $\mathbf{Exp}^{anon\text{-}0}_{\mathsf{ePCAS},\mathcal{A}}(\eta)$ and $\mathbf{Exp}^{anon\text{-}1}_{\mathsf{ePCAS},\mathcal{A}}(\eta)$ have the same probability distribution. So for any ppt adversary $\mathcal{A}$, the advantage $\mathbf{Adv}^{anon}_{\mathsf{ePCAS},\mathcal{A}}(\eta) = \left|\Pr[\mathbf{Exp}^{anon\text{-}0}_{\mathsf{ePCAS},\mathcal{A}}(\eta) = 1] - \Pr[\mathbf{Exp}^{anon\text{-}1}_{\mathsf{ePCAS},\mathcal{A}}(\eta) = 1]\right|$ is obviously a negligible function, i.e. the ePCAS is third-party anonymous.

C.2 Proof of Theorem 2

Proof. By definition, the adversary $\mathcal{A}$ wins the unforgeability game either $\mathcal{A}$ produces a certificate on some public pk that had not been involved in an execution with the CA (i.e. $\mathcal{A}$ produced the certificate on his own) or $\mathcal{A}$ managed to produce a self certificate which is a signature on epk_l under sk however the short-key key pair $(\mathsf{pk}, \mathsf{sk})$ does not belong to the TPM t_l.

Technically, we prove that for any adversary $\mathcal{A}$ against the ePCAS protocol, there exists adversaries $\mathcal{B}$ and $\mathcal{C}$ against the signature scheme such that:

$$\mathbf{Adv}^{unforge}_{\mathsf{ePCAS},\mathcal{A}}(\eta) \leq \frac{1}{p(\eta)} \cdot \mathbf{Adv}^{\mathsf{eucma}}_{\mathsf{DSIG},\mathcal{B}}(\eta) + \frac{1}{p'(\eta)} \mathbf{Adv}^{\mathsf{eucma}}_{\mathsf{DSIG},\mathcal{C}} \tag{2}$$

Fix an adversary $\mathcal{A}$ for the experiment $\mathbf{Exp}^{unforge}_{\mathsf{ePCAS},\mathcal{A}}(\eta)$. Let NoCert be the event that for the tuple $(\mathsf{cpk}_{j^*}, \mathsf{pk}^*, \mathsf{cer}^*)$ output by $\mathcal{A}$ there is no entry of the form $(\mathsf{epk}, \mathsf{cpk}_{j^*}, \mathsf{pk}^*, \mathsf{cer}^*)$ in $\mathsf{RegList}$, and let $\mathsf{CertInvKey}$ be the event that $(\mathsf{epk}_l, \mathsf{cpk}_{j^*}, \mathsf{pk}^*, \mathsf{cer}^*)$ for some epk_l, and $\mathsf{ValidKey}(\mathsf{epk}_l, \mathsf{pk}^*) = 0$. Then we have that:

$$\Pr[\mathbf{Exp}^{unforge}_{\mathsf{ePCAS},\mathcal{A}}(\eta) = 1] =$$
$$\Pr[\mathbf{Exp}^{unforge}_{\mathsf{ePCAS},\mathcal{A}}(\eta) = 1 \wedge \mathsf{NoCert}] +$$
$$\Pr[\mathbf{Exp}^{unforge}_{\mathsf{ePCAS},\mathcal{A}}(\eta) = 1 \wedge \mathsf{CertInvKey}]$$

Next we upper bound each of the terms above. The intuition is as follows. If event NoCert occurs, then cer^* is not produced by any oracle $\mathrm{CA}(\mathsf{cpk}_{j^*}, \mathsf{epk}_{l^*}, \mathsf{pk}^*)$, so the adversary $\mathcal{A}$ must have produced this signature on his own, hence he forged a signature under csk^*. This intuition is behind the construction of the following adversary $\mathcal{B}$ for $\mathbf{Exp}^{\mathsf{eucma}}_{\mathsf{DSIG},\mathcal{B}}(\eta)$ out of an adversary $\mathcal{A}$ for $\mathbf{Exp}^{unforge}_{\mathsf{ePCAS},\mathcal{A}}(\eta)$.

The adversary $\mathcal{B}$ is for $\mathbf{Exp}^{\mathsf{eucma}}_{\mathsf{DSIG},\mathcal{B}}$ so, by the notion of EU-CMA signature schemes as shown in the Appendix B, $\mathcal{B}$ has as input some verification key pk and access to a signing oracle under the corresponding secret key sk. The adversary $\mathcal{B}$ runs adversary $\mathcal{A}$ internally and simulates for $\mathcal{A}$ all of the oracles to which $\mathcal{A}$ has access in $\mathbf{Exp}^{unforge}_{\mathsf{ePCAS},\mathcal{A}}(\eta)$. The keys for all of the TPM and $\mathsf{CorrTPM}$ oracles are obtained by running the key generation algorithm of the encryption scheme: $(\mathsf{epk}_l, \mathsf{esk}_l) \leftarrow \mathsf{A.KG}(\eta)$ (for all $1 \le l \le p(\eta)$). The keys for all but one randomly selected CAs are obtained using the key generation algorithm $(\mathsf{csk}_j, \mathsf{cpk}_j) \leftarrow \mathsf{KG}(\eta)$ (for all $1 \le j \ne j_0 \le p(\eta)$, where j_0 is selected uniformly at random from $1, 2, \ldots, p(\eta)$). The public key of CA_{j_0} is set to be the verification key pk that $\mathcal{B}$ has as input. Adversary $\mathcal{B}$ can therefore simulate perfectly all of the oracles: for TPM^n_l oracles he simply executes the code defined by TPM (Figures 2). For any oracle CA^m_j with $j \ne j_0$ the adversary executes the code defined by CA (Figures 2). For all oracles $\mathrm{CA}^m_{j_0}$ the adversary $\mathcal{B}$ executes the same code with the difference that any signature σ that such an oracle needs to produce on some message m is obtained from the signing oracle to which $\mathcal{B}$ has access. Adversary $\mathcal{B}$ can also answer corruption queries for all of the $\mathsf{CorrTPMs}$ and $\mathsf{CorrCAs}$ except for c_{j_0}; if $\mathcal{A}$ ever queries j_0 to his CorrCA oracle, then $\mathcal{B}$ aborts its execution. Provided that j_0 is not submitted by $\mathcal{A}$ to his decryption oracle, the simulation that $\mathcal{B}$ offers to $\mathcal{A}$ is therefore perfect. When $\mathcal{A}$ produces his forgery $(\mathsf{cpk}^*, \mathsf{pk}^*, \mathsf{cer}^*)$ adversary $\mathcal{B}$ proceeds as follows. If $\mathsf{cpk}^* \ne \mathsf{pk}$ then $\mathcal{B}$ aborts. Otherwise $\mathcal{B}$ outputs $(\mathsf{pk}^*, \mathsf{cer}^*)$ as his forgery.

Since the simulation that $\mathcal{A}$ provides is perfect (if $\mathcal{B}$ does not abort), cpk_{j^*} in the output of $\mathcal{A}$ equals cpk_{j_0} (i.e. pk) with probability $\frac{1}{p(\eta)}$. It remains to determine when the forgery that is output by $\mathcal{B}$ is valid (if the guess j_0 is correct, that is, it does correspond to the forgery). This is the case when the message/signature pair $(\mathsf{pk}^*, \mathsf{cer}^*)$ is valid under sk, the signature cer^* had not been produced by the oracle to which $\mathcal{B}$ has access in response to a query pk^* by $\mathcal{B}$, and $\mathcal{B}$ did not abort due to a CorrCA query. Whenever adversary $\mathcal{A}$ wins the triple $(\mathsf{cpk}_j^*, \mathsf{pk}^*, \mathsf{cer}^*)$ is such that cer^* had not been produced by some oracle cpk_j^* as a signature on pk^*, since otherwise, a tuple of the form $(\mathsf{epk}_l, \mathsf{cpk}_{j^*}, \mathsf{pk}^*, \mathsf{cer}^*)$ would appear in $\mathsf{RegList}$ since $\mathsf{RegList}$ contains all tuples $(\mathsf{epk}, \mathsf{pk}, m, \mathsf{cer})$ where pk is the verification key that $\mathcal{B}$ has as input and cer had been obtained from the signing oracle of $\mathcal{B}$. In this case, j^* had also not been queried by $\mathcal{A}$ to its corruption oracle (as otherwise the output of $\mathcal{A}$ would not lead to a successful break), so $\mathcal{B}$ does not abort. To conclude, when $\mathcal{A}$ produces his output $(\mathsf{cpk}^*, \mathsf{pk}^*, \mathsf{cer}^*)$, with probability $\frac{1}{p(\eta)}$ the forgery is with respect to the public key of CA_{j_0} so $\mathsf{pk}^* = \mathsf{pk}$. Furthermore, if event NoCert occurs in the simulation of $\mathbf{Exp}^{unforge}_{\mathsf{ePCAS},\mathcal{A}}(\eta)$, then $(*, \mathsf{pk}, \mathsf{pk}^*, \mathsf{cer}^*)$ does not appear in $\mathsf{RegList}$. According to the observation above cer^* has not been obtained by sending pk^* to the signing oracle under sk, hence $(\mathsf{pk}^*, \mathsf{cer}^*)$ is a successful forgery for $\mathbf{Exp}^{\mathsf{eucma}}_{\mathsf{DSIG},\mathcal{B}}(\eta)$. We therefore obtain that

$$\Pr[\mathbf{Exp}^{unforge}_{\mathsf{ePCAS},\mathcal{A}}(\eta) = 1 \wedge \mathsf{NoCert}] \leq \frac{1}{p(\eta)} \cdot \Pr[\mathbf{Exp}^{\mathsf{eucma}}_{\mathsf{DSIG},\mathcal{B}}(\eta) = 1] \qquad (3)$$

Next we bound the probability $\Pr[\mathbf{Exp}^{unforge}_{\mathsf{ePCAS},\mathcal{A}}(\eta) = 1 \wedge \mathsf{CertInvKey}]$. Assume that event $\mathsf{CertInvKey}$ occurs so for some corrupted esk_l the tuple $(\mathsf{epk}_l, \mathsf{cpk}_{j^*}, \mathsf{pk}^*, \mathsf{cer}^*)$ appears in $\mathsf{RegList}$ and $\mathsf{ValidKey}(\mathsf{epk}_l, \mathsf{pk}^*) = 0$. Then, there exists some oracle $\mathcal{O} = \mathrm{CA}(\mathsf{cpk}_{j^*}, \mathsf{epk}_l, \mathsf{pk}^*)$ such that $(\mathsf{epk}_l, \mathsf{pk}^*, \mathsf{scer}^*)$ is the first message received by $\mathcal{O}$. The oracle then outputs an asymmetric encryption d of $k^*||pk^*$ under epk_l and symmetric encryption b^* of scer^* under k^* to the adversary. The adversary who can access $\mathsf{CorrTPM}$ oracle to obtain esk_l can consequently get a certification cer^* on pk^*. Since TPM oracle first checks whether $\mathsf{ValidKey}(\mathsf{epk}_l, \mathsf{pk}^*) = 1$ and then returns scer^* if it holds, this contradicts that $\mathsf{ValidKey}(\mathsf{epk}_l, \mathsf{pk}^*) = 0$. Thus, $\mathcal{A}$ cannot get such tuple $(\mathsf{epk}_l, \mathsf{cpk}_{j^*}, \mathsf{pk}^*, \mathsf{cer}^*)$ by querying TPM oracle. The only way to send such tuple is to produce it on his own. Therefore, if event $\Pr[\mathsf{CertInvKey}]$ occurs, then the adversary $\mathcal{A}$ must have produced a valid self certificate which the CA oracle accepted , hence he forged a signature on epk_l under sk^* which is corresponding to pk^* and $\mathsf{ValidKey}(\mathsf{epk}_l, \mathsf{pk}^*) = 0$. This intuition is behind the construction of the following EU-CMA adversary $\mathcal{C}$ for $\mathbf{Exp}^{\mathsf{eucma}}_{\mathsf{DSIG},\mathcal{C}}(\eta)$ out of an adversary $\mathcal{A}$ for $\mathbf{Exp}^{unforge}_{\mathsf{ePCAS},\mathcal{A}}(\eta)$.

The adversary $\mathcal{C}$ is for $\mathbf{Exp}^{\mathsf{eucma}}_{\mathsf{DSIG},\mathcal{C}}$ so, by the notion of EU-CMA signature schemes as shown in the Appendix B, $\mathcal{C}$ has as input some verification key pk and access to a signing oracle under the corresponding secret key sk. The adversary $\mathcal{C}$ runs adversary $\mathcal{A}$ internally and simulates for $\mathcal{A}$ all of the oracles to which $\mathcal{A}$ has access in $\mathbf{Exp}^{unforge}_{\mathsf{ePCAS},\mathcal{A}}(\eta)$. The keys for all of the TPMs are obtained by running the key generation algorithm of the encryption scheme: $(\mathsf{epk}_l, \mathsf{esk}_l) \leftarrow \mathsf{A.KG}(\eta)$ (for all $1 \leq l \leq p(\eta)$). The keys for all CAs are obtained using the key generation algorithm $(\mathsf{csk}_j, \mathsf{cpk}_j) \leftarrow \mathsf{KG}(\eta)$ (for all $1 \leq j \leq p(\eta)$). The short term public keys for all but one are obtained using the key generation algorithm $(\mathsf{pk}^*, \mathsf{sk}^*) \leftarrow \mathsf{KG}(\eta)$ and the special one is set to be the verification key pk that $\mathcal{B}$ has as input. Assume there are $p'(\eta)$ short-term public keys for the $p(\eta)$ TPMs.

Adversary $\mathcal{C}$ can therefore simulate perfectly all of the oracles: for TPM_l^n oracles he simply executes the code defined by TPM (Figures 2). For any oracle CA_j^m the adversary executes the code defined by CA (Figures 2). Adversary $\mathcal{C}$ can also answer corruption queries for all of the $\mathsf{CorrTPM}$ and CorrCA oracles, the simulation that $\mathcal{B}$ offers to $\mathcal{A}$ is therefore perfect. If $\mathcal{A}$ with corrupted esk_{l^*} sends $(\mathsf{pk}^*, \mathsf{epk}_{l^*}, \mathsf{scer}^*)$ to CA oracle such that $1 \leftarrow \mathsf{VER}(\mathsf{pk}^*, \mathsf{epk}_{l^*}, \mathsf{scer}^*)$, then the CA oracle will generate cer^* and then append $(\mathsf{epk}_{l^*}, \mathsf{cpk}_{j^*}, \mathsf{pk}^*, \mathsf{cer}^*)$ to $\mathsf{RegList}$. In this case, the adversary $\mathcal{A}$ with esk_{l^*} can obtain cer^* and then consequently win the game. When $\mathcal{A}$ outputs $(\mathsf{epk}_{l^*}, \mathsf{cpk}_{j^*}, \mathsf{pk}^*, \mathsf{cer}^*)$, $\mathcal{B}$ proceeds as follows. If $\mathsf{pk}^* \neq \mathsf{pk}$ then $\mathcal{C}$ aborts. Otherwise $\mathcal{C}$ outputs $(\mathsf{pk}^*, \mathsf{scer}^*)$ as his forgery.

If $\mathcal{C}$ does not abort, the simulation that $\mathcal{C}$ provides ti $\mathcal{A}$ is perfect. pk^* in the output of $\mathcal{A}$ equals pk with probability $\frac{1}{p'(\eta)}$. When the the event $\Pr[\mathsf{CertInvKey}]$ occurs and the adversary $\mathcal{A}$ wins, the message/signature pair $(\mathsf{epk}^*, \mathsf{scer}^*)$ should be valid under pk. According to the observation above scer^* has not been obtained by sending pk^* to the signing oracle under sk, hence $(\mathsf{pk}^*, \mathsf{scer}^*)$ is a successful forgery for $\mathbf{Exp}^{\mathsf{eucma}}_{\mathsf{DSIG},\mathcal{C}}(\eta)$.

We therefore obtain that

$$\Pr[\mathbf{Exp}^{unforge}_{\mathsf{ePCAS},\mathcal{A}}(\eta) = 1 \wedge \mathsf{CertInvKey}] \leq \frac{1}{p'(\eta)} \cdot \Pr[\mathbf{Exp}^{\mathsf{eucma}}_{\mathsf{DSIG},\mathcal{C}}(\eta) = 1] \quad (4)$$

Together with the previous bounds, we obtain that:

$$\mathbf{Adv}^{unforge}_{\mathsf{ePCAS},\mathcal{A}}(\eta) \leq \frac{1}{p(\eta)} \mathbf{Adv}^{\mathsf{eucma}}_{\mathsf{DSIG},\mathcal{B}} + \frac{1}{p'(\eta)} \mathbf{Adv}^{\mathsf{eucma}}_{\mathsf{DSIG},\mathcal{C}} \quad (5)$$

C.3 Proof of Theorem 3

Proof. The idea of the proof is to introduce a simulator $\mathcal{S}$ that imposes all corrupted CA (but must not interact with any TPM), uses $\mathcal{A}$ as a black-box and simulates the oracles that $\mathcal{A}$ can access. Then $\mathcal{S}$ can produce indistinguishable transcripts from $\mathcal{A}$'s realistic outputs in interaction with real TPMs and CAs. In fact, anyone can produce realistic transcripts for ePCAS protocol by using the simulator $\mathcal{S}$.

We construct the required simulator $\mathcal{S}$ as follow: The simulator $\mathcal{S}$ runs $\mathcal{A}$ and simulates $\mathrm{TPM}'_{\mathcal{S}}$ oracle. When $\mathcal{A}$ makes TPM' queries, then $\mathcal{S}$ answers $\mathcal{A}$ according to the simulation that shown in Figure 8. When $\mathcal{A}$ queries TPM' oracle, the simulator first generates a new short-term key pair $(\mathsf{pk}, \mathsf{sk})$, signs epk under sk and finally sends a self certificate scer. The simulator $\mathcal{S}$ works as in Figure 9.

Now observe the simulated $\mathrm{TPM}'_{\mathcal{S}}$ oracle, from $\mathcal{A}$'s point of view, the generation of the output of $\mathrm{TPM}_{\mathcal{S}}$ and that of $\mathrm{TPM}'_{\mathcal{S}}$ are identical and these outputs are indistinguishable except that the adversary has the knowledge of $\mathsf{ValidKey}$. Thus, the simulated oracle and the original oracle that $\mathcal{A}$ can access are indistinguishable from $\mathcal{A}$'s point of view. Obviously, the adversary $\mathcal{A}$ is in an perfect simulation. Once $\mathcal{A}$ outputs a transcript $\tau_{\mathcal{S}}$, the simulator $\mathcal{S}$ uses it as its output

$\text{TPM}'_S(\mathsf{epk}_l, \mathsf{pk})$
  $(\mathsf{pk}, \mathsf{sk}) \leftarrow \mathsf{KG}(\eta)$
    $\mathsf{scer} \leftarrow \mathsf{SIG}(\mathsf{sk}, \mathsf{epk})$
    send scer

Fig. 8. The simulated TPM'_S oracle

Algorithm $\mathcal{S}(\mathbf{epk}, \mathbf{cpk}, \mathbf{csk}, \mathsf{ValidTPM})$
  run $\mathcal{A}$ and answer $\mathcal{A}$'s queries according to Figure 8.
  $\tau_S \leftarrow \mathcal{A}^{\text{TPM}'_S}(\mathbf{epk}, \mathbf{cpk}, \mathbf{csk}, \mathsf{ValidTPM})$.
  $\tau_1 \leftarrow \tau_S$.
  output τ_1.

Fig. 9. The behaviour of the simulator $\mathcal{S}$

τ_1. Since $\mathcal{A}$ is used in a perfect simulation, the output τ_1 of $\mathcal{S}$ is essentially indistinguishable from $\mathcal{A}$'s output τ_0 in interaction with real TPM$'$ oracle. Thus, for any ppt distinguisher $\mathcal{D}$, its advantage $\mathbf{Adv}^{s\text{-}deni}_{\mathsf{ePCAS},\mathcal{D}}(\eta)$ is a negligible function. Therefore, the ePCAS is strongly deniable.

Context Aware Specification and Verification of Distributed Systems*

Liliana D'Errico and Michele Loreti

Dipartimento di Sistemi e Informatica
Università di Firenze

Abstract. Distributed and mobile systems are typically composed of heterogeneous computational units that interact with each other following a predefined protocol. Process algebras and modal logics have been largely used as tools for specifying and verifying such kind of systems. However, to use these tools a complete system description has to be provided. This is not always possible. Indeed, even if the protocol governing the interactions among the system components is completely specified, the precise implementation of each component, as well as the number of network elements, is generally unknown. In this paper we present a set of formal tools that permits specifying systems by means of *mixed specifications*: a system is not considered in isolation, but under the assumption that the enclosing environment satisfies a given set of properties. A model-checking algorithm is also defined to verify whether considered specifications satisfy or not the expected properties. In the former case, it is also guaranteed that whenever the context is instantiated with components satisfying the assumptions, property satisfaction is preserved.

1 Introduction

Distributed and mobile systems are typically composed of heterogeneous computational units that interact with each other following a predefined protocol. For this class of systems it is crucial to have tools that can be used to predict and avoid unexpected behaviours. One of the most successful technique to specify and verify properties of concurrent and distributed systems is the one based on process algebras.

Process algebras are a set of mathematically rigorous languages, with well defined semantics, that provide a number of constructors for system descriptions which follow an algebraic approach. Moreover, process algebras are equipped with formal tools, like modal and temporal logics, that can be used to specify expected properties of the modeled system. Model-checking algorithms can also be used to verify whether a given process algebraic specification satisfies or not the expected properties expressed in a modal logic.

However, to use process algebras and modal logics, a complete system description has to be provided. Unfortunately, this is a strong requirement when

* This work has been partially supported by the EU project ASCENS 257414.

R. Bruni and V. Sassone (Eds.): TGC 2011, LNCS 7173, pp. 142–159, 2012.

distributed and, more in general, open-ended systems are considered. Indeed, even if the protocol governing the interactions among the system components is completely specified, the precise implementation of each component, as well as the number of network elements, is generally unknown.

In [12] an assume-guarantee approach has been introduced to support analysis of concurrent systems. A system is not considered in isolation, but in conjunction with assumptions on the behaviour of the environment where it is executed. A specification consists of two parts: the first one (the process) accurately defined, the second one (the environment) more abstract and formalized by means of logical formulae.

In this paper we extend the approach proposed in [12,13] to a process algebra specifically thought for modeling mobile and distributed concurrent systems. Indeed, while in [12,13] the framework was based on CCS [18], in this paper we consider KLAIM [19]. This is a process algebra designed to provide programmers with primitives for handling physical distribution, scoping and mobility of processes. KLAIM is based on process algebras but makes use of Linda-like asynchronous communication and distribution is modeled via multiple shared tuple spaces [15]. Properties of KLAIM systems can be specified by means of MoMo [11], a modal logic equipped with primitives for assessing properties concerning distributions of resources within localities.

A model-checking algorithm is also defined to verify whether considered specifications satisfy or not the expected properties. In the former case, it is also guaranteed that whenever the context is instantiated with components satisfying the assumptions, property satisfaction is preserved.

Running Example. A running example will be used to describe the proposed framework. We consider a *distributed information system* where mobile agents are used to search data in the network. The system is composed of a set of nodes each of which contains some data and that is able to resolve client requests.

To recover information, mobile agents can be used. These agents are first evaluated locally to resolve the client's queries. The result of these operations can be either the data, which is then sent to the client, or a reference to a remote site where an agent has to migrate to continue the computation. If, after a given set of hops, requested data are not found a negative result is reported to the client location.

Related Works. Many works have been proposed in the literature for supporting contextual specification of concurrent and distributed systems. In [9,10] the logic is equipped with specific operators (*spatial implication*) for relating the satisfaction of a formula to the properties satisfied by the context. *Mixed specifications* [2] have been also introduced to describe a system where transitions *must* or *may* happen. In [1] intuitionistic and linear time logics are used to specify reactive systems and for studying compositional rules.

In [17] an operational framework has been proposed to describe concurrent processes that are immersed into an *open context*, i.e. a context that can contain holes. More recently, in [3] the same approach has been generalized in order to obtain a general methodology for analysing open systems. These approaches follow a complementary approach with respect to the methodology presented in the present paper. Indeed, they aim at identifying the most general assumptions that has to be imposed on the environment in order to guarantee some properties. On the contrary, in the present paper we are interested on verifying wether a property is satisfied when we guarantee that the hosting environment enjoys a set of assumptions.

Another related approach is the one based on compositional model-checking. This is a technique that aims at overcoming the problem of state explosion. In compositional model-checking, each system component is individually verified and the obtained results are merged without analyzing the whole system [4,5,8]. When a component is checked in isolation, it is often necessary to incorporate some knowledge about the context in which each component is expected to operate correctly. However, to apply these techniques, a complete description of a system has to be provided.

Finally, the framework proposed in this paper is somehow reminiscent of the one presented in [7], where a language for supporting abstract descriptions of the protocol governing the interactions between a client and a service is presented. However, the framework considered in this paper, besides possible interactions, permits taking into account other properties of enclosing environments like, for instance, name mobility and spatial structure.

Structure of the Paper. In Section 2 and Section 3 Klaim and MoMo are recalled. In Section 4 a logic for specifying contexts of Klaim nets is defined together with a model checking algorithm for verifying if a system (specified by means of the introduced assume-guarantee approach) satisfies or not a given property. Section 5 concludes the paper.

2 Klaim

In this section we present μKlaim [6], a simplified version of Klaim (Kernel Language for Agent Interaction and Mobility), that abstracts from some linguistic mechanisms (e.g. high-level communication, logical and physical localities,...) provided by Klaim, while preserving basic communication primitives. Moreover, for the sake of simplicity, in this paper we do not take the creation of *new nodes* into account. This allow us to define the framework without considering all the technicalities needed to handle new names while simplifying the presentation of the considered framework.

A μKlaim system, called a *net*, is a set of *nodes*, each of which is identified by a *locality*. *Localities* can be seen as the addresses of nodes. We shall use Loc to denote the set of localities $l, l_1, \ldots$. Every node has a computational component (a set of processes running in parallel) and a data component (a tuple space). A special locality `self` is used to refer to the node where a process is running. Moreover, we let LVar be the set of *locality variables* $u, u_1, \ldots$. In the rest of this paper, we let ℓ denote an element Loc $\cup$ LVar.

Table 1. μKLAIM syntax

$N ::= 0 \mid l :: C \mid N_1 \parallel N_2$	NETS
$C ::= P \mid \langle t \rangle$	COMPONENTS
$P, Q ::= \mathbf{nil} \mid P \vert Q \mid P + Q \mid A(t) \mid act.P$	PROCESSES
$act ::= \mathbf{out}(t)@\ell \mid \mathbf{in}(T)@\ell \mid \mathbf{eval}(P)@\ell$	ACTIONS
$t ::= f \mid f, t$	TUPLES
$f ::= \ell \mid e$	FIELDS
$T ::= F \mid F, T$	TEMPLATES
$F ::= f \mid !u \mid !\mathrm{x}$	TEMP. FIELDS

Processes interact with each other either locally or remotely inserting and withdrawing tuples from tuple spaces. A tuple is a sequence of *actual* fields. Each actual field can be either a locality (ℓ) or an expression e. The precise syntax of expressions is not specified here, we assume that expressions contain, at least, values $v, v_1, v' \ldots$ in the set of *basic values* Val (not specified here) and variables $x, x_1, x', \ldots$ in the set of *value variables* Var.

Tuples are retrieved from tuple spaces via *pattern matching* using *templates* (T). Templates are sequences of *actual* and *formal* fields. The second ones are *variables* that will get a value when a tuple is retrieved. Formal fields are signalled by a '!' before the variable name.

The *pattern-matching* predicate *match* is as expected: a template T matches against a tuple t if both have the same number of fields and the corresponding fields do match; two *actual* fields match only if they are identical, while formal fields match any value of the same type. For instance, template $\langle \mathsf{QUERY}, !u, !x \rangle$ matches against tuple $\langle \mathsf{QUERY}, l, 3 \rangle$ and the match yields the substitution mapping u to l and x to 3. In the rest of this paper we let $\sigma, \sigma', \sigma_1, \ldots$ range over substitutions in SUBST, that is finite partial functions mapping locality variables in localities and value variables in values. We let: *(i)* $[]$ denote the empty substitution; *(ii)* $\sigma \cdot [l/u]$ (resp. $\sigma \cdot [v/x]$) denote the substitution associating l (resp. v) to u (resp. v) and $\sigma(u')$ (resp. $\sigma(x')$) to every $u' \neq u$ (resp. $x' \neq x$); *(iii)* and $\sigma'[\sigma]$ denote the standard function composition of substitutions σ' and σ.

The syntax of μKLAIM nets is defined in Table 1. Term 0 denotes the *empty net*, i.e. the net that does not contain any node. Terms $l :: P$ (*located process*) and $l :: \langle t \rangle$ (*located tuple*) are used to describe basic μKLAIM nodes: the former states that process P is running at l whilst the latter that the tuple space located at l contains tuple $\langle t \rangle$. μKLAIM nets are obtained by parallel composition ($\parallel$) of located processes and tuples. Let N be a net, we let $\mathsf{nodes}(N)$ denote the set of nodes in N[1].

The syntax of μKLAIM processes is also defined in Table 1. There **nil** identifies the process that cannot perform any action, $P|Q$ denotes the parallel composition of P and Q while $P + Q$ identifies the process that can nondeterministically

[1] $\mathsf{nodes}(\mathbf{0}) = \emptyset$, $\mathsf{nodes}(l :: C) = \{l\}$, $\mathsf{nodes}(N_1 \parallel N_2) = \mathsf{nodes}(N_1) \cup \mathsf{nodes}(N_2)$.

behave either like P or like Q. Process invocation $A(t)$ is used to model recursive behaviour, where we assume a definition $A(T) \stackrel{\text{def}}{=} P$ for each process constant A. Finally, $act.P$ stands for the process that executes action act and then behaves like P. Possible actions are $\mathbf{out}(t)@l$, $\mathbf{in}(T)@l$ and $\mathbf{eval}(P)@l$.

Action $\mathbf{out}(t)@\ell$ adds the evaluation of t to tuple space located at ℓ. To resolve target locality ℓ (that can be $\mathtt{self}$) function $\mathcal{E}(\ell, l)$ is used, where the second parameter is the locality identifying the node where the action is performed: $\mathcal{E}(\mathtt{self}, l) = l$ and $\mathcal{E}(l_1, l) = l_1$ if $l_1 \neq \mathtt{self}$.

Function $\mathcal{T}[\![\cdot]\!]$ is used to evaluate tuples and templates. This function takes a tuple t (resp. a template T) and a locality l, which indicates the nodes where the action is performed, and returns a tuple obtained from t (resp. from T) by replacing each expression with its evaluation and each occurrence of $\mathtt{self}$ with l. For instance, $\mathcal{T}[\![2, 2+3, \mathtt{self}]\!]_l = (2, 5, l)$ while $\mathcal{T}[\![!u, \mathtt{self}]\!]_l = (!u, l)$. In the rest of this paper we will use et to denote *evaluate tuples*, i.e. tuples that only contain basic values and localities different from $\mathtt{self}$.

Action $\mathbf{in}(T)@\ell$ is used to retrieve tuples from tuple spaces. Differently from **out** this is a blocking operation: the computation is blocked until a tuple matching the template $\mathcal{T}[\![T]\!]_l$, that is the evaluation of T at locality l, is found in the tuple space located at ℓ. Action **in** acts as a binder for the variables occurring as formal fields in T. Finally, action $\mathbf{eval}(P)@\ell$ spawns process P at locality ℓ.

In the sequel we use $\mathsf{fn}(N)$ (resp. $\mathsf{fn}(P)$, $\mathsf{fn}(t)$) to denote the set of *free names* in N (resp. in P and in t). We also write $l \in N$ (resp. $l \in P$, $l \in t$) to denote that $l \in \mathsf{fn}(N)$ (resp. $l \in \mathsf{fn}(P)$, $l \in \mathsf{fn}(t)$), For any term X, we let $X\sigma$ denote the result of the capture-avoiding substitution of each free occurrence of a variable u/x by the corresponding value $\sigma(u)/\sigma(x)$. Finally, we let $\textsc{Net}$ denote the set of μKLAIM nets. Elements in $\textsc{Net}$ are considered to be structurally equivalent by means of the *structural congruence* $\equiv$ induced by the laws in Table 3.

Operational semantics of μKLAIM is defined by means of a *labelled transition relation* $\longrightarrow \; \subseteq \textsc{Net} \times \Lambda \times \textsc{Net}$ inductively defined in Table 2 where Λ is the set of transition labels λ defined by the following grammar:

$$\lambda ::= \; t \triangleright l \mid t \triangleleft l \mid \; \blacktriangleright l \mid \tau$$

Label $t \triangleright l$ denotes that a tuple t can be inserted at l and it is originated when an **out** action is performed (rule OUT). A transition with lable $t \triangleleft l$ is performed when tuple t can be retrieved from tuple space located at l (rule IN). A system evolves with a transition labelled $\blacktriangleright l$ whenever a process is evaluated at l (rule EV). Label τ denotes silent transitions, these are originated by rules S-OUT, S-IN or S-EV that model synchronizations related to **out**s, **in**s or **eval**s, respectively. Other rules are standard.

In the sequel we will write $N \xrightarrow{\lambda}$ to denote that there exists N' such that $N \xrightarrow{\lambda} N'$, while $N \not\xrightarrow{\lambda}$ denotes that no net is reachable from N with a λ. Moreover, let $L \subseteq \textsc{Loc}$, we will say that λ *operates on* L ($\lambda \downarrow L$) if $\lambda = \tau$ or λ is $t \triangleright l$, $t \triangleleft l$, or $\blacktriangleright l$ and $l \in L$.

Example 1 (Information Seeker in μKLAIM). The considered distributed information system can be easily described in μKLAIM by associating to each

Table 2. μKLAIM operational semantics

$$\frac{et = \mathcal{T}[\![t]\!]_{l_1} \quad l_2 = \mathcal{E}(\ell, l_1)}{l_1 :: \mathbf{out}(t)@\ell.P \xrightarrow{et \triangleright l_2} l_1 :: P}\ \textsc{Out} \qquad \frac{\sigma = match(\mathcal{T}[\![T]\!]_{l_1}, t) \quad l_2 = \mathcal{E}(\ell, l_1)}{l_1 :: \mathbf{in}(T)@\ell.P \xrightarrow{t \triangleleft l_2} l_1 :: P\{\sigma\}}\ \textsc{In}$$

$$\frac{l_2 = \mathcal{E}(l_1, \ell)}{l_1 :: \mathbf{eval}(Q)@\ell.P \xrightarrow{\blacktriangleright l_2} l_1 :: P \parallel l_2 :: Q}\ \textsc{Ev} \qquad \frac{N_1 \xrightarrow{t \triangleright l} N_1' \quad l \in \mathsf{nodes}(N_2)}{N_1 \parallel N_2 \xrightarrow{\tau} N_1' \parallel l :: \langle t \rangle) \parallel N_2}\ \textsc{S-Out}$$

$$\frac{N_1 \xrightarrow{t \triangleleft l} N_1'}{N_1 \parallel l :: \langle t \rangle \xrightarrow{\tau} N_1'}\ \textsc{S-In} \qquad \frac{N_1 \xrightarrow{\blacktriangleright l} N_1' \quad l \in \mathsf{nodes}(N_2)}{N_1 \parallel N_2 \xrightarrow{\tau} N_1' \parallel N_2}\ \textsc{S-Ev}$$

$$\frac{l :: P \xrightarrow{\lambda} N}{l :: (P + Q) \xrightarrow{\lambda} N}\ \textsc{Ch} \qquad \frac{A(T) \stackrel{\text{def}}{=} P \quad \sigma = match(T, \mathcal{T}[\![t]\!]_{l}) \quad l :: P\sigma \xrightarrow{\lambda} N}{l :: A(t) \xrightarrow{\lambda} N}\ \textsc{Call}$$

$$\frac{N_1 \xrightarrow{\lambda} N_1'}{N_1 \parallel N_2 \xrightarrow{\lambda} N_1' \parallel N_2}\ \textsc{Par} \qquad \frac{N_1 \equiv N \quad N \xrightarrow{\lambda} N' \quad N' \equiv N_2}{N_1 \xrightarrow{\lambda} N_2}\ \textsc{Str}$$

component a μKLAIM node. We assume one of these nodes be server_0. The latter is the *entry point* for the considered *distributed information system*.

Queries are modeled as tuples of the form (QUERY, l): The first field is a value identifying the query while the second field is a locality playing the role of query identifier. Each node operates as follows. When a query (QUERY, l) is received either a tuple of the form (DATA, l), containing the requested data, or, when the query cannot be resolved locally, a tuple $(\mathsf{FWD}, l, \mathsf{server}_j)$ are produced. In the latter case, server_j indicates the address of the server that may be able to resolve the query.

We let terminal be a node that is used to collect clients requests. When a request is received, a mobile agent, that will perform the query, is evaluated at server_0. This process is defined as follows:

$$\mathsf{QHandler}(\,) \stackrel{\text{def}}{=} \mathbf{in}(\mathsf{QUERY}, !u)@\mathtt{self}.\mathbf{eval}(\mathsf{Search}(u, 3))@\mathsf{server}_0.\mathsf{QHandler}(\,)$$

when a query (QUERY, l) is received at terminal (for some locality l), $\mathsf{Search}(l, 3)$ is evaluated at server_0. Search, defined below[2], is an agent that takes two parameters: a locality, that is a client request identifier, and an integer indicating the maximum number of *hops* the agent can perform to execute the query.

$$\begin{aligned}\mathsf{Search}(!u, !x) \stackrel{\text{def}}{=}\ & \mathbf{out}(\mathsf{QUERY}, u)@\mathtt{self}.\\ & \quad \mathbf{in}(\mathsf{DATA}, u)@\mathtt{self}.\mathbf{out}(\mathsf{DATA}, u)@\mathsf{terminal}.\mathbf{nil}\\ & \quad + \mathbf{in}(\mathsf{FWD}, u, !u_2)@\mathtt{self}.\\ & \qquad \mathbf{if}\ x > 0\ \mathbf{then}\ \mathbf{eval}(\mathsf{IS}(u, x-1))@u_2.\mathbf{nil}\\ & \qquad \mathbf{else}\ \mathbf{out}(\mathsf{FAIL}, l)@\mathsf{terminal}.\mathbf{nil}\end{aligned}$$

[2] In Search we use **if then else** as a macro in the language.

Table 3. Structural congruence

$$N_1 \parallel N_2 \equiv N_2 \parallel N_1 \qquad (N_1 \parallel N_2) \parallel N_3 \equiv N_1 \parallel (N_2 \parallel N_3) \qquad l :: C \equiv l :: C \parallel l :: \mathbf{nil}$$

$$l :: (P_1 | P_2) \equiv l :: P_1 \parallel l :: P_2 \qquad N_1 \parallel 0 \equiv N_1 \qquad l :: (P + Q) \equiv l :: (Q + P)$$

This is a process that first tries to resolve the query locally and, in the case of success, reports the result at terminal. When the query cannot be resolved, Search evaluates itself at the obtained reference. If after x jumps the query has not be resolved, a failure is reported at terminal

Notice that in the specification outlined above we have a part of the system completely specified and another, the one containing node server_0, for which only some assumptions about the behaviour are known.

3 MoMo: A Modal Logic for Mobility

To specify properties of μKLAIM systems modal logic MoMo [11] can be used. This is a modal logic that extends Hennessy-Milner logic [16] with modal operators specifically thought for specifying properties of mobile and distributed systems. In particular, MoMo formulae can be used to specify possible interactions of a net with the environment where it is executed. These interactions are described in terms of tuples and processes that can be added/retrieved and evaluated to/from a given site. Moreover, MoMo also provides operators for reasoning about distribution of resources. The syntax of MoMo formulae (φ, φ_1, φ_2,...,φ',...) is defined by the following grammar:

$$\varphi ::= \mathbf{T} \mid \{l_1 = l_2\} \mid \varphi \vee \varphi \mid \neg\varphi \mid \langle t\rangle@l \rightarrow \varphi \mid \langle t\rangle@l \leftarrow \varphi \mid \langle\lambda\rangle\varphi \mid \forall u.\varphi \mid \text{И} u.\varphi \mid \mathcal{A}.\{\sigma\}$$
$$\mathcal{A} ::= \nu\kappa.\phi \mid \kappa$$

In Table 4 we present a set of derivable operators that we will use as macros of the logic.

In the sequel, the intuitive meaning of MoMo operators is illustrated. *Name matching* ($\{l_1 = l_2\}$) permits verifying whether two names are equals: every net satisfies $\{l = l\}$ while no net satisfies $\{l_1 = l_2\}$ if $l_1 \neq l_2$. The consumption operator is used to specify properties concerning the availability and distribution of *resources* in the net. Resources in μKLAIM are located tuples $\langle t\rangle@l$, that is tuple t at location l. A net N satisfies $\langle t\rangle@l \rightarrow \varphi$ if and only if $N \equiv N' \parallel l :: \langle t\rangle$ and N' satisfies formula φ. To describe how a system reacts to cretion of new resources, *production* can be used. A net N satisfies $\langle t\rangle@l \leftarrow \varphi$ whenever $N \parallel l :: \langle t\rangle$ satisfies φ.

Temporal properties are specified using the *diamond* operator. This is parameterized with respect to a transition label λ. A net N_1 satisfies $\langle\lambda\rangle\varphi$ if and only if there exists N_2 such that $N_1 \xrightarrow{\lambda} N_2$ and N_2 satisfies φ.

Operator $\text{И} u.\varphi$ [14] acts as a quantifier over all names that do not occur free either in the formula φ or in the state. A net N satisfies $\text{И} u.\varphi$ if there exists l

Table 4. Derivable operators

$\mu\kappa.\varphi \stackrel{\text{def}}{=} \neg\nu\kappa.\neg\varphi[\neg\kappa/\kappa]$	$\varphi_1 \wedge \varphi_2 \stackrel{\text{def}}{=} \neg(\neg\varphi_1 \vee \neg\varphi_2)$
$\{l_1 \neq l_2\} \stackrel{\text{def}}{=} \neg\{l_1 = l_2\}$	$[\lambda]\,\varphi \stackrel{\text{def}}{=} \neg\langle\lambda\rangle\neg\varphi$
$\exists u.\varphi \stackrel{\text{def}}{=} \neg\forall u.\neg\varphi$	$Always(\varphi) \stackrel{\text{def}}{=} \nu\kappa.\varphi \wedge [\tau]\,\kappa\ (\kappa \notin \varphi)$
$Never(\varphi) \stackrel{\text{def}}{=} Always(\neg\varphi)$	$Eventually(\varphi) \stackrel{\text{def}}{=} \neg Never(\varphi)$

not occurring neither in φ nor in N such that N satisfies $\varphi[l/u]$. Moreover, N satisfies $\forall u.\varphi$ if and only if N satisfies $\varphi[l/u]$ for each $l \in$ Loc.

Recursive properties are specified by means of *abstractions* $\mathcal{A}.\{\sigma\}$, where $\mathcal{A}$ can be either a *maximal fixed point* ($\nu\kappa.\varphi$) or a *logical variable* (κ). A net N satisfies $(\nu\kappa.\varphi).\{\sigma\}$ if and only if N satisfies $(\varphi\sigma)[\nu\kappa.\varphi/\kappa]$. Formally, the interpretation of $\nu\kappa.\varphi$ is defined as the maximal fixed point of the interpretation of φ. To guarantee well-definedness of the interpretation function, it is assumed that in every formula $\nu\kappa.\varphi$, logical variable κ is positive within φ (i.e. it appears within the scope of an even number of negations)[3].

Example 2. For the system of Example 1 one could be interested in guaranteeing that whenever a query is received at node terminal, eventually a result will be obtained. This property can be specified in MoMo as follows:

$$\not\!\!|\!\!\nearrow\! u.\langle \mathsf{QUERY}, u\rangle @\mathsf{terminal} \leftarrow$$
$$Eventually(\langle \mathsf{DATA}, \mathsf{u} \triangleright \mathsf{terminal}\rangle\mathbf{true} \vee \langle FAIL, u \triangleright \mathsf{terminal}\rangle\mathbf{true})$$

This formula states that if the tuple $\langle \mathsf{QUERY}, l\rangle$ is inserted in the tuple space located at terminal, for some new name l, then either $\langle \mathsf{DATA}, l\rangle$ or $\langle \mathsf{FAIL}, l\rangle$ will be eventually sent at terminal. Notice that to verify whether this property is satisfied or not by the system of Example 1, a complete description of the system has to be provided. In the next section we will introduce a formalism that can be used to specify the properties we assume satisfied by the context where node terminal operates. This approach can be used to verify the behaviour of the considered example while abstracting from the concrete specification of the environment.

4 Compositional Analysis of μKlaim Nets

In this section we extend the syntax of μKlaim in order to take *mixed specifications* into account. Following the same approach proposed in [12], we consider a specification consisting of two parts: the first one (a μKlaim net) accurately defined, the second one (the environment) more abstract and formalized by means of logical formulae. The latter identifies the set of properties we *assume* satisfied by the environment where the part of the system we completely know operates.

[3] This permits defining interpretation of logical formulae as the composition of monotonic functions in a complete lattice and Tarski's Fixed Point Theorem guarantees existence of a unique *maximal* fixed point.

The proposed temporal logic permits describing all the interactions the enclosing environment can have with the known part of the system and the spatial structure of the environment. The former properties are specified by means of an adaptation of MoMo diamond operator, while the latter are defined by means of an adaptation of spatial operators proposed in [9,10].

4.1 A Logic for μKlaim contexts

We let $\mathcal{L}_K^\chi$ be the set of formulae χ, $\chi_1, \chi', \ldots$ defined by the syntax in Table 5 where ι, ι_1 are used to specify possible interactions performed by the environment, while $\delta, \delta_1, \delta', \ldots$ identify recursive assumptions.

Semantics of $\mathcal{L}_K^\chi$ formulae is defined by means functions $\mathbb{C}[\![]\!]^L$ and $\mathbb{I}[\![]\!]^L$ formally defined inTable 6. These function are parametrized with respect to a set of localities L. This set contains all the localities we assume used by the environment to interact with the part of the system that is completely specified:

Definition 1. *A net N only interacts with L ($N \bowtie L$) if and only if for any N', t and l such that $N \equiv N' \parallel l :: \langle t \rangle$, $l \notin L$. In the sequel we let* $\textsc{Net}_L$ *be* $\{N | N \bowtie L\}$.

Function $\mathbb{C}[\![\cdot]\!]^L\varepsilon\sigma$ (resp. $\mathbb{I}[\![\cdot]\!]^L\varepsilon\sigma$) takes an assumption χ (resp. an interaction ι), a *logical environment* ε, a substitution σ and yields the set of nets in satisfying χ. A logical environment is a function in $\textsc{LVar} \rightarrow \textsc{Subst} \rightarrow 2^{\textsc{Net}_L}$, i.e. a function associating to each logical variable $\kappa \in \textsc{LVar}$ a function associating to each substitution a subset of $\textsc{Net}_L$. We let ε_0 bet the logical environment associating the empty set constant function to each logical variable. We will also use $N \models_\sigma^L \chi$ to denote that $N \in \mathbb{C}[\![\chi]\!]^L\varepsilon_0\sigma$ and $N \models^L \chi$ when $N \models_{[\,]}^L \chi$.

Interactions. Basic interactions are: $\mathbf{0}$ and $(\!|\ \lambda\ |\!)\chi$. The former identifies an environment that cannot perform any action: indeed $\mathbb{I}[\![\mathbf{0}]\!]^L\varepsilon\sigma$ is the set of N such that $N \not\xrightarrow{\lambda}$ for any transition label λ. Conversely, $(\!|\ \lambda\ |\!)\chi$ identifies a context where a transition λ can be performed always leading to a configuration satisfying χ[4]: $N \in \mathbb{I}[\![(\!|\ \lambda\ |\!)\chi]\!]^L\varepsilon\sigma$ if and only if $N \xrightarrow{\lambda\sigma}$ and for each N' such that $N \xrightarrow{\lambda\sigma} N'$, $N' \in \mathbb{C}[\![\chi]\!]^{L\cup\mathsf{n}(\lambda\sigma)}\varepsilon\sigma$. When λ is an output ($t \triangleright l$) we also require that $\mathsf{fn}(t) \subseteq \mathsf{nodes}(N) \cup L$. The latter condition guarantees that if a locality name is received from the environment then it refers to a node that actually exists.

Universal quantification over localities $\forall u.\iota$ has the usual meaning: $N \in \mathbb{I}[\![\forall u.\iota]\!]^L\varepsilon\sigma$ if and only if for each $l \in \textsc{Loc}$, N satisfies $N \in \mathbb{I}[\![\iota]\!]^L\varepsilon\sigma \cdot [l/u]$. Finally, $\iota_1 \oplus \iota_2$ is satisfied when both the interactions described by ι_1 and ι_2 are provided. Hence, $N \in \mathbb{I}[\![\iota_1 \oplus \iota_2]\!]^L\varepsilon\sigma$ if and only if N belongs to both $\mathbb{I}[\![\iota_1]\!]^L\varepsilon\sigma$ and $\mathbb{I}[\![\iota_2]\!]^L\varepsilon\sigma$.

Given an interaction ι, we let $\mathsf{first}(\iota)$ be the set of initial transition labels in ι and it is inductively defined as follows: $\mathsf{first}(\mathbf{0}) = \emptyset$, $\mathsf{first}((\!|\ \lambda\ |\!)\chi) = \{\lambda\}$, $\mathsf{first}(\forall u.\iota) = \cup_{l \in \textsc{Loc}} \mathsf{first}(\iota[l/u])$, and $\mathsf{first}(\iota_1 \oplus \iota_2) = \mathsf{first}(\iota_1) \cup \mathsf{first}(\iota_2)$. A formula

[4] $(\!|\ \lambda\ |\!)\cdot$ can be expressed in MoMo as $\langle\lambda\rangle\mathbf{true} \wedge [\lambda]\cdot$

Table 5. Syntax of formulae for environments

$\chi ::= \iota \mid \chi_1 \vee \chi_2 \mid \chi_1 \otimes \chi_2 \mid \{\chi\}_l\chi \mid {\not\!\!\mid\!\!\!\lambda} u.\chi \mid \delta.\{\sigma\}$	ASSUMPTIONS
$\iota ::= \mathbf{0} \mid (\!\mid \lambda \mid\!)\chi \mid \forall u.\iota \mid \iota \oplus \iota$	INTERACTIONS
$\delta ::= \nu\kappa.\chi \mid \kappa$	ABSTRACTIONS

ι is *well formed* if and only if for each sub-formula of the form $\iota_1 \oplus \iota_2$ we have that $\mathsf{first}(\iota_1) \cap \mathsf{first}(\iota_2) = \emptyset$. In the rest of this paper we will only considered *well formed* formulae.

We will see in the next section that the specific operators used to formalize assumptions about possible interactions are crucial for defining an operational semantics of logical formulae.

Assumptions. A net N fulfill assumption ι ($N \in \mathbb{C}[\![\iota]\!]^L\varepsilon\sigma$) if N only interacts with the part of the system that is completely specified by means of actions considered in ι. Namely, if and only if $N \in \mathbb{I}[\![\iota]\!]^L\varepsilon\sigma$ and if $N \xrightarrow{\lambda}$ and $\lambda \downarrow L$ then $\lambda \in \mathsf{first}(\iota)$.

Conjuction $\chi_1 \vee \chi_2$ has the expected meaning: $N \in \mathbb{C}[\![\chi_1 \vee \chi_2]\!]^L\varepsilon\sigma$ if $N \in \mathbb{C}[\![\chi_1]\!]^L\varepsilon\sigma$ or $N \in \mathbb{C}[\![\chi_2]\!]^L\varepsilon\sigma$

To formalize assumption about spatial structure of the environment formulae $\{\chi\}_l$ and $\chi_1 \otimes \chi_2$ are used. Formula $\{\chi\}_l$ states that a node identified by locality l is available in an environment satisfying χ. This node l can only be used for interactions. Hence, no tuples can be located at l (unless these are explicitly produced via an output). Formally: $N \in \mathbb{C}[\![\{\chi\}_l]\!]^L\varepsilon\sigma$ if and only if $N \equiv N' \parallel l :: \mathbf{nil}$ and $N' \in \mathbb{C}[\![\chi]\!]^{L\cup\{l\}}\varepsilon\sigma$.

Formula $\chi_1 \otimes \chi_2$ states that the environment is composed of two parts, one satisfying χ_1 and the other satisfying χ_2. These two parts do not share any locality name but the ones considered in the concrete specification. Indeed, $N_1 \parallel N_2 \in \mathbb{C}[\![\chi_1 \otimes \chi_2]\!]^L\varepsilon\sigma$ if and only if $N_1 \in \mathbb{C}[\![\chi_1]\!]^L\varepsilon\sigma$, $N_2 \in \mathbb{C}[\![\chi_2]\!]^L\varepsilon\sigma$ and $\mathsf{fn}(N_1) \cap \mathsf{fn}(N_2) \subseteq L$. Since both N_1 and N_2 only interact with L, it is guaranteed that N_1 and N_2 cannot interfere with each other.

Like in MoMo, ${\not\!\!\mid\!\!\!\lambda} u.\chi$ and $\delta.\{\sigma\}$ are used for *fresh name quantification* and for *recursive invocation.*

Example 3. In Example 1 we have assumed that a node, named server_0 is available in the environment. Here, we can use the following formula in $\mathcal{L}_K^{\chi}$ to formalize the properties we assume satisfied by the environment where node $\mathsf{terminal}$ operates:

$$\{\delta_1.\{\mathsf{server}_0/u_1\}\}_{\mathsf{server}_0} \tag{1}$$

where:

$$\delta_1 = \nu\kappa_1.\forall u_2.(\!\mid \langle \mathsf{QUERY}, u_2\rangle \lhd u_1 \mid\!)(\!\mid \langle \mathsf{DATA}, u_2\rangle \rhd u_1 \mid\!)\kappa_1.\{\ \} \vee {\not\!\!\mid\!\!\!\lambda} u_3.(\!\mid \langle \mathsf{FWD}, u_2, u_3\rangle \rhd u_1 \mid\!)\{\kappa_1.\{u_3/u_1\}\}_{u_3} \otimes \delta_2.\{\ \}$$

$$\delta_2 = \nu\kappa.\forall u_2.(\!\mid \langle \mathsf{QUERY}, u_2\rangle \lhd u_1 \mid\!)((\!\mid \langle \mathsf{DATA}, u_2\rangle \rhd u_1 \mid\!)\kappa_2 \vee (\!\mid \langle \mathsf{FWD}, u_2, u_3\rangle \rhd u_1 \mid\!)\kappa_2)$$

Table 6. $\mathcal{L}_K^{\chi}$ interpretation functions

$$\mathbb{C}[\![\iota]\!]^L\varepsilon\sigma = \{N | N \in \mathbb{I}[\![\iota]\!]^L\varepsilon\sigma \text{ and } \forall\lambda.N \xrightarrow{\lambda} \text{ and } \lambda \downarrow L \Longrightarrow \lambda \in \mathsf{first}(\iota\sigma), \}$$
$$\mathbb{C}[\![\chi_1 \vee \chi_2]\!]^L\varepsilon\sigma = \mathbb{C}[\![\chi_1]\!]^L\varepsilon\sigma \cup \mathbb{C}[\![\chi_2]\!]^L_\varepsilon\sigma$$
$$\mathbb{C}[\![\nu\kappa.\chi]\!]^L\varepsilon\sigma = \nu\mathcal{C}^L_\varepsilon\sigma \qquad \text{where } \mathcal{C}^L_\varepsilon(f) = \mathbb{C}[\![\chi]\!]^L\varepsilon[\kappa \mapsto f]$$
$$\mathbb{C}[\![\kappa]\!]^L\varepsilon\sigma = \varepsilon(\kappa)\sigma$$
$$\mathbb{C}[\![\delta.\{\sigma'\}]\!]^L\varepsilon\sigma = \mathbb{C}[\![\delta]\!]^L\varepsilon(\sigma[\sigma'])$$
$$\mathbb{C}[\![\{\chi\}_l]\!]^L\varepsilon\sigma = \{N \parallel l :: \mathbf{nil} | N \in \mathbb{C}[\![\chi]\!]^{L\cup\{l\}}\varepsilon\sigma\}$$
$$\mathbb{C}[\![\text{И} u.\chi]\!]^L\varepsilon\sigma = \{N | \exists l.l \notin \mathsf{fn}(\chi) \cup L \text{ and } N \in \mathbb{C}[\![\chi[l/u]]\!]^L\varepsilon\sigma\}$$
$$\mathbb{C}[\![\chi_1 \otimes \chi_2]\!]^L\varepsilon\sigma = \{N_1 \parallel N_2 \mid N_1 \in \mathbb{C}[\![\chi_1]\!]^L\varepsilon\sigma, N_2 \in \mathbb{C}[\![\chi_2]\!]^L\varepsilon\sigma \text{ and } (\mathsf{fn}(N_1) \cap \mathsf{fn}(N_2)) \subseteq L\}$$

$$\mathbb{I}[\![\mathbf{0}]\!]^L\varepsilon\sigma = \{N \in \textsc{Net}_L | \forall\lambda : N \not\xrightarrow{\lambda}\}$$
$$\mathbb{I}[\![(\!|\, \lambda \,|\!)\chi]\!]^L\varepsilon\sigma = \{N \in \textsc{Net}_L \mid (1)\ N \xrightarrow{\lambda\sigma} \text{ and } \forall N' : N \xrightarrow{\lambda\sigma} N', N' \in \mathbb{C}[\![\chi]\!]^{L\cup n(\lambda)}\varepsilon\sigma; \ (2) \text{ if } \lambda = t \rhd l \text{ then } n(\lambda) \subseteq \mathsf{nodes}(N) \cup L\}$$
$$\mathbb{I}[\![\iota_1 \oplus \iota_2]\!]^L\varepsilon\sigma = \mathbb{I}[\![\iota_1]\!]^L\varepsilon\sigma \cap \mathbb{I}[\![\iota_2]\!]^L\varepsilon\sigma$$
$$\mathbb{I}[\![\forall u.\iota]\!]^L\varepsilon\sigma = \bigcap_{l \in \textsc{Loc}} \mathbb{I}[\![\iota]\!]^L\varepsilon\sigma \cdot [l/u]$$

Assumption (1) states that there exists a node named server_0 and δ_1, where u_1 is replaced by server_0, is satisfied. Formula δ_1 states that whenever tuples of the form $(\langle \mathsf{QUERY}, l\rangle)$ can be retrieved from u_1 (in our case u_1 is server_0) one of the following two behaviours can be experienced: tuple $(\langle \mathsf{DATA}, l\rangle)$ will be inserted at u_1 and δ_1 is again satisfied; tuple $(\langle \mathsf{FWD}, l, u_3\rangle)$ will be inserted at u_1 and $\delta_1.\{u_3/u_1\} \otimes \delta_2$ is satisfied. In the latter case, we have that a new part of the context (the one containing u_3) has been discovered. Indeed, formula $\delta_1.\{u_3/u_1\} \otimes \delta_2$ identifies a context where two parts are available: one satisfying $\delta_1.\{u_3/u_1\}$ and the other satisfying δ_2. The component satisfying $\delta_1.\{u_3/u_1\}$ contains a node named u_3 that behaves exactly like server_0. The part satisfying δ_2 contains the node server_0 that now we know it redirects unsatisfiable queries to u_3.

Mixed Specifications. We extend μKlaim syntax by considering specifications composed of two parts: a μKlaim net and an $\mathcal{L}_K^{\chi}$ formula. We let Mix be the set of *mixed specifications* have the following form: $\chi \rhd N$.

Operational semantics is extended in order to take mixed specifications into account. New rules, reported in Table 7, are straightforward: $(\!|\, \lambda \,|\!)\chi$ works as an action prefixing (rule Nec); $\oplus$ works similarly to a choice (rule Sel); while $\otimes$ and $\rhd$ have the same meaning of a parallel composition. Indeed, rules CompL, CompR, MixL and MixR are the ones for *interleaving* while rules MOut, MIn and MEv regulate synchronizations. Notice that after a MOut, besides the produced tuple, a new component, $\textsc{n}(\mathsf{fn}(t))$, is composed in parallel in the reduced net[5]. This component instantiates in the concrete specification the nodes

[5] Let L be a finite set of locality names, $\textsc{n}(L)$ is $\mathsf{0}$ when $L = \emptyset$ and $l :: \mathbf{nil} \parallel \textsc{n}(L')$ when $L = \{l\} \cup L'$.

Table 7. Operational semantics of mixed specifications

$$\frac{}{(\!| \lambda |\!)\chi \xrightarrow{\lambda} \chi}\ \textsc{Nec} \qquad \frac{\iota_i \xrightarrow{\lambda} \chi \quad i \in \{1,2\}}{\iota_1 \oplus \iota_2 \xrightarrow{\lambda} \chi}\ \textsc{Sel}$$

$$\frac{\chi_1 \xrightarrow{\lambda} \chi'}{\chi_1 \otimes \chi_2 \xrightarrow{\lambda} \chi' \otimes \chi_2}\ \textsc{CompL} \qquad \frac{\chi_2 \xrightarrow{\lambda} \chi'}{\chi_1 \otimes \chi_2 \xrightarrow{\lambda} \chi_1 \otimes \chi'}\ \textsc{CompR} \qquad \frac{\chi \xrightarrow{\lambda} \chi'}{\chi \rhd N \xrightarrow{\lambda} \chi' \rhd N}\ \textsc{MixL}$$

$$\frac{N \xrightarrow{\lambda} N'}{\chi \rhd N \xrightarrow{\lambda} \chi \rhd N'}\ \textsc{MixR} \qquad \frac{\chi \xrightarrow{t \rhd l} \chi' \quad l \in \mathsf{nodes}(N)}{\chi \rhd N \xrightarrow{\tau} \chi' \rhd N \parallel l :: \langle t \rangle \parallel \mathrm{N}(\mathsf{fn}(t))}\ \textsc{MOut}$$

$$\frac{\chi \xrightarrow{\blacktriangleright l} \chi' \quad l \in \mathsf{nodes}(N)}{\chi \rhd N \xrightarrow{\tau} \chi' \rhd N}\ \textsc{MEv} \qquad \frac{\chi \xrightarrow{t \lhd l} \chi'}{\chi \rhd N \parallel l :: \langle t \rangle \xrightarrow{\tau} \chi' \rhd N}\ \textsc{MIn}$$

referenced in t. Indeed, according to the semantics of $(\!| \lambda |\!)\cdot$, it is guaranteed that these nodes actually exist in the environment. Structural congruence is also extended to take mixed specification into account: $\chi \rhd N_1 \equiv \chi \rhd N_2$ if and only if $N_1 \equiv N_2$. Notice that a transition can be derived only from assumptions that are composition of modal operators. We will refer to this kind of assumptions as *modal*:

Definition 2. *We say that an assumption χ is* modal *if $\chi = \iota$ or $\chi = \chi_1 \otimes \chi_1$ and both χ_1 and χ_2 are* modal. *Similarly, we say that $\chi \rhd N$ is* modal, *if χ is modal.*

The following lemma guarantees that all the computations associated to an assumption χ are performed also by all the net satisfying χ.

Lemma 1. *If χ is modal and $\chi \xrightarrow{\lambda} \chi'$ then for each $N \models \chi$, $N \xrightarrow{\lambda} N'$ and $N' \models \chi'$.*

Proof Sketch. By induction on rules of Table 7.

Example 4. Combining specification of Example 1 with assumptions proposed in Example 3 we obtain a mixed specification of the form:

$$\{\delta_1.\{\mathsf{server}_0/u_1\}\}_{\mathsf{server}_0} \rhd \mathsf{terminal} :: \mathsf{QHandler}(\ )$$

4.2 Compositional Model Checking of μKLAIM Nets

In this section, we introduce an algorithm that, given a mixed specification $\chi \rhd N$, permits verifying whether N satisfies φ whenever it is composed with a net satisfying χ. The model checking algorithm is based on functions Sat_K and check defined in Table 8 and Table 9. There the syntax of MoMo maximal fixed-point is extended in order to consider *recursive assumptions* [20]. Let $\mathcal{N} \subseteq$

MIX × SUBST, $\chi \triangleright N$ satisfies $(\nu\kappa\{\mathcal{N}\}.\varphi).\{\sigma\}$ if and only if either $(\chi \triangleright N, \sigma) \in \mathcal{N}$ or $\chi \triangleright N$ satisfies $(\varphi\sigma)[\nu\kappa\{\mathcal{N}, (\chi \triangleright N, \sigma'[\sigma])\}.\varphi/\kappa]$. Standard MOMO recursive operator is obtained by considering $\mathcal{N} = \emptyset$.

Function $\mathsf{Sat}_K(\chi \triangleright N, \varphi)$ is used to move on top non-modal operators of χ and relies on relation $\chi_1 \succ \chi_2$ be inductively defined as follows:

$$\chi_1 \vee \chi_2 \succ \chi_1 \vee \chi_2 \qquad \{\chi\}_l \succ \{\chi\}_l \qquad И l.\chi \succ И l.\chi$$

$$\frac{(\chi_1\sigma)[\nu\kappa.\chi/\kappa] \succ \chi_2}{(\nu\kappa.\chi_1).\{\sigma\} \succ \chi_2} \qquad \frac{\chi_1 \succ \chi_1^1 \vee \chi_1^2}{\chi_1 \otimes \chi_2 \succ (\chi_1^1 \otimes \chi_2) \vee (\chi_1^2 \otimes \chi_2)} \qquad \frac{\chi_1 \succ \{\chi_1^1\}_l}{\chi_1 \otimes \chi_2 \succ \{\chi_1^1 \otimes \chi_2\}_l}$$

$$\frac{\chi_1 \succ И x.\chi_1^1 \quad y \notin \chi_2}{\chi_1 \otimes \chi_2 \succ И y.(\chi_1^1[y/x] \otimes \chi_2)} \qquad \frac{\chi_2 \otimes \chi_1 \succ \chi}{\chi_1 \otimes \chi_2 \succ \chi}$$

When $\chi \succ \chi_1 \vee \chi_2$, we have to check function Sat_K recursively on both $\mathsf{Sat}_K(\chi_1 \triangleright N, \varphi)$ and $\mathsf{Sat}_K(\chi_2 \triangleright N, \varphi)$ and returns the conjunction of the two obtained results. Indeed, N satisies φ under the assumption $\chi_1 \vee \chi_2$ if and only if φ is satisfied by N when both χ_1 and χ_2 are assumed separately.

If $\chi \succ И u.\chi_1$ then Sat_K is recursively invoked with parameters $\chi[l/u] \triangleright N$ and φ where $l = sup(\mathsf{fn}(\chi \triangleright N) \cup \mathsf{fn}(\varphi))$. For each $L \subset$ LOC, $sup(L)$ identifies the smallest element in LOC that does not belong to L[6]. The use of function *sup* permits univocally identifying a new name to use in the rest of the verification. When $\chi \succ \{\chi_1\}_l$ node l is considered in the concrete part of the specification and function $\mathsf{Sat}_K(\chi_1 \triangleright N \parallel l :: \mathbf{nil}, \varphi)$ is recursively invoked.

Finally, if χ is a modal assumption, function $\mathsf{check}(\chi \triangleright N, \varphi)$ is invoked. This extends standard *on-the-fly* algorithm for Hennessy-Milner Logic [20] by taking into account MOMO operators and the assumptions imposed on the environment. When ϕ is one of the standard boolean operators, name matching, production of consumption the algorithm proceeds as expected.

Verification of recursive properties relies on *recursive assumptions*. These guarantee that the algorithm never enters into an infinite loop while handling recursive formulae. Indeed, to check whether $\chi \triangleright N$ satisfies $(\nu\kappa\{\mathcal{N}\}.\varphi).\{\sigma\}$, first the algorithm verifies if the pair $(\chi \triangleright N, \sigma)$ belongs to $\mathcal{N}$. In Table 9 we use $(\chi \triangleright N, \sigma) \in \mathcal{N}_\equiv$ to denote that there exists $(\chi' \triangleright N', \sigma) \in \mathcal{N}$ such that $\chi \triangleright N \equiv \chi' \triangleright N'$. If $\chi \triangleright N \in \mathcal{N}_{/\equiv}$ then value **true** is returned otherwise function Sat_K is recursively invoked on $(\varphi\sigma)[\nu\kappa\{\mathcal{N}, (\chi \triangleright N, \sigma)\}.\varphi/\kappa]$. Function check works similarly for $(\mu\kappa\{\mathcal{N}\}.\varphi).\{\sigma\}$. However, in this case value **false** is yielded when $\chi \triangleright N \in \mathcal{N}_{/\equiv}$.

When ϕ is a new name quantification $И u.\phi_1$ (similarly for $И u.\phi_1$), function Sat_K is recursively invoked with parameters $\chi \triangleright N$ and $\phi_1[l/u]$ where $l = sup(\mathsf{fn}(\chi \triangleright N) \cup \mathsf{fn}(\varphi))$. Function *sup* is also used when $\exists u.\varphi_1$ or $\forall u.\varphi_1$ have to be verified. In both the cases the algorithm check for any l in $\mathsf{fn}(\chi \triangleright N) \cup \mathsf{fn}(\varphi) \cup \{sup(\mathsf{fn}(\chi \triangleright N) \cup \mathsf{fn}(\varphi))\}$ if $\chi \triangleright N$ satisfies or not $\varphi_1[l/u$. When φ is $\exists u.\varphi_1$ (resp. $\forall u.\varphi_1$), **true** (resp. **false**) is returned as soon as an l for which $Sat_K(\chi \triangleright N, \varphi[l/u]) =$ **true** (resp. $=$ **true**) is found. The final result is **false**

[6] We assume a total order over the set of localities LOC with a minimum element.

Table 8. Compositional model-checking: function Sat_K

```
SatK(χ ▷ N, φ)=
  if (χ is modal) return check(χ ▷ N, φ)
  else if χ ≻ χ1 ∨ χ2 then return SatK(χ1 ▷ N, φ) and SatK(χ2 ▷ N, φ);
  else if χ ≻ И l.χ1 then
      let l = sup(fn(χ) ∪ fn(N) ∪ fn(φ)) in
        return SatK(χ[l/x] ▷ N, φ);
  else if χ ≻ {χ'}l then
        return SatK(χ' ▷ N || l :: nil, φ);
```

(resp. **true**) when such a l does not exists. The following Lemma guarantees that, even if we limit our attention to a finite set of names, no information is lost:

Lemma 2. *For any* $l_1, l_2 \notin \mathsf{fn}(N)$, $N \models \varphi$ *if and only if* $N \models \varphi[l_2/l_1]$

Proof Sketch. By induction on the syntax of φ.

Finally, when φ is $\langle\lambda\rangle\varphi_1$ (resp. $[\lambda]\varphi_1$), the algorithm verifies if there is an element (resp. all elements) in $next(\chi \triangleright N, \lambda)$ that satisfies φ_1. There $next(\chi \triangleright N, \lambda)$ denotes the set of mixed specifications reachable from $\chi \triangleright N$ via a transition labeled λ.

Theorem 11 (Soundness). *Let* χ, N, φ *be respectively an assumption, a net, and a formula. For each set of localities* L *such that* $\mathsf{fn}(\chi) \cup \mathsf{fn}(\varphi) \cup \mathsf{fn}(N) \subseteq L$*:*

$$\mathsf{Sat}_K(\chi \triangleright N, \varphi) = \textbf{\textit{true}} \Rightarrow \forall N_1 \in \mathbb{C}[\![\chi]\!]^L \varepsilon_0[] : N_1 \parallel N \models \varphi$$

Proof Sketch. The proof proceeds by induction on the number of recursive invocations of Sat_K and from the Lemma 1 and Lemma 2.

In general, completeness cannot be guaranteed. Indeed, the algorithm may not terminate when the reachability graph associated to $\chi \triangleright N$ contains infinite elements. However, if we limit our attention to *invariants* we are also guaranteed that whenever $\mathsf{Sat}(\chi \triangleright N, \varphi) = \textbf{false}$ then there exists N_1 satisfying χ such that $N \parallel N_1$ does not satisfy φ.

Definition 3. *A* MoMo *formula* φ *is an invariant if it is generated by the following grammar:*

$$\varphi ::= \mathbf{T} \mid \varphi \wedge \varphi \mid \nu\kappa\{\mathcal{N}\}.\phi \mid \langle t\rangle@l \rightarrow \varphi \mid \langle t\rangle@l \leftarrow \varphi \mid [\lambda]\varphi \mid \{l_1 = l_2\} \mid Иx.\varphi$$

Theorem 12. *Let* χ, N, L, φ *be respectively an environment, a Net, a set of localities and an invariant where* $\mathsf{fn}(\varphi), \mathsf{fn}(N) \subseteq L$*:*

$$\mathsf{Sat}_K(\chi \triangleright N, \varphi) = \textbf{\textit{false}} \Rightarrow \exists N_1 \in \mathrm{NET}_L : N_1 \models \chi,\ N_1 \parallel N \models_\sigma \neg\varphi$$

Table 9. Compositional model-checking: function check

$\mathsf{check}(\chi \triangleright N, \varphi)=$
match
  φ
with
| $\mathbf{T} \to$ return **true**;
| $\mathbf{F} \to$ return **false**;
| $\neg\neg\varphi \to$ return $\mathsf{Sat}_K(\chi \triangleright N, \varphi)$;
| $\varphi_1 \vee \varphi_2 \to$ return $\mathsf{Sat}_K(\chi \triangleright N, \varphi_1)$ or $\mathsf{Sat}_K(\chi \triangleright N, \varphi_2)$;
| $\varphi_1 \wedge \varphi_2 \to$ return $\mathsf{Sat}_K(\chi \triangleright N, \varphi_1)$ and $\mathsf{Sat}_K(\chi \triangleright N, \varphi_2)$;
| $\{l_1 = l_2\} \to$ return $l_1 = l_2$;
| $\{l_1 \neq l_2\} \to$ return $l_1 \neq l_2$;
| $(\nu\kappa.\{\mathcal{N}\}\varphi).\{\sigma\} \to$ if $(\chi \triangleright N, \sigma) \in \mathcal{N}_{/\equiv}$ then return **true**;
  else return $\mathsf{Sat}_K(\chi \triangleright N, \varphi\sigma[\nu\kappa\{\mathcal{N}, (\chi \triangleright N, \sigma)\}\varphi/\kappa])$;
| $(\mu\kappa.\{\mathcal{N}\}\varphi).\{\sigma\} \to$ if $(\chi \triangleright N, \sigma) \in \mathcal{N}_{/\equiv}$ then return **false**;
  else return $\mathsf{Sat}_K(\chi \triangleright N, \varphi\sigma[\mu\kappa\{\mathcal{N}, (\chi \triangleright N, \sigma)\}\varphi/\kappa])$;
| $\langle t\rangle@l \to \varphi \to$ if $N \equiv (N' \parallel l :: \langle t\rangle)$ then return $\mathsf{Sat}_K(\chi \triangleright N', \varphi)$;
  else return **false**;
| $\neg\langle t\rangle@l \to \varphi \to$ if $N \equiv (N' \parallel l :: \langle t\rangle)$ then return $\mathsf{Sat}_K(\chi \triangleright N', \neg\varphi)$;
  else return **true**;
| $\langle t\rangle@l \leftarrow \varphi \to$ return $\mathsf{Sat}_K(\chi \triangleright N \| l :: \langle t\rangle, \varphi)$;
| $\neg\langle t\rangle@l \leftarrow \varphi \to$ return $\mathsf{Sat}_K(\chi \triangleright N \| l :: \langle t\rangle, \neg\varphi)$;
| $\mathsf{И}x.\varphi \to$ let $l = sup(\mathsf{fn}(\chi \triangleright N) \cup \mathsf{fn}(\varphi))$ in return $\mathsf{Sat}_K(\chi \triangleright N, \varphi[l/x])$;
| $\neg\mathsf{И}x.\varphi \to$ let $l = sup(\mathsf{fn}(\chi \triangleright N) \cup \mathsf{fn}(\varphi))$ in return $\mathsf{Sat}_K(\chi \triangleright N, \neg\varphi[l/x])$;
| $\exists u.\varphi \to$ let $L = \mathsf{fn}(\chi \triangleright N) \cup \mathsf{fn}(\varphi)$ in
  for each $l \in L \cup \{sup(L)\}$ do
    if $(Sat_K(\chi \triangleright N, \varphi[l/u]))$ then return **true**;
  done;
  return **false**;
| $\forall u.\varphi \to$ let $L = \mathsf{fn}(\chi \triangleright N) \cup \mathsf{fn}(\varphi)$ in
  for each $l \in L \cup \{first(L)\}$ do
    if $(\neg Sat_K(\chi \triangleright N, \varphi[l/u]))$ then return **false**;
  done;
  return **true**;
| $\langle\lambda\rangle\varphi \to$ for each $\chi' \triangleright N' \in next(\chi \triangleright N, \lambda)$ do
    if $(Sat_K(\chi' \triangleright N', \varphi))$ then return **true**;
  done;
  return **false**;
| $[\lambda]\varphi \to$ for each $\chi' \triangleright N' \in next(\chi \triangleright N, \lambda)$ do
    if $(\neg Sat_K(\chi' \triangleright N', \varphi))$ then return **false**;
  done;
  return **true**

Proof Sketch. The proof proceeds by induction on the number of recursive invocations of Sat_K.

Using function Sat_K we can verify that mixed specification of Example 4 satisfies the properties of Example 2. Moreover, the proposed framework naturally induces a notion of *refinement*. Indeed, $\chi_2 \triangleright N_2$ refines assumption χ_1 if and only if $\chi_2 \triangleright N_2$ satisfies χ_1. At the same time, if $\chi_1 \triangleright N_1$ satisfies φ the same holds for $\chi_2 \triangleright N_1 \parallel N_2$. By iterating the proposed approach we obtain a methodology that permits obtaining a complete description of a system starting from a high level logical based specification. In each step of the refinement procedure the satisfaction of the expected properties is preserved. Two possible refinements for assumptions of Example 3 are:

- $\mathbf{0} \triangleright \mathbf{server}_0 :: \mathsf{SHandler}(\,)$
- $\{\delta_1.\{\mathsf{server}_1/u_1\}\}_{\mathsf{server}_1} \triangleright \mathbf{server}_0 :: \mathsf{Proxy}(\,)$

where:

$$\mathsf{SHandler}(\,) \stackrel{\text{def}}{=} \mathbf{in}(\mathsf{QUERY}, !u)@\mathtt{self}.\mathbf{out}(\mathsf{DATA}, u)@\mathtt{self}.\mathsf{SHandler}(\,)$$

$$\mathsf{Proxy}(\,) \stackrel{\text{def}}{=} \mathbf{in}(\mathsf{QUERY}, !u)@\mathtt{self}.\mathbf{out}(\mathsf{FWD}, u, \mathsf{server}_1)@\mathtt{self}.\mathsf{Proxy}(\,)$$

In the first case, server_0 is always able to resolve any query while in the second one, server_0 always relies on another node, named server_1, that satisfies the same assumptions considered in Example 3 for server_0.

5 Conclusions and Future Work

In this paper we have described a methodology for supporting compositional specification of mobile and distributed and open-ended systems specified in KLAIM. The proposed methodology is based on an assume-guarantee approach: a system is not considered in isolation, but in conjunction with assumptions on the behaviour of the environment where it is executed. A specification consists of two parts: the first one (the process) accurately defined, the second one (the environment) more abstract and formalized by means of logical formulae. The proposed framework extends the one introduced in [12,13] for supporting rely-guarantee based analysis of concurrent systems specified in CCS [18].

Assumptions on the environment are specified by means $\mathcal{L}_K^{\chi}$ a modal logic that permits describing all the interactions the enclosing environment can have with the known part of the system and the spatial structure of the environment.

A model-checking algorithm has been also defined to verify whether, under the given assumptions on the environment, a KLAIM nets enjoys expected properties specified with MoMo logic. At the same time, it is guaranteed that whenever the environment is replaced with a net satisfying the assumptions, property satisfaction is preserved. The complexity of the considered algorithm, as in standard model-checking algorithms, is exponential in the size of the considered specification. However, differently from the standard approach where a complete description is considered, in our approach the system "size" can be limited by the fact that assumptions on environment permit abstracting from many of the details of large part of the system.

As a future work we plan to identify a common language that could be used to specify both the expected properties and the assumption on the operating environment of a KLAIM system. To achieve this goal, we plan to study the use of new modal operators that permit specifying properties related to specific localities. Indeed, in MoMo each KLAIM net is considered as an *undivided world* and properties have a *global meaning*. Specific operators can be introduced to see a net as the composition of *many worlds* each of which is associated to a KLAIM locality. Using this approach, both assumptions and investigated properties could be seen as the composition of *localized* properties.

Moreover, we also plan to develop an automatic tool for supporting context-aware specification of KLAIM systems. This will permit applying the considered framework to a larger class of systems that could be specified and verified in an incremental way. We also plan to apply methodology proposed in [17] and in [3] to identify the most general assumption in $\mathcal{L}_K^{\chi}$ that we have to impose on the environment to see a KLAIM net N satisfying a MoMo formula φ. When possible, this will support semi-automatic refinement of systems specification. Indeed, starting from the expected properties and from a small part of the system, a set of requirements for the enclosing environment could be generated and refined each time a new system component is taken into account.

Finally, we plan to study if an approach similar to the one considered in this paper can be applied to process algebras where quantitative aspects (like time or costs) are taken into account.

Acknowledgments. We would like to thank the anonymous reviewers for fruitful comments that enabled us to improve the presentation of our work.

References

1. Abadi, M., Plotkin, G.D.: A logical view of composition. Theoretical Computer Science 114(1), 3–30 (1993)
2. Antonik, A., Huth, M., Larsen, K.G., Nyman, U., Wasowski, A.: 20 years of modal and mixed specifications. Bulletin of the EATCS 95, 94–129 (2008)
3. Baldan, P., Bracciali, A., Bruni, R.: A semantic framework for open processes. Theoretical Computer Science 389(3), 446–483 (2007)
4. Bensalem, S., Bozga, M., Nguyen, T.-H., Sifakis, J.: Compositional verification for component-based systems and application. IET Software, Special Issue on Automated Compositional Verification: Techniques, Applications and Empirical Studies 4(3), 181–193 (2010)
5. Berezin, S., Campos, S., Clarke, E.M.: Compositional Reasoning in Model Checking. In: de Roever, W.-P., Langmaack, H., Pnueli, A. (eds.) COMPOS 1997. LNCS, vol. 1536, pp. 81–102. Springer, Heidelberg (1998)
6. Bettini, L., Bono, V., De Nicola, R., Ferrari, G., Gorla, D., Loreti, M., Moggi, E., Pugliese, R., Tuosto, E., Venneri, B.: The Klaim Project: Theory and Practice. In: Priami, C. (ed.) GC 2003. LNCS, vol. 2874, pp. 88–150. Springer, Heidelberg (2003)

7. Beyer, D., Chakrabarti, A., Henzinger, T.A.: Web service interfaces. In: Ellis, A., Hagino, T. (eds.) Proceedings of the 14th International Conference on World Wide Web, WWW 2005, pp. 148–159. ACM (2005)
8. Gheorghiu Bobaru, M., Păsăreanu, C.S., Giannakopoulou, D.: Automated Assume-Guarantee Reasoning by Abstraction Refinement. In: Gupta, A., Malik, S. (eds.) CAV 2008. LNCS, vol. 5123, pp. 135–148. Springer, Heidelberg (2008)
9. Caires, L., Cardelli, L.: A spatial logic for concurrency (part I). Information and Computation, 1–37 (2001)
10. Caires, L., Cardelli, L.: A Spatial Logic for Concurrency (Part II). In: Brim, L., Jančar, P., Křetínský, M., Kučera, A. (eds.) CONCUR 2002. LNCS, vol. 2421, pp. 209–225. Springer, Heidelberg (2002)
11. De Nicola, R., Loreti, M.: MoMo: A Modal Logic for Reasoning About Mobility. In: de Boer, F.S., Bonsangue, M.M., Graf, S., de Roever, W.-P. (eds.) FMCO 2004. LNCS, vol. 3657, pp. 95–119. Springer, Heidelberg (2005)
12. D'Errico, L., Loreti, M.: Assume-Guarantee Verification of Concurrent Systems. In: Field, J., Vasconcelos, V.T. (eds.) COORDINATION 2009. LNCS, vol. 5521, pp. 288–305. Springer, Heidelberg (2009)
13. D'Errico, L., Loreti, M.: Property-Preserving Refinement of Concurrent Systems. In: Wirsing, M., Hofmann, M., Rauschmayer, A. (eds.) TGC 2010. LNCS, vol. 6084, pp. 222–236. Springer, Heidelberg (2010)
14. Gabbay, M., Pitts, A.M.: A new approach to abstract syntax involving binders. In: Proceedings of 14th IEEE Symposium on Logic in Computer Science, pp. 214–224 (1999)
15. Gelernter, D.: Multiple Tuple Spaces in Linda. In: Odijk, E., Rem, M., Syre, J.-C. (eds.) PARLE 1989. LNCS, vol. 366, pp. 20–27. Springer, Heidelberg (1989)
16. Hennessy, M., Milner, R.: Algebraic laws for nondeterminism and concurrency. Journal of ACM 32(1), 137–161 (1985)
17. Larsen, K., Xinxin, L.: Compositionality through an operational semantics of contexts. Journal of Logic and Computation 1(6), 761–795 (1991)
18. Milner, R.: Communication and Concurrency. Prentice Hall (1989)
19. De Nicola, R., Ferrari, G.L., Pugliese, R.: KLAIM: A kernel language for agents interaction and mobility. IEEE Transactions on Software Engineering 24(5), 315–330 (1998)
20. Winskel, G.: Topics in concurrency. Lecture notes. University of Cambridge (2008), `http://www.cl.cam.ac.uk/~gw104/TIC08.ps`

Orchestrating Tuple-Based Languages*

Rocco De Nicola[1,2], Andrea Margheri[1], and Francesco Tiezzi[2]

[1] Univeristà degli Studi di Firenze, Dipartimento di Sistemi e Informatica
[2] IMT - Institute for Advanced Studies Lucca
{rocco.denicola,francesco.tiezzi}@imtlucca.it, margheri.a@alice.it

Abstract. The World Wide Web can be thought of as a global computing architecture supporting the deployment of distributed networked applications. Currently, such applications can be programmed by resorting mainly to two distinct paradigms: one devised for orchestrating distributed services, and the other designed for coordinating distributed (possibly mobile) agents. In this paper, the issue of designing a programming language aiming at reconciling orchestration and coordination is investigated. Taking as starting point the orchestration calculus ORC and the tuple-based coordination language KLAIM, a new formalism is introduced combining concepts and primitives of the original calculi. To demonstrate feasibility and effectiveness of the proposed approach, a prototype implementation of the new formalism is described and it is then used to tackle a case study dealing with a simplified but realistic electronic marketplace, where a number of on-line stores allow client applications to access information about their goods and to place orders.

Keywords: Global computing, Orchestration, Coordination, Tuple-based languages, Formal methods, Software tools.

1 Introduction

In recent years, the growing success of e-business, e-learning, e-government, and similar emerging models, has led the World Wide Web, initially thought of as a tool supporting humans in looking for information, to evolve towards a service-oriented architecture, where more and more networked applications, the so-called *services*, are deployed. This has promoted the rising of a novel programming paradigm for the *orchestration* of concurrent and distributed services. There are by now some successful and well-developed technologies supporting this paradigm, like e.g. WS-BPEL [33], the standard language for orchestration of web services. However, current software engineering technologies remain at the descriptive level and lack rigorous formal foundations. Hence, many researchers have tackled the problem at a more foundational level, by developing formal languages for designing and programming service orchestrations.

Among the many proposed formalisms (see, e.g., [28,8,10,23,11,7]), we will focus on ORC [31,40], a task orchestration language with applications in workflow, business process management, and web service orchestration. ORC is the result

* This work has been partially sponsored by the EU project ASCENS, 257414.

R. Bruni and V. Sassone (Eds.): TGC 2011, LNCS 7173, pp. 160–178, 2012.

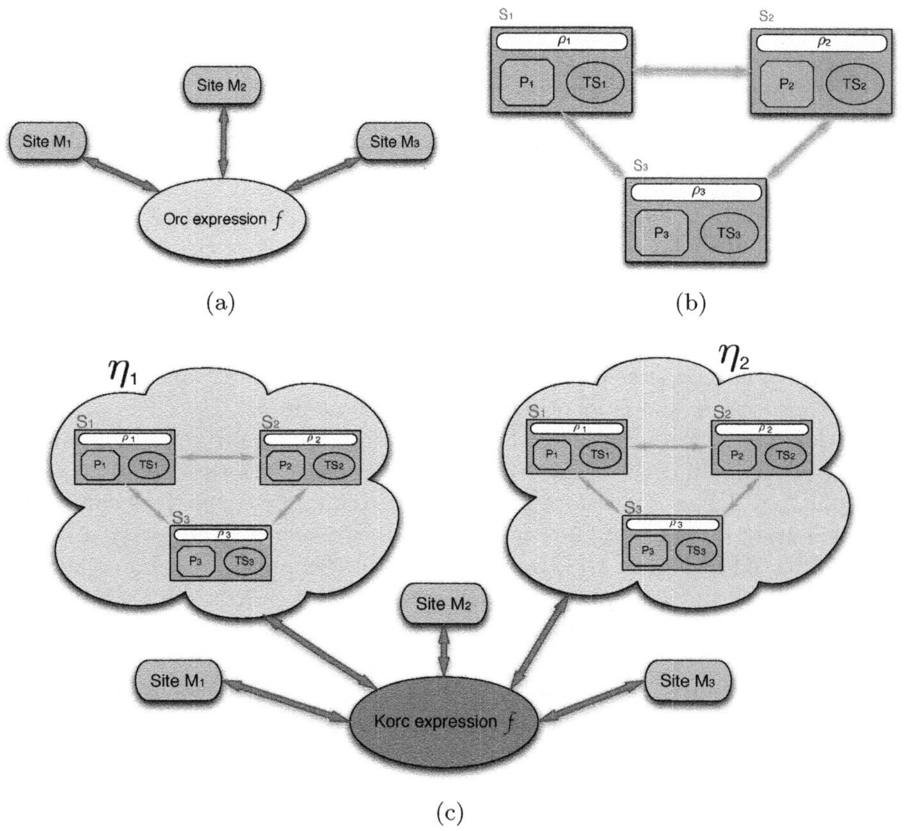

Fig. 1. The ORC (a), KLAIM (b) and KORC (c) approaches

of a tension between simplicity and expressiveness, and its primitives, differently from most the formalisms mentioned above, focus on orchestration rather than on communication. An ORC program, graphically depicted in Figure 1(a), is an *expression* that orchestrates concurrent invocations of a number of services, called *sites* in the ORC's jargon, by means of three operators modelling sequential and parallel composition.

The small numbers of ORC's operators have been proved to be sufficiently expressive to model the most common orchestration patterns (e.g. those identified in [38]). However, they do not provide adequate and flexible mechanisms for distributed *coordination*, which may possibly refer and exploit the structures of the network. *Tuple-based* languages have, instead, been effectively used to implement coordination mechanism in a distributed setting. Among the many proposals (see, e.g., [22,37,35,17,14,36]), here, we would like to focus on KLAIM [15,6,16], a coordination language specifically designed to program distributed systems consisting of mobile components interacting through multiple distributed tuple spaces. The KLAIM's communication model builds over, and extends, Linda's notion of generative communication through a single shared tuple space [22] and

Table 1. ORC syntax

(Expressions)	f, g	::=	$M(\bar{p}) \mid E(\bar{p}) \mid f > \bar{p} > g \mid f \mid g \mid f < \bar{p} < g$
(Parameters)	p	::=	$x \mid m$

its primitives allow programmers to distribute and retrieve data and processes to and from the nodes of a net. Localities are first-class citizens that can be dynamically created and communicated over the network and can be handled via sophisticated scoping rules.

A KLAIM specification, graphically depicted in Figure 1(b), can be thought of as a net of interconnected nodes, each of which hosts data tuples and (possibly mobile) processes, and is identified by a unique name.

In this paper, we investigate the issue of designing a programming language aiming at reconciling the orchestration paradigm with the tuple-based coordination one and define a new formalism, called KORC, that combines composition patterns and primitives of ORC and KLAIM. Intuitively, a KORC program, graphically depicted in Figure 1(c), consists of an ORC expression and a collection of KLAIM nets. Expressions are enriched with primitives for acting on the tuple spaces within the KLAIM nets, the latter are named and can be referred within the expressions.

The choice of using ORC and KLAIM as theoretical basis for KORC has been mainly motivated by the fact that they are compact formalisms and are already supported by software tools for programming networked applications. Such tools are Java-based and, hence, easily integrable. Indeed, to demonstrate effectiveness of the programming paradigm fostered by KORC and to experiment with it, we have developed a prototype implementation of the new language that builds upon the implementations of ORC and KLAIM.

The rest of the paper is structured as follows. Section 2 presents the design and the formal definition of KORC, by introducing concepts and definitions of ORC and KLAIM. Section 3 introduces an e-commerce scenario that illustrates the relevant and specific aspects of KORC. Section 4 provides an overview of the prototype implementation of KORC and describes an excerpt of the e-commerce scenario written in the syntax accepted by the tool. Finally, Section 5 draws a few conclusions and reviews some strictly related work.

2 From Orc and Klaim to Korc

In this section, we first recap the basic notions of ORC and KLAIM, borrowed from [40] and [16], then we use them to define KORC.

Orc: *An Orchestration Language.* An ORC program consists of a goal *expression* and a set of *definitions*; the goal expression is evaluated in order to run the program. The definitions can be used in the expression and in other definitions. Formally, the ORC syntax is defined in Table 1, where M ranges over *site* names, E over *expression* names, x over variables, and m over values. It is assumed that the sets of site names, expression names, variables and values are countable and pairwise disjoint.

Since we aim at merging ORC with a tuple-based coordination language, we consider the polyadic variant of ORC informally described in [26] that permits using tuples as parameters rather than single values. The overbar $\bar{}$ over a name denotes tuples of parameters, thus $\bar{m}$ is the compact notation for the tuple of values $\langle m_1, \ldots, m_n \rangle$ (with $n \geq 0$). Variables in the same tuple are pairwise distinct. The empty tuple, written $\langle\rangle$, corresponds to a *signal*, i.e. the ORC unit value that has no additional information. When convenient, we shall regard tuples simply as sets.

Expressions can be composed by means of sequential composition $\cdot > \bar{p} > \cdot$, symmetric parallel composition $\cdot \mid \cdot$, and asymmetric parallel composition $\cdot < \bar{p} < \cdot$, starting from site calls $M(\bar{p})$ and expression calls $E(\bar{p})$. The variables within $\bar{p}$ are *bound* in g for the expressions $f > \bar{p} > g$ and $g < \bar{p} < f$. We use $\text{fv}(f)$ to denote the set of variables that are not bound (i.e. which occur *free*) in f. Each expression name E has a unique declaration of the form $E(\bar{x}) \triangleq f$, where $\bar{x} = \text{fv}(f)$, i.e. only the variables $\bar{x}$ are free in f. The evaluation of an expressions may call a number of sites and returns, i.e. *publishes* in ORC's jargon, a (possibly empty) stream of (tuple of) values.

Informally, the semantics of ORC expressions is as follows:

Site call: a site call can have the form $M(\bar{p})$, where the site name M is known statically, and $\bar{p}$ are the parameters of the call. A site call returns at most one response and, hence, a site might also not respond. If $\bar{p}$ contains variables, then they must be instantiated before the call.

Expression call: an expression call has the form $E(\bar{p})$ and executes the expression defined by $E(\bar{x}) \triangleq f$ after replacing $\bar{x}$ by $\bar{p}$ in f (of course, the tuples $\bar{x}$ and $\bar{p}$ must have the same length). Here $\bar{p}$ is passed by reference. Expression definitions can be recursive.

Symmetric parallel composition: the composition $f \mid g$ executes both f and g concurrently, assuming that there is no interaction between them. It publishes the interleaving of the two streams of tuples published by f and g.

Sequential composition: the composition $f > \bar{p} > g$ executes f and, for each tuple of values $\bar{m}$ returned by f, it checks if $\bar{p}$ and $\bar{m}$ match. If this is the case, an instance of g is executed with variables in $\bar{p}$ replaced by the corresponding values in $\bar{m}$. Otherwise the publication is ignored and no new instance of g is executed. The composition publishes the interleaving of the streams of tuples published by the different instances of g.

Asymmetric parallel composition: the composition $g < \bar{p} < f$ starts in parallel both f and the parts of g that do not need the variables in $\bar{p}$. When f publishes a tuple, let say $\bar{m}$, if $\bar{p}$ and $\bar{m}$ do match the evaluation of f terminates and the variables within $\bar{p}$ are replaced by the corresponding values in $\bar{m}$ (in this way, the suspended parts of g can proceed). The composition publishes the stream obtained from g (instantiated with values in $\bar{m}$).

Table 2. KLAIM syntax

$$
\begin{array}{rrcl}
\text{(Nets)} & N & ::= & \mathbf{0} \quad | \quad s ::_{\rho} C \quad | \quad N_1 \parallel N_2 \quad | \quad (\nu s)N \\
\text{(Components)} & C & ::= & P \quad | \quad \langle t \rangle \quad | \quad C_1 \mid C_2 \\
\text{(Processes)} & P & ::= & \mathbf{nil} \quad | \quad \alpha.P \quad | \quad P_1 \mid P_2 \quad | \quad A(\bar{p}) \\
\text{(Actions)} & \alpha & ::= & \mathbf{out}(t)@\ell \quad | \quad \mathbf{in}(T)@\ell \quad | \quad \mathbf{read}(T)@\ell \\
 & & | & \mathbf{eval}(P)@\ell \quad | \quad \mathbf{newloc}(s) \\
\text{(Tuples)} & t & ::= & e \quad | \quad \ell \quad | \quad P \quad | \quad t_1, t_2 \\
\text{(Templates)} & T & ::= & e \quad | \quad \ell \quad | \quad !\,x \quad | \quad !\,l \quad | \quad !\,X \quad | \quad T_1, T_2
\end{array}
$$

More formally, the operational semantics of ORC is given in terms of a labelled transition relation and an auxiliary function for pattern-matching on semi-structured data. Due to space limitations, we refer the interested reader to [29] for a full account of the ORC's operational semantics considered in this paper.

Klaim: *A Language for Agents Interaction and Mobility.* KLAIM is a formal language equipped with primitives for network-aware programming that combines a process algebraic approach with a coordination-oriented one. The syntax of KLAIM is reported in Table 2, where s, s',... range over *locality names* (i.e. network addresses); **self**, l, l',... range over *locality variables* (i.e. aliases for addresses); ℓ, ℓ',... range over locality names and variables; x, y,... range over *value variables*; X, Y,... range over *process variables*; e, e',... range over *expressions*[1]; A, B,... range over *process identifiers*[2]. We assume that the set of variables (i.e. locality, value and process variables), the set of values (locality names and basic values) and the set of process identifiers are countable and pairwise disjoint.

Nets are finite plain collections of nodes where *components*, i.e. processes and evaluated tuples, can be allocated. In the net $(\nu s)N$, the scope of the name s is restricted to N; the intended effect is that if one considers the net $N_1 \parallel (\nu s)N_2$ then locality s of N_2 cannot be referred to from within N_1.

A *node* is a triple $s ::_{\rho} C$, where the locality s is the address of the node, ρ is the allocation environment and C are the hosted components. An *allocation environment* binds the locality variables occurring free in the processes allocated in the corresponding node. Basically, allocation environments provide a name resolution mechanism by mapping locality variables l into localities s. The dis-

[1] The precise syntax of expressions is deliberately not specified, but we assume that they contain basic values (ranged over by v, v', ...) and variables.

[2] We assume that each process identifier A has a unique definition, visible from any locality of a net, of the form $A(\bar{f}) \triangleq P$, where the formal parameters in $\bar{f}$ are pairwise distinct. Like for ORC, $\bar{p}$ in the call $A(\bar{p})$ is the tuple of actual parameters.

Table 3. KORC syntax

(Expressions)	f, g	$::=$	$M(\bar{p}) \quad \mid \quad E(\bar{p}) \quad \mid \quad f > \bar{p} > g \quad \mid \quad f \mid g \quad \mid \quad f < \bar{p} < g$
		$\mid$	$\mathbf{out}(t)@\eta : \ell \quad \mid \quad \mathbf{eval}(P)@\eta : \ell$
		$\mid$	$\mathbf{in}(T)@\eta : \ell \quad \mid \quad \mathbf{read}(T)@\eta : \ell$
(Named nets)	$\mathcal{K}$	$::=$	$\{\eta_i ::_{\rho_i} N_i\}_{i \in I}$

tinguished locality variable **self** is used by processes to refer to the address of their current hosting node.

Processes are the KLAIM active computational units. They are built up from the special process **nil**, which does not perform any action, and from the basic actions by means of action prefixing $\alpha.P$, parallel composition $P_1 \mid P_2$ and process definition. Process may be executed concurrently either at the same locality or at different localities and can perform five different basic actions.

Actions **out**, **in** and **read** manage data repositories by adding/withdrawing/accessing data to/from node repositories. Action **eval** activates a new thread of execution, i.e. a process, in a (possibly remote) node. Action **newloc** permits creating new network nodes. All actions, apart for **newloc**, are indexed by the (possibly remote) locality where they will take place. Actions **in** and **read** are blocking actions and exploit templates as patterns to select data in shared repositories. *Templates* are sequences of actual and formal fields, where the latter are written $!\,x$, $!\,l$ or $!\,X$ and are used to bind variables to basic values, locality names or processes, respectively. Actions **out** and **eval** are non-blocking and implement *static* and *dynamic scoping* disciplines, respectively (see [16,29]).

Names and variables occurring in KLAIM processes and nets can be *bound.* More precisely, prefix $\mathbf{newloc}(s).P$ binds name s in P, and, similarly, net restriction $(\nu s)N$ binds s in N. The sets $\mathrm{fn}(\cdot)$ and $\mathrm{bn}(\cdot)$ of, respectively, free and bound locality names of a term are defined accordingly. Prefixes $\mathbf{in}(\ldots, !\_, \ldots)@\ell.P$ and $\mathbf{read}(\ldots, !\_, \ldots)@\ell.P$ binds variable $\_$ in P. A name/variable that is not bound is called *free.*

The operational semantics of KLAIM is given in terms of a structural congruence relation and a reduction relation expressing the evolution of nets. Due to space limitations, we refer the interested reader to [29] for a complete account of the KLAIM's semantics considered in this paper.

Korc: *A Language for Orchestrating* Klaim *Agents.* We now show how the orchestration approach of ORC and the network-aware one of KLAIM can be combined in order to define a new formalism for orchestrating concurrent processes coordinated via distributed tuple spaces. More specifically, in this section we present the syntax and the operational semantics of the new calculus, that we call KORC.

A KORC program consists of a configuration $(f, \mathcal{K})$, where f is an extended ORC expression (possibly equipped with a set of expression definitions) and $\mathcal{K}$ is a set of *named* KLAIM *nets*. To execute a program, f is evaluated while the nets are concurrently running. The KORC syntax is defined in Table 3, where f is an ORC expression (like in Table 1) extended with KLAIM actions; η ranges over *net names*. Parameters p are defined in Table 1, and N, P, t and T are defined in Table 2.

We assume that the KORC set of values, ranged over by m, includes the KLAIM set of values. Symbol $\uplus$ is used to denote disjoint union of sets.

A KORC expression can interact with different KLAIM nets that can be referred (and distinguished) by means of net names. A *named net* is a triple $\eta ::_\rho N$, where η is the name of the net, ρ is the allocation environment used to bind location variables within KORC expressions, and N is a KLAIM net. Besides site and expression calls, a KORC expression can perform **out**, **eval**, **in** and **read** actions over named nets within the associated set $\mathcal{K}$. The actions have an additional argument η that explicitly indicates the target net. Action **newloc** cannot be directly executed by a KORC expression, because it only acts locally to a KLAIM node. However, it can be indirectly performed via **eval** actions.

A KORC program $(f, \{\eta_i ::_{\rho_i} N_i\}_{i \in I})$ is *well-formed* if names η_i are pairwise distinct and for each $i \in I$ we have that **self** is not in the domain of ρ_i and N_i is a well-formed net (see [16] and [29, Section 2.2]). Hereafter, we will only consider well-formed programs. Notably, we consider named nets, rather than unnamed ones, to avoid requiring locality names of all nets to be pairwise distinct. In fact, while this is reasonable when considering a single net, it becomes a too strong requirement in a distributed, loosely coupled, environment where different and independent subnets co-exist. The requirement on **self** is due to the fact that ρ_i are used to evaluate actions executed by a KORC expression and that, hence, are not hosted by any KLAIM node.

The operational semantics of KORC is given in terms of a labelled transition relation $\xrightarrow{a}$ over configurations, which relies on the standard reduction relation $\longmapsto$ over KLAIM nets (see [29, Table 7]). As in the semantics of ORC, label a is generated by the following grammar:

$$a \;::=\; \tau \quad | \quad !\bar{m}$$

Label τ indicates an *internal event*, while label $!\bar{m}$ indicates a *publication event* corresponding to the communication of the tuple of values $\bar{m}$ after the evaluation of an expression. The operational rules defining the labelled transition relation are those in Table 4 together with those defining the ORC semantics (see [29, Table 3]) extended to KORC configurations in standard way[3]. For example, the rule for the left component of symmetric parallel composition extends to configurations as follows:

$$\frac{(f, \mathcal{K}) \xrightarrow{a} (f', \mathcal{K}')}{(f \mid g, \mathcal{K}) \xrightarrow{a} (f' \mid g, \mathcal{K}')}$$

Notably, site and expression calls cannot modify the set $\mathcal{K}$, only the KORC actions **out**, **eval**, **in** and **read** can.

[3] Since KORC inherits pairwise disjoint variables sets from KLAIM, the definition of the ORC pattern-matching function $\mathcal{M}(\cdot,\cdot)$ has been revised to guarantee that each variable only matches with values of the corresponding category (see [29, Section 2.3]).

Table 4. KORC operational semantics (additional rules)

$$\frac{\rho(\ell) = s' \qquad \mathcal{E}[\![\, t \,]\!]_\rho = t' \qquad (\mathrm{fn}(t') \cup \{s'\}) \not\subseteq (\mathrm{bn}(N) \cup \bar{s})}{\begin{array}{l}(\mathbf{out}(t)@\eta : \ell, \mathcal{K} \uplus \{\eta ::_\rho (\nu\bar{s})(N \parallel s' ::_{\rho'} \mathbf{nil})\}) \\ \quad \xrightarrow{!\langle\rangle} (\mathbf{0}, \mathcal{K} \uplus \{\eta ::_\rho (\nu\bar{s})(N \parallel s' ::_{\rho'} \langle t' \rangle)\})\end{array}} \ \textit{(Korc-out)}$$

$$\frac{\rho(\ell) = s' \qquad (\mathrm{fn}(P) \cup \{s'\}) \not\subseteq (\mathrm{bn}(N) \cup \bar{s})}{\begin{array}{l}(\mathbf{eval}(P)@\eta : \ell, \mathcal{K} \uplus \{\eta ::_\rho (\nu\bar{s})(N \parallel s' ::_{\rho'} \mathbf{nil})\}) \\ \quad \xrightarrow{!\langle\rangle} (\mathbf{0}, \mathcal{K} \uplus \{\eta ::_\rho (\nu\bar{s})(N \parallel s' ::_{\rho'} P)\})\end{array}} \ \textit{(Korc-eval)}$$

$$\frac{\rho(\ell) = s' \qquad \mathit{match}(\mathcal{E}[\![\, T \,]\!]_\rho, t) = \sigma \qquad (\mathrm{fn}(T) \cup \{s'\}) \not\subseteq (\mathrm{bn}(N) \cup \bar{s})}{\begin{array}{l}(\mathbf{in}(T)@\eta : \ell, \mathcal{K} \uplus \{\eta ::_\rho (\nu\bar{s})(N \parallel s' ::_{\rho'} \langle t \rangle)\}) \\ \quad \xrightarrow{!\langle t\rangle} (\mathbf{0}, \mathcal{K} \uplus \{\eta ::_\rho (\nu\, \bar{s} \backslash \mathrm{fn}(t))(N \parallel s' ::_{\rho'} \mathbf{nil})\})\end{array}} \ \textit{(Korc-in)}$$

$$\frac{\rho(\ell) = s' \qquad \mathit{match}(\mathcal{E}[\![\, T \,]\!]_\rho, t) = \sigma \qquad (\mathrm{fn}(T) \cup \{s'\}) \not\subseteq (\mathrm{bn}(N) \cup \bar{s})}{\begin{array}{l}(\mathbf{read}(T)@\eta : \ell, \mathcal{K} \uplus \{\eta ::_\rho (\nu\bar{s})(N \parallel s' ::_{\rho'} \langle t \rangle)\}) \\ \quad \xrightarrow{!\langle t\rangle} (\mathbf{0}, \mathcal{K} \uplus \{\eta ::_\rho (\nu\, \bar{s} \backslash \mathrm{fn}(t))(N \parallel s' ::_{\rho'} \langle t \rangle)\})\end{array}} \ \textit{(Korc-read)}$$

$$\frac{N \longmapsto N'}{(f, \mathcal{K} \uplus \{\eta ::_\rho N\}) \xrightarrow{\tau} (f, \mathcal{K} \uplus \{\eta ::_\rho N'\})} \ \textit{(Korc-net)}$$

The rules in Table 4, like those in the semantics of KLAIM, expolit two auxiliary functions: $\mathcal{E}[\![\, \_ \,]\!]_\rho$ for evaluating tuples/templates using the allocation environment ρ, and $\mathit{match}(\cdot,\cdot)$ for verifying the compliance of a tuple w.r.t. a template and associating basic values, locality names and processes to corresponding variables in templates.

Let us now comment on the rules in Table 4. All actions evolve to expression $\mathbf{0}$ (which has no observable transitions), act on a net named η, require the existence of the target node s' (which must not be restricted in η) and exploit the environment ρ for evaluating their arguments. We abbreviate $(\nu s_1)\ldots(\nu s_n)$ to $(\nu\bar{s})$ with $\bar{s} = \langle s_1, \ldots, s_n \rangle$. Actions **out** and **eval**, rules *(Korc-out)* and *(Korc-eval)*, can be performed only if the components they intend to insert in s' (i.e. the tuple $\langle t' \rangle$ or the process P) do not contain locality names restricted in η. If such actions can be performed, a signal $\langle\rangle$ is published. It has been decided to emit a signal and not to perform a τ event, to use the signal in further sequential or asymmetric parallel compositions (see rules *(Seq1)* and *(Asym2)* in [29, Table 3]). Similarly, actions **in** and **read**, rules *(Korc-in)* and *(Korc-read)*, can be performed only if the template T does not contain locality names restricted in η, because a private name cannot be matched by any name used outside the net (private names cannot be 'guessed'). Instead, these actions can be performed if the tuple t

they intend to withdraw/read contains some locality names restricted in η; in this case, the restriction of such names is removed. If a matching datum t exists in the target node, actions **in** and **read** can proceed and publish the withdrawn/read tuple $\langle t \rangle$. Notice that, to properly integrate **in** and **read** actions with the binding operators of ORC, in rules *(Korc-in)* and *(Korc-read)* the generated substitution σ is not applied and the complete withdrawn/read tuple is published. The values in the returned tuple can be then caught via pattern-matching through sequential or asymmetric parallel compositions. Finally, rule *(Korc-net)* says that KLAIM nets in $\mathcal{K}$ can freely evolve w.r.t. the evolution of expression f.

As mentioned above, the execution of actions **in** and **read** in KORC does not yield a substitution, but simply the publication of the involved tuple. However, **in** and **read** actions *à la* KLAIM can be easily modelled in KORC: e.g., an expression $\mathbf{in}(5, !x)@\,\eta : \ell\,.f$, where a substitution for x is applied to f, can be rendered in KORC as $\mathbf{in}(5, !y)@\,\eta : \ell > \langle 5, x \rangle > f$, where y is a fresh local variable. Moreover, in KLAIM, locality names can be private, i.e. restricted with operator (νs) and their freshness can be guaranteed by a middleware supporting the execution of a KLAIM net. Instead, the loosely coupled nature of the service-oriented architecture underlying KORC makes it more difficult to guarantee names freshness over a global net consisting of many independent KLAIM subnets. Therefore, in KORC, when a private name is extracted from a KLAIM net, through an **in**/**read** action, the name becomes public (like in the *(open)* rule of π-calculus [30]).

It is worth noticing that KORC is not equipped with specific linguistic primitives for composing programs, which are indeed designed to be separately executed. However, KORC programs can be easily composed by resorting to the three ORC orchestration operators. More specifically, if two programs act on the same set $\mathcal{K}$ of named KLAIM nets, their composition is the program consisting of the set $\mathcal{K}$ and the expression obtained by applying the composition operator to the two expressions of the argument programs. As an example, consider the two KORC programs $(f, \mathcal{K})$ and $(g, \mathcal{K})$, the program corresponding to their sequential composition is $(f > \bar{p} > g, \mathcal{K})$. If the two programs act on different sets of nets, the composition is done similarly, except that the two sets must be composed by means of an appropriate union operator that guarantees the well-formedness of the resulting KORC program.

3 Korc at Work on an e-commerce Case Study

In this section, we illustrate an application of KORC to a simplified but realistic electronic marketplace scenario, where a number of on-line stores allow client applications to read data about items availability and to place orders. We assume that each store has an on-line portal and relies on many 'realworld' stores, each of which with its own warehouse. Specifically, here we consider a client application that aims at finding a store that has in stock a given quantity of a specific item, by concurrently accessing different stores, and placing an order to the first store found. For the sake of presentation, we shall consider a scenario consisting of only three on-line stores. The outlined scenario can be rendered in KORC by:

$$(f, \{\eta_{store1} ::_\rho N_1,\ \eta_{store2} ::_\rho N_2,\ \eta_{store3} ::_\rho N_3,\ \eta_{client} ::_\rho (s ::_{\{\mathbf{self}\mapsto s\}} \mathbf{nil})\})$$

where ρ stands for $\{l \mapsto s\}$ and each net N_i has the following form

$$\begin{array}{l} s_1 ::_{\{\mathbf{self}\mapsto s_1, l\mapsto s, l_{next}\mapsto s_2, l_{end}\mapsto s_e\}} \langle t_{i1}^1\rangle \mid \ldots \mid \langle t_{i1}^{k_i}\rangle \\ \parallel\ s_2 ::_{\{\mathbf{self}\mapsto s_2, l\mapsto s, l_{next}\mapsto s_3, l_{end}\mapsto s_e\}} \langle t_{i2}^1\rangle \mid \ldots \mid \langle t_{i2}^{w_i}\rangle \\ \parallel\ \ldots\ \parallel\ s_{m_i} ::_{\{\mathbf{self}\mapsto s_{m_i}, l\mapsto s, l_{next}\mapsto s_e, l_{end}\mapsto s_e\}} \langle t_{im}^1\rangle \mid \ldots \mid \langle t_{im}^{r_i}\rangle \\ \parallel\ s ::_{\{\mathbf{self}\mapsto s, l_{start}\mapsto s_1\}} \mathbf{nil} \end{array}$$

In KORC, each store *store i* consists of a site $M_{store\,i}$, representing the on-line portal to place orders to the store (see expression g below), and a named net $\eta_{store\,i} ::_\rho N_i$ whose nodes s_j represent the data storages of its warehouses while node s is used for computational support. Each tuple t_{ij}^u represents the data of a specific item stored inside the warehouse s_j of the store *store i*. Specifically, such tuples have the form $\langle id, q, p\rangle$, where id is the item identifier, q (with $q > 0$) is the quantity available at the warehouse, and p is the price (which can be different from a warehouse to another). We assume that each node contains at most one tuple for each item identifier. Finally, the client application is rendered in KORC as the expression f and the net η_{client}. The latter contains a node s, initially empty, to elaborate the retrieved data. The expression f is defined as follows:

$$\begin{array}{l} \mathbf{eval}(FindItem(\text{“}itemId3\text{”}, 20, \text{“}reqId12\text{”}))@\,\eta_{store1} : l \\ \mid\ \mathbf{eval}(FindItem(\text{“}itemId3\text{”}, 20, \text{“}reqId12\text{”}))@\,\eta_{store2} : l \\ \mid\ \mathbf{eval}(FindItem(\text{“}itemId3\text{”}, 20, \text{“}reqId12\text{”}))@\,\eta_{store3} : l \\ \mid\ f_{moveFromStore1}\ \mid\ f_{moveFromStore2}\ \mid\ f_{moveFromStore3}\ \mid\ g \end{array}$$

Basically, it represents a client's search request for 30 items[4] of type “*itemId*3” whose maximum price per item that the client is willing to pay is less or equal to 20. To avoid that data of different search requests are erroneously mixed together, a request identifier, say “*reqId*12”, is provided by the client and inserted into each tuple. Of course, the above expression could be parameterized w.r.t. item identifier, price, request identifier and quantity, but we prefer to leave it as it is for the sake of presentation.

Specifically, by means of three **eval** actions, the client expression spawns three copies of the process *FindItem* into the locality s of each store net. Such process looks for tuples having as arguments the item identifier “*itemId*3” and a price less or equal to 20. A copy of each tuple (extended with the request identifier “*reqId*12”) that meets this requirement is stored in the locality s of the net. Then, by means of three expression calls $f_{moveFromStore\,i}$, as tuples are inserted into the node s of each store's net, they are moved to the node s of the client's net. Each expression $f_{moveFromStore\,i}$ is defined as a recursive expression performing a sequence of **in** and **out** actions:

[4] As it will be clearer later, the check of the availability of 30 items is performed by the subexpression g of f (to be more precise, by the three components g_i of g).

$$
\begin{aligned}
f_{moveFromStore\,i} \triangleq\; & \mathbf{in}(\text{“}itemId3\text{”}, !x_q, !x_p, \text{“}reqId12\text{”})@\,\eta_{store\,i} : l \\
& > \langle \text{“}itemId3\text{”}, x_q, x_p, \text{“}reqId12\text{”} \rangle > \\
& \mathbf{out}(\text{“}store\,i\text{”}, \text{“}reqId12\text{”}, x_q)@\,\eta_{client} : l \gg f_{moveFromStore\,i}
\end{aligned}
$$

where $f_1 \gg f_2$ is used as short-hand for $f_1 > \langle\rangle > f_2$. Notably, in performing such movements, information about prices and item identifiers are left out, while information about the source stores are added.

The KLAIM process *FindItem* is defined as follows:

$$
\begin{aligned}
& FindItem(itemId, maxPrice, reqId) \triangleq \\
& \quad \mathbf{eval}(Find(itemId, maxPrice, reqId))@l_{start}
\end{aligned}
$$

It simply activates a mobile process *Find* (i.e. an *agent*) in the 'start' locality of the hosting net. This mobile process, defined below, will visit all nodes of the net to find the availability of the wanted item:

$$
\begin{aligned}
& Find(itemId, maxPrice, reqId) \triangleq \\
& \quad \mathbf{read}(itemId, !q, !p)@\mathbf{self}. \\
& \qquad \mathbf{if}\ (p \leqslant maxPrice)\ \mathbf{then}\ \mathbf{out}(itemId, q, p, reqId)@l \\
& \quad \mid\ \mathbf{if}\ (l_{next} \neq l_{end})\ \mathbf{then}\ \mathbf{eval}(Find(itemId, maxPrice, reqId))@l_{next}
\end{aligned}
$$

The process simply checks if a tuple for the given item is present locally; if the price per item is not greater than the maximum price then it adds a corresponding tuple to the node s of the hosting net (referred by means of the locality variable l). Moreover, if there exists a next node to be visited, then a new copy of the process is spawned on such node. This second check exploits the locality variables l_{next} and l_{end}, which are properly bound by the allocation environment of each net node. For the sake of simplicity, in defining the above agent we have used a conditional construct (which can be easily programmed by exploiting the dynamic creation of new nodes and the parallel composition operator) and we have omitted trailing occurrences of **nil**.

The expression g is defined as follows:

$$
\begin{aligned}
g \triangleq\; & \mathbf{out}(\text{“}sum\text{”}, \text{“}store1\text{”}, \text{“}reqId12\text{”}, 0)@\,\eta_{client} : l \\
& \mid \mathbf{out}(\text{“}sum\text{”}, \text{“}store2\text{”}, \text{“}reqId12\text{”}, 0)@\,\eta_{client} : l \\
& \mid \mathbf{out}(\text{“}sum\text{”}, \text{“}store3\text{”}, \text{“}reqId12\text{”}, 0)@\,\eta_{client} : l \\
& \mid (\, (\, if(x = \text{“}store1ok\text{”}) \gg M_{store1}(\text{“}itemId3\text{”}, 30)\,) \\
& \qquad \mid (\, if(x = \text{“}store2ok\text{”}) \gg M_{store2}(\text{“}itemId3\text{”}, 30)\,) \\
& \qquad \mid (\, if(x = \text{“}store3ok\text{”}) \gg M_{store3}(\text{“}itemId3\text{”}, 30)\,)\,) \\
& \quad < \langle x \rangle < (\, g_1 \mid g_2 \mid g_3\,)
\end{aligned}
$$

It adds to the node s of the client's net three tuples containing the partial sum of the quantity of the requested item available at each store (initially set to 0). It also starts the concurrent evaluation of three expressions g_i, each of which computes the sum of the item quantity for a store and publishes the string "*store i ok*" if the store has in stock at least 30 items of the requested type. The asymmetric parallel composition operator is used here to bind the variable x with the (first published) string "*store i ok*" and to terminate the evaluation of the other functions g_j, with $j \neq i$. Then, according to the published string, the corresponding site $M_{store\,i}$ is called to place an order. We have exploited here the fundamental[5] ORC site $\mathit{if}(b)$, which returns a signal $\langle\rangle$ if b evaluates to true, otherwise it does not respond.

Finally, an expression g_i is defined as follows:

$$
\begin{aligned}
g_i \triangleq\ & \mathbf{in}(\text{“}\mathit{store\,i}\text{”}, \text{“}\mathit{reqId12}\text{”}, !y_q)@\,\eta_{client} : l \\
& > \langle \text{“}\mathit{store\,i}\text{”}, \text{“}\mathit{reqId12}\text{”}, y_q \rangle > \\
& \mathbf{in}(\text{“}\mathit{sum}\text{”}, \text{“}\mathit{store\,i}\text{”}, \text{“}\mathit{reqId12}\text{”}, !y_{sum})@\,\eta_{client} : l \\
& \\
& > \langle \text{“}\mathit{sum}\text{”}, \text{“}\mathit{store\,i}\text{”}, \text{“}\mathit{reqId12}\text{”}, y_{sum} \rangle > \\
& (\ (\ \mathit{if}(y_q + y_{sum} \geqslant 30)\ \gg\ \mathit{let}(\text{“}\mathit{store\,i\,ok}\text{”})\,) \\
& \quad \mid\ (\ \mathit{if}(y_q + y_{sum} < 30)\ \gg \\
& \qquad\quad (\,\mathbf{out}(\text{“}\mathit{sum}\text{”}, \text{“}\mathit{store\,i}\text{”}, \text{“}\mathit{reqId12}\text{”}, y_q + y_{sum})@\,\eta_{client} : l \gg\ g_i\,)\,)\,)
\end{aligned}
$$

Basically, this a recursive expression that, at each recursive call, consumes a tuple containing an item availability and a tuple containing the actual sum, computes the sum between the read values and, if the sum is less than the desired number (i.e. 30) it produces a new 'sum' tuple and calls itself, otherwise publishes the string "*store i ok*" and terminates. Notably, to publish the string "*store i ok*", expression g_i exploits the fundamental ORC site $\mathit{let}(x, y, \ldots)$, which returns the argument values as a tuple.

4 Implementation Issues

In this section, we first provide a brief overview of the implementations of the programming languages derived from ORC and KLAIM, then we give a glimpse of the proof-of-concept implementation of KORC.

Although ORC was originally conceived as a process calculus, it has then evolved into a complete language for programming orchestration-based concurrent applications [26]. Such a programming language provides the ORC's orchestration operators and the site call construct with their original syntax, while expression definitions take the form `def f(x1,...,xn)` $= f_{body}$. The language is also equipped with arithmetic and logical operators, data structures, a conditional construct, and a variable binder construct `val` (e.g., `val x = 5` binds `x` to `5`). Moreover, Java classes can be accessed by an ORC expression as sites. To make a class available to an expression, a `site` declaration and a variable binding must be used like in the following example

```
site orcNode = com.orcNode
val client = orcNode(...)
```

where the variable `client` can be then used for calling functionalities provided by the Java class `com.orcNode`. To be accessed as an ORC site, a Java class

[5] To effective programming in ORC, the language is equipped with a few 'fundamental' sites (e.g. $\mathit{if}(b)$, $\mathit{let}(x, y, \ldots)$) that have to be considered local and whose behavior is predefined and predictable [40].

must extend one of the specific classes provided with the ORC's libraries (e.g. EvalSite). We refer the interested reader to [1] for a complete account of the ORC programming language and its supporting libraries[6].

Similarly to ORC, also the process calculus KLAIM has been extended with high-level features, such as variable declarations, assignments, and (standard) control flow constructs, to effectively program distributed networked applications. The implementation of the resulting programming language, called X-KLAIM (eXtended KLAIM [5]), is based on a compiler, which generates Java code, and on the Java library KLAVA [4], which provides the run-time support for X-KLAIM actions within the generated code[7]. The KLAIM net N_1 belonging to *store*1 of the e-commerce case study introduced in Section 3 can be rendered in X-KLAIM as follows:

```
nodes
  shop11::{nextl ~ localhost:11002, endl ~ localhost:11005, l ~ localhost:11004}
    port 11001
    begin
    out("itemId1",10,11)@self; ...
    end;

  shop12::{...}
    port 11002 ...
  ...
endnodes
```

A net, as expected, is a collection of node definitions, which must be included within nodes and endnodes. A node, e.g. the first one in the net above, is defined by specifying its name (shop11), its allocation environment (containing, e.g., the mapping from the locality variable nextl to the locality localhost : 11002), the port (11001) where it is listening, and a set of processes running on it (out("itemId1", 10, 11)@self; ...). It is worth noticing that the (physical) locality of a node is not defined by its name, but by the IP address of the computer where the node will run (in our example, this always is localhost) together with its port number. Instead, as an example of process definition, consider the process *FindItem* exploited in the e-commerce case study:

```
rec FindItem [itemId:str, maxPrice:int, reqId:str]
  declare locname startl
  begin
    eval(Find(itemId,maxPrice,reqId))@startl
  end
```

To speed up the experimentation with the programming paradigm fostered by KORC, we have exploited the compile- and run-time support tools for ORC and KLAIM presented above to implement KORC. The underlying idea is the following: KORC expressions are rendered as standard ORC expressions that rely on ad-hoc sites for performing the KLAIM actions. Specifically, we have developed a Java class com.orcNode, extending EvalSite, that can be used to define a

[6] We consider here the version 1.1.0 of the ORC's implementation, whose source code and binaries can be downloaded from http://orc.csres.utexas.edu.

[7] Complete documentation of X-KLAIM and KLAVA, together with source and binary files can be found at http://music.dsi.unifi.it/klaim.html.

new type of ORC site and that relies on the KLAVA library for performing the KLAIM actions. Since KLAVA uses types for values different from those of ORC, e.g. `KString`, `KInteger`, etc., and allows patterns to use both actual and formal parameters, we have also developed another kind of ORC site, `com.orcTuple`, that can be used to create objects having the correct types for invoking the KLAVA methods.

As an example of how a KORC expression is rendered in our implementation, the expression f of the e-commerce case study is written as follows

```
site orcNode = com.orcNode
site orcTuple = com.orcTuple

val client = orcNode("client",15000,"localhost",9999)
val store1 = orcNode("store1",15001,"localhost",9998)
val store2 = orcNode("store2",15002,"localhost",9997)
val store3 = orcNode("store3",15003,"localhost",9996)
val c = orcTuple()

def addLocality() =
   client.addEnv("lClient",14000) >> store1.addEnv("l",11004) >> ...

def moveFromStore1() =
   store1.in(c.tuple("id3",c.intFormal(),c.intFormal(),"reqId12"),c.locality("l"))
   > x > c.get(x,1) > z >
   client.out(c.tuple("store1","reqId12",z),c.locality("lClient")) >> moveFromStore1()

def ...

addLocality()
>> ( startSearch() >> (moveFromStore1() | moveFromStore2() | moveFromStore3() | g()) )
```

At the beginning, our sites `com.orcNode` and `com.orcTuple` are declared and assigned to some variables. Each `com.orcNode` site permits interfacing with a KLAIM net; thus, the corresponding variable can play the role of net name in the subsequent KORC actions. For example, the action $\mathbf{out}(\text{“}store1\text{”}, \text{“}reqId12\text{”}, z)@\eta_{client} : l$ is rendered as `client.out(c.tuple("store1","reqId12",z),c.locality("l"))`, where `client` represents η_{client}.

It is worth noticing that a `com.orcNode` site corresponds to a node belonging to the corresponding KLAIM net (in the example above, for the `client` net such node has name `client` and locality `localhost : 9999`). Thus, specific methods have been provided to set the allocation environment of such nodes and to load processes into them: `addEnv` and `loadProcess`, respectively. Notice also that formal parameters are unnamed in `com.orcTuple` tuples and, hence, a `get` method has to be used after **in**/**read** actions to extract the values associated to the formal parameters by pattern-matching.

We refer the interested reader to [29] for the Java code of classes `com.orcNode` and `com.orcTuple`. Such classes can be downloaded from `http://cse.lab.imtlucca.it/korc/` and can be installed in ORC as any other Java class defining an external site. The KORC implementation has been tested with ORC 1.1.0, X-KLAIM 2.b9 and KLAVA 2.b1. Due to lack of space, also the complete specification of the e-commerce case study, written in the syntax accepted by our tool, is relegated to [29].

5 Concluding Remarks

We have introduced KORC, a formalism aiming at reconciling the orchestration paradigm of ORC with the coordination one of KLAIM. Specifically, we have formally defined syntax and operational semantics of KORC, and we have developed a prototype implementation supporting KORC programming.

As witnessed by the case study presented in Section 3, the combined approach that we propose is very convenient to program distributed networked applications. In fact, on the one hand, the KLAIM approach alone does not permit exploiting the powerful ORC's orchestration operators and interacting with external sites. On the other hand, the ORC approach used alone is not suitable for distributed coordination tasks. This would require the use of dummy sites and would make programming complex and awkward.

In particular, while the operators for sequential composition and for symmetric parallel composition could be rendered in KLAIM by properly exploiting action prefixing and parallel composition, it would be tricky to express ORC asymmetric parallel composition $\cdot < \bar{p} < \cdot$ in terms of KLAIM constructs. Indeed, $f < \bar{p} < g$ permits immediately terminating the evaluation of g when a given event occurs (i.e. g publishes a tuple) while KLAIM lacks primitives for interrupting processes. In general, as seen in the case study, asymmetric parallel composition is very suitable for orchestration purposes, e.g. to implement transactional behaviours and fault handling. Another relevant aspect where KORC improves on KLAIM concerns the capability of interacting with external ORC sites, which may act as proxies for different kinds of services and applications. This enables the possibility of contacting and, hence, coordinating web services.

Some of the drawbacks of relying only on ORC approach are evident from our case study. There, the data storages of the warehouses of a store are rendered in a natural way as nodes of a KLAIM net. In this way, in KORC, to check the availability of items of type "*itemId3*", it is sufficient to perform the action **read**("*itemId3*", $!q, !p$)**@self** on the nodes; among all information stored in the tuple spaces about different kinds of items, by exploiting the pattern-matching mechanism, this action directly accesses the information for "*itemId3*". If we would use ORC alone to model this aspect, we would have to create a site, for each data storage, that publishes all items available at the corresponding warehouse and, then, use the pattern-matching provided by sequential composition to identify "*itemId3*" among all published values. Another solution would be to implement the search completely at site-side, thus leaving just site calls at expression-side; the programmer would then be forced to use another language (i.e. Java) to complete the implementation of the case study rather than simply using ORC. Notice also that, unless a single site would handle the data of all warehouses (which would not be reasonable in a distributed setting), the ORC program has to contact separately all warehouse sites and then to elaborate the retrieved information. In KORC, all the data storages associated to a given store can be visited through a single mobile process.

Related work. From the theoretical point of view, the formalisms closest to ours are ORC and KLAIM. In fact, to define KORC, we have chosen them as representative of the broader classes of orchestration calculi (as, e.g., [28,10,23,11,7]) and coordination calculi for network-aware and mobility programming (as, e.g., [21,24,12,39]). Relatively to these calculi, KORC does not provide new primitives, but it permits experimenting and reasoning on a novel programming paradigm combining orchestration and coordination operators.

In the web services literature [34], the terms *orchestration* and *choreography* are used to describe composition of web services. Orchestration describes how services can interact from the perspective of one party (*local descriptions*), while choreography tells of the sequence of messages according to a global perspective, where each party describes the part that plays in the choreography (*global descriptions*). Means to check conformance of local and global descriptions have been defined in [9,10,27], by relying on bisimulation-like relations, and in [25], by relying on session types. In KORC, the ORC part describes the orchestration, while the KLAIM part represents a form of collaborative coordination that can be used to enforce the involved parties to adhere to a given protocol, which can be thought of as a sort of choreography. Notably, both components of a KORC program play an active role, i.e. represent running programs, and describe different parts of the same system. This makes our approach different from the above mentioned works, where a choreography is intended to be either checked for conformance w.r.t. an orchestration of the different parties, or projected onto individual parties; in both cases, only orchestration is actually executed.

From the technological point of view, our work falls within the line of research that aims at developing programming frameworks based on process calculi. Among the several proposals, we want to mention below those designed for programming distributed networked applications. JCaSPiS [3] is a Java implementation of the service-oriented calculus CaSPiS [7] that, as well as KORC, takes inspiration by ORC (in particular, for the use of the sequential composition operator, called *pipeline*, over value streams). CaSPiS's implementation is based on the generic Java framework IMC [2] that provides recurrent mechanisms for network applications and, hence, can be used as a middleware for the implementation of different process calculi. JOLIE [32] is an interpreter written in Java for a programming language based on the process calculus SOCK [23], which is a formalism inspired by the WS-BPEL language for formalizing some fundamental concepts of Service-Oriented Computing, such as the design of a service behaviour, its deployment, and the composition of services within a system. JSCL [20] is a Java-based coordination middleware for services based on the event notification paradigm of the Signal Calculus [19], a variant of the π-calculus with explicit primitives to deal with event notification and component distribution. Finally, `PiDuce` [13] is a distributed run-time environment that implements a variant of the asynchronous π-calculus extended with native XML values, datatypes and patterns. The environment also permits interacting and experimenting with web services technologies.

Ongoing and future work. At foundational level, we intend to investigate the extension of KORC with name passing communication. Indeed, the ORC's formalization considered in this paper, drawn from [40], does not allow expressions to receive site names and use them in site calls, e.g. the term $M() > x > x(5)$ is not an ORC expression since the variable x cannot occur as a site name in the call $x(5)$. However, in other formalizations of ORC, see e.g. [31], sites are intended to be published as values by other sites and then called or used as parameters. Moreover, in KORC, besides site name passing, also net name passing is disallowed. In fact, a language for programming networked applications that permits passing net names but not site names would not be particularly meaningful.

We intend also to revise the programming language based on KORC presented in Section 6 to make it more usable by programmers. For example, KLAIM actions should have a syntax more similar to that shown in Table 3 and permit the direct use of named formal parameters. This could be realized, e.g., by means of a pre-compiling step. To further simplifying the task of writing KORC programs, we also intend to provide programmers with an Eclipse-based development environment relying on the Xtext framework [18]. Finally, while KORC is basically an extension of ORC with KLAIM actions and nets, we are also currently investigating a sort of reverse extension, i.e. KLAIM with mechanisms for calling sites (specifically, web services via SOAP over HTTP). Such extension mainly involves the KLAIM middleware (i.e. X-KLAIM and KLAVA) rather than the process calculus itself, since we would still rely on standard **out**/**in** actions for interacting with web services.

References

1. Orc Reference Manual. Technical report, University of Texas at Austin (2011), `http://orc.csres.utexas.edu/documentation.shtml`
2. Bettini, L., De Nicola, R., Falassi, D., Lacoste, M., Loreti, M.: A Flexible and Modular Framework for Implementing Infrastructures for Global Computing. In: Kutvonen, L., Alonistioti, N. (eds.) DAIS 2005. LNCS, vol. 3543, pp. 181–193. Springer, Heidelberg (2005)
3. Bettini, L., De Nicola, R., Loreti, M.: Implementing Session Centered Calculi. In: Wang, A.H., Zavattaro, G. (eds.) COORDINATION 2008. LNCS, vol. 5052, pp. 17–32. Springer, Heidelberg (2008)
4. Bettini, L., De Nicola, R., Pugliese, R.: Klava: a Java Package for Distributed and Mobile Applications. Software - Practice and Experience 32(14), 1365–1394 (2002)
5. Bettini, L., De Nicola, R., Pugliese, R.: X-Klaim and Klava: Programming Mobile Code. In: TOSCA 2001. ENTCS, vol. 62. Elsevier (2001)
6. Bettini, L., Bono, V., De Nicola, R., Ferrari, G.-L., Gorla, D., Loreti, M., Moggi, E., Pugliese, R., Tuosto, E., Venneri, B.: The Klaim Project: Theory and Practice. In: Priami, C. (ed.) GC 2003. LNCS, vol. 2874, pp. 88–150. Springer, Heidelberg (2003)
7. Boreale, M., Bruni, R., De Nicola, R., Loreti, M.: Sessions and Pipelines for Structured Service Programming. In: Barthe, G., de Boer, F.S. (eds.) FMOODS 2008. LNCS, vol. 5051, pp. 19–38. Springer, Heidelberg (2008)

8. Buscemi, M.G., Montanari, U.: CC-Pi: A Constraint-Based Language for Specifying Service Level Agreements. In: De Nicola, R. (ed.) ESOP 2007. LNCS, vol. 4421, pp. 18–32. Springer, Heidelberg (2007)
9. Busi, N., Gorrieri, R., Guidi, C., Lucchi, R., Zavattaro, G.: Choreography and Orchestration: A Synergic Approach for System Design. In: Benatallah, B., Casati, F., Traverso, P. (eds.) ICSOC 2005. LNCS, vol. 3826, pp. 228–240. Springer, Heidelberg (2005)
10. Busi, N., Gorrieri, R., Guidi, C., Lucchi, R., Zavattaro, G.: Choreography and Orchestration Conformance for System Design. In: Ciancarini, P., Wiklicky, H. (eds.) COORDINATION 2006. LNCS, vol. 4038, pp. 63–81. Springer, Heidelberg (2006)
11. Carbone, M., Honda, K., Yoshida, N.: Structured Communication-Centred Programming for Web Services. In: De Nicola, R. (ed.) ESOP 2007. LNCS, vol. 4421, pp. 2–17. Springer, Heidelberg (2007)
12. Cardelli, L., Gordon, A.D.: Mobile ambients. Theoretical Computer Science 240(1), 177–213 (2000)
13. Carpineti, S., Laneve, C., Padovani, L.: PiDuce - a project for experimenting Web services technologies. Science of Comput. Program. 74(10), 777–811 (2009)
14. Ciancarini, P., Rossi, D.: Jada - Coordination and Communication for Java Agents. In: Tschudin, C.F., Ryan, M. (eds.) MOS 1996. LNCS, vol. 1222, pp. 213–226. Springer, Heidelberg (1997)
15. De Nicola, R., Ferrari, G., Pugliese, R.: KLAIM: A Kernel Language for Agents Interaction and Mobility. Trans. on Software Engineering 24(5), 315–330 (1998)
16. De Nicola, R., Gorla, D., Pugliese, R.: On the expressive power of KLAIM-based calculi. Theor. Comput. Sci. 356(3), 387–421 (2006)
17. Denti, E., Natali, A., Omicini, A.: On the expressive power of a language for programming coordination media. In: SAC, pp. 169–177. ACM (1998)
18. Behrens, H., et al.: Xtext 1.0 (2010), `http://www.eclipse.org/xtext`
19. Ferrari, G., Guanciale, R., Strollo, D.: Event Based Service Coordination over Dynamic and Heterogeneous Networks. In: Dan, A., Lamersdorf, W. (eds.) ICSOC 2006. LNCS, vol. 4294, pp. 453–458. Springer, Heidelberg (2006)
20. Ferrari, G., Guanciale, R., Strollo, D.: JSCL: A Middleware for Service Coordination. In: Najm, E., Pradat-Peyre, J.-F., Donzeau-Gouge, V.V. (eds.) FORTE 2006. LNCS, vol. 4229, pp. 46–60. Springer, Heidelberg (2006)
21. Fournet, C., Gonthier, G., Levy, J.J., Maranget, L., Remy, D.: A Calculus of Mobile Agents. In: Sassone, V., Montanari, U. (eds.) CONCUR 1996. LNCS, vol. 1119, pp. 406–421. Springer, Heidelberg (1996)
22. Gelernter, D.: Generative Communication in Linda. ACM Transactions on Programming Languages and Systems 7(1), 80–112 (1985)
23. Guidi, C., Lucchi, R., Gorrieri, R., Busi, N., Zavattaro, G.: SOCK: A Calculus for Service Oriented Computing. In: Dan, A., Lamersdorf, W. (eds.) ICSOC 2006. LNCS, vol. 4294, pp. 327–338. Springer, Heidelberg (2006)
24. Hennessy, M., Riely, J.: Resource access control in systems of mobile agents. Information and Computation 173(1), 82–120 (2002)
25. Honda, K., Yoshida, N., Carbone, M.: Multiparty asynchronous session types. In: POPL, pp. 273–284. ACM Press (2008)
26. Kitchin, D., Quark, A., Cook, W., Misra, J.: The Orc Programming Language. In: Lee, D., Lopes, A., Poetzsch-Heffter, A. (eds.) FMOODS 2009. LNCS, vol. 5522, pp. 1–25. Springer, Heidelberg (2009)

27. Lanese, I., Guidi, C., Montesi, F., Zavattaro, G.: Bridging the Gap between Interaction- and Process-Oriented Choreographies. In: SEFM, pp. 323–332. IEEE (2008)
28. Lapadula, A., Pugliese, R., Tiezzi, F.: A Calculus for Orchestration of Web Services. In: De Nicola, R. (ed.) ESOP 2007. LNCS, vol. 4421, pp. 33–47. Springer, Heidelberg (2007)
29. Margheri, A., De Nicola, R., Tiezzi, F.: Orchestrating Tuple-based Languages (full version). Technical report, IMT Advanced Studies Lucca (2011), `http://cse.lab.imtlucca.it/korc/`
30. Milner, R., Parrow, J., Walker, D.: A Calculus of Mobile Processes, I and II. Information and Computation 100(1), 1–40, 41–77 (1992)
31. Misra, J., Cook, W.R.: Computation Orchestration: A Basis for Wide-Area Computing. Journal of Software and Systems Modeling 6(1), 83–110 (2007)
32. Montesi, F., Guidi, C., Lucchi, R., Zavattaro, G.: JOLIE: a Java Orchestration Language Interpreter Engine. In: MTCoord. ENTCS, vol. 181, pp. 19–33. Elsevier (2007)
33. OASIS WSBPEL TC. Web Services Business Process Execution Language Version 2.0. Technical report, OASIS (April 2007)
34. Peltz, C.: Web Services Orchestration and Choreography. Computer 36(10), 46–52 (2003)
35. Picco, G.P., Murphy, A.L., Roman, G.: Lime: Linda meets mobility. In: ICSE, pp. 368–377. ACM (1999)
36. Rowstron, A.I.T.: WCL: A Co-ordination Language for Geographically Distributed Agents. World Wide Web 1(3), 167–179 (1998)
37. Tolksdorf, R.: Laura: A Coordination Language for Open Distributed Systems. In: ICDCS, pp. 39–46. IEEE (1993)
38. van der Aalst, W.M.P., ter Hofstede, A.H.M., Kiepuszewski, B., Barros, A.P.: Workflow Patterns. Distributed and Parallel Databases 14(1), 5–51 (2003)
39. Wand, M., Siveroni, I.: Constraint systems for useless variable elimination. In: POPL, pp. 291–302. ACM (1999)
40. Wehrman, I., Kitchin, D., Cook, W.R., Misra, J.: A timed semantics of orc. Theoretical Computer Science 402(2-3), 234–248 (2008)

Transactional Correctness for Secure Nested Transactions
(Extended Abstract)

Dominic Duggan and Ye Wu

Department of Computer Science, Stevens Institute of Technology
Hoboken, New Jersey 07030, USA
dduggan@cs.stevens.edu

Abstract. Secure Nested Transactions are an adaptation of traditional nested transactions to support the synergy of language-based security and multi-level database security. They have application in security for enterprise applications, where transactional semantics are a critical feature in middleware systems. This article considers correctness in terms of transactional properties for secure nested transactions. Correctness is expressed in terms of a labeled transition system, the TauZero calculus.

1 Introduction

Security is a hard problem, one that cuts across many disciplines. Providing a yardstick for the correctness of secure systems is equally hard. Information flow control has a long history as a mechanism for stating end-to-end security policies. Noninterference and other properties are stated for the correctness of information flow in secure systems.

Information flow control was investigated for database systems in the context of multilevel database systems. One avenue for investigation has been the interaction of information flow with transaction processing in multilevel databases. Database transactions are partitioned into "low" and "high" transactions, with the understanding that "low" transactions can only read "low" database variables, and "high" transactions can only write "high" database variables. Nevertheless, for example, a high transaction might attempt to read a low variable, and therefore need to synchronize with low transactions that are reading and writing those variables. The particular issue of interest has been the potential for transactions with "high" security level to implicitly signal to transactions with "low" security level using the synchronization mechanisms provided to ensure proper isolation levels for concurrent transactions. In the example in Fig. 1(a), if transactions T_1^{High} and T_2^{Low}, which have high and low security levels respectively, use locking to synchronize access to "low" variables X and Y, then even though T_1^{High} may be unable to write to these low variables, it may signal to T_2^{Low} by locking one variable and not the other. In this example, $||$ denotes parallel composition, and `X` and `Y` are both low security variables. The high transaction implicitly sets `Z` to 1 by locking `X` and not `Y`. Why might the two transactions need to synchronize on variables at all? The high transaction may be monitoring a database being updated by low transactions, and

R. Bruni and V. Sassone (Eds.): TGC 2011, LNCS 7173, pp. 179–196, 2012.

the isolation property of transactions dictates that it should only be able view consistent states of the database, not an intermediate inconsistent state due to other uncompleted transactions.

This problem has been fairly extensively researched, and for at least one or two decades, it has been understood that in a situation such as this, a low transaction should be able to preemptively abort a high transaction that holds locks that it requires to proceed [1]. This avoids *termination leaks* such as exemplified above.

More recently information flow control has received attention in programming language security. Here much of the focus has been on reasoning about implicit control flow by relating control flow to data flow. For example, the program in Fig. 1(b) is rejected by type-based security analysis, since it would allow the setting of the "low" security level variable `Y` based on the value of the high security level variable `X`.

Secure nested transactions comprise an extension of transactions that synthesizes secure transaction processing, as exemplified by multilevel databases, and programming languages security.

Why should we care about synthesizing these two strands of research? The motivation is the interaction of language-based information flow control and concurrency. If we simply add the ability to fork concurrent threads in a sequential language, we allow leaks that subvert the information flow guarantees provided by type-based analysis. This is demonstrated by the example in Fig. 1(c). It is certainly possible to extend type systems for sequential programs to prevent low security level threads to depend on the termination behavior of high security threads [19,5,18]. However this misses the point, as demonstrated by the example in Fig. 1(c), that there is a need for synchronization between threads at different security levels. If mechanisms such as locks are not provided, then applications must implement their own using test-and-set and busy waiting.

$\texttt{int}^{\mathsf{Low}}$ `X, Y, Z;`
T_1^{High}: `lock(X); while (1) ;`
T_2^{Low}: `(lock(X); Z=0;)` $\|$ `(lock(Y); Z=1)`

(a) Transaction Processing

$\texttt{int}^{\mathsf{High}}$ `X;` $\texttt{int}^{\mathsf{Low}}$ `Y;`
`if (X==0) Y=0; else Y=1;`

(b) Sequential Programs

$\texttt{int}^{\mathsf{High}}$ `X, Y;` $\texttt{int}^{\mathsf{Low}}$ `Z;`
`(X=0; Y=1;)`
$\|$ `(while (X==0); Z=0;)` $\|$ `(while (Y==0); Z=1;)`

(c) Concurrent Programs

Fig. 1. Implicit Information Leaks

The obvious synthesis of these approaches is to have each thread in a concurrent programming language execute as a transaction, and allow "low" threads to pre-empt "high" threads that hold resources that the latter requires. This is an obvious idea, and simple to state. However if we assume that transaction aborts are now visible, either via language primitives for interrogating the state of transactions, or via the scheduler, then each transaction must have just one security level, High or Low. This is analogous to the situation in multilevel databases. However this rules out a class of examples that have been the raison d'etre for language-based information flow control, *viz.* situations where low-level programs wish to test high-level variables and then perform high-level actions in a temporary high context, before resuming execution as low-level code. In the "flat" transaction model, there is no facility for allowing this. Middleware environments such as Java Enterprise Edition allow transactional RPC calls to start new transactions that are independent of any transaction for the caller bean. However if the caller transaction subsequently aborts, we are left with an "orphan" transaction that by all rights should not exist. The preferred behavior is that the callee should execute as part of the same transaction as the caller. The problem if one is concerned with information flow control is that abort of the callee can force abort of the caller transaction. Therefore low security code cannot call into high security code. Ever.

Nested transactions were proposed by Moss [16] as an extension of the flat transaction model to support transactional remote procedure calls. The nesting of transactions is intended to model a call tree of nested RPCs. The abort of a transaction forces the abort of all transactions descended from that transaction, undoing that RPC and any effects arising from it. On the other hand, abort of a child transaction does not mandate failure of the parent transaction.

Secure nested transactions are an adaptation of nested transactions to support synthesize multilevel transaction processing and language-based information flow control. Secure nested transactions provide the same level of synchronization as provided by transactions, while avoiding implicit information leaks such as termination leaks. They also allow the mixing of high and low parts in transactional computations, as demonstrated by the example in Fig. 1(b). Here secure nested transactions leverage the fact that abort of a child transaction does not force abort of the parent. So, as in the sequential case, a "low" computation may test high variables and perform "high" effects in a temporary "high" context.

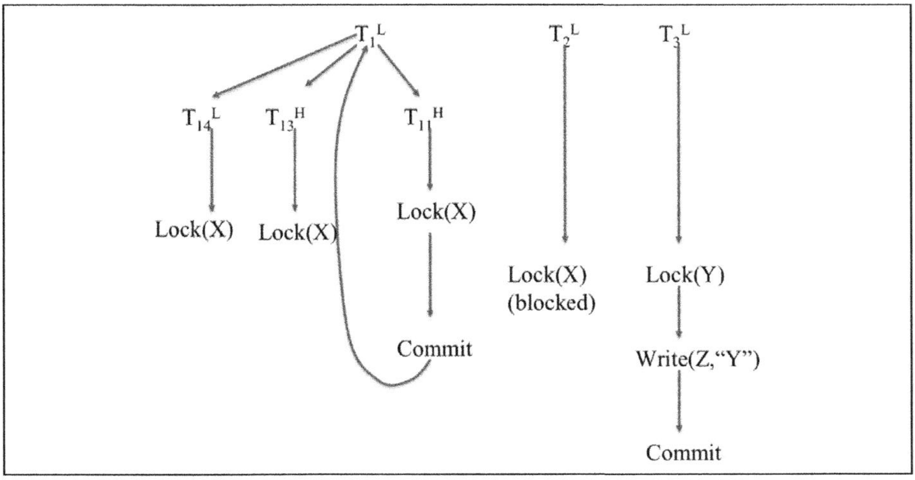

Fig. 2. The need for retroactive abort

Fig. 2 illustrates the challenges that may arise. In this example, the low transactions T_1^L, T_2^L and T_3^L are cooperating with the high transaction $T_{1.1}^H$ in order to create a covert channel that bypasses the level restrictions on information flow. $T_{1,1}^H$ is a child of T_1^L. The high child transaction $T_{1,1}^H$ acquires the lock for the variable X, in order to establish a covert channel to a low transaction. This high transaction commits, releasing the lock on the variable to its parent (since its commitment must be tentative). The low transactions T_2^L and T_3^L attempt to acquire locks on variables X and Y, respectively. T_3^L acquires the lock on Y, prints a message to this effect, and commits. Since it is outside of any other transaction, its effects are now publicly visible. On the other hand, T_2^L is blocked on attempting to lock X, which was originally locked by $T_{1,1}^H$. Were the latter still active, it would be forced to abort by T_2^L and the lock released. However the lock is now held by the parent of the high transaction, T_1^L, even if this low parent is unaware of the lock it has acquired via the actions of its child. To fix this problem, we require that the high child transaction $T_{1,1}^H$ of T_1^L be *retroactively* aborted. This is possible because the effects of any successful transactions cannot be made visible outside a nested transaction until the root transaction succeeds, and the low parent of a high transaction obviously cannot be aware of whether its high child aborted or committed.

Fig. 2 illustrates two other scenarios related to this. Suppose another high child transaction of $T_{1,3}^H$ has inherited the lock (from its parent T_1^L) that was originally acquired by $T_{1,1}^H$. In this case, $T_{1,3}^H$ will be aborted when the low transaction T_2^L attempts to lock X. Suppose on the other hand that the low child $T_{1,4}^L$ of T_1^L has acquired the lock on X that was originally acquired by $T_{1,1}^H$. If we allow T_2^L to pre-emptively abort $T_{1,4}^L$, then this is caused indirectly by $T_{1,1}^H$, so this is a form of abort dependency from high to low transactions that we are claiming to avoid. In this case, we can say that the low transaction $T_{1,4}^L$ is oblivious of the fact that the lock has been acquired due to inheritance and anti-inheritance from a high sibling, and this amounts to a scenario where a low transaction is blocked due to a resource being held by another low transaction. In this case, there is no information leak and the participation of high transactions in the overall computation is unknown to the low transaction.

Describing the semantics of retroactive abort imposes some challenges. Recent descriptions of transactional semantics for programming languages [4,12,15] describe transactional computations where the underlying transactional "machinery" is hidden in the language semantics. We have two reasons for not adopting this approach. First, our intention is to reason about security properties using techniques of observational equivalence from concurrency theory, since we are concerned about information leaks in potentially nonterminating concurrent execution. Second, rather than providing an operational semantics that effectively suggests a particular implementation of retroactive abort, we decouple the details of state management from the operational semantics using an abstraction of *logs*. One may consider logs as a collection of logical statements describing transaction state, and certain operations in the language are predicated on properties being deducible from the logs. For example, once a transaction has aborted, that property enables the restoration of messages that it has consumed. Logs are also not far removed from practical implementations, and protocols such as two-phase commit can be leveraged to check required log properties during the commit of a root transaction.

Our approach is based on a kernel language that has a straightforward implementation. We term our language **Tau$_{\mathbf{Zero}}$**. Its description is in three parts: a core language derived from the asynchronous pi-calculus, a global collection of logs, and a context of global names (including channel names and transaction identifiers). We use this language to reason about transactional properties of secure nested transactions.

This language is based on the asychronous pi-calculus, a variant of Milner's pi-calculus that accommodates non-blocking message-passing[1]. However our language is *not* a process calculus. Because all channel names are given global scope, there is no way to reason compositionally about the observational equivalence of processes. Neverthess this language is good enough to provide a trace-based semantics that is useful for reasoning about transactional properties such as serializability.

Furthermore, in other work [7] we have developed a processed calculus called **Tau$_{\mathbf{One}}$**, and used it to verify the security correctness of secure nested transactions. Moreover we are able to relate computations in **Tau$_{\mathbf{Zero}}$** and **Tau$_{\mathbf{One}}$**, using a notion of contextual constraint entailment that is novel. We provide more discussion of **Tau$_{\mathbf{One}}$** in Sect. 6.

Several bodies of work demonstrate how higher-level languages may be compiled to various process calculi, and we regard the translation of higher-level languages, extended with retroactive abort, into our calculus as a worthy topic for further research.

We introduce **Tau$_{\mathbf{Zero}}$** in Sect. 2. We describe our operational semantics in Sect. 3. We consider transactional correctness in Sect. 4. We consider related work in Sect. 5, while Sect. 6 provides our conclusions.

2 Tau$_{\mathbf{Zero}}$: A Calculus for Secure Nested Transactions

The **Tau$_{\mathbf{Zero}}$** language is a two-dimensional calculus of transactions and dependencies, based on Milner's pi-calculus. We assume a core language of asynchronous message-passing, and we extend this familiar idea with a transactional semantics. Our calculus can be viewed as a formal representative for asynchronous messaging systems that are at the core of modern service oriented architectures, providing a transactional semantics for adding messages to, and removing messages from, message queues. Example systems include Java Messaging System (JMS), Microsoft Queuing System (MSQS) and IBM's MQSeries.

The syntax of the language is provided in Fig. 3. We assume the following spaces of variables and names:

$$a,b,c,\ldots,\in \text{Channel name},\quad x,y,z,w \in \text{Variable},\quad \overrightarrow{t} \in \text{Transaction id},\quad k \in \text{Event id}$$

The only values in the language are channel names, represented by constants $a,b,c,\ldots$. Some channels have special significance in their use as locks: they have the property that they are always released by a transaction, whether that transaction commits or aborts.

[1] It is worth noting that asynchronous message-passing alone does not support "write-ups" from low to high processes, because of the possibility of traffic analysis of low messages if they can be consumed by high processes. Therefore our semantics includes a special form of message for supporting such communication, that is handled in a linear fashion by the semantics.

$C \in$ Channel Type ::=	$(\vec{C})^{\ell}$	Message channel
	$\mid \mathsf{Lock}(\vec{C})^{\ell}$	Lock
	$\mid \mathsf{Unit}^{\ell}$	Unit
$\ell \in$ Security Level ::=	$\mathsf{High} \mid \mathsf{Low}$	
$T \in$ Type ::=	C	Channel type
	$\mid \mathsf{Trans}(\ell)$	Transaction type
	$\mid \mathsf{Event}(\vec{t}, \ell)$	Event type
$w \in$ Name ::=	$a \mid \vec{t} \mid k$	
$v \in$ Value ::=	$a \mid x \mid ()$	
$A \in$ Agent ::=	$\vec{t}P$	Agent process
	$\mid A_1 \mid A_2$	Composition of agents
$P \in$ Proc ::=	$\hat{v}\vec{v}$	Send message
	$\mid \check{a}\vec{x}P$	Receive message
	$\mid (v_1{=}v_2) \rightarrow P_1 [] P_2$	Internal choice
	$\mid P_1 + P_2$	External choice
	$\mid \vec{t}[P]$	Launch transaction
	$\mid P_1 \mid P_2$	Fork process
	$\mid (\nu a{:}C)P$	New channel
	$\mid \mathsf{repl}\ P$	Replicate
	$\mid \mathsf{stop}$	Stopped
	$\mid \Box$	Commit or abort
	$\mid \mathsf{await}\ t[\Box]\ \mathsf{then}\ P$	Test status
$\Box \in$ Status ::=	$\boxdot$	Commit
	$\mid \boxtimes$	Abort
$V \in$ Env ::=	ε	Empty env
	$\mid (a : C)$	Channel decl
	$\mid (t : \mathsf{Trans}(\ell))$	Transaction decl
	$\mid (k : \mathsf{Event}(\vec{t}, \ell))$	Event declaration
	$\mid V_1.V_2$	Append envs
$\mathscr{L} \in$ Log ::=	true	Empty log
	$\mid \mathscr{L}_1 \wedge \mathscr{L}_2$	Join logs
	$\mid k{::}\,\vec{t}\,\hat{a}\,\vec{c}$	Log send
	$\mid k{::}\,\vec{t}\,\check{a}\,\vec{c}$	Log receive
	$\mid k_1 \searrow k_2$	Mesg exchanged
	$\mid k\ \mathsf{undone}$	Undone receive
	$\mid k_1 \curvearrowright k_2$	Lock transferred
	$\mid \vec{t}\boxdot$	Trans commit
	$\mid \vec{t}\boxtimes$	Trans abort

Fig. 3. **Tau$_{\text{Zero}}$** Syntax

Channels and locks have security levels. These security levels stratify channels into high and low channels, with high channels only usable by high processes and similarly for low channels and low processes. Locks are similarly stratified into high and low, but *low locks may be acquired by high processes.*

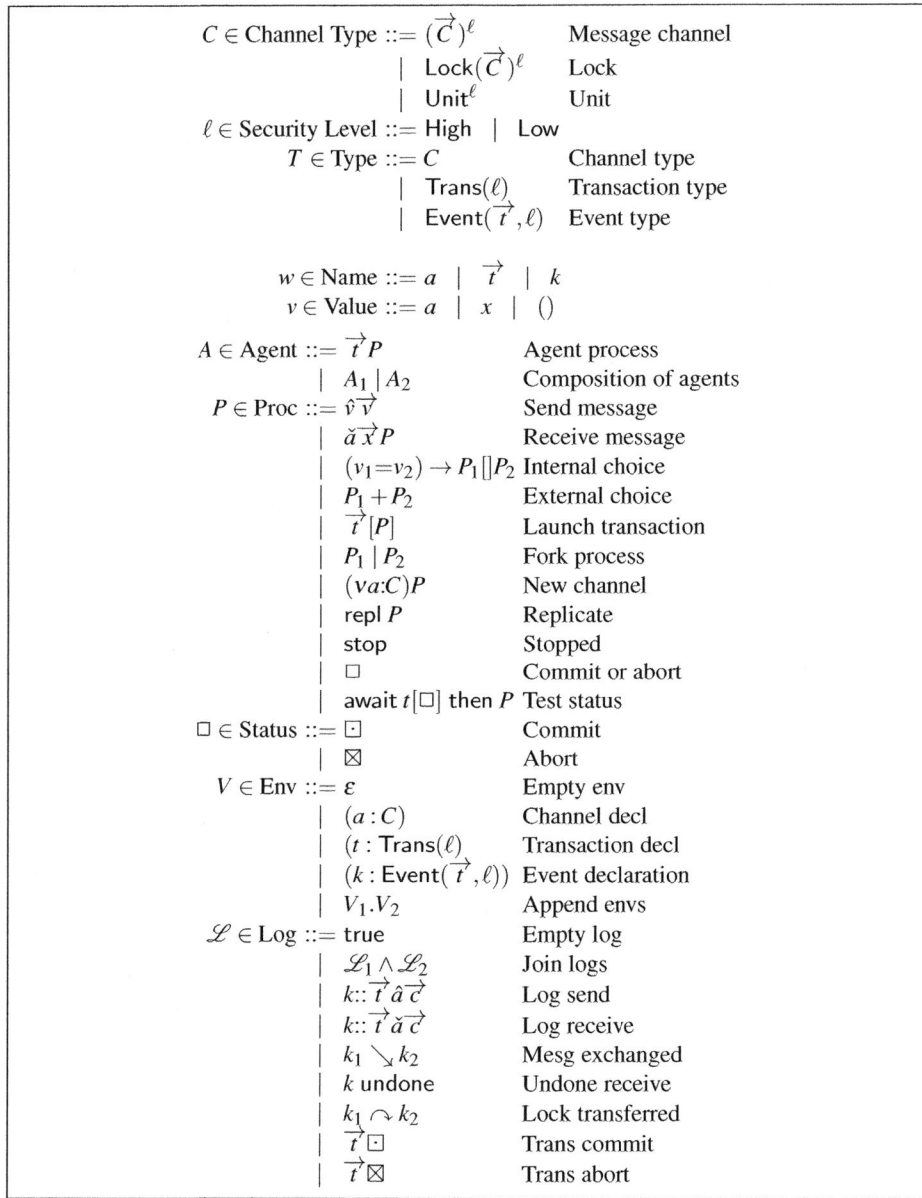

Each transaction is identified by a sequence of transaction identifiers $\overrightarrow{t} = (t_1, \ldots, t_k)$ for some k. Here t_1 is intended to be the root transaction, and the complete path identifies a nested transaction and all of its ancestors. We denote the prefix relation between sequences by $\leq$, so we have: $\overrightarrow{t_1} \leq \overrightarrow{t_2}$ iff $\overrightarrow{t_2} = \overrightarrow{t_1} . \overrightarrow{t_1'}$ where the period denotes sequence concatenation. Note that $\overrightarrow{t_1} \leq \overrightarrow{t_2}$ means that the former transaction is an ancestor of the latter. This is used extensively in the sequel.

The semantics of the language needs to track dependencies between transactions. In one dimension of this two-dimensional calculus, the dependency is from parent transactions to child transactions. Failure of the parent transaction forces failure of the child, even if the child has tentatively committed. This is to be consistent with the view that no updates propagate from an aborted transaction, including from any of its child transactions. Therefore a transaction type includes the name of its parent transaction, to record this dependency.

There are richer dependencies in our calculus than parent-child. Even when a high transaction commits and its effects are consumed by other transactions, it is possible for the original high transaction to be retroactively aborted and any high successors be subsequently aborted along with it. This requires that **Tau_{Zero}** track dependencies between transactions due to exchange of messages.

Fig. 4 explains why this is necessary for secure nested transactions, but not for classical nested transactions. Fig. 4(a) demonstrates an example where t_0, t_1 and t_2 are sibling transactions. If t_2 consumes a message output by t_0, then the abort of t_0 would mandate the abort of t_2, indicating a failure dependency. However the only way that t_2 can receive a message output by t_0 is if the latter commits. If t_0 tentatively commits, then it can only be forced to abort if its parent aborts. But if the latter aborts, then t_2 must also be forced to abort. Therefore for classical nested transactions, there is no need to track failure dependencies between transactions (beyond parent-child relationships).

Fig. 4(b) demonstrates how secure nested transactions complicate matters. In this example, t_0 is a high transaction that has acquired a lock a, and subsequently (tentatively) committed.. The sibling t_2 has consumed a message c produced by t_0. The parent transaction has not yet committed. If a low transaction now preemptively aborts t_0 in order to obtain the lock a, this will induce an abort of t_2. The failure dependency of t_2 on t_0 is due to the message produced by t_0 and consumed by t_2. Meanwhile the intermediate low transaction t_1 is (necessarily) unaffected. This demonstrates the need to track dependencies due to message exchanges in the semantics. Specifically these dependencies are recorded in the logs.

Therefore we need to track dependencies to propagate cascading aborts of high transactions (although aborts will only cascade within the scope of a parent transaction that contains the high transactions that abort). In order to track dependencies as a result of message-passing and synchronization, we use event identifiers k to uniquely identify significant events in the logs.

The syntax of types is provided in Fig. 3. We assume a security type system to prevent information flow leaks, by classifying data as High or Low. The details of this type system are provided in a technical report [7], that also considers a non-interference result for this system using a related system (**Tau_{One}**, discussed in Sect. 6). These security levels ℓ decorate the types of message channels $(\overrightarrow{C})^\ell$ and locks $\mathsf{Lock}(\overrightarrow{C})^\ell$, and reflect

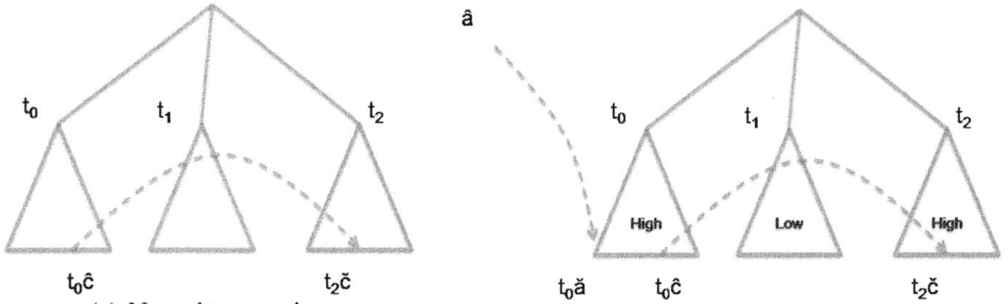

(a) Nested transactions (b) With retroactive abort

Fig. 4. Failure dependencies

restrictions on information that can be exchanged as a result of synchronization. Transactions are either "high" or "low," as reflected by their types, and can only have effects (sending and receiving of messages) based on their allowed security level. Whereas in sequential languages, a low thread can raise its security level to high in order to make high side effects, in our language a low transaction must spawn a high child transaction to have high effects. As discussed earlier, if high and low processes occupied the same transaction, a covert channel would be available by having the high process abort the shared transaction. This type systems distinguishes ordinary messages and "locks." Unlike messages, locks are always released by a transaction when it completes, whether it aborts or commits. This prevents a high transaction from consuming a lock (acquiring and never releasing it). Because of this, it is possible for high transactions to acquire locks with a low level, that may be shared with low transactions.

Although message-passing is asynchronous, we only allow messages to be exchanged between processes of the same security level. Allowing a high security level process to receive a message sent by a low security level process would allow information leaks due to low processes being able to detect contention between high and low processes for such messages. This is because of our choice of observational equivalence as a basis for reasoning about noninterference. We could allow asynchronous sending of messages from low to high processes if we instead used may-testing equivalence, which is equivalent to trace equivalence. It should be said that in this article, we are only using traces to reason about atomicity of transactional execution, in a manner similar to I/O automata. Instead we provide explicit locks to enable synchronization between high and low security level processes. There is a great deal of overlap between the semantics of messages and locks, except in the treatment of lock release for a committed process.

3 Operational Semantics

In this section we consider the operational semantics for $\mathbf{Tau}_{\mathbf{Zero}}$. The syntax of the language is provided in Fig. 3. The language includes asynchronous message sending and blocking message receive operations. The message send operation $\hat{a}\overrightarrow{v}$ outputs values $\overrightarrow{v}$ on channel a, where the latter may be sent as part of another message between processes. The message receive operation $\check{a}\,\overrightarrow{x}\,P$ unpacks a message received on channel a into local variables $\overrightarrow{x}$, and then executes the continuation process P. The accent on the channel names is intended to suggest "upload" and "download" respectively. We enrich these basic message-passing operations with both internal and external choice operations ($(v_1{=}v_2) \rightarrow P_1 [] P_2$ and $P_1 + P_2$, respectively), as well as a replication operation repl P. The latter is useful for defining recursive processes. We assume that all processes that are ready to input a message have the form $\overrightarrow{t}\,\Sigma\{\check{a}\,\overrightarrow{x}\,P\}$. In other words, a process may use external choice to select between different input channels. A facility for timeouts could easily be added. A process may launch a new transaction $\overrightarrow{t}\,[P]$ that executes nested within any transaction that encompasses the launching process. The language includes parallel composition and name scoping constructs for each of the forms of constants in the language, as well as a stopped process stop.

The semantics includes a log $\mathscr{L}$. The latter holds information both for reasoning about the status of transactions (e.g. committed or aborted), and also for recovering from the abort of a transactional by undoing any visible effects it has had. The latter take the form of messages consumed or locks acquired during the execution of the transaction. The sending or receiving of a message, and the transfer of a lock, is recorded with a unique event identifier k in the log. The type of this event identifier reflects the transaction in which event occurred. The transaction in turn has an associated security level.

Logs are an important part of controlling the complexity of the transaction calculus. In general configurations in the semantics have components of the form $\overrightarrow{t}\,P$, reflecting that every process P executes with respect to a (nested) transaction $\overrightarrow{t}$. We refer to components of this form as *agents* A. The operational semantics are made relatively simple by separating the evolution of process execution from the meta-reasoning about when operational steps are enabled, and what information must be logged to enable the computation.

There are various forms of log rules added during evaluation:

1. A log entry of the form $k{::}\,\overrightarrow{t}\,\hat{a}\,\overrightarrow{c}$ requires the sending of a message or generation of a lock. If the former, the message is sent by a transaction operating within the transaction $\overrightarrow{t}$. If the latter, the type system requires that the lock be generated at top-level, outside the scope of any transaction ($|\,\overrightarrow{t}\,| = 0$).
2. A log entry of the form $k{::}\,\overrightarrow{t}\,\check{a}\,\overrightarrow{c}$ records the receipt of a message or acquisition of a lock by a process executing in the transaction $\overrightarrow{t}$.
3. A log entry of the form $k_1 \searrow k_2$ relates a receive event k_2 to the corresponding send event k_1. It has several purposes. One is to establish a failure dependency from the sending to the receiving transaction: If the former is aborted, the latter is required in turn to abort. Another purpose is to relate a receive event to the corresponding send event, so that if the latter is undone in the process of aborting a transaction, the corresponding message to be restored is identified.
4. A log entry of the form k undone denotes that the action logged with event identifier k in the logs has been undone. This corresponds to a message receive or lock acquisition event that has been undone because the corresponding transaction has aborted. This type of log entry is used to ensure that message receives are only undone once in the event that a transaction aborts.

$$\frac{\mathscr{L} \equiv \mathscr{L}_0 \wedge k{::}\,\vec{t}\,P}{V,\mathscr{L} \vdash k{::}\,\vec{t}\,P} \qquad \text{(LOGJ ENTRY)}$$

$$\frac{V,\mathscr{L} \vdash k{::}A}{V,\mathscr{L} \vdash A} \qquad \text{(LOGJ ANON)}$$

$$\frac{\begin{array}{c}\forall \vec{t_0}.\vec{t_0} \leq \vec{t} \supset V,\mathscr{L} \not\vdash \vec{t_0}\boxdot \\ \forall \vec{t_0}.V,\mathscr{L} \vdash \vec{t_0} \rightsquigarrow \vec{t} \supset V,\mathscr{L} \not\vdash \vec{t_0}\boxtimes\end{array}}{V,\mathscr{L} \vdash \vec{t}\ \mathsf{running}} \qquad \text{(LOGJ RUNNING)}$$

$$\frac{\begin{array}{c}\vec{t_0}.t' \leq \vec{t} \qquad V,\mathscr{L} \vdash \vec{t_0}.t'\boxdot \\ \forall \vec{t_1}.V,\mathscr{L} \vdash \vec{t_1} \rightsquigarrow \vec{t} \supset V,\mathscr{L} \not\vdash \vec{t_1}\boxtimes\end{array}}{V,\mathscr{L} \vdash \vec{t}\ \mathsf{committed}\ \vec{t_0}} \qquad \text{(LOGJ COMMITTED)}$$

$$\frac{V,\mathscr{L} \vdash \vec{t_0}\boxtimes \qquad V,\mathscr{L} \vdash \vec{t_0} \rightsquigarrow \vec{t}}{V,\mathscr{L} \vdash \vec{t}\ \mathsf{aborted}} \qquad \text{(LOGJ ABORTED)}$$

$$\frac{\begin{array}{c}V,\mathscr{L} \vdash k{::}\,\vec{t}\,\breve{a}\,\vec{c} \\ \forall k_0.k \neq k_0 \wedge V,\mathscr{L} \vdash k \overset{*}{\curvearrowright} k_0 \supset V,\mathscr{L} \vdash tid(V,k_0)\ \mathsf{aborted}\end{array}}{V,\mathscr{L} \vdash k{::}\,\vec{t}\,\breve{a}\,\vec{c}\ \mathsf{terminal}} \qquad \text{(LOGJ TERMINAL)}$$

$$\frac{\begin{array}{c}V,\mathscr{L} \vdash k{::}\,\vec{t}\,\breve{a}\,\vec{c}\ \mathsf{terminal} \\ V,\mathscr{L} \vdash \vec{t}\ \mathsf{aborted} \qquad V,\mathscr{L} \not\vdash k\ \mathsf{undone}\end{array}}{V,\mathscr{L} \vdash k{::}\,\vec{t}\,\breve{a}\,\vec{c}\ \mathsf{undoable}} \qquad \text{(LOGJ UNDOABLE)}$$

$$\frac{V,\mathscr{L} \vdash k{::}\,\vec{t}\,\breve{a}\,\vec{c}\ \mathsf{terminal} \qquad V,\mathscr{L} \vdash \vec{t}\ \mathsf{committed}\ \vec{t_0}}{V,\mathscr{L} \vdash k{::}\,\vec{t}\,\breve{a}\,\vec{c}\ \mathsf{transferable}\ \vec{t_0}} \qquad \text{(LOGJ TRANSFERABLE)}$$

$$\frac{\begin{array}{c}V,\mathscr{L} \vdash k_0{::}\,\vec{t_0}\,\breve{a}\,\vec{c}\ \mathsf{terminal} \\ V,\mathscr{L} \vdash \vec{t_0}\ \mathsf{committed}\ \vec{t_0'} \qquad \vec{t_0'} \not\leq \vec{t_1} \qquad V,\mathscr{L} \vdash \vec{t_0'}\ \mathsf{running} \\ lev(V,\vec{t_1}) = \mathsf{Low} \qquad \vec{t_2} = min\,\{\vec{t} \leq \vec{t_0} \mid lev(V,\vec{t}) = \mathsf{High}\}\end{array}}{V,\mathscr{L} \vdash k_0{::}\,\vec{t_0}\,\breve{a}\,\vec{c}\ \mathsf{preemptible}\ \vec{t_2} \curvearrowright \vec{t_1}} \qquad \text{(LOGJ PREEMPTIBLE)}$$

Fig. 5. Reasoning From Logs

5. A log entry of the form $k_2 \curvearrowright k_1$ denotes that the lock acquired in the event labelled with k_2 has been released (or "anti-inherited") from a transaction to one of its ancestor transactions, as a result of the former transaction having committed. The lock was then acquired by a descendant of that ancestor transaction, in a lock acquisition event labelled k_1. The actual anti-inheritance of locks up the transaction tree is implicit in the committal of ancestor transactions, and fresh log entries for a lock are only added when descendant of one of these ancestors (a "cousin" transaction) acquires the lock. A log entry reflecting the ownership of this lock by the cousin transaction is recorded in the logs with an event identifier k_1. It is the counterpart to the $k_2 \searrow k_1$, but where the lock has already been acquired in the transaction tree and now its ownership is being transferred within that tree.

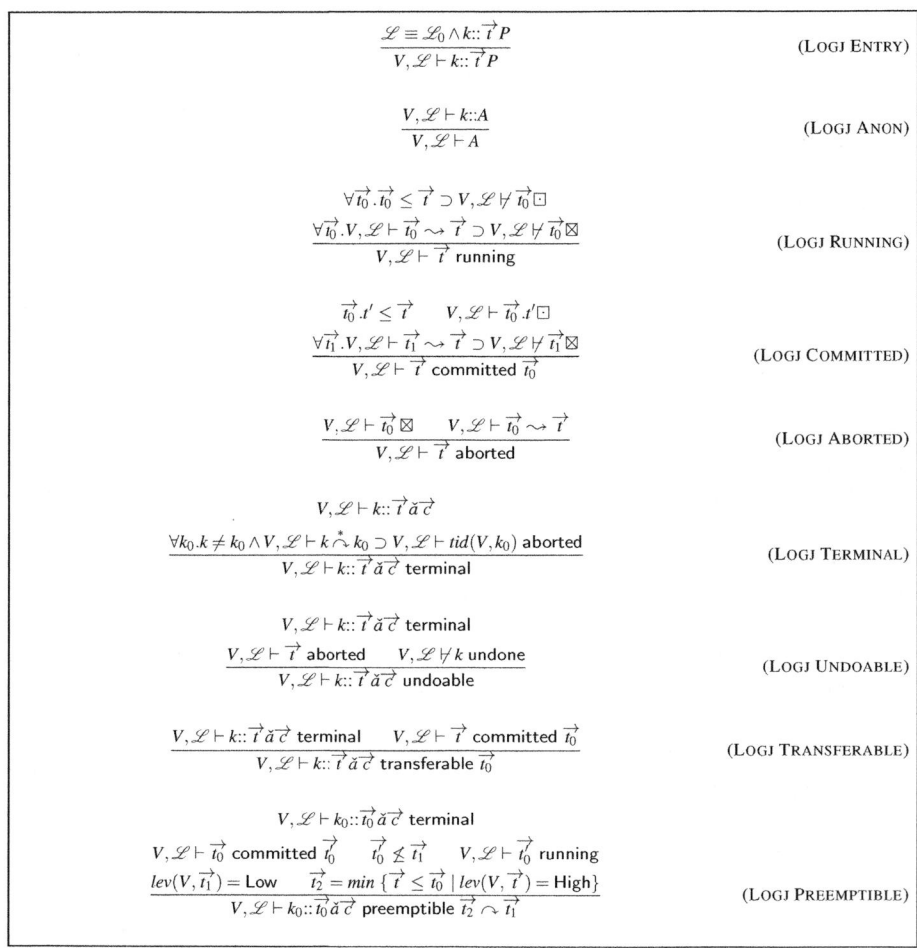

$$V,\mathscr{L} \vdash X \rightsquigarrow X \quad \text{(FDep Refl)}$$

$$\frac{V,\mathscr{L} \vdash k_1 \searrow k_2}{V,\mathscr{L} \vdash k_1 \rightsquigarrow k_2} \quad \text{(FDep SentTo)}$$

$$\frac{\overrightarrow{t_1} \leq \overrightarrow{t_2}}{V,\mathscr{L} \vdash \overrightarrow{t_1} \rightsquigarrow \overrightarrow{t_2}} \quad \text{(FDep Tid)}$$

$$\frac{V(k) = \mathsf{Event}(\overrightarrow{t},\ell) \qquad V,\mathscr{L} \vdash k \rightsquigarrow Y}{V,\mathscr{L} \vdash tid(V,k) \rightsquigarrow Y} \quad \text{(FDep ELeft)}$$

$$\frac{V(k) = \mathsf{Event}(\overrightarrow{t_2},\ell) \qquad V,\mathscr{L} \vdash X \rightsquigarrow k}{V,\mathscr{L} \vdash X \rightsquigarrow tid(V,k)} \quad \text{(FDep ERight)}$$

$$\frac{V,\mathscr{L} \vdash X \rightsquigarrow Y \qquad V,\mathscr{L} \vdash Y \rightsquigarrow Z}{V,\mathscr{L} \vdash X \rightsquigarrow Z} \quad \text{(FDep Trans)}$$

(a) Failure Dependency

$$V,\mathscr{L} \vdash k \overset{*}{\curvearrowright} k \quad \text{(XFer Refl)}$$

$$\frac{V,\mathscr{L} \vdash k_1 \searrow k_2}{V,\mathscr{L} \vdash k_1 \overset{*}{\curvearrowright} k_2} \quad \text{(XFer Acquire)}$$

$$\frac{V,\mathscr{L} \vdash k_1 \curvearrowright k_2}{V,\mathscr{L} \vdash k_1 \overset{*}{\curvearrowright} k_2} \quad \text{(XFer Transfer)}$$

$$\frac{V,\mathscr{L} \vdash k_1 \overset{*}{\curvearrowright} k_2 \qquad V,\mathscr{L} \vdash k_2 \overset{*}{\curvearrowright} k_3}{V,\mathscr{L} \vdash k_1 \overset{*}{\curvearrowright} k_3} \quad \text{(XFer Trans)}$$

(b) Ownership Dependency

Fig. 6. Failure and Ownership Dependencies

The reduction rules use various judgements to check preconditions by reference to the log:

$V,\mathscr{L} \vdash k{::}A$	Identifiable log entry
$V,\mathscr{L} \vdash A$	Anonymous log entry
$V,\mathscr{L} \vdash k_1 \searrow k_2$	Mesg or lock acquired
$V,\mathscr{L} \vdash k_1 \curvearrowright k_2$	Lock released
$V,\mathscr{L} \vdash k \ \mathsf{undone}$	Action undone
$V,\mathscr{L} \vdash \overrightarrow{t} \ \mathsf{running}$	Transaction still running
$V,\mathscr{L} \vdash \overrightarrow{t} \ \mathsf{aborted}$	Transaction aborted
$V,\mathscr{L} \vdash \overrightarrow{t} \ \mathsf{committed} \ \overrightarrow{t_0}$	Transaction committed
$V,\mathscr{L} \vdash k{::}A \ \mathsf{terminal}$	Terminal lock ownership
$V,\mathscr{L} \vdash k{::}A \ \mathsf{undoable}$	Undoable receive
$V,\mathscr{L} \vdash k{::}A \ \mathsf{transferable} \ \overrightarrow{t}$	Transferable lock
$V,\mathscr{L} \vdash k{::}A \ \mathsf{preemptible} \ \overrightarrow{t_2} \curvearrowright \overrightarrow{t_1}$	Preemptible trans
$V,\mathscr{L} \vdash k_1 \rightsquigarrow k_2$	Failure dependency
$V,\mathscr{L} \vdash k_1 \overset{*}{\curvearrowright} k_2$	Transfer of ownership

The first five judgements correspond to simply looking up a log entry, while the remaining judgements are based on inferences drawn from the contents of the log. The inference rules for these judgements are provided in Fig. 5, Fig. 6(a) and Fig. 6(b).

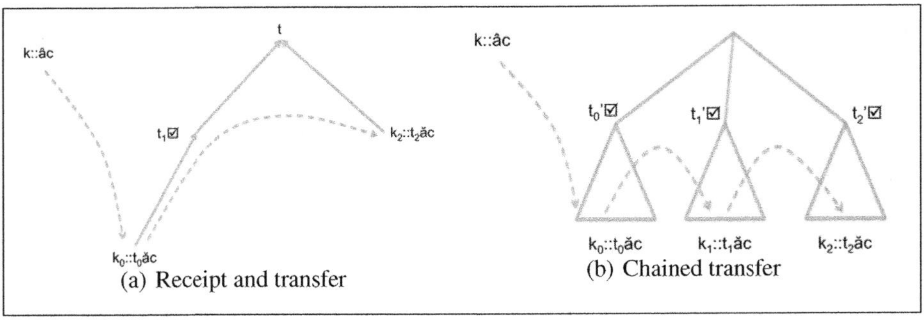

Fig. 7. Receipt of message/lock and transfer of ownership

The operational semantics of **Tau$_{\text{Zero}}$** are specified in Fig. 9(b) using reduction rules of the form:

$$(V_1, \mathscr{L}_1, A_1) \Rightarrow (V_2, \mathscr{L}_2, A_2) \text{ Internal reduction}$$

and in Fig. 8 using reaction rules of the form

$$(V_1, \mathscr{L}_1, A_1) \xrightarrow{\vec{t}} (V_2, \mathscr{L}_2, A_2) \text{ Visible reaction}$$
$$(V_1, \mathscr{L}_1, A_1) \longrightarrow (V_2, \mathscr{L}_2, A_2) \text{ Internal reaction}$$

The reduction steps correspond essentially to local unfolding in the semantics: unrolling loops where necessary, unfolding conditionals, forking new threads, launching new transactions, etc. The reaction rules correspond to interactions between transactions: message and lock exchange, (Rules (REACT SYNC) and (REACT TRANSFER)), preemption of all processes in a transaction, (Rule (REACT PREEMPT)), as well as committing or aborting a transaction, (REACT FINISH), and testing to see if a child transaction has committed or aborted. (REACT AWAIT).

Both reduction and reaction steps potentially modify the context V and the log $\mathscr{L}$. Hence the context and log are outputs from as well as inputs to each reduction step. The visible reaction rules expose the transaction in which the computation step happens. These rules include: a message receive or lock acquisition step (which may consume a message from an ancestor transaction or from the "top level"), a transaction commit step (that releases messages and locks that heretofore had been confined to a child transaction), and a transaction abort step (that releases messages and locks that had been consumed by the transaction before it aborted). We use the notation

$$(V_1, \mathscr{L}_1, A_1) \xrightarrow{[\vec{t}]} (V_2, \mathscr{L}_2, A_2)$$

to denote a reaction step that may be either visible or internal, with the label $\vec{t}$ optional.

4 Correctness

Define the following notions of repeated reaction steps:

$$(V,\mathscr{L},A) \Longrightarrow (V',\mathscr{L}',A') \text{ iff } \begin{cases} V = V_0, \mathscr{L} = \mathscr{L}_0, A = A_0, \\ V' = V_n, \mathscr{L}' = \mathscr{L}_n, A' = A_n \\ \text{and } (V_j,\mathscr{L}_j,A_j) \longrightarrow (V_{j+1},\mathscr{L}_{j+1},A_{j+1}) \\ \text{for } j = 0,\ldots,n-1 \end{cases}$$

$$(V,\mathscr{L},A) \overset{\vec{t}}{\Longrightarrow} (V',\mathscr{L}',A') \text{ iff } \begin{cases} (V,\mathscr{L},A) \Longrightarrow (V_0,\mathscr{L}_0,A_0), \\ (V_0,\mathscr{L}_0,A_0) \overset{\vec{t}}{\longrightarrow} (V',\mathscr{L}',A') \end{cases}$$

$$(V,\mathscr{L},A) \overset{(\vec{t_1},\ldots,\vec{t_n})}{\Longrightarrow} (V',\mathscr{L}',A') \text{ iff } \begin{cases} V = V_0, \mathscr{L} = \mathscr{L}_0, A = A_0, \\ V' = V_n, \mathscr{L}' = \mathscr{L}_n, A' = A_n \\ \text{and } (V_j,\mathscr{L}_j,A_j) \overset{\overrightarrow{t_{j+1}}}{\Longrightarrow} (V_{j+1},\mathscr{L}_{j+1},A_{j+1}) \\ \text{for } j = 0,\ldots,n-1 \end{cases}$$

The first of these corresponds to a sequence of zero more invisible reaction steps (one for which we do not record transaction interactions, such as testing whether a transaction has succeeded or failed). The second of these corresponds to a sequence of zero or more invisible reaction steps, followed by a visible reaction step. The last of these corresponds to a sequence of zero or more visible reaction steps, where there may be invisible reaction steps between each one of these visible steps.

To state a correctness theorem for nested transactions we need some auxiliary definitions. We first define a notion of equivalence between final configurations, based on the output messages that configurations are ready to offer.

Definition 1. *Define that $(V,\mathscr{L},A)$ can output $\vec{t}\,\hat{a}\,\vec{c}$, written $(V,\mathscr{L},A) \Uparrow \vec{t}\,\hat{a}\,\vec{c}$ if and only if:*

1. *a is a message channel: $V(a) = (\vec{C})^{\ell}$.*
2. *$(V,\mathscr{L},A) \Longrightarrow (V',\mathscr{L}',\vec{t_0}\,\hat{a}\,\vec{c} \mid A')$.*
3. *$V',\mathscr{L}' \vdash \vec{t_0}$ $\mathsf{committed}$ $\vec{t}$.*
4. *$\mathscr{L}' \not\vdash \vec{t}$ $\mathsf{aborted}$.*

Recall that an internal reaction step cannot include a transaction commit or abort operation. We use this to define a notion of final state equivalence between configurations of the operational semantics:

$$(V_1,\mathscr{L}_1,A_1) \approx (V_2,\mathscr{L}_2,A_2)$$

if and only if

1. $V_1(X) = V_2(X)$ for $X \in dom(V_1) \cap dom(V_2)$, and
2. $(V_1,\mathscr{L}_1,A_1) \Uparrow \vec{t}\,\hat{a}\,\vec{c}$ if and only if $(V_2,\mathscr{L}_2,A_2) \Uparrow \vec{t}\,\hat{a}\,\vec{c}$.

Definition 2. *Assume $(V,\mathscr{L},A) \overset{\vec{\vec{t}}}{\Longrightarrow} (V',\mathscr{L}',A')$. We say that $\vec{\vec{t}}$ is a* weakly nested trace *if, for all i_1, j and i_2 such that $i_1 < j < i_2$ and $\vec{t_{i_1}} = \vec{t_{i_2}}$, we have that $\vec{t_{i_1}} \le \vec{t_j}$ or $\vec{t_j} \le \vec{t_{i_1}}$. We say that $\vec{\vec{t}}$ is a* nested trace *if, for all i_1, j and i_2 such that $i_1 < j < i_2$ and $\vec{t_{i_1}} = \vec{t_{i_2}}$, we have that $\vec{t_{i_1}} \le \vec{t_j}$..*

$$\frac{\begin{array}{c} V,\mathscr{L} \vdash k_1{::}\overrightarrow{t_1}\,\breve{a}\,\overrightarrow{c} \text{ undoable} \qquad V,\mathscr{L} \vdash k_2 \searrow k_1 \\ V,\mathscr{L} \vdash k_2{::}\overrightarrow{t_2}\,\hat{a}\,\overrightarrow{c} \qquad \mathscr{L}' = \mathscr{L} \wedge k_1 \text{ undone} \end{array}}{(V,\mathscr{L},A) \Rightarrow (V,\mathscr{L}',\overrightarrow{t_2}\,\hat{a}\,\overrightarrow{c} \mid A)} \quad (\text{Red Undo})$$

$$\frac{V,\mathscr{L} \vdash \overrightarrow{t} \text{ running}}{(V,\mathscr{L},\overrightarrow{t}\,\Box \mid A) \xrightarrow{\overrightarrow{t}} (V,\mathscr{L} \wedge \overrightarrow{t}\,\Box, A)} \quad (\text{React Finish})$$

$$\frac{V,\mathscr{L} \vdash \overrightarrow{t}.t_0[\Box]}{(V,\mathscr{L},\overrightarrow{t}(\text{await } t_0[\Box] \text{ then } P) \mid A) \longrightarrow (V,\mathscr{L},\overrightarrow{t}\,P \mid A)} \quad (\text{React Await})$$

$$\frac{\begin{array}{c} A_1 = \overrightarrow{t_1}(\breve{a}\,\overrightarrow{x}P_1 + P_2) \qquad A_2 = \overrightarrow{t_2}\,\hat{a}\,\overrightarrow{c} \\ \overrightarrow{t_0} \le \overrightarrow{t_1} \text{ and } \overrightarrow{t_0} \le \overrightarrow{t_2} \text{ for some } \overrightarrow{t_0} \qquad V,\mathscr{L} \vdash \overrightarrow{t_1} \text{ running} \qquad V,\mathscr{L} \vdash \overrightarrow{t_2} \text{ committed } \overrightarrow{t_0} \\ V' = V.(k_1 : \text{Event}(\overrightarrow{t_1}, lev(V,\overrightarrow{t_1}))).(k_2 : \text{Event}(\overrightarrow{t_2}, lev(V,\overrightarrow{t_2}))) \\ \mathscr{L}' = \mathscr{L} \wedge k_1{::}\overrightarrow{t_1}\,\breve{a}\,\overrightarrow{c} \wedge k_2{::}\overrightarrow{t_2}\,\hat{a}\,\overrightarrow{c} \wedge k_2 \searrow k_1 \end{array}}{(V,\mathscr{L},A_1 \mid A_2 \mid A) \xrightarrow{\overrightarrow{t_1}} (V',\mathscr{L}',\overrightarrow{t_1}\{\overrightarrow{c}/\overrightarrow{x}\}P_1 \mid A)} \quad (\text{React Sync})$$

$$\frac{\begin{array}{c} A = \overrightarrow{t_1}(\breve{a}\,\overrightarrow{x}P_1 + P_2) \qquad V,\mathscr{L} \vdash \overrightarrow{t_1} \text{ running} \qquad V(a) = \text{Lock}(\overrightarrow{C})^{\ell} \text{ for some } \overrightarrow{C},\ell \\ \overrightarrow{t_0} \le \overrightarrow{t_1} \text{ and } \overrightarrow{t_0} \le \overrightarrow{t_2} \text{ for some } \overrightarrow{t_0} \qquad V,\mathscr{L} \vdash k_2{::}\overrightarrow{t_2}\,\breve{a}\,\overrightarrow{c} \text{ transferable } \overrightarrow{t_0} \\ V' = V.(k_1 : \text{Event}(\overrightarrow{t_1}, lev(V,\overrightarrow{t_1}))) \qquad \mathscr{L}' = \mathscr{L} \wedge k_2 \curvearrowright k_1 \wedge k_1{::}\overrightarrow{t}\,\breve{a}\,\overrightarrow{c} \end{array}}{(V,\mathscr{L},A \mid A_0) \xrightarrow{\overrightarrow{t_1}} (V',\mathscr{L}',\overrightarrow{t_1}\{\overrightarrow{c}/\overrightarrow{x}\}P_1 \mid A_0)} \quad (\text{React Transfer})$$

$$\frac{\begin{array}{c} A = \overrightarrow{t_1}(\breve{a}\,\overrightarrow{x}P_1 + P_2) \mid A_0 \qquad V,\mathscr{L} \vdash \overrightarrow{t_1} \text{ running} \qquad V(a) = \text{Lock}(\overrightarrow{C})^{\ell} \text{ for some } \overrightarrow{C},\ell \\ V,\mathscr{L} \vdash k_0{::}\overrightarrow{t_0}\,\breve{a}\,\overrightarrow{c} \text{ preemptible } \overrightarrow{t_2} \curvearrowright \overrightarrow{t_1} \qquad \mathscr{L}' = \mathscr{L} \wedge \overrightarrow{t_2}\boxtimes \end{array}}{(V,\mathscr{L},A) \xrightarrow{\overrightarrow{t_1}} (V,\mathscr{L}',A)} \quad (\text{React Preempt})$$

$$\frac{(V_1,\mathscr{L}_1,A_1) \Rightarrow (V_1',\mathscr{L}_1',A_1') \qquad (V_1',\mathscr{L}_1',A_1') \xrightarrow{[\overrightarrow{t}]} (V_2',\mathscr{L}_2',A_2') \qquad (V_2',\mathscr{L}_2',A_2') \Rightarrow (V_2,\mathscr{L}_2,A_2)}{(V_1,\mathscr{L}_1,A_1) \xrightarrow{[\overrightarrow{t}]} (V_2,\mathscr{L}_2,A_2)} \quad (\text{React Struct})$$

Fig. 8. Reaction Rules

Define a transaction to be *flat* if it contains no subtransactions. Say that a transaction is *proper* if lock acquisitions and message exchanges between transactions only occur within flat transactions.

Theorem 1 (Serializability). *Suppose* $(V_1,\mathscr{L}_1,A_1) \stackrel{\overrightarrow{t}}{\Longrightarrow} (V_2,\mathscr{L}_2,A_2)$. *Then there is some* $V_3,\mathscr{L}_3,A_3$ *such that:*

1. $(V_1,\mathscr{L}_1,A_1) \stackrel{\overrightarrow{t'}}{\Longrightarrow} (V_3,\mathscr{L}_3,A_3)$.
2. $(V_2,\mathscr{L}_2,A_2) \approx (V_3,\mathscr{L}_3,A_3)$.
3. $\overrightarrow{t'}$ *is a weakly nested trace.* $\overrightarrow{t'}$ *is a nested trace if all transactions in* A_1 *are proper transactions.*

Proof. We verify the result by induction on the length of the trace. For the step, assume $j = i_1 + 1$ in the definition of nested trace (the more general case follows from another

$$A \equiv A \mid \mathsf{stop}$$
$$\vec{t}\,\mathsf{stop} \equiv \mathsf{stop}$$
$$A_1 \mid A_2 \equiv A_2 \mid A_1$$
$$A_1 \mid (A_2 \mid A_3) \equiv (A_1 \mid A_2) \mid A_3$$
$$A \equiv A$$
$$\frac{A_1 \equiv A_2}{A_2 \equiv A_1}$$
$$\frac{A_1 \equiv A_2 \qquad A_2 \equiv A_3}{A_1 \equiv A_3}$$
$$\mathscr{L} \equiv \mathscr{L} \wedge \mathsf{true}$$
$$\mathscr{L}_1 \wedge \mathscr{L}_2 \equiv \mathscr{L}_2 \wedge \mathscr{L}_1$$
$$\mathscr{L}_1 \wedge (\mathscr{L}_2 \wedge \mathscr{L}_3) \equiv (\mathscr{L}_1 \wedge \mathscr{L}_2) \wedge \mathscr{L}_3$$
$$\mathscr{L} \equiv \mathscr{L}$$
$$\frac{\mathscr{L}_1 \equiv \mathscr{L}_2}{\mathscr{L}_2 \equiv \mathscr{L}_1}$$
$$\frac{\mathscr{L}_1 \equiv \mathscr{L}_2 \qquad \mathscr{L}_2 \equiv \mathscr{L}_3}{\mathscr{L}_1 \equiv \mathscr{L}_3}$$

(a) Structural Equivalence

$$\frac{\mathscr{L}_1 \equiv \mathscr{L}_2 \qquad P_1 \equiv P_2}{(V,\mathscr{L}_1,P_1) \Rightarrow (V,\mathscr{L}_2,P_2)} \quad \text{(RED REFL)}$$

$$\frac{(V,\mathscr{L}_1,P_1) \Rightarrow (V,\mathscr{L}_2,P_2) \qquad (V,\mathscr{L}_2,P_2) \Rightarrow (V,\mathscr{L}_3,P_3)}{(V,\mathscr{L}_1,P_1) \Rightarrow (V,\mathscr{L}_3,P_3)} \quad \text{(RED TRANS)}$$

$$(V,\mathscr{L},\vec{t}((a{=}a) \rightarrow P_1 [] P_2) \mid A) \Rightarrow (V,\mathscr{L},\vec{t}P_1 \mid A) \quad \text{(RED IFTRUE)}$$

$$\frac{a_1 \neq a_2}{(V,\mathscr{L},\vec{t}((a_1{=}a_2) \rightarrow P_1 [] P_2) \mid A) \Rightarrow (V,\mathscr{L},\vec{t}P_2 \mid A)} \quad \text{(RED IFFALSE)}$$

$$(V,\mathscr{L},\vec{t}(\mathsf{repl}\,P) \mid A) \Rightarrow (V,\mathscr{L},\vec{t}(P \mid \mathsf{repl}\,P) \mid A) \quad \text{(RED REPL)}$$

$$(V,\mathscr{L},\vec{t}(P_1 \mid P_2) \mid A) \Rightarrow (V,\mathscr{L},\vec{t}P_1 \mid \vec{t}P_2 \mid A) \quad \text{(RED FORK)}$$

$$(V,\mathscr{L},\vec{t}(\vec{t_0}[P]) \mid A) \Rightarrow (V,\mathscr{L},(\vec{t},\vec{t_0})P \mid A) \quad \text{(RED SPAWN)}$$

$$\frac{\begin{array}{c} V,\mathscr{L} \vdash k_1{::}\vec{t_1}\vec{a}\vec{c}\ \mathsf{undoable} \qquad V,\mathscr{L} \vdash k_2 \searrow k_1 \\ V,\mathscr{L} \vdash k_2{::}\vec{t_2}\vec{a}\vec{c} \qquad \mathscr{L}' = \mathscr{L} \wedge k_1\ \mathsf{undone} \end{array}}{(V,\mathscr{L},A) \Rightarrow (V,\mathscr{L}',\vec{t_2}\vec{a}\vec{c} \mid A)} \quad \text{(RED UNDO)}$$

$$\frac{a \notin fn(A) \qquad V' = V.a:C}{(V,\mathscr{L},\vec{t}((\nu a{:}C)P) \mid A) \Rightarrow (V',\mathscr{L},\vec{t}P \mid A)} \quad \text{(RED NEW)}$$

(b) Reduction Rule

Fig. 9. Structural Equivalence and Reduction Rules

induction argument). If the $\vec{t_{i_1}}$ action and the $\vec{t_j}$ actions both involve message receives, a case analysis verifies that the two message receive actions can be permuted. The difficult case would be if the $\vec{t_{i_1}}$ action acquired a message that was then acquired by $\vec{t_j}$ nested within $\vec{t_{i_1}}$, since permuting these actions would no longer make it possible (in general) for the $\vec{t_{i_1}}$ action to acquire the message. However this case is ruled out by the assumption that neither $\vec{t_{i_1}}$ nor $\vec{t_j}$ are prefixes of each other. The other problematic case would be if $\vec{t_{i_1}}$ was a commit or abort action that released a message then acquired by $\vec{t_j}$. But this case is ruled out by the fact that there is another action of $\vec{t_{i_1}} = \vec{t_{i_2}}$ after $\vec{t_j}$, so the action at i_1 cannot be a commit or abort (the transaction is still running at i_2).

5 Related Work

Birgisson and Erlingsson in [3] present the semantics and implementation for transactional memory introspection (TMI) that supports to enforce security policies under a multiple transaction context. Cohen, Meyden and Zuck [6] develop an access control model based on Rushby's work [17] to reason about information flow security in their extended system, caused by transaction aborting. All of these works essentially extend work in multilevel databases to software transactional memory.

Transactions have at various points received interest from the programming languages community. The Argus, Camelot and Avalon languages, among several others, incorporated nested transactions to support a transactional semantics for nested RPC [14,20,9]. Black et al [4] provide an equational characterization of the ACID properties of transactions. Atomicity, isolation and durability are characterized in terms of appropriate categories of actions, while consistency is characterized as an induction rule for reasoning about overall system consistency. Jagannathan et al [12] provide an operational semantics for transactions in terms of an extension of Featherweight Java [11]. Their calculus supports both nested and multi-threaded transactions, and is agnostic as to whether concurrency control is optimistic or pessimistic. Their main result is the verification of serializability for their semantics. Harris et al [10] provide an operational semantics for software transactional memory abstractions in Haskell, using a monadic semantics to ensure isolation, although without nested transactions. Wojciechowski [21] verifies isolation for a language with nested transactions, extending lock types to ensure that concurrency control is properly attained. Moore and Grossman [15] provide a higher-level operational semantics for nested transactions, one that allows them to investigate several variations on transactional semantics. They use an effect system to ensure isolation of transactions, analogous to the use of monads [10] or extended lock types [21], but abstracting from the operational details of synchronization. This approach is in that respect similar to that of Jaganathan et al.

The concerns for the current article are clearly very different. Our concern is providing an operational semantics for secure nested transactions, in particular with retroactive abort. While the aforesaid approaches are motivated by the need for operational models for software transactional memory, our concern is in reasoning about both transactional and security properties. Thus for example the approach of Moore and Grossman is too high-level for our purposes: They model aborted transactions as transactions that never start in a non-deterministic semantics, which elides many operational details that may be the source of attack vectors. The reliance on type systems in many of the aforesaid approaches to ensure isolation mitigates their usefulness for our purposes. Indeed, it is already known how to use linear type systems to ensure isolation in concurrent program, without information leaks [13]. The motivation for this work is to consider approaches to controlling information flow that shift the focus from static approaches (beyond a security type system) to the dynamic approach of transactional execution.

Bertino et al [2] consider noninterference for nested transactions. They are principally concerned with the issue of starvation of high transactions in multi-level databases. They only consider nested transactions where parent and child transactions have the same security level. A synthesis of our mixed level transactions with their notion of security locks would be an interesting topic for future work.

6 Conclusions

We have described the semantics of secure nested transactions in terms of a language inspired by a process calculus, though it is not in fact a process calculus. In particular, the fact that all channels names are globalized in the semantics makes this inappropriate for reasoning about observational equivalence. In other work [7], we have developed a true process calculus, $\mathbf{Tau}_{\mathbf{One}}$, that extends $\mathbf{Tau}_{\mathbf{Zero}}$ with local scoping of channel names. The motivation for this work is exactly to reason about security properties, in particular, to draw on results in process equality theory to reason about noninterference independent of transactional properties. This result has profound implications for the system, however. In $\mathbf{Tau}_{\mathbf{Zero}}$, all logs are global, and so reaction and reduction rules for computation can interrogate those logs for preconditions that are required for rules to fire. In $\mathbf{Tau}_{\mathbf{One}}$, on the other hand, compositionality requires that log entries be distributed amongst processes descriptions. Since reaction and reduction rules no longer have global logs to interrogate, they instead fire in the semantics with logical constraints on the surrounding log context. These constraints propagate upwards through the context of a rule firing, constraining the forms of log entries that can appear in the context. The point of $\mathbf{Tau}_{\mathbf{One}}$ is to use stronger notions of process equivalence, in particular observational equivalence, to reason about security properties independent of transactional properties such as serializabiity. We report on this relationship between $\mathbf{Tau}_{\mathbf{Zero}}$ and $\mathbf{Tau}_{\mathbf{One}}$, and further details on the semantics of $\mathbf{Tau}_{\mathbf{Zero}}$, in a longer version of this article [8].

References

1. Atluri, V., Jajodia, S., George, B.: Multilevel Secure Transaction Processing. Kluwer Academic Publishers (1999)
2. Bertino, E., Catania, B., Ferrari, E.: A nested transaction model for multilevel secure database management systems. ACM Trans. Inf. Syst. Secur. 4, 321–370 (2001)
3. Birgisson, A., Erlingsson, Ú.: An implementation and semantics for transactional memory introspection in haskell. In: PLAS, pp. 87–99 (2009)
4. Black, A., Cremet, V., Guerraoui, R., Odersky, M.: An Equational Theory for Transactions. In: Pandya, P.K., Radhakrishnan, J. (eds.) FSTTCS 2003. LNCS, vol. 2914, pp. 38–49. Springer, Heidelberg (2003)
5. Boudol, G., Castellani, I.: Noninterference for concurrent programs and thread systems. Theor. Comput. Sci. 281(1-2), 109–130 (2002)
6. Cohen, A., van der Meyden, R., Zuck, L.D.: Access Control and Information Flow in Transactional Memory. In: Degano, P., Guttman, J., Martinelli, F. (eds.) FAST 2008. LNCS, vol. 5491, pp. 316–330. Springer, Heidelberg (2009)
7. Duggan, D., Wu, Y.: Security correctness for secure nested transactions. Technical Report, Stevens Institute of Technology (2012)
8. Duggan, D., Wu, Y.: Transactional correctness for secure nested transactions. Technical report, Stevens Institute of Technology (2012)
9. Eppinger, J., Mummert, L., Spector, A. (eds.): Camelot and Avalon: A Distributed Transaction Facility. Morgan Kaufmann (1993)
10. Harris, T., Marlow, S., Peyton-Jones, S., Herlihy, M.: Composable memory transactions. In: ACM Conference on Principles and Practice of Parallel Programming (2005)
11. Igarashi, A., Pierce, B., Wadler, P.: Featherweight Java: A core calculus for Java and GJ. In: Proceedings of ACM Symposium on Object-Oriented Programming: Systems, Languages and Applications, Denver, CO. ACM Press (1999)
12. Jagannathan, S., Vitek, J., Welc, A., Hosking, A.: A transactional object calculus. Science of Computer Programming (2005)
13. Kobayashi, N.: Type-based information flow analysis for the pi-calculus. Acta Informatica (2003)
14. Liskov, B.: Distributed programming in Argus. Communications of the ACM 31(3) (March 1988)

15. Moore, K., Grossman, D.: High-level small-step operational semantics for transactions. In: Proceedings of ACM Symposium on Principles of Programming Languages (2008)
16. Moss, J.E.B.: Nested Transactions: An Approach to Reliable Distributed Computing. MIT Press (1985)
17. Rushby, J.M.: Noninterference, transitivity and channel-control security policies. Technical report, SRI (1992)
18. Sabelfeld, A.: Semantic Models for the Security of Sequential and Concurrent Programs. PhD thesis, Chalmers University of Technology and Gothenburg University, Gothenburg, Sweden (May 2001)
19. Smith, G., Volpano, D.: Secure information flow in a multi-threaded imperative language. In: Proceedings of ACM Symposium on Principles of Programming Languages, pp. 19–21 (1998)
20. Spector, A., Swedlow, K.: Guide to the Camelot distributed transaction facility: Release 1. Technical report, Carnegie Mellon University (1987)
21. Wojciechowski, P.: Isolation-only transactions by typing and versioning. In: ACM Conference on Principles and Practice of Declarative Programming (2005)

Orchestrating Unreliable Services: Strategic and Probabilistic Approaches to Reliability*

Joaquim Gabarro[1], Maria Serna[1], and Alan Stewart[2]

[1] ALBCOM. LSI Dept. Universitat Politècnica de Catalunya, Barcelona
[2] School of Computer Science. The Queen's University of Belfast, Belfast
{gabarro,mjserna}@lsi.upc.edu, a.stewart@qub.ac.uk

Abstract. The robustness of orchestrations of unreliable web-services to failure can be analysed using Angel Daemon ($\mathcal{A}/\mathcal{D}$) games. A measure of the reliability of an orchestration O can be determined by characterising a user's perception of underlying services and, additionally, making assumptions about the number of services that will fail during an evaluation of O (here such characterisations are called *uncertainty profiles*). The Nash equilibria of games associated with *uncertainty profiles* provide *a posteriori* information about the probability of orchestration success. In this approach probabilities are second class objects since they are derived from calculated Nash equilibria. Alternatively, probabilistic characterisations of failing services can be given from the outset (*probabilistic profiles*). Uncertainty profiles and probabilistic profiles provide complementary techniques for investigating the robustness of web-based orchestrations. In this paper the relationship between the two approaches is investigated. A means of adding probabilistic information to an uncertainty profile is proposed – hybrid profiles give rise to bayesian variations of $\mathcal{A}/\mathcal{D}$ games. The main result of the paper is to align $\mathcal{A}/\mathcal{D}$ games with bayesian $\mathcal{A}/\mathcal{D}$ games. When the probabilistic information retrieved by the angel is consistent with a Nash equilibrium, the corresponding bayesian Nash equilibrium mimicks the original Nash equilibrium.

Keywords: Web orchestrations, zero-sum games, angel-daemon games, uncertainty profile, probabilistic profiles, bayesian games.

1 Introduction

An orchestration can be viewed as the way "in which one web service invokes other web-services in order to realize some useful function" [13]. The reliability and the performance characteristics of web-services and orchestrations are difficult to formalise: service performance can fluctuate wildly between times of over-demand and idle times. In extreme situations services can fail. Analysing orchestration behaviour is also complex; services which superficially appear to be unrelated can in practice utilise the same infrastructure (located within in the same data centre). Thus, the performance of one service may be unexpectedly related to that of another. Cloud providers and application

* J. Gabarro and M. Serna are partially supported by TIN-2007-66523 (FORMALISM), and SGR 2009-2015 (ALBCOM). Alan Stewart is partially supported by EPSRC project EP/I03405X/1 (ECHO).

R. Bruni and V. Sassone (Eds.): TGC 2011, LNCS 7173, pp. 197–211, 2012.

developers often utilise third-party infrastructures or software services – heuristics are often employed to provide guidance on which resources or services are most cost effective (or reliable). In this paper the reliability of application orchestrations is analysed when a number of underlying services fail: robust orchestrations contain a degree of redundant computation to counteract unreliability. Uncertainty profiles [3,4] can be used to analyse the uncertainty associated with web orchestrations. An uncertainty profile $\mathcal{U}$ gives rise to a strategic game which can be assessed as, $\nu(\mathcal{U})$, using Nash equilibria, to give a posteriori information about orchestration reliability [3]. In [4] a partial ordering for uncertainty profiles is shown to be monotonic – that is: $\mathcal{U} \sqsubseteq \mathcal{U}'$ implies $\nu(\mathcal{U}) \leq \nu(\mathcal{U}')$. The goal of this paper is to compare the probabilistic information obtained from uncertainty profiles with probabilistic information obtained in other ways. It is possible to augment the strategic approach of uncertainty profiles with additional probabilistic information. This approach gives rise to a special class of bayesian games, called *one-site* $\mathcal{A}/\mathcal{D}$ bayesian games.

This paper advocates game-based assessments of orchestration reliability in preference to probabilistic approaches because of the difficulty in providing meaningful *a priori* reliability measures of services. In Section 2 formal models of orchestrations and service failures are given while section 3 introduces uncertainty profiles in order to analyze orchestration reliability. Section 4 introduces probabilistic profiles as an alternative way to assess orchestration reliability. In section 5 a new class of bayesian games, *one-site* $\mathcal{A}/\mathcal{D}$ bayesian games, is introduced by augmenting uncertainty profiles with relevant probabilistic information. Some reflections on analysing orchestration reliability are given in Section 6.

2 Orchestrations, Failures

An orchestration is a user-defined program that utilises web services. Typical examples of services might be: an eigensolver, a search engine or a database. A *service* accepts an argument and *publishes* a result value[1]. For example, a call to a search engine, $\mathit{find}(s)$, may publish the set of sites which *currently* offer service s. A service is said to be *silent* if it does not publish a result when called. Service calls may induce *side effects*. A service call can publish *at most one response*. A service s may fail to respond when it is called in an unreliable environment. The orchestration language Orc [8] contains a number of inbuilt services: 0 is always silent whereas $1(x)$ always publishes x. Two Orc expressions P and Q can be combined using the following operators:

- Sequence $P > x > Q(x)$: Orchestration P is evaluated: for each output v, published by P, an instance $Q(v)$ is invoked. If P publishes the stream of values, $v_1, v_2, \ldots, v_n$, then $P > x > Q(x)$ publishes some interleaving of the set $\{Q(v_1), Q(v_2), \ldots, Q(v_n)\}$. The abbreviation $P \gg Q$ is used in situations where Q does not depend on x.
- Symmetric Parallelism $P \mid Q$: The independent orchestrations P and Q are executed in parallel; $P \mid Q$ publishes *some* interleaving of the values published by P and Q.

[1] The words “publishes”,“returns” and “outputs” are used interchangeably.

- Asymmetric parallelism $P(x) < x < Q$: The dependent orchestrations P and Q are evaluated in parallel; P may become blocked by a dependency on x. The first result published by Q is bound to x, the remainder of Q's evaluation is terminated and evaluation of the blocked residue of P is resumed.

Example 1. Example orchestrations for distributing digital newspapers by email are:

$$\begin{aligned}
&Two_Each = (CNN \mid BBC) > x > (EmailAlice(x) \mid EmailBob(x))\\
&One_Each = ((CNN > x > EmailAlice(x)) \mid (BBC > x > EmailBob(x)))\\
&Any_One = (EmailAlice(x) \mid EmailBob(x)) < x < (CNN \mid BBC)
\end{aligned}$$

Two_Each delivers digital newspapers from both CNN and BBC to both Alice and Bob. One_Each delivers the CNN paper to Alice and the BBC paper to Bob. Any_One delivers the same newspaper, either BBC or CNN, to both Alice and Bob. □

In order to make connections between probabilistic approaches and strategic games a restrictive class of orchestrations, *basic orchestrations*, are introduced. *Basic orchestrations* are non-recursive and underlying sites are parameterless. Non-vacuous sites are assumed to return results when called. As sites are parameterless orchestrations cannot model selection (normally site *if* is called with a boolean parameter, *b*, to specify choice). In a parameterless environment, the asymmetric construct $P < x < Q$ degenerates to $P \mid (Q \gg 0)$ (see 6.2 in [8])– if Q is stateless this degenerates further to P, since $(Q \gg 0) = 0$. In order to model asymmetry in this parameterless framework the operator $<!$ is introduced:

Definition 1 (blocked until). *Execution of the orchestration $P <! Q$ is blocked until Q publishes – at which point Q is terminated and P is activated.*

$P <! Q$ can be encoded in Orc as $(1(x) \gg P) < x < Q$.

Definition 2 (basic orchestrations). *In a basic orchestration all services are parameterless; services are composed using the operators $|, \gg, <!$. Basic orchestrations are non-recursive.*

The following are examples of basic orchestrations:

$$Par(P_1, \ldots, P_n) = (P_1 \mid \cdots \mid P_n), \qquad Seq(P_1, \ldots, P_n) = (P_1 \gg \cdots \gg P_n)$$

Web environments are unreliable. Sites evolve and a user has little (or no) control over the execution environment. When a complex orchestration E is evaluated it is *unrealistic* to assume that all necessary services will be working. We make the following reliability assumption: *Service performance is variable and services can fail. A failed service remains silent when called.* The behaviour of a working service is assumed to be consistent with its specification. Let E be an orchestration and $\alpha(E)$ (the alphabet of E) be the set of services called within E. $\alpha_+(E)$ denotes external web-services ($\alpha_+(E) = \alpha(E) \setminus \{0, 1\}$). Suppose that the set of unreliable services used in E is $\mathcal{F}$ where $\mathcal{F} \subseteq \alpha_+(E)$. Services in $\alpha_+(E) \setminus \mathcal{F}$ are assumed to be completely reliable. In an execution of E, services in $\mathcal{F}$ can either fail or function normally. Assume that all sites in $f \subseteq \mathcal{F}$ fail while the remaining sites $\overline{f} = \mathcal{F} \setminus f$ function normally. An orchestration with multiple threads (and built-in redundancy) may still return partial results even if some services fail. Let $\mathsf{fail}_f(E)$ denote the effect of evaluating E in an environment where services in f fail; $\mathsf{fail}_f(E)$ is found by replacing all occurrences of services s, where $s \in f$, by 0.

Definition 3 (resilience measure). *The behaviour of E in an environment where services in $f \subseteq \alpha_+(E)$ fail is denoted by $\mathsf{fail}_f(E)$. A measure of the resilience of $\mathsf{fail}_f(E)$ is $\mathsf{out}(\mathsf{fail}_f(E))$, the number of outputs,* out*, published by E where the* out *verifies $0 \leq \mathsf{out}(\mathsf{fail}_f(E)) \leq \mathsf{out}(E)$.*

Let the threshold function θ be such that $\theta(n) = 1$ if $n > 0$ and $\theta(0) = 0$. Functions fail and out satisfy:

Lemma 1. *Consider E_1 with $\mathcal{F}_1 \subseteq \alpha_+(E_1)$ and E_2 with $\mathcal{F}_2 \subseteq \alpha_+(E_2)$ where $\mathcal{F}_1 \cap \mathcal{F}_2 = \emptyset$. Any $f \subseteq \mathcal{F}_1 \cup \mathcal{F}_2$ can be factored uniquely into $f = f_1 \cup f_2$ where $f_1 = f \cap \mathcal{F}_1$ and $f_2 = f \cap \mathcal{F}_2$. Then:*

$$
\begin{aligned}
\mathsf{fail}_f(E_1 \mid E_2) &= \mathsf{fail}_{f_1}(E_1) \mid \mathsf{fail}_{f_2}(E_2)\\
\mathsf{fail}_f(E_1 \gg E_2) &= \mathsf{fail}_{f_1}(E_1) \gg \mathsf{fail}_{f_2}(E_2)\\
\mathsf{fail}_f(E_1 <! E_2) &= \mathsf{fail}_{f_1}(E_1) <! \mathsf{fail}_{f_2}(E_2)\\
\mathsf{out}(\mathsf{fail}_f(E_1 \mid E_2)) &= \mathsf{out}(\mathsf{fail}_{f_1}(E_1)) + \mathsf{out}(\mathsf{fail}_{f_2}(E_2))\\
\mathsf{out}(\mathsf{fail}_f(E_1 \gg E_2)) &= \mathsf{out}(\mathsf{fail}_{f_1}(E_1)) \cdot \mathsf{out}(\mathsf{fail}_{f_2}(E_2))\\
\mathsf{out}(\mathsf{fail}_f(E_1 <! E_2)) &= \mathsf{out}(\mathsf{fail}_{f_1}(E_1)) \cdot \theta(\mathsf{fail}_{f_2}(E_2))
\end{aligned}
$$

Example 2. Reconsider Example 1 in the risky environment $\mathcal{F} = \{CNN, EmailAlice\}$. If no failures arise $\mathsf{out}(Two\_Each) = 4$, $\mathsf{out}(One\_Each) = 2$. If $f = \{CNN\}$ then $\mathsf{out}(\mathsf{fail}_f(Two\_Each)) = 2$ and $\mathsf{out}(\mathsf{fail}_f(One\_Each)) = 1$. □

An evaluation of an orchestration E in the risky environment $\mathcal{F} \subseteq \alpha_+(E)$ is modelled using failure sets. $\delta = (f, \overline{f})$ where $f \subseteq \mathcal{F}$ denotes the set of failing services and $\overline{f} = \mathcal{F} \setminus f$ denotes the set of operational services. The set of all possible failure sets is the power set $\wp(\mathcal{F}) = \{f \mid f \subseteq \mathcal{F}\}$. A failure in $\mathcal{F} = \{s_1, \ldots s_\ell\}$ can be represented by the tuple $(\delta_1, \cdots, \delta_i, \ldots, \delta_\ell)$ where $\delta_i = 0$ if service s_i is in f and $\delta_i = 1$ otherwise. Sets containing exactly k failing services are $\wp_k(\mathcal{F}) = \{f \subseteq \mathcal{F} \mid \#f = k\}$.

Example 3. Consider an assessment of $E = (s_1 \mid s_2 \mid s_3) \gg (s_4 \mid s_5)$ in an environment in which all services can potentially fail: $\mathcal{F} = \{s_1, s_2, s_3, s_4, s_5\}$. If there is 1 failure then $\wp_1(\mathcal{F}) = \{\{s_1\}, \{s_2\}, \{s_3\}, \{s_4\}, \{s_5\}\}$. The failure set for the case where s_2 fails is $(\{s_2\}, \{s_1, s_3, s_4, s_5\})$ or $(1, 0, 1, 1, 1)$. □

Let E be an orchestration and $\mathcal{F} \subseteq \alpha_+(E)$. The *publications function* $\mathsf{pubs}(E, \mathcal{F}) : \wp(\mathcal{F}) \to \mathbb{N}$ when applied to any $f \in \wp(\mathcal{F})$, returns the number of publications produced by a call to E when the underlying services in f fail. Formally $\mathsf{pubs}(E, \mathcal{F})(f) = \mathsf{out}(\mathsf{fail}_f(E))$. Using notations from Lemma 1 it follows that:

$$
\begin{aligned}
\mathsf{pubs}(E_1 \mid E_2, \mathcal{F}_1 \cup \mathcal{F}_2)(f) &= \mathsf{pubs}(E_1, \mathcal{F}_1)(f_1) + \mathsf{pubs}(E_2, \mathcal{F}_2)(f_2)\\
\mathsf{pubs}(E_1 \gg E_2, \mathcal{F}_1 \cup \mathcal{F}_2)(f) &= \mathsf{pubs}(E_1, \mathcal{F}_1)(f_1) \cdot \mathsf{pubs}(E_2, \mathcal{F}_2)(f_2)\\
\mathsf{pubs}(E_1 <! E_2, \mathcal{F}_1 \cup \mathcal{F}_2)(f) &= \mathsf{pubs}(E_1, \mathcal{F}_1)(f_1) \cdot \theta(\mathsf{pubs}(E_2, \mathcal{F}_2)(f_2))
\end{aligned}
$$

Given E and $\mathcal{F} \subseteq \alpha_+(E)$ the failure set $\wp(\mathcal{P})$ can be taken as a sample space and $\mathsf{pubs}(E, \mathcal{F})$ can be treated as a random variable.

3 Uncertainty Profiles and $\mathcal{A}/\mathcal{D}$ Games

Suppose that the alphabet $\alpha_+(E)$ is partitioned, according to a user's *perception* of the services, into two disjoint sets, $\mathcal{A}$ (angelic services) and $\mathcal{D}$ (daemonic services) such that $\mathcal{A} \cup \mathcal{D} \subseteq \alpha_+(E)$. Services in $\alpha_+(E) \setminus \{\mathcal{A} \cup \mathcal{D}\}$ are reliable. Resilience is analysed by assuming that service failures in $\mathcal{A}$ *minimise damage to* E whereas service failures in $\mathcal{D}$ *maximise damage to the application*.

An uncertainty profile [3,4] defines $\mathcal{A}$ and $\mathcal{D}$ together with the number of service failures that can be expected to occur within both $\mathcal{A}$ and $\mathcal{D}$ ($f_{\mathcal{A}}$, and $f_{\mathcal{D}}$, respectively). Initially it may appear to be unusual that the angel player makes "moves" that may damage an application. However, the aim of reliability games is to provide a *mixed assessment* of the effects of service failures to an orchestration. Given an expected number of site failures the angel must choose a designated set of "broken" services in a way that minimizes damage to the application. For example, if service S is operational then the angel may choose service T to fail in the orchestration $R <! (S \mid T)$ since T is a redundant computation. In contrast the daemon has the opposite motivation – in the orchestration $P \gg (Q \mid R \mid S)$ the daemon may choose P to fail in order to crash the application (since $0 \gg E = 0$, see [8] Subsection 6.1). In this way angel daemon games provide a mixed assessment of orchestration reliability. The notion of uncertainty profile is formally defined as:

Definition 4 (uncertainty profile). $\mathcal{U} = \langle E, \mathcal{A}, \mathcal{D}, f_{\mathcal{A}}, f_{\mathcal{D}} \rangle$ *is an uncertainty profile for orchestration* E *where* $\mathcal{A} \cup \mathcal{D} \subseteq \alpha_+(E)$, $\mathcal{A} \cap \mathcal{D} = \emptyset$, $f_{\mathcal{A}} \leq \#\mathcal{A}$ *and* $f_{\mathcal{D}} \leq \#\mathcal{D}$.

Uncertainty profiles can be analysed using zero-sum games [11] as developed by John von Neumann and Oskar Morgenstern [9]. Here a class of zero-sum games called angel-daemon games [3] is used to provide a mixed analysis of uncertainty, lying between over-optimism and over-pessimism.

Definition 5 (angel-daemon game). *The profile* $\mathcal{U} = \langle E, \mathcal{A}, \mathcal{D}, f_{\mathcal{A}}, f_{\mathcal{D}} \rangle$ *has an associated zero-sum* angel-daemon game $\Gamma(\mathcal{U}) = \langle \{\mathfrak{a}, \mathfrak{d}\}, A_{\mathfrak{a}}, A_{\mathfrak{d}}, u_{\mathfrak{a}}, u_{\mathfrak{d}} \rangle$*: the players,* $\mathfrak{a}$ *and* $\mathfrak{d}$ *have the following sets of actions,*

- *The angel* $\mathfrak{a}$ *selects* $f_{\mathcal{A}}$ *distinct failing services from* $\mathcal{A}$*. Calls to remaining services in* $\mathcal{A} \setminus a$ *are successful. The actions are* $A_{\mathfrak{a}} = \wp_{f_{\mathcal{A}}}(\mathcal{A}) = \{a \subseteq \mathcal{A} \mid \#a = f_{\mathcal{A}}\}$.
- *The daemon* $\mathfrak{d}$ *selects* $f_{\mathcal{D}}$ *distinct failing services from* $\mathcal{D}$*. Calls to remaining services in* $\mathcal{D} \setminus d$ *are successful. Then* $A_{\mathfrak{d}} = \wp_{f_{\mathcal{D}}}(\mathcal{D}) = \{d \subseteq \mathcal{D} \mid \#d = f_{\mathcal{D}}\}$.

Sites which are not in either $\mathcal{A}$ *or* $\mathcal{D}$ *are assumed to be working. A strategy profile* $s = (a, d)$ *defines a set of failing sites* $a \cup d$*. The resilience of* E *under* s *is measured by the angel's utility* $u_{\mathfrak{a}}(s) = \mathsf{out}(\mathsf{fail}_{a \cup d}(E))$*. As the game is zero-sum:* $u_{\mathfrak{d}}(s) = -u_{\mathfrak{a}}(s)$.

Angel-daemon games are zero sum because $u_{\mathfrak{a}}(a, d) + u_{\mathfrak{d}}(a, d) = 0$. As usual (in zero-sum games) all Nash equilibria (pure or mixed) are assessed using player 1's utility [9] (i.e. $\mathfrak{a}$'s utility). The value of this utility $\nu(\Gamma)$ is called the *value of* Γ. A player's choice of action can be defined probabilistically. A mixed strategy for player $\mathfrak{a}$ is a probability distribution $\alpha : A_{\mathfrak{a}} \to [0, 1]$ and, similarly, a mixed strategy for $\mathfrak{d}$ is a probability distribution $\beta : A_{\mathfrak{d}} \to [0, 1]$. A mixed strategy profile is a tuple (α, β) and

$$u_{\mathfrak{a}}(\alpha, \beta) = \sum_{(a,d) \in A_{\mathfrak{a}} \times A_{\mathfrak{d}}} \alpha(a)\beta(d)u_{\mathfrak{a}}(a, d) = \mathbb{E}_{\mathsf{prod}(\alpha,\beta)}(\mathsf{pubs}(E, \mathcal{A} \cup \mathcal{D}))$$

Let $\Delta_{\mathfrak{a}}$ and $\Delta_{\mathfrak{d}}$ denote the set of mixed strategies for $\mathfrak{a}$ and $\mathfrak{d}$, respectively. It is well known [9] that there is always a mixed saddle point (α, β) satisfying

$$\nu(\Gamma) = u_{\mathfrak{a}}(\alpha, \beta) = \max_{\alpha' \in \Delta_{\mathfrak{a}}} \min_{\beta' \in \Delta_{\mathfrak{d}}} u_{\mathfrak{a}}(\alpha', \beta') = \min_{\beta' \in \Delta_{\mathfrak{d}}} \max_{\alpha' \in \Delta_{\mathfrak{a}}} u_{\mathfrak{a}}(\alpha', \beta')$$

The set of saddle points (pure or mixed) coincides with the set of Nash equilibria (pure or mixed). The following property is adapted from Proposition 116.2 in [11]. A mixed strategy profile (α, β) is a mixed Nash equilibrium iff:

- for any $a \in A_{\mathfrak{a}}$ such that $\alpha(a) > 0$ it holds $u_{\mathfrak{a}}(a, \beta) = u_{\mathfrak{a}}(\alpha, \beta)$,
- for any $d \in A_{\mathfrak{d}}$ such that $\beta(d) > 0$ it holds $u_{\mathfrak{a}}(\alpha, d) = u_{\mathfrak{a}}(\alpha, \beta)$,
- for any $a \in A_{\mathfrak{a}}$ such that $\alpha(a) = 0$ it holds $u_{\mathfrak{a}}(a, \beta) \leq u_{\mathfrak{a}}(\alpha, \beta)$,
- and, for any $d \in A_{\mathfrak{d}}$ such that $\beta(a) = 0$ it holds $u_{\mathfrak{a}}(\beta, d) \geq u_{\mathfrak{a}}(\alpha, \beta)$.

The *assessment* $\nu(\mathcal{U})$ of an uncertainty profile $\mathcal{U}$ is defined to be the value of its associated angel-daemon $\Gamma(\mathcal{U})$ (i.e. $\nu(\Gamma(\mathcal{U}))$).

Example 4. Consider the profile $\mathcal{U} = \langle E, \mathcal{A}, \mathcal{D}, f_{\mathcal{A}}, f_{\mathcal{D}} \rangle$ for the orchestration $E = (P \mid Q \mid R) \gg (S \mid T)$ where $\mathcal{A} = \{P, S\}$, $\mathcal{D} = \{Q, R, T\}$, $f_{\mathcal{A}} = 1$, $f_{\mathcal{D}} = 2$. $\mathcal{U}$ is associated with the following angel-daemon game:

		Player $\mathfrak{d}$	
	$\{Q,R\}$	$\{Q,T\}$	$\{R,T\}$
Player $\mathfrak{a}$ $\{P\}$	0	1	1
Player $\mathfrak{a}$ $\{S\}$	1	0	0

Nash equilibria satisfy $\alpha(\{P\}) = \alpha(\{S\}) = 1/2$, $\beta(\{Q,T\}) + \beta(\{R,T\}) = 1/2$ and $\beta(\{Q,R\}) = 1/2$. Let δ and μ be choosen so that $0 \leq \delta, \mu \leq 1$ and $\delta + \mu = 1$. Then $\beta(\{Q,T\}) = \delta/2$, $\beta(\{R,T\}) = \mu/2$ and $\nu(\mathcal{U}) = 1/2$. □

4 Probabilistic Profiles

Probability is widely used to analyse risk – see [6] and [2]. Here a probabilistic treatment of reliability is developed in several steps. In Subsection 4.1 we give the definition of *probabilistic profile* $\mathcal{P} = \langle E, \mathcal{F}, \gamma \rangle$ such that for any $f \subseteq \mathcal{F}$, $\gamma(f)$ is the probability that an execution of E involves only the services in f failing. Moreover we consider the constructions $\mathcal{P}_1 \mid \mathcal{P}_2$, $\mathcal{P}_1 \gg \mathcal{P}_2$ and $\mathcal{P}_1 <! \mathcal{P}_2$. Subsection 4.2 is devoted to a special class of probabilistic profiles called *site probabilistic profiles*. In $\mathcal{S} = \langle E, \mathcal{F}, \sigma \rangle$, $\sigma(s)$

give the probability of s failing for a site $s \in \mathcal{F}$. In Subsection 4.3 we classify orchestrations under progressive failures using Taleb's [12] ideas. Situations in which an extra site failure does not seriously domage the application are called *mediocristran*; dual situations are called *extremistan*. Subsection 4.4 develops conections between probabilistic and site probabilistic profiles. Subsection 4.5 links uncertainty profiles with probabilistic profiles.

4.1 Basic Definitions and Operations

A probabilistic treatment of reliability is formalized using the following assumptions. First, given an orchestration it is possible to determine the set of services, $\mathcal{F}$, that may potentially fail. Second, the probability of any set of failures $f \subseteq \mathcal{F}$ that can arise in practice can be measured.

Definition 6 (probabilistic profile, value and crash probability). *A* probabilistic profile *of an orchestration E is a tuple $\mathcal{P} = \langle E, \mathcal{F}, \gamma\rangle$ where $\mathcal{F} \subseteq \alpha_+(E)$ denotes the set of* potentially failing sites. *The probability $\gamma : \wp(\mathcal{F}) \to [0,1]$ is defined so that $\sum_{f\in\wp(\mathcal{F})} \gamma(f) = 1$ with $\gamma(f)$ being the probability that an execution of E involves only the services in f failing. The expected number of publications in $\mathcal{P}$ is given by $\mathbb{E}_\gamma(\mathsf{pubs}(E,\mathcal{F})) = \sum_{f\in\wp(\mathcal{F})} \mathsf{pubs}(E,\mathcal{F})(f)\gamma(f)$. The value of $\mathcal{P}$ is $\nu(\mathcal{P}) = \mathbb{E}_\gamma(\mathsf{pubs}(E,\mathcal{F}))$. The probability of a complete failure for $\mathcal{P}$, which is called a* crash probability, *is defined as $\mathsf{crash}(\mathcal{P}) = \sum_{\{f\subseteq\mathcal{F}\mid \mathsf{pubs}(E,\mathcal{F})(f)=0\}} \gamma(f)$.*

As $\wp(\mathcal{F})$ is finite $\mathbb{E}_\gamma(\mathsf{pubs}(E,\mathcal{F})) = \sum_{0\le k\le \#\mathcal{F}} \sum_{f\in\wp_k(\mathcal{F})} \mathsf{pubs}(E,\mathcal{F})\gamma(f)$.

Definition 7 (profile operations). *Given two sets of failures $\mathcal{F}_1$, $\mathcal{F}_2$ and two probabilities $\gamma_1 : \wp(\mathcal{F}_1) \to [0,1]$, $\gamma_2 : \wp(\mathcal{F}_2) \to [0,1]$, such that $\mathcal{F}_1 \cap \mathcal{F}_2 = \emptyset$, we define $\mathsf{prod}(\gamma_1,\gamma_2) : \wp(\mathcal{F}_1 \cup \mathcal{F}_2) \to [0,1]$ such that, for every $f \in \mathcal{F}_1 \cup \mathcal{F}_2$, $\mathsf{prod}(\gamma_1,\gamma_2)(f) = \gamma_1(f_1)\gamma_2(f_2)$ where $f_1 = f \cap \mathcal{F}_1$ and $f_2 = f \cap \mathcal{F}_2$. Consider $\mathcal{P}_1 = \langle E_1, \mathcal{F}_1, \gamma_1\rangle$ and $\mathcal{P}_1 = \langle E_2, \mathcal{F}_2, \gamma_2\rangle$ where $\mathcal{F}_1 \cap \mathcal{F}_2 = \emptyset$. Then*

$$\mathcal{P}_1 \mid \mathcal{P}_2 = \langle E_1 \mid E_2, \mathcal{F}_1 \cup \mathcal{F}_2, \mathsf{prod}(\gamma_1,\gamma_2)\rangle$$
$$\mathcal{P}_1 \gg \mathcal{P}_2 = \langle E_1 \gg E_2, \mathcal{F}_1 \cup \mathcal{F}_2, \mathsf{prod}(\gamma_1,\gamma_2)\rangle$$
$$\mathcal{P}_1 <! \mathcal{P}_2 = \langle E_1 <! E_2, \mathcal{F}_1 \cup \mathcal{F}_2, \mathsf{prod}(\gamma_1,\gamma_2)\rangle$$

Theorem 1. *Given $\mathcal{P}_1 = \langle E_1, \mathcal{F}_1, \gamma_1\rangle$ and $\mathcal{P}_1 = \langle E_2, \mathcal{F}_2, \gamma_2\rangle$ we have the following crash properties:*

$$\mathsf{crash}(\mathcal{P}_1 \gg \mathcal{P}_2) = \mathsf{crash}(\mathcal{P}_1 <! \mathcal{P}_2) = \mathsf{crash}(\mathcal{P}_1) + \mathsf{crash}(\mathcal{P}_2)$$
$$\mathsf{crash}(\mathcal{P}_1 \mid \mathcal{P}_2) = \mathsf{crash}(\mathcal{P}_1) \cdot \mathsf{crash}(\mathcal{P}_2)$$
$$\nu(\mathcal{P}_1 \mid \mathcal{P}_2) = \nu(\mathcal{P}_1) + \nu(\mathcal{P}_2)\ , \nu(\mathcal{P}_1 \gg \mathcal{P}_2) = \nu(\mathcal{P}_1) \cdot \nu(\mathcal{P}_2)$$
$$\nu(\mathcal{P}_1 <! \mathcal{P}_2) = \nu(\mathcal{P}_1) \cdot (1 - \mathsf{crash}(\mathcal{P}_2))$$

4.2 Site Probabilistic Profiles

It is likely to be problematic to find accurate estimates for $\gamma(f)$, for each $f \in \wp(\mathcal{F})$. Instead it may be more realistic to give estimates for the independent failure probability $\sigma(s)$ for each site $s \in \mathcal{F}$.

Definition 8 (site probabilistic profile). *A* site *probabilistic profile of an orchestration E is a tuple $\mathcal{S} = \langle E, \mathcal{F}, \sigma \rangle$ such that $\mathcal{F} \subseteq \alpha_+(E)$ and $\sigma : \mathcal{F} \to [0,1]$ gives, for each site s, the probability $\sigma(s)$ of s failing.*

From $\sigma : \mathcal{F} \to [0,1]$, the probability $\mathsf{prod}(\sigma) : \wp(\mathcal{F}) \to [0,1]$, is defined (as usual in the case of independence) as $\mathsf{prod}(\sigma)(f) = \prod_{s \in f} \sigma(s) \prod_{s \in \mathcal{F} \setminus f}(1 - \sigma(s))$. The probabilistic profile associated with a $\mathcal{S}$ is $\mathcal{P}(\mathcal{S}) = \langle E, \mathcal{F}, \mathsf{prod}(\sigma) \rangle$. $\nu(\mathcal{S})$ is used as shorthand for $\nu(\mathcal{P}(\mathcal{S}))$.

Given $\mathcal{S}_1 = \langle E_1, \mathcal{F}_1, \sigma_1 \rangle$ and $\mathcal{S}_2 = \langle E_2, \mathcal{F}_2, \sigma_2 \rangle$ such that $\mathcal{F}_1 \cap \mathcal{F}_2 = \emptyset$, the mapping $\mathsf{union}(\sigma_1, \sigma_2) : \mathcal{F}_1 \cup \mathcal{F}_2 \to [0,1]$ is defined as

$$\mathsf{union}(\sigma_1, \sigma_2)(s) = \begin{cases} \sigma_1(s) \text{ if } s \in \mathcal{F}_1 \\ \sigma_2(s) \text{ if } s \in \mathcal{F}_2 \end{cases}$$

and

$$\begin{aligned} \mathcal{S}_1 \mid \mathcal{S}_2 &= \langle E_1 \mid E_2, \mathcal{F}_1 \cup \mathcal{F}_2, \mathsf{union}(\gamma_1, \gamma_2) \rangle \\ \mathcal{S}_1 \gg \mathcal{S}_2 &= \langle E_1 \gg E_2, \mathcal{F}_1 \cup \mathcal{F}_2, \mathsf{union}(\gamma_1, \gamma_2) \rangle \\ \mathcal{S}_1 <!\, \mathcal{S}_2 &= \langle E_1 <!\, E_2, \mathcal{F}_1 \cup \mathcal{F}_2, \mathsf{union}(\gamma_1, \gamma_2) \rangle \end{aligned}$$

From the factorization $f = f_1 \cup f_2$, $f_1 = f \cap \mathcal{F}_1$ and $f_2 = f \cap \mathcal{F}_2$ in Lemma 7 we have $\mathsf{prod}(\mathsf{union}(\sigma_1, \sigma_2))(f) = \mathsf{prod}(\sigma_1)(f_1) \cdot \mathsf{prod}(\sigma_2)(f_2)$. From Theorem 1 we have

$$\begin{aligned} &\nu(\mathcal{S}_1 \mid \mathcal{S}_2) = \nu(\mathcal{S}_1) + \nu(\mathcal{S}_2),\ \nu(\mathcal{S}_1 \gg \mathcal{S}_2) = \nu(\mathcal{S}_1) \cdot \nu(\mathcal{S}_2) \\ &\nu(\mathcal{S}_1 <!\, \mathcal{S}_2) = \nu(\mathcal{S}_1) \cdot (1 - \mathsf{crash}(\mathcal{S}_2)) \end{aligned}$$

where $\mathsf{crash}(\mathcal{S})$ is shorthand for $\mathsf{crash}(\mathcal{P}(\mathcal{S}))$.

4.3 Mediocristan and Extremistan

Risks are sometimes classified into high, moderate and low risk categories -see [1,10]. The following table summarises recommendations given by the National Institute of Standards and Technology of the U.S. Department of Commerce [10] ,

Likelihood Level	Likelihood Definition
High	The threat-source is highly motivated and sufficiently capable; and controls to prevent vulnerability are ineffective.
Medium	The threat-source is motivated and sufficiently capable; controls that are in place may impede vulnerability.
Low	The threat-source lacks motivation or capability; alternatively, controls are in place to prevent, or significantly impede vulnerability.

Consider the analysis of the behaviour of an orchestration E in two extreme cases: sites in $\mathcal{H}$ fail with probability $1 - \epsilon$ (i.e. close to 1), sites in $\mathcal{L}$ fail with probability ϵ (i.e. close to 0). Orchestrations can be classified roughly in two types,

- *Mediocristan orchestrations.* Consider a highly resilient orchestration E which has a "gentle behaviour under failures" (an extra site failure only damages the system a little bit more). Following Taleb [12], these orchestrations are in a *mediocristan* where a single failure cannot seriously damage the application. Intuitively, an assessment would follow a Taylor expansion; informally, for small ϵ the assessement verifies $\nu(\langle E, \mathcal{H}, 1-\epsilon\rangle) \approx \mathsf{out}(\mathsf{fail}_{\mathcal{H}}(E))$ and $\nu(\langle E, \mathcal{L}, \epsilon\rangle) \approx \mathsf{out}(E)$.
- *Extremistan orchestrations.* Certain types of orchestration E are such that a single failure has a very destructive effect on the application. Even worse, such failures can occur with very small probability. In such cases $\mathsf{out}(E)$ is a poor approximation to $\nu(\langle E, \mathcal{L}, \epsilon\rangle)$. These orchestrations are in *extremistan* [12] and the failing site (or sites), which occur with small probability and seriously damage the application, are called a *black swan*.

Consider a partition of $\mathcal{F}$ into three sets $\mathcal{H}$, $\mathcal{M}$ and $\mathcal{L}$, where the elements of each set have a fixed probability:

Definition 9 (high, moderate and low probability). *Let $\epsilon > 0$ be an infinitesimal value. Given a mediocristan-extremist profile $\langle E, \mathcal{H}, \mathcal{M}, \mathcal{L}, \epsilon\rangle$ we define the associated site probabilistic profile $\mathcal{ME}(E, \mathcal{H}, \mathcal{M}, \mathcal{L}, \epsilon) = \langle E, \mathcal{F}, \sigma\rangle$ where $\mathcal{F} = \mathcal{H} \cup \mathcal{M} \cup \mathcal{L}$ and $\sigma(s) = 1-\epsilon$ if $s \in \mathcal{H}$, $\sigma(s) = 1/2$ if $s \in \mathcal{M}$ and $\sigma(s) = \epsilon$ if $s \in \mathcal{L}$.*

An orchestration E in a highly unreliable environment can be analysed by the profile $\langle E, \mathcal{H}, \emptyset, \emptyset, \epsilon\rangle$ where any failure $s \in \mathcal{H}$ occurs with high probability. It might be expected that the failure set $(\mathcal{H}, \emptyset)$ with highest probability dominates the behaviour, giving rise to an expansion such as $\nu(\mathcal{P}(\langle E, \mathcal{H}, \emptyset, \emptyset, \epsilon\rangle)) = \mathsf{out}(\mathsf{fail}_{\mathcal{H}}(E)) + \cdots$ In such expresion, ν is dominated by the behaviour where all the sites in $\mathcal{H}$ fail.

Example 5. Consider $Par(P_1, \ldots, P_n)$ where all the sites $\mathcal{H} = \{P_1, \ldots, P_n\}$ fail with high probability: $\mathcal{P} = \langle Par(P_1, \ldots P_n), \mathcal{H}, \emptyset, \emptyset, \epsilon\rangle$. Assuming that the highest probability term dominates then $\nu(\mathcal{P}) = \mathsf{out}(\mathsf{fail}_{\mathcal{H}}(Par(P_1, \ldots P_n)) + \cdots \approx 0$. More exactly $\nu(\mathcal{P}) = \sum_k \binom{n}{k}(1-\epsilon)^k \epsilon^{h-k}(h-k) = \epsilon n$. If $\epsilon = 1/2^n$, then 0 is a reasonable approximation to $\nu(\mathcal{P})$. □

The following example demonstrates that a low probability event can dominate behaviour.

Example 6. The orchestration $Blowup(P, n)$ is an example of a situation in which a single event with very low probability can dominate proceedings:

$$Blowup(P, n) = P \gg (P \mid P) \gg (P \mid P \mid P \mid P) \gg \cdots \gg \underbrace{(P \mid \cdots \mid P)}_{2^n \text{ times}}$$

For $n \geq 0$, $\mathsf{out}(Blowup(P, n)) = 2^0 2^1 \cdots 2^n = 2^{n(n+1)/2}$. Assume $\sigma(P) = 1-\epsilon$, where the probability of success ϵ is tiny. Consider $\mathcal{P} = \langle Blowup(P, n), \{P\}, \emptyset, \emptyset, \epsilon\rangle$. We might expect, for small ϵ, an assessment to be $\nu(\mathcal{P}) \approx 0$, as whp P will fail. This is not realistic, since $\nu(\mathcal{P}(\langle Blowup(P, n), \{P\}, \emptyset, \emptyset, \epsilon\rangle)) = \epsilon 2^{n(n+1)}$. For $\epsilon = (1/2)^{n^2}$ we have $\nu(\mathcal{P}) = 2^{n/2}$. Now consider

$$SecuredBlowup(Q_1, \ldots, Q_m, P, n) = Seq(Q_1, \ldots, Q_m) \gg Blowup(P, n)$$
$$\nu(\mathcal{P}(\langle SecuredBlowup(Q_1, \ldots, Q_m, P, n), \{Q_1, \ldots Q_m\}, \emptyset, \emptyset, \epsilon\rangle)) = \epsilon^{m+1} 2^{n(n+1)/2}$$

Note that n is independent of ϵ. Therefore we can have a situation in which a very unlikely event can dominate expectations.[2] □

An orchestration with medium reliability is $\langle E, \emptyset, \mathcal{M}, \emptyset, \epsilon\rangle$ where all sites in $\mathcal{M}$ have reliability $1/2$ and $\nu(\mathcal{P}(\langle E, \emptyset, \mathcal{M}, \emptyset, \epsilon\rangle)) = \left(\sum_{f\subseteq\mathcal{M}} \mathsf{pubs}(E, \mathcal{F})(f)\right)/2^{\#\mathcal{M}}$. A highly reliable profile is modalized as $\langle E, \emptyset, \emptyset, \mathcal{L}, \epsilon\rangle$ where all sites succeed with high probability. We might expect that $\nu(\mathcal{P}(\langle E, \emptyset, \emptyset, \mathcal{L}, \epsilon\rangle)) = \mathsf{out}(E) + \cdots$ but it is easy to find cases where this approximation is very poor.

Consider the sets $\mathcal{H} = \{H_1, \ldots, H_h\}$, $\mathcal{M} = \{M_1, \ldots, M_m\}$ and $L = \{L_1, \ldots, L_l\}$ which have failure probabilitites $1 - \epsilon$, $1/2$ and ϵ, respectively. Consider

$$Par(\mathcal{H}, \mathcal{M}, \mathcal{L}) = (H_1 \mid \cdots \mid H_h \mid M_1 \mid \cdots \mid M_m \mid L_1 \mid \cdots \mid L_l)$$
$$Seq(\mathcal{H}, \mathcal{M}, \mathcal{L}) = (H_1 \gg \cdots \gg H_h \gg M_1 \gg \cdots \gg M_m \gg L_1 \gg \cdots \gg L_l)$$

It holds $\nu(Par(\mathcal{H}, \mathcal{M}, \mathcal{L})) = l + m/2 + \epsilon(h-l)$, $\nu(Seq(\mathcal{H}, \mathcal{M}, \mathcal{L})) = \epsilon^h(1/2)^m(1-\epsilon)^l$.

4.4 From Probabilistic Profiles to Site Probabilistic Profiles

Now consider the problem of going in the opposite direction from probabilistic profiles to site probabilistic profiles. Suppose that we have $\gamma : \wp(\mathcal{F}) \to [0,1]$ and we want to estimate individual probabilities of failure. We use cumulative probabilities:

Definition 10 (fails probability). *Given a probabilistic profile $\mathcal{P} = \langle E, \mathcal{F}, \gamma\rangle$ event "s fails" corresponds to $\{f \in \wp(\mathcal{F}) \mid s \in f\}$. The probability of individual failure $\mathsf{fails}(\gamma) : \mathcal{F} \to [0,1]$ is $\mathsf{fails}(\gamma)(s) = \sum_{\{f\in\wp(\mathcal{F})\mid s\in f\}} \gamma(f)$. The site probabilistic profile associated with $\mathcal{P}$ is $\mathcal{S}(\mathcal{P}) = \langle E, \mathcal{F}, \mathsf{fails}(\gamma)\rangle$.*

Normally $\mathsf{fails}(\gamma) : \mathcal{F} \to [0,1]$ is not a lottery and so $\sum_{s\in\mathcal{F}} \mathsf{fails}(\gamma)(s) \neq 1$. Usually $\mathsf{fails}(\gamma)(s) \neq \gamma(\{s\})$ because s refers to different events on both sides: In $\gamma(\{s\})$ the event corresponds to the unique $(\{s\}, \mathcal{F} \setminus \{s\})$ representing "just site s fails". In $\mathsf{fails}(\gamma)(s)$ the site represents "s fails in any context" and corresponds to $\{(f, \overline{f}) \mid s \in f\}$. Due to independence $\mathsf{fails}(\mathsf{prod}(\mathsf{fails}(\gamma)))(s) = \mathsf{fails}(s)$.

Example 7. Reconsider Example 4 with $\mathcal{F} = \{Q, R, T\}$ and $s = Q$. Then the set $\{(f, \overline{f}) \mid s \in f\}$ corresponds to

$$\{(f, \overline{f}) \mid Q \in f\} = \{(\{Q\}, \{R, T\}), (\{Q, R\}, \{T\}), (\{Q, T\}, \{R\}), (\{Q, R, T\}, \emptyset)$$

Consider the distribution $\beta : \wp(\mathcal{F}) \to [0,1]$ given by $\beta(\{Q, R\}) = 1/2$, $\beta(\{Q, T\}) = \delta/2$ and $\beta(\{R, T\}) = \mu/2$ with $0 \leq \delta, \mu \leq 1$ with $\delta + \mu = 1$. From Definition 10 we have $\mathsf{fails}(\beta)(Q) = (1+\delta)/2$, $\mathsf{fails}(\beta)(R) = (1+\mu)/2$ and $\mathsf{fails}(\beta)(T) = 1/2$. Note that $\beta(\{Q\}) \neq \mathsf{fails}(\beta)(Q)$ and similarly for R and T. The probability $\mathsf{fails}(\beta)(Q)$ tries to model the likelihood of Q failing when called during a execution with failures. This differs from $\mathsf{prod}(\{\mathsf{fails}(\gamma))(\{Q\}) = (1+\delta)(1-\mu)/8$. □

[2] Rephrasing N. Tabeb [12], chapter 3, the behaviour of $Blowup(P, n)$ corresponds to "the strange country of extremistan": uncertainly profiles such as $\langle SecuredBlowup(Q_1, \ldots, Q_m, P, n), \{Q_1, \ldots Q_m\}, \emptyset, \emptyset, \epsilon\rangle$ give rise to black swans.

Given E and $\mathcal{F}$ we can bound the number of failures to give bounded probabilistic profiles. Given E a *k-bounded probabilistic profile* is a tuple $\mathcal{B} = \langle E, \mathcal{F}, \gamma, k\rangle$ such that $\gamma : \wp_k(\mathcal{F}) \to [0,1]$ is the probability of (exactly) k sites failing in $\mathcal{F}$. The assessement is $\nu(\mathcal{B}) = \mathbb{E}_\gamma(\mathsf{pubs}(E,\mathcal{F}))$. What happens when we have several types of unreliability? In this case we have bounded probabilistic profiles with several unreliable sets. Let us consider the case of Given $\mathcal{B} = \langle E, \mathcal{F}, \mathcal{F}', \gamma, \gamma', k, k'\rangle$ with $\mathcal{F} \cap \mathcal{F}' = \emptyset$ such that $\gamma : \wp_k(\mathcal{F}) \to [0,1]$ and $\gamma' : \wp_{k'}(\mathcal{F}') \to [0,1]$, the assessement is given by $\nu(\mathcal{B}) = \mathbb{E}_{\mathsf{prod}(\gamma,\gamma')}(\mathsf{pubs}(E, \mathcal{F}\cup\mathcal{F}'))$.

Example 8. Reconsider Example 7. Consider the bounded probabilistic profile $\mathcal{B} = \langle E, \mathcal{F}, \beta, 2\rangle$ with $E = (P \mid Q \mid R) \gg (S \mid T)$, $\mathcal{F} = \{Q, R, T\}$ and $\beta : \wp_2(\mathcal{F}) \to [0,1]$ such that $\beta(\{Q,R\}) = 1/2$, $\beta(\{Q,T\}) = \delta/2$ and $\beta(\{R,T\}) = \mu/2$ with $0 \le \delta, \mu \le 1$ and $\delta + \mu = 1$. We have $\nu(\mathcal{B}) = 2$. □

4.5 From Uncertainty Profiles to Probabilistic Profiles

Uncertainty profiles can be used to impose restrictions on corresponding probabilistic profiles.

Lemma 2. *Given $\mathcal{U} = \langle E, \mathcal{A}, \mathcal{D}, f_\mathcal{A}, f_\mathcal{D}\rangle$, let (α,β) be Nash equilibrium in $\Gamma(\mathcal{U})$ the probabilistic profile is $\mathcal{B}(\mathcal{U},(\alpha,\beta)) = \langle E, \mathcal{A}, \mathcal{D}, \alpha, \beta, f_\mathcal{A}, f_\mathcal{D}\rangle$ verifies $\nu(\mathcal{B}(\mathcal{U},(\alpha,\beta)) = \nu(\mathcal{U})$.*

Example 9. Using (α,β) from Ex. 4 and $\mathcal{B} = \langle E, \mathcal{A}, \mathcal{D}, \alpha, \beta, 1, 2\rangle$, $\nu(\mathcal{B}) = \nu(\mathcal{U})$. □

Definition 11 (site probabilistic profile associated to an uncertainty profile). *Given an uncertainty profile $\mathcal{U} = \langle E, \mathcal{A}, \mathcal{D}, f_\mathcal{A}, f_\mathcal{D}\rangle$, let (α,β) be mixed strategy profile in $\Gamma(\mathcal{U})$. We define the site probabilistic profile $\mathcal{S}(\mathcal{U},(\alpha,\beta)) = \langle E, \mathcal{A}\cup\mathcal{D}, \mathsf{fails}(\alpha,\beta)\rangle$ with $\mathsf{fails}(\alpha,\beta)(s) = \mathsf{fails}(\alpha)(s)$ if $s \in \mathcal{A}$ and $\mathsf{fails}(\alpha,\beta)(s) = \mathsf{fails}(\beta)(s)$ if $s \in \mathcal{D}$.*

Lemma 3. *Given $\mathcal{U} = \langle E, \mathcal{A}, \mathcal{D}, f_\mathcal{A}, f_\mathcal{D}\rangle$, the probabilities in $\mathcal{S}(\mathcal{U},(\alpha,\beta))$ verifies*

$$\sum_{s\in\mathcal{A}} \mathsf{fails}(\alpha,\beta)(s) = f_\mathcal{A},\ \sum_{s\in\mathcal{D}} \mathsf{fails}(\alpha,\beta)(s) = f_\mathcal{D}$$

Example 10. Consider profile $\mathcal{U}$ from Example 4. Let (α,β) be any mixed strategy corresponding to a Nash equilibrium and consider $\mathcal{R}(\mathcal{U},(\alpha,\beta))$. According to Example 7, $\mathsf{fails}(\alpha,\beta)(s) = \sigma(s)$ for $s \in \{P,Q,R,S,T\}$ where

$$\sigma(P) = \sigma(S) = \sigma(T) = 1/2,\ \sigma(Q) = (1+\delta)/2,\ \sigma(R) = (1+\mu)/2$$

and δ and μ can be though as perturbations, then

$$\begin{aligned}\mathbb{E}_{\mathsf{prod}(\sigma)}(\mathsf{pubs}(E,\mathcal{F})) &= 20\frac{1}{2^5}(1-\delta)(1-\mu) + 12\frac{1}{2^5}(1+\delta)(1-\mu)\\ &+12\frac{1}{2^5}(1-\delta)(1+\mu) + 4\frac{1}{2^5}(1+\delta)(1+\mu)\end{aligned}$$

Consider some special cases. If we assume $\delta = \mu = 0$ the expectation is $3/2$. With the constraint $\delta + \mu = 1$ then we check that the expectation is 1. We check $\sigma(\alpha,\beta)(Q) + \sigma(\alpha,\beta)(R) + \sigma(\alpha,\beta)(T) = 2$ according to Lemma 3. □

5 One Site $\mathcal{A}/\mathcal{D}$ Bayesian Games

Consider the uncertainty profile $\mathcal{U} = \langle E, \mathcal{A}, \mathcal{D}, f_\mathcal{A}, f_\mathcal{D}\rangle$. Assume that $\mathfrak{a}$ has extra information (or belief) about the behaviour of $\mathfrak{d}$ with respect to a particular site $s \in \mathcal{D}$. For example, $\mathfrak{a}$ might believe that $\mathfrak{d}$ will choose site s with probability $\sigma(s)$. This complementary information can be combined with uncertainty profiles to give a bayesian approach.

5.1 Angelic Uncertainty about Daemonic Behaviour

The uncertaintity of $\mathfrak{a}$ with respect to $\mathfrak{d}$'s behaviour can be formalized using two different types of uncertainty profile "for $\mathfrak{d}$".

- Suppose that $\mathfrak{d}$ is certain to choose $s \in \mathcal{D}$. A new uncertainty profile which captures this situation is $\langle \mathsf{fail}_{\{s\}}(E), \mathcal{A}, \mathcal{D} \setminus \{s\}, f_\mathcal{A}, f_\mathcal{D} - 1\rangle$.
- Suppose that $\mathfrak{d}$ does not choose s. A new uncertainty profile which captures this situation is $\langle E, \mathcal{A}, \mathcal{D} \setminus \{s\}, f_\mathcal{A}, f_\mathcal{D}\rangle$.

Definition 12 (daemonic types). *Profile $\mathcal{U} = \langle E, \mathcal{A}, \mathcal{D}, f_\mathcal{A}, f_\mathcal{D}\rangle$ with $f_\mathcal{D} > 1$ has the following uncertainty profiles with respect to $s \in \mathcal{D}$ (so called types for $\mathfrak{d}$):*

$$\textit{noFail}(\mathcal{U}, s) = \langle E, \mathcal{A}, \mathcal{D} \setminus \{s\}, f_\mathcal{A}, f_\mathcal{D}\rangle$$
$$\textit{Fail}(\mathcal{U}, s) = \langle \textit{fail}_{\{s\}}(E), \mathcal{A}, \mathcal{D} \setminus \{s\}, f_\mathcal{A}, f_\mathcal{D} - 1\rangle$$

Consider the relationship between the strategies $A'_\mathfrak{d}$ in $\Gamma(\mathsf{Fail}(\mathcal{U}, s))$ and $A_\mathfrak{d}$ in $\Gamma(\mathcal{U})$. Any $d' \in A'_\mathfrak{d}$ must have the form $d' = \{s_1, \dots, s_{f_\mathcal{D}-1}\}$ where each $s_i \in d'$, $1 \le i \le f_\mathcal{D} - 1$, satisfies $s_i \in \mathcal{D} \setminus \{s\}$. A profile $d' \in A'_\mathfrak{d}$ can be transformed into a profile in $A_\mathfrak{d}$ by adding s, $d = d' \cup \{s\}$, since $\mathsf{fail}_{d'}(\mathsf{fail}_{\{s\}}(E)) = \mathsf{fail}_{d' \cup \{s\}}$. Then $A'_\mathfrak{d} \subseteq A_\mathfrak{d}$.

Example 11. The orchestration $E = (P \mid Q \mid R) \gg (S \mid T)$ is used to provide an example of angelic uncertainty about the daemonic behaviour. Consider the profile $\mathcal{U} = \langle E, \mathcal{A}, \mathcal{D}, f_\mathcal{A}, f_\mathcal{D}\rangle$ where $\mathcal{A} = \{P, S\}$, $\mathcal{D} = \{Q, R, T\}$, $f_\mathcal{A} = 1$, $f_\mathcal{D} = 2$ (see Example 4). $\mathfrak{a}$ view of $\mathfrak{d}$'s behaviour with respect to site T are given by the following uncertainty types:

$$\mathsf{noFail}(\mathcal{U}, T) = \langle E, \{P, S\}, \{Q, R\}, f_\mathcal{A}, f_\mathcal{D}\rangle$$
$$\mathsf{Fail}(\mathcal{U}, T)) = \langle \mathsf{fail}_{\{T\}}(E), \{P, S\}, \{Q, R\}, f_\mathcal{A}, f_\mathcal{D} - 1\rangle$$

Following the previous remark about strategy profiles, we represent the game $\Gamma(\mathsf{Fail}(\mathcal{U}, T)))$ by adding the failing site T. The games associated with the different types are

$\mathfrak{a}$ \ $\mathfrak{d}$	$\{Q,R\}$
$\{P\}$	0
$\{S\}$	1

$\Gamma(\mathsf{noFail}(\mathcal{U}, T))$

$\mathfrak{a}$ \ $\mathfrak{d}$	$\{Q,T\}$	$\{R,T\}$
$\{P\}$	1	1
$\{S\}$	0	0

$\Gamma(\mathsf{Fail}(\mathcal{U}, T))$

$\mathfrak{a}$ \ $\mathfrak{d}$	$\{Q,R\}$	$\{Q,T\}$	$\{R,T\}$
$\{P\}$	0	1	1
$\{S\}$	1	0	0

$\Gamma(\mathcal{U})$

These games are compared with with $\Gamma(\mathcal{U})$ given in Example 4. □

Definition 13 (Bayesian profile). *Consider* $\mathcal{U} = \langle E, \mathcal{A}, \mathcal{D}, f_{\mathcal{A}}, f_{\mathcal{D}} \rangle$ *be an uncertainty profile. If* $\mathfrak{a}$ *believes that* $\mathfrak{d}$ *will choose site* $s \in \mathcal{D}$ *with probability* $\sigma(s)$ *then the scenario is described by the bayesian profile* $\mathsf{Bayesian}(\mathcal{U}, s, \sigma) = \sigma(s) \cdot \mathsf{Fail}(\mathcal{U}, s) + (1-\sigma(s)) \cdot \mathsf{noFail}(\mathcal{U}, s)$*. The bayesian game associated to the bayesian profile is*

$$\Gamma(\mathsf{Bayesian}(\mathcal{U}, s, \sigma)) = \sigma(s) \cdot \Gamma(\mathsf{Fail}(\mathcal{U}, s)) + (1 - \sigma(s)) \cdot \Gamma(\mathsf{noFail}(\mathcal{U}, s))$$

Consider the strategy profiles for $\mathsf{Bayesian}(\mathcal{U}, s, \sigma)$. The angel $\mathfrak{a}$ is uncertain about the type of $\mathfrak{d}$. Thus, a profiles has the form $(a, (d_1, d_2))$ where the angel chooses an action and the daemon makes a choice for each type. From the angelic point of view $\mathfrak{d}$ chooses d_1 with probability $\sigma(s)$ and q_2 with probability $1 - \sigma(s)$. The uncertainty of $\mathfrak{a}$ about $\mathfrak{d}$'s behaviour is represented by the lottery $\sigma(s) \cdot d_1 + (1 - \sigma(s)) \cdot d_2$ with

$$u_{\mathfrak{a}}(a, (d_1, d_2)) = \sigma(s) u_{\mathfrak{a}}(a, d_1) + (1 - \sigma(s)) u_{\mathfrak{a}}(a, d_2)$$

In a pure Bayesian Nash equilibrium [5,11,7] $(a, (d_1, d_2))$

- The angel $\mathfrak{a}$ chooses a best response to $\sigma(s) \cdot d_1 + (1 - \sigma(s)) \cdot d_2$.
- From daemonic point of view there is no uncertainty: both d_1 and d_2 have to be best responses to $\mathfrak{a}$.

The same definition also applies to mixed Nash equilibria, say $(\alpha, (\beta_1, \beta_2))$.

Example 12. Reconsider Example 4. Assume that $\mathfrak{a}$ considers *dae*'s behaviour with respect to site T. Suppose that $\mathfrak{a}$ believes that site T will fail with probability $\sigma(T) = p$ and T will succeed with probability $1 - p$. This situation is modeled by the bayesian profile:

$$\mathsf{Bayesian}(U, T, p) = p \cdot \mathsf{Fail}(\mathcal{U}, T) + (1 - p) \cdot \mathsf{noFail}(\mathcal{U}, T)$$

In $\Gamma(\mathsf{Bayesian}(U, T, p))$ consider $(a, (d_1, d_2)) = (\{P\}, (\{Q, T\}, \{Q, R\}))$. In such a profile $\mathfrak{a}$ choses P as a failing site but the failures choosen by $\mathfrak{d}$ depends on the type. When T fails $\mathfrak{d}$ has freedom to choose between Q or R. In the current strategy $\mathfrak{d}$ chooses Q – we represent this situation by the pair $\{Q, T\}$. When T works $\mathfrak{d}$ is forced to choose the pair $\{Q, R\}$. Therefore $\mathfrak{d}$ behaves according to the lottery $p\{Q, T\} + (1-p)\{Q, T\}$ and the utility for $\mathfrak{a}$ is

$$u_{\mathfrak{a}}(\{P\}, (\{Q, T\}, \{Q, R\})) = p u_{\mathfrak{a}}(\{P\}, \{Q, T\}) + (1 - p) u_{\mathfrak{a}}((\{P\}, \{Q, R\}) = p$$

By similar means we have:

$$u_{\mathfrak{a}}(\{P\}, (\{Q, T\}, \{Q, R\})) = u_{\mathfrak{a}}(\{P\}, (\{R, T\}, \{Q, R\})) = p_{\mathcal{F}}$$
$$u_{\mathfrak{a}}(\{S\}, (\{Q, T\}, \{Q, R\})) = u_{\mathfrak{a}}(\{S\}, (\{R, T\}, \{Q, R\})) = 1 - p_{\mathcal{F}}$$

The best response for $\mathfrak{a}$ denoted $B_{\mathfrak{a}}(\{Q, T\}, \{Q, R\}) = B_{\mathfrak{a}}(\{R, T\}, \{Q, R\})$ is $\{S\}$ if $p < 1/2$, $\{\{P\}, \{S\}\}$ if $p = 1/2$ and $\{P\}$ if $p > 1/2$. Therefore, when $p < 1/2$ we have that both $(\{S\}, (\{Q, T\}, \{Q, R\}))$ and $(\{S\}, (\{R, T\}, \{Q, R\}))$ are bayesian pure Nash equilibria. In this case the orchestration is assessed by the angelic utility $u_{\mathfrak{a}}(\{S\}, (\{Q, T\}, \{Q, R\})) = 1 - p$. When $p > 1/2$ the pure bayesian Nash equilibria are $(\{P\}, (\{Q, T\}, \{Q, R\}))$, $(\{P\}, (\{R, T\}, \{Q, R\}))$ and in this case $u_{\mathfrak{a}} = p$. When $p = 1/2$ there are 4 bayesian pure Nash equilibria and $u_a = 1/2$. □

Note that in a bayesian Nash equilibrium $(\alpha, (\beta_1, \beta_2))$ we do not ask (α, β_1) and (α, β_2) to be Nash equilibria in $\Gamma(\mathsf{Fail}(\mathcal{U}, s))$ and $\Gamma(\mathsf{noFail}(\mathcal{U}, s))$.

Example 13. Take Example 12 with $p < 1/2$, the profile $(\{S\}, (\{Q,T\}, \{Q,R\}))$ is a bayesian Nash equilibrium. Neither $(\{S\}, \{Q,T\})$ is a Nash in the game $\Gamma(\mathsf{Fail}(\mathcal{U}, s))$ nor $(\{S\}, \{Q,R\})$ is a Nash equilibrium in $\Gamma(\mathsf{noFail}(\mathcal{U}, s \mid s \in \mathcal{D}))$. □

5.2 From Uncertainty Profiles to Bayesian Games

From Definition 10 we have that $\mathsf{fails}(\gamma)(s) = \sum_{\{f \in \wp(\mathcal{F}) \mid s \in f\}} \gamma(f)$. Given a pair (β, s), $s \in \mathcal{D}$ we adapt β to deal with the angelic uncertainty inherent in bayesian games.

Definition 14. *Let $\beta : A_\mathfrak{d} \to [0,1]$ be a strategy for $\mathfrak{d}$ in $\Gamma(\mathcal{U})$ such that $\mathcal{U} = \langle E, \mathcal{A}, \mathcal{D}, f_\mathcal{A}, f_\mathcal{D}\rangle$. Given $s \in \mathcal{D}$ such that $\mathsf{fails}(\beta)(s) \neq 0$, consider daemonic strategies corresponding to each type of bayesian game. For $\Gamma(\mathsf{Fail}(\mathcal{U}, s))$ define the strategy $\mathsf{failSite}(\beta, s) : \{d \in A_\mathfrak{d} \mid s \in d\} \to [0,1]$ as*

$$\mathsf{failSite}(\beta, s)(d) = \beta(d) / \sum_{\{d' \in A_\mathfrak{d} \mid s \in d\}} \beta(d') = \beta(d) / \mathsf{fails}(\beta)(s)$$

For $\Gamma(\mathsf{noFail}(\mathcal{U}, s))$ define $\mathsf{nofailSite}(\beta, s) : \{d \in A_\mathfrak{d} \mid s \notin d\} \to [0,1]$ as

$$\mathsf{nofailSite}(\beta, s)(d) = \beta(d) / \sum_{\{d' \in A_\mathfrak{d} \mid s \notin d\}} \beta(d') = \beta(d) / (1 - \mathsf{fails}(\beta))(s)$$

Note $\sum_{\{d \in A_\mathfrak{d} \mid s \in d\}} \mathsf{failSite}(\beta, s)(d) = 1$ and $\sum_{\{d \in A_\mathfrak{d} \mid s \notin d\}} \mathsf{nofailSite}(\beta, s)(d) = 1$.

Example 14. Consider Example 4 with the distribution $\beta(\{Q,R\}) = 1/2$, $\beta(\{Q,T\}) = \delta/2$, $\beta(\{R,T\}) = \mu/2$ and focus on site T. From Example 10, $\mathsf{fails}(T) = 1/2$ and therefore we have $\mathsf{nofailSite}(\beta, T)(\{Q,R\}) = 1$, $\mathsf{failSite}(\beta, T)(\{Q,T\}) = \delta$ and $\mathsf{failSite}(\beta, T)(\{R,T\}) = \mu$. □

Theorem 2. *Given $\mathcal{U} = \langle E, \mathcal{A}, \mathcal{D}, f_\mathcal{A}, f_\mathcal{D}\rangle$, a mixed strategy profile (α, β) for $\Gamma(\mathcal{U})$ and $s \in \mathcal{D}$ such that $\mathsf{fails}(\beta)(s) \neq 0$, in the bayesian game $\Gamma(\mathsf{Bayesian}(\mathcal{U}, s, \mathsf{fails}(\beta)))$ the angelic utility verifies $u_\mathfrak{a}(\alpha, (\mathsf{failSite}(\beta, s), \mathsf{nofailSite}(\beta, s))) = u_\mathfrak{a}(\alpha, \beta)$. When (α, β) is a Nash equilibrium $(\alpha, (\mathsf{failSite}(\beta, s), \mathsf{nofailSite}(\beta, s)))$ is a bayesian Nash equilibrium.*

6 Conclusions

Typically providers and application developers utilise a number of underlying resources (both hardware and software) to implement a service. Providers buy resources according to their reliability, their performance and their cost. At present services are selected using a number of heuristics about their behaviour. The approach presented in this paper offers alternative means for service providers to formalise the behaviour of web orchestrations.

In this paper it is shown how the reliability of orchestrations of services can be analysed by means of both uncertainty and probabilistic profiles. An uncertainty profile models a personal (or team) *perception* of possible service failures within a system and measures the consequences to an application when a number of service failures occur. An uncertainty profile classifies services according to a users perception of service behaviour together with placing bounds on the number of expected service failures. In practice the reliability of an application could be analysed using a number of different profiles in which the number of failures is varied from one to severe breakdown. Classification of services as angelic or daemonic is entirely based on a users perception of these services; it is conceivable that one user's perception of a service may differ from another's, based on different patterns of usage (e.g. time of day that services are called).

In a probabilistic profile, probabilities need to be given a priori. However, it is debatable if it is possible to adequately characterise, using probability, the performance of a service which includes multiple (and sometimes unpredictable) spikes and dips in demand (think of the *ludic fallacy* of N. Taleb). It may be the case that Bayesian games might provide links between the approaches – this remains an open reseach field.

Acknowledgement. We thank the referees for pointing out an error in a preliminary draft of the paper and for several suggestios which help us to improve the paper.

References

1. Carpenter, M.: How to Better Understand and Manage Risk, The Risk-Wise Investor. John Wiley & Sons (2009)
2. Clint, M., Gabarro, J., Harmer, T., Kilpatrick, P., Perrott, R., Stewart, S.: Assessing the Reliability and Cost of Web and Grid Orchestrations. In: Availability, Reliability and Security, ARES, pp. 428–433 (2008)
3. Gabarro, J., García, A., Serna, M., Stewart, A., Kilpatrick, P.: Analysing Orchestrations with Risk Profiles and Angel-Daemon Games. In: Grid Computing Achievements and Propects, pp. 121–132. Springer, Heidelberg (2008)
4. Gabarro, J., Serna, M., Stewart, A.: Web Services and Incerta Spiriti: A Game Theoretic Approach to Uncertainty. In: Liu, W. (ed.) ECSQARU 2011. LNCS, vol. 6717, pp. 651–662. Springer, Heidelberg (2011)
5. Gibbons, R.: A primer on Game Theory. Harvester-Wheatsheaf (1992)
6. Kokash, N., D'Andrea, V.: Evaluating Quality of Web Services: A Risk-Driven Approach. In: Abramowicz, W. (ed.) BIS 2007. LNCS, vol. 4439, pp. 180–194. Springer, Heidelberg (2007)
7. Mas-Colell, A., Whinston, M., Green, J.: Microeconomic Theory. Oxford University Press (1995)
8. Misra, J., Cook, W.: Computation Orchestration: A basis for wide-area computing. Software and Systems Modeling 6(1), 83–110 (2007)
9. von Neumann, J., Morgenstern, O.: Theory of Games and Economic behaviour, Princeton (1944)
10. NIST, Risk Management Guide for Information Technology Systems (July 2002), `http://csrc.nist.gov/publications/nistpubs/800-30/sp800-30.pdf`
11. Osborne, J.: An Introduction to Game Theory, Oxford (2004)
12. Taleb, N.: The Black Swan, 2nd edn. Penguin Books (2010)
13. W3C, Web Services Glossary, `http://www.w3.org/TR/ws-gloss/`

On Correlation Sets and Correlation Exceptions in ActiveBPEL*

Hernán Melgratti[1,2] and Christian Roldán[1]

[1] Departamento de Computación, FCEyN, Universidad de Buenos Aires
[2] CONICET

Abstract. Correlation sets are a programming primitive that allows instance identification in orchestration languages. A correlation set is a set of properties (i.e., values carried on by messages) that are used to associate each received message with a process instance: every time a service receives a message, it explores its content and determines a service instance that should handle the received message. Based on a concrete implementation, this paper proposes a formal model for correlation sets accounting for correlation exceptions. We also investigate different type systems aimed at ensuring that orchestrators are free from some kind of correlation exceptions.

1 Introduction

Service instances are a key concept when dealing with service composition. Typically, a service may have several instances that concurrently interact with different partners. Each service provides a template definition used to create process instances (all instances interact by using the same operations). Instances are created when the service receives a message that matches one of the start activities of its definition. For instance, a service that handles purchase orders creates a new instance any time it receives a new purchase order. All subsequent messages directed to the newly created instance should precisely identify the target instance. For example, when the client sends the payment details, the corresponding message should arrive to the correct instance (i.e., the one created when the client placed the purchase order). Orchestration languages (like the standard BPEL [4]) provide different alternatives to facilitate instance identification: they may rely on external mechanisms like dynamic endpoint references (as defined by WS-ADDRESSING [3]) or may use built-in primitives, like correlation sets. The main idea behind correlations sets is that messages carry on the identification of the instance they are targeted for, i.e., any service defines a set of properties that it will use to identify instances. Then, any instance is associated to a particular assignment of values to those selected properties. Consequently, any time a service receives a message, it compares the values of the received message against the values associated to any of its instances. The incoming message is routed to the matching instance.

Few approaches appeared in the literature have proposed a formal account for correlation sets, namely core correlation calculus [13], SOCK [6], COWS [9], and BLITE [10].

* Research supported by ANPCyT Project BID-PICT-2008-00319, and UBACyT 20020090300122.

R. Bruni and V. Sassone (Eds.): TGC 2011, LNCS 7173, pp. 212–226, 2012.

Each of these approaches proposes process calculi enriched with correlation primitives. Nevertheless, none of them includes a definition for correlation exceptions as defined in BPEL. In this paper, we aim at studying the relationship between correlation sets and correlation exceptions. We start by proposing a process calculus with a correlation mechanism, called Corr. Although Corr shares similarities with both SOCK, COWS, and BLITE, it is very different in scope. Basically, Corr is not aimed at providing a formal account for a complete orchestration language, consequently, several features that are usually present in composition languages, like scopes, compensations, fault and termination handlers, state, two-way operations, are not included in the calculus. For the sake of simplicity, we have preferred to focus on a minimal language exhibiting correlations and correlation exceptions and to leave orthogonal features outside of the model.

It has been shown in [10] that different implementations of BPEL exhibit discrepancies on the implementation of different primitives. In this paper, we follow the interpretation made by ActiveBPEL for setting the semantics of the correlation mechanism. The choices made during the design of Corr have been based on the runs of toy examples of BPEL orchestrators (such examples can be found at `http://www.di.unipi.it/~melgratt/activebpel`). Then, we use Corr to reason about exceptions originated by the correlation mechanism. We also propose a type system that singles out services that are free from different kind of correlation exceptions. The main result of this paper shows that well-typed services are free from correlation exceptions.

2 Correlation Language

We assume the countable sets of operation names $\mathcal{O}$ ranged over by $o, o_1, \ldots$; service names $\mathcal{S}$ ranged over by $s, s', \ldots$; data variables $\mathcal{V}$ range over by $x, y, \ldots$, data constants $\mathcal{A}$ ranged over by $a, a', \ldots$. We write v for either a data variable or constant, i.e., $v \in \mathcal{A} \cup \mathcal{V}$.

A correlation set C is a finite set of data variables, i.e., $C \subset \mathcal{V}$, and a correlation instance is a partial function $c : \mathcal{V} \to \mathcal{A} \cup \{\perp\}$. For any correlation set C, we denote with $C_\perp$ the uninitialized correlation instance, i.e., $dom(C_\perp) = C$ and $C_\perp(x) = \perp$ for all $x \in C$. We will say that two correlation instances c_1 and c_2 do not *collide* if and only if $\forall x \in dom(c_1) \cap dom(c_2).(c_1(x) \neq \perp \wedge c_2(x) \neq \perp \Rightarrow c_1(x) \neq c_2(x))$. We will explicitly write correlation instances as sets of pairs, for instance $c = \{x \mapsto \perp, y \mapsto b\}$. We will also use correlation instances as substitutions. When a correlation instance is applied to a term, we only substitute the variables that are mapped to values different from $\perp$. For instance, when $c = \{x \mapsto \perp, y \mapsto b\}$, $(\overline{o}\langle x,y\rangle;P)c = (\overline{o}\langle x,y\rangle;P)[b/y] = \overline{o}\langle x,b\rangle;P[b/y]$. Let c_1 and c_2 be correlation instances, we define the update operator $\_[\_]$ such that $dom(c_1[c_2]) = dom(c_1)$ and

$$c_1[c_2](x) = \begin{cases} c_1(x) & \text{if } x \notin dom(c_2) \vee (x \in dom(c_2) \wedge (c_1(x) = c_2(x) \vee c_2(x) = \perp)) \\ c_2(x) & \text{if } c_1(x) = \perp \wedge x \in dom(c_2) \\ \textit{undefined} & \text{Otherwise} \end{cases}$$

Definition 2.1 (Corr). *The syntax of flows, service instances and systems is given by the following grammar*

$$
\begin{array}{ll}
(\text{FLOW}) & P ::= 0 \mid \sum_i o_i(\vec{x_i});P_i \mid \overline{o}\langle\vec{v}\rangle \mid P|P \mid P;P \mid \textbf{if } v = v' \textbf{ then } P \textbf{ else } P \mid \textbf{rec}_X\ P \mid X \\
(\text{INST}) & I ::= 0 \mid c \triangleright [P] \mid I|I \\
(\text{SYS}) & N ::= 0 \mid s^O_C\{P,I,M\} \mid N \| N \\
(\text{MSG}) & M ::= \emptyset \mid \overline{o}\langle\vec{v}\rangle|M
\end{array}
$$

Flows are processes of value-passing CCS [11] with guarded choices, conditional if-then-else, and without any form of restriction. We include the operator ";" for sequential composition because we are not able to encode this primitive with the remaining ones (we do not have restriction). We only consider closed guarded recursive terms. The set of instances of a service can be either the empty set denoted by 0, the singleton containing the instance $c \triangleright [P]$ or the union of instances $I_1|I_2$. The instance $c \triangleright [P]$ denotes a service instance whose correlation variables have been initialized as described by c and its execution state is described by P. The simplest system is a service $s^O_C\{P,I,M\}$, where s is the name of the service, O is the set of ports or operations it provides, C is the set of correlated variables that it uses, P is the definition of the service, I are the active instances and M is the bag of all the received messages that are still pending.

We will refer to the set of input and output operations of a flow P (respectively, instances I and systems N), denoted $in(P)$ and $out(P)$ (respectively $in(I)$ and $out(I)$, and $in(N)$ and $out(N)$) as the sets of operation names that are subjects of the input and output prefixes occurring in P. We will write $subj(M)$ for the set of all operation names that appear as subjects of messages in M.

We remark that any name $x \in C$ acts as a binder in $s^O_C\{P,I,M\}$. For instance, all occurrences of x in $N = s^O_{\{x\}}\{o(x,y).P, \{x \mapsto a\} \triangleright [Q], M\}$ are bound to the correlation variable x. Note that x in $o(x,y).P$ is also bound to correlation name and cannot be α-renamed without renaming the correlation variable, i.e., $N \equiv_\alpha s^O_{\{z\}}\{o(z,y).P[z/x], \{z \mapsto a\} \triangleright [Q[z/x]], M\}$ for any fresh z. Contrastingly, $N \not\equiv_\alpha s^O_{\{x\}}\{o(z,y).P[z/x], \{x \mapsto a\} \triangleright [Q], M\}$. In what follows we consider only systems in which any two different input prefixes of a flow only share correlation variables (this constraint is analogous to Barendregt's hygiene convention).

We will restrict our attention to systems satisfying a well-formedness condition defined below. We first introduce some auxiliary notions.

Definition 2.2 ($C \blacktriangleright I$). *A set of service instances I is correlated by a correlation set C, written $C \blacktriangleright I$, iff*

$$
C \blacktriangleright 0 \qquad \frac{dom(c) = C}{C \blacktriangleright c \triangleright [P]} \qquad \frac{C \blacktriangleright I_1 \quad C \blacktriangleright I_2}{C \blacktriangleright I_1|I_2}
$$

Definition 2.3 (Input-blocked). *We say a flow P is input blocked iff one of the following conditions holds*

$$
\begin{array}{l}
P = \sum_i o_i(\vec{x_i});P_i \\
P = P_1|P_2 \textit{ with } P_1 \textit{ and } P_2 \textit{ input blocked} \\
P = P_1;P_2 \textit{ with } P_1 \textit{ input blocked}
\end{array}
$$

The well-formedness condition is formally stated by the next definition.

Definition 2.4 (Well-formedness). *A flow P is well-formed if $in(P) \cap out(P) = \emptyset$. An instance $c \triangleright [P]$ is well-formed iff P is well-formed. A system $s_C^O\{P,I,M\}$ is well-formed iff all the following conditions hold:*

1. *The service definition P is well-formed and input-blocked;*
2. *All instances in I are well-formed;*
3. *Instances I are correlated by C, i.e., $C \blacktriangleright I$;*
4. *The input operations appearing in service instances I and service definition P are declared as operations provided by the service, i.e., $in(I) \cup in(P) \subseteq O$.*
5. *The bag of pending messages consists of messages for the operations provided by the service, i.e., $subj(M) \subseteq O$.*

A system $N \| N'$ is well-formed iff there are not input conflicts among different services, i.e., $in(N) \cap in(N') = \emptyset$.

The well-formedness condition states assumptions underlying business process models. Well-formed flows use input and output operations for communicating with third parties and not to establish intra service synchronization (i.e., $in(P) \cap out(P) = \emptyset$). This is a standard assumption implicit in most orchestration languages because each operation is associated to a particular partner link, which is different from the service itself. Our model does not include partner links explicitly but we require a consistent usage of operations by imposing a well-formed condition over systems. Orchestration languages provide particular primitives for internal synchronization, like links. (For simplicity's sake we do not include links in our model since this primitive is somehow orthogonal to correlation and exceptions). For services, we require all definitions to be input blocked (condition 1), which relates to the fact that activities should causally depend on start activities. Conditions 2, 3 and 4 stand for a relaxed form of a condition requiring instances to actually describe partial executions of service definitions.

2.1 Operational Semantics

In order to describe the dynamics of a system, we will consider an extended form of flows, which denotes the fact that an exception has been thrown. We add two additional forms of processes to account for the two different correlation exceptions defined by BPEL, namely, *ambiguous receive*($\dagger$) and *conflicting receive*($\ddagger$).

$$(\text{FLOW}) \quad P ::= \ldots \mid \dagger \mid \ddagger$$

The operational semantics of Corr is defined by a labeled transition system over well-formed terms, up-to the structural congruence defined below.

Definition 2.5 (Structural Congruence). *The structural congruence is the smallest congruence over the extended form of systems such that $|$, $+$, $\|$ are associative, commutative and have 0 as identity, ; is associative and have 0 as identity and the following axioms hold (P below does not contain $\dagger$ nor $\ddagger$).*

$$0;P \equiv P \qquad \dagger;P \equiv \dagger \qquad \ddagger;P \equiv \ddagger \qquad \dagger \mid P \equiv \dagger \qquad \ddagger \mid P \equiv \ddagger$$

Parallel composition of messages $|$ is associative, commutative and have $\emptyset$ as identity.

The labeled transition system considers the following actions, whose meaning is standard.

$$\alpha ::= o(\vec{v}) \mid \overline{o}\langle\vec{v}\rangle \mid \tau$$

We usually refer to $o(\vec{v})$ as a receive action instead of as an input and $\overline{o}\langle\vec{v}\rangle$ as an invoke instead of as an output.

The semantics of Corr is given by a Labeled Transition System (LTS) defined by structural induction on the syntax of the process, following Plotkin's Structural Operational Semantics (SOS) scheme [12]. Transitions for systems and instances are labeled by actions α as usual, while transitions for flows are labeled by pairs α, c, where α is an action and c is a correlation instance. A transition $P \xrightarrow{\alpha,c} P'$ denotes that P becomes P' by performing α and assigning variables as described by c. The semantics for flows is defined by using the auxiliary reduction relation $P \overset{\alpha,c}{\longmapsto} P'$. The meaning of labels is analogous to $\xrightarrow{\alpha,c}$. The main difference between $\overset{\alpha,c}{\longmapsto}$ and $\xrightarrow{\alpha,c}$ is that the latter accounts for correlation exceptions while the former does not (as explained below).

Definition 2.6. *The label transition system for Corr flows, instances and systems is defined by the rules in Figure 1.*

Rule (IN) is standard except for the fact that the label contains also the partial function $\vec{x_i} \mapsto \vec{v}$ recording the assignment of received values (this information is used by other rules to ensure that the use of correlated variables is consistent). Note that the function is set to $\emptyset$ in rule (OUT) because no variable is instantiated when a process performs an invoke. Rules (PAR), (SEQ), (REC), (THEN), (ELSE) are standard. Rule (NO-EXCP) states that a flow P can perform an action α without throwing any exception only when P can perform the action α (first premise) and there is no way (i.e., any other computation) for P to raise a correlation exception by performing the same action α (second and third premises). Rule (AMB-REC-EXCP) states that a flow that concurrently activates two receive operations for handling the same input action raises the ambiguous-receive exception. Differently, rule (CONF-REC-EXCP) states that a flow P raises the conflicting-receive exception after performing an action α if the residual of P after α enables two different input actions that are indistinguishable. There are two main differences between (AMB-REC-EXCP) and (CONF-REC-EXCP). Firstly, ambiguous-receive exception is raised when a flow attempts to perform an input action that can be handled in different ways while the conflicting-receive exception is raised when a flow performs an action α (note that it can be any action) and the residual enables at least two input actions for handling the same request. Secondly, the rules differ also on the conditions imposed over the instantiation of received variables. Rule (CONF-REC-EXCP) requires the same usage of received variables on conflicting inputs (i.e., last two premises require the same instantiation c_1) while (AMB-REC-EXCP) allows for different instantiation (note that premises use different correlations c_1 and c_2). These rules are aligned with BPEL specification statement that reads: "*If a business process instance simultaneously enables two or more IMAs [inbound message activities] for the same partnerLink, portType, operation but different correlationSet(s), and the correlations of multiple of these activities match an incoming request message, then the bpel:ambiguousReceive standard fault MUST be thrown by all IMAs whose correlation set(s) match the incoming message*". This makes clear that ambiguous-receive is raised when considering

FLOW

(IN)
$$\textstyle\sum_i o_i(\vec{x_i});P_i \xmapsto{o_i(\vec{v}),\vec{x_i}\mapsto\vec{v}} P_i\{\vec{x_i}/\vec{v}\}$$

(OUT)
$$\overline{o_i}\langle\vec{d}\rangle \xmapsto{\overline{o_i}\langle\vec{d}\rangle,\emptyset} 0$$

(PAR)
$$\frac{P_1 \xmapsto{\alpha,c} P_1'}{P_1|P_2 \xmapsto{\alpha,c} P_1'|P_2}$$

(SEQ)
$$\frac{P_1 \xmapsto{\alpha,c} P_1'}{P_1;P_2 \xmapsto{\alpha,c} P_1';(P_2c)}$$

(REC)
$$\frac{P[^{\mathbf{rec}_X\, P}/_X] \xmapsto{\alpha,c} P'}{\mathbf{rec}_X\, P \xmapsto{\alpha,c} P'}$$

(THEN)
$$\mathbf{if}\ a=a\ \mathbf{then}\ P_1\ \mathbf{else}\ P_2 \xmapsto{\tau,\emptyset} P_1$$

(ELSE)
$$\frac{a\neq b}{\mathbf{if}\ a=b\ \mathbf{then}\ P_1\ \mathbf{else}\ P_2 \xmapsto{\tau,\emptyset} P_2}$$

(NO-EXCP)
$$\frac{P\xmapsto{\alpha,c}P' \quad P \not\xmapsto{\alpha,c_1} \dagger \quad P\not\xmapsto{\alpha,c_1}\ddagger}{P\xrightarrow{\alpha,c}P'}$$

(AMB-REC-EXCP)
$$\frac{P_1 \xmapsto{o(\vec{v}),c_1} P_1' \qquad P_2 \xmapsto{o(\vec{v}),c_2} P_2' \qquad c_1\neq c_2}{P_1|P_2 \xrightarrow{o(\vec{v}),\emptyset}\dagger}$$

(CONF-REC-EXCP)
$$\frac{P\xmapsto{\alpha,c}P' \quad P'\equiv P_1|P_2 \quad P_1\xmapsto{o(\vec{v}),c_1}P_1' \qquad P_2 \xmapsto{o(\vec{v}),c_1} P_2'}{P\xrightarrow{\alpha,c}\ddagger}$$

INSTANCES

(CORR)
$$\frac{P\xrightarrow{\alpha,c'}P' \qquad c[c'] \text{ defined}}{c\rhd[P] \xrightarrow{\alpha} c[c']\rhd[P']}$$

(I-PAR)
$$\frac{I_1\xrightarrow{\alpha}I_1'}{I_1|I_2 \xrightarrow{\alpha} I_1'|I_2}$$

SYSTEMS

(SVC-IN)
$$\frac{o\in O}{s_C^O\{P,I,M\} \xrightarrow{o(\vec{v})} s_C^O\{P,I,\overline{o}\langle\vec{v}\rangle|M\}}$$

(NEW)
$$\frac{C_\perp \rhd [P] \xrightarrow{o(\vec{v})} c\rhd[P']}{s_C^O\{P,I,\overline{o}\langle\vec{v}\rangle|M\} \xrightarrow{\tau} s_C^O\{P, I \mid c\rhd[P'],M\}}$$

(DISPATCH)
$$\frac{I\xrightarrow{o(\vec{v})}I'}{s_C^O\{P,I,\overline{o}\langle\vec{v}\rangle|M\}\xrightarrow{\tau}s_C^O\{P,I',M\}}$$

(SVC-NON-IN)
$$\frac{I\xrightarrow{\alpha}I' \qquad \alpha\neq o(\vec{v})}{s_C^O\{P,I,M\}\xrightarrow{\alpha}s_C^O\{P,I',M\}}$$

(S-PAR)
$$\frac{N_1\xrightarrow{\alpha}N_1'}{N_1\|N_2 \xrightarrow{\alpha} N_1'\|N_2}$$

(COMM)
$$\frac{N_1 \xrightarrow{o(\vec{v})} N_1' \quad N_2 \xrightarrow{\overline{o}\langle\vec{v}\rangle} N_2'}{N_1\|N_2 \xrightarrow{\tau} N_1'\|N_2'}$$

Fig. 1. Labeled Transition System for Corr

different correlation sets (i.e., variables). For conflicting-receive, BPEL specification says: "*if two or more receive actions for the same partnerLink, portType, operation and correlationSet(s) are simultaneously enabled during execution, then the standard fault bpel:conflictingReceive MUST be thrown*". Consequently, conflicting-receive is thrown when considering the same correlation set. Moreover, ActiveBPEL implements this requirement as referring to IMAs of the same instance (as for ambiguous-receive) and does not impose restrictions over simultaneous enabling on different instances.

We also remark that our calculus does not provide exception handling and hence we make the whole instance to raise the exception. Models accounting for exception handling should keep track of the places in which exceptions are raised.

Rule (CORR) states that a service instance $c \triangleright [P]$ can perform an action only when the instantiation of variables induced by the execution of such action (i.e., the assignments described by c') is consistent with the correlation values of the instance (condition $c[c']$ defined). In this case, both P evolves to P' and the correlation is updated to $c[c']$. Since $c' = \emptyset$ when α is either τ or an invoke action, the correlation update has effect only for receive actions. Rule (I-PAR) deals with the behaviour of a set of multiple instances. Note that instances are independent from each other, which corresponds to the fact that ActiveBPEL does not impose correlation constraints between different instances.

We remark that services interact asynchronously and received messages are kept in a bag of received messages (rule (SCV-IN)) and then they are used either for creating a new instance (rule (NEW)) or in a received action of an existing instance (rule (DISPATCH)). Differently from other approaches such as COWS, rule (NEW) have no side conditions ensuring that it has less priority than (DISPATCH). This accounts for the fact that ActiveBPEL may create new instances even when some other instance may handle the received message. This behaviour appears related to an implementation aspect that introduces delay in the registration of ready inputs. For this reason, ActiveBPEL may create a new instance when an input action of an instance has not completed its registration. The semantics of Corr abstracts away from timing issues and specifies this kind of behaviours by introducing non-determinism for handling received messages. Rule (SCV-NON-IN) lifts non-input actions (i.e., outputs or silent moves) of an instance to the service level. Rules (PAR) and (COM) are standard. We only remark here that communication is possible only between two different services.

Notation. We will write $\Rightarrow$ to denote the relation $\Rightarrow = \bigcup_\alpha \xrightarrow{\alpha}$. By abusing notation, we also write $\Rightarrow$ for $\Rightarrow = \bigcup_{\alpha,c} \xrightarrow{\alpha,c}$. As usual we write $\Rightarrow^n$ for the sequential composition of n steps of $\Rightarrow$ and $\Rightarrow^*$ for the reflexive and transitive closure of $\Rightarrow$.

We use the following examples to illustrate the main features of Corr.

Example 2.1 (Simple Correlation). Consider the following system built-up from two different services:

$$\begin{aligned} N = \quad & s^{\{o_1,o_2\}}_{\{x\}}\{o_1(x,y);o_2(x,z);\overline{o}\langle y,z\rangle,0,\emptyset\} \\ & \parallel s'^{O}_{C}\{Q, c \triangleright [\overline{o_1}\langle a,b\rangle;\overline{o_1}\langle d,e\rangle;\overline{o_2}\langle d,f\rangle;\overline{o_2}\langle a,c\rangle],M\} \end{aligned}$$

Service s provides two operations, namely o_1 and o_2, it has no active instances and uses x as the only correlation variable. The two receive actions contained in the definition of s (i.e., o_1 and o_2) use the same correlation property x (x is the first parameter in both input prefixes). Service s' has only one active instance with correlation c —the particular values are uninteresting because all actions are outputs. The instance of s' is sending the request $\overline{o_1}\langle a,b\rangle$. Since o_1 is an operation provided by s, this request will be added to the message bag of s, as shown below.

$$\begin{aligned} N \xrightarrow{\tau} \quad & s^{\{o_1,o_2\}}_{\{x\}}\{o_1(x,y);o_2(x,z);\overline{o}\langle y,z\rangle,0,\overline{o_1}\langle a,b\rangle\} \\ & \parallel s'^{O}_{C}\{Q, c \triangleright [\overline{o_1}\langle d,e\rangle;\overline{o_2}\langle d,f\rangle;\overline{o_2}\langle a,c\rangle],M\} \end{aligned}$$

At this point, s may consume the message $\overline{o_1}\langle a,b\rangle$ in its message bag to create a new instance (by using rule DISPATCH), as shown below.

$$\begin{array}{ll}\xrightarrow{\tau} & s^{\{o_1,o_2\}}_{\{x\}}\{o_1(x,y);o_2(x,z);\overline{o}\langle y,z\rangle,\{x\mapsto a\}\triangleright[o_2(x,z);\overline{o}\langle b,z\rangle],\emptyset\}\\ & \parallel s'^{O}_{C}\{Q,c\triangleright[\overline{o_1}\langle d,e\rangle;\overline{o_2}\langle d,f\rangle;\overline{o_2}\langle a,c\rangle],M\}\end{array}$$

After two reduction steps s will activate a new instance to handle the request $\overline{o_1}\langle d,e\rangle$. Note that $\{x\mapsto a\}\triangleright[o_2(x,z);\overline{o}\langle b,z\rangle]$ is not able to perform $o_1(d,e)$ and hence the creation of a new instance is the only possibility. Then, the system evolves as follows.

$$\begin{array}{ll}\xrightarrow{\tau}\xrightarrow{\tau} & s^{\{o_1,o_2\}}_{\{x\}}\{o_1(x,y);o_2(x,z);\overline{o}\langle y,z\rangle,\ \{x\mapsto a\}\triangleright[o_2(x,z);\overline{o}\langle b,z\rangle]\ |\\ & \qquad\qquad \{x\mapsto d\}\triangleright[o_2(x,z);\overline{o}\langle e,z\rangle],\quad \emptyset\}\\ & \parallel s'^{O}_{C}\{Q,c\triangleright[\overline{o_2}\langle d,f\rangle;\overline{o_2}\langle a,c\rangle],M\}\end{array}$$

After two communication steps the system reduces to

$$\begin{array}{ll}\xrightarrow{\tau}\xrightarrow{\tau} & s^{\{o_1,o_2\}}_{\{x\}}\{o_1(x,y);o_2(x,z);\overline{o}\langle y,z\rangle,\{x\mapsto a\}\triangleright[o_2(x,z);\overline{o}\langle b,z\rangle]\ |\\ & \qquad\qquad \{x\mapsto d\}\triangleright[o_2(x,z);\overline{o}\langle e,z\rangle],\ \overline{o_2}\langle d,f\rangle|\overline{o_2}\langle a,c\rangle\}\\ & \parallel s'^{O}_{C}\{Q,c\triangleright[0],M\}\end{array}$$

Now, the message $\overline{o_2}\langle d,f\rangle$ will be handled by the instance correlated by $\{x\mapsto d\}$, and the message $\overline{o_2}\langle a,c\rangle$ by the instance correlated by $\{x\mapsto a\}$, as below

$$\begin{array}{ll}\xrightarrow{\tau} & s^{\{o_1,o_2\}}_{\{x\}}\{o_1(x,y);o_2(x,z);\overline{o}\langle y,z\rangle,\ \{x\mapsto a\}\triangleright[o_2(x,z);\overline{o}\langle b,z\rangle]\ |\\ & \qquad\qquad \{x\mapsto d\}\triangleright[\overline{o}\langle e,f\rangle],\quad \overline{o_2}\langle a,c\rangle\}\\ & \parallel s'^{O}_{C}\{Q,c\triangleright[0],M\}\\ \xrightarrow{\tau} & s^{\{o_1,o_2\}}_{\{x\}}\{o_1(x,y);o_2(x,z);\overline{o}\langle y,z\rangle,\ \{x\mapsto a\}\triangleright[\overline{o}\langle b,c\rangle]\ |\\ & \qquad\qquad \{x\mapsto d\}\triangleright[\overline{o}\langle e,f\rangle],\quad \emptyset\}\\ & \parallel s'^{O}_{C}\{Q,c\triangleright[0],M\}\end{array}$$

Example 2.2 (Multiple correlations). Orchestration languages provide the possibility of defining multiple correlation sets. This is especially useful for defining services that interact with different partners. These scenarios usually require the usage of one correlation value for each partner. Multiple correlation sets are a built-in feature of Corr as shown by the following example.

$$\begin{array}{rl}N = & s^{\{o_1,o_2\}}_{\{x,y\}}\{P,\{x\mapsto a,y\mapsto b\}\triangleright[(o_1(x,z)\mid o_2(y,w))],\emptyset\}\\ & \parallel s1^{0_1}_{C_1}\{P_1,c_1\triangleright[\overline{o_1}\langle a,d\rangle;R_1],M_1\}\\ & \parallel s2^{0_2}_{C_2}\{P_2,c_2\triangleright[\overline{o_2}\langle b,e\rangle;R_2],M_2\}\end{array}$$

The instances of the service s can be identified by using indistinctly x, y or a combination of both of them. In particular, the communication between the instance of s_1 and the instance of s takes place by using operation o_1 and the correlation set x, while the communication with the instance of s_2 will take place over operation o_2 in combination with correlation set y.

Example 2.3 (Colliding instances). In Corr (as in ActiveBPEL), some or all correlation values of two different instances may coincide, i.e., there is not a unique association of correlation values and instances. For example, the following system

$$N = s_{\{x\}}^{\{o_1,o_2\}}\{o_1(x);o_2(x),0,\emptyset\} \parallel s1_{C_1}^{O_1}\{P_1, c_1 \triangleright [\overline{o_1}\langle a\rangle;\overline{o_1}\langle a\rangle], M\}$$

may reduce after two communication steps as below

$$N \xrightarrow{\tau}\xrightarrow{\tau} s_{\{x\}}^{\{o_1,o_2\}}\{o_1(x);o_2(x),0,\overline{o_1}\langle a\rangle|\overline{o_1}\langle a\rangle\} \parallel s1_{C_1}^{O_1}\{P_1, c_1 \triangleright [0], M\}$$

At this time, s may create a new instance with correlation $\{x \mapsto a\}$, as below

$$\xrightarrow{\tau} s_{\{x\}}^{\{o_1,o_2\}}\{o_1(x);o_2(x),\{x \mapsto a\} \triangleright [o_2(x)],\overline{o_1}\langle a\rangle\} \parallel s1_{C_1}^{O_1}\{P_1, c_1 \triangleright [0], M\}$$

In the state above, service s has an instance associated with the correlation $\{x \mapsto a\}$ and an available message $\overline{o_1}\langle a\rangle$. Note that the message cannot be handled by the only instance of s, but s may create a new instance because its definition starts with receive o_1. Hence, the system reduces to

$$\xrightarrow{\tau} s_{\{x\}}^{\{o_1,o_2\}}\{o_1(x);o_2(x),\{x \mapsto a\} \triangleright [o_2(x)]|\{x \mapsto a\} \triangleright [o_2(x)],\emptyset\} \parallel s1_{C_1}^{O_1}\{P_1, c_1 \triangleright [0], M\}$$

Now s contains two instances with exactly the same correlation values. Assume that s receives a message $\overline{o_2}\langle a\rangle$. Then it evolves as follows

$$\xrightarrow{o_2(a)} s_{\{x\}}^{\{o_1,o_2\}}\{o_1(x);o_2(x),\{x \mapsto a\} \triangleright [o_2(x)]|\{x \mapsto a\} \triangleright [o_2(x)],\overline{o_2}\langle a\rangle\} \parallel \ldots$$

We remark here that the available message $\overline{o_2}\langle a\rangle$ is non-deterministically dispatched to one of the existing instances. It should be noted that correlation mechanism in ActiveBPEL does not ensures univocal identification of a session. Hence, clients of a service cannot rely only on correlation values to identify a particular instance of a service.

Example 2.4 (Exception due to ambiguous receive). Consider the following system

$$N = s_{\{x,y\}}^{\{o_1,o_2\}}\{o_1(x,y);(o_2(x)|o_2(y)),0,\emptyset\}$$

Then, the following computation is allowed

$$\begin{array}{ll}
\xrightarrow{o_1(a,a)} & s_{\{x,y\}}^{\{o_1,o_2\}}\{o_1(x,y);(o_2(x)|o_2(y)),0,\overline{o_1}\langle a,a\rangle\} \\
\xrightarrow{o_2(a)} & s_{\{x,y\}}^{\{o_1,o_2\}}\{o_1(x,y);(o_2(x)|o_2(y)),0,\overline{o_2}\langle a\rangle|\overline{o_1}\langle a,a\rangle\} \\
\xrightarrow{\tau} & s_{\{x,y\}}^{\{o_1,o_2\}}\{o_1(x,y);(o_2(x)|o_2(y)),\{x \mapsto a, y \mapsto a\} \triangleright [o_2(x) \mid o_2(y)],\overline{o_2}\langle a\rangle\}
\end{array}$$

At this time, the service s may dispatch the message $\overline{o_2}\langle a\rangle$ to its unique instance, which will raise an exception. Note that the flow of the instance will reduce as follows

$$\text{(AMB-REC-EXCP)}\ \frac{o_2(x) \xmapsto{o_2(a),\{x\mapsto a\}} 0 \qquad o_2(y) \xmapsto{o_2(a),\{y\mapsto a\}} 0 \qquad \{x \mapsto a\} \neq \{y \mapsto a\}}{o_2(x)|o_2(y) \xrightarrow{o_2(a),\emptyset} \dagger}$$

and hence, the complete system will evolve as shown below

$$\xrightarrow{\tau} s^{\{o_1,o_2\}}_{\{x,y\}}\{o_1(x,y);(o_2(x)|o_2(y)),\{x\mapsto a,y\mapsto a\}\triangleright[\dagger],\emptyset\}$$

Example 2.5 (Exception due to conflicting receive). The simplest system exhibiting a conflicting receive can be written as follows

$$N = s^{\{o_1,o_2\}}_{\{x\}}\{o_1(x);(o_2(x)|o_2(x)),0,\emptyset\}$$

Then, N can reduce as follows

$$\xrightarrow{o_1(a)} s^{\{o_1,o_2\}}_{\{x,y\}}\{o_1(x);(o_2(x)|o_2(x)),0,\overline{o_1}\langle a\rangle\}$$

Then, the exception is raised when the service attempts to create a new instances for the message $\overline{o_1}\langle a\rangle$. In fact,

$$\text{(CONF-REC-EXCP)}\quad \frac{o_1(x);(o_2(x)|o_2(x)) \xmapsto{o_1(a),x\mapsto a} o_2(x)|o_2(x) \quad o_2(x) \xmapsto{o_1(a),x\mapsto a} 0 \quad o_2(x) \xmapsto{o_1(a),x\mapsto a} 0}{P \xrightarrow{o_1(a),x\mapsto a} \ddagger}$$

Example 2.6 (No exception for undetermined receiver). An invoke that neither matches an existing instance nor creates a new instance will remain blocked instead of raising an exception. For example,

$$\begin{array}{rcl} N & = & s^{\{o_1,o_2\}}_{\{x,y\}}\{o_1(x);o_2(x),\{x\mapsto a\}\triangleright[0],\emptyset\} \parallel s_1{}^{O_1}_{C_1}\{P_1,c\triangleright[\overline{o_2}\langle a\rangle],M\} \\ & \xrightarrow{\tau} & s^{\{o_1,o_2\}}_{\{x,y\}}\{o_1(x);o_2(x),\{x\mapsto a\}\triangleright[0],\overline{o_2}\langle a\rangle\} \parallel s_1{}^{O_1}_{C_1}\{P_1,c\triangleright[0],M\} \end{array}$$

Note that N is blocked because the unique instance of s has terminated and the message $\overline{o_2}\langle a\rangle$ cannot create a new instance of the service definition (operation o_2 is not a start activity of the service definition). Although BPEL does not prescribe the behaviour of implementations, there are some engine implementations (like WEBSPHERE) that choose to raise ad hoc exceptions in these cases. For the sake of simplicity, we prefer to keep operational semantics simple and do not include such behaviour. Our choice reflects also the behaviour of ActiveBPEL.

3 Correlation Exceptions

As illustrated in the examples above, there are situations in which a system may raise an exception. These exceptions are due to the fact that the flow concurrently activates several input actions over the same operation. In cases in which the concurrent actions use exactly the same variables in the same position, then the raised exception is a conflicting-receive. Otherwise, the exception is ambiguous-receive.

Definition 3.1. *A service $s^O_C\{P,0,M\}$ is free from ambiguous-receive exception iff $\forall I$ such that $s^O_C\{P,0,\emptyset\} \Rightarrow^* s^O_C\{P,I,M\}$, then $I \not\equiv c\triangleright[\dagger]\|I'$. Similarly, it is free from conflicting-receive when $I \not\equiv c\triangleright[\ddagger]\|I'$. We say that the service is free from correlation exceptions when it is free from ambiguous- and conflicting-receive exceptions.*

Following section introduces a simple type system characterizing those services that are free from correlation exceptions.

(ZERO)
$$\Gamma \vdash 0 : \emptyset$$

(INPUT)
$$\frac{\Gamma \vdash P : \mathcal{T}}{\Gamma \vdash o(\vec{x});P : \mathcal{T} \oplus \{o \mapsto \vec{x}\}}$$

(SUM)
$$\frac{\Gamma \vdash o_1(\vec{x_1});P_1 : \mathcal{T}_1 \quad \dots \quad \Gamma \vdash o_n(\vec{x_n});P_n : \mathcal{T}_n}{\Gamma \vdash \Sigma_i o_i(\vec{x_i});P_i : \bigoplus_i \mathcal{T}_i}$$

(OUTPUT)
$$\Gamma \vdash \bar{o}\langle\vec{v}\rangle : \emptyset$$

(PAR)
$$\frac{\Gamma \vdash P_1 : \mathcal{T}_1 \quad \Gamma \vdash P_2 : \mathcal{T}_2 \quad \mathcal{T}_1 \circledcirc \mathcal{T}_2}{\Gamma \vdash P_1|P_2 : \mathcal{T}_1 \oplus \mathcal{T}_2}$$

(SEQ)
$$\frac{\Gamma \vdash P_1 : \mathcal{T}_1 \quad \Gamma \vdash P_2 : \mathcal{T}_2}{\Gamma \vdash P_1;P_2 : \mathcal{T}_1 \oplus \mathcal{T}_2}$$

(REC)
$$\frac{X \mapsto \mathcal{T}, \Gamma \vdash P : \mathcal{T}}{X \mapsto \mathcal{T}, \Gamma \vdash \mathbf{rec}_X\, P : \mathcal{T}}$$

(X)
$$X \mapsto \mathcal{T}, \Gamma \vdash X : \mathcal{T}$$

(IF)
$$\frac{\Gamma \vdash P_1 : \mathcal{T}_1 \quad \Gamma \vdash P_2 : \mathcal{T}_2}{\Gamma \vdash \mathbf{if}\ v = v'\ \mathbf{then}\ P_1\ \mathbf{else}\ P_2 : \mathcal{T}_1 \oplus \mathcal{T}_2}$$

Fig. 2. Typing rules

3.1 Type System for Correlation-Exception-Free Services

We will consider the following type judgements for flows: $\Gamma \vdash P : \mathcal{T}$. The type $\mathcal{T}$ assigned to a flow is a partial function from operation names to a set of tuples of variables, i.e., $\mathcal{T} : O \to \mathcal{P}_f(\mathcal{V}^*)$. Basically, the type of a flow P associates any input name occurring in P with a set containing the formal parameters of all its occurrences in P. Moreover, Γ is a partial function from process variables to types, i.e., Γ assigns a type to any process variable in P. For example, $\mathcal{T}(o) = \{\langle x,y\rangle, \langle z,x\rangle\}$ means that all input actions for the operation o have parameters $\langle x,y\rangle$ or $\langle z,x\rangle$. With abuse of notation, we use use $\mathcal{T}$ also to denote the obvious total function defined such that $\mathcal{T}(o) = \emptyset$ when o is not in the domain of the corresponding partial function. We define also type composition as follows $(\mathcal{T}_1 \oplus \mathcal{T}_2)(o) = \mathcal{T}_1(o) \cup \mathcal{T}_2(o)$.

Typing rules are shown in Figure 2. The main idea behind typing rules is that of collecting all tuples used as formal parameters of input actions. Note that rule (INPUT) adds a tuple corresponding to the formal parameters of the input prefix to the type of the continuation of the process. Differently, an output prefix has no effect over the type of a flow (see rule OUTPUT). Rule (PAR) takes into account the compatibility of the types assigned to parallel branches. Note that any input action that takes place in one branch may be concurrently enabled with an input action occurring in the other branch. Hence, type compatibility states sufficient conditions for avoiding exceptions. Our type system is parametric with respect to the definition of the compatibility operation $\circledcirc$. We will actually consider the following three alternative definitions for compatibility:

$$\mathcal{T}_1 \circledcirc_c \mathcal{T}_2 = \forall o. \mathcal{T}_1(o) \cap \mathcal{T}_2(o) = \emptyset$$
$$\mathcal{T}_1 \circledcirc_a \mathcal{T}_2 = \forall o. \#(\mathcal{T}_1(o) \cup \mathcal{T}_2(o)) > 1 \Rightarrow (\mathcal{T}_1(o) = \emptyset \vee \mathcal{T}_2(o) = \emptyset)$$
$$\mathcal{T}_1 \circledcirc_e \mathcal{T}_2 = \forall o. \mathcal{T}_1(o) = \emptyset \vee \mathcal{T}_2(o) = \emptyset$$

Definition for $\circledcirc_c$ requires that input actions for a particular operation taking place in different branches use different parameters (actually, we require different tuples, which implies that there is at least one formal parameter that differs). Differently, $\circledcirc_a$ states that concurrently enabled input actions for a particular operation must use exactly the same parameters. Finally, $\circledcirc_e$ forbids the concurrent enabling of two or more input actions for the same operation. We will show that each of these definitions can be associated with different notions of correlation exception freeness. Remaining rules are straightforward (note that they do not check compatibility since they do not introduce concurrent enabling of input prefixes).

The following result states that the type of a flow captures the actual parameters of all ready input actions of a flow.

Proposition 3.1. *Let P be a flow. If $\Gamma \vdash P : \mathcal{T}$ and $P \xmapsto{o(v_1,\ldots,v_n),c'} P'$, then there exists $\langle y_1,\ldots,y_n\rangle \in \mathcal{T}(o)$ s.t. $dom(c') = \langle y_1,\ldots,y_n\rangle$.*

Proof (Sketch). The proof follows by induction on derivation $P \xmapsto{o(v_1,\ldots,v_n),c'} P'$. When last applied rule is (IN) $P = \Sigma_i o_i(\vec{x}_i);P_i$ and $P' = P_i$ for some i. By typing rules, we know that $\mathcal{T}(o) = \bigoplus_i \mathcal{T}_i(o)$ where $\Gamma \vdash o_i(\vec{x}_i);P_i : \mathcal{T}_i$. Moreover, $\Gamma \vdash o_i(\vec{x}_i);P_i : \mathcal{T}_i' \oplus \{o_i \mapsto \vec{x}_i\}$. Clearly, $\vec{x}_i \in \mathcal{T}(o)$ because $\vec{x}_i \in \mathcal{T}_i(o)$. Other cases follows using inductive hypothesis.

Proposition 3.2. *Let P be a flow. If $\Gamma \vdash P : \mathcal{T}$ and $P \xrightarrow{o(v_1,\ldots,v_n),c'} P'$, then there exists $\langle y_1,\ldots,y_n\rangle \in \mathcal{T}(o)$ s.t. $dom(c') = \langle y_1,\ldots,y_n\rangle$.*

Proof. By analysis of the applied rule for $P \xrightarrow{o(v_1,\ldots,v_n),c'} P'$ and Proposition 3.2.

Proposition 3.3 (Subject reduction for $\xmapsto{\alpha,c}$). *Let P be flow. If $\Gamma \vdash P : \mathcal{T}$ and $P \xmapsto{\alpha,c'} P'$, then there exists $\mathcal{T}'$ such that (i) $\Gamma \vdash P' : \mathcal{T}'$ and (ii) $\forall o.\mathcal{T}'(o) \subseteq \mathcal{T}(o)$.*

Proof (Sketch). It follows by induction on the derivation $P \xmapsto{\alpha,c'} P'$. Interesting cases are rules (PAR) and (REC). For (PAR), $P = Q_1|Q_2$ and $P' = Q_1'|Q_2$ with $Q_1 \xmapsto{\alpha,c'} Q_1'$. Since P is well-typed, $\Gamma \vdash Q_1 : \mathcal{T}_1$, $\Gamma \vdash Q_2 : \mathcal{T}_2$, $\mathcal{T}_1 \circledS \mathcal{T}_2$ and $\mathcal{T} = \mathcal{T}_1 \oplus \mathcal{T}_2$. Then, by inductive hypothesis we know that there exists $\mathcal{T}_1'$ such that $\Gamma \vdash Q_1' : \mathcal{T}_1'$ and $\mathcal{T}_1'(o) \subseteq \mathcal{T}_1(o)$ for all o. It is easy to check that for any compatibility operator $\circledS_c$, $\circledS_a$ or $\circledS_e$ the following statement holds: $\mathcal{T}_1 \circledS \mathcal{T}_2$ and $\mathcal{T}_1'(o) \subseteq \mathcal{T}_1(o)$ for all o implies $\mathcal{T}_1' \circledS \mathcal{T}_2$, hence $\Gamma \vdash Q_1'|Q_2 : \mathcal{T}_1' \oplus \mathcal{T}_2$. Moreover, $\mathcal{T}_1'(o) \subseteq \mathcal{T}_1(o)$ implies that $\mathcal{T}_1'(o) \cup \mathcal{T}_2(o) \subseteq \mathcal{T}_1(o) \cup \mathcal{T}_2(o)$, and hence $\mathcal{T}'(o) \subseteq \mathcal{T}(o)$. For (REC) we rely on an auxiliary property stating that $\Gamma \vdash \mathbf{rec}_X\, Q : \mathcal{T}$ implies $\Gamma \vdash Q[^{\mathbf{rec}_X\, Q}/_X] : \mathcal{T}$ and inductive hypothesis.

Following result states that the type of a flow captures all formal parameters of the input operations that a process may execute.

Lemma 3.1. *Let P be a flow. If $\Gamma \vdash P : \mathcal{T}$ and $c \triangleright [P] \Rightarrow^* c_n \triangleright [P_n] \xrightarrow{o(v_1,\ldots,v_n),c'} c[c'] \triangleright [P']$, then there exists $\langle y_1,\ldots,y_m\rangle \in \mathcal{T}(o)$ s.t. $dom(c') = \langle y_1,\ldots,y_n\rangle$.*

Proof. The proof follows by induction on the length of the derivation $\Rightarrow^*$.

- **n=0**. This case follows immediately by Proposition 3.2.
- **n=k+1**. $c \triangleright [P] \xrightarrow{\alpha,c_0} c'' \triangleright [P''] \Rightarrow^k c_{k+1} \triangleright [P_{k+1}] \xrightarrow{o(v_1,\ldots,v_n),c_{k+1}} c' \triangleright [P']$. We proceed by case analysis on the structure of P. When $P = \Sigma_i o_i(\vec{x}_i);P_i$, $c \triangleright [P] \xrightarrow{o_i(\vec{v}),\vec{x}_i \mapsto \vec{v}} c[\vec{x}_i \mapsto \vec{v}] \triangleright [P_i']$. By Proposition 3.3 we know that there exists $\mathcal{T}_1$ such that $\Gamma \vdash P_i' : \mathcal{T}_1$ and $\forall o.\mathcal{T}_1(o) \subseteq \mathcal{T}(o)$. By inductive hypothesis (applied over $c'' \triangleright [P''] \Rightarrow^k c_{k+1} \triangleright [P_{k+1}] \xrightarrow{o(v_1,\ldots,v_n),c_{k+1}} c' \triangleright [P']$) we know that there exist $\langle y_1,\ldots,y_m\rangle \in \mathcal{T}_1(o)$ s.t. $dom(c') = \langle y_1,\ldots,y_n\rangle$. Since, $\forall o.\mathcal{T}_1(o) \subseteq \mathcal{T}(o)$ we conclude that $\langle y_1,\ldots,y_m\rangle \in \mathcal{T}_1(o)$. Remaining cases follow analogously.

Lemma 3.2 (Subject reduction). *Let P be a flow and c a correlation instance. If $\Gamma \vdash P : \mathcal{T}$ and $P \xrightarrow{\alpha,c'} P'$, then one of the following holds*

1. *there exists $\mathcal{T}'$ such that $\Gamma \vdash P' : \mathcal{T}'$ and $\forall o.\mathcal{T}'(o) \subseteq \mathcal{T}(o)$,*
2. *if $P' = \dagger$ then compatibility operator is $\circledcirc_c$, or*
3. *if $P' = \ddagger$ then compatibility operator is $\circledcirc_a$.*

Proof (Sketch). The proof follows by analysis of the rule applied for $P \xrightarrow{\alpha,c'} P'$. For rule (NO-EXCP) we show that 1 holds by using Proposition 3.2. For rule (AMB-REC-EXCP) there are two cases. (i) When compatibility is $\circledcirc_c$ then $P = \dagger$ and 2 holds. (ii) For $\circledcirc_e$ and $\circledcirc_a$ we show by contradiction that this rule cannot be applied. Since $P = Q_1 | Q_2$ is well-typed, $\Gamma \vdash Q_1 : \mathcal{T}_1$, $\Gamma \vdash Q_2 : \mathcal{T}_2$ and $\mathcal{T}_1 \circledcirc \mathcal{T}_2$. Moreover, $Q_1 \xrightarrow{o(\vec{v}),c_1} Q_1$ and $Q_2 \xrightarrow{o(\vec{v}),c_2} Q_2$ with $c_1 \neq c_2$. For Proposition 3.2, $dom(c_1) \in \mathcal{T}_1$ and $dom(c_2) \in \mathcal{T}_2$. It is easy to check that this implies that neither $\mathcal{T}_1 \circledcirc_a \mathcal{T}_2$ nor $\mathcal{T}_1 \circledcirc_e \mathcal{T}_2$ holds, which contradicts the fact that P is well-typed. For rule (AMB-REC-EXCP) we proceed as in the previous case.

Next theorem states the main result of the paper, saying that services with well-typed definitions do are free from correlation exceptions.

Theorem 3.1. *Let P be a flow s.t. $\Gamma \vdash P : \mathcal{T}$, then the well-formed service $s^O_C\{P,0,\emptyset\}$ is*

1. *free from ambiguous-receive exception if type compatibility is taken as $\circledcirc_a$.*
2. *free from conflict-receive exception if type compatibility is taken as $\circledcirc_c$.*
3. *free from correlation exception if type compatibility is taken as $\circledcirc_e$.*

Proof. 1. We prove by induction on the length of the derivation $\Rightarrow^n$ that $s^O_C\{P,0,\emptyset\} \Rightarrow^n s^O_C\{P,I,M\}$ implies (i) $I \not\equiv c \triangleright [\dagger] || I'$ and $I \equiv c \triangleright [Q] || I'$ implies Q is well-typed. Case **n=0** is immediate since $I \equiv 0$. For **n=k+1**, $s^O_C\{P,0,\emptyset\} \Rightarrow^k s^O_C\{P,I_k,M_k\} \Rightarrow s^O_C\{P,I,M\}$. By inductive hypothesis, $I_k \not\equiv c \triangleright [\dagger] || I'_k$. We show that exception cannot be raised in the last step by case analysis on the reduction $s^O_C\{P,I_k,M_k\} \Rightarrow s^O_C\{P,I,M\}$.

- $s^O_C\{P,I_k,M_k\} \xrightarrow{\tau} s^O_C\{P,I,M\}$. There are three possibilities. For rule (DISPATCH) it should be $I' \equiv c \triangleright [Q] || I_2 \xrightarrow{o_1(v_1),c'} I = c' \triangleright [Q'] || I_2$ with $Q \xrightarrow{o_1(v_1),c'} \dagger$, but this contradicts Lemma 3.2. Hence, $Q' \neq \dagger$ and Q is well-typed. Rule (NEW) follows analogously. Rule (SVC-NON-IN) follows immediately since τ actions in flow do not introduce $\dagger$.
- $s^O_C\{P,I_k,M_k\} \xrightarrow{\overline{o}\langle v\rangle} s^O_C\{P,I,M\}$ and $s^O_C\{P,I_k,M_k\} \xrightarrow{o(v)} s^O_C\{P,I,M\}$. These cases follow by noticing that these reductions do not introduce exceptions.

Cases 2. and 3. follow analogously.

4 Related Works and Concluding Remarks

This paper introduces Corr, which is a process calculus with correlation primitives. The formal definition of the correlation mechanism exhibited by Corr has been greatly inspired by SOCK [6]. However, we do not include two-way operations, state manipulation and assignment to keep the language simple. We are convinced that the proposed approach smoothly extends to a calculus containing those features (this is left as a future work). We remark that the semantics of SOCK blocks computations that generate correlation instances that collide, while Corr does not impose restrictions among different instances. Differently from SOCK, Corr has a mechanism that automatically raises exceptions when instances activate receive actions that may handle the same request non-deterministically. Although some extensions of SOCK (like [5]) provide primitives for exception handling, exceptions in those approaches are thrown by the execution of a particular primitive but not as a consequence of some correlation violation.

BLITE [9] is a process calculus aimed at explaining most of BPEL features. As a consequence, it contains several primitives that are not included in Corr. With respect to the subset of BLITE that corresponds to Corr we remark that: (i) a BLITE service chooses the receiver of a message by using "the most specific instance principle", i.e., if several instances can handle an incoming message, then the message is directed to the instance associated with the correlation instance that have more initialized values matching the incoming message. If there are several ones, then BLITE chooses non-deterministically one of them. On the contrary, Corr does not have control over different instances and raises an exception when non-determinism is internal to an instance.

Corr does not model explicitly partner links (as done in BLITE and SOCK) because the correlation mechanism is usually used in combination with static endpoints. Consequently, if partner links cannot change dynamically, we see no reason for including them into the model (the study of correlation mechanism in combination with dynamic endpoint identification is out of the scope of this paper).

COWS [9] relies on a pattern matching mechanism to deal with correlation sets. In this sense, COWS describes correlations at a lower level of abstraction — although it has been shown in [10] that it is expressive enough for encoding the correlation mechanism of BLITE.

As already mentioned, the distinctive feature of Corr when compared against previous proposals like SOCK, COWS, and BLITE is that Corr accounts for exceptions raised as a consequence of incorrect usage of correlation sets. None of the previous proposals accounts for the interaction between correlations and exceptions.

We also mention that a completely different approach for structuring interactions among service instances is related to the concept of sessions [2,8,1,7]. Sessions are a more abstract way of thinking about service interaction, which facilitates the analysis of the interaction between instances.

Acknowledgements. The authors thank the anonymous reviewers for their valuable comments and suggestions.

References

1. Bonelli, E., Compagnoni, A.: Multipoint Session Types for a Distributed Calculus. In: Barthe, G., Fournet, C. (eds.) TGC 2007. LNCS, vol. 4912, pp. 240–256. Springer, Heidelberg (2008)

2. Boreale, M., Bruni, R., Caires, L., De Nicola, R., Lanese, I., Loreti, M., Martins, F., Montanari, U., Ravara, A., Sangiorgi, D., Vasconcelos, V., Zavattaro, G.: SCC: A Service Centered Calculus. In: Bravetti, M., Núñez, M., Zavattaro, G. (eds.) WS-FM 2006. LNCS, vol. 4184, pp. 38–57. Springer, Heidelberg (2006)
3. Web services addressing (ws-addressing) (August 2004), http://www.w3.org/Submission/ws-addressing/
4. Web services Business Process Execution L anguage (BPEL). version 2.0 (April 2007), http://docs.oasis-open.org/wsbpel/2.0/wsbpel-v2.0.pdf
5. Guidi, C., Lanese, I., Montesi, F., Zavattaro, G.: On the interplay between fault handling and request-response service invocations. In: Proceedings of 8th International Conference on Application of Concurrency to System Design (ACSD 2008), pp. 190–198. IEEE (2008)
6. Guidi, C., Lucchi, R., Gorrieri, R., Busi, N., Zavattaro, G.: SOCK: A Calculus for Service Oriented Computing. In: Dan, A., Lamersdorf, W. (eds.) ICSOC 2006. LNCS, vol. 4294, pp. 327–338. Springer, Heidelberg (2006)
7. Honda, K., Vasconcelos, V.T., Kubo, M.: Language Primitives and Type Discipline for Structured Communication-Based Programming. In: Hankin, C. (ed.) ESOP 1998. LNCS, vol. 1381, pp. 122–138. Springer, Heidelberg (1998)
8. Lanese, I., Vasconcelos, V.T., Martins, F., Ravara, A.: Disciplining orchestration and conversation in service-oriented computing. In: Proc. of SEFM 2007, pp. 305–314. IEEE Computer Society Press (2007)
9. Lapadula, A., Pugliese, R., Tiezzi, F.: A Calculus for Orchestration of Web Services. In: De Nicola, R. (ed.) ESOP 2007. LNCS, vol. 4421, pp. 33–47. Springer, Heidelberg (2007)
10. Lapadula, A., Pugliese, R., Tiezzi, F.: A Formal Account of WS-BPEL. In: Wang, A.H., Zavattaro, G. (eds.) COORDINATION 2008. LNCS, vol. 5052, pp. 199–215. Springer, Heidelberg (2008)
11. Milner, R.: A Calculus of Communication Systems. LNCS, vol. 92. Springer, Heidelberg (1980)
12. Plotkin, G.: A structural approach to operational semantics. Technical Report DAIMI FN-19, Aarhus University, Computer Science Department (1981)
13. Viroli, M.: A core calculus for correlation in orchestration languages. J. Log. Algebr. Program. 70(1), 74–95 (2007)

Conditional Information Flow Policies and Unwinding Relations*

Chenyi Zhang

School of Computer Science and Engineering
The University of New South Wales

Abstract. Noninterference provides a control over information flow in systems for ensuring confidentiality and integrity security properties. In general, user A is not allowed to interfere with user B if A's behaviour cannot cause any difference in B's observation. Unwinding relations are useful verification techniques for noninterference-based properties. This paper defines a framework for the notion of conditional noninterference, which allows to specify information flow policies based on the semantics of action channels. To verify the properties, we present unwinding relations that are both sound and complete for the new policies.

1 Introduction

Information flow security policies are concerned with both confidentiality and integrity requirements of a system. The seminal work by Goguen and Meseguer introduces a way of defining information flow security policies by a set of *noninterference* assertions [15]. Each assertion specifies that a given set of actions are *not allowed to interfere with* a user. The follow-up works often interpret a noninterference policy as a *binary relation* "$\rightsquigarrow$" over a set of users indicating *permitted flow* of information. Such relations are assumed to be *reflexive*, since naturally every user should be allowed to pass information to himself. If a policy relation is *transitive*, it has a natural correspondence to the classical multilevel security policies of Bell and LaPadula [3,4].

A typical transitive policy on a three user system is depicted in Fig. 1(a), where permissions are given for information to flow from L to M, from M to H and from L to H. (We omit the reflexive arrows as they are always assumed.) If we only allow a policy to be transitive, there is no way to let H pass information to L. Fig. 1(b) shows a policy that is not transitive: a trusted downgrader D is allowed to declassify information received from H to later be forwarded to L. In this case, H cannot directly send messages to L, but all information flowing from H to L must pass through D (i.e., D must first acquire the information and then send it to L). It is possible to further relax the policy, by allowing H to conditionally pass information to L, as shown in Fig. 1(c). The dashed arrow specifies that information flow is allowed from H to L only if φ is satisfied (i.e.,

* A major part of the work was done when the author was a postdoc researcher in the SaToSS group, University of Luxembourg.

R. Bruni and V. Sassone (Eds.): TGC 2011, LNCS 7173, pp. 227–241, 2012.

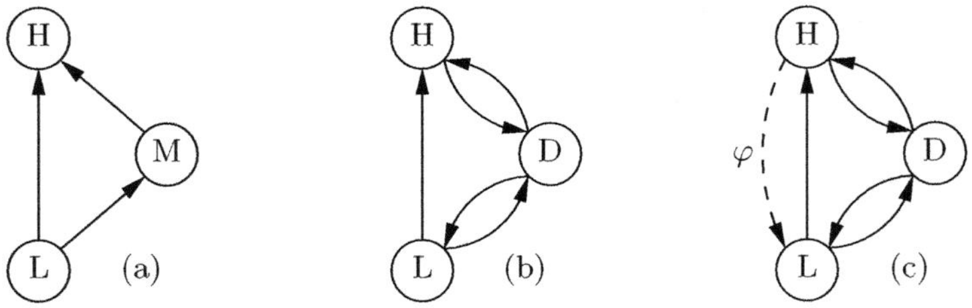

Fig. 1. Example policies

conditional to φ). Such a policy is usually not expressible in a framework with only a binary flow relation "$\rightsquigarrow$".

This paper presents a framework of *conditional noninterference* in order to express some general information flow policies. Conditional noninterference is a term overloading a notion presented in [15]. A number of interesting security requirements are expressible in our framework (see Sect. 2.3). In particular we study two subclasses, *pre-conditional control* policies and *channel control* policies. We present unwinding relations as verification techniques for both classes of policies which are both sound and complete with respect to the policies we study. In the literature, the classical *weak unwinding relations* [26] are sound but *not* complete for *intransitive noninterefernce* [18,26]. Our work is a one-step-forward since intransitive noninterference can be encoded as a special class of *channel control* policies. The outline of the paper is as follows. Sect. 2 defines the system model and presents conditional noninterference, Sect. 3 presents unwinding techniques to characterise the properties, and for a particular class of policies, we reduce their verification to safety. Sect. 4 discusses related work. Sect. 5 concludes the paper and suggests possible future research directions. All the proofs for the results in the paper are available in the version at `http://arxiv.org/abs/1003.3893`.

2 Notions of Noninterference

We define a state machine model similar to those that one can find in the literature [15,26]. We assume a finite set of *users* (or *security domains*) $\mathbb{U}$, a set of actions $\mathcal{A}$, and a function $dom : \mathcal{A} \to \mathbb{U}$ that maps each action to a user who performs it. In our model, each action is associated with a unique security domain, since in practice if there is an action that is available to more than one user, we add distinct user-names as subscripts to produce different actions. The tuple $(\mathcal{A}, \mathbb{U}, dom)$ is called a *signature*, based on which we write $\mathcal{A}_u$ as the set $\{a \in \mathcal{A} \mid dom(a) = u\}$ for $u \in \mathbb{U}$. We write $a, b, a_1, \ldots$ to range over $\mathcal{A}$.

A *machine* for a given signature $(\mathcal{A}, \mathbb{U}, dom)$ is a tuple of the form $M = \langle S, s_0, step, obs, O\rangle$ where S is a set of states, $s_0 \in S$ the initial state, $step : S \times \mathcal{A} \to S$ the transition function, $obs : \mathbb{U} \times S \to O$ the observation function, and O is a set of outputs. The function *step* describes the (asynchronous) system transition, such that $step(s, a)$ is the unique next state when action a is applied on state s. The function *obs* gives a (partial) observation made in each state by a user. For readability, we 'curry' the function *obs* by obs_u of type $S \to O$ given $u \in \mathbb{U}$. Note that such a machine is always *input enabled* by the definition of function *step*, so that every input action is enabled on every state. Also, a machine is always *deterministic* in the sense that given a state s and sequence of actions $\alpha \in \mathcal{A}^*$, a run of state sequence can be uniquely determined. To denote the final state after the execution of a sequence of actions, define the operation $\bullet : S \times \mathcal{A}^* \to S$, by $s \bullet \epsilon = s$, and $s \bullet (\alpha \cdot a) = step(s \bullet \alpha, a)$ for $s \in S$, $a \in \mathcal{A}$ and $\alpha \in \mathcal{A}^*$. We assume every state in a machine is reachable.

In this model we define observation on states, which is different from the definitions of Rushby [26] where observations are associated with actions. This distinction is not essential for many security notions [31], including noninterference. In the literature, the state-observed machines have also been used by a number of authors, such as Goguen and Meseguer [15] and Bevier and Young [5]. Our choice on the modelling of a machine is arbitrary.

2.1 Security Policies

The security policy we are to define assumes a partition on the set of actions. Given a signature $(\mathcal{A}, \mathbb{U}, dom)$, define a partition $\texttt{Part}$ over $\mathcal{A}$ satisfying the following conditions. (1) For all $P \in \texttt{Part}$, there exists $u \in \mathbb{U}$ such that $P \subseteq \mathcal{A}_u$, (2) $\bigcup \texttt{Part} = \mathcal{A}$, (3) $P_1 \cap P_2 = \emptyset$ for all distinct $P_1, P_2 \in \texttt{Part}$. We define a function $part : \mathcal{A} \to \texttt{Part}$ that assigns each action a unique partition. Obviously *part* refines *dom*.

A *conditional noninterference assertion* T is of the form $\langle P \not\rightsquigarrow u \, [\![\varphi]\!] \rangle$ for $u \in \mathbb{U}$ and $P \in \texttt{Part}$, referring to a security requirement that partition P is not allowed to interfere with a user u under condition φ. In this case, we say T *controls* P and *is associated with* u. An assertion is *condition-free*, or a *strict assertion*, if its condition does not impose any constraints, in which case we drop φ and write it as $\langle P \not\rightsquigarrow u \rangle$. This definition seems finer than what is presented by Rushby [26] who defines interference (the complement of noninterference) as a relation over the set of users. We choose this structure to define a policy because it allows a policy to express finer and more reasonable controls. For example, a user, who is in charge of downgrading but also has to maintain other functionalities, can avoid unnecessary downgrading of information by choosing actions not in the downgrading partition.[1] A *conditional noninterference policy* is a set of (conditional noninterference) assertions, which we simply call a *policy* if it is clear from the context, and use symbols such as Π, Π' to range over.

Every information flow policy as a binary relation $\rightsquigarrow$ on $\mathbb{U}$ is expressible by a set of strict assertions that include pairs of users that are missed out in the relation $\rightsquigarrow$. For example, assuming *part* equivalent to *dom*, the policy in Fig. 1(a) can be expressed as $\Pi_a = \{\langle A_H \not\rightsquigarrow L \rangle, \langle A_H \not\rightsquigarrow M \rangle, \langle A_M \not\rightsquigarrow L \rangle\}$. For the policy in Fig. 1(b) we have $\Pi_b = \{\langle A_H \not\rightsquigarrow L \rangle\}$.

[1] As in the case of a channel control policy [18,26] where $u \rightsquigarrow v$ and $v \rightsquigarrow w$, it seems more realistic to let only a subset of $\mathcal{A}_v$ act as a channel passing information from u to w. Such a finer-grained treatment is also advocated by Roscoe and Goldsmith [25].

2.2 Conditional Noninterference

For a policy consisting of only strict assertions, the notion of *noninterference*, as introduced in [15], requires a function $purge_{\Pi} : \mathcal{A}^* \times \mathbb{U} \rightarrow \mathcal{A}^*$ to clear away actions that are not allowed to interfere with a security domain. This is inductively defined by $purge_{\Pi}(\epsilon, u) = \epsilon$, and

$$purge_{\Pi}(a \cdot \alpha, u) = \begin{cases} purge_{\Pi}(\alpha, u) & \text{if } \langle part(a) \not\rightarrowtail u \rangle \in \Pi \\ a \cdot purge_{\Pi}(\alpha, u) & \text{otherwise.} \end{cases}$$

A system satisfies noninterference, if for all $u \in \mathbb{U}$ and $\alpha \in \mathcal{A}^*$, $obs_u(s_0 \bullet \alpha) = obs_u(s_0 \bullet purge_{\Pi}(\alpha, u))$. Plainly, if removing all the actions not allowed to interfere with a user is not noticeable by that user, the security property should be satisfied, since arbitrarily inserting or removing actions in P does not alter the view of u to the system.

For *conditional noninterference*, we consider a condition φ as a function of type $\mathcal{A}^* \times \mathcal{A} \times \mathcal{A}^* \rightarrow \{true, false\}$ that assigns more flexibility to *purge*. Given sequences of actions $\alpha, \alpha' \in \mathcal{A}^*$ and a single action $a \in \mathcal{A}$, $\varphi(\alpha, a, \alpha')$ answers whether the current action a is allowed to interfere with user u within the sequence $\alpha \cdot a \cdot \alpha'$, i.e., whether it needs to be 'purged'. If φ is always evaluated true in $T = \langle P \not\rightarrowtail u \ [\![\varphi]\!] \rangle$, then T is a strict assertion. We revise the *purge* function in the following definition.

Definition 1. *Given a policy Π, the function $purge_{\Pi} : \mathcal{A}^* \times \mathbb{U} \rightarrow \mathcal{A}^*$ is defined as for all $\alpha \in \mathcal{A}^*$ in the form of $a_1 a_2 \dots a_n$, $purge_{\Pi}(\alpha, u) = a'_1 a'_2 \dots a'_n$, such that for every $i \in \{1, \dots, n\}$,*

$$a'_i = \begin{cases} \epsilon & \text{if there exists } \langle part(a_i) \not\rightarrowtail u \ [\![\varphi]\!] \rangle \in \Pi \text{ such that } \varphi(\alpha_{-i}, a_i, \alpha_{+i}), \\ a_i & \text{otherwise.} \end{cases}$$

where $\alpha_{-i} = a_1 \dots a_{i-1}$, $\alpha_{+i} = a_{i+1} \dots a_n$, and ϵ denotes the empty sequence.

A system is secure with respect to a policy Π, if for all $u \in \mathbb{U}$ and $\alpha \in \mathcal{A}^*$, $obs_u(s_0 \bullet \alpha) = obs_u(s_0 \bullet purge_{\Pi}(\alpha, u))$.

In the following we define two subclasses of *conditional assertions*. A *pre-conditional assertion* provides a control when a decision on permitted information flow needs to be made ahead of time. For example, in a system with discretionary access control, if a user wishes to receive information from another user, he may create a file which he can read, and delegate the 'write' access of the file to that particular user. He may also revoke this access in the future. A *channel assertion* controls flow of information after an action with intended flow is performed. An example is that a secret message must be followed by an encrypting action before it is allowed to be sent out.

We start with a simple language Φ^- for expressing the constraints (or conditions) as shown in Fig. 2. The superscripts '*pre*' and '*chan*' denote whether a constraint is defined in a pre-conditional or channel assertion, and the arrows '$\nearrow$' and '$\searrow$' denote whether the effect of the constraint is to upgrade or to downgrade information, respectively. A channel assertion asserts a condition under which an already-taken action is allowed to produce effect. For example, the

$$C := P \mid P \cup C \qquad P := P_1 \mid P_2 \mid \ldots \mid P_n$$
$$\overleftarrow{C} := C \mid C\Diamond \mid \overleftarrow{C}\, C \mid \overleftarrow{C}\, C\Diamond \qquad \overrightarrow{C} := C \mid \Diamond C \mid C\,\overrightarrow{C} \mid \Diamond C\,\overrightarrow{C}$$
$$\varphi_{pre} := [\overleftarrow{C}_1 \cup \overleftarrow{C}_2 \cup \cdots \cup \overleftarrow{C}_n]^{pre}_{\nearrow} \mid [\overleftarrow{C}_1 \cup \overleftarrow{C}_2 \cup \cdots \cup \overleftarrow{C}_n]^{pre}_{\searrow}$$
$$\varphi_{chan} := [\overrightarrow{C}_1 \cup \overrightarrow{C}_2 \cup \cdots \cup \overrightarrow{C}_n]^{chan}_{\rightarrow} \qquad \text{where } P_i \in \texttt{Part} \text{ for } 1 \leq i \leq n \text{ for some } n$$

Fig. 2. syntax of the constraints in Φ^-

assertion $\langle P \not\rightarrowtail u \; [\![[P_1P_2]^{pre}_{\searrow}]\!] \rangle$ disallows partition P to interfere with u unless it is immediately preceded by an action in P_1 followed by an action in P_2, and the assertion $\langle P \not\rightarrowtail u \; [\![[\Diamond(P_1 \cup P_2)]^{chan}_{\rightarrow}]\!] \rangle$ allows actions from P to be detectable by u only if somewhere in the future an action in $P_1 \cup P_2$ is performed. In this case, the symbol '$\Diamond$' resembles its usage in temporal logics, in the sense that the actions in the next partition (or union of partitions) are not necessarily to happen immediately after, but *within a finite distance* in the action sequence. We define the channel assertions in the way of controlled release of information, and such release is regarded as *irreversible*.[2]

Every $\varphi \in \Phi^-$ is interpreted as a regular expression. Let $[\![.]\!]$ be a function from Φ^- to regular expressions. For a pre-conditional constraint $\overleftarrow{C}_i = W_1W_2 \ldots W_n$ (or $\overrightarrow{C}_i$ for channel constraints) where $W_i \in \{\Diamond\} \cup \mathcal{P}(\mathcal{A})$, define $[\![\overleftarrow{C}_i]\!]$ as the regular language represented by $W_1'W_2' \ldots W_n'$ where $W_i' = \mathcal{A}^*$ if $W_i = \Diamond$ and $W_i' = W_i$ otherwise. Given $\varphi = \overleftarrow{C}_1 \cup \overleftarrow{C}_2 \cup \ldots \overleftarrow{C}_n$, we have $[\![\varphi]\!] = [\![\overleftarrow{C}_1]\!] \cup [\![\overleftarrow{C}_2]\!] \cup \ldots [\![\overleftarrow{C}_n]\!]$, i.e., the union of the languages of all the constraints. The semantics for channel constraints are defined in a similar way. Given an assertion $\langle P \not\rightarrowtail u \; [\![\varphi]\!] \rangle$, $\alpha, \alpha' \in \mathcal{A}^*$ and $a \in \mathcal{A}$,

- if φ is in the form of $[\varphi']^{pre}_{\nearrow}$, then $\varphi(\alpha, a, \alpha') = true$ iff $\alpha \in \mathcal{A}^*[\![\varphi']\!]$,
- if φ is in the form of $[\varphi']^{pre}_{\searrow}$, then $\varphi(\alpha, a, \alpha') = false$ iff $\alpha \in \mathcal{A}^*[\![\varphi']\!]$,
- if φ is in the form of $[\varphi']^{chan}_{\rightarrow}$, then $\varphi(\alpha, a, \alpha') = false$ iff $\alpha' \in [\![\varphi']\!]\mathcal{A}^*$.

Note that the formal interpretations over upgrading and downgrading are different. For an upgrading assertion $\langle P \not\rightarrowtail u \; [\![[\varphi]^{pre}_{\nearrow}]\!] \rangle$, if a pre-conditional sequence α matches the pattern, i.e., $\alpha \in \mathcal{A}^*[\![\varphi]\!]$, the following action (if in P) must be purged. However in the case of downgrading that action must not be purged. The channel assertions only downgrade information.

The usage of the terms 'upgrading' and 'downgrading' are intuitive. An upgrading assertion $\langle P \not\rightarrowtail u \; [\![[\varphi]^{pre}_{\nearrow}]\!] \rangle$ allows actions in P to interfere with u, as default, until a (regular) pattern in $[\![\varphi]\!]$ occurs, after which the policy becomes more strict. An interpretation for downgrading assertions could be made in a similar way. Plainly, every conditional assertion is weaker than its corresponding strict assertion that is generated by removing its conditional part.

---

[2] On the other hand, pre-conditional assertions can be used to revoke a "permission" that may cause flow, as long as the actions (which can be regarded as the information source) under control are not yet performed.

2.3 Two Examples

We give the following two examples to show that conditional policies can be used to express several useful security requirements related to information flow.

Example 1. (book-keeping) We present a simple example of *well-formed* transactions to ensure data integrity by Clark and Wilson [8]. Assume there is a company with a number of employees. A shared database $\mathbb{B}$ is in the company's IntraNet from which every user is allowed to retrieve information. A user can modify $\mathbb{B}$, but this is only allowed immediately after he has registered (or authenticated) himself into the system. This is a basic integrity requirement.

Database $\mathbb{B}$ is modelled as a user with no actions, and its observation on the system is just its contents. For a user E, his action set $\mathcal{A}_E$ can be partitioned into the set of reading operations $\mathcal{A}_E^r$, the set of writing operations $\mathcal{A}_E^w$ and the book-keeping action $\{a_E^{bk}\}$. The security requirement thus can be stated as follows for each user E.
(1) E's reading actions are not allowed to change $\mathbb{B}$, which is the assertion

$$\langle \mathcal{A}_E^r \not\rightarrowtail \mathbb{B} \rangle$$

(2) E's writing actions are allowed to modify $\mathbb{B}$ only if that action occurs immediately after a book-keeping action. An assertion for this rule is

$$\langle \mathcal{A}_E^w \not\rightarrowtail \mathbb{B} \; [\![[\{a_E^{bk}\}]_{\searrow}^{pre}]\!] \rangle$$

(3) Finally, the action a_E^{bk} also needs to be constrained. If it is not immediately followed by a write operation, it should not affect any part of the database. So we have

$$\langle \{a_E^{bk}\} \not\rightarrowtail \mathbb{B} \; [\![[\mathcal{A}_E^w]_{\rightarrow}^{chan}]\!] \rangle$$

□

The above example illustrates how actions need to be bundled together in order to become a *well-formed* transaction. The book-keeping operation serves as a downgrading action on the integrity level of $\mathbb{B}$, after which the employee E is allowed to modify $\mathbb{B}$. The next example presents an upgrading policy.

Example 2. (conflict of interest) In a small town two sales companies u and v, which compete with each other, are seeking advices on their business strategies. There is only one consulting company available in that town. If both u and v connect themselves to the consulting company, it raises the requirement that for each individual consultant c, once he contacts one company of u and v, he will not be allowed to consult the other, so that he cannot play two-sides. This requirement resembles the Chinese Wall security policy [7]. We regard both u and v as users with action sets $\mathcal{A}_u$ and $\mathcal{A}_v$. For each consultant c, we assume the set of actions he can do is fixed as $\mathcal{A}_c$, which can further be split into disjoint sets $\mathcal{A}_c^u$ and $\mathcal{A}_c^v$ which are supposed to be used to exchange messages with u and v, respectively.

(1) Initially, it is required that the companies u and v are not allowed to leak information to each other, which can be sketched as

$$\langle \mathcal{A}_u \not\rightarrowtail v \rangle \text{ and } \langle \mathcal{A}_v \not\rightarrowtail u \rangle.$$

(2) The actions for c to communicate with u are not supposed to have any effect on v, so that v's view over the system should not be changed by actions in $\mathcal{A}_c^u$. Similarly, $\mathcal{A}_c^v$ is not allowed to alter u's view. Therefore we have the following assertions.

$$\langle \mathcal{A}_c^u \not\rightarrowtail v \rangle \text{ and } \langle \mathcal{A}_c^v \not\rightarrowtail u \rangle.$$

(3) Once c starts consulting u (or tries to access u), he should be immediately disallowed to communicate with v. This is defined over the action partition $\mathcal{A}_c^u$ to company v. For the effect from partition $\mathcal{A}_c^v$ on company u, we define the same assertion.

$$\langle \mathcal{A}_c^u \not\rightarrowtail u \; [\![[\mathcal{A}_c^v \Diamond]_{\nearrow}^{pre}]\!] \rangle \text{ and } \langle \mathcal{A}_c^v \not\rightarrowtail v \; [\![[\mathcal{A}_c^u \Diamond]_{\nearrow}^{pre}]\!] \rangle$$

(4) However, it is also possible that c listens to u before he starts to communicate with v, so that he can pass information from u to v in an undesirable way. Therefore we disallow actions by u to reveal information to c before c shows his intention to consult u. This can be sketched by the following assertions.

$$\langle \mathcal{A}_u \not\rightarrowtail c \; [\![[\mathcal{A}_c^u \Diamond]_{\searrow}^{pre}]\!] \rangle \text{ and } \langle \mathcal{A}_v \not\rightarrowtail c \; [\![[\mathcal{A}_c^v \Diamond]_{\searrow}^{pre}]\!] \rangle$$

In this example the actions in $\mathcal{A}_c^u$ upgrade the information flow policy on $\mathcal{A}_c^v$ to v, i.e., once an action in $\mathcal{A}_c^u$ is performed, the policy becomes more strict on the actions in $\mathcal{A}_c^v$, and vice versa. A reasonable consequence of this policy is that once a consultant tries to communicate with both companies, he will be forbidden to consult both companies thereafter. □

2.4 Avoiding Inconsistencies

It is possible that two assertions associated with the same user and controlling the same partition disagree on whether an action needs to be purged. This is handled by Def. 1 which insists that an action be purged from a sequence if there *exists* an assertion that returns *true*.

Nevertheless there is another form of conflict. For example, let a channel assertion $T_1 = \langle P_1 \not\rightarrowtail u \; [\![[\Diamond P_2]_{\rightarrow}^{chan}]\!] \rangle$ be an assertion that allows P_1 to interfere with u only via a channel provided by P_2. This assertion is intuitively conflicting the assertion $T_2 = \langle P_2 \not\rightarrowtail u \rangle$ which disallows P_2 to interfere with u in all circumstances. Since P_2 is allowed to control information from P_1 to u in T_1, information passed from P_1 to u carries a 'permission' from P_2, which seems undesirable. The following conditions monitor this type of inconsistencies in policies.

Definition 2. *Given a signature* $(\mathcal{A}, \mathbb{U}, dom)$*, a partition* $\mathtt{Part}$ *and a policy* Π*,*

- Π *is* left-consistent, *if for all* $u \in \mathbb{U}$ *and for all* $\alpha, \alpha' \in \mathcal{A}^*$, $purge_\Pi(purge_\Pi(\alpha, u) \cdot \alpha', u) = purge_\Pi(\alpha \cdot \alpha', u)$,

- Π *is* right-consistent, *if for all* $u \in \mathbb{U}$ *and for all* $\alpha, \alpha' \in \mathcal{A}^*$, $purge_\Pi(\alpha \cdot purge_\Pi(\alpha', u), u) = purge_\Pi(\alpha \cdot \alpha', u)$.

Intuitively, suppose the effect of action a depends on the existence of action b, then the conditions that determine the effect of b should be consistent with the conditions that determine the effect of a. A policy being left-consistent (right-consistent) requires that the existence of every action in a purged sequence is consistent with the existence of every other action appearing to the left (right) of that action in the sequence.

2.5 Encoding Intransitive Noninterference

Intransitive noninterference [18,26] assumes a flow policy $\rightsquigarrow$ as a (reflexive binary) relation on $\mathbb{U}$. It interprets $u \rightsquigarrow v \rightsquigarrow w$ in the way that u is allowed to interfere with w only with v's intervention. Its definition is as follows.

Given $u \in \mathbb{U}$ and $\alpha \in \mathcal{A}^*$ in the form of $a_1 a_2 \dots a_n$, $ipurge(\alpha, u) = a'_1 a'_2 \dots a'_n$, such that for every $i \in \{1, \dots, n\}$,

$$a'_i = \begin{cases} a_i \text{ if } a_{i+1}a_{i+2}\dots a_n \text{ contains an } \textit{interference chain}, \\ \epsilon \text{ otherwise.} \end{cases}$$

where an interference chain is a subsequence $b_1 b_2 \dots b_m$ that is contained in $a_{i+1}a_{i+2}\dots a_n$, satisfying that $dom(a_i) \rightsquigarrow dom(b_1)$, $dom(b_j) \rightsquigarrow dom(b_{j+1})$ for all $1 \leq j \leq m-1$, and $dom(b_m) \rightsquigarrow u$. A system is secure with respect to intransitive noninterference (of policy $\rightsquigarrow$), if for all $u \in \mathbb{U}$ and $\alpha \in \mathcal{A}^*$, we have $obs_u(s, \alpha) = obs_u(s, ipurge(\alpha, u))$.

We encode intransitive noninterference policies as a consistent subclass of channel control policies. Given a signature $(\mathcal{A}, \mathbb{U}, dom)$ and an intransitive noninterference policy $\rightsquigarrow \subseteq \mathbb{U} \times \mathbb{U}$, we construct a policy $\Pi(\rightsquigarrow)$ as follows. First we let $\texttt{Part} = \{\mathcal{A}_u \mid u \in \mathbb{U}\}$. For every pair of users $u, v \in \mathbb{U}$, we construct the set $\texttt{Interf}(u,v) = \{v_1 v_2 \dots v_n \in \mathbb{U}^* \mid u \rightsquigarrow v_1 \rightsquigarrow v_2 \rightsquigarrow \dots \rightsquigarrow v_n \rightsquigarrow v\}$. In this set we enumerate all possible *interference chains* from user u to user v. (This set could be infinite.) Define a condense operator $Cond : 2^{\mathcal{A}^*} \rightarrow 2^{\mathcal{A}^*}$ by $Cond(TSet) = \{\alpha \in TSet \mid \forall \alpha' \in TSet : \alpha \text{ contains } \alpha' \Rightarrow \alpha = \alpha'\}$, where a sequence $a_1 a_2 \dots a_n$ is *contained* in sequence α if there exists $\alpha_0, \alpha_1, \dots \alpha_n \in \mathcal{A}^*$ such that $\alpha_0 \cdot a_1 \cdot \alpha_1 \cdot a_2 \cdot \alpha_2 \dots a_n \cdot \alpha_n = \alpha$. This operator is to remove all redundant and cyclic chains in a set $\texttt{Interf}(u,v)$, so that the remaining condensed set is *minimal.* For instance if $u \rightsquigarrow v$ is in the policy, then neither the chain $u \rightsquigarrow w \rightsquigarrow v$ nor the chain $u \rightsquigarrow w \rightsquigarrow u \rightsquigarrow v$ provides more information on purging actions in A_u with respect to user v. Moreover, such a condensed set is always finite provided that $\mathbb{U}$ is finite. We define $\Pi(\rightsquigarrow)$ as a set consisting of the following assertions. For all distinct $u, v \in \mathbb{U}$,

1. if $\texttt{Interf}(u,v) = \emptyset$, then $\langle \mathcal{A}_u \not\rightarrow v \rangle$ is in $\Pi(\rightsquigarrow)$,
2. if $\texttt{Interf}(u,v) \neq \emptyset$ and $Cond(\texttt{Interf}(u,v)) \neq \{\epsilon\}$, then $\langle \mathcal{A}_u \not\rightarrow v\ [\![[\lambda_1 \cup \lambda_2 \cup \dots \cup \lambda_n]^{chan}_{\rightarrow}]\!] \rangle$ is an assertion in $\Pi(\rightsquigarrow)$, where $\{\lambda_1, \lambda_2, \dots, \lambda_n\} = Cond(\texttt{Interf}(u,v))$.

The correctness of the above construction of $\Pi(\rightsquigarrow)$ is by the following result.

Proposition 1. *Given an intransitive noninterference policy* $\rightsquigarrow$, *for all* $u \in \mathbb{U}$ *and* $\alpha \in \mathcal{A}^*$, $ipurge(\alpha, u) = purge_{\Pi(\rightsquigarrow)}(\alpha, u)$.

Intuitively, intransitive noninterference is right-consistent: if $u \rightsquigarrow v \rightsquigarrow w$ is in the policy where v controls u's information to w, then v is obviously allowed to interfere with w.

Proposition 2. *Every intransitive noninterference policy is right-consistent.*

Since the effect of *ipurge* on the policy $\rightsquigarrow$ is the same as that of $purge_{\Pi(\rightsquigarrow)}$, every policy $\Pi(\rightsquigarrow)$ encoding an intransitive noninterference policy $\rightsquigarrow$ is right-consistent. Together with the unwinding characterisation for policies of channel assertions in Sect. 3, this makes it possible to reason about security with respect to intransitive noninterference by unwinding theorems that are both *sufficient* and *necessary.* Moreover, our policy language on channel assertions is strictly more expressive, even in the case of `Part` $= \{\mathcal{A}_u \mid u \in \mathbb{U}\}$. An example can be a four-user system with $\mathbb{U} = \{H, D_1, D_2, L\}$, on which we have a policy of a single assertion $\langle \mathcal{A}_H \not\rightsquigarrow L \; [\![[\Diamond \mathcal{A}_{D_1} \Diamond \mathcal{A}_{D_2}]^{chan}_{\rightarrow}]\!] \rangle$, but neither $\mathcal{A}_{D_1}$ nor $\mathcal{A}_{D_2}$ is restricted from interfering with L. This policy asserts that an action from H must be approved by both D_1 and D_2 in the particular order before being passed on to L. Note D_1 is allowed to interfere with L in a way independent to the actions from D_2. This policy is not expressible by intransitive noninterference. Moreover, it is not hard to show that such a policy is also right-consistent.

3 Unwinding Relations

Unwinding provides a verification technique on noninterference-related security requirements. An unwinding theorem reduces the verification of an information flow security problem into the existence of a set of relations satisfying certain properties, which is thus easier to be formalised and verified by existing proof assistants (e.g. [9,32]). We present unwinding theorems for the two classes of conditional noninterference assertions introduced in the previous section.

The unwinding relations for policies specified as transitive relations have been discussed by Goguen and Meseguer [16] and further adapted as a verification technique by Rushby et. al [26,9]. Rushby's unwinding relation is a set $\{\sim_u\}_{u \in \mathbb{U}}$ of equivalence relations for each $u \in \mathbb{U}$, satisfying output consistency (OC), step consistency (SC), and local respect $\rightsquigarrow$ (LR).

OC $s \sim_u t$ implies $obs_u(s) = obs_u(t)$.
SC $s \sim_u t$ and $a \in A$ implies $step(s, a) \sim_u step(t, a)$.
LR $s \sim_u step(s, a)$ if $\langle part(a) \not\rightsquigarrow u \rangle \in \Pi$.

The intuition behind the relation $\sim_u$ is that it represents strong indistinguishability between states to u's observation, which cannot be disturbed by the actions that are not allowed to interfere with u (as asserted by a policy), so that u can never deduce any information from the actions. The existence of a set of relations $\{\sim_u\}_{u \in \mathbb{U}}$ that satisfy the above three properties is both sufficient and necessary for a system to be secure with respect to a policy of strict assertions. For a detailed proof methodology we refer to [26].

Theorem 1. *A system M is secure with respect to Π consisting of only strict assertions iff there exist a set of unwinding relations $\{\sim_u\}_{u\in\mathbb{U}}$.*

3.1 Unwinding for Pre-conditional Assertions

We present an unwinding technique that is sound for policies consisting of pre-conditional assertions. Since the policy language produces a regular set of sequences, for each assertion T, we write $A(\varphi)^{P,u}$ for the (deterministic) finite automaton accepting $L(\varphi)$ (which is the regular set $\mathcal{A}^*[\![\varphi']\!]$ if φ is of the form $[\varphi']^{pre}_{\nearrow}$, or $\mathcal{A}^* \setminus \mathcal{A}^*[\![\varphi']\!]$ if φ is of the form $[\varphi']^{pre}_{\searrow}$), and regard $A(\varphi)^{P,u}$ as the assertion automaton of T.

We define a new rule for the unwinding relations on pre-conditional assertions. Given a machine M and a policy Π, a set of unwinding relations $\{\sim_u\}_{u\in\mathbb{U}}$ are equivalence relations satisfying OC, SC, and the new condition $\mathrm{LR}^{\leq}$ which is specified as follows.

$\mathrm{LR}^{\leq}$ $s \sim_u \mathit{step}(s,a)$ if $\langle \mathit{part}(a) \not\rightarrowtail u\ [\![\varphi]\!]\rangle \in \Pi$ and there exists $\alpha \in L(\varphi)$ such that $s = s_0 \bullet \alpha$.

The condition $\mathrm{LR}^{\leq}$ ensures that if a state is reachable by an action sequence within the language defined by an assertion controlling $\mathit{part}(a)$, then the transition from s made by a must not be noticeable by u. We prove that this characterisation is sufficient for a system to be secure with respect to a policy consisting of only pre-conditional assertions.

Theorem 2. *Given a system M and a policy Π consisting of pre-conditional assertions, M is secure if there exists a set of equivalence relations $\{\sim_u\}_{u\in\mathbb{U}}$ satisfying OC, SC and $\mathrm{LR}^{\leq}$.*

If a given policy is left-consistent, then this characterisation is also complete.

Theorem 3. *Given a system M and a policy Π consisting of pre-conditional assertions, if M is secure and Π is left-consistent, then there exist a set of equivalence relations $\{\sim_u\}_{u\in\mathbb{U}}$ satisfying OC, SC and $\mathrm{LR}^{\leq}$.*

The regularity of the assertion language allows us to apply assertion automata for pre-conditional assertions to place marks on the states where $\mathrm{LR}^{\leq}$ needs to be applied to purge an action. This can be done by a parallel composition of the machine M with the $A(\varphi)^{P,u}$ for every $\langle P \not\rightarrowtail u\ [\![\varphi^{pre}]\!]\rangle \in \Pi$, which may be automated in a model checker. Since assertion automata usually do not have many states, a local model checking algorithm is able to detect violations of security on-the-fly when exploring the state space even if the system is very large. We have the following reduction from noninterference security properties with policies consisting of pre-conditional assertions to safety properties.

For an assertion $T = \langle P \not\rightarrowtail u\ [\![\varphi^{pre}]\!]\rangle \in \Pi$, we assume that an assertion automaton $A(\varphi)^T = \langle S_T, s_{(T,0)}, \rightarrow, \mathcal{F}_T\rangle$ is deterministic, and accepts the language $L(\varphi)$. We assume Π is a finite set $\{T_1, T_2, \ldots, T_n\}$. Given a machine $M = \langle S, s_0, \mathit{step}, \mathit{obs}, O\rangle$, for each $u \in \mathbb{U}$, we define a machine

$M_u^\Pi = \langle S^u, s_0^u, step^u, obs^u, dom\rangle$ to be the system with identical actions and domains, and states $S^u = S \times S \times S_{T_1} \times \dots S_{T_n}$, initial state $s_0^u = (s_0, s_0, s_{(T_1,0)}, \dots s_{(T_n,0)})$, and the observation function $obs^u : S^u \to (O \times O)$ is defined as $obs^u(s_1, s_2, t_1, \dots t_n) = (obs_u(s_1), obs_u(s_2))$ for $s_1, s_2 \in S$, and transition function $step^u : S^u \times \mathcal{A} \to S^u$ is given by $step^u((s_1, s_2, t_1, \dots t_n), a) = (s_1', step(s_2, a), t_1', \dots t_n')$ with $a \in \mathcal{A}$ and $t_i \xrightarrow{a} t_i'$ for all i, and
$s_1' = \begin{cases} s_1 & \text{if there is } T_i = \langle part(a) \not\rightsquigarrow u\ [\![\varphi^{pre}]\!]\rangle \text{ and } t_i \in \mathcal{F}_{T_i}, \\ step(s_1, a) & \text{otherwise.}\end{cases}$

Intuitively, in every transition, an action a is not allowed to be applied on the left part of a state pair, if the assertion automaton controlling $part(a)$ and associated with u is in its final state. A proof by induction shows that for every sequence of actions $\alpha \in A^*$, if $s_0^u \bullet \alpha = (s, t, \dots)$ in M_u^Π, then in M we have $s = s_0 \bullet purge_\Pi(\alpha, u)$ and $t = s_0 \bullet \alpha$. We therefore obtain the following.

Proposition 3. *A machine M is secure with respect to a left-consistent policy Π iff for all $u \in \mathbb{U}$ and for all states s in M_u^Π reachable from s_0^u, we have that $obs^u(s) = (o, o')$ implies $o = o'$.*

3.2 Unwinding for Channel Assertions

We present the unwinding relations for policies consisting of channel assertions given in Fig. 2. The design of unwinding for this class of policies is rather involved, which allow possibly more than one equivalence relations for each user. The underlying intuition is as follows. If action a is allowed to interfere with u only if it is followed by action b, then for each state s, we need to have s and $step(s, a)$ indistinguishable by u after any sequence of actions that does not contain b. Based on that, we define a binary relation $\overset{[b]}{\sim}_u \subseteq S \times S$ and let $s \overset{[b]}{\sim}_u step(s, a)$ represent the effect that state s and state $step(s, a)$ are indistinguishable by u as long as b is not performed (i.e., $s \overset{[b]}{\sim}_u t$ implies $step(s, c) \overset{[b]}{\sim}_u step(t, c)$ if $c \neq b$). Such a relation must be an *equivalence* relation.

Let Π be a policy of channel assertions. For a user $u \in \mathbb{U}$, write the set of assertions associated with u as a subpolicy $\Pi_u \subseteq \Pi$. Let $Q = \mathcal{P}(\texttt{Part}) \cup \{\Diamond C \mid C \subseteq \texttt{Part}\}$. Define the set of terms which are suffixes of the given constraints in Π_u as $\Delta_u^\Pi = \{\lambda \in Q^* \mid \exists \lambda' \in Q^*, \langle P \not\rightsquigarrow u\ [\![[C_1 \cup C_2 \cup \dots \cup C_n]_{\to}^{chan}]\!]\rangle \in \Pi_u : \lambda' \cdot \lambda = C_i \wedge i \in [1 \dots n]\}$. Intuitively, this is the suffix closure of the set of channels that allow to downgrade information from some partition to u. The unwinding relations for a user $u \in \mathbb{U}$ is $\{\overset{\delta}{\sim}_u \mid \delta \subseteq \Delta_u^\Pi\}$, which satisfy the following rules.

OC $s \overset{\delta}{\sim}_u t$ and $\epsilon \notin \delta$ implies $obs_u(s) = obs_u(t)$.

SC$^+$ If $s \overset{\delta}{\sim}_u t$ and $a \in \mathcal{A}$, then $step(s, a) \overset{sc(\delta,a)}{\sim}_u step(s, a)$.

LR $\langle part(a) \not\rightsquigarrow u\rangle \in \Pi$ implies $s \overset{\emptyset}{\sim}_u step(s, a)$.

LR$^\geq$ $\langle part(a) \not\rightsquigarrow u\ [\![[\lambda_1 \cup \lambda_2 \cup \dots \lambda_n]_{\to}^{chan}]\!]\rangle \in \Pi$ implies $s \overset{\{\lambda_1,\lambda_2,\dots\lambda_n\}}{\sim}_u step(s, a)$.

SUB For all $\delta_1, \delta_2 \in \mathcal{P}(\Delta_u^\Pi)$, $\delta_1 \subseteq \delta_2$ implies $\overset{\delta_1}{\sim}_u \subseteq \overset{\delta_2}{\sim}_u$.

The function $sc : \mathcal{P}(\Delta_u^{\Pi}) \times \mathcal{A} \to \mathcal{P}(\Delta_u^{\Pi})$ is defined as $sc(\delta) = \bigcup_{\lambda \in \delta} cut(\lambda, a)$, where the cut function is defined by: (1) $cut(\epsilon, a) = \{\epsilon\}$ for all $a \in \mathcal{A}$, (2) $cut(P \cdot \lambda, a) = \{\lambda\}$ if $a \in P$, (3) $cut(P \cdot \lambda, a) = \emptyset$ if $a \notin P$, (4) $cut(\Diamond P \cdot \lambda, a) = \{\lambda\}$ if $a \in P$, (5) $cut(\Diamond P \cdot \lambda, a) = \{\Diamond P \cdot \lambda\}$ if $a \notin P$.

The condition OC asserts that all such relations containing only unfinished downgrading channels to u (i.e., $\epsilon \notin \delta$) must not be distinguishable by u. The definition of the SC$^+$ rule follows the mechanism of pattern matching which simulates the process of purging. For example, if $s \overset{\{\Diamond P \lambda\}}{\sim}_u t$, then after an action $a \in P$ is performed, $step(s, a)$ and $step(t, a)$ needs to be related by the relation $\overset{\{\lambda\}}{\sim}_u$, indicating that an action in P has been performed and that the rest of the downgrading channel is λ. The states can be related by two downgrading channels, e.g. $s \overset{\{\lambda, \lambda'\}}{\sim}_u t$, indicating the two possible ways to affect the view (or to relax the indistinguishability relation) of u. When two states are related by a set that contains a completed channel, e.g., $s \overset{\delta}{\sim}_u t$ with $\epsilon \in \delta$, then s and t need not be indistinguishable to u any more. Plainly $\overset{\delta}{\sim}_u = S \times S$ if $\epsilon \in \delta$, where S is the state space of a machine. Informally, condition SUB indicates that the more channels a relation carries, the weaker policies that relation represents. As $\overset{\emptyset}{\sim}_u$ is the smallest such relation for user $u \in \mathbb{U}$, which represents strict noninterference, a system is secure if $s_0 \overset{\emptyset}{\sim}_u s_0$ for all u.

Theorem 4. *Given a system M, a user $u \in \mathbb{U}$, and a policy Π with only channel assertions, if there exists a set of relations $\{\overset{\delta}{\sim}_u\}_{\delta \subseteq \Delta_u^{\Pi}, u \in \mathbb{U}}$ satisfying OC, LR, LR$^{\geq}$, SC and SUB, then M is secure with respect to Π.*

Similar to the pre-conditional case, the existence of such unwinding relations is also necessary for a system to be secure, provided that the given policy consisting of channel assertions is right-consistent. Interested readers are referred to the full version of the paper for the proofs.

Theorem 5. *Given a system M with a right-consistent policy Π consisting of channel assertions, if M is secure with respect to Π, then there exists a set of relations $\{\overset{\delta}{\sim}_u\}_{\delta \subseteq \Delta_u^{\Pi}}$ satisfying OC, LR, LR$^{\geq}$, SC$^+$ and SUB for all $u \in \mathbb{U}$.*

4 Related Work

Noninterference and intransitive noninterference were proposed by Goguen and Meseguer [15] and Haigh and Young [18], respectively, and both were revised by Rushby [26]. The weak unwinding relation in [26] fails to be complete for intransitive noninterference. The unwinding technique of Mantel [20] is sound for a spectrum of trace-based properties [19]. A few other works extend Rushby's weak unwinding in nondeterministic language-based settings [22,21]. Bossi et al. extended the unwinding-based characterization for the security properties in SPA [13,14] to support downgrading [6]. They described a policy for three security levels including H (High level), D (Downgrader) and L (low level) by applying unwinding to disallow information flow from H to L without putting any constraint on D. Their policy is basically an intransitive version of [15] in a nondeterministic environment with silent system moves. Roscoe and Goldsmith [25] generalized the determinism-based notion of noninterference [24] to intransitive noninterference with three security levels in process algebra CSP. Backes and Pfitzmann introduced a number of intransitive policies in terms of computational probabilistic non-interference [1].

Van der Meyden developed a new set of intransitive noninterference properties to reason about information flow epistemically [29]. As it was identified that Haigh and Young's intransitive flow property [18] may allow a downgrader to pass information from high level to low level without knowing what is to be downgraded, a number of new intransitive noninterference properties are introduced to catch the idea that a downgrader's knowledge about the secret information should be no less than what the low level user is able to get. Our framework lies in an orthogonal direction, in that we extend the framework of [15,26] to support more flexible policies without much concern on a downgrader's knowledge.

Different versions of downgrading have been studied in the domain of language-based information flow, which have been surveyed in [27]. Four different dimensions are proposed: (1) *who* releases information, (2) *what* information is released (3) *where* in the system information is released and (4) *when* information can be released. Informally, our policy design supports the *who* dimension, by assigning a partition of a user in a policy to control information flow (to another user), and also the *where* and *when* dimensions, by controlling information release only after a downgrading channel is fully established. However, unwinding is not a common approach in the language-based community, which usually applies type systems or program analysis as tools. Most of their downgrading methods rely on particular settings or language semantics. Since every program can be interpreted as a (possibly infinite) transition system, our work focuses on a more fundamental level by defining security notions in an automata-based model.

Hadj-Alouane et al. studied verification of intransitive noninterference property in finite state systems [17]. They reduce a system into an automaton accepting the reversed language, which consumes space exponential to the size of the system. A new algorithm for intransitive noninterference is proposed by Eggert et al. [12] which has a complexity bound polynomial to the size of a machine but exponential to the number of users. Verification on our unwinding relations for channel assertions can be done in-place, therefore it is also polynomial time to the size of a system, but it could be exponential to the size of a policy (as shown in the subset construction on the set of channel assertions when constructing unwinding relations). It will also be interesting to investigate algorithmic verification methods on generating unwinding relations in more general systems (i.e., systems that are not necessarily finite state), as it has been shown that verification of Mantel's BSPs [19] in push-down systems is undecidable [11]. The methodologies on reducing information flow properties to safety by self-composition have been discussed in the literature [2,28,10,30], in a variety of system models.

5 Conclusion and Future Work

This work introduces a framework of information flow policies by conditional noninterference assertions which generalises existing work in the literature. Although noninterference is supposed to be a static security notion, we applied our policy language to express a number of dynamic security requirements including upgrading, downgrading and channel control. Our unwinding theorems on both pre-conditional and channel assertions are novel, and they are more precise and more general than the existing results in the literature, to our knowledge.

The result in this paper is based on systems with deterministic transition functions, but it will be possible to extend the definitions in nondeterministic systems, possibly by revising the unwinding rule SC (or SC^+) in the way of bisimulation [23]. There are plenty of extensions of noninterference in nondeterministic and probabilistic systems, so this will be an interesting future work for conditional noninterference. Also we believe that it will be of interest to find real cases where our unwinding theorems (or any suitable extensions) can be applied to verify their corresponding security requirements in more general systems.

Acknowledgement. The author thanks Peter Ryan and the anonymous reviewers for their helpful comments to improve the presentation of the paper.

References

1. Backes, M., Pfitzmann, B.: Intransitive non-interference for cryptographic purpose. In: Proc. S&P, pp. 140–152 (2003)
2. Barthe, G., D'Argenio, P.R., Rezk, T.: Secure information flow by self-composition. In: Proc. CSFW, pp. 100–114 (2004)
3. Bell, D.E., LaPadula, L.J.: Secure Computer System: Vol.I—mathematical foundations, Vol.II—a mathematical model, Vol.III—a refinement of the mathematical model. Technical report MTR-2547 (three volumes), The MITRE Corporation (March-December 1973)
4. Bell, D.E., LaPadula, L.J.: Secure computer system: unified exposition and MULTICS interpretation. Technical report MTR-2997 Rev. 1, The MITRE Corporation (March 1976)
5. Bevier, W.R., Young, W.D.: A state-based approach to noninterference. In: Proc. CSFW, pp. 11–21 (1994)
6. Bossi, A., Piazza, C., Rossi, S.: Modelling downgrading in information flow security. In: Proc. CSFW, pp. 187–201 (2004)
7. Brewer, D.F.C., Nash, M.J.: The Chinese Wall security policy. In: Proc. S&P, pp. 206–214 (1989)
8. Clark, D., Wilson, D.: A comparison of commercial and military computer security policies. In: Proc. S&P, pp. 184–193 (1987)
9. Crow, J., Owre, S., Rushby, J., Shankar, N., Srivas, M.: A tutorial introduction to PVS. In: Proc. Workshop on Industrial-Strength Formal Specification Techniques (1996)
10. Darvas, Á., Hähnle, R., Sands, D.: A Theorem Proving Approach to Analysis of Secure Information Flow. In: Hutter, D., Ullmann, M. (eds.) SPC 2005. LNCS, vol. 3450, pp. 193–209. Springer, Heidelberg (2005)

11. D'Souza, D., Holla, R., Kulkarni, J., Ramesh, R.K., Sprick, B.: On the Decidability of Model-Checking Information Flow Properties. In: Sekar, R., Pujari, A.K. (eds.) ICISS 2008. LNCS, vol. 5352, pp. 26–40. Springer, Heidelberg (2008)
12. Eggert, S., van der Meyden, R., Schnoor, H., Wilke, T.: The complexity of intransitive noninterference. In: Proc. S&P, pp. 196–211 (2011)
13. Focardi, R., Gorrieri, R.: A classification of security properties for process algebras. Journal of Computer Security 3(1), 5–33 (1995)
14. Focardi, R., Rossi, S.: Information flow security in dynamic contexts. In: Proc. CSFW, pp. 307–319 (2002)
15. Goguen, J.A., Meseguer, J.: Security policies and security models. In: Proc. S&P, pp. 11–20 (1982)
16. Goguen, J.A., Meseguer, J.: Unwinding and inference control. In: Proc. S&P, p. 75 (1984)
17. Ben Hadj-Alouane, N., Lafrance, S., Lin, F., Mullins, J., Yeddes, M.: On the verification of intransitive noninterference in mulitlevel security. IEEE Transactions on Systems, Man and Cybernetics 35(5), 948–958 (2005)
18. Haigh, J.T., Young, W.D.: Extending the noninterference version of MLS for SAT. IEEE Transactions on Software Engineering 13(2), 141–150 (1987)
19. Mantel, H.: Possiblistic definitions of security – an assembly kit. In: Proc. CSFW, pp. 185–199 (2000)
20. Mantel, H.: Unwinding Security Properties. In: Cuppens, F., Deswarte, Y., Gollmann, D., Waidner, M. (eds.) ESORICS 2000. LNCS, vol. 1895, pp. 238–254. Springer, Heidelberg (2000)
21. Mantel, H., Reinhard, A.: Controlling the What and Where of Declassification in Language-Based Security. In: De Nicola, R. (ed.) ESOP 2007. LNCS, vol. 4421, pp. 141–156. Springer, Heidelberg (2007)
22. Mantel, H., Sands, D.: Controlled Declassification Based on Intransitive Noninterference. In: Chin, W.-N. (ed.) APLAS 2004. LNCS, vol. 3302, pp. 129–145. Springer, Heidelberg (2004)
23. Milner, R.: Communication and concurrency. Prentice-Hall (1989)
24. Roscoe, A.W.: CSP and determinism in security modelling. In: Proc. S&P, pp. 114–221 (1995)
25. Roscoe, A.W., Goldsmith, M.H.: What is intransitive noninterference ? In: Proc. CSFW, pp. 228–238 (1999)
26. Rushby, J.: Noninterference, transitivity, and channel-control security policies. Technical report, SRI international (December 1992)
27. Sabelfeld, A., Sands, D.: Dimensions and principles of declassification. In: Proc. CSFW, pp. 255–269 (2005)
28. Terauchi, T., Aiken, A.: Secure Information Flow as a Safety Problem. In: Hankin, C., Siveroni, I. (eds.) SAS 2005. LNCS, vol. 3672, pp. 352–367. Springer, Heidelberg (2005)
29. van der Meyden, R.: What, Indeed, Is Intransitive Noninterference (Extended Abstract). In: Biskup, J., López, J. (eds.) ESORICS 2007. LNCS, vol. 4734, pp. 235–250. Springer, Heidelberg (2007)
30. van der Meyden, R., Zhang, C.: Algorithmic verification on noninterference properties. ENTCS 168, 61–75 (2007)
31. van der Meyden, R., Zhang, C.: A comparison of semantic models for noninterference. Theoretical Computer Science 411(7), 4123–4147 (2010)
32. von Oheimb, D.: Information Flow Control Revisited: Noninfluence = Noninterference + Nonleakage. In: Samarati, P., Ryan, P.Y.A., Gollmann, D., Molva, R. (eds.) ESORICS 2004. LNCS, vol. 3193, pp. 225–243. Springer, Heidelberg (2004)

Author Index

GPSR Compliance

The European Union's (EU) General Product Safety Regulation (GPSR) is a set of rules that requires consumer products to be safe and our obligations to ensure this.

If you have any concerns about our products, you can contact us on ProductSafety@springernature.com

In case Publisher is established outside the EU, the EU authorized representative is:

Springer Nature Customer Service Center GmbH
Europaplatz 3
69115 Heidelberg, Germany

Batch number: 09490872

Printed by Printforce, the Netherlands